COLLISION COURSE

COLLISION COURSE

Admiral Sir Raymond Lygo, KCB

The Book Guild Ltd
Sussex, England

First published in Great Britain in 2002 by
The Book Guild Ltd
25 High Street
Lewes, East Sussex
BN7 2LU

Typesetting in Times by
Acorn Bookwork, Salisbury, Wiltshire

Printed in Great Britain by
Bookcraft (Bath) Ltd, Avon

A catalogue record for this book is available from
The British Library.

ISBN 1 85776 514 1

To Pepper, whose love, understanding and loyalty I can never hope to repay – leave alone deserve.

CONTENTS

Part Two   British Aerospace

FOREWORD

Sir Raymond Lygo is one of the great achievers of the last half century and he has written an autobiography of rare quality with wit and style.

Chapter after chapter is a record of endeavour and excitement, vicissitude and success often in faraway places and more often in difficult conditions, but always displaying his determination to give more than his best, however difficult the task.

Ray Lygo's early career as a Royal Navy aviator was something special; ordered to fly indifferent aircraft to land on ships not always equipped to take them required courage and skill, which laid the foundations of the distinguished flying career that followed.

The period set out in the chapter called 'Fighter Pilot', when the author was posted to the Far East and the war against Japan, is written with great modesty. The battle was long and hard and the conditions aboard the carriers, lacking in air-conditioning as they did, were harsh indeed. Reading between the lines it is clear that Raymond Lygo fought with great bravery, fully aware of what would happen to those who fell into the hands of the Japanese. The reference to the memorial to the Fleet Air Arm in the churchyard at Yeovilton is a poignant reminder of the price that some of the Royal Naval fighter pilots paid.

Throughout his career as a Naval Aviator in various appointments of flying commands, Flying Instructor, Staff Officer Ray Lygo was moving steadily up the snakes and ladder board of a distinguished career in the Royal Navy. But his future changed dramatically when he removed the 'A' from the rings on his sleeve to become a sea-going officer in command of ships of varying types and ultimately to command *Ark Royal*. The adventures, emergencies and anecdotes of those sea-going years are riveting reading.

The years of training and practical experience built the character of Ray Lygo, and with it the commanding objective of his life: efficiency and attention to detail in everything he has done. Equally important was his requirement for the highest standard of competence in all those he led, whether in the navy or later in his industrial career.

Two examples of this came when commanding *Ark Royal*. On collision with a Russian destroyer in the Mediterranean, confident that his crew knew their job in recovering their own men thrown overboard, his great compassion to ensure that the Russian survivors should be saved was leadership that no one who was there could ever forget.

Again in *Ark Royal,* faced with difficulty in manoeuvring so large a vessel through very confined water to the open sea, he took the trouble to explain the complexity of the operation to the Engineers below deck on whose reactions success and safety depended. Leadership, teamwork and efficiency writ large.

With all the qualities demanded of one of the youngest officers since Nelson to be promoted to the rank of Admiral, Ray Lygo has one above all others: integrity – uncompromising with the truth, uncompromising in his opinions formed from his training, experience and great intellectual ability, and uncompromising with fudge. These qualities were also to have great impact during Lygo's second career. At the age of 51 Ray Lygo retired from the Navy and was appointed as Managing Director of the Dynamics Group, a wholly owned subsidiary of British Aerospace.

The story which is set out in Part 2 of this book is required reading for anybody who is interested in management, corporate governance and industrial leadership. It is also the history of one of the worst periods of failure of British industry in the last century, with the awful employee relationships, and the major enterprises for national economic growth – eg. railways, gas, shipbuilding and much else – nationalised without regard for profit or cost control, only for maximising employee numbers thus with scant regard for productivity.

British Aerospace was no exception and Ray Lygo found an organisation at the Dynamics Group leaderless, divisive and unfocused. Worse, the relations between the various divisions of British Aerospace with their major customers, namely the vast departmental bureaucracy of Whitehall engaged in defence equipment procurement for all three services, lacked mutual confidence and the sense of urgency in decision-making. The lack of political will and even ability of the Government to provide the enormous sums of money for research and development of new defence equipment all added enormously to the problem.

Ray Lygo set out to change this. From his position in the Dynamics Group he rose steadily to become Chief Executive of British Aerospace. It was a long hard road; to revitalise the style of management, to introduce the profit motive, to combine many diverse organisations within British Aerospace into a coherent whole and, above all, to build a viable, credible British aircraft enterprise which would compete with any and every foreign producer in the world was not a task for the faint-hearted.

Of course there were many disappointments and many man-made failures and other obstacles to be overcome but at the end British Aerospace achieved a premier place in British industry.

Some examples of extreme difficulty stand out. How and why did the Westland imbroglio have such devastating results? Bad faith or misunderstanding? Indecision or lack of clarity of objective? Political ambition or disregard for the national interest? Even with the benefit of hindsight who can tell?

After privatisation British Aerospace started to flex its muscles and look for suitable acquisitions, a not unusual corporate ambition. The takeover of Sperry Gyroscape, Royal Ordnance and Rover were not unalloyed successes for reasons which the experienced reader will recognise – namely that each had large contractual, financial or management liabilities not identified during the pre-acquisition investigations. Such disappointments were not mortal and were entirely offset by the long list of successes Ray Lygo achieved, almost single-handed, over the years of his leadership.

I doubt whether the author himself could claim which were the most important single actions which contributed to the prime reputation and success of British Aerospace which it has become today.

The decision to negotiate fixed price contracts with the Ministries in Whitehall for the development and supply of defence equipment instead of the outdated method of 'cost plus' was a major contribution to the ultimate success. This single imaginative step had an enormous effect on British Aerospace and indeed British industry as a whole. It became competitive against foreign suppliers and productivity was forced to improve for cost over-runs and failures to meet delivery dates fell on the manufacturers. It was revolutionary and salutary.

The second major step was the decision to join or rejoin the European Consortium (Airbus Industrie) after long periods of patient negotiation with the foreign partners and considerable reorganisation and rationalisation of manufacturing capability. It required too the courage and foresight to back the first Airbus Industrie product, the A300, from which came a brand of civilian aircraft to become world beaters and the lifeblood of British Aerospace today.

To build a business with ever increasing demand for new developments, using indifferent manufacturing capability with an organisation which had become almost moribund and defeatist was an enormous task. If this were not enough, the need to change the whole enterprise at the same time into a modern, dynamic and profitable industrial force required a great-hearted man.

This book is about honour and service exemplified by Sir Raymond

Lygo's outstanding career in the Royal Navy. Those qualities are manifested again in his outstanding career in Industry. Sir Raymond Lygo writes, 'it was my ambition to make British Aerospace the greatest aerospace company in Europe'. He did.

Sir Denis Thatcher
August 2001

ACKNOWLEDGEMENTS

To my family, always there for me.
My secretary, Linda Mills, for deciphering my writing, correcting my spelling and typing it several times.
The FAA Museum
The Naval Historical Branch
The Beatys – the first to read the draft, who encouraged me to complete it.
Lieutenant Commander 'Crash' Leggott, MBE
Commander Charles Lamb, DSO, DSC
Those whose tolerance and support both in the Navy and industry made my life a happy one.
Denis Thatcher for taking the time, effort and trouble to write the Foreword. Flattery will get him nowhere!

PART 1

THE NAVY

1

The Westland Affair and the Collision

It had been a relatively quiet afternoon. Things appeared to be falling
into place; we were beginning to put together the consortium of
European companies that would bid for Westland, and although I had
been most reluctant to partake in such a bid, either alone as British
Aerospace or collectively, after the last meeting with John Cuckney
both Arnold Weinstock and Tin Pearce, the CEO and Chairman
respectively of GEC and British Aerospace at the time, had both
elected me to lead the band. How we had arrived at this situation I
shall come to later.

I was on my way to an evening meeting – well, late afternoon
actually – with Geoffrey Pattie, the then Minister of Technology in the
Department of Trade and Industry, where Leon Brittan had just taken
over. I went through security at the DTI and was told to proceed up
to the seventh or eighth floor, whichever it was, where I would be met.
I really had little idea of what lay in store for me, but then one rarely
does when things happen that you're not expecting. Even though one
may be prepared for something similar it always seems to come as a
surprise, no sense of foreboding, no signals in the system to warn you.

It had been the same when, as Captain of the *Ark Royal*, I sat alone
in my sea cabin eating my supper before the commencement of night
flying south of Crete, on a calm, still, moonlit night. The Officer of the
Watch had said 'Permission to come round on to the flying course,
Sir.' And I'd replied, 'Yes, approved if we are clear to do so. Where's
the Russian?' 'He is well clear on the starboard quarter, some five
miles away, and he will be clear when we come round.' 'Approved,' I'd
said. And then it began.

*   *   *   *   *

Geoffrey Pattie was in his usual friendly and expansive mood. We had
known each other and worked together on various programmes and
prospects during his time at the Ministry of Defence. A competent,
straightforward man who seemed to understand industry and who had
had to suffer under some not dreadfully superior bosses in his previous

job. We got on well together; at least, I thought we did! We talked about various programmes that British Aerospace had in the offing in which government support was necessary, or certainly government understanding was necessary. We went over some of the space programmes and ambitions we shared in what had become one of a series of regular meetings that I held with ministers who were interested and involved in the affairs of British Aerospace. It's been called 'walking the corridors of power' and I suppose I had been doing it for many years, previously in my Naval days and more recently since becoming involved in British Aerospace. 'Corridors of power' sometimes conjures up an image of large, impressive Victorian passageways. They do exist. The old Admiralty building was blessed with quite a number of them, and that was interesting. The Foreign Office is cavernous and gloomy and has the same kind of tiling on the floor as the Admiralty building and makes you wonder about those who had worn the bare patches before you. In some of the more modern buildings, however, it was far less interesting and in all of them a slightly grubby, run-down look prevailed. They had one thing in common: a need for a fresh lick of paint, a good clean and slightly less sombre colours. Why is it so often lavatory green?

Anyway, we had exchanged our views on the subjects I had come to discuss and I had to get back for a Board meeting that had been called to discuss our involvement in the Westland affair, to explain to the whole Board, including the non-executive directors, what it was we were planning to do. As I was getting ready to leave, Geoffrey Pattie said, 'Oh, by the way, Leon Brittan knows that you are in the building and wonders if you could pop in and have a word with him while you are here.'

*   *   *   *   *

The next call I got from the bridge was, 'We're steady on the flying course but the Russian appears to have altered, Sir, and he now appears to be on a steady bearing.' (We were about to commence night flying and first off was to be a pair of Phantoms.) I laid down the book I had been reading, left my meal and stepped out on to the darkened bridge, trying to adjust to the complete darkness, even though my sea cabin had the minimum of illumination to enable me to read a book while I was eating – alone, of course, as all Captains do.

Captains of ships live lonely lives; they are not members of the Wardroom, or Officers' Mess as it would be called in the Army or RAF. They are members of no Mess, they eat alone under the watchful eye of their steward. They live alone. They have no equals with whom to share their thoughts until they are in harbour and talking over a glass of gin or Coca-Cola to a fellow Captain. *Ark Royal* was my third ship command and my sixth command, including squadrons of Fleet Air Arm aircraft, and I had become used to being alone. I am, I suppose, naturally a loner anyway, so being alone was not a tremendous burden. You were alone and kept separate because you had to administer the law, and when you had to administer the law at sea it was fairly arbitrary and it was necessary that the Captain should be seen to be totally independent.

Sometimes when a case was brought and the evidence was not sufficiently substantial and you had dismissed it, the Commander or First Lieutenant, as the case may be, would be rather upset. The administration of Naval justice in the fifties, sixties and seventies hadn't really changed very much from when it all began, but I had changed the way I conducted it because I didn't consider it to be entirely fair to the defence. The burden of proof should lie on the accuser and it was customary in my ship for the Rating to be asked, as is now the general rule, 'Do you understand the charge and how do you plead in answer to the charge, guilty or not guilty?' You then listen to the evidence on behalf of the prosecution brought by, of course, the First Lieutenant or Commander, the Executive Officer. The Rating was entitled to have his Divisional Officer, or some other Officer, to defend him or to defend himself if he wished. In the case of a guilty plea there were statements to be made in mitigation.

In one ship, the *Lowestoft*, we had a well-known 'skate'. A 'skate' is a Rating who manages to slip through life sailing very close to the wind but never being caught and always getting away with it. A bit irritating for the First Lieutenant on this particular occasion. The charge this time was an aggravated offence (in other words, he had done it before) of absence over leave – being late on board – but this time made more serious by the fact that the ship was under sailing orders. He could therefore have missed the ship altogether. A serious charge, and Number One believed he had got his man!

'You have heard the charge,' I said. 'How do you plead in answer to the charge? Guilty or not guilty?' Mind you, there couldn't have been much of an answer other than 'guilty' because he had been late. 'Guilty but with mitigating circumstances, Sir,' he replied. The details of the offence and previous offences were then read out and I asked, 'And what are the mitigating circumstances?' 'My wife', said the Rating, 'has a budgie, Sir.' The whole Table – as the court is known in the navy – the Captain's Table, officers and witnesses all became attentive. 'And she is very fond of this budgie, Sir, and won't go anywhere

5

without it, she takes it with her wherever she goes. And when we go to bed at night, Sir, she takes it into the bedroom with her, Sir.' You could have heard a pin drop. 'Well, I knew I had to get back to the ship on time, Sir, and so I set the alarm in plenty of time so that I could get up and be here prompt, Sir.' 'Go on,' I said. 'Well, in the night, Sir, the budgie must have got out of its cage and it flew around the room, sir, and it must have landed on the little knob on top of the alarm clock, Sir, and held it down and as a consequence, Sir, it didn't go off and I overslept, and I was late on board.' I hesitated, trying to keep a straight face. 'Case dismissed,' I said.

The First Lieutenant came to see me afterwards and said, 'You didn't believe that story, Sir, did you?' 'Of course I didn't,' I said, 'but it was a bloody good story.' 'It will go round the ship like wildfire,' said Number One, 'and we shall be seen to be guilty of letting this chap get away with it.' 'No, we shall not, Number One,' I said. 'We shall be guilty of having a sense of humour and being seen to have a sense of humour, and the whole Ship's Company will know it. It will do no harm at all and he will not be able to use that excuse again; he knows it, and next time he is for it.'

*   *   *   *   *

As my eyes became accustomed to the light I took my binoculars and trained them on the Russian ship. I checked the bearing of the Russian from the binnacle. He was, indeed, on a steady bearing, in other words, on a collision course. The first Phantom was running up on the port catapult ready for launch.

The Phantom was to be the last fixed-wing aircraft that the Royal Navy was to have in its inventory since the loss of the 'carrier battle' during the Healey Defence Review, and *Ark Royal* was the last aircraft carrier we possessed. The biggest aircraft carrier we possessed – indeed, the biggest ship we had ever had – and it was all mine. But these pilots who were flying this very sophisticated aircraft that night off a not too large deck, despite the fact that it was our largest ship, were doing so knowing that they would not be required any more after *Ark Royal* had finished its last commission. They were then to be expended. Not wanted any more. Yet night after night they and their contemporaries in the Buccaneer Squadron and the Gannet Squadron did their duty faithfully without regard for what lay ahead and the unsatisfactory way in which the whole event had been handled. I admired them, I felt responsible. As a Naval Aviator I was one of them.

What a strange breed Naval Aviators are, neither fish nor fowl really. At the end of the First World War the Royal Navy Air Service was the largest air force in the world. It had been responsible for the air defence of the United Kingdom, which is how Sub-Lieutenant Warneford won his VC, destroying the first Zeppelin. Logical, really; because the Navy was responsible for the sea defence of the United Kingdom so Naval Air must be responsible for the air defence! These early Naval Aviators had pioneered sea-borne aviation at great cost to themselves. A gallant band of men who started flying at their own expense in order to try to persuade Their Lordships of the value of air power at sea. *Campania*, a seaplane tender with a new forward flying off deck, although part of the Grand Fleet, failed to receive the sailing signal for Jutland. Having chased after the Fleet she was ordered back by Jellicoe because she had no escorts, and thus her air assets were never employed. It would appear that in the minds of the command, the risk to the ship sailing unescorted outweighed the enormous importance her aircraft could have had to the battle.

Engerdine, the other seaplane tender, sailed from Rosyth with Beatty and managed to fly one useful sortie which actually sighted the van of the German Fleet, which was reported to *Engerdine*. However, she could not communicate with the rest of the Fleet! These events seem to indicate that the value of air reconnaisance was neither appreciated nor understood. Find, Fix and Strike – the motto of Naval Aviation had not reached the C-in-C!

At the end of the war this vast Naval air armada was allowed to be taken away by Their Lordships to help form the Royal Air Force. I am certain that history has vindicated the formation of the Royal Air Force and I doubt whether the Battle of Britain would have been as successfully fought by the Navy as it was by this new, young and independent Air Force under the brilliant leadership of Dowding. Nevertheless, that is not the point; the point is that Their Lordships failed to realise the value of their tremendous asset.

The first Phantom was launched in a ball of fire. The Phantom went into after burner to be launched from the catapult of *Ark Royal*, and this on a dark night looked as though the whole aeroplane's back end was on fire. It certainly illuminated the darkness of the night! Surely there could be little doubt in the minds of the Russian shadower that we were launching aircraft? However, I decided to check that we were displaying the correct signals. 'Have we got the flying signals hoisted?' I asked. 'Yes, Sir.' 'Go outside, Yeoman, and check that they are burning brightly,' I said. He returned after a moment: 'Yes, Sir, they are burning brightly' – a rather old-fashioned term nowadays, but why change a term to be contemporary if it still served its purpose?

The Russian was still coming at us on a steady course. He was

7

closing on my starboard bow. As an operating aircraft carrier displaying the correct signals to indicate that I was operating aircraft I had the right of way, and the rule of the road was clear. Vessels having the right of way should hold their course and speed until a collision appears unavoidable, when they should then take such actions as might avoid it!

'Start flashing "Uniform" to him, yeoman,' I ordered. 'Uniform' in international code means 'You are standing into danger'.

The Russians had been harassing us for months. No more harassing, I suppose, than some of the other harassments I had had and those that were yet to come, but they were acting in the classic way of an emerging power, flexing their muscles so that we could see them. Trying to force us off course, making us climb down; arrogant, Teutonic, stupid, illegal, dangerous.

The second Phantom was now running up on the catapult. He reached full power, the front end of the flight deck illuminated by the afterburner. By now we were using the 20-inch signal lantern flashing the international code 'Uniform' which was illuminating the whole upper structure of the Russian ship, now clearly visible as a Kotlin Class destroyer, bearing down on to the starboard bow. How could the man not realise what he was doing? I stopped the launch. A frightening anticlimax for any pilot on the catapult at night. Having run up to full power and just waiting for the signal indicating that you are ready to go, by flashing your wing-tip lights, when suddenly you get the 'cross batons' and then the 'slow down' to cancel the launch. It is a tremendous let-down. You are geared up, the adrenaline has all been pumping round the system and you were ready to go. You are doing something which you know how to do but which you do not particularly relish doing! You have set your mind on it and have come to terms with it. You have expected it and now, suddenly, No! Why not? What was wrong? What had gone wrong? What if the catapult fired when you had throttled back; it had happened before – known as a 'cold shot' – and into the sea (the oggin, in naval slang) you would go. There was no way that the pilot on the catapult could have known what was wrong. No way the observer sitting in the back could have known what was wrong, although it might by now have been possible for him to see the top light of the Russian appearing over the edge of the flight deck on the starboard side. We weren't steaming that fast, it wasn't necessary in order to get the 35 knots of wind over the deck that we needed for launching the Phantom. There was a fair natural wind, and so we were steaming into it at about 20 knots. The Russian ship looked very large even when viewed from the bridge of the *Ark Royal*. It was coming at us at a good speed and was about to disappear under the flare of the starboard bow – I mean literally. Collision now looked unavoidable.

*   *   *   *   *

When we entered Leon Brittan's room it seemed to me to be packed; it probably wasn't, but anyway there were a large number of people there. The conference table, which was at the foot of his desk, was full. There was a place for me at the top, on the side from which I entered the door. Leon himself was sitting at the head of the table, at the foot of his desk. Those around the table, apart from the Private Secretary, were a whole range of officials, but not the Permanent Under-Secretary; he was away on a visit. I didn't recognise them all but I remember them now. Geoffrey went to perch on the radiator in front of the window facing me.

Leon opened the conversation in the somewhat naturally unctuous way that he has, thanking me for coming in to see him and saying that he wanted to explain to me the difficult position in which he was finding himself. He began by explaining that he was being put in some difficulty in the trade talks that were taking place with the Americans, particularly by the allegations that Airbus Industrie was being unfairly funded and supported by the partner governments, including the UK Government, against the principles of free trade, and contrary to GATT. He went on to say that he found the consortium of companies we were leading, that is to say Agusta, Aérospatiale, MBB, GEC and British Aerospace, as being hostile to the attempt by a US company – United Technologies – to take control of Westland and thus helping to solve the problems that Westland faced. He thought it very unwise for British Aerospace to be associated with such a team in view of its involvement in Airbus Industrie and the importance to the company of Airbus Industrie, and we should not be seen to be taking an anti-American stance.

I could scarcely believe my ears. I countered at once: 'I can't really understand how you or anybody else could think of me as leading an anti-American band, my whole family are Americans; I'm the only Brit in the family' (which was almost true at that time). 'I served for two years in the United States Navy and have a great affection for that country and you really are barking up the wrong tree. There is nothing anti-American in being pro-European, and if you believe that that is so then I really don't understand what we are trying to do. We have been encouraged by the Secretary of State for Defence to take a role in this matter of trying to save Westland, and it is not unnatural that our continental partners should expect the British to take the lead in negotiating what terms we can with Westland; after all, it is a British company.'

9

I did have some supporters! (© *The Daily Telegraph*)

'I think it is extremely unwise,' he went on to counsel. 'It puts me in an extremely difficult position.' 'I can't understand how it could put you in a difficult position,' I countered, 'the Government's policy is in favour of competition; that market forces should prevail; what we are doing is in accordance with that policy. There is nothing we are going to do that is anti-competitive, or designed to damage the British economy, or anybody else's economy for that matter.'

The officials, for the most part, remained silent, just looking at me occasionally, making notes. The Private Secretary was, of course, taking the record. Geoffrey said little or nothing. I continued, 'I find it

10

extraordinary that one great department of state should be urging us to do one thing and it would appear that the other great department of state is now urging us to do something else.' I explained that I had to get back, I had a Board meeting to attend which had been called to debate this very issue of our involvement in Westland, and I noted what he had to say. In truth I had noted it, but the impact of what he had said had not yet hit me. It did, however, as the meeting broke up.

As I started to get up to leave he leaned across to me and pointing a stubby finger in my direction said, 'You should withdraw.' His words hit me like a sledgehammer but I was already preparing to depart, others were rising or had risen from the table. He did not make the remark in an overly loud fashion but to me as the meeting was breaking up. '*You should withdraw*' – those words are engraved on my memory. I left the meeting and went to the lift, led by one of the secretaries, got into the lift, went down, got into my car and was driven back to Pall Mall. Slowly, the truth of what had happened dawned on me and I didn't like it. The more I thought of it the more I resented the way I had been treated. It was now my duty to report this matter to the Board. Whilst in the car and on the way to the Board meeting I tape-recorded the conversation we had had, and the events that had led up to it, so that the words and the situation should not be distorted by the passage of time. I had been alone – the Secretary of State had not!

The Board meeting was not an easy affair. Tin Pearce was not a strong Chairman; he preferred to rely on consensus, and some of the non-executive directors had become restless at the idea of our being involved in Westland without formal Board endorsement. As is often the case, events had moved very fast and it is not always possible for non-executive directors to be brought together at short notice, and sometimes it is difficult to keep them fully informed on every issue. This was the earliest opportunity we had had to bring them up to date. I sat opposite Harold Hitchcock who said subsequently, 'I've never seen a senior member of the Establishment so shattered by an experience as Ray has demonstrated tonight.' He proposed that I should receive the Board's full support. I had asked, with a touch of the melodramatic, I suppose, for the protection of the Board. I shall now try to explain how we had got into this mess – what the events were leading up to it. That night I telephone Geoffrey Pattie at home; the phone was answered by Tuëma, his wife, whom I knew quite well. 'Poor Ray,' she said, after recognising who it was, 'I understand you have had a difficult day.' 'You can say that again,' I replied, 'it was more than difficult, it was most unpleasant.' 'Oh dear, I am so sorry,' she said, 'did you wish to speak to Geoffrey?' 'Yes please,' said I, and Geoffrey came on the other end of the line. 'I really can't believe the

11

way I was treated by Leon Brittan today and the way in which the meeting was conducted; the things that were said, and to tell me that we should withdraw, were really outrageous.' Geoffrey remained silent and then, after a pause, said, 'I don't think you should make too much of it, Ray, he has boxed himself into a corner and he is doing what he believes to be right.'

'That is not the point,' I said, 'he may be doing what he thinks is right but it is not in accordance with good government/industry relations or commercial practice and, furthermore, I just don't believe that a Chief Executive of a major British company should be dealt with in this manner.' 'Oh, I shouldn't be too upset about it,' said he, 'I think you'll find it will all blow over.' 'Well, I don't think it will,' I said, 'I think it is more serious than that, Geoffrey.' 'What do you want me to do?' he said. 'Well, nothing really,' I replied, 'except to understand my position and how strongly we feel about this problem and how strongly the company and the Board feel about this matter; you should be aware of that.' 'All right,' said he, 'I take note of what you say.' And on this somewhat disinterested note the conversation was terminated and was never resumed.

It had all stated some months before. I had received a visit from John Treacher, who was then Deputy Chairman (I believe) of Westland, at my office in Pall Mall, just the two of us, at which he had said that Westland was in trouble. They needed an injection of capital to keep them going and they were looking for a partner who would be prepared to take up a substantial shareholding in the company, but not a controlling interest. He suggested something in a region of £20 million. I was not particularly enthusiastic. 'I can see', I said to him (as I said so often to people who came to us with offers like that) 'what it can do for you, but I cannot see really what it could do for us.' The reputation of Westland in the aerospace industry had never been high, and its attempts to go it alone and do things by itself had generally ended in failure. Its greatest successes had been when it had taken Sikorsky licences and added weapon systems developed by government establishments, as had been the case with the Sea King which had the Wessex 3 weapon system installed in it.

John persisted, however, and although I really had little sympathy for his case or for his request I said that I would discuss it with my colleagues. I did discuss it with Tin Pearce and Bernard Friend, the Finance Director, and we all agreed that it was something we should not do, nor even consider. In fact we took the view that, if Westland was in trouble and if it went belly-up, it was better to wait until that happened and then try to salvage some of the pieces. It was agreed that I should go to see the Permanent Under-Secretary and the Chief

12

of Defence Procurement to make clear to them that, if they were worried about the viability and support of helicopter programmes for the British services in the event of a collapse of Westland, then we would be prepared to step in and take over the responsibility. As I said to them, 'We could put the Westland helicopter operation in the corner of one of our hangars and hardly notice it was there.'

There the matter rested, although the turmoil at Westland continued, until some months later John Cuckney, who had taken over as Chairman, came to see Tin Pearce and me, accompanied by John Treacher, to make the same pitch. He said that the Company was in trouble but that it was a viable company, it could be saved, but it needed an injection of capital and some substantial backers, and he was looking for ways in which this could be achieved. We listened to him politely but he received the same answer that I had previously given to John Treacher. As he left he said to us, 'Well, I didn't expect anything more than tea and sympathy and that's what I've got.' That is how it was left until I came in one morning and was asked to go round to see our Chairman. When I got there, Bernard Friend was already in with him.

The previous night I had been invited to attend a parliamentary dinner at the House of Commons, organised by the Society of British Aerospace Companies, one of a series that were given from time to time for the aerospace industry in order to have a general discussion with interested Members of Parliament. I had not been able to go but Tin Pearce had and attended the dinner. Tin recounted how the dinner the evening before had gone. The Permanent Under-Secretary of the MOD had asked whether there were any companies interested in providing support for Westland in their present difficulties, since no one had volunteered. Tin Pearce had said that we might be prepared to put up some financial support. I exploded. 'You did what?' I asked. He repeated it, but said that he only meant a few million. 'Do you realise what you have done?' I asked him. Both he and Bernard looked surprised at my vehemence. 'You have now opened up the possibility of the Secretary of State being able to say that you are prepared to put money into Westland, and as a result I shall be sent for before this day is out; I shall be put up against the wall and told that, since the Chairman of British Aerospace is prepared to put up some money, can we come to some agreement on terms for this. Then I shall be told about all the other programmes that are of importance to British Aerospace which, of course, could be affected by our attitude to this. Putting it bluntly, I am going to be raped.' Both Bernard and Tin looked very surprised at this, but I was shattered. We had agreed that we would not get involved; we had no Board authority for getting

13

involved, and yet our Chairman had apparently given a commitment. Although Tin tried to pretend that it wasn't a commitment, I said, 'You just don't understand the jungle you are operating in.' I then left them in order to chair a meeting of my executive committee of management.

The executive committee of management for British Aerospace at that time consisted of the functional directors and the various heads of the individual plants and activities. It was a very experienced bunch of operators. I recounted briefly what had occurred and asked if there was anybody there who believed that we should get involved with Westland in any way, shape or form. They all shook their heads; no, we should not. I said that that was my view also, but nevertheless, in view of the statement that the Chairman had made the night before, it was going to be difficult, if not impossible, to back down. What we would have to do was to think of what compensation we could try to extract from the Ministry of Defence for any involvement. There are always issues that a large company has with the MOD that are generally to its disadvantage. There may be some argument abut payment of certain contracts or the terms of payment and, although these can be resolved by persistent discussion over a period of time, a favourable wind from the top of the MOD would sometimes help to clear these blockages without committing any impropriety, if it is merely a question of getting issues resolved quickly rather than through the lengthy bureaucratic processes that sometimes those at lower levels were content to use in order to protect their jobs. I told them what I had told the Chairman: that before the meeting was over I would be asked to go to see the Secretary of State for Defence, Michael Heseltine.

At eleven o'clock precisely my secretary came in and passed me a message which read, 'The Secretary of State has asked whether it would be possible for you to pop in and see him sometimes this morning, preferably as soon as possible.' I said that I would go as soon as I was able.

At first Michael Heseltine, the Secretary of State for Defence, had been, as I understood it, hesitant about the value of trying to save Westland. If Westland couldn't survive then let it go to the wall and have its affairs picked up by somebody else: 'We are not in the business of saving lame ducks,' etc. During the course of events, however, and his increasing involvement in European defence projects, he had come to change his mind and now believed that the way ahead would be for a European helicopter industry, much as he believed in many other European ventures. He was therefore promoting the idea of a European venture, but we had stayed absolutely clear of it and I wanted nothing to do with it – I could see nothing but trouble. Our belief, quite simply, was that the future of Westland lay inside British Aerospace but not at the kind of premium prices that were being discussed. Michael, however, had become more and more enthusiastic about the idea of trying to create a European industry and saw, I think, that his relations with his European counterparts in other programmes, notably the European fighter aircraft (EFA) project, would be more difficult if he were seen to lack support for this initiative.

As far as the motives of the continental Europeans were concerned, the motives of Aérospatiale as a prime mover were, of course, very straightforward. They did not wish to see Westland fall into the hands of a US manufacture; they wanted to see Westland as a passive or neutral part of a European helicopter industry in which they would be in the lead. They also thought that there was a possibility of getting the British Government to join the programme for the support helicopter that they were engaged in with MBB for the German and French services; their motivation was quite clear. MBB was there for the ride. Agusta, on the other hand, had a long relationship with Westland and, of course, with Sikorsky, and saw that their position would be strengthened by being part of a European industry. However, Michael wasn't getting anywhere with this pitch because, without a British company to lead the bandwagon, not much could happen. This formed the background for the meeting that morning.

*   *   *   *   *

We were now sounding the letter 'U' on the ship's siren. A fairly dreadful sound on a still night from a large ship, and by now the Russian was so close that there could be no doubt in his mind, if indeed he had a mind or he knew what was happening, that he was going to collide with *Ark Royal*. I proceeded to obey rule 49 of the rules for the prevention of collision at sea and went half astern both engines, and as the Russian disappeared from sight under the starboard bow I went full astern. The astern power of a warship is much greater than a comparable merchantman, and therefore when you go full astern the ship really comes up all standing. Unbeknown to me it was a dining-in night in the wardroom that evening – I say unbeknown because I may have been told about it but it hadn't registered very much with me as it was a routine affair. The wardroom was situated in the stern of the ship, low down, directly over the propellers, and when the engines were put to full astern the whole back end of the ship vibrated violently! Glasses and silver were soon leaving the tables and so were the officers attending, realising that something very serious was afoot.

I put the ship to collision stations and waited. As the klaxon sounded the ship came to a halt and I went out on to the side of the bridge and dropped overboard some bits of broomstick called 'Dutch logs'. (These are dropped down on to the surface of the sea and an Aldis lamp shone on them. If the pieces of wood are sitting stationary alongside the ship then you are stopped!) We were stopped! At that moment the Kotlin hit us.

It was customary at that time to have a plane guard destroyer when you were operating aircraft at night in order to be there in case an aircraft ditched. The correct station for the plane guard destroyer when aircraft were being launched was on the port quarter of the carrier. My consort, *HMS Yarmouth*, had been watching the events with some considerable surprise and, of course, they saw the Russian ship disappear under the bulk of the *Ark Royal*. The next thing he saw, or I saw, was the Russian emerging from under my bow, keeled right over on his starboard side by the force of the collision, coming back down the port side of *Ark Royal*, having struck my starboard anchor with his missile housing. His propeller guard had taken a piece out of the stem of *Ark Royal*, which had keeled him right over, and 13 seamen, who for some unknown reason were on his quarterdeck, were thrown into the sea. All this had put him on a collision course with the escorting destroyer, which took immediate evading action.

Suddenly, all was calm except for the hiss of steam from the Kotlin. Steam and smoke were belching from her and I thought she was on fire. My Commander appeared on the Bridge, having come from the wardroom aft. He was quickly appraised of the situation and told to get boats away to look for survivors and to prepare to provide any other support the Russian might need. Commander Air was already up in FLYCO for night flying and I ordered him to get the helicopters ready to provide assistance. I had one Russian interpreter on board, Sub Lt Philip Broom, who was the assistant secretary. I sent for him and briefed him that he was to get into a boat and make his way over to the Russian ship to see whether we could render any assistance.

The flight deck of *Ark Royal* was now fully illuminated and alive with action as helicopters were being brought up in readiness to survey the area. Boats were being lowered and, of course, the ship's company was agog to find out what had happened. I said to the signal officer, who had also appeared on the Bridge, 'Make a flash signal to the Admiralty saying that I have been in collision with the Kotlin. Give the position of the ship and say that a further report will follow.' You

16

can imagine the consternation that arose when this reached the Admiralty and the Commander-in-Chief!

I now sent the Commander forward with the Shipwright Officer to assess any damage that we might have sustained. The answer came back that there was a hole in the ship's stem just about two feet above the waterline that was not letting in water but would if we got underway again. Therefore they were proposing to put a 'coffer dam' or cement box over the hole to plug it until such time as we could make proper repairs in Malta. This was the only visible damage, and I was then able to send an amplifying report saying that the Kotlin was stopped in the water emitting smoke and steam but that I had suffered only minor damage, and that we were investigating and remaining in the area.

The Russian had by this time lowered one boat. It was under oars, having three oars on one side and two on the other, thus it went round in an ever diminishing circle until it finally went back and was hoisted. That was the Russians' total contribution to the search for any survivors which might result from the 13 men he had lost overboard. Of

How close can you get?
The shadower taking a close look the day before the collision

17

course, at this time we didn't know that he had lost 13 men, or that 13 men had gone overboard, and it was not until the Sub Lieutenant reached the Kotlin and tried to board that we began to understand what the problem was. He was met at the gangway by the political commissar; the Captain came running down later. He subsequently passed me a message saying that he had had 13 men working on the quarterdeck and that they had all gone over the side at the time of the collision. The next sentence, translated literally by the interpreter, was, 'He pleads with you with all his heart, please do not leave him.' I said that we had no intention of leaving him and to tell him so and ask if he wanted any assistance – firefighting equipment or generators, or men to come and help – just let me know what he wanted, and in the meantime we would mount a massive search for any survivors.

It was about this time that I got a message from one of the boats which said, 'We have found a Russian, Sir, in the water, but he will not get into the boat.' This, to me, was the most staggering moment of the whole, rather trying, episode. Here we were, miles south of Crete,

The first Phantom to be launched from *Ark Royal*

18

on a black night and in a black sea, and this young man who had been doing something, God knows what, on the quarterdeck of his ship – perhaps he was under punishment – suddenly, without warning, finds himself in the sea. Here he was swimming about and a boat comes up, but instead of being grateful he refuses to get in! What kind of people did they believe we were? What kind of animals did he think existed in our ships? If it had happened to me and a boat manned by gorillas had come along, I'd have been grateful to get in! Why had the Captain pleaded with all his heart that I should stay? Was it conceivable that the common law of seamen's behaviour would induce me to do anything else? I thought for a moment and then said, 'Tell him to wait until the chap is exhausted and then heave him in, whether he likes or not.' This duly occurred – he was pulled into the boat and brought back to the ship.

My Sub Lieutenant subsequently told me that as survivors were picked up and brought back they were counted back on to the ship's books, and it was quite clear that any survivors that we had taken into *Ark Royal* would still be counted as missing until they were actually returned on board. So, having given our survivors new clothes and some hot beverage, and checked that they were not injured, I decided that they should be returned to their ship as quickly as possible. None of them would give more than their name, rank and number, and would not tell us the name of their ship or its number, even though the number was clearly visible on the side of the ship, which was only a couple of cables away from us. One young man from east of the Urals was a nice farm-boy and we finally elicited from him that he had been a tractor-driver before he joined the navy and had joined up because it was a duty to his Mother Country. We dressed them in clean, dry clothes and despatched them back. Then an amazing thing happened. As they were returned on board they were stripped of all the clothes we had given them; these were taken away, presumably so that no one could make a comparison as to the quality, and nobody could see that we had acted in a compassionate way. What I didn't know was that the wet clothes of the survivors had been put into aircrew bags, and with the usual sense of humour that our sailors exhibit at all times they had attached 'Fly Navy' stickers to them!

By now the engine-room telephone was ringing and I knew what it would be. Chief, Commander Guy Crowden, who had gone down to the engine room when I had rung down 'full astern', said to me, 'I'll have to start turning the engines fairly soon because the turbine temperatures are rising very steeply.' One of the problems of stopping a steam-powered ship from relatively high power is that there is nowhere for the spare heat to go in the turbines unless they are kept

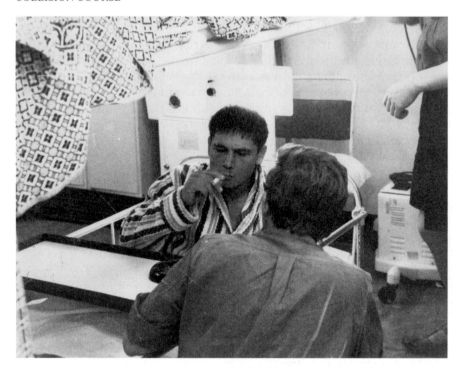

Russian survivor in *Ark Royal* Sick Bay

turning. This meant that I had to turn the engines and then the propellers and start getting under way. I therefore passed a message to the Russian, saying, 'In order to keep my turbines cool I shall have to slowly circle you, but I am not leaving.' The difficulty which the Sub Lieutenant had in translating some of these technical terms, he told me later, was tremendous.

Helicopters were now circling the area with searchlights, and we had four boats away looking for survivors. As I have said, the Russian contribution was one under oars. It became clear to us, after an hour or so, that the helicopter contribution was not perhaps as great as it might have been because of the noise they were making. On a still night at sea probably one of the best ways of finding somebody is to hear them calling, and when there is an enormous din of helicopters flying around, of course nobody could hear anything. I therefore decided to recall the helicopters and just leave it to the boats to lay about, shouting out in the stillness to try to hear any replies.

During the course of this episode the Commander had detailed off a young Sub Lieutenant with instructions to 'Write down everything the Captain says.' I didn't know that he had been told this, but every time I turned round on the darkened bridge I saw this young man with his pencil poised and his pad at the ready. Finally I asked him, 'What are you doing, sub?' 'I've been told by the Commander to write down everything you say.' 'Well, you can forget it,' I said; 'If you don't, you will get in my way and hear some language I doubt you'll be able to record. So forget it.' I then settled down to write a despatch to the Admiralty giving further details of what had happened and a brief outline of events. This was completed by about midnight.

We began to wonder where the Kotlin would have entered the side of *Ark Royal* had I not gone full astern. It was very clear that she would have gone in about 100 feet aft of the bow, straight into a Petty Officers' Messdeck which was full at the time. The carnage and destruction that could have resulted had we not taken action was clear for everyone to see. The danger of the kind of manoeuvres the Russians had been undertaking in harassing and shadowing us must now be clear to the whole world. It was a sobering experience. I turned over and over in my mind why he had acted in this way, and I could only conclude that it may have been that, at the same time as I was having my frugal supper on the bridge, the Captain of the Kotlin may have gone off the Bridge somewhere to have his supper and an inexperienced officer of the watch had not realised what was happening and had somehow become mesmerised by events. I could not believe that it was a deliberate act, but only that it could have been the act of someone who had very little experience. There was no way they could win in a confrontation with *Ark Royal*, so it couldn't have been deliberate! It must have been accidental, but caused by a history of shadowing and harassing that was becoming all too common and was bound to end in tragedy.

In order to mitigate or to reduce the damage that might result from a misunderstanding in similar circumstances, the United States Navy had recently instructed its ships to open up a dialogue with the Russians to make sure that each side knew what the other was doing. We, quite rightly, had refused to follow suit. The rules of the road for the prevention of collisions at sea were perfectly clear; if the Russians wished to abide by those rules then there would be no collisions; if they wished to disobey them then there might be. To suddenly open up a dialogue would mean that you were about to compromise the rules of the road, the law of the sea. In my view that was totally unacceptable, and I would never have agreed to it whatever our politicians might have thought.

My mind now started to prepare me for the inevitable Board of

21

After the collision. You can just see the nick in the stem

Enquiry. To this extent it was important that I understood what the chart of the escorting destroyer showed, as well as our own chart which showed quite clearly that after we had turned on to the flying course the Russian had altered course. If she had stayed on her original course and speed she would have passed clear astern. Imagine my relief when the Captain of HMS *Yarmouth*, Cdr Nichol, came over with his charts, which showed an exact replica of the tracks that we had obtained ourselves.

By now it was getting light and it was fairly clear that we were not going to find any more survivors, but we continued to look and, as we looked, every Russian warship in the Mediterranean began to converge on this particular point: cruisers, destroyers and, I have no doubt, submarines were in the vicinity. It was an interesting position to be in – the honeypot to which the whole of the Russian Mediterranean fleet was approaching.

I had instructed our escorting destroyer to stop engines at the place

22

One of the best cartoons (© *The Sun*)

where the collision occurred and, having taken a careful fix, to just allow herself to drift in the current. This, of course, meant that she was in the sea position of the collision at dawn, and we could actually carry out a search in the area where survivors were most likely to be present. Regrettably, there were none, and the Russians have never, to my knowledge, reported how many were lost. I calculate that there must have been five or seven young men who gave their lives because of a rather stupid policy decision to flex muscles in the face of potential adversaries.

When dawn broke it was clear to see that the aft missile housing on the Kotlin had been badly damaged. How badly it was difficult to say, because they had drawn a great canvas all over it and, although we had helicopters filming and photographing the extent of the damage, it was impossible to see what lay inside the missile housing. What was more clear was the fact that *Ark Royal*'s starboard anchor had had its paint chipped off and this was the point which had hit the housing! She couldn't have hit a stronger point if she had tried, and it was also clear that it was her propeller guard that had nicked the stem of *Ark Royal*. I have the piece that was subsequently cut off mounted on teak in my study to this day. The shipwrights had waggishly inscribed it, 'Creation Sam Kotlin'.

The Kotlin with canvas over the damage

*　　*　　*　　*　　*

Michael Heseltine was positively beaming. He opened up by saying that he was pleased to learn that we were prepared to help in saving Westland, and that he had now been in touch with Arnold Weinstock at GEC and that they were prepared to come in as well. I told him quite frankly that I was not a supporter of the idea and that, though the Chairman had said we might be prepared to make some financial contribution or assistance, he had not spelt this out and we still had to talk to our Board in order to get approval. He seemed to take all this for granted, and went on to say how helpful it would be in relation to the discussions that were taking place on the EFA, if we were seen to be acting in a genuine European fashion in other areas.

It was very important for British Aerospace to obtain the support of the MOD in moving forward its plans for a new-generation fighter for NATO/European air forces. It was the central plank in the strategy of our military aircraft division and one of immense importance for the company. To have had a Secretary of State for Defence, therefore, to whom we had not offered support when he needed it, would have been bad news. I said that we would need to discuss matters with our continental partners and to establish what, if anything, we could do. He said he was delighted that we had come forward and that we would stay in touch. Clive Whitmore, the Permanent Under-Secretary, was present, and I said to the Secretary of State, in front of Clive, 'I shall now go outside and talk to your Permanent Under-Secretary about ways in which you can help us, we having agreed to help you, and Clive will know what I mean by that.' Outside, I outlined to Clive several areas in which the company would welcome MOD support, and he agreed that they would look sympathetically at those issues that I had raised without, of course, any commitment, which he could not give.

When I got back to my office I rank Cuckney and asked him what the situation with Westland now was with regard to the approach he had made to us, and said that I had been asked to go to see the Secretary of State. I didn't explain why, but I thought it was to do with Westland and how did the situation stand? He said that it was very interesting and that they had some substantial offers from other sources and there was nothing more he could tell me.

The next thing to do was to discuss what it was our colleagues on the continent were prepared to do and how far they were prepared to go. A meeting was therefore called of the executives of Aérospatiale, MBB and Agusta, together with GEC. It transpired that Aérospatiale had already involved Lloyds Financial Services in the undertaking to look at their involvement and, although this was not the strongest financial support that we could normally have expected to bring to bear, since they were already there, we proceeded to work through them. It didn't take long to put together a package in which the percentage share of each of the partners was agreed, but our involvement, of course, was always subject to board approval which we still did not have, although Tin had been trying to keep the non-executive directors informed of what was going on.

At this point Alan Bristow arrived on the scene. He had started Bristow Helicopters after leaving Westland, and had developed the most successful independent helicopter operation probably in Europe, if not in the world. He had sold his interest and was now no longer associated with the company which bore his name but had, it subsequently appeared, tried to get involved in Westland at an earlier stage. He came to see me in Pall Mall, introduced by Alan Curtis, and we met for the first time. We got on well together and there was no difficulty in our communicating. He told me of his previous involvement in Westland and of his attempt to gain control and of some curious things that had occurred at that time, and that he would be interested in joining the consortium in some way. He certainly held no brief for the existing management.

It occurred to me that with his drive, determination and knowledge of the helicopter business he could make, potentially, a good Chairman of the company should we acquire control. Furthermore, he was prepared to put in money to back up his own desire to see Westland Helicopters come under better and stronger management and financial control.

It was now time to seek a meeting with John Cuckney and his Board to try to establish what it was that they would find acceptable and how we might be able to come together. Arnold Weinstock, Malcolm Bates (I believe), Tin Pearce and I therefore sought a meeting and obtained one with John Cuckney at the Westland headquarters in Carlton House Terrace. It was a strange meeting, or to me it was strange, in that there was very little dialogue. John Cuckney's line was simple and in retrospect correct. It was that they had had an offer from Sikorsky to pick up shares in Westland, or Sikorsky had bought some shares, and he wanted to know what offer we were prepared to make. We, on the other hand, were merely there to establish what the prospects for Westland might be and how we could become involved. Treacher was with John Cuckney, as was another non-executive director, and the most important statement they made was that, as a result of the involvement with Sikorsky, they would be able to make sales of Blackhawk helicopters that they would manufacture under licence.

26

I wanted to know where these sales might be, but there was no answer to that. I pointed out that the MOD had said that they had no requirement for such a helicopter and therefore it couldn't be through the MOD. I was told that, nevertheless, they had large orders in view and this would enable Westland to become much more profitable in a relatively short space of time. This was the deal that the association with Sikorsky produced, and what did we have to offer? We said that our only offer was to retain the independence of Westland within a European future. John Cuckney then went on to say that Sikorsky had offered a package of work to Westland which was necessary in order to keep the company in business, and could we do likewise? We said that we would examine this with our partners and would come back to him.

As we left the meeting and went down the stairs, Arnold expressed the view that we had now got to start looking seriously at how to acquire shares in Westland in order to have any effect on the outcome. It was also agreed between Tin and Arnold that I should be the chap who would lead the team and present our views both to the City and to the Press.

We called our first briefing for the Press. There was a large turnout because the event was already attracting considerable interest. The representatives of Aérospatiale, GEC and Agusta were ranged up on the stage with me in the middle, flanked by our merchant bank advisers. I took the opportunity to introduce my partners and to say that British Aerospace was leading the consortium approach to Westland, and to outline the strength of each of the companies and what they could bring to Westland and how the consortium would provide for Westland a secure and independent future within a European package. I was asked whether I was aware that Sikorsky was already involved with the company and was likely to want to become further involved, and was this not likely to lead to competition? I replied that we were all in favour of competition and didn't mind it at all. If that is what the Government wanted in relation to helping Westland, we would participate and relish the competition itself.

The more I thought about the proposal the more I began to believe that it could be viable; that we, in conjunction with Aérospatiale, Agusta and MBB could actually involve Westland in a European collaborative venture that would yield long-term security for Westland and give it some work in the shorter term, but there was one considerable fly in this particular ointment. It was clear that Westland had a great suspicion of Aérospatiale's intentions and Aérospatiale's word. They had, in their own view, been seen off by Aérospatiale unfairly in previous ventures and were reluctant to place any reliance on them. This was most vocally expressed by John Treacher, who was very much in favour of US collaboration as opposed to collaboration with the French. He had, in a previous existence, been the champion of the sub-launched Harpoon for the submarines of the Royal Navy and backed it against the proposal that British Aerospace had made, together with Matra, for an Anglo-French weapon. It was natural, therefore, that he should look with disfavour upon the intervention of a European consortium at this time, especially one including Aérospatiale.

We sought another meeting with John Cuckney, and this was even shorter and more to the point than the other. He merely asked one question: 'What offer are you making for Westland? If you have an offer to make for Westland tell me what it is, otherwise we are wasting our time.' Of course, we had no desire to make a complete offer for Westland but wanted to secure a substantial shareholding which we could then enlarge as time passed. This was not acceptable to him and he made it very clear to us that he was interested in nothing other than a firm offer of money for the whole company. It now came down to who was going to be able to pick up enough shares to outbid the other, and we authorised Lloyds Financial Services to go into the market to pick up shares.

During this period there was an extraordinary meeting which took place at Stanhope Gate, which amused me no end. It was the first time that Tin Pearce had actually seen Arnold in action, and the meeting was with Jim Prior, Arnold, Malcolm Bates, Tin Pearce, Bernard Friend and myself. Arnold's style of conducting business was always amusing to me – very sharp and astute – but his ability to go into side issues without detracting from his concentration on the main one was extremely confusing to Tin. At one stage Arnold had asked for a list of shareholders in Westland and Malcolm Bates had produced an enormous volume which Arnold proceeded to flip through, page by page. Tin just could not believe this. The meeting had a rather inconclusive outcome, except to say that we should go on trying to pick up shares. Tin said, after we had left the meeting, 'I really don't understand that chap at all.' They were totally unalike as potential partners, not the easiest problem for me to resolve, who worked for one and admired the other!

The political temperature was now beginning to heat up. The press was taking a keen interest in what was going on, but it still seemed to me that if market forces prevailed then no harm would come of it. Bernard Friend and I then began to visit various institutional holders of shares in Westland in order to convince them that committing to the European solution would be in the best interest of their share-holders. We went to the Pearl and also to the Prudential, which enabled me to say to Bernard, as we got out of our chauffeur-driven car in Holborn and walked in the front entrance, 'This is the first time I have been in the front entrance of the Pru. When I used to work here, before the war, I was only allowed in the back entrance!'

Most listened carefully to what we had to say but, to the question of which way they would vote on the future direction of Westland they were, for the most part, non-committal. Not so United Scientific Holdings, whose Chairman was the former Permanent Under-Secretary of the MOD, Sir Frank Cooper. It had shares in Westland and was fully committed to the European solution, and so was easy to convince that ours was the right option.

About this time we sought another meeting with Michael Heseltine at which Arnold, Tin and myself were present. Michael was really quite upset. He told us that his endeavour to rationalise this part of the industry and to come to a European solution was being blocked and he was having great difficulty with his colleagues. He was clearly very concerned about it, so much so that Arnold, quite astutely, said to him, 'I do hope that you are not considering this to be an issue over which you would resign.' Michael didn't answer directly, but said that we had no idea of the kinds of things that were going on, and if any of this came out it would be incredible. Arnold reminded him of the consequences that would fall to those he left behind, and that it would not be good for us should he resign because we had now got ourselves committed to this programme. We left on that note. Soon after this, my fateful meeting with Leon Brittan took place.

*   *   *   *   *

At about midday, after the collision, I signalled to the Admiralty my intention of leaving the scene and of leaving our destroyer behind, stopped and drifting, so that insofar as was possible she would remain in the same position as the collision. I set course for Malta and started to prepare myself for the inevitable Board of Enquiry. I had received a message from the Commander-in-Chief of the Fleet stating that such a Board was to be set up to look into the event when the ship arrived in Malta, and that the President of the Board would be Captain Peter Scott who was then Captain of HMS *Fife*, a guided-missile destroyer. Peter Scott was an old submariner friend of mine whom I had known for many years, and as we proceeded towards Malta he overtook us from astern with his destroyer escort and requested permission to join my task force for replenishment from the tanker we had with us. In

HE SAYS HE'S SORRY SIR! BUT HE HAS NOTHING SMALLER THAN A TEN ROUBLE NOTE!

Cartoon in *Noah's News*, the ship's newspaper

my reply I said, 'Anything for you, Mr President,' and he duly replenished and departed ahead of us for Malta.

As flying had been cancelled in order to make our original ETA, we had sufficient time in hand before we were due to arrive in Malta to start a boiler clean while still at sea. This was a procedure that had been started some years before in ships with multiple boiler capacity so that the rather dirty job of cleaning boilers could be done at sea instead of in harbour which, of course, affected the ability of giving leave to the engine-room staff. It meant that we would close down one engine rom and the two associated boilers would be cleaned. It also meant, of course, that it reduced our top speed of over 30 knots down to 24 knots.

The *Fife* and its escort of destroyers had disappeared long before and the sun was setting when I became involved in the second flash signal in 48 hours. It was from *Fife*: 'Flash. Am on fire in position blank.' I was stunned. What on earth had gone wrong? Had he been in a collision? Her position was, of course, dead ahead some 60 miles or so. We immediately brought the Sea King helicopters to readiness and I asked Peter Scott what it was he most required. The answer was simple – fire-fighting foam. It was fortunate that he had an aircraft carrier close to him because no ship carries more fire-fighting foam than an aircraft carrier. I sent for the Sea King Squadron Commander, Lt. Hallett, and told him of the problem, and that we would now have to start ferrying foam over to the *Fife* which was way over the horizon. I asked about the clearance for operating the Sea King off the deck of a County Class destroyer at night and he said it was not cleared but that, in his opinion, in view of the emergency, there would be enough room to operate safely.

We then started one of the biggest foam lifts in the history of fire-fighting. Because of the boiler clean, of course, I was unable to ring on more than 24 knots; we were proceeding towards the scene of the fire as fast as we could but it was clear that it was going to take us something in the order of two to three hours before we got there. As we got closer Peter signalled that if the temperature in *Fife*'s magazines got any higher as a result of the fire he would have to start launching his Sea Slug missiles in order to get them clear of the magazines. This was the official way of clearing the rounds in the event of fire in the magazine. I was asked to keep his stern clear of all shipping when I arrived. It was a great testimony to Peter's sense of humour that, as I had him in sight, he flashed up to me, 'Good evening, Mr President,' accurately foreseeing that he now would be the subject of his own Board of Enquiry!

It was some hours before *Fife* got the fire under control and, although the temperature in the magazine, I understand, had reached within one or two degrees of the limit at which he would have had to start discharging his Sea Slug missiles, they managed to get it under control and keep the temperature within bounds so that that eventuality was not required. What a staggering evening, and what an excellent job those Sea Kings of 824 did that evening.

Our arrival in Malta was bound to have been well reported, and entry into harbour of a capital ship was always a stimulating experience. As you pass through the breakwaters into that super Grand Harbour, the buildings rise up all round you, many of them naval establishments, standing out clearly against the general background of Malta with its church spires and its steep streets leading away from the harbour up to the top of the hills that surround it. A stirring and spectacular occasion; the Royal Marine band playing on the flight deck and the ship's company drawn up for entering harbour.

The ship looked as smart as it could look after a period at sea and, on this occasion, was an object of curiosity from all the locals to see what the damage had been. The news of the collision had been flashed around the world and carried in most of the world's newspapers. It had made a particular impact on our own newspapers at home which had, I am glad to say, all reacted in a favourable way and in a way which reflected no criticism on the conduct of *Ark Royal*. For this I was very grateful although, at the moment of entering Grand Harbour, I was not aware of the details of this, but just that my public relations officer was able to report to me, that from a preliminary look at the newspapers which had been flown out to us as we approached Malta, we had received a favourable coverage in the UK Press. It always seems to me that, more often than not, entering harbour is not as straightforward an affair as you would like to believe. The winds and sea conditions around the British Isles, particularly in winter, are well known, but of course it could hardly be avoided, that the climax to our arrival should be the tail-end of a *gregale*, a wind that blows fiercely around Malta at that time of the year. It meant that the limits for entering, as far as a large ship was concerned, were being breached by my coming in and I could have been justified in waiting outside until the wind had abated. It is, however, always the case that there is so much hanging on the programme that the Captain is under enormous pressure to bring the ship in even if the limits are going to be exceeded. This was no exception and my nerves, which were not exactly settled after the events of the previous two evenings, were to be tested once again on this particular occasion. The problem was the entry itself; once you are inside Grand Harbour the whole anchorage was well protected from the wind, although eddies and currents blowing around the houses sometimes made it difficult.

Anyway, we entered, with the band's music echoing back to us from the steeply rising battlement of that truly named Grand Harbour, with a great crowd lining the galleries to cheer us in, well-wishers, families and friends. The ship had arranged that, for this period of self-mainte-nance in Malta, a number of the wives and girlfriends of the ship's company were coming out to spend some time with their loved ones. This arrangement, which was usually done through a package tour operator, had proved to be extremely good in helping to keep up morale in the ship, as well as in the families, so it was natural that they should be relieved to see their loved ones entering safely in a ship which had been in 'Collision with a Russian Warship' but only had a slight nick in the stem! One of the first vessels to come out was the Queen's Harbourmaster's launch in which was my Admiral, John Treacher – strange how some names keep cropping up. He took a close look at the bow as we turned and came into our berth and, after I had secured to the buoy for capital ships, just off the entrance to Dockyard Creek, he came on board.

We had known each other, John and I, for many years and had served together as Lieutenants when we first met at the Naval Air

Fighter School at Culdrose. I had followed him in some appointments although we had not actually served together until he became my Admiral as Flag Officer Aircraft Carriers and Amphibious Ships, and therefore had responsibility for *Ark Royal*. I outlined to him the events of the two previous evenings, and then it was time for the press conference which had been called to make clear what the story really was. We held it in the wardroom of *Ark Royal* and a large number of press assembled. I gave an unexpurgated account of what had happened in language that I hoped the Press would understand. There is no point, in my view, of hiding your light under a bushel when it came to dealing with the Press; it was best to be as clear and straightforward as possible and to give them information in a way which they could use it, hopefully, to your advantage.

It must have been quite an interesting episode for them and as we left John Treacher turned to me and said, 'So much for the Board of Enquiry, you have just dealt with it!' By this, of course, he meant that if we received the kind of publicity and favourable comment from the Press that we hoped for, then the Board of Enquiry would merely cover some of the same ground with a result which could be reasonably predicted. I was less certain. I was concerned. I knew from bitter experience, and nothing has changed my views since, that there is a tendency for us to be critical of the actions of someone whom we think might have failed, even though it is by no means certain that he or she has. It is a tendency all too prevalent in our society at the present time. This is particularly so if the person has always lived dangerously – by taking chances and acting in a way that people could criticise as being, perhaps, too bold, too aggressive. Or if you had been sharp in some of your remarks, no matter how genuine and justified they may have been, then there were bound to be people who would see this as an opportunity to rub your nose in it.

The rules for the conduct of Boards of Enquiry had only recently been changed to allow the officer whose conduct was being investigated to be present and not just to appear as a witness – that is to say, if he wished to be present. I elected to be present and duly sat through the Board of Enquiry which, of course, had to be conducted under the chairmanship of a different officer since Peter Scott had problems of his own.

*   *   *   *   *

The question of getting Board approval for us to participate in any buying of shares of Westland was not going to be easy, because the Board of British Aerospace was taking a particularly cautious view of this event and it was difficult to see how we were going to get any authority to go any further. The events of my involvement with Leon Brittan, of course, and the Board meeting which followed, left the Board with little appetite to pursue the matter. The Board, furthermore, said that I should no longer lead the consortium and that British Aerospace should take a back seat. This was extremely difficult for our continental partners because it meant that one of them would have to take the lead in an essentially British undertaking. Much as I argued that we should continue to take the lead, although perhaps not with such a high profile, this was not supported by my colleagues and I was quite clearly told that British Aerospace should keep a low profile. Having discussed this among ourselves it was clear that the merchant bank would have to take the lead, with us supporting them as necessary. Unfortunately, this was not the best way to conduct the campaign on which we had embarked, as I have explained, by accident. We had fallen between the two stools of two Secretaries of State who were promoting opposite views.

Events in relation to the European Fighter Programme were steadily moving ahead, and I was required to attend an important meeting in Germany at the headquarters of MBB to discuss the progress that we were making and about the approaches we should be making to our respective governments. This was a tri-nation meeting. I flew over to Munich in a British Aerospace 125, and as we landed in Munich the co-pilot came back to me and said, 'It has just been passed to us from Hatfield, Sir, that Michael Heseltine has resigned.' I was dumbfounded. Although we had feared that this might happen it was something that none of us who were involved would have wished to happen. He was proving to be a good and successful Secretary of State for Defence, he had established good working relationships with industry and our continental partners, and it was a blow to see him go. Worse was to come.

It wasn't until I got back that evening that I was able to read the statement he had made after his resignation, in which he said that the final blow had come when he had been told that the Chief Executive of British Aerospace had been told by Leon Brittan that British Aerospace should withdraw. He thus used words which in fact were not entirely accurate. What had been said to me was, '**YOU** should withdraw.' Michael had translated this as meaning, not unreasonably, that British Aerospace should withdraw. Quite clearly the crisis had deepened and we, British Aerospace, and I, Lygo, were right in the middle of it. I rang Clive Whitmore at home that evening because I needed to know how the Secretary of State had been informed of what had transpired the night before, at my interview with Leon Brittan. I

34

had spoken to only two people, apart from my colleagues on the Board, when I returned that evening from the DTI; one was Clive Whitmore to inform him of what I had been told, because it was quite clearly a matter of some importance to his department, and the other was Arnold Weinstock, our partner in the enterprise. It was clear that the information to the Secretary of State must have come from the Permanent Under-Secretary, and Clive confirmed that this was the case. He had called and told him what had transpired, but of course the exact words used in transmitting messages sometimes gets blurred. The inference, of course, was that I had deliberately blown the whistle on Leon Brittan. In fact, the thing was developing like some Greek tragedy with events over which the players seem to have little control. The fat was really on the fire!

We did not know what the Prime Minister's view would be, and it was therefore decided that the chairman should write to the Prime Minister outlining what had happened and seeking some guidance as to which way the company was supposed to be proceeding. A letter was drafted, Tin signed it and it was hand-delivered to Downing Street. To our consternation we were told that the Prime Minister's office had decided that the letter would have to be published. I really felt that this could not do anything to help the situation, only make it worse and be extremely embarrassing for the Government. I therefore rang Charles Powell in the Cabinet Office to ask whether it really was essential that the letter, which had been marked 'Confidential', should be made public. He said the view was that it would have to be made public and therefore it was.

The howl in the Press now rose to a crescendo, and in a conversation with Arnold, he said that matters looked extremely grave for the Government and that the matter could well cause the Government to fall. I was shocked beyond belief. I had always been and continued to be a strong supporter of the Government and what it was doing to sort out the sorry state of British industrial relations and create a new environment in which business could thrive. The thought of all this being set back was more than I could stand. Leon Brittan, meantime, denied that he had ever said that British Aerospace should withdraw. I was standing by my guns but, of course, we were not doing anything to make the situation worse – it was bad enough already.

About this time an old friend of mine, Michael Marshall, the Member of Parliament for Arundel, who had been abroad, returned to the UK to read of all the events that had transpired and got on the phone to me to ask for a meeting to say, 'Really, Ray, I cannot believe that we have got ourselves into this situation.' I, of course, told him that neither could I; it wasn't a situation of my making, but that

A very small sample of the press coverage of the Westland Affair

Another small sample of the press coverage of the collision

didn't improve matters. As a result of this meeting and the consternation that the whole episode was causing with Government, I decided that with my colleagues' help we should try to find a way of mitigating, or limiting, the damage by doing a damage-control exercise, in Naval terms, to get ourselves clear of this embarrassing situation which certainly was not going to do any good for British Aerospace or its shareholders.

As a result of conversations with Michael, it was decided that he should arrange for a meeting to take place between representatives of Leon Brittan and me to see if we could find some way of extricating ourselves from the situation and thus avoid the possibility of great damage being done to the Government. Arnold Weinstock's words weighed heavily on my mind. The representatives who were chosen for Leon Brittan were his PPS, assisted by an assistant Under-Secretary in the Department of Trade and Industry, and on our side by the Company Secretary, Brian Cookson, with Michael Marshall acting as a kind of referee. The meeting was to take place in Brown's Hotel, the venue of so many of the meetings I had during my time in and around British Aerospace.

*   *   *   *   *

After the press conference in Malta and the Board of Enquiry, I was able to read the newspaper reports that had been published on the collision; one of the leader writers who was most supportive and clear-thinking about the whole episode was Chapman Pincher, then writing for the *Daily Express*. I had only met Chapman Pincher once but none of the many other people who had written about me and my behaviour had supported me more solidly. I decided to drop a line to Harry Chapman Pincher to thank him, and used a simile which I had used before to get the message across to the great British public as to what it was like to be harassed by these Russian destroyers and escorts when you were operating a large ship. I used the example of a double-decker London bus which was on a main road proceeding along its course on its proper business, full of passengers, when it was subject to constant harassment by small cars which cut in front of it, tried to drive it off the road, actually crossed the dividing line between the two carriageways to come at it head-on to see if they could deflect it, to play the game of 'chicken'. I hoped that this would give an impression of the kinds of problems we had been having with the Russians at sea for the last several years and how dangerous a game it was; leading, inevitably, to the kind of situation I had had to face on that dark night south of Crete. It seemed to work, and as a result of this

38

encounter I remained on very good terms with a lot of the Press people for many years afterwards, and still do.

The Board of Enquiry's investigation into the event rested heavily on the evidence of the escorting destroyer and the track charts of both ships, which matched identically. This showed that had the Russian not altered course, she would have passed well clear astern, and therefore showed that the action which she took in the circumstances led directly to the cause of the accident. The report cleared *Ark Royal* and all of us involved in any responsibility for the accident, and commended the action that I took at the last moment, which undoubtedly avoided a very much more serious event.

When the report of the Board of Enquiry into the collision of the *Ark Royal* and the Kotlin reached Their Lordships and had been debated and deliberated on by them, it was clear that there was no evidence to suggest that I had acted in any way other than that which was appropriate in the circumstances. Nevertheless, it is always natural to be somewhat sceptical of such a clean bill of health, and I believe that one distinguished officer actually said, 'Can it be that Lygo made no mistakes at all?'

The matter was resolved, however, by an incident which took place far from the scene of the actual occurrence – in Tokyo. An old friend of mine, Ted Anson, had made Captain and his first appointment was to go as Naval and Air Attaché, I believe, in Tokyo. Ted had been in my Squadron 800 in the Sea Hawk days when we were the first squadron to embark in *Ark Royal*, and subsequently he had progressed through command of a Buccaneer Squadron and as Commander Air of a carrier up to the position of Captain. Strange to relate, he would go on to command *Juno* – my old ship – and then straight on to *Ark Royal*, as I had done. However, at this point in the story he was Naval Attaché in Tokyo where a reception was held for Naval Attachés which the Russian Naval Attaché attended. Ted waited until late in the evening and then, approaching his Russian colleague, asked him confidentially what had been the cause of this collision in the Mediterranean. The answer he got surprised him and, of course, put the final touch to the whole episode. He was told that the Russian Captain was a fool and was now in Siberia. Whether this was true or false was of little consequence, but a signal was soon flashed to Their Lordships informing them of this interview, which put QED on the Board of Enquiry and the whole episode.

After we had arrived back in Malta after the event, the Flag Officer Malta gave a dinner party to which I was invited as was Peter Kirk (the Minister for the Navy in the new Conservative Government). Before dinner he said to me, 'Ray I'd like to have a quiet word with you,' and we went out on the balcony overlooking Sliema Creek, whereupon he said, 'Ray, you've won.' 'What have I won?' I said. 'Well,' he said, '*Ark Royal* is going to continue in commission.' To which I replied, 'What about *Eagle*?' He said, 'No, I'm talking about *Ark Royal*.' I said, 'I know you're talking about *Ark Royal*, you couldn't have done anything else but what are you going to do about *Eagle*?' He said, 'Well, no ...' I said, 'If you're serious we need both these carriers to continue in service.'

I'm sure he took the point on board, but so often in these discussions with politicians they think that the first move is the last, but since they have often never been told the whole story beforehand it's not unusual for them to be taken by surprise when you straight away come back and say that this must mean something else. Sadly, it didn't happen, although *Eagle* in many respects was a much better ship – more modern, with more modern equipment than was *Ark Royal*.

As I said before, I have often pondered on what happened that night in the Russian ship and why it happened, and I believe that it could not have been a deliberate act; I never believed it was at the time and do not now. Maybe the Captain, like me, was having his supper; maybe an inexperienced Officer of the Watch got mesmerised by events and did not understand what was going on. However, whether it was deliberate or by accident is not the point. It was inevitable that such a collision, or worse, was bound to take place sooner or later if the Russians persisted with their aggressive ways. Fortunately, the message was received. The conduct of Russian ships at sea after this episode changed completely and unnecessary harassment ceased. As I said publicly at the time, my one regret at the end of all this was that the lives of innocent Russian sailors were lost. My great consolation was to know that I had not placed any of my sailors in similar danger.

* * * * *

The meeting at Brown's Hotel started badly with a somewhat pompous and unctuous opening statement by the Under-Secretary in which he said that the Secretary of State completely refuted my statement that he had made a remark to me that I should withdraw, and that the only solution was a complete withdrawal and apology on my part. This produced the expected explosion from our side, and Michael Marshall said that in this case there was no point in continuing the meeting. Furthermore, the company secretary said that if that was the view of the Secretary of State, British Aerospace would stand by my statements and that would be the end of the matter as far

40

as this meeting was concerned. We proceeded to collect our papers, preparing to leave. This brought the other side to its senses; they realised that if we were to have any agreement at all there would have to be something other than an outright statement of the kind they had already made. It was not a pleasant meeting – it was a fairly unpleasant one – but once we had established the fact that if a compromise was to be reached then an understanding also had to be reached, things began to settle down.

By about ten o'clock the meeting in Brown's Hotel was not really getting anywhere, and I suggested that sandwiches should be obtained and some soft drinks so that we could sustain ourselves for the obviously longer time that was going to be necessary – unless we were going to terminate the thing and forget all about it. It was not an easy evening, but it became clear to me at a fairly early stage that one possible way out was to hang the compromise on the words that Michael Heseltine had himself used. He had said that Leon Brittan had said to me that 'British Aerospace' should withdraw. Those were not the words that I recalled; the words in my mind were perfectly

"That reminds me—were you at the Palladium the night Dorothy Squires took it over?"

This summed it all up!

(By kind permission of *Private Eye*)

clear and it was that '**YOU** [I]' should withdraw. There was, therefore, in essence the possibility of a 'misunderstanding', shallow as it might be, transparent as it might be, but it might serve the purpose. Discussion then centred around whether this could be framed in such a way as to provide Leon Brittan with a hook to hang it on and also enable me to maintain my position without embarrassing him further. At the end of the night it was decided that an exchange of letters would take place in which I would use the words, 'if, in his expression, he meant that I personally should withdraw ...' then, of course, I understood that. The inference that British Aerospace should withdraw was one that had been taken from it and that he might not have meant. It was left to our lawyers to arrange an exchange of letters, and I went back to report next morning to my colleagues what had happened.

The letter which arrived from Leon Brittan's office, for us to send to him, was unacceptable. It reverted to the original position of his saying that he had never made such a statement and this, of course, we completely disputed. It was, therefore, necessary to have further legal exchanges to get the words amended in the light of what we wanted; I was told that this upset Leon Brittan considerably, for he thought that we were reneging on what we had agreed the night before. In fact, as I recall, there was no intention to renege but merely to stand firmly by the position that British Aerospace had taken all along: that the conversation did take place and that the words that I said were used were, in fact, used. The only change would be what those words meant. It is interesting that, while my recording of the conversation that we had had was taken on tape within ten minutes of my departing from the Department of Trade and Industry, it took them something like five working days to produce an agreed minute of what transpired! Perhaps the fact that they had so many witnesses became an embarrassment!

So it was that we released the letter. It was immediately seized upon by the Prime Minister's Press Office and Bernard Ingham, and I understand that the statement was made, quite simply, to journalists, 'He [I] has withdrawn.' This was a sadness for me because I had not withdrawn, I had merely allowed an interpretation of the words to be used in order to save the Government embarrassment. Subsequently, in a television interview, the Prime Minister was asked if she was satisfied about the misunderstanding and she expressed satisfaction that the misunderstanding had been cleared up.

It left an unpleasant taste in my mouth, an unpleasant taste in the mouth of British Aerospace and, I suspect, an unpleasant taste in the mouths of all those who had been involved and knew something of my character and of the circumstances. It was comforting to see at one stage three Members of Parliament interviewed, who, when asked about the likelihood of my being truthful, were able to say that they knew me and very much doubted whether it was possible for me, in such circumstances, to be other than truthful.

The debate in the House was due to be broadcast and I went round to listen to the broadcast at Tin Pearce's house. The Opposition had the Government on the rails. As the cover-up for Leon progressed there had been a further, more damaging, revelation about a letter from the Attorney-General. Neil Kinnock had the opportunity to bring the Government down; instead, he missed it by his desire for Welsh oratory. A direct question to the Prime Minister was avoided and Margaret's parliamentary skill won the day. But it was a close-run thing. It didn't save Leon, however. He had to resign. It was a sad affair, and extremely distressing for me – so much so that I seriously considered whether I should resign my position as Chief Executive of British Aerospace, and I said as much to Tin. His response was generous. He said, 'If you go, I go as well, Ray, and I don't know that that would be in the best interests of the Company.' The relationship between Tin and myself was never easy, as we were two totally different characters. In some ways, however, it should have been a strength; perhaps in retrospect it was, but I remember this occasion with particular gratitude.

And so we sweated out the next days and weeks. Arnold's only remark to me was, 'You should never have compromised at all, you should have talked to your friends' – but that was easier said than done. The attempt by the consortium to outbid Sikorsky carried on, though not very excitingly or confidently, and in the end the consortium failed to get enough of the shares that were required. The Board of British Aerospace had ruled that we should not enter the market to buy any shares in Westland, and in any case it was difficult to pick them up. People were looking for a premium as a result of the fight that had been joined between the two contending parties. Some very mysterious buying and selling took place during this period!

Alan Bristow was naturally disappointed that we had given up our leadership role, as were, of course, all our partners. I am bound to say that they were all most understanding of the reasons why and were sympathetic to my own position. Alan had himself acquired some shares and this was the subject of some interesting debate between himself and other parties who were interested in acquiring those shares. The full story of this episode would be worth another chapter, but not in my book – that is a matter for Alan. Suffice it to say, he was very upset by the allegations that were made against him at that time, and quite rightly so. But as Denis Thatcher remarked to me sometime later, when he had debated the issue with the Prime Minister privately, they neither of them could conceive of how the thing had developed into the crisis that it had and could not understand how quickly it had got out of hand! Join the club!

I had always been dismissive of stress up to then. I had preferred to use the old service description of it as 'LMF' (lack of moral fibre), but I have to confess that, as I shuttled backwards and forwards on those tense evenings between my office on one side of Pall Mall and Tin's office on the other, I felt stress for the first time in my life. At one of the Board meetings in which this matter was discussed I suddenly felt a slight pain in one eye, and subsequently discovered that I had suffered a thrombosis in that eye which affected its ability to see clearly. Although it is much recovered, and that is another story, it is still affected and is a permanent reminder of the Westland affair. The whole of the campaign, the whole of our extrication from it, the whole of the event, the whole of the business had fallen on my shoulders and, while I had the utmost support from my subordinates I was never totally sure of how much the Board ever understood what had happened. I believe that there was a feeling that in some way I had been the instigator of the whole affair. Never did Tin ever explain to the Board in clear and concise language that it was the steps he had taken that led us into this situation, and never did I remind the Board or any of my colleagues of this fact. It is a strange and different world that one enjoys in the services, where loyalty is taken for granted and expected and you expect loyalty in return. It is a strange and different world in business, where loyalty is rarely given without reward and seldom sustained in times of crisis. Certainly my relations with my Board colleagues from then on, I felt – whether correctly or no – to have been disturbed, and they were never really restored.

In the end, the consortium did not muster enough votes and Sikorsky won its interest in Westland only to divest itself of those shares some years later; one wonders what it was all about. One thing became clear, of course. The opportunity to sell the Black Hawk helicopter was only to be valid if the US Congress refused permission for Sikorsky to sell Black Hawk direct to Saudi Arabia, and therefore it was seen as a way round this particular embargo.

The whole of the Al Yamama programme was, and is run by British Aerospace, and therefore it was for the Saudis to decide what their priorities were for equipment, all of which was organised on their behalf by British Aerospace. It might have been a better outcome for Westland if the consortium had won.

*　　　*　　　*　　　*　　　*

The stem of *Ark Royal* was repaired while we were in Malta, a new plate placed over it, and we were ready to continue with our work. We sailed out of Malta to the cheerful waves of the families and friends we had made, and I took with me a silver model of a *dhaisa* presented to me by the Maltese NATO Society for my contribution to the defence of Malta. I was touched at the little ceremony that we had on board when the presentation was made. It must be remembered that at that time a large Russian presence was anchored in some shallow water off the Maltese Islands, where they kept a watchful eye on events and established for themselves a presence in that area. It must also be remembered that, at that time, Mr Mintoff's government was looking in various directions, to Libya and to Russia, for assistance, and the old British connections were beginning to look a bit well worn. There

Secretary of the Maltese NATO Society presents me with a silver Dhaisa

were, however, many Maltese who were very concerned about developments and very anxious to maintain the historic ties between the two countries. Their loyalty was touching.

The press coverage and the general level of interest which had been displayed in the aftermath of the collision had made me a recognised character and, since I had always been lucky enough to have the encouragement of that extraordinary man Michael Le Fanu, now First Sea Lord, in my career in its latter stages, I was considered to be a perfect candidate, at the expiration of my time in *Ark Royal*, to become the Director of Naval Public Relations. I did not find this too distasteful – after all, I had started my original career with the intention of finishing up in Fleet Street, or in public relations in some way, and this was yet another opportunity. On my return to the UK I was asked to pay the usual visit to see the Naval Appointer. This time it was my old friend Captain David Dunbar-Nasmith who was the Naval Appointer and David it was who suggested to me that I should become the next Director of Public Relations. I did not dissent. I was sent from his office to talk to Captain Harry Home-Cook who was then holding the position. It would have been the second time I had relieved Harry, since I had taken over from him as Commander of Greenwich.

Harry was surprised to find me in his office informing him that I was to replace him as Director of Public Relations; obviously it was the first that he had heard of it! However, we had lunch together and reminisced a bit and chatted about Naval affairs before I returned to my ship. Sadly, Michael Le Fanu was not a fit man and one of those tragedies was about to overtake the Ministry of Defence when a man at the top has to retire because of ill health. The shuffling and changes that can go on have a profound effect on the whole structure, and thus it was that Admiral Peter Hill-Norton became Chief of Naval Staff. Peter obviously didn't have the kind of feeling that I might be as successful as a DPR as Michael Le Fanu may have had, and the change at the top meant that, after *Ark Royal*, I was something of an embarrassment to Their Lordships. Here I was with six and a half years' seniority, having done the one thing most Naval officers would have loved to have done, commanded the *Ark Royal*, and yet I was some little way off the top of the Captains' list and eligible for promotion; what, then, should they do with me?

About this time someone, I don't know who, had the good idea of starting the Naval Presentation Team, a small team of officers and ratings whose job was to tour the country and to pass the Naval message to people of influence and standing in the community in order to uphold the Naval image in the eyes of the population at large, and it was decided that I should be the first to lead this team.

47

After I had paid off from *Ark Royal* and had been carried ceremoniously away in a helicopter from the flight deck, back to West Malling to join my family, I received a message that the First Sea Lord (Hill-Norton having gone on to be Chief of Defence Staff because of Michael Le Fanu's illness) wished to see me. This was Michael Pollock.

*   *   *   *   *

Had it not been for some people who had an interest in my career (as opposed to those who had an interest in making sure that I did not have a career) it would have been the end of a chapter. I had had a collision, not my fault, but it had nevertheless happened and with the Russians to boot. No, better perhaps to write Lygo off. Another life lost!

It was the same after the Westland affair. People looked at me somewhat askance. Was I really one of theirs? Oh yes, I was, but it was not plain to see. For what I believe was an act that was designed to help save the Government I had paid a fairly high price. Was there to be a future? We shall see.

2

In the Beginning

I was born at 41 Richmond Road, Ilford, Essex, on the Ides of March 1924. My father was a compositor with *The Times* and my mother a housewife. I had one older brother, nine years older than me, and it was always made clear to me (at least it seemed to be) that I was a bit of an afterthought, and in fact I remember on one occasion my mother saying, 'I could have had you all taken away', which perhaps you might conclude would have been the best outcome for all concerned. However it didn't happen, and there I was. Because of the gap between my brother and me, I suppose I was virtually an only child. I looked up to my brother as somebody vastly older and far more worldly than I, and in later years I have often said to people, 'Do you know my brother?' and if they said No, I'd say, 'What a pity because you missed the nice one.' He was one of the nicest men I've ever met, simple, straightforward, direct, and in later years be became very proud of me, although why that should have been only he could tell you. Unfortunately he can't; he died a few years back.

My father had been one of two brothers born to his father Henry Lygo, who had married a Miss Thomas – hence my father's name Edward Thomas Lygo. He had an elder brother Frank, who was at one time manager of the Prince of Wales Theatre, but my grandfather, on the death of his first wife and my father's mother, married again, one Salome, whose pictures indicate that she was aptly named.

My father went to what was called a 'penny' school in Victorian times and did very well. One of his prizes (which we have to this day) is a book entitled *In the Wilds of Florida*, and little could he have realised that many years later I was to get married to a Floridian in Florida, by which time Florida had changed quite a bit! Unfortunately, his new stepmother decided not to afford the one penny a week that he required for schooling and so at the age of twelve he had to leave and find employment. He could not stand his stepmother and did the only thing that was proper: he left home, and was lucky to have somewhere to go. He went and stayed with his brother Frank. Through the intervention of the father of a friend of his, he was apprenticed as a compositor in London to a company called Waterlows. He served his apprenticeship and then proceeded to work as a compositor, joining *The Times* newspaper just before the First World War, which was a great step forward because it was very highly paid in relation to the general trade. My parents lived in Bromley, and then at some stage in the early 1920s moved to Richmond Road, Ilford, where I was born on 15 March 1924.

It was, as I recall, a happy home. We were well off, by the standards of our time; my father's pay of £500 or so a year was more than adequate to provide us with a decent house, a car and holidays (although we sometimes had to take them camping, more I suspect because my brother became enthusiastic with the idea of camping than did my mother). Finally, in about 1929, we moved to Wycombe Road,

Is it a fella?
The author aged 18 months

also in Ilford, a new housing development, and it was from there that I went to Valentine's School, the local elementary school.

I passed my eleven-plus by dint of learning by rote. My father was a self-taught scholar – he had to be, having left school at twelve – and a great reader who left me his collection of books including the Penny Poets, a series of books of the great English poets that he bought for a penny each. He recognised that if I was to get through this eleven-plus I would have to have something better than the others, and so he taught me to learn compositions that he had written. They covered a fair multitude of things since in those days (and I suspect in exams to this day) familiar subjects constantly recur; he reckoned that if I mastered four or five of these, one was bound to come up that could be used at the dreaded eleven-plus to my great advantage. And so it turned out. One was entitled 'The Motor Car', it started, 'In the early days of 1890, a German inventor named Daimler conceived the idea of the first internal combustion engine which led to the motor car, an invention that has influenced trade and commerce throughout the world more than any other means of transport.' How about that for memory! When I got to the eleven-plus, I found that there was no composition to be written about the motor car but one about the steam engine, so I quickly modified it to, 'In the early days of 1800, an English inventor named Watt conceived the idea of the first steam engine which he applied to a locomotive and the steam engine has influenced trade and commerce throughout the world more than any other means of transport.' So there you are.

Six hundred boys, because it was divided between boys and girls in those days, sat the examination for entrance to the Ilford County High School and 120 were chosen, and I think I was no. 104. So I just made it. So it was with the eleven-plus safely under my belt, I went to Ilford County High School for Boys, to the newly opened site of the school at Chigwell. It was a lovely school with excellent facilities and good educational procedures, and to the best of my ability I enjoyed it. I remember few things about it. I remember Selwyn Lowe, the music teacher, who introduced me to a love of classical music on the firm foundation that my father had set by buying records for the newly bought radiogramophone for which we were all allowed to choose one record each week to add to our collection. Strangely enough, mine was military band music. I loved military band music. I remember Selwyn Lowe because he is the only man I have ever known who wore a plastic 'dicky', a fake shirt front, which in hot weather he would unveil and use to fan himself!

In 1937 we moved to Orpington for what today would be a very strange reason: that my brother had formed a liaison with a married

51

woman. She was separated from her husband but divorce in those days took a long time, and she was also considerably older than he was. It was a massive family scandal, and my mother insisted that we move clean away from the neighbourhood so that nobody should make any connection. Can you believe it in today's world? Anyway, we finished up in Orpington in Melbourne Close, at a very nice house, better than the one we had left, with a nice big garden where I was, for the first time, to begin my love of gardening.

By 1938 it was clear that something was going very wrong in Europe. I remember reading an article by Stefan Geddes in the *Daily Express* in which he talked of 'the fallen bastions' which he described as the Ruhr and Austria, and then of course, latterly, the Sudenten-land in Czechoslovakia. My family were staunch Conservatives (although my father was by this time rising high in the Trade Union movement, later to become Imperial Father of the Chapel for the whole combined Union activity of *The Times*), yet I was brought up in a house where the rights of workers and the important essence of Conservatism were intertwined. There was no conflict; my father was both a Trade Unionist and a staunch Conservative, and so was my brother.

In 1938 I joined the local Air Defence Cadet Corps, which was part of the Air League of the British Empire. I don't recall why I joined it but I must have had some strong patriotic feelings for so doing. This, combined with my love of military music, I suppose would have me branded today as an out-and-out nationalist.

My father wanted me to follow him into the printing trade as a compositor, and in those days, you had to be apprenticed before the age of sixteen and serve a seven-year apprenticeship. It was also a rule of the union that there could only be one apprentice for every four qualified journeymen. My father had known a man in his early days at Waterlows who had gone on to found his own printing business, and Dad looked him up, made contact, and I found myself employed at A. S. Atkinsons, 154 Clerkenwell Road, at the tender age of fourteen and a half in September 1938, at the time of the Munich crisis. I was employed for the princely sum of twelve shillings per week, minus fourpence which was deducted for National Insurance, as a reader's boy: in other words, I read the proofs to the reader who was correcting them. A more slap-up title was 'copy holder'. My fare from Orpington to London was a workman's return of elevenpence, which meant that I had to catch a train that got me into London before 8 o'clock in the morning, and we worked a forty-five-hour week which was modest in those days and this was arranged in five days of nine hour shifts. So it was eight in the morning until six in the evening with an hour's break for lunch. At the end of one week when I collected my wages, I discovered that one penny had been deducted because I had been collectively 15 minutes late for work during the week. Perhaps my liking for punctuality started then!

It was to be a very salutary experience for me. Hitherto I had been the centre of attention in the family and elsewhere whenever I cared to disport myself, but here it was very clear to me that I was absolutely nothing. I was the bottom of the pile and suddenly became aware for the first time in my life of the stratified nature of British society; furthermore, it was clear to me that I had been cast into the lower section. The chap I had relieved had indeed become apprenticed as a compositor, and in the two years that remained it was difficult for me to see how I was going to find a space in such a small company when there were already two apprentices and only eight journeymen. It just was not possible. I learned something while I was there, however. We printed the *Gamekeeper*, and by reading proofs of that I learned something about an aspect of life I had never really come across before and found some of the stories quite fascinating. We also printed the *Anti-Vivisectionist*, so I learned something about that although I was not persuaded. We printed insurance forms, in ghastly small 6-point (or Ruby in those days) print that were used by Pearl Assurance and also the Prudential, and we printed a miscellany of bits and pieces which all had to be proof-read to Mr Double.

Mr Double was an almost Dickensian character. He wore a bowler hat which perched rather than fitted on to his rather large head. He wore a black coat and pinstriped trousers and carried an umbrella. He was by trade a compositor, a member of the London Society of Compositors, and therefore able to be employed as a proof-reader. We sat in a small, screened-off caboose just inside the door of the composing room, and in the confines of this somewhat restricted area I was subjected to the philosophies of Mr Double and also to his habit of snuff-taking. Snuff-taking was prevalent among compositors and people who worked with lead type in those days, and I was despatched at regular intervals to the tobacconist across the road to get a quarter of an ounce, as I recall, of some particular snuff that Mr Double especially enjoyed.

He would take this in large pinches from time to time and then blow noisily into a handkerchief which, during the course of the day, turned from a misty grey into a definite brown. I didn't like the habit and particularly didn't like his habit of spitting down the side of his chair. There was a knothole in the floor and I think his idea was to get his gob through this hole, not always successfully, and so a pile of this rather revolting green slime would accumulate during the course of the day, or indeed week. It somehow managed to dry out over the weekend, I suppose, so that there was room for another load. He wasn't all bad; he was a kindly man, he just had these rather disgusting habits, and so I decided that I would try to break him of this habit by going to a novelty shop and buying a large packet of sneezing powder. While he was off to the heads one day, I carefully mixed a large quantity of the sneezing powder into his snuff. Imagine my disappointment when Mr Double returned, took a large pinch, drew it carefully up the left nostril and then, another pinch as he kind of wiggled his nose, and then another pinch up the starboard nostril. It had no effect on him whatsoever, and then he turned to me and said, 'This snuff is getting stale, you'd better go over and get me some more.'

The people in the firm were, by and large, kindly and tolerated what I was, I suppose, to them my rather strange behaviour. For example, I insisted that when I made the tea for the entire workforce it was made with proper milk, not condensed milk. They just looked at me with amazement and said, 'Well, you won't get any more money.' Of my 11s 8d a week, a shilling a day went on fares, and a shilling a day was allowed for my lunches, which left me with 1s 8d. I wasn't exactly contributing to the family home!

Mr Atkinson himself was a florid gentleman who lived upstairs, and smoked Passing Clouds cigarettes which I thought was very exotic because I had to go out to buy them for him. Another of my chores was to deliver some of the printed material, particularly a thing called the *Theatre Guide* to a Mrs Sneyd who lived in a kind of garret in St Martin's Court. By delivering these and other papers I began to find my way round London, and well remember on one of the early deliveries of the *Theatre Guide*, coming back past the statue of Florence Nightingale towards St Martin-in-the-Fields, where the news vendor stood (and still stands) on the corner there, and seeing the placard 'Peace in our Time'. Neville Chamberlain had just returned form Munch!

The atmosphere at that time was quite ecstatic. War, which after all had only finished some twenty years before, had been averted and Neville Chamberlain was the hero of the hour. But young as I was, I remember how quickly the mood was changing in the country as the details of what he had done became apparent. He had sold the Czechs down the river, or up the creek if you wish, and very quickly the electorate sensed this and braced itself for the inevitable consequences of his actions.

Business picked up but unemployment was still high. We were girding our loins for war. It must have been early in 1939 that A. S. Atkinsons was bought by W. P. Griffiths of Prujean Square in Old

Bailey, which has now disappeared. This was a much larger printing works, very old-fashioned and Victorian, bare board floors, and I remember vividly coming in one Monday morning after the rat-catchers had been in the building to see all the rats laid out in serried ranks indicating their prowess. It was, however, well-known to all of us that a couple of the best mating pairs would have been let go so that the ratcatchers could come back in six months' time! Here should have been a better opportunity for me to become apprenticed, but time was beginning to run out. If this hadn't happened by March in 1940, I wasn't going to be able to make it, but I was then to have another experience. I was loaned, can you believe it, to a company that was photostatting the Prudential Assurance Company's documents to be taken away and buried in some remote colliery in Wales for protection during the war that everybody knew now was coming.

Here I met a different situation altogether because we were working not a five-day week but a five-and-a-half-day week, and although my wages had shot up from 12s. a week to 14s. when I was at W. P. Griffiths, and now I was to be offered 16s. a week to go in this new place, it was yet another experience. The Prudential Assurance Company were offering 50s. a week for men to come and work a 48-hour week in this temporary job – it was expected to last about three months – down in the basement of their main office in High Holborn. The queue of men to apply for the job stretched down High Holborn and round the corner into Hatton Garden – they were queuing four deep for a job paying 50s. a week. I was entering my socialist phase, and no wonder.

I had realised that I was in the bottom layer of society and that the opportunity to escape from this was not going to be easy. One Saturday, very early on, I arrived home at about three o'clock. My father, who, as I have explained, was a staunch Trade Unionist, asked me where I'd been. 'I haven't been anywhere,' I said, 'I've come straight home.' 'What time did you finish?' he asked. 'One-fifteen,' I replied. He then said, 'You must go and look at the copy of the Factory Act, that you'll find hanging somewhere in the space in which you are working, and if there isn't one, you are to tell the foreman that you wish to see it and to have it displayed because that is the law. When it is displayed and you have had a look at it, read it thoroughly and read the section that applies to juniors.' On the Monday morning, I duly approached the foreman, whose name I think strangely enough was Mr Foreman, and asked, where was the Factory Act? He looked at me, this 15-year-old youth, in amazement. 'The Factory Act?' he growled. 'Yes,' I said, 'it is required to be displayed by law in all work spaces.' He glowered at me and said nothing, but that morning a copy of the Factory Act was pasted on the wall. I read it, particularly the section on juveniles, where I saw: 'juveniles are not to be worked after one o'clock on Saturday.' I could hardly wait for next Saturday to roll around. At one o'clock precisely I put on my coat, picked up my belongings and marched towards the door. 'Where are you going?' asked the foreman. 'I am going home.' 'It's not time to finish yet,' he said. 'Read the Factory Act,' said I, and stalked out of the door. I was becoming a budding Trade Unionist.

The war came, that terrible day of the 3rd September with the bleating voice of Chamberlain apologising for the fact that we were now at war with Germany, and the wailing of the air-raid sirens, which I fear set me all a-trembling because I was quite certain we were going to be gassed.

In March 1940 the tragic events in Norway began to unfold, and my father got me a job as a messenger boy at *The Times* because it was clear that I was not going to become a compositor in spite of the fact that he had actually bought me a frame (that is the box in which types were set for composing) and also constructed a proof-pulling device so that I could set up type and have proof pulls at home. I had my own 'stick' and so on, but all to no avail – some things are not meant to happen. Another failure?

I was recruited at *The Times* by Mr Hoare, the company secretary, who hired all the messenger boys in those days. He also ran the Widows and Orphans Fund (that is to say, the pension funds). My job was to be an indoor messenger, there being two varieties of messengers: the outdoor, who wore a uniform with a little pill box hat, and the indoor, who were allowed to wear civilian clothes as long as they were smart. We resided in Room 3, on the first floor overlooking Queen Victoria Street, which was later to receive a direct hit right through the window (but not while I was there, thank goodness). The Editor of *The Times*, who had the office opposite, was Mr Geoffrey Dawson, a man of great influence within the Chamberlain clique. Next to him, the Deputy Editor, Barrington Ward; there was an Admiral Thursfield, the Naval correspondent, who strutted up and down the corridor with his hands firmly clasped behind his back like a ship in full sail. Next door was a leader writer called Dermot Morrah, who later became Head of the College of Heraldry and whom I was to meet many years later. One of the jobs we had when the leader writers or senior people came in was to light their fires. The fires were laid by the cleaners the night before, and our job was to strike a match and set fire to them, which wasn't too difficult since they were well laid. There was no central heating, and each room had its own fireplace and fire. The one thing that was clear to me as a messenger boy was that the avenues of advancement were not entirely closed. There were examples of messenger boys who had actually made it into junior positions in journalism in the home affairs department. One of my predecessors was Louis Heron, who later became Deputy Editor of *The Times*, so it could be done.

The war was not going well, to say the least. After the débâcle of Norway came the collapse of France, and the whole building of *The Times* was put on to a war footing. My father, I remember, was despatched to the Midlands to find a suitable factory where *The Times* could be printed in the event that the building was destroyed. Meantime, it was decided to move us all down below into the machine room. I was now a night messenger, that is to say, I started about four and stayed until the main edition had gone to press, normally about ten. Geoffrey Dawson was put in the machine minder's office, the manager's office which was a kind of room on stilts so that the manager had a good view of all the machines. Unfortunately, of course, as Editor he had absolutely no means of communication down there except for a telephone, and so needed a messenger to run all his messages for him. I was appointed to sit in this room with Geoffrey Dawson to run his errands.

Geoffrey Dawson did not appeal to me. He had reinforced my socialist tendencies by allowing a swing door to go straight into my face as I followed him through on one occasion, and I have always believed that good manners are the hallmark of a gentleman and that a failure to observe them casts one into a quite different role. But I was allocated to him as his personal messenger. It must have made him more uncomfortable than me to have this callow youth sitting gawping at him while he was trying to write some erudite piece for the newspaper or have a good look over what other people were producing. So it came to pass that I happened to be there on the great day when Chamberlain resigned and Churchill took over, and I remember very well the conversations he had on the telephone with people like Halifax and Samuel Hoare, commiserating with them over what had happened as a result of the departure of Chamberlain. Geoffrey Dawson and *The Times* had been appeasers, and now it was very clear that appeasement with a man like Hitler was just not going to work. Of course, there was nothing very new about this. Appeasing a bully never works. Soon after this episode it was made clear to me that I was not required in the room and that I should sit outside in a chair on the balcony, which I duly did, or on a form at the foot of the stairs that led to his office. There I remained throughout 1940, throughout the Battle of Britain, and through to the period when the raids on London started.

I was becoming more and more involved in the Air Training Corps, as it had now become, and this was my abiding interest outside *The Times*. Because I was on night work I was able to observe the Battle of Britain being fought during the day, or the vapour trails of it, and the aircraft and the noises which I carry in my mind to this day.

I had now been promoted within the system, first into the intelligence department which was a section of *The Times* devoted to really answering questions that people inside the office might have about any subject and also in keeping a record, an index, of all the things that happened in the newspaper. I was only there for a short time, however, before again I was moved, this time back into the reading room and back into my old job of proof-reading to a very nice man called Mr Benest (sadly killed later in the War). The plan now was for me to become a 'Corrector of the Press' by taking the necessary exam. My spelling – ask my secretaries – has never been my strong suit and so my father had insisted I read *The Times* every morning and he used to test my spelling by reading to me the fourth leader!

I was still on night duty when the night raids on London began, and I became obsessed with getting home. It seemed to me to be one of the ways in which I could demonstrate that I was actually beating the Germans at their game. If they could not, with their air raids on London, prevent me from getting home to Orpington and my bed every night, that was a success.

The raids on London were at their height and I have vivid memories of St Paul's illuminated during the great fire raids, standing out stark against the red, burning sky. Buildings were being demolished at regular intervals and the scream of bombs dropping was intermittent, whereas the screaming, whirling noise of shrapnel coming down was almost continuous. It came at you like some kind of firework, whirring, whizzing and then, with a deep thud hit the ground at whatever distance it was by which it had decided to miss you.

To its great credit the Southern Railway kept operating right through the Blitz on London. If one station was out of action, then there would be the possibility that another would manage to have a train or so running. *The Times* building was right opposite Blackfriars Station, which then connected to Holborn Viaduct, a terminus from which trains ran to Orpington and Wimbledon. I remember one night trying to get up the stairs of Blackfriars station with water from the Fire Brigade activities cascading down it, wondering vaguely where my brother might be who was by this time in the London Fire Brigade. On another occasion, walking up Queen Victoria Street and sheltering in one of the doorways on the river side of the street as bombs hurtled into the various buildings, most of which, of course, are no longer standing and have been replaced. Miraculously the telephone exchange and the College of Heraldry survived, as did *The Times* until of course it got that direct hit I referred to earlier. Even that only made a hole which was soon patched up. There was always Cannon Street as well, with the possibility of trains from there, or even Charing Cross, and somehow it always seemed to work; although one might be delayed and it took a long time, eventually one got to Orpington.

On one of the worst nights, however, there was obviously no way in which we were going to be able to get a train, so I borrowed a bicycle from one of my colleagues who, like most of them, had decided not to try to go home but to stay in the comparative safety of the basement of *The Times* where they could sleep on canvas beds. Cycling home was not easy because the roads were likely to be somewhat pockmarked, and furthermore, in the worst-hit areas, there would be Fire Brigade hosepipes and the ambulancemen and people in the Salvage Corps going about their business. One night, however, I failed to get home as I was stuck on Nunhead Station for the whole night in a train. Nunhead is very high and gives you a marvellous view of the whole of London, and the train had stopped there because a bomb had fallen on the track just ahead and there was no way the train could get through. We stayed there all night, talking to other passengers and trying to get some rest while observing the extraordinary scene of the attacks on London from this very good vantage point. When it was light, the train reversed back down to Loughborough Junction and proceeded down the alternate main line, thus skirting the Catford loop line which had been damaged. Please don't get me wrong, nobody was being brave or acted as though they were being brave, and indeed in some respects what I was doing was pretty selfish. It was just the determination not to be beaten that was important and yet somehow it was enough.

3

We Joined the Navy

I had joined the Air Defence Cadet Corps of the British Empire in 1938 when I was 14 and eligible to join. In those days we paid sixpence a week in order to be members of the Cadet Corps, which was a privately organised charitable organisation. It was designed to train young men for a career in the Royal Air Force, or the other services if the Royal Air Force was not available for them. The Squadron I joined was 173 Orpington Squadron and we paraded in the cinema car park every Sunday and then went off to one of the school rooms for lectures and general instruction in various aspects of airmanship. We wore a uniform similar to that worn in the First World War but in Royal Air Force blue.

The Squadron was run by a bunch of worthies who devoted their weekends to trying to teach us some rudiments of air force organisation and, most importantly, discipline and parade drill which I quite enjoyed. It was not, however, a totally absorbing activity and, as I had started work in 1938 and in view of the fact that I worked a five-day week, my weekends were fairly precious to me. My membership therefore lapsed to some extent but when the war broke out in 1939 I rejoined, and soon afterwards the Air Defence Cadet Corps was taken over officially by the Royal Air Force and became the Air Training Corps. The uniforms were changed slightly to a less severe model, the curriculum expanded and extended, and I became an enthusiastic member of the Squadron.

During 1941 we started to have regular visits to Biggin Hill, the famous fighter base south of London, and there we were allowed to 'help' the squadrons of Battle of Britain fame generally by sweeping up the hangars or crew rooms, or cleaning the aeroplanes or just hanging about and looking admiringly at the crews when they were visible. I remember particularly spending some time on the Blenheim Squadron that was then based at one side of Biggin Hill, the Spitfires and Hurricanes being on the other side.

The Battle of Britain was now more or less over and so the aircrew could relax a bit more, and it was in early 1941 that I had my first flight. The RAF pilots were kind enough to spend some of their spare time in taking chaps like me for a quick trip around the local area in a Tiger Moth. It was something we sought after and strove to achieve and by this time I had, with the expansion of the Squadron caused by war, leapt the rank of corporal to be made a sergeant and was therefore high up on the list of those who could get a flight.

Little did I realise at the time that this flight was to change the focus and shape of my entire life but, looking back on that event, I suppose it did. The thing that impressed me most was the very unassuming and friendly nature of the pilot who took me flying, whose mind was probably a long way away. We flew in that famous little aeroplane with the wind whistling through the rigging and the gritty little noise of the engine as we took off, and I gained my first sight of the land from the air. How different everything looked, how detached one felt and separate from, and not a part of, the earth we had just left. All this must have had an effect upon me. I was profuse, in my stumbling way, in my thanks to the pilot and never will I forget his generosity, amid so much stress for him, for taking me into a new dimension.

There was a particular award for service in the Air Training Corps which was called 'proficiency'. To obtain this we were examined in various aspects of airmanship, air navigation, Morse code, meteorology, general knowledge of aeroplanes etc., and if you passed this exam then you got a 'proficiency' star. I worked hard and got this and was promoted to Flight Sergeant. Here, I was able to exercise my now considerable enjoyment in square-bashing and I became extremely proficient in organising my squad and enjoyed being part of parade training. We started a magazine called *The Flaming Onion* which had some reference to the colour of my hair, and we started concert parties, which I compered and took round to local establishments, Army and Air Force, to entertain the troops. All pretty amateur stuff with simple sketches and well rehearsed jokes, but it went down well enough in those difficult days of 1941. It was all to provide the grounding which was necessary for whatever else I was going to achieve – although this was not clear to me at the time. Exposure to standing on a stage and compering a show, to being a stand-up comic, to speaking in public, to being theatrical if you like or an embryo star, was all to be of enormous benefit to me as life unfolded.

It was after a Morse exam on Sunday morning that I realised for the first time the power of the English language spoken reasonably properly; something that has continued to surprise me wherever I have been, particularly in the United States where a well-spoken English delivery can still have them all swooning. It was as I read out the results of the Morse code test, using the alphabetic numerals of the time, that I noticed that the audience of youngsters (all of my own age or thereabouts) was very quiet and listening intently; and it was then that I first recognised the sound of my own voice. As I have already explained, I had done some amateur dramatics before and I had had some experience of public speaking, but it was at that moment that I realised that, if I cultivated my accent and if I projected my voice in a certain way, people would listen. It was a profound and new experience, and I suppose it did more for my self-esteem and my ability to make progress than anything before. I was, after all, an absolute rabbit at any sport, but suddenly I found something that I could do that others could not do and which put me into a rather different category. In short, I had begun to discover one of the basic qualities of leadership – how to project yourself.

It must have been about this time that I came across my first piece of literature about the Fleet Air Arm. It fascinated me. Here were a bunch of people who had had the extraordinary success of Taranto, who were part of that great Senior Service to which we all, in our heart of hearts, belonged in some strange way, and they were different. They were more than just pilots, they were in the Navy, they were part of our great tradition of the sea. I began to look more closely at entering the Fleet Air Arm, but the problem was that I had no recognised educational qualifications. I had left school at 14 and therefore, although I had passed my eleven-plus and had been to a grammar school, I had no qualifications, no bits of paper that I could show.

As the war worsened and the situation blackened, by 1941 the Navy had lowered the standards of entry into training for the Fleet Air Arm to a point which I am quite certain has never been reached since. The Navy had introduced the 'Y' Scheme which stipulated that, if you didn't have two matriculation passes to qualify for the interview but you had passed the Air Training Corps proficiency exam, were recommended by your Squadron commander and had evidence of adequate schooling, then you could apply.

In order to reinforce these scant qualifications I went off to my old school, the Ilford County High School (for Boys) and found people who actually remembered me and were kind enough to get the Head Master to write a letter explaining that if I had stayed at school, I would almost certainly have gained what was then known as the Intermediate exam passes (equivalent to A levels) – but, of course, I hadn't! I also went to Clarke's College where I had also studied and they gave me a similar piece of paper. What these were worth I am never sure because they were not actually taken into account as far as I can recall. Nevertheless it was the best I could do.

There was, however, a more serious problem. I had worn glasses since the age of five and when I realised that I wished to become

62

aircrew, I knew that I certainly could not do it wearing glasses! I therefore proceeded to discard them. My job at the time was as a proof-reader, or copyholder, at *The Times* and consequently I spent a great deal of time reading. I had no difficulty reading and no difficulty seeing but when I left the glasses off I did get very severe headaches, which I put up with, believing that if I could see perfectly well the headaches were acceptable.

I knew that in the examination I would be put through for the interview board, I would be asked questions on trigonometry and mechanics. As I had not the faintest idea of either of them because mathematics was never my strongest subject at school, I bought two books – *Teach Yourself Mechanics* and *Teach Yourself Trigonometry* – and on the train into London to work and back and during the time when I wasn't actually reading proofs, I read and studied both. I learned how to use logarithms and became reasonably proficient in the kind of quality of work that the books enshrined. Armed with this flimsy evidence of capability, I duly volunteered and was eventually called to present myself, aged nearly 18, at the nearest Royal Naval Recruiting Office which was near Kent House Station in Kent.

I remember getting off the train and finding my way to the Naval Recruiting Office where I joined a fairly motley collection of youths who were attempting to join the Royal Navy – I suspect mostly because they did not want to go into the Army! Queuing up, I presented myself eventually in front of a very bored Chief Petty Officer who had the job of categorising the applicants and starting them down the road towards whatever career they thought they were going to have in the Royal Navy. I remember being very amused, as I stood in the queue, by the chap in front of me who was asked first of all what was his job or profession? To which he replied, 'A plasterer's improver, sir.' The Chief Petty Officer had a large volume at his elbow in which, presumably, all recognised categories of employment were catalogued. He looked through it and obviously could not find 'plasterer's improver'. He said, 'Plasterer's mate, that's what you are,' and entered him accordingly. He then turned to the next question, 'What denomination are you?' he enquired. The lad in front of me looked a bit stunned. 'Well, what denomination are you?' said the Chief, 'Religion, lad?'

'Oh,' said the lad, 'I'm a Christian.'

'Yes, yes, yes, yes,' said the Chief Petty Officer, 'but you can't just be a Christian, you have to be either a Catholic, or a Methodist, or a Baptist, or something else, or Church of England, now what are you?' The lad, who had presumably heard of the Church of England even where he had come from, said, grasping at a straw, 'Church of England.'

'That's what most of them are,' said the Chief with obvious relief, and duly entered it.

When he asked me my religious denomination I said that I was a Rationalist, which threw him a bit, but as it was listed in the large book at his elbow I was allowed to be registered as a Rationalist, although perhaps not too wisely. Then, as far as my profession was concerned, when I said 'Copyholder' he looked it up and, since it appeared in the book, I was duly entered as a copyholder. We next looked at what I wanted to do. I told him that I wanted to join as a Fleet Air Arm pilot under the 'Y' scheme. He turned up the regulations and said, 'Do you have your School Certificates?' 'No, sir, I don't have them.' 'Well, you are not eligible,' said he. 'With respect, Sir [how often was I to use that introduction!], I am,' I said. 'Under the "Y" entry scheme, Chief, you will find that if I have an Air Training Corps proficiency certificate I am eligible for consideration.' He thumbed through some latest Admiralty Fleet Orders on the subject and finally confirmed that indeed I could just scrape an interview with those bare qualifications. So I was duly entered to await the call to go before the Admiralty Interview Board. I remember leaving the recruiting office elated and getting the train, thinking to myself, well, that's the first hurdle crossed – one step at a time.

On the great day I duly presented myself at 54 Cockspur Street at the side of Trafalgar Square in my Flight Sergeant's uniform. I thought, I have little enough to impress them with, I had better make the best of what I've got! As I entered the room I remember a large table with four gentlemen seated on the other side; one, who was the Admiral, was in the centre. Probably a retired Admiral brought back for this onerous duty but, as it turned out, a man with a sense of humour, thank God. He was aided by an Instructor Captain from the naval Education Branch, who was not very much to my liking as he looked fairly gaunt and was wearing spectacles. To the left of the Admiral was a young Sub Lieutenant, Sub Lieutenant Rose of the Fleet Air Arm with Fleet Air Arm wings (one of the few survivors of the Channel Dash) and I sensed a friendly face, and to his left the secretary who was taking down the record.

In front of the Admiral was a selection of model battleships or warships. I had studied these as I had studied my aircraft recognition, but my aircraft recognition was better than my ship recognition. However, the Admiral pointed to one ship which in fact turned out to be the Rodney, one of those ships that had been truncated by the Washington Treaty. He looked at it and said, 'Right, what are these?'

I said, 'They are Battle Cruisers, Sir.' 'Yes, and what are these?' 'Oh, those are destroyers.' 'And what is that?' 'It is a County Class cruiser.' 'Yes,' he said, 'which way is this Battle Cruiser going?' Well, it was a toss of a coin: I got it wrong. 'That way,' I said. He burst out laughing. 'No, no, no,' he said, 'you might think so but actually it's going the other way.' The Instructor Captain now started the educational ordeal, asking me about sines, cosines and about mechanics, talking about fulcrums and balance and pressures. I answered reasonably well, I thought; after all, I knew what a sine and a tangent, and a cosine were, which was more than I had known before I read *Teach Yourself Trigonometry*, that's for sure. Then it was the turn of Sub-Lieutenant Rose who, looking up to the ceiling where were suspended aircraft models, asked me what these various aeroplanes were. There was a Walrus, a Swordfish, a Fulmar, a Skua, a Seafire and a Hurricane and, of course, I knew them all. So that part, was not too diffi-

Flt. Sgt. Squadron 173 – note the Naval flash

cult. Then I was asked, of course, the usual question,' Why do you want to join the Fleet Air Arm?' I said, 'I suppose, quite honestly, because most of my friends wanted to join the Royal Air Force and I wanted to do something which was, to me, more interesting and more all embracing than just flying. I wanted to be part of the great Naval Service.' Bullshit, you may say, but it might have swung the day. I was asked to wait outside.

I had volunteered for aircrew, which embraced both observer and pilot, I hadn't indicated that I wanted to be a pilot – perhaps it never occurred to me that there was a difference. On the other hand, in all the Naval publications I had read, the observer was the captain of the aircraft and therefore had a higher standing than the mere 'throttle jockey'. So I contented myself with being satisfied with either, but preferably an observer. How fortunate I was to be wrong! I was called back in and, standing stiffly to attention, the Admiral said, 'Well, Lygo, we have reviewed your qualifications and we don't think that you have adequate qualifications to become an observer, but we are prepared to take you as a pilot.' I could hardly believe my ears; I stuttered out a 'thank you,' turned as smartly as I could, about turn, and left the office. I was exhilarated. I had received the biggest lift I'd ever had in my life since I had passed my eleven-plus, I suppose. I was going to be trained as a Fleet Air Arm pilot. Of course, I had very little idea of what that meant, but it was good, it was something I had achieved, it was something that set me apart from the others, and in due course I got that very important blue flash with the red 'Y' on it, which my mother stitched on to my uniform, which indicated that I had been accepted for entry into the Royal Navy as a pilot under training. My parents were very pleased and proud, although I suspect that my mother was somewhat concerned about this aviating business, but it was enough that I wanted to do it and that I had been successful. I was full of myself.

There was, however, one further hurdle to be jumped that I have already mentioned – the aircrew medical. Time passed and eventually the notice came for me to present myself for the medical. This again was in Cockspur Street and the medical was carried out by a Naval Surgeon Lieutenant, RNVR. All went well until the great moment of the eye test. Of course, I could see the various characters that were displayed before me, I had no trouble with the test on judgement of relative distance which was conducted, as I recall, by holding two strings in a long tunnel and trying to get two objects to line up. A kindly Wren Petty Officer had pointed out to me that I took the strings where they were dirtiest, that was where most people brought them together and that would get me passed, which it did! But at the end of the eye examination the doctor said, 'Well, Lygo, I'm afraid your eyes aren't quite up to standard. Do you play tennis?' I looked at him in amazement. I said, 'No, Sir, I don't play tennis.' In fact,I had never even held a tennis racquet. 'Well,' said he, 'go off and play a bit of tennis and come back in a month's time and see how you get on.' I was stunned. I walked out, got the train home and was debriefed by my parents. They could understand it no better than I could, so they said that I should go to see the local doctor and have a word with him. This was a kindly gentleman by the name of King Hutton, who was I believe, the uncle of Hutton the famous cricketer. I duly presented myself to him and told him what had happened. He asked me to read some letters on the wall and said he could not understand it either, but the only thing he could suggest was that he would give me a letter to go to see an eye specialist at the Royal Westminster Ophthalmic Hospital.

Considering that it was wartime it was amazing that an appointment was arranged within a week. I duly presented myself at the hospital and proceeded to go through the stages, which were common at that time, of sitting on long wooden forms in front of a stage upon which the great man was conducting his examinations. You shuffled your bum along the bench, and then on to the next bench and shuffled in the other direction, one at a time until you reached the front and were bidden on to the stage. The great man read the letter and said, 'What's the problem?' and I said 'Well, I've failed an eye test to become a pilot in the Fleet Air Arm.' 'Oh,' he said, 'read those letters over there.' I did so. He looked into my eyes with a light and then he said, 'I don't understand why you have failed, tell me what else he did.' I said, 'One thing he did was to put a thing like a ruler with a peg in it under my nose and moved it towards me. He then moved it towards my eyes and either side. 'Ah yes, I see,' he said and took his pen out of his pocket and asked me to follow it. 'Yes, well, of course, your eyes aren't good enough to be aircrew but you can join the Navy or the Army and you will be perfectly fit for ordinary service.' 'But, sir,' said I, 'I wish to become a pilot in the Fleet Air Arm.' 'Well, you can't,' he said, 'your eyes aren't good enough.' 'But I wish them to be good enough,' said I. He looked at me for a moment and said, 'Are you serious?' 'Yes, Sir,' said I. 'Then', said he, 'you shall be a pilot in the Fleet Air Arm.' And he gave me a written note to take downstairs to a department where I should start receiving treatment.

It was not until I was going down the steps to the basement that I saw that I was going to the 'Squint Department.' In fact, all that was wrong with my eyes, and presumably all that ever had been, was that I was not able to focus them, to bring them together close to the end of my nose; they just would not do it. So for the next week I exercised, along with a lot of cross-eyed looking children, in the Squint Department looking at pink rabbits and blue rabbits in a machine which gradually got my eyes to meet at a point in front of my nose. In fact, so good did I become that I could actually start moving my eyes out from the centre, apart. I was delighted, and particularly delighted since the great man had said, 'And when you go back for your eye test, if there is anything wrong you can refer the gentleman to me.' That was good enough.

So I presented myself to the Surgeon Lieutenant again in Cockspur Street one month after he had failed me. He went straight to the point, put the ruler under my nose, produced the peg and, to his astonishment, I was able to follow it right down to the end of his wretched calibration. He tried it again, no problem. 'Ah,' said he, 'I see you must have been playing quite a lot of tennis.' 'No, Sir,' said I, 'I didn't play any tennis at all. I went and saw ...' and I quoted the great man's name, 'and he has treated me and he has asked me to tell you that if there is anything wrong with my eyes now he would like to know.' At that point the Surgeon Lieutenant swallowed, looked at me again and said, 'Ah, yes, well, I think that will do.' I had passed my medical! Now all I had to do was wait for the dreaded day to be called up to join the Fleet Air Arm. My calling-up papers invited me to present myself at Lee-on-the-Solent on 2 November 1942 to join No. 45 Pilots' Course. I have never forgotten the debt I owe to the Air Training Corps for giving me the opportunity to join the Navy, and for the subsequent events in that career. Many years later, I was invited to become the honorary patron of 173 Orpington Squadron, which I did with great pleasure.

The railway warrant and instructions for joining told me that I should take the train to Portsmouth Harbour Station, cross to Gosport on the Gosport Ferry and then by bus, getting off at the pier and then walking to the gates of Lee-on-Solent. I packed a somewhat meagre bag, since the Navy was to provide me with the wherewithal from then on, and, smartly dressed in my Flight Sergeant's uniform replete with proficiency bade and 'Y' entry scheme insignia, I bade a fond farewell to my parents. I remember little of the trip except stepping on to the Gosport Ferry, this being the first nautical experience of my life, and that I arrived practically the first of my intake, to go into hut 49 at Lee-on-the-Solent. Being first, at least I had the choice of which bed I should occupy and chose one next to one of the pot-bellied stoves, so that (it being winter) I should at least have a warm bed. Eventually the rest of my companions joined – 120 of us in all on that one course – and I suppose 30 or 40 to a hut. Over that bed now is a plate which says that I slept in that particular bunk; what will happen to it when Lee-on-the-Solent disappears I am not quite sure. Such is fame!

My companions were drawn from all sorts of backgrounds, some from public schools, some from a broken university course, some from very ordinary backgrounds – like me – and most of us were in the age bracket 17 to 19. To be any older than that was considered to be very old indeed. The following morning we were issued with our uniforms, very new, very dark blue, not at all bleached or well worn, and with our round hats with the white band that signified that we were officer candidates. The Petty Officers and Chief Petty Officers at Lee, as I recall, were a kindly lot who looked after us well and grounded us in the basic requirements for squad drill and so on, for which, of course, I was only too well versed, and the way in which to look after ourselves.

I remember one particular episode (it is strange how you remember the little things) when a very large, fatherly Chief Petty Officer stopped me after I had fallen out on the parade ground one day and said, 'Don't forget to wash the back of our neck, lad, it's stained blue.' My low-cut jumper, brand new and full of dye, had indeed coloured the back of my neck and I had not noticed it. I was extremely embarrassed, almost as embarrassed as I was subsequently to get my first attack of dhobi itch, brought on by wearing woollen underpants together with Naval serge trousers! I really thought that I had got something quite unbelievably contagious, and I remember the cure was Whitfields ointment. To this day I have that engraved on my memory. I was still sending my laundry home in a parcel for my poor mother to deal with and send back to me. Trying to wash a Naval collar in a way which stopped the blue running into the white lines was something which even she never managed to master, and I do not know if many people did.

The days at Lee passed easily enough, there was plenty of food, plenty of exercise and therefore not much inclination to do anything other than study or sleep at the end of a hard day. Soon a month had passed and we were due to go to HMS *St Vincent*, about which so many stories of the rigours and stress of this particular establishment had been passed down to us. The gates of *St Vincent* are still there in Gosport but the establishment itself has gone, apart from the swimming pool. I had come to enjoy swimming since I had taught myself to swim while with the Air Training Corps, and it is interesting to recall that in those days many joined the Navy unable to swim, to serve their lives in a service surrounded by water without the ability to survive if anything happened to them.

No. 45 Course. I'm 5th from the right, second row

Much has been written about *St Vincent*, and I shall not dwell on it. One or two of the things that both surprised and impressed me, however, I shall recall. First, we were put in dormitories in a building which I am told had been built to house French prisoners of war, but perhaps that was just one of the stories. There were something like 40 or so in a dormitory, which had two lavatories and four washbasins. The two lavatories had had the doors removed so that there could be no lingering in that particular hideaway. I was shocked by this, as I had never before had to perform in semi-public with a queue of my compatriots waiting to use the same facility – not one of the easiest things to overcome. Operating in a common shower was no problem, but operating in an open loo was something quite different!

The other thing I remember was going as cooks of the galley, which in those days was the norm since we ate in what was called 'broadside messing'. That is to say, a group of some 16 of you would mess together at a scrubbed wooden table with a bench on either side. You would take your turn to become the 'cook of the mess' and when the meal was piped you would proceed to the galley, stand in a queue and collect the victuals for your particular mess for that day – bread, cheese, butter, sugar – and at the main mealtime you would collect a large tray of whatever was going. The day it came my turn to go as cook of the mess I stood in a long queue in the galley in HMS *St Vincent* and watched, with increasing fascination and horror, the movement on the walls. The place was alive with cockroaches, and it was perfectly clear that some of the cockroaches must be finding their way into the shepherd's pie that I was about to collect for my messmates. A story is told of a chap who was similarly horrified and when, he had got the food back to the table, discovered there was a cockroach in his portion. He took it back to the Petty Officer Ship's Cook and said, 'There's a cockroach in our tray of dinner,' to which the Petty Officer replied, 'Oh, dear, only one?' and grabbing two more from the wall he threw them into the chap's plate and said, 'Now you've got a proper ration.' True or false, it really held my attention and made me rather curious as to what I was eating when I started to attack it.

The man who was responsible for running the routine for all of us who were there was a man whose name is held in high esteem, or not as the case may be, by every Fleet Air Arm chap who has ever passed through *St Vincent*. That man was Chief Petty Officer Wilmott, who addressed us on arrival, and apparently addressed every course in the same way, by throwing his head back with his cap slightly perched on the back of his head and displaying a set of not too attractive teeth. He would utter the immortal words over and over again, 'Naval airmen live in filth and squalor and it is our job to train you in more sanitary ways.' He was an object of terror but, as it turned out in my case, he had a softer side. Towards the end of our two-month stay there we had exams in order to go on to the next stage, which was basic flying training. Exams in navigation, meteorology, seamanship, Morse code, semaphor, the rudiments of theory of flight and airmanship. Within the last week of our course I came down with what must have been a bad cold which turned into flu and rapidly developed into pleurisy, but I had no intention of baling out at this point. However, after one morning parade CPO Wilmott walked over to me and said, 'Are you feeling all right, lad?' to which I said, 'Well, yes, Sir.' 'You report to Sick Bay at once, lad,' and as I fell out I said, 'But Chief, I've got my exams.' 'Don't worry about those, my boy, I'll arrange for you to take them in Sick Bay,' where I did them and passed. So the awesome man had a more humane side after all.

I suppose the thing that most impressed me at *St Vincent* and changed my entire attitude, however, was that on the third or fourth day I was walking across the parade ground into the portico which fronted the building where we were accommodated when I saw, standing with his back to one of the pillars, my Divisional Officer,

Warrant Officer Woolven, talking to another officer. As Dunning, my companion on that occasion, and I passed we saluted smartly and as he returned my salute my Division Officer said, 'Good morning, Lygo.' I was astonished. Here was a chap who had known me for less than a week, and of 120 different guys he had remembered my name. It was the first time that I could remember someone actually taking that kind of interest in me as an individual, certainly since leaving school. In the work I had done in the intervening years no one had taken that much notice of me, or had bothered to learn my name unless I had pushed it down their throats. This, thought I, was an organisation I could relate to. Here was an organisation that took an interest in me as an individual with a name; it began a love affair with the Royal Navy which was to last for 36 years.

What other memories? The memories of the Royal Marine Band coming on the parade ground every morning to play as we all fell in for Divisions and the routine, the ceremony, the pageantry of the occasion, the thrill it gave me and gives me still. There is nothing in the world that quite compares with a Royal Marine Band.

While at *St Vincent* we were asked to state our preference as to where we would go for the continuation of our training. The most popular was to go to the United States, to Pensacola, Florida, and to be trained by the United States Navy. The second choice was to go to Elmden at Birmingham for elementary flying training school (EFTS) and then on to Canada. The least favoured, presumably because it was further away, was to go to Sealand in the Wirral near Chester and then on to FTS in Canada. Although the least desirable, this was considered to be the fastest route and Dunning and I both elected for it. Since it was the least favourite there was no doubt that we would get our choice, as indeed we did. The great day came, the end of the *St Vincent* course, we were promoted to Acting Leading Naval Airmen with the associated rise in pay, which was substantial to us in those days, and then off on leave pending appointment to our new stage of training, when the real tests would begin.

I am now the Patron of the St Vincent Society!

4

Flying Training

We were now all set to start the most exciting part of our training, flying.

I had chummed up with Gordon Dunning, who remains a friend of mine to this day, a strange combination really because although I was a Rationalist and fairly severe in my views on religion, he was a born-again Christian but we got on extremely well together, perhaps because neither of us drank at that time and we shared many of the same interests.

I duly arrived at Sealand which was a grass field operated by Airwork, I seem remember, a civilian firm, but the flying instructors were RAF. We were stationed in quite good accommodation, after what we had been used to, and good sound RAF flying training food.

There was not much ground instruction, as I recall, but a great deal of attention and waiting around in the crew room for flying, which of course depended mainly on the state of the weather. I do recall one lesson, however, which was on the theory of flight. Whether the chap had read Air Commodore Kermode's book on the subject I am not quite sure and in later years, when I was an instructor myself, I remembered the lecture very well because the chap made the point that when you turn the aircraft on its side the rudder became the elevators. I don't think this theory would have gone down very well at CFS. My instructor was a Warrant Officer by the name of Gadd who had been on operations and was now having a rest, teaching new-entry young-sters to fly the Tiger Moth.

The Tiger Moth is a delightful little aeroplane which has not really suffered the effects of time because it still remains an excellent basic trainer. I enjoyed my flying experience very much and very quickly came to terms with the peculiarities of the aircraft and the way in which you needed to handle it to operate it safely. We had, of course, been issued with flying gear, in itself a somewhat sobering experience because quite a lot of it had been turned in by previous trainees who had failed the course! So when you were issued with a piece of kit that had somebody's name on it, rather badly blacked out, it gave you a slightly worrying feeling about what might happen to you. However, my prowess with the Tiger Moth was sufficient for me to be put up for a solo check by the Flight Commander after only eight hours, which was pretty good stuff. Unfortunately, I failed this test (I do not know why, and my instructor was as mystified as I was) but the Flight Lieutenant who took me up was an elderly and somewhat severe gentleman and there it was, so I had to do another couple of hours' flying before I could be put up again for a test, which was quite important, as since I'd failed the first one it wasn't going to be entirely satisfactory if I had failed the second.

My next test passed, I proceeded with the flying training but confidence and over-confidence are always followed by some kind of disaster and sure enough when I returned from a solo flight, in trying to park my aircraft quite tidily next to another one I managed to hit it. Turning the Tiger Moth into wind, or out of wind or against the wind, was an extremely difficult operation because you had no brakes, you just opened the throttle, banged on full rudder and hoped the aircraft would turn under the effects of the rudder and the tailplane. On this occasion it failed to do so and I collided with the other aircraft. There was a certain amount of damage, not a tremendous amount but enough to have me terrified at what the prospects might be. But thank goodness, my flying instructor stuck by me and obviously had a few words with the Wing Commander (Flying) by whom I was interviewed, and the only punishment I received was 14 days stoppage of leave. I would happily have taken two months' or a year's stoppage of leave to have remained on the course, so I was extremely lucky to get away with it.

At the end of our course we were sent to Blackpool, there to await shipment to the United States. In due course we were ordered to report to an assembly point where we were transported to the *Queen Mary* in Liverpool to await one of the fast passages that those ships then made on a regular basis with troops backwards and forwards to the United States.

It's strange to look back and think that really at that time, we weren't worried too much about the prospects of being torpedoed (and ships were being torpedoed fairly regularly at that time), but not the *Queens* or the fast Atlantic passenger liners which, if they were capable of something approaching 30 knots, were routed independently. They somehow always managed to avoid the concentration of U-boats and thus arrived safely at the other end. Perhaps the breaking of the German Code played a part.

The ship was crowded mainly with RAF and army personnel going off to the United States for training for various reasons, and the food of course was provided in the United States and therefore was by our standards unbelievably good. I can remember that there was an abundance of Herschey chocolate bars, and with all sweets being rationed at that time in England we all promptly made ourselves jolly nearly sick on a surfeit of Herschey's chocolate. Accommodation was in three or four racked high bunks with not much space that you could use for reading, but we didn't mind and the passage was bearable and in fact enjoyable. We arrived in New York to see the famous Statue of Liberty, and then to be whisked away by train up north to Monkton, New Brunswick, which was the assembly point for dispersing new arrivals to their various training activities in Canada.

Each of the courses had with it their Divisional Officer – that is to say an officer who was actually in charge of us all – and in our case this was one Mike Hayward, a Lieutenant Engineer who was also undergoing flying training. Mike was an extremely nice, charming man and very tolerant of all of us but I don't think we gave him too much trouble because we were too much in awe of where we were and who he was.

On the way over in the *Queens*, we had been aware of a new game (to us, at any rate) called Crown & Anchor and this was where most of the passengers on board managed to lose most of their money to the Ship's Company, who were quite versed at playing this game and skimming off the savings of the airmen who were being transported. One of our number thought it might be a good idea to acquire a Crown & Anchor board and try to do the same with his companions on the train journey to Monkton and from there to Kingston, Ontario. He didn't seem to have much luck and I think at the end of the time, to his amazement, he was actually in debt rather than in profit!

During our stay in Monkton, which was two or three weeks, we were royally entertained by some Canadian families, all of whom seemed to have the most gorgeous daughters and it was not an entirely unpleasant stay. But soon we were to be moved south to Kingston and once again boarded one of those trains with those marvellous wailing hooters as they roared through the night spitting out cinders, which came with great frequency through the carriage windows into the compartments themselves, a somewhat gritty experience but for us stunning and enjoyable. I remember going down to the observation car at the end of the train and seeing the endless lines disappearing into the distance as we sped through part of the wilderness of Canada on our way down to the more civilised parts. The train had to stop to change engines in Montreal and was going to be there for something like two hours and four of us therefore enquired of Mike Hayward whether we could go ashore, hire a cab and have a look round the town, and he said, 'as long as you're back here by such and such a time then off you go.'

We duly disappeared out of the station and there found a rather sombre looking taxi driver who told us that it was not allowed, with the petrol shortage in Canada, to take people on joy rides but he would pretend he was going in the direction of some place or the other so that we could have a look at some of the landmarks, and proceeded to show us various places of interest in Montreal. Then, without much ado, we drew up in front of a house, one of a number of terraced houses with tall steps, I seem to remember leading up to the front door. We said, 'What's this?' and he said, 'I'd like you to come in and meet somebody and you might enjoy this.' My forebodings began to worry me slightly but we rather sillily got out of the car and mounted the steps and went into the house, which of course was a brothel. As we sat there in the waiting room, the madame produced the ladies of the night (or was it morning, in this case?) who proceeded to stand in front of us holding tea towels which they lifted up and lowered down to reveal piece by piece the total extent of their anatomy, but not all together, as it were. There was a look of horror on the faces of my companions who leapt up and proceeded to leave and I was left looking at the madame who said to me, 'What's the matter? Don't you know your own mind?' to which I replied quite accurately, 'Well, yes I think we do but I don't think the taxi driver knows it!' We piled back in the taxi and the somewhat sombre man took us back to the station where we boarded the train in plenty of time to depart, but of course it gave us an excuse for embellishing a most marvellous story of how we had actually been into Montreal, in and out of a brothel, and back on the train during the stopover.

Kingston was a rather super air station, as far as we were concerned, and our task there was to be taught to fly the Harvard (which was quite an advance on the Tiger Moth) as a preparation to going on to our operational types when we returned to the UK. If we passed this course, we would be awarded our wings. Many are the stories one can tell about advanced flying training, about the course and what we did and the instruction and everything else, but this has all been well recorded elsewhere. Suffice it to say that I managed to pass the course and was quite good at aerobatics as was my instructor and I managed never to be sick no matter how many times he spun me. He was a frustrated fighter pilot and clearly saw me in the same light.

We had quite reasonable pay for our age and for the various alternatives that were open to us and a couple of other guys and I clubbed together and bought a motor car for $45 to give us wheels to visit the local area. This turned out to be a 1928 (can you believe it?) Studebaker

Erskine, a make that I had never heard of before or since but I can assure you it was true. Tyres were a problem in Canada at that time and ours had just enough tyre tread on them to make them serviceable, but I am afraid brakes were somewhat lacking and one had to be a bit careful how one anticipated coming to a stop. However, it started all right and it ran all right and it was sold to us by one of the enlisted airmen on the base who was a mechanic of some kind and obviously made his money by selling used motor cars to unsuspecting students. It did serve however to get us around and gave us an opportunity to see bits of Canada that otherwise we might not have seen.

The most exciting experience was when we went over the border into Watertown to sample the delights of an American town. On leaving, as I came down a hill towards the traffic lights they changed to red just before I arrived and, even by standing hard on the brakes, I could not stop the car from rolling across the lights. Whistles blew and a policeman came over and told me that I'd better take the car into the local cop shop, which I duly did. The man got in the car, pressed on the brakes and said, 'these are no good'. So I asked for a spanner and I adjusted the brakes up so tight that they were on solid. When he came out to test them again he said, 'Ah, that's much better.' I then had to slacken them off a bit so that we could actually get under way again and creep out of Watertown and back over the border into Canada.

Studebaker Erskine – I kid you not!

77

We duly qualified and earned our wings which, in our case, were stitched on the side of the sleeves of our Naval ratings uniform, where the golden embellishments look suitably impressive to anybody who knows what to look for. Our RAF colleagues were all rated up to officer status or Sergeant Pilot as the case may be, changed their uniforms accordingly, and had their wings blazoned on their chests.

The last episode in Canada was a trip I took with two of my friends, Bert Alder (sadly murdered many years later by his son) and Michael Levitt, whom I still see to this day. We hitch-hiked from Kingston, through Gananoque, down through Watertown, Syracuse and into New York where we stayed courtesy of the USO and then back up to Niagara, Hamilton (where we stayed with the editor of the *Hamilton Spectator*, who had been a colleague of my father's many years before) and eventually back to Kingston to catch the train off to Monkton once again and then Halifax and home in the *Aquitania*.

My memories of the United States and that trip are all extremely pleasant. We had a marvellous time, and the people were extremely kind to us. The one thing we learned in hitching around the United States was to explain to whoever was driving the car who we were and

83rd Pilots' Course. I'm 2nd from right, second row down

where we came from. There wasn't much point in saying England because they associated this with New England, and Great Britain or the United Kingdom seemed to mean nothing. Finally we hit on the phrase, 'we come from over there' and that did it; they knew then where we came from. One forgets, and the British particularly forget to this day, how insular the Americans are because of the vast continent they inhabit, which to them is the whole world.

We eventually arrived at Lee-on-the-Solent and here happened one of the most inglorious moments that I have ever witnessed in my Naval career. We were fallen in as a body in the gutter outside the regulating office at Lee, and it was raining. As we waited patiently, the window of the office at last opened (it was a Crittall window, I remember, so firmly is this whole episode engrained on my mind) and a Petty Officer proceeded to call out our names in alphabetical order. Alder was the first one; he stepped up and was given a piece of what looked from the distance like lavatory paper which, when he opened it and read it, said, 'This rating is entitled to purchase officer's uniform.' He then proceeded down through the alphabetical list and the next chap was Barrow, whose name was not called and that meant he was going to be a Petty Officer Pilot, and so on through the list. Levitt, my friend on the trip around the United States who was next ahead of me, was not called, I was and so on. Can you imagine a worse way of handling a bunch of newly-qualified pilots than this episode? It reminded me of our return to the UK in the *Aquitania* when, because we were still lower deck (in other words, ratings), we were detailed off to wait table in the large dining room on Pilot Officers in the RAF who, of course, were no different from us but had been rated up in Canada. Life in the Fleet Air Arm can sometimes be very hard!

The purchase of the officer's uniform was accomplished, and we presented ourselves next to the RAF station at Errol where we were to be converted back to British aircraft. This meant flying Magister I's and III's. It was an interesting course and quite enjoyable, except that the accommodation was somewhat rudimentary once again and, it being Scotland and winter, it was fairly cold. We were supposed to fall in every morning for PT and as we had no plimsolls and had not been issued with any we had an alternative of either falling in with our working shoes or, as the Sergeant Instructor said, 'If you don't have them you can fall in barefooted.' This caused me to exercise my union upbringing and to seek an interview with the Group Captain. I protested that we could not be expected to do PT in the morning in the cold outside, unless we were given proper footwear.

This gentleman, who sat in an office which was like an oven, in front of a pot-bellied stove which was roasting away burning up huge amounts of coal, chastised us for being weaklings. I thought, 'coming from you, mate this is really a good lecture'. However we were not required to continue to do PT in the open; indeed we didn't do any PT at all because we hadn't got the right gear.

I had a nice instructor at Errol, a pleasant man who sadly later was killed flying with a student at night when the weather closed in and they finally had to bail out and they landed in the sea and both perished. Luck plays an enormous part in one's career.

5

Fighter Pilot

In the early part of 1944 I found myself at the Naval Air Fighter School at Yeovilton, Somerset. My arrival there confirmed the fact that I was destined for the role of a fighter pilot in the Royal Navy, despite the fact that I didn't really wish to be one, since most of my friends had gone off to Craill to fly torpedo spotter bomber reconnaissance aircraft (TSRs). As I recall, about 24 pilots had come together from Kingston, Ontario, where I had been trained, together with some who had come from the US Naval Air Station at Pensacola in Florida in order to be trained as fighter pilots at No. 1 NAFS.

The standard fighters of that time were either the Seafire, which was a Naval version of the Spitfire, or the Grumman Martlet, later to be replaced by the Hellcat. Of the two aircraft, the Spitfire was much the more romantic and desirable from a pure fighter pilot's point of view, and it subsequently appeared that we were to be streamed, so that six of us would go on to the Seafire and the rest would be on Martlets.

The Seafire and me

81

Since I was a bit disappointed to be at Yeovilton in the first place, I was, therefore, not particularly interested in which aircraft I was going to be asked to fly. My selection as a fighter pilot had presumably been decided on the basis of never having been sick during aerobatics! On the other hand, I did quite enjoy aerobatics or, put more correctly, my Flying Instructor did, so I had become reasonably proficient at them. As a result, as we queued up outside the office of the Chief Flying Instructor – a gentleman who rejoiced in the name of Major Bird, a distinguished Royal Marine aviator – I hung back from going in for my interview and, in fact, was the last one to be interviewed.

I was asked by the Major if I had any preference for the type of aircraft I was going to fly at Yeovilton. 'No, Sir,' I said, 'I have none.' 'Why not?' said he. 'Well, Sir, I didn't want to come here in the first place. I really would have preferred to have gone flying TSRs; in fact, my original request was to be put on to seaplanes.' I had formed the impression that to be a seaplane pilot in a cruiser would be much more nautical! He and his fellow interviewers looked at me in astonishment; how could anyone not want to fly Seafires? and Seaplanes? 'Well, you are here and you have to express a preference; which would you prefer?' 'Well, Seafires I suppose, Sir,' I said. In a somewhat exasperated way he stared at me and said, 'Well, you are very fortunate, Lygo, because that is what you have been selected for.' And so I became an embryonic Seafire pilot.

The dispersal area, I recall, was quite near the church, which has now been dedicated as the Fleet Air Arm Church, St Bartholomew's, in the old village of Yeovilton because the airfield had not by then been extended to the size it is today. Our dispersal was a collection of Nissen huts with a blister hangar in which the aircraft were stowed, and most of the surroundings, other than the taxiway or peri-track, were a sea of mud. The weather was normal Somerset weather, which meant that it was not very good at that time of the year! Yeovilton itself is a fairly low-lying airfield and it was rumoured that, when it was being selected as an airfield by the Navy, and being built, the locals believed it would probably be a seaplane base because the area was subject to flooding!

The Seafires used for training were various early models, including one Spitfire Mark 1 which had a pump undercarriage – you pulled up a long handle on the right-hand side, selected your gear down, and then pumped – and, since the Spitfire was fairly light on elevator control, as you pumped with your right hand, your left hand on the stick tended to follow the motion and you could see chaps on a down-wind leg who were flying this aircraft, going up and down as if they were on a big dipper! Four-channel radio VHF was only just coming

82

into service then, and most of the aircraft had the old TR9D transmitter/receiver single-channel radio. However, in wartime one was encouraged not to use it and so radio silence was the norm.

Our crew room was heated by one pot-bellied stove, the normal heating arrangement at that time, and we spent many hours sitting there when the weather was too bad to fly, 'shooting the breeze' with one another and telling stories, overheard to some extent by the instructors who inhabited the other part of the Nissen hut with their own pot-bellied stove, only just a matchboard away from us. I cannot remember who the CO was, and I can barely remember my instructor except that he was tall, dark and, as I recall, good-looking; a dashing type of chap who you would expect to be a fighter pilot. However, his instructional technique was almost non-existent! I don't recall being given anything but the most superficial briefings, and for my first operational training flight, after only three familiarisation flights, I was told just to follow him and stay close, tucked in under his wing, which I did. We flew at low level around the area, including flying round the aerials at Sparkford which was where his current girlfriend lived! I was too paralysed with fear to know what we were doing, except to see the wires flash by every now and again, and I was only too relieved to get back and land. What that had taught me I am not quite sure. Stay tucked in, I suppose!

Another training feature was to take you in close formation, flying around the local are at low level and then suddenly, by visual signals, indicate that you were to lead your instructor back to base. Fortunately, Somerset is endowed with a number of monuments sitting on top of hills which give some rough idea of where you are, but you were still mightily afraid that you would be unable to find the airfield and be thus disgraced and failed on the course. I suppose this was called pilot navigation training!

In parallel with this type of flying was an instrument flying course which we took on Airspeed Oxfords. This was held at a separate part of the Naval Air Fighter School and attempted to bring us up to some kind of standard on instruments. The instructors here, by contrast, seemed elderly and staid and probably were. I duly undertook and passed this course. In fact, I quite liked instrument flying. Apart from formation flying and simulated air combat, the most important aspect of the course was air-to-air firing which was carried out over the English Channel, in Lyme Bay. We would fly down and pick up a Corsair which would be towing a drogue for us over the Channel, and after many simulated attempts we would finally be allowed to fire. I am afraid my firing results were never very good – in fact, I seem to recall that I never hit the drogue once while under training! This was a cause of considerable concern to a very nice instructor called Lieutenant Constable who tried very hard to explain to me the finer points of how to get your bullets into the target on a curve of pursuit. The fact is, most aircraft were shot down from dead astern anyway, and if you could get yourself into that position you were generally guaranteed a kill. Not much good for hitting a drogue, however.

As the course progressed, the final act was to carry out simulated carrier landings, 'Addls' – aerodrome dummy-deck landings. The 'batsman' was the chap who controlled the approach and landing by the use of a pair of 'paddles' or bats like large ping-pong bats. If he held them straight to each side it meant you were, in his opinion, in the correct attitude at the correct point on the approach path. If he held them down like an inverted 'V' you were too low. Up in the air above his head in a 'V', too high. Right arm only straight out, too fast. Rolling both bats like oars, too slow. Got it? Well, just to confuse you and me, in the US Navy, the up and down signals were reversed! These signals were instructions to *go* lower or *go* higher! Anyway, he would stand at the end of the runway and we would make low-level circuits at low speed, simulating an approach to land on a carrier or, if you missed the deck, ditch! Part of the routine for landing in a Seafire was to open the hood and then lock it back by opening the door on the side of the aircraft one notch; this jammed the hood from coming forward in the event of a ditching or a heavy landing, or into the arrester wires in the case of landing on a carrier.

The Seafires we were flying at that time had what were called 'kidney' exhaust, that is to say, the exhaust pipes came out and then flared. It was extremely difficult to see round them because they stuck out about six inches directly in your line of view on the approach. The Seafire was not designed for deck landings. It was merely a Spitfire to which had been added a belly hook which dropped down when you pulled a toggle in the cockpit. Once down it could not be raised except by the ground crew on the deck. I seem to recall that it was alleged that 60 per cent of the shock of landing in the Seafire was taken by the tyres and only 40 per cent by the oleos, whereas an aircraft designed for deck landing absorbed most of the shock in large, spongy, hydraulic oleos. As a result, the Seafire, if it was not put down in a three-point attitude fairly gently, would bounce back into the air off its pneumatic tyres and deposit you either into the barrier or over the top of the barrier, which was even worse. The trick, therefore, was to get the attitude right; the nose well up with the speed as low as possible.

I discovered that by putting my seat down and resting my cheek on the door I could actually get the nose up high enough to squint under the kidney exhaust and just get the batsman framed in that setting.

This guaranteed a very good nose-up attitude, which could only be achieved at slow speed with a fair amount of throttle, and brought the aeroplane in only just above the stall. We are talking here of a landing speed of somewhere between 55 and 60 knots on the clock.

Of social activity during the course there was not a lot, except going down to the pub and drinking quantities of watery beer, or drinking in the Wardroom. Since I have never been able to drink large quantities of beer, this did not attract me and fortunately I had not really been converted to alcohol and so drank very little. In fact at that time I was virtually a teetotaller when required for flying, which probably saved me from going the way of some of my more liquid companions whose judgement was thus impaired, causing some fatal flying mistakes.

Despite my not very good gunnery results, my ability to unerringly find the airfield and get back to it, to execute safely most things I was asked to do and to be competent at aerodrome dummy-deck landings, helped me to pass the course and I duly set off with my six Seafire companions to carry out our first deck-landing exercise up in the Firth of Clyde on a carrier which was, as it turned out, aptly named HMS *Ravager*. We travelled up by train in a state of agitation and expectation. The great moment had come: all this training was to be put to good effect and we were to undertake the most difficult task in a Fleet Air Arm pilot's assembly of skills, deck landing.

HMS *Ravager* in the Firth of Clyde

85

We arrived in Glasgow and then took a ferry to Rothesay, where we reported to the Naval Movements Officer and awaited a launch which was to come out from *Ravager* to take us to the ship. *Ravager* was a new escort carrier built in the United States and acquired under Lend-Lease; not large, basically a merchant ship type of construction but properly conceived as a carrier, not converted like so-called Woolworth Carriers. She had a straight axial deck which was the norm in those days, a wooden surface to it, as was common with American carriers, six arrester wires (or was it four?) and two barriers. She had a proper bridge and 'fly-co' (flying control) position and had a flight-deck length of 450 feet. Not a lot, one might say, but sufficient if there were 15 or 20 knots of wind over the deck to enable a Spitfire or Seafire, without long-range tanks or external armament, to be spotted at something like 400 feet and be quite comfortable for take-off.

Perhaps I should explain the layout of an axial-deck carrier. Axial because you landed along the axis of the ship, in other words from the stern, straight towards the bow, and you took off in precisely the same direction. The ship normally steamed into the wind for take-offs and landings, although sometimes it would give you a little wind on the port bow so that the smoke from the funnel, which was normally situated in the starboard side of the carrier, could be kept clear of the approach path of the aircraft. As a result of the combination of ship's speed, wind speed and aircraft landing speed, the approach speed of some aircraft was relatively very slow. Take, for example, the Seafire – a hot ship in those days – at an approach speed of, say, 60 knots. If the ship was steaming at 20 knots into a 15-knot wind you were actually approaching the deck at something in the region of 25 knots, or some 30 miles an hour. The problem was more with the control of the aircraft at this very low speed, very close to the stall, and if, of course, the aircraft had stalled on the approach, particularly if there was any turbulence that was being caused astern of the carrier by its passage through the water, then it could fall short and miss the carrier and plough into the sea, or crash into the quarter-deck, or hit the round-down. All of these events, I am afraid, were not uncommon.

The aircraft was arrested by lowering a hook which engaged wires that were laid across the flight deck, attached to hydraulic rams and which pulled out at a pre-arranged tensioning speed to draw the aircraft to a stop in something in the nature of 50 feet or so. So it was quite a sudden stop and you needed to be tightly strapped in if you were not to be jolted forwards, particularly dangerous as the gunsight in a fighter was only a few inches away from your face and you would almost certainly hit it! This was all long before the invention of 'bone domes' and we flew in leather helmets, just the same kind as Biggles was supposed to use, with goggles which were not dissimilar.

At the end of the arresting area of the deck there were normally two barriers. These were arrester wires which were attached to large hinged metal girders which raised up when aircraft were landing to produce a kind of fence, so that in the event of you missing the wires you would engage the barrier head-on, the aircraft would be arrested, but somewhat violently, and you would almost certainly break the prop, if not most of the aircraft. Most of our props were wooden and would fracture, although the American ones were metal and bent under the impact. The engine would then be shock-loaded and there would be some stress damage to the aircraft as well, but it would prevent you from going right forward into the deck park of aircraft which had been landing ahead of you and which had taxied over the barriers, when they were lowered, and had been parked in the forward part of the ship. The actual area of touch-down, therefore, was quite limited and so the degree of precision required was quite high.

Then there was the problem of a pitching deck. If the ship was in a rough sea and the deck was rising and falling, then of course a great deal more skill would be required, particularly on the part of the batsman, to get the pilot into a position where, when he gave you the cut, the aircraft would settle on to the deck and engage a wire. If the deck was falling away you might miss it completely; if it was rising at that point it could come up and strike the aircraft quite forcibly, causing a heavy landing and damage to the undercarriage. However, most practices were carried out in sheltered waters and so, for your initial training, you did not have the problem of pitch to contend with.

The trip out was exciting; we saw on the horizon the ship, getting larger and larger as we came closer until the final moment of climbing the gangway and saluting the quarterdeck, which we had been taught to do – after all it was the first quarterdeck we had ever been on, apart from the Gosport ferry! Then being shown to our quarters in this brand new ship; smelling new, warm, humming with activity, the fans, the whole atmosphere different and exciting, vibrant.

After supper and a good night's rest we were briefed on what we had to do. The procedure was to carry out a series of six deck landings, four in one session and then a break while we were debriefed, and then two. Then you were qualified and would be sent on leave pending an appointment to a Squadron. We duly assembled next morning on the 'goofers', that is to say, the platform by the funnel which allowed you to look at what was going on on deck, to see the start of flying. The first pilot to go, as we steamed along in the Firth of Clyde near the Isle of Arran, was to us a very elderly chap, a

Lieutenant-Commander – obviously an acting Lieutenant-Commander, RNVR – Air Engineer, who was going to do his first deck landing in a Seafire. We watched as the aircraft was spotted.

The night before my companions and I had walked up and down on that deck, pacing it out, looking at it. It seemed quite wide when you stood on it and the length didn't seem to be too frightening, just a large expanse, and we had thought about how we would cope with it the following day.

The Lieutenant-Commander manned the aircraft and the engine started. The Flight Deck Officer 'wound him up ' – that is to say, the procedure was to hold the aircraft on its brakes whilst you opened the throttle until the tail came up, then you let the brakes go and with full throttle the aircraft would roar off down the deck, hopefully getting airborne before it fell over the bows. We stood watching with intense interest as the engine was started and the moment came for the pilot to be 'wound up' prior to take-off. The Launching Officer rotated the flag and the Lieutenant-Commander opened the throttle. He continued to open the throttle, the tail came up, but he did not release the brakes. The aircraft just proceeded to tip straight over on to its nose and the wooden propeller fractured on contact with the deck and was shattered into a thousand pieces. The aeroplane finished up drilling holes in the deck with the boss of the propeller, the engine roaring, and the Flight Deck Officer scurrying to avoid being hit by the flying bits, as did the rest of the chaps on the flight deck. The pilot was then told – presumably over the RT – to shut down the engine, which he duly did, and rather shamefacedly got out of an aeroplane that was now sitting on its nose having gone nowhere – a complete wreck in the middle of the flight deck. Well, well, we thought, that will teach you to let go of the brakes! However, next one up was Lygo.

I changed into my flying gear and manned the aircraft. I was spotted in the same place as the ill-fated Lieutenant-Commander. I was 'wound up' in more ways than one – opened the throttle, let go of the brakes, piled on the power and raced down the deck, and as we came to the end of the flight deck I eased back the stick and to my delight we floated clear. I had 15 degrees of flap down and, for those people who are used to flying modern aircraft with selective flaps, let me tell you that the Seafire only had two-position pneumatic flaps – they were either up or fully down. In order to get 15 degrees of flap it was necessary, therefore, before take-off, to lower the flaps to allow the ground crew to place two wooden wedges in between the flap surface (it being a spilt flap) and the wing. You would then retract the flaps and they would come up and be held 15 degrees down by the wooden blocks. When airborne, to get the flaps up, you selected down momentarily, the wooden blocks flew out as they were released from the pressure of the flaps holding them in, and then you retracted the flaps and there you were!

I went through this routine, climbed up and looked down at the carrier; it was tiny, it was frightening, it looked like a postage stamp. How was I expected to get this thing back on board? It didn't bear thinking about. So I went into the routine: height 600 feet, turn across wind, that's too high, get her down to 400 feet; 400 feet, throttle back, down-wind checks, brakes, undercarriage down, mixture fully rich, pitch fully fine. Now, towards the end of the downward leg, flaps down fully – well, there was only one place they could go and they were pneumatic and went down quite quickly – readjust the trim, turn on a kind of curve of pursuit towards the stern of the carrier. It was automatic, it was what we had been taught to do. Get the nose up, get the throttle back, get the speed off, crouch down, open the hood, open the door one notch, get my cheek on the top of the door and, as we rounded out, straight approach towards the carrier, there was the batsman framed inside the kidney exhaust! Marvellous! I was getting a steady, I was getting a slight high, ease her down, a little bit of low, ease her up, steady, you are looking good, cut the throttle and there I was with a jerk that threw me forward towards the gunsight only inches from my face, into the gear. I had caught a wire and made my first deck landing. As I sat there recovering my composure the batsman came over to me and said, 'That was very nice, very nice indeed. Let's have another one like that.' Puffed up with pride I was respotted, pushed back to the stern, opened the throttle and took off once again.

Unbeknown to me, the Commander Air had gone on to the 'goofers', which was just aft of his fly control position, and had addressed the rest of my team as follows: 'There you are. Here's a chap whose never done a deck landing before in his life, and look at that, absolutely immaculate.' I zoomed around feeling quite an old hand by this stage, fell into the groove as usual, nose up, pictured the batsman inside the kidney exhaust. In I came, hardly any movement from the batsman, it was steady all the way down, 55, 56, 58 knots, something in that region, then cut. There I was again, bang. The batsman came over. 'That was excellent,' he said, 'Do one more and if you go on like this you are all set for an above-average deck landing qualification.' I was thrilled. It was the first time I had been offered an above-average assessment. I had had high average, I had had low average, I had had average, but above average – this was my great moment. I was respotted and shot off again. Again I came round and again I made the same kind of approach, same kind of routine, no problem, cut, into the wires. The batsman came over. 'That was excellent,' he said. 'One more like that and you are all set for an exceptional assessment as you really have got it absolutely buttoned; just keep doing that.'

Off I went again, this time puffed up with so much pride that the fall was almost inevitable. I came around, same again. As I flattened out and came up towards the round-down there was a slight hint of a stall, just a slight flutter of the wings as she wobbled a bit. No, no, I thought, I'll go round again, I don't want to make a heavy landing, I wanted it to be as immaculate as the last. I applied full throttle but unbeknown to me, at precisely that moment the batsman was about to give me the cut. The aircraft caught a wire at full throttle and shot out of control, pulling the wire with it to the port side of the ship where the funnel came out, and landed on top of it and broke in two! There I was in a state of disaster having semi-concussed myself as my head went forward and hit the gunsight. Now they really did have a problem, because fuel from my aircraft was pouring down the funnel and we had a slight fire hazard.

I was hauled out of the cockpit by willing hands and staggered across the flight deck, bleeding from the blow I had received on the bridge of my nose and a cut over my right eye. I was shattered in more ways than one! Here I had come to within an ace of an 'exceptional' and had blown the whole blooming thing. I was probably going to be grounded, thrown off the course and finished. Apart from the kind of stress that must have occurred I was obsessed with just one thing. I must get back and do it again. Not exactly what I had just done, but demonstrate that I could do it properly! Commander Air came to see me, a nice man.

'I want to go off and do it again,' I said.

'Well, you can't,' he said, 'not just yet. You've got to get patched up and steady down, Lygo.'

'Yes,' I said, 'but you know, Sir, I really do want to get on with this.'

'You'll be all right,' he said, 'you just need to have a rest and go back and do a few more aerodrome dummy-deck landings and then come back again.'

And so it was. I packed my bags somewhat ignominiously, left without my companions who were there qualifying, and slowly made my way back to Yeovilton where I was told to go on leave, pending reappointment.

Now, of course, I had to break the news to my parents that I was coming home, somewhat unexpectedly, but also to ensure that my mother should not be put off too much by my appearance which was

90

slightly black and blue from bruising, and also with stitches over my eye and a broken nose. I 'phoned her from the station at Orpington before I set off down Lynwood Grove to our house in Melbourne Close. She received the news calmly. I suppose, in wartime, parents who are told that their children are returning are glad to have them in more or less whatever condition they might arrive!

I was sent off back to the Naval Air Fighter School to do some more dummy-deck landings. It was a somewhat sheepish Lygo who appeared but no one seemed to take too much notice. People were quite used to this kind of thing happening and I was allocated a Squadron and given time to do some more Addls, which of course I was quite capable of doing. However, the knack of looking under the kidney exhaust and framing the batsman was no longer possible for me. I had lost my nerve as far as that particular activity was concerned and I did what most people did, craned my head out and looked – or tried to look – round the side of the kidney exhaust, coming in slightly crab fashion so that I could get a better view. The result, of course, was that you came in slightly faster with the risk of ballooning and going into the barrier, or having too much crab or not getting it off and damaging the very frail undercarriage on the Seafire. Nevertheless, my efforts seemed to suffice, and I was given a clean bill of health and told that I would have to go back and do my deck-landing practices once more.

Once again I set out for Rothesay, once again to the *Ravager*, with not quite such an air of expectation; I was really much more nervous this time than I had been the first time, but I succeeded. This time I did my four landings, not exceptionally good but adequate, and then the break and the final two, and I was qualified as a deck-landing Seafire pilot. I have often wondered, in later years, whether that accident was in a way to save my life. I believe that, had I gone on flying the aircraft so close to the stall by looking under the exhausts and that very exaggerated nose-up attitude, sooner or later with a badly pitching deck I might well have come to grief, but who knows? I had survived my collision course.

Before I joined a front-line Squadron, it was decided that I should get a little more general flying practice under my belt, and I was sent to a Squadron based at Speke, near Liverpool, which was a Fleet Requirements Unit, towing drogues and doing general communication duties. It was a bit of a comedown for a budding fighter pilot but it was good in that it was the first time I actually flew as a pilot in a Squadron; it enabled me to get my confidence back, and also gave me an opportunity to fly many different types of aeroplanes.

I remember, without affection, the Skua which was being used for target towing. The first time I took off in a Skua was on the short runway straight towards the gasworks in Liverpool. This extraordinary aeroplane had a strange appearance in that the undercarriage pointed vertically downwards when the aircraft was on the ground so that the aeroplane looked as if it was in the landing, three-point attitude, when it was coming in to land. This didn't really help since I gather the aircraft was originally designed, as most Fleet Air Arm aircraft were, for stronger or larger more powerful engines but these all went to the RAF and so the Skua was fitted with a Bristol Taurus engine. In order to get the centre of gravity right with the smaller less powerful engine, the Skua had a long extension between the front end of the occupied part of the fuselage and the engine which was held out on a series of tubes. It was not uncommon if you landed the aeroplane terribly heavily to find that the whole engine, the whole of the front of the aircraft, would droop down!

It had a two-speed propeller and I had never flown such an aeroplane but as I lined up on the short runway at Speke and looked at the gasworks I thought, well, once again boys, this is it. Full power in fine pitch produced a scream from the engine and we started to roll steadily down the runway eventually lurching airborne in this three-point attitude and starting to climb away. I retracted the undercarriage and once safely clear of the gasworks and clear of Liverpool, heading out towards Morecambe Bay, I decided to go into coarse pitch; I pushed the lever, a kind of plunger, which stuck out of the dashboard, to change into coarse pitch and nothing happened for a few moments, and then it seemed as if the whole engine had stopped. When it had settled down I could hear clonkity clonk, clonkity clonk, clonkity clonk; I was now in coarse pitch and I could almost see the propeller turning in front of me. The ailerons were so stiff in this aircraft, that how anybody ever fought with it or did anything operational was beyond my belief, especially after I had flown such a hot ship as the Spitfire. But there it was, the standard aircraft that the Fleet Air Arm had for dive bombing which had been used successfully against targets in Norway. Those pilots had carried out the unenviable task of flying all the way from Hatston across the Norwegian Sea to Bergen to attack German ships, and then back again, carrying one 500lb. bomb; an extraordinary performance.

Another aeroplane was the Boulton Paul Defiant, which was again converted for target towing. This aircraft's engine had a propensity to boil, and it was often overheating before you got to the end of the runway! It was a very, very heavy aeroplane pulled by one Merlin engine, so the Merlin found itself struggling. It had been successful on one occasion, I believe, during the Battle of Britain when it first appeared because it looked to the Luftwaffe like a Hurricane and as they swooped down to attack seeing this aircraft on a fairly straight and level course, they were met with a barrage of fire from the four-barrelled turret at the rear. However, once the Luftwaffe had got the measure of this they proceeded to attack it from underneath and that was the end of the Boulton Paul Defiant and I don't think it was ever used operationally again. It was a heavy, clunking aeroplane but it did well enough for target towing. We also had the ubiquitous Miles Master III which was quite a nice aeroplane for target towing, and also some aircraft for communications flying, typically the Oxford, and various others. By the time I had got these few types under my belt and had mastered the art of being one's own boss in the air, even though it was only target towing, I enjoyed it. I did a detachment to Squires Gate, just north of Blackpool where it was quite amusing to fly out to sea towing drogues just north of Blackpool Tower. I was billeted in a house on the outskirts of Liverpool, which was shared by some RAF types, Pilot Officers, who were actually working on the LMS Railway because there was no work for them in the RAF. They were stoking on the trains! There were also some Americans with lots of American loot who were based at a large US Air Force base not too far away. But life there did not last long because after a month or so I was drafted to my first first-line Squadron, 887, at Englinton, Northern Ireland.

I got my things together to be flown to Northern Ireland in an Airspeed Oxford by one of the pilots in the squadron. I remember sitting somewhat uncomfortably in the back of the aeroplane with my bag and baggage as we took off in dreadful weather. The pilot elected to fly at low level across the Irish Sea and eventually came across the Isle of Man; when I say came across it, he literally came across it – suddenly saw it rearing up in front of him out of the sea! By applying full throttle and heaving back on the control column he managed to scrape over the top of the hill and clear the Isle of Man. Had this not been the case I would have ended my Naval career very smartly there and then. He somewhat nervously let down the other side and finally we arrived at Belfast and crept round the coast to Eglinton, which was one of three or four aerodromes that were then operating in Northern Ireland. It was a classic wartime Nissen-hutted dispersed airfield, literally in the middle of nowhere. The nearest town was Londonderry which was, I suppose, about an hour's drive away in a 'tilly', and it rained almost incessantly, or it seemed to.

It was dark by the time I checked in at the wardroom to be told that I was in hut 43 which was miles away in some dispersed campsite. Having had supper, I proceeded to get myself there in the duty tilly and was dumped in a desolate, unlit hutted campsite which was a sea of mud. I found my way across to the hut in which I had been allocated a cabin and there found myself in a classic iron-cotted, one-bed cabin with the usual pot-bellied stove for which we were allowed one bucket of coal a week – hardly enough to keep you going for one night, let alone one week! But there was nothing for it. No one appeared to be around, and I settled down for my first night as a member of a front-line Squadron at Eglinton.

At about midnight or soon after there was a lot of noise, lights began to be turned on and it was clear to me that the 'Squadron' had returned from a run ashore in Londonderry. It was with some trepidation that I lay there wondering how soon it was going to be before they realised they had a new boy and required him to be turned out to be inspected; it wasn't long. There were, in fact, two Squadrons based at Eglinton at the time, forming 24 Fighter Wing, 894 Squadron and 887. The moment arrived which I feared would, when a voice said, 'We've got a new pilot here somewhere, let's turn him out.' And I was turned out in my pyjamas to be introduced to a drunken bunch of fellow aviators who had just returned from a run ashore in various states of inebriation. I remember one chap, and incidentally they were all in mess undress, who had blood all over the top of his shirt and front of his uniform and innocently asking, 'How did this happen?' I was told that he had gone into a chemist shop asking for condoms and when he was told they didn't sell them he exited via the plate glass window! Eventually the activity subsided sufficiently for me to get back to bed and early next morning I was up in the company of a sullen bunch of hung-over chaps on their way up to the Wardroom for breakfast and then down to the Squadron dispersal.

The Squadron was equipped with Seafire F3s, which I had never flown, so after a while I approached someone and asked him if he would be kind enough to give me a cockpit check. The guy looked at me with surprise. 'Well, we're certainly not flying today,' he said, looking out of the window – it was absolutely clamped down and raining. 'Well, nevertheless ...' I said. 'You can find somebody else, I'm not going to do it.' And so it went on. In the end I walked out and got into the aeroplane, one that was sitting outside, shut the hood to keep the rain off, and examined the contents. It was the first time I had seen a gyro gunsight, for example, and this intrigued me. It had a large cable that led from the throttle to the graticule adjuster in the sight. These were opened and closed by turning the barrel of the throttle. I found my way around the cockpit fairly easily, but found this large gunsight even more difficult for deck landing, as far as head movement was concerned, than the old GS8.

At the end of the first morning we embarked in the tilly and went up to the wardroom where for the most part it seemed the Squadron was going to have some of the hair of the dog that had bitten them the night before. The bar was in the corner on the left as you entered the Ante-Room. I strode to the other end of the room by the fire and sat in a chair, picking up a copy of *The Times*. I drank hardly at all in those days, and certainly didn't want to drink at lunchtime if there was any prospect of flying. However, shortly the chap I was relieving in the Squadron came over and touched me on the shoulder and said, 'Oh Ray, when you're ready, from the CO, come over and join us, we've been buying for you.' I rose slowly, put the paper down and proceeded, my worst fears rising in my bosom, to walk towards the bar in the corner of the Ante-Room where my Squadron mates were grouped together. There on the bar stood two pints of black liquid which I recognised as being Guinness. I was about to say, 'I'm sorry, Sir, I don't drink,' when the Squadron Commander, a chap by the name of Wiggington, said, 'Well, Lygo, welcome to 887, it's nice to have you. They sent us somebody else but he only lasted two weeks.' In my innocence, of course, I rose to the bait immediately and said, 'Oh really, Sir, why was that?' 'He didn't drink,' he said, and my hand stretched out for my first glass of Guinness. How I managed to get through that lunch without collapsing I shall never know, and Dicky Reynolds, who sat opposite me, has told me since that I showed no visible signs of what was going on inside me, which would be hard to describe. I was therefore well able to join the rest of the Squadron in getting my head down in the afternoon, which seemed to be the normal occupation if there was no flying.

I seem to recall that the Squadron was actually going off to do something else, and as I was new it wasn't considered appropriate for me to go with them. I think they went off to do fighter sweeps over Europe, and were away for about two weeks, so I was attached to the other Squadron on the station, 894, for my familiarisation flying. I found them a very congenial bunch of chaps, some of whom, Dick Reynolds, now sadly dead, and Ken Ward, have been lifelong friends.

The days in 887 rolled by and soon it was time for us to embark in the new aircraft carrier HMS *Indefatigable* to go on a shakedown cruise off the coast of Norway. The idea in those days was to embark in Scapa Flow itself, just as Squadron Commander Dunning had done when he made the first ever deck landing on *Furious* in those same waters 27 years before. The carrier would steam up and down as the aircraft were recovered until it had reached its full load, and when that was done all was secured until night when it would make a night departure from the Flow. Life aboard the carrier was for me fascinating and interesting, and I met for the first time one of the most effective and efficient Naval Officers I have ever met in my career, Commander Whitfield, the Commander of the ship. He was a traditional good old-fashioned RN Commander, a seaman from the tips of his toes to the top of his head, who did much to keep the whole ship together in what became an extremely difficult cruise and commission.

Indefatigable's task was to cover a Russian convoy that was proceeding round the top of Norway. Our task was to maintain fighter readiness on deck to go off and intercept any shadowers that came out to try to find either us or attack the convoy, or plot the position of the convoy. This was a fairly boring task because it meant being strapped into your aircraft for four-hour stints. You started the engine every thirty minutes just to warm it through because it got extremely cold – in fact, the upper parts of the ship were beginning to get covered in ice as we proceeded further and further north. Such flying as we did was generally on the basis of a scare of one sort or another – an echo would be detected, perhaps, and it would be decided to scramble the four aircraft that were in readiness. If you were lucky you were one of those at readiness and got airborne; if you were unlucky you could spend a week or a fortnight without flying and then suddenly find yourself shot off the deck on some fairly abortive mission, to come back and attempt a deck landing which perhaps was the first time you had tried it for weeks, on a deck that was pitching and a sea that was freezing cold.

The Captain was Q.D. Graham, again a traditional and experienced Naval officer but it was the first time he had come across the aviation fraternity. Our Commander Air was Pat Humphries, who was an old and solid pilot, and we had an Ops Officer called Buchanan Dunlop.

After an operation of this kind we would return to Scapa Flow, the ship would refuel and we would start out again on the next operation. Sometimes it would be to cover attacks on the *Tirpitz*, the battleship that was holed up in Norway. On other occasions it would be to carry out fighter sweeps against German airfield as far north as Bardafoss which was the most northerly airfield in Norway. I remember particularly, as one does when one is young, one of the briefings which indicated that there was a certain building at Bardafoss that we should not strafe as we ran in on our fighter sweep, because that was where some Norwegian women were being kept as comforts for the northerly based Luftwaffe pilots. Somehow that brought the brutality and horror of war to me, closer than anything that had touched me thus far, and if I needed inspiration to be determined to do my duty this was one of the little things that helped. I remember also on one particular strafing run being told that the position I was in, flying number two now to the Senior Pilot, would take me right over the heaviest defence guns. 'Don't worry,' said the SP, 'it's a good thing that, they'll never hit you if you fly straight over them.' Nevertheless, it didn't help me to sleep easy the night before, waiting for the sortie to take place.

We always went in at a very low level to escape detection and would hope to hit a particular landmark on the Norwegian coast. This would lead us in to our first target, which we would attack and then proceed to an alternate or down the 'leads' where German ships would hide up during the day, taking passage at night to keep their supply routes open, and open fire with our remaining ammunition on any ship we could find sheltering. All the time, of course, we had to be alert to the hornet's nest we had raised behind us, the Messerschmitt 109s that would get airborne and come belting after us. Somehow they never caught us.

On about the third sortie up north we hit a slight technical snag. The Seafire was particularly prone to bursting tyres; as I mentioned earlier, 60 per cent of the shock of landing was taken by the tyres, so even a moderately heavy landing would be accompanied by a loud pop as the tyre burst and the aircraft was forcibly taxied forward on a flat tyre. As a result we used up quite a number of tyres and eventually the moment arrived when there were no more tyres left! Someone then had to go and tell the Captain that we had to stop flying the Seafires because they were running out of tyres. The Captain was absolutely horrified. 'I can't stop flying just for that,' he said. And then, turning to the Commander Air, he said, 'Bind the wheels with rope. We'll use rope instead of inflatable tyres.' Well, it was a splendid piece of seamanship no doubt, but it would have driven the oleos, brittle as they were, straight up through the mainplane of the aircraft. This was, however, a difficult technical point to get across to a Captain who was determined to do well with his ship on its first operational series of engagements. We had to stop flying, nevertheless, and we just kept the aircraft that still had tyres at standby until we returned to Scapa and were able to replenish our stocks!

My deck-landing ability was not of the highest order. I had gone from almost exceptional to almost below average, and on one occasion fairly early on I landed with drift on and broke the under-carriage; that is to say, it collapsed on me and my crew had to spend that night repairing it. I went down to offer them my commiserations and, as is always the case with ground crew on these occasions, they were more than supportive. 'Good heavens, Sir, that's nothing, we'll soon get this fixed for you.' I was mortified, but worse was to come. We were flying on a dusk patrol; it was a clear evening and we would be landing into the sun. However, I decided that, although I

A particularly nasty accident off Norway, when a Seafire floated over the barrier and landed on top of the previous aircraft taxiing forward killing the pilot

had with me my clear lenses to put into my goggles, we would be landing sufficiently ahead of sunset for me not to worry too much about keeping my dark lenses in. Remember, we were only flying 1h30-minute sorties and that was with 30-gallon drop tanks. Incidentally, I should tell you that when we went on low-level missions flying at 50 feet or so, the normal routine was to start the engines on the main tanks, bring the drop tank into action, turn off the main tank to make sure that the engine didn't quit and then return to main tank for take-off. As soon as we were airborne and safely on our way we would turn on the drop tank, switch off the main tank, and if the engine did not cut – and usually it didn't – we ran on for the 40 minutes or so that the drop tank lasted and waited until the engine stopped. Having drunk all the fuel it would suddenly stop and you would drop back; then, perhaps, number three would drop back, or the Leader would drop back, and then we would switch on our main tanks, the engine would burst into life again, we would catch up and on we would go. A fairly hairy way of ensuring that you were using all the fuel that was available, but we needed to because the Seafire was not designed for long endurance.

On this particular occasion we had with us *Nabob* and *Trumpeter*, two escort carriers that were equipped with Avengers to be used for attacks on the Norwegian mainland. When we returned after this particular sortie towards sunset, just as we let down to come back to recover at our due time, when we would normally have about 15 minutes' worth of fuel remaining, to our horror we saw our carrier, instead of turning into wind to recover us, turn out of wind, rev up for full speed and disappear with its destroyer escort away from the main body as fast as possible. The reason for this was that HMS *Nabob* had been torpedoed; there was therefore a submarine somewhere in the vicinity of the force and the Captain was determined to get *Indefatigable* as far away from it as possible. Our recovery was therefore delayed. As we waited the sun got lower and lower until it became apparent that we would be landing in the dusk if we got on at all. So I proceeded to fiddle with my dark lenses to put the clear lenses into my goggles so that I would be ready for landing in dusk. I just could not manage to do it and stay in formation, however, so I was stuck with dark glasses! We were delayed and delayed and our gauges were now reading something ridiculously low; finally, the SP led us back over the ship, waggling his wings to indicate that if we were not brought aboard we would all be in the oggin. With some reluctance, therefore, the Captain decided that he would turn the ship into wind and bring us on.

We fell into line astern up the starboard side as the ship was turning and came round the circuit. The SP, Andrew Thompson, was too close in to get aboard as the ship was still turning with full helm; as I came round as number two the ship was still turning but 'Wings' apparently said, 'Bring him on.' I was duly brought on with the ship still turning, not quite understanding why I had difficulty lining up, only to find that when I did straighten out, with the ship turning, splat ... I bust an undercarriage. Not popular when other aircraft were trying to get on with as little fuel as I had. They quickly dragged me forward out of the way and the others came aboard safely. Although this accident was not technically my fault, it came on top of the two others I have already mentioned and for which on each occasion I had had to render an A25, the accident report form which all pilots have to fill in after they have had a flying accident in the Fleet Air Arm.

The Squadron Staff Officer Admin. at that time was a particularly unpleasant character who was a bully; he was other things too, it turned out, but that is for a later part of the story. And when I had to render an A25, I had to go to him to get the form and every time, sometimes in front of other people, he would make remarks about my flying ability and the fact that I had had to render one of these forms.

Over she goes. A damaged beyond repair Seafire is ditched

On the last occasion it really was too much and I knew that the only way to deal with a bully would be to confront him. I am not a physically strong person, neither am I particularly physically aggressive, but I knew that something had to be done. I therefore waited and just before changing for dinner went down to this chap's cabin, knocked on the door and went in. 'Oh, yes,' he said looking up, 'What do you want?' 'I've come to tell you', I said, 'that if you don't stop making remarks about my flying ability and in particular my deck-landing ability, I'm going to strike you and I shall strike you in public.' He looked at me for a moment and then said, visibly shaken, 'I didn't realise that it was getting to you so much.' 'Well, it is,' I said, 'and you had better stop it because otherwise I shall not be responsible for my actions and you will suffer at least a broken nose. What will happen to me I have no idea but I couldn't care less.' The ribbing ceased. The only way to deal with bullies is to stand up to them, and the sooner the better because no matter what the consequences may be, it never gets any better.

After the episode with *Nabob* and *Trumpeter*, we went back into Scapa Flow where fuel was transferred from the stricken escort carrier, which had limped back into Scapa, into lighters and subsequently into

Indefatigable. Each time the ship returned to Scapa, the squadron was disembarked to a shore station and we manage to be based at each one of the four stations in the Orkneys at that time – Hatston, Grimsetter, Skeabrae and Twatt – and I had also by this time been made the Squadron Staff Officer, presumably because I had some ability to string a few words together.

On arrival at one of these stations it was time to pay the Squadron Ratings and so I flew from Grimsetter in a Seafire, across to Hatston to collect their money. I landed at Hatston which was in itself an experience because the main runway, or rather the only runway, had been the road out of Kirkwall and the only way in a Seafire, with its difficulty of seeing straight ahead, that you knew you were actually lined up and on the runway, was when you couldn't see it! If as you came into land you saw grass on either side of the nose you knew you were on the runway. Anyway I landed, taxied in and strolled nonchalantly over to the Paymaster Commander's office to draw the Squadron pay; it was, of course, even in those days several hundred pounds. 'Do you wish to count it?' said the rather pompous Purser looking at me through his glasses, and unfortunately for me I said, 'No, Sir, no that's quite all right, I'll just sign for it.' I signed for it and stuffed it in the back of the seat in my Seafire and off I took and flew back to Grimsetter. Can you imagine such a performance today!

The moment then came for me to pay the men. A regulating Petty Officer called each man by name and in those days the call was 'off-caps' and the cap was laid in front of you and the money laid on top. I believe the theory was that at some stage, a Rating who had been dissatisfied with his pay had used his cap to take a swipe at the officer concerned. After that, it was decided that the cap having been removed should be placed on the table and the money put on top of it so that if anybody decided to take a swipe at the Paying Officer with their cap, they would lose their money! Incidentally, if a Rating turned his hat over the other way after being paid it meant he was asking for a condom! The Navy has a method for everything! Sailors' pay in those days varied from £2 to £6, depending on how much allotments they were making, and we had just over a hundred men in the Squadron. When it came to the last man I didn't have any money left! He had to be paid out of my own pocket which for me was an experience not to be repeated – always count the money before you sign the receipt!

We then set sail on what was to be another trip up the Norwegian coast. The first aircraft to be launched was a Barracuda; it went rolling down the deck, got to the end of the deck, just got airborne, the engine stopped and it fell gracefully into the oggin. The one thing a Barracuda could do beautifully was ditch! The crew stepped out, no problems, and we then proceeded to carry on flying. The first episode with a Seafire occurred when a chap went roaring down the deck and the engine stopped after about a hundred feet. He did a neat ground loop just on the edge of the flight deck, stopping the aircraft from going over the front, and then was towed back. 'What happened?' we asked. 'The engine stopped,' he said. The CO said to me, 'Ray, when we are back in Scapa tonight I would like you to do an engine run on that aircraft. I am quite certain the chap turned off his main fuel cock to check his drop tank and forgot to turn it on again.' So on a particularly wild night in Scapa Flow, when we were safely back, I went up to do an engine run on this particular Seafire. I remember it very well because I was in Mess Undress which I thought was a rather unusual way of doing an engine run. It was to be repeated many years later, but that's another story!

However, I could not start the aircraft and finally had to report back to the CO, saying, 'I can't start it, Sir, and I have told the Squadron air artificer to start having a look to see what can be the matter.' When they removed the carburettor from the aircraft, what was the matter was pretty obvious – it was full of water. It transpired that the fuel that had been transferred to the ship from the stricken *Nabob* was contaminated with sea water. Sea water had been drawn off in lieu of petrol and put into our tanks, and we had drawn off the sea water. All the aircraft in all the Squadrons, therefore, had to be inspected for salt water contamination and most, if not all, were found to be suffering and had to be worked on and cleaned, which meant no flying on that particular operation.

We had suffered our losses on this series of operations, mostly caused by accidents, some caused by enemy action: chaps being shot down over enemy territory or having engine failures over enemy territory. It is difficult with a Seafire to be quite certain, because it needed only one bullet in the radiator to cause the engine to lose coolant and stop, so whether that was a natural cause or whether it had been caused by enemy action was sometimes difficult to determine after you had been flying low level over heavily defended airfields.

I remember now how I became the Squadron Staff Officer. We had join the Squadron after I joined, the one and only RN officer. He was a Lieutenant RN and he obviously told the CO that he thought he should be the Squadron Admin. Officer and was duly appointed as such, replacing the unpleasant chap referred to earlier. He was not a particularly likeable chap, as I recall, and we were all fallen in, all the Sub Lieutenants that is, soon after he arrived, to get a lecture by – it was still Wiggington in those days – the Squadron CO, on the extreme dignity and standing of a Lieutenant in the Royal Navy. Obviously this chap didn't like the way we had been treating him, as if he was one of the lads. It was pointed out to us that a Lieutenant was Wardroom status whereas we were not and that if the ship had a big enough Gun Room, which it didn't, that is where we would be. There were too many of us, of course, because all the pilots for the most part in the Squadrons were Sub Lieutenants and so it was only the Midshipmen who went into the Gun Room. I must say the lecture signally failed to impress us or endear the RN to us.

I remember sitting at breakfast one morning when a chap came in and said, 'Lieutenant Blank has spun in on the approach.' 'Oh dear,' I said, and finished my cornflakes. It was then that the new CO – it was Andrew Thompson by now – appointed me to become Staff Officer. The point I am making is that death was taken for granted. People didn't come back, or spun in, or failed to make it in some way, and although, particularly if it was your personal friend, you were very upset at the loss and saddened by it, nevertheless the terrible thought was always present that since something like 50 per cent of us were not going to make it anyway, everyone who was knocked off and not you, lengthened the chance of your survival! Nonsense, ridiculous, macabre, uncaring – that is the way it was. I was asked during an interview when I retired from the Navy, 'What was it like, what were your feelings?' and I said, 'Well, we didn't have many feelings except one of trepidation every time we walked out on to the Flight Deck to fly, and I always felt that if I ever walked out there thinking this is a piece of cake I would have bought it the next flight. Nevertheless, the thing that motivated me was survival, I lived from day to day and hoped to live from day to day, and if I lived for another week then that was a week closer to the time when I would be released from the kind of purgatory in which I was serving. I did my duty as everybody else did but it was a callous business and one was concerned solely for one's self, at least I was; after all, I was a fighter pilot and that is a single-seat occupation.'

One rather more pleasant experience was that we were called upon to embark in HMS *Implacable*, a new carrier but the same class as *Indefatigable* that was working up and wished to borrow some experienced Squadrons to take with her for an operation off Northern Norway. I am bound to say it was rather a different experience. I do not know why but things seemed to go much better. The ship was cleaner, it seemed to me, more well organised than *Indefatigable* was, and we enjoyed our embarked time. During the course of that embarkation I am pleased to say that my deck-landing prowess improved considerably. It was during this embarkation that I met Lt Cdr. Lamb, the flight deck officer, who told me of his experiences during the loss of the *Courageous* which I recount in another chapter.

At length the time came for the final disembarkation from *Indefatigable*, while she went back to have a refit to prepare her for the next major event. Her next operation was to join the Indian Ocean Fleet and then out to the Pacific to fight the Japanese. With most of the German Navy bottled up and the U-boat war largely won there was no longer a great threat in the North Atlantic, and we were to be spared to go out to the Far East. I had joined 887 some five months previously as the fourteenth pilot. When we got back to disembark at Grimsetter for the last time I was the seventh pilot in the Squadron, and as two were going to be relieved in the normal course of duty it left five of us as the 'old hands' to welcome the new pilots.

We arrived at Lee-on-Solent, the aircraft were put away for servicing and overhaul to prepare them for re-embarkation for the Far East, and we went on leave. My first experience in the North Atlantic, on Russian convoys, attacks on the *Tirpitz*, and the fighters sweeps over Norway, had ended. I do not know what damage we had actually inflicted on the enemy but we had inflicted quite a lot of damage on ourselves, that is for certain! But I suppose that is war. War is a muddle and it is not the chaps who get it absolutely right who win, it is the ones who get it least wrong!

Lee was a fairly uneventful affair, it usually was. I managed to make a date with a rather attractive girl who lived not too far away, and that brief romance was all there was to it, really. I am afraid my background and upbringing had not really conditioned me to making the best of social opportunities. It was a long time before I could believe that you could get tea in a first class hotel for little more than you would have to pay for it in a Lyons Tea Shop, or that you could use it for something more pressing. I really wasn't couth in the ways of the world at that time but that was hardly surprising. My background and the War, and what I had done so far in it, really left me little time for socialising and even though my ambitions were considerable they remained largely unfulfilled.

When I got back to Lee-on-Solent, it was to find that Lieutenant-Commander Wiggington had been relieved by Andrew Thompson, an entirely different character. Andrew, a tall, lanky and languid redhead, with an almost permanent cigarette hanging out of his mouth and an almost permanent glass of gin in his other hand, was only four years my senior but to us at that stage, when six months' seniority meant so much, a kind of father figure. He was kind, he was considerate, and he was a great help to me. 887 Squadron was to be increased from a 12-aircraft squadron to a 24-aircraft squadron, and to do this we were given two courses out of Henstridge, the secondary Naval Air Fighter School. Can you really imagine doing that at that time? It was an enormous task for the most robust of Squadron Commanders, and Andrew was never that. In addition, we were only given something like two weeks in which to sort ourselves out with all the new aeroplanes and new pilots before we were to take off to Mona, in Anglesey, prior to embarking in *Indefatigable* which was coming to pick us up in the Irish Sea. The other squadron, 894, was increased from 12 aircraft to 18 but it had a much more stable core to build on. Andrew was made wing leader of 24 Wing, now comprising some 40 Seafires.

Little flying was achieved from Lee during that period because of the problems of getting the aeroplanes ready, and ourselves sorted out; I was now made a Section Leader to Andrew Thompson, and we acquired in our flight, Red Flight, two brand-new pilots. On the day we were due to fly to Anglesey, the weather was a classic winter's day with a south-westerly wind and a depression with its fronts moving steadily across the British Isles. To my considerable surprise, Andrew decided that the Squadron would fly to Anglesey in formation, (the well known Balbo), six flights of four Seafires. We duly set off from Lee and proceeded in a north-westerly direction towards Anglesey. We were below cloud and the cloud base got lower, and the ground began to rise, until it became obvious that there was only one way to go and that was up through it, and so up we went.

We had not been closed in particularly close for the penetration of cloud and it was therefore soon after entering cloud that we all became dispersed. It was a miracle there was not a massive number of air collisions but I climbed up through the cloud, having waggled my wings to tuck my number two in close to me. However, I was then busy concentrating on my flying and instruments up through the cloud and not too concerned about whether he was with me or not. When I finally broke out at the top, he was not there and there were no other aircraft in sight. In those days, one had only basic radio information and it was therefore not possible to determine exactly where one was, or even where one might be going. Therefore I flew on a steady north-westerly course until I saw the clouds thinning and a hole open up and some ground appear below. I descended through the hole until I got contact with the ground and, to my great relief, saw a large four-engined aircraft with its wheels down, which was a good enough indication for me that there was an airfield somewhere around. I tucked in beside it and then, much to the pilot's horror, I am sure, as soon as I saw the airfield ahead, darted in and landed ahead of him. I don't think it would have been wise to have followed him in a Seafire anyway, so it was better for him to follow me.

The airfield turned out to be Chipping Warden and there I found Andrew Thompson and one other Seafire pilot. Andrew decided that we would return to Lee-on-the-Solent, which we did; then, having refuelled and repaired our morale a bit, he decided that we would continue north but this time indicating to the scattered brood that were all over the country, that everyone should make their own way to Mona. Our own flight was not together, except for one Sub-Lieutenant who had tragically collided with a Halifax, I believe, in cloud and they had all been lost. This was my Number Two who had been separated from me. I was given another Number Two, the flight re-formed, and we got airborne for Mona once again, this time landing at Cosford to refuel. We duly arrived at Mona, the rest of the Squadron arriving in dribs and drabs, and set about preparing ourselves for embarkation in *Indefatigable* the same day, 21st November 1944.

Having landed on, I was old enough and wise enough in the ways of carrier flying to vacate my aircraft promptly and disappear into the island to find my cabin and get myself sorted out. We now had a very crowded ship and most of the Midshipmen and Junior Sub-Lieutenants were sleeping on bunks in the passageways, outside the cabins. I went down to the Wardroom to be greeted by another Squadron mate, who said, 'Did you realise that your number two had spun in downwind?' 'No,' I said, 'I hadn't realised that.' I had last seen him as I waved goodbye as I broke from the bows of the ship to turn downwind in the normal routine of breaking, one, two, three, four, and assumed that he had followed me round. Clearly, he hadn't followed very far. So my second number two was lost in a matter of days, both by tragic accidents, and we had hardly embarked!

There was little flying on the way out to the Indian Ocean because the ship was required to make a fairly fast passage. I see that in fact I flew just three hours before we arrived off Ceylon, and I completed three deck landings in just under a month, which was not a high rate of flying. The first port we called at, and my first foreign visit, was Port Said, where we were allowed to go ashore. Then it was off to Trincomalee, Ceylon, with a short stop for some flying practice off Massawa on the Red Sea. I rapidly learned why we were not loved by the natives very much and also why we didn't particularly like them. Three of us went ashore to savour the delights of Port Said, and like any youngster, I suppose, at that time I was open-eyed and open-eared and prepared for more or less anything, but generally speaking had a benign attitude towards everybody concerned. I was no great drinker, and so at one stage I found myself with my companions sitting, while I was drinking some kind of soft drink, when a small Arab boy appeared and offered me a newspaper. I thought it might be a good idea to read the local paper so I paid him whatever he asked for, only to discover within a few minutes after he departed that he'd charged me three times the going rate for the day before yesterday's paper!

My next experience was when another youngster arrived to clean my shoes, which didn't need cleaning, but the waiter advised me that it was probably sensible to get my shoes cleaned otherwise they would make them very dirty indeed. And the third episode was when a cart, drawn by a donkey with a bunch of chaps cheering, came along the street. When I asked the waiter what this was all about, he replied, 'It is for Farouk. They shout for Farouk. Today he is up, tomorrow,' he said with a shrug of his shoulders, 'he may be down.' It seemed to me that within a very short space of time, I had managed to be briefed on the commercial realities of where I was, the system of patronage that existed, and a snapshot of the political situation! Later that evening, we joined up with a bunch of the more boisterous members of the Squadron, and it was decided that we would engage a garry each to go back to the Dockyard, and to have a race. Two garries were forthwith commandeered and we proceeded off down the road. The game here was to draw lots beforehand as to the order in which we would abandon the garry and the ultimate success would be if the garries arrived at the Dockyard gates with no passengers left on board at all. The job of the last man was to set fire to the bundle of hay that was hanging under the garry. Now you may have understood my attitude had been hardened towards the natives, but you can now begin to understand why their attitude was fairly hard against us. Yes, I am sad to say, one sat helplessly in the road rocking with laughter as the garry roared away with the hay blazing. It was not long of course before the driver realised something was amiss and stopped, and had to detach his bucket of hay lest it set fire to the garry.

So much for the run ashore in Port Said, but soon we were off again, moving through the Canal and looking at that scene which I suspect has not changed very much over the years. I do remember one episode, one always remembers one and it's never the most important, but these things stick in your memory. Waving in a friendly fashion to a couple of Arabs who were on the bank, we received a return greeting which was that they turned round and threw their robes back over their heads, revealing two bare behinds. Well, I've heard of a sailor's farewell but this was slightly different! We entered the Red Sea, and then we were going to do some flying with a diversion airfield at Masawa.

It just so happened that my cousin, who was my only remote

Indefatigable in the Suez Canal

connection with the Navy, was a Surgeon Lieutenant Commander, and having done his stint at sea in a cruiser in the Mediterranean had been appointed as PMO to the Naval hospital in Masawa, which had been the capital of Italian Eritrea but of course which had now been captured by the British. I therefore addressed a letter to Surgeon Lieutenant Commander Sutton, telling him as best as one could in those days, when one wasn't allowed to give information, that I might be able to see him in the not too distant future and would certainly avail myself of such an opportunity should it occur.

As we approached Massawa, I therefore asked the CO if I could take a Seafire ashore just to visit him, and then come back and rejoin the ship. Whilst he was sympathetic, the Ops Officer decided that it wasn't a good thing for Lygo to do because if the aeroplane went unserviceable I should be left in Masawa and not where I was supposed to be going. However we did fly off Masawa, and in the course of that exercise one Sub Lieutenant Jones couldn't get his hook down and therefore was diverted ashore, somewhat short of fuel, and arrived at this long coastline with two options – he could either turn left or he could turn right. He decided to turn right (in fact, he should have turned left) so he ran out of fuel and ditched in the desert.

Imagine my cousin's surprise when he not only had received a letter from me saying that I might visit him, but then was told that a Seafire from *Indefatigable* had force-landed somewhere to the North of Masawa and that a search party was to be sent out to try to recover the pilot.

My cousin and I enjoyed a similar form of parentage, in that our respective mothers were two of the three formidable Cushing sisters, who were not to be messed with on any account, and he told me afterwards that the thought of Aunt Ada dealing with him if he hadn't done his best to recover her precious son from the desert was something that spurred him to even greater endeavour. So he joined the party on camels that proceeded to look for what he thought to be me. They found Sub Lieutenant Jones unharmed and in due course he was returned to us in Ceylon. So much for flying in the Red Sea, but mine had been uneventful and it was the last flying we were to get before the ship arrived in Trincomalee in Ceylon.

At Trincomalee we went through the usual routine of being disembarked before the ship actually entered port, and all the Seafires, indeed the whole of the air group – Seafires, Avengers, Fireflies – went to a new airfield that had been bulldozed out of the jungle at Katakurunda, south of Colombo. The airfield was literally sunk amid the coconut palms, and the buildings consisted of wooden bamboo structures which served as cabin accommodation for the officers and a kind of barrack accommodation for the lads, as well as a Wardroom and a Chief Petty Officers' Mess and all the usual kinds of facilities for a Naval Air Station. It had, however, only recently opened and we were rapidly approaching Christmas. The Station officers had organised themselves a Christmas Ball, and of course this was somewhat swamped by a shower of mostly Sub Lieutenant aviators who descended upon them. As usual, there were a few Wren officers around – the Wren headquarters were, I think, in Colombo itself, and there was a Communications Centre at Kandy – but the few Wrens that were available were not, clearly, going to be enough to make a ball a really sensible occasion. It was bound to degenerate into something more akin to a booze-up. This turned out to be the case but it was instrumental in some really rather amusing songs being composed by 820 Squadron (the Avenger squadron) which was the source of so many excellent Fleet Air Arm songs. The one that I remember particularly was the one that they sang at the ball to the Executive Officer of the Air Station, to the tune of Blaze Away, the opening lines of which read: 'Insanitary bogs, thieving wogs, Got no time for A boys'. The evening, I seem to remember, culminated with one or two of the more boisterous officers firing, allegedly, at snakes and various other things that might be seen crawling around inside the huts, and which occasioned me and several others to lie flat on the floor under our beds as the bullets whistled through the somewhat flimsy fabric of our accommodation.

The aircraft, as usual, needed quite a bit of work having been disembarked. Many of the things that were very difficult to do on board ship, like alignment of guns and calibration, needed to be carried out. Very early on, I remember going with a particular friend of mine, Winston Ostegaard, to a tea house quite near to the airfield on the beach where we spent a quite idyllic afternoon drinking innumerable cups of delicious Ceylon tea, the like of which I couldn't remember having had before, swimming and generally enjoying the sun, although with my very gingery complexion sun was not something I could take too much of. During that afternoon, as we mucked about on the beach, I remember Winston running along dragging his feet behind him and leaving trail marks in the sand. He was one of the more mature members of the Squadron, a sensible and sober individual, not given to too much drink, and therefore I found him a congenial companion.

The next morning I went down to the squadron with the CO in the tilly and there we saw a message from Winston, who was the Squadron Duty Officer, which said, 'Most of the aeroplanes are unserviceable; I can't get any sense out of anybody; I'm fed up and I'm going off to do a test flight.' At that moment we heard the roar of an engine as a Seafire took off and then a sickening silence followed by a bang and a ball of flame and smoke. We leapt into the tilly to go off to see what had happened and if we could render any assistance. I have never forgotten the scene as we arrived. He had cut a swathe through the coconut palms and there were the remains of the Seafire with the incinerated body of my friend clearly visible, the smoke and flames still playing around the wreckage. There was absolutely nothing that could be done, but I had lost a friend and it touched me more deeply than so many of the other tragedies that befell us with people I knew less and cared less about. To this day, I cannot on the beach in Florida bear to trail my feet through the sand to make the kind of marks that he left such a short time before his death. But life went on. Subsequently, months later there was a rumour that his death had been caused by sabotage – whether this was true or not I am not sure, but it didn't help.

We were not to spend long in Ceylon, however; although we were able to get in some flying and gunnery practice, we were soon to embark again for operations against Sumatra. We had now formed into what was to become the British Pacific Fleet under Admiral Vian:

110

four carriers – *Indomitable, Indefatigable, Formidable* and *Victorious* – together with two battleships – the *Duke of York* and the *King George V* – numerous cruisers and a big escort of destroyers. Not until recently did I realize how difficult it was for Admiral Bruce Fraser, who was commanding the whole operation, to keep this large force replenished at sea with no forward bases. The US Navy had managed to build up a Fleet Train to meet its every need at sea when a thousand miles or more from a shore base, and was expert at replenishment at sea; this was not something we in the British Fleet had yet exercised to any extent, so some completely new evaluations and exercises were required by the ships involved. Replacement spares, aircraft engines, parts, ammunition, fuel, all these things were going to be required on a massive scale, and provided from a Fleet Train; it is amazing, looking back, that this was managed as well as it was.

The Seafire Squadrons were divided into two. In 887 we had F3s, which were designed for high-altitude intercept work, so most of our time was spent between 15,000 and 30,000 feet, on oxygen most of the time, denying the skies to the enemy. Whether the enemy wished to be there is something that I never really figured out, but we did spend an awful lot of time doing what was called 'combat air patrol', high above the fleet. 894, on the other hand, was equipped with L3s which were designed for low-level work; they were required to box the fleet in, literally in a square box with two aircraft in each side, flying patrols at 500 to 1000 feet up and down, to protect it from low-flying aircraft. It just so happened that the aircraft the Japanese chose to attack the fleet were, for the most part, Sallys (twin-engined torpedo attack aircraft) and then later, with the Kamikazes, anything they could really lay their hands on. All these aircraft came in at low level, so it was thus somewhat disappointing for us in 887 to find our peers in 894 getting all the action while we sat solemnly up above waiting to be directed on to something that never materialised. Our shakedown target for Operations Lentil and Meridian was to be the oil refineries at Palembang and Pangkalan Brandan in Sumatra, and our role in the attacks was exactly as I have described. The Seafires first justified their existence when Sallys attacked the force and were massacred by the Seafires of 894 Squadron, several of which gained two or three victories in one single sortie.

To be perfectly honest, it was fairly boring in 887 to be patrolling at 30,000 feet for an hour at a time (our total endurance being one hour forty minutes from take-off to landing), and seeing nothing but your wingman or your flight companions as we solemnly patrolled and countered at the end of each patrol line back and forth over the fleet. It was not long, however, before we began to face problems. The

111

A Seafire taking off in Pacific markings

Seafire was never an aeroplane designed for deck landing and, unless one put it down very carefully, it would either leap back off the deck and go into the barrier, or worse still over the top of the barrier (as had happened at one tragic accident that took place when we were up off Norway), in which case the aircraft then landed flat into the deck park for'ard with catastrophic results and carnage everywhere. Or, if it got too slow, it would stall on the approach (we had lost one or two pilots that way), or it would drift slightly and break an undercarriage, or it would burst tyres and then have to be towed or manoeuvred forward with some difficulty. All this caused the recovery of the Seafires to be a more lengthy process than was the case with Avengers or Hellcats. *Indefatigable* was the only carrier with Seafires. The advantage that the specifically designed American aircraft had in deck landing was pretty obvious. They had enormous undercarriages with soft oleos which absorbed the shock and for the most part, apart from the Corsair, they had excellent vision – they could look straight ahead at the deck. It was not until some years later, when I started deck landing jet aircraft, that I began to see how very simple it was to land an aircraft if only you could see where you were going!

Admiral Vian, however, flying his flag in *Indomitable* with US aircraft, did not really understand the technicalities involved in the different aeroplanes and only saw *Indefatigable* as the carrier that was taking longer to recover its aircraft than any of the others, thus causing the whole fleet to stay into wind longer than the other carriers would have liked. If you were trying to make good a PIM (point of intended movement) along a track towards a certain objective while operating aircraft, and if the wind was contrary to the direction you wished to go, then you can see that every time the fleet turned to operate or recover aircraft, it was going in the opposite direction to that which was intended. This situation was further compounded by the fact that, even with our longer-range tanks (45 gallons in all, which were certainly larger than the 30-gallon tanks with which we had originally been fitted), we were still really only capable of staying airborne for a total of just under two hours. Our normal length of sortie was therefore one hour forty minutes, whereas the American aircraft were all capable of staying up for three and a half to four hours, so the fleet was required to turn into wind twice as often for Seafires as it was for any of the other aircraft. Hence the rapidly building dislike of the Seafire by operating Admirals. It was fortunate for us that 894 was able to demonstrate the advantages of the Seafire in a combat role by really destroying the attacking Japanese aircraft that came out from Sumatra, and doing it so effectively and promptly. But of course, these things are soon forgotten in a long-running battle.

The briefing for the attacks on Sumatra I recall very well. They were, of course, directed mainly at the Avenger and Fireflies that were going in to attack the oil refinery, whereas we in the Seafires were not to be involved in the actual attack but in the defence of the fleet. From our high position off Sumatra, however, it was easy to see the coast of Sumatra and indeed the lake, which was en route on one of the attacking paths, into which the Walrus (our Seaplane) was going to be launched if anybody got into trouble. The aircrew were told to try to make the lake if they were slightly disabled and ditch there where they would be picked up by the Walrus. All fairly hairy, if you ask me, but then it was something I could look at with a somewhat detached view.

The attacks went extremely well and great damage was done to both oil refineries, which were then very important to the Japanese. It was a good bloodletting for the newly arrived aircrew, particularly of the strike and attack aircraft, and a highly successful operation to boot. Thus we were able to return to Trincomalee and disembark back to Katakurunda, feeling that we had actually earned our spurs in this new area of war, and that we could hold our heads up fairly high. We had lost some aircraft, shot down by the Japanese during that attack, and we learned later that the crews had been taken prisoners of war. Sadly, wickedly, they were executed after the war had ended. If you visit the Fleet Air Arm Church at Yeovilton, there is a plaque on the floor commemorating this tragic, savage event. We didn't think of them at the time except to hope that they had been captured and were at least safe. Little were we to imagine the kind of fate that waited for them when the war, in fact, was already over.

The shakedown exercise off Sumatra reminded me when, in much later life as Chief Executive of British Aerospace, I called on President Suharto of Indonesia. He asked me if I had ever been to Indonesia before, to which I was able to reply, 'In a manner of speaking.' He asked me what I meant. 'Well,' I said, 'I was involved in the attacks on the oil refineries at Palembang and Pangkalan Brandan during the war, but it would not have been advisable for me to have landed in your country at that time.' He smiled and said he remembered the attacks and the effect that they had had on the Japanese at that time.

It was then another fast passage, this time to Perth where we refuelled, and then on to Sydney where the ship arrived in great style into Sydney Harbour but, as usual, before that happened we had taken off and arrived at Schofields, the Naval Air Station just outside Sydney, which was to be our main operating base.

So we had completed the first operation in the Far East and it had been a great success. In order to overcome some of the difficulties the Seafires were having in their short operating cycles, we were now pushing the sortie length out to just over two hours and, with careful use of the throttle, one was able to stretch the endurance a little so that we could fit in better with the longer sorties of the American aircraft. They were on a standard four to four and a half hour sortie and we were stretching ourselves to just over two hours perhaps two and a quarter. Soon, however, we were ready to re-embark off Sydney Heads to be recovered on board *Indefatigable* and start our trips north to cover the American landings on the Sakishima-guntō and for attacks on Formosa.

The attack on Formosa was designed as a shakedown for us against specific military targets, but once again the high-flying Seafires were consigned to air defence of the fleet and no high-level attacks developed. The briefing included some escape and evasion instructions for the attacking aircrew, which stated that if damaged and they could not make the carrier, they should try to reach the mountains in the centre of Formosa which were inhabited, it was alleged, by headhunters. We were briefed that it would be preferable to land among the headhunters and take our chance of buying our freedom with our 'goolie' chits (which consisted of 50 gold Dutch guilders, which we carried in a small pouch) rather than risk capture by the Japanese which might lead, and as events showed afterwards almost certainly did lead, to immediate decapitation. Quite a choice! I never understood how these 'goolie' chits were supposed to work. If you were landed among a bunch of very primitive people, was it not likely that they would remove both the gold guilders and your 'goolies' in one clean swipe? Or perhaps it was just a morale-boosting gimmick to cause us fewer sleepless nights!

We were issued with jungle survival kit which consisted of jungle greens, a large machete, an Australian-type bush hat, a 0.5-calibre revolver with the necessary webbing, medical packs (quinine etc.), jungle survival kit – all most impressive, but if you tried to get this into a Seafire cockpit it was almost certain that you would have to vacate it yourself. So most of us opted, in view of the kind of flying we were doing, for leaving this stuff behind. The ship became very, very hot; we had no air-conditioning, except some limited amount in the operations room, and since we were shut down for most of the time (that is to say, no scuttles or ventilators were allowed to be open) life on board became very sticky indeed. As a result, prickly heat became a constant source of irritation; it was much worse for the stokers, the chaps down in the engine room, and I remember seeing one chap come up on deck on one occasion who was literally bright red from prickly heat. Upset stomachs were not entirely unusual, which was hardly surprising when you think of the amount of time we were spending at sea in ships that were never designed for prolonged operations in a tropical climate, with food going off. I remember being given some cold ham one day, and as I turned it over various things started to wriggle out from underneath. Our bread was always full of weevils, which infested the flour, and if you held the slice of bread up to the light you could actually see them baked in it. I am sure they were quite nutritious.

While we had been in Ceylon, some of the chaps had been buying opals and I remember one story of a chap coming back saying how he'd spent all day in some jeweller's shop bidding and negotiating with the chap for a necklace that he wanted for his girlfriend back home and how delighted he was when at the end of the negotiation the jeweller had said he would throw in a pair of earrings free! Obviously a good deal.

There occurred another episode which sticks in my memory. The unpleasant character I have referred to before had also been ashore in Ceylon, and had bought a pair of very high-heeled patent leather ladies' shoes. He had told us that he was engaged and intended to marry when he returned to the UK and with clothes rationing as it was he thought these would be ideal for his bride-to-be. Time passed and he was killed; I can't remember how or under what circumstances but as Squadron Admin. Officer it was my painful duty to muster the kit of those who went missing or killed, and this I usually did in company with the Padre who shared this unpleasant duty with me. When we mustered this chap's kit, we found of course the high-heeled black patent leather shoes but more significantly we found a pair of handcuffs, a whip and some shackles. The Padre and I looked at each other with some surprise at this collection of stuff, but all was made clear when we found a short story this chap had written in which he described in lurid details how the hero of this particular story used to like shackling his girlfriends to the bed and having first paraded them naked with nothing to wear but a pair of black patent leather high-heeled shoes, which gave him the opportunity to exercise the whip. The chaplain and I having read the story and looked at the evidence, decided that this was not something that should be sent back to the grieving relatives but we consigned it via the scuttle to the great big deep garbage bin of the Pacific Ocean. We both agreed that though she might grieve the loss of her fiancé, little did she know how well rid she was of him.

The combined fleets, under the command of Admiral Halsey, were spread over some hundreds of miles and we, the British, occupied the southern end, attacking the islands to the south of the Sakishima-guntō, and patrolling the area off the southern tip. Now was the time for the Kamikazes to come and attack, and attack they did, but it was here that the superiority of the British design in terms of withstanding direct hits came to bear fruit. By having an armoured box around the hangar, with four inches of steel on the flight deck between the lifts and the sides of the hangar and the hangar deck itself, the Royal Corps of Naval Constructors had introduced a very damage-resistant hull, though unfortunately it did mean that it very much restricted the ability of the carriers to have side deck elevators. Nevertheless, whereas when American carriers were struck by Kamikazes their thin wooden-clad decks were quite easily penetrated, with enormous carnage resulting when the bomb or the aircraft itself went off in the hangar below, no British ship was penetrated. Many of the Kamikazes literally bounced off the deck and went over the side. Those that did the most damage struck the unarmoured portions aft or for'ard of the lifts and, in the case of *Indefatigable*, when we were struck the aircraft went straight into the base of the island.

Luck plays an enormous part in our affairs, and I very well remember the occasion when we were struck because I was in the crew room being briefed with those who were ready to man the aircraft that were already spotted for the next launch. We heard over the ship's broadcast that a raid was closing on the fleet at something in the region of 30 miles or so, and at that moment one of the pilots due to get airborne in the flight to go off with 894 Squadron came in and told Jimmy Crossman, the CO, that he wasn't feeling well and really didn't think he should fly. Jimmy was clearly annoyed with this and, turning to the pilot in question, said, 'Get yourself to Sick Bay then, straight away.' The Sick Bay was, of course, down in the bowels of the ship but there was an emergency station in the Island, which was just aft of our crew room, and the pilot concerned departed for the Sick Bay in the Island. I, in common with my companions, went out and manned the aircraft – I was flying then, I think, the section in Yellow Flight and so was number three to be launched. After I had started and been spotted at about 250 feet, which was normal in those days, I opened the throttle and took off. Just as I was pulling my wheels up I looked up and saw a great red spot on the side of a Japanese Zero, literally about a 100 feet or so above me, pulling up into a stall turn from which he dived into the ship. I had my gunsight on at the same time as I had my undercarriage up, but even with a Seafire there was no way at full throttle I could pull up to do anything to engage this chap. By the time I had gained height and enough speed to turn to come round behind him, he was already on his way down on his final dive. He hit the ship at the base of the Island, smack into the Sick Bay, and a great flash of flame spread up the side of the ship and around the flight deck. Those that were in the vicinity were killed, including the doctor and his patients. There was nothing I could do but continue to turn away and join the rest of the flight and continue with the patrol, trying to avoid the mass of bullets that were flying in all directions at the same time from the ship's defensive armament.

Again, the selfish thoughts of young Lygo I remember very well. 'Well,' thought I to myself, 'if they don't get that deck sorted out within two hours when we're due to come back and land on, there's three other carriers we can land on, so we'll be all right.' In fact, to the great credit of *Indefatigable*, we landed at our due time after two hours and fifteen minutes. They only had two wires operating and one barrier, but we weren't told this because there was RT silence. As far as we were concerned it was a normal recovery, and it was only when I got out of the aeroplane and saw the blackened sides of the ship that I realised what she had been through. It was a remarkable effort. She had not lost a moment's operating time, but I shall never forget the smell as I walked through the shattered entrance to the island and down the ladder, that mixture of blood, and steam, and oil; that is the common mixture that assails one in any experience of that kind. We had been extremely lucky to have got all the aircraft off from that particular launch; there was just one behind me before the Kamikaze actually struck and thus we had lost no aircraft on deck because the deck was clear, waiting for the recovery of the aircraft that were coming back. These aircraft had also been recovered, with only a delay of something like thirty minutes, a truly amazing testimony to the ruggedness of the British carrier fleet at that time.

Our Captain's frustration at the continuous bollockings he must have been receiving from the Admiral was beginning to run him a bit ragged. The primary blame for this was put upon the shoulders of the luckless Andrew Thompson who really, as, Wing Commander of the Seafires, could do little but explain the facts of life to anybody who was inclined to listen, so he was the fall guy. In the end, on one occasion, the Captain announced that he intended to brief the pilots himself before they went off. I went up to the bridge to be briefed personally by Q.D. Graham; on this particular occasion I was leading my own flight. I remember his words very clearly. Pointing out at the horizon abeam the ship he said, 'After you break, Lygo, and you get about there,' pointing roughly abeam, 'put your helm hard over and come round.' 'Aye, aye, Sir,' I replied. It was, of course, what we were always doing, but it only required one chap to get a bit long in the groove, or for something to happen on deck, to have the whole thing degenerate, and take longer than in an ideal world would have been desirable. Soon after this poor Andrew Thompson was relieved and Buster Hallett, who had been previously the Squadron Commander in 887, came out to join us as the new Wing Commander. Buster was an experienced and capable Seafire pilot, but I doubt that he was able to do anything to change the Seafire from being a converted land-based fighter plane into something that could compete with the specifically designed naval aircraft of the US Navy.

Life went on, however, and we duly joined up with the American fleet in Ulithi in the Carolines. As we approached the main American operating base we were flying combat air patrols as usual, when one of my flight mates had an engine failure and put his Seafire down on the beach on one of the islands around the lagoon of Ulithi. Quite unthinkingly, I took the rest of the flight in to see that he was safe and found myself flying over the lagoon which was filled with American warships. Why they didn't open fire on what, to them, must have been a very strange-looking group of aeroplanes approaching I have no idea, but I can only assume that our own air defence organisation in Indefat had managed to alert them.

After we'd anchored in the lagoon, it was decided that a party should be sent ashore to try to recover some spare parts from the aircraft that were in short supply because we certainly wouldn't have been able to recover the aircraft. An LST was borrowed from the Americans, who took a party ashore which was led by our senior pilot and included me, the pilot who had been flying the aircraft and an Air Engineer Officer and some Ratings to do the necessary work. After we'd landed and found the Seafire concerned, which was in pretty good shape but clearly could not be recovered, (we had no suitable recovery gear), action was taken to take from it the spare parts that were in short supply on board. The sun was blazing down and we had all of us been incarcerated in this large metal box which was now sitting out in the middle of the Ulithi lagoon with hardly any exposure to the sun's rays, and I therefore cautioned the Air Engineer who was leading the party to keep covered up and to keep the lads covered up, much as they might have wished to strip off and take the sun. He did not choose to take my advice, and since he was a Lieutenant and I merely a Sub Lieutenant it was really up to him. For our part, the senior pilot and I with revolvers strapped around us walked into the nearest village where we encountered the only inhabitants that remained in Ulithi and where the only women were to be found. As a result, it had been placed strictly out of bounds by the US Navy! My imagination about the way in which grass skirts were designed and worn was quickly demolished when I saw that they were in fact extremely thick and largely impenetrable, as far as I could determine.

The unmarried men all lived together in a separate long-house where it was interesting to see a kind of social system had been established and the loot, of which there was an abundance because a lot of stuff was being thrown up on shore from ships and cargos of ships that had sunk, was all neatly stacked and packets of Lucky Strike and various other desirable trinkets were rationed out by the Head Man in an orderly fashion. The diet, apart from coconuts, seemed to consist of fish and pork, pigs being fed themselves on coconut and fish, and this together with a few vegetables that were grown in vegetable gardens provided their main food. Communication was difficult and the best that could be achieved was to talk to the Head Man with some words of German because the Carolines had once been a German controlled territory prior to the Treaty of Versailles, after which it had been given over to the Japanese. He managed to convey to us that all the young men had been taken away by the Japanese to work in various places and one wonders how many returned to these idyllic surroundings. So we bid them farewell and returned to the aircraft and that evening the LST came and took us off with the loot which we had taken from the downed Seafire, and returned us to *Indefatigable*. Within twenty four hours the appearance of the Air Engineer Officer, who had refused to take my advice, was like nothing I had ever seen then nor have I seen since. His swollen features were not a pretty sight.

As I have mentioned before, replenishment at sea on the scale at which it was now required was something new to the British Pacific Fleet and various innovations were tried, not all of them terribly successful. I used to volunteer to go over and collect replacement aircraft that were coming out on the escort carriers, for the main reason that, because they were American built and had been equipped in America, they had the best coffee that I had tasted! And so during the period when we were replenishing, I would often find myself being jackstayed over to a destroyer and from the destroyer to the escort carrier to pick up the replacement Seafire and then, at a suitable moment, bring it back and land it on board the *Indefatigable*. On one such occasion, when quite a number of us were going over to collect aircraft for various ships in the Force (remember, there were four

Jimmy Hayes being recovered, having been shot down

carriers to be fed with replacement aircraft), I found that the escort carrier had decided to invent a new way of getting pilots across more expeditiously by arranging a RSJ (a short piece of girder) to be attached to the running block on the transfer gear, from both ends of which they had attached a large, squareish canvas bag with four strops that led up to the attachment point, and into each canvas bag they proceeded to install four pilots! Thus they were able to transfer eight at a time. I watched with horror when the first transfer was being made, and with even more horror when the line on which this device was travelling parted. The whole lot fell into the sea and was rapidly dragged astern by the passage of the ship to alongside its screws, where the men struggled to get out of the bags in which they found themselves encapsulated. Needless to say, they then reverted to using a single transfer in a bosun's chair, which was the conventional method. On my return to the ship I reported the whole of this matter to the Commander; in due course the Captain informed the Admiral and the Admiral had the unkindest of words conveyed to the Captain of the ship concerned. It was indeed an extremely dangerous way of trying to save time, and could have cost us very dearly.

Time passed, the endless days, the endless weeks, the flying, the replenishment, the flying, the replenishment, on, on, on, with little alteration or break. The Kamikaze attacks, the raids on the fleet, the difficulty of the living conditions, the problem of maintaining morale, of getting adequate sleep, of getting adequate food, all these things became part and parcel of the daily, weekly routine. In the end, however, after the longest deployment of a British fleet at sea in the whole war, we had to return to Sydney, which was our supporting base, to replenish before returning north for attacks on mainland Japan. By this time, however, my embarked tour of duty had expired; this, I think at that time, lasted fifteen months embarked and then you were entitled to six months' shore time to refresh you before returning for another bash. So I was to leave the ship on her return to Sydney, and the first part of my shore duty was to carry out trials of using napalm dropped from Corsairs. This I duly did, creating some quite horrendous fireballs in the process. At the same time, at Schofields, the first pilots to form the Royal Australian Naval Air Arm had been recruited from the RAAF, where they changed their light blue uniforms for dark blue and were being indoctrinated in the ways of the Navy and flying Seafires. I, meantime, was to be sent down to Nowra, south of Sydney, to join a fleet requirements unit there, flying the usual miscellany of aircraft – Hellcats, Corsairs, Martlets and so on – and the days passed pleasantly enough. I was busily dating various girls I had met, and one in particular who lived in the Uplands as it's called, or Highlands at Moss Vale, I used to visit by travelling up from Nowra on my 2 stroke Velocette motorcycle, which I had bought from a chap in the ship, through the delightful Kangaroo Valley where the noise of the kookaburras sometimes caused me to stop my motorbike thinking that something had gone wrong with it!

The six months was all too quickly up and during this time came, fairly early on, VJ Day. The war was finally over, and the celebrations at Nowra took the form of setting fire to the Wardroom with the spectacle of the Commander dressed in a nightshirt wearing a nightcap (can you believe it) trying to put the fire out with the aid of a stirrup pump and being passed buckets of 100 octane by some inebriated aviators, which turned his stirrup pump into a flame thrower! Another worthy, on the same night, started up a tractor which was steam driven by pouring 100 octane underneath the boiler and throwing in a match. Afterwards he said, 'steam was raised very quickly!' He then proceeded to drive this steam tractor up to the Wardroom, failing to notice that it had behind it a large furrow, by means of which he tore up not only the peritrack but all the main road leading to the Wardroom! However, all this jollity came to a fairly rapid end and I was sent off to join 801 Squadron back at Schofields, due to embark once again in HMS *Implacable*. This time we were flying Seafire 17s, a more advanced version of the Seafire with a sting hook, that is to say, a hook that came out of the rear of the aeroplane as opposed to being attached to the fuselage underneath. It gave you a much better chance of grabbing a wire, and was an easier aeroplane to fly and very nice to boot, with its Griffin engine. Life embarked in *Implacable*, however, was nothing compared with what had gone before since it was merely exercise flying as the carrier, together with some of the others, made her farewell visits to Melbourne and finally Sydney, and then the aircraft were struck down and we were on our way home.

Lend-Lease had ended, and the Americans demanded that those aeroplanes that had been supplied to foreign services should either be returned to them or bought from them or disposed of. The first two courses were impractical for an impoverished Britain, and so a carrier was devoted solely to loading these brand-new aeroplanes, Hellcats, Corsairs, Avengers, steaming out of Sydney Heads and solemnly pushing them over the side, or firing them off the catapult. Somewhere off Sydney Heads lies an enormous amount of aluminium. How often I was think back to those aircraft in the few years that followed when the Royal Navy was still trying to make do with some of the aeroplane that were not entirely satisfactory for its purpose.

The war having ended, most of my companions were now looking to what was their release date from the service but, having survived the War and found myself in a service where it had been made clear to me that, if I could survive, my progress would be determined by what I did, not by what anybody else might do for me, I decided to try to stay in. I did, however, make one attempt to return to civilian life when I received a letter form the Company Secretary at *The Times*, the same Mr Hoare, who said that my job was open for me should I wish to return. You will recall that that job, at the time I left, was reading proof in the reading room of *The Times* newspaper. I wrote back to him saying that I would love to return on the basis that, in view of the way in which communications had changed in the world, *The Times* news service would no doubt need its own aeroplane and I would be perfectly prepared to return to work for them as the pilot of that aircraft. I received a polite letter in reply which said quite simply that, in view of my response, he assumed that I did not wish to return to *The Times*, and there the matter was closed!

I therefore applied for, and obtained, a short-service four-year commission in the Royal Navy and changed my one wavy stripe with an 'A' in the sleeve to a straight stripe with an 'A' in the sleeve, but soon this was to be replaced by another stripe as I made Lieutenant. I think there were some four or five hundred of us that were allowed to extend to a four-year short service commission while the Navy sorted out what its requirement for the Fleet Air Arm might be, and I was therefore asked what I wanted to do when I returned to the United Kingdom. My answer to this was to volunteer to go on a flying instructors' course which was to be at the Central Flying School at Little Rissington. Meantime, I busied myself in *Implacable* when not flying by taking over the editing of the ship's magazine called the *Eighth Wire*. Looking back on it, it was quite an ambitious under-taking to get it printed and circulated monthly, in particular the 'paying-off' copy in which I decided to have all the more risqué jokes included in a pink-page supplement which went in the middle. I gather that from the Admiral downwards, the pink pages were the first things that were read when the magazine was distributed.

My new Captain was C.C. Hughes-Hallett, who had had a distin-guished war record, as indeed had my previous Captain, Q.D. Graham. Hughes-Hallett was much more of a father figure and proceeded to take a considerable interest in young Lygo. I volunteered to start learning seamanship and was put on the roster for second officer of the watch for the trip home, so at least I was beginning to show willing. In due course I was selected to go on the second post-war instructors' course at Little Rissington and, after some leave, went as a newly promoted Lieutenant (A)RN.

6

Immediately After the War

Little Rissington was a purpose-built RAF station on top of a hill. Apparently, before the war, it had been decided that some should be built on top of hills, to get above the fog, and some should be built in the lowlands, to get below low cloud, so that there would always be a usable airfield available. Unfortunately, some of the best airfields were built on the top of hills, and when it came time to extend the runways for more modern aeroplanes they became impossible. Rissington had not quite reached this stage; it was quite a good airfield for the kind of aeroplanes that we were then flying. Basic instruction was still being given on Tiger Moths, Advanced Flying Training on the Harvard and then Operational Flying on Mosquitoes, Vampires, Lancasters, at a later stage, but my course consisted of teaching me to be an instructor on Tiger Moths and Harvards.

My Flight Lieutenant Flying Instructor was a nice man who very quickly had me adopting the right kind of attitude towards my new job. After the first instrument flight in the back of a Harvard, as we walked in, I turned to him and said, 'I must apologise for that appalling performance, I had never realised that my instrument flying was quite as bad as it was.' He turned to me and smiled and said, 'No, it wasn't bad at all by Royal Naval standards.' Well, he obviously meant it, and it was a severe lesson for me. I realised very quickly for how long I had been living on borrowed time. When I came to think of it, the kind of flying I had been doing had really been 'at risk'. CFS gave me an opportunity to polish up my flying and become much more professional and proficient.

There were long period when we didn't fly because there were no aircraft serviceable. The RAF had gone into this centralised planned maintenance operation, which I will talk about in a later chapter, which is great for the Engineers but bad for producing flying aeroplanes. In the times when we couldn't fly, if the weather was quite good, we were sent farming and I remember sitting with German prisoners of war, who were also out farming, loading hay and drinking cider and generally having a healthy time in the open air.

Having finished the course, I was sent to join 799 Squadron at Lee-on-Solent where our primary job was in refresher flying, particularly chaps coming back who had been prisoners of war and who had not flown for a very long time. My first student had been in the bag for quite a long time and having briefed him carefully in my most professional and newly-qualified manner, I then said, 'Right, get yourself ready and we'll go off and have our first flight'. To my astonishment, he appeared in a full Irvine suit, which was leathers lined with sheepskin. He was a big man to start with and by the time he'd got all this gear on, he was quite enormous. I looked at this with some surprise but didn't say anything and put him in the front seat of a Harvard, while I got in the back as the instructor. We taxied out, we took off, it was winter and it was cold and I then said to him, 'Would you please shut the hood'. With the mass of the Irvine jacket around him, he couldn't reach round far enough with his right hand to grasp the handle to pull the hood forward. So we spent the whole of that hour's flight with the hood open and me freezing to death in the back. After we landed I said to him, 'I don't think you'll find it necessary to wear a full Irvine suit because we have a heater in the aircraft and as long as we can close the hood, we'll be reasonably warm'.

'Oh', said he, 'I don't like flying in enclosed cockpits'.

'Well,' said I, 'I'm afraid you're going to have to, with me in the back otherwise all flying as far as you and I are concerned will cease'.

On the next flight, with snow on the ground, we again took off; this time he was not encased in an Irvine suit and managed to shut the hood. We carried out some normal flying and then I asked him to return and join the circuit at Lee-on-Solent. To my surprise, he returned me to the airfield at Gosport, which was a grass airfield in those days but even more surprising, instead of attempting to land at Gosport, he proceeded to do a circuit and made an approach to land in a field outside the Wardroom mess. I allowed the aircraft to descend to about 200 feet whereupon I said, 'Now, open up please, I have control' and I took the aeroplane and put it in the circuit at Lee and landed at Lee, where I debriefed him. I asked him where he thought he was going. He apologised and said, 'I'm sorry, I mistook Gosport for Lee'.

'Yes', I said, 'I can understand that that might be possible even though one's got runways and the other hasn't, but why were we attempting to land not at the airfield but in front of the Wardroom?'

'Oh', he said 'because in 1938 when I was flying there, that's where we used to operate from'. There was no answer to this.

It was an interesting job, meeting interesting people, refreshing senior officers who wanted to get back into flying practice, one of whom was to be my future Captain of the *Ark Royal*, Dennis Cambell.

I think he was then in the Admiralty and just wanted to get some flying to keep his hand in, but I insisted that he stayed for a couple of weeks, in order to become fully proficient again. I don't think he particularly liked the idea at the time, but probably enjoyed being able to spend a couple of weeks flying which otherwise would not have been possible.

It was a happy time, I was now back into the dating circuit and life for a young bachelor, just after the war, who had managed to save some money, was reasonably bearable. In the early stages of the War, I had my brother buy for me from the local garage for £10 a 1933 Morris 10, for the purpose solely of my learning to take it to pieces and put it together again, so that I understood how motor cars worked. With his supervision, this I duly did but at the end of the War, when vehicles were at a premium, this thing became a very desirable item and I later sold it for £150 which enabled me to move on to bigger and better things via a Sunbeam Talbot to an AC.

It was while I was flying in 799 down at Lee that I had my only serious forced-landing experience. I was on a training flight with a student in a Harvard, doing stall turns over the Isle of Wight at about four or five thousand feet, and after he had conducted the first one I said, 'Open up, climb back up, and let's do another one.' After a pause he said, 'The throttle won't open.' I became alert and, putting my hand down on the throttle, found that indeed it was stuck in the closed position. When you get to the top of the climb for a stall turn you throttle right back and bring the aircraft over by use of the rudder into a stall turn into the opposite direction. 'Right,' I said, 'we now have the opportunity for me to demonstrate to you a forced landing. Put out a Mayday call and alert Lee to the fact that we are about to make a forced landing and give them our position.' While he proceeded to do this, I looked around for a suitable field. There really wasn't one. The fields in the Isle of Wight at that time were even smaller than I suspect they are today, but I found one and proceeded to circuit round to come in, make an approach and land. To my horror, as I turned on to the approach and was coming in low, I discovered, first, that the field was on the side of a valley and I was coming in over the lowest point, and second, that there was a string of cables across the field obstructing my approach. As a result, I was high as I came over the hedge to miss the cables; pushing the nose down I drilled the aeroplane into the ground but, despite my best endeavours, we still hit the hedge at the other end. Since I was at the back of the aircraft and had to look out over the side in order to see where we were going, the harness restraint did not prevent my head, before the days of bone domes, from going forward and cracking itself on the forward part of the canopy and then, with the reaction, jerking back and hanging it on the back part. I had shut everything down, so there was little risk of fire, but I was bleeding fairly badly as my student, who had been able to brace himself for the impact in the front and had suffered no damage whatsoever, clambered out and helped me out of the back cockpit.

It transpired I was outside the back garden of the local vicar of the village, who very kindly rushed me into Ryde Hospital where I was stitched up and placed in good care. Meantime, back at Lee-on-Solent the Mayday had been received but unfortunately my student had given a reciprocal of our position from Ryde and they had decided that I had ditched in the sea and launched the Otter. It was later discovered that the throttle butterfly on all Harvards had been modified because backfires in the engine had been found to cause it to weld shut. The modification consisted of reducing the diameter of the butterfly so that when it became heated through a backfire it would not weld itself to the choke. Although mine had been stamped as modified, in fact the modification had not been carried out. I carry the scars to this day!

After a year at Lee-on-Solent, the appointers told me that the RAF had asked if I could go back to the Central Flying School on the staff as an instructor, which was a very flattering invitation, so I duly departed to join CFS staff. By this time, CFS was not only training instructors in basic flying training instructional techniques but also qualifying and checking out those who were going to operational flying schools to instruct, so we had the opportunity to fly Vampires, Mosquitos and Lancasters as well as Beaufighters. It was a fascinating time to be in the Royal Air Force and at the CFS, with such a variety of aeroplanes to be able to fly.

My first flight in a Mosquito with my instructor Graham Hulse, came to an early end, as they usually did, so I later learned. In attempting to take off with two very powerful engines, with the propellers both turning in the same direction, the swing was quite vicious and most students, including me, opened up the throttles and practically did a ground loop as they swung off the runway. The second time round it was easier and I learned to enjoy flying the Mosquito very much indeed and spent many hours instructing on it.

One thing we were doing at the time was Limit Flying. This involved flying the aircraft to its limits and in furtherance of this, an immense amount of time was spent learning to fly and land and operate the Mosquito on a single engine. I was later to discover that this was not the policy of the United States Navy and I think they were right. I fear that despite our best efforts, we probably caused more casualties and loss of aircraft teaching students to fly on one engine, than would have occurred if we had left it to the day when this might actually have happened with nothing but verbal instructions to go on after that.

It became an intriguing possibility for me to become qualified on the Lancaster, (the 4-engined World War II bomber) and one day it was decided that they could spare an aeroplane for me to do my first flight. I climbed aboard the aircraft and, together with a stoical and extremely brave flight engineer, started the engines and readied myself to taxi to the end of the runway. Most casual flying of this kind was done during the lunch break when the students were off eating and aircraft were relatively freely available, but as I called for clearance to taxi, the tower asked me what I was going to do. I said, 'Local flying,' omitting to say that it was my first solo, whereupon I was asked if I would mind taking the Little Rissington rugby team to Hulavington. 'Certainly,' I replied, and 15 strong, stalwart men climbed in the back of the aeroplane. I then took off with this lot on my first solo, grasping a handleful of throttles as we thundered down the runway, and proceeded to point myself in the general direction of Hulavington. As we continued on our way at about 2,000 feet the visibility began to decrease until it was only about, I suppose, two or three miles. On calling to join for landing instructions, I was told, 'Join for right-hand circuit for runway whatever, Buckmaster downwind single engine left-hand circuit'.

Now, flying a Lancaster (which was a big aeroplane, with a handful of throttles), after being used to something much smaller, was an interesting experience to start with. To be asked to do a right-hand circuit, which meant that visibility, since the pilot sits on the left-hand side of an aircraft, is restricted, and with 15 rugger players in the back in poor visibility, and finding a runway on which I hadn't landed before, was almost bound to be exciting. However, with good instructional technique, I found the runway, flew up it, did a timed right-hand circuit and sure enough, as I rolled out, there was the runway. It wasn't a very long runway, so I pulled the throttles back before we reached its threshold and, with a large clatter, the Merlins began to shut down and the aeroplane settled firmly on to the runway. The end of the runway was approaching fast, however, and by standing on the brakes, I managed to stop the dreaded thing before it rolled off the end. I turned off onto the peri-track, nonchalantly told the tower that I had cleared the runway, raised my flaps, taxied in, and 15 grateful chaps got out thanking me profusely, waving to me and disappearing off to their rugger game. Little did they know how close they had been to missing it!

I enjoyed CFS. Amateur Dramatics came into play once again and this time I produced *Dangerous Corner* for the local Society and then produced and performed in *Rookery Nook*, a play made famous by Tom Walls and Ralph Lynn and guess which part I played? It was a happy time and I enjoyed myself. I became an acting Flight Commander while I was there and in those days I had a brindle bull terrier, Buck, who accompanied me everywhere. One of my biggest mistakes was to actually take him flying one day and put him on the shelf behind the pilot in a Mosquito. He thoroughly approved of this exercise and used to sit there barking at the clouds if I flew in and out of them, really enjoying himself. It was, however, a mistake because he was now so keen to fly that, whenever he saw me getting into my flying gear, he would become hysterical waiting to go outside and leap into an aeroplane. Unfortunately, the aeroplanes all had large propellers, or 'mincemeat machines', on the front end and, if he had tried to follow me out to man an aircraft in the blind, dashing way of bull terriers, he might have finished as an early version of a hamburger. So I had to chain him to some fixed object with a very strong collar to prevent this happening. Nevertheless, when I was away he started to howl pitifully, so I had to take to leaving him back in the Officers' accommodation rather than letting him see that I was going down to the Squadron.

On one occasion, I was asked by the Flight Sergeant to deal with an airman who had been late in turning out for early morning duty. Buck at this time was asleep in his basket in the corner of the office and the man was fallen in in front of me by the Flight Sergeant in the correct RAF manner. The charge was read and I proceeded to give the chap a stiff talking to, during the course of which Buck woke up and seeing that, as he thought, I was dealing with some difficult situation, decided to be helpful and leapt out of his basket and attacked the airman. As the Flight Sergeant said to me afterwards, 'I don't think he'll be late again, Sir!'

During my time at CSF Their Lordships decided that they would offer some permanent commissions to aviators who had signed on for the four-year commission. The others were to be given extensions of a further four years. I can't remember how many permanent commissions were to be issued but I applied for and got one, so I was now a regular RN fellow. Soon after this I was told by the appointers in London that I was to leave CSF and go on the Empire flying course at Hulavington, of pleasant Lancaster memories! With some sadness, I packed my bags and went down to Hulavington, where the course was on Meteors, so my rudimentary jet experience on Vampires was rapidly expanded as this very advanced course progressed. In addition to the Meteors, we had the famous Aries Lancastrian aircraft which was used for long range navigational flights, one of which during my time was to fly the aeroplane down across France towards Nice and then along the coast, avoiding Spain, and landing at Gibraltar where we spent the night before returning to Hulavington. Nowadays it is a common experience, but then they were fairly long flights and very valuable from a practical point of view. Remember, there were really no navigation aids to speak of.

During this course I was given the opportunity of qualifying as an A1 Instructor, the highest grade that is available and for which you have to be assessed as exceptional under several headings. I duly underwent the test and qualified – I imagine that I was one of the few who has actually flown and qualified on four engines in the Royal Navy as an A1! Except of course later I did have 4 engines in the Ark Royal!

Towards the end of my time at EFS the appointer called me again with two choices – I could either go back to the RAF as an instructor on the new course being set up at RAF Manby, called the College of Knowledge, or I could go and serve in the United States Navy on exchange for twelve months. I could hardly wait to call him back to say, 'It's the US Navy for me, if you please.' And so, my immediate postwar period ended. I had been fortunate to spend much of that time with the Royal Air Force and, when that was taken together with the flying I had done during training, I had now spent more time flying with the RAF than with the Royal Navy. Much as I love the Royal Navy and the Fleet Air Arm, at that time I was lucky to spend so much time in a service where the flying standards by and large, not the operational qualifications, don't misunderstand me, were of a different order. I learned a lot and remain eternally grateful to the Royal Air Force, as I was to be grateful to the US Navy.

7

Brown Shoes

In the United States there is a term of classification which describes aviators as 'Brown Shoes' because they wear brown shoes with their khaki uniforms ashore, or embarked for that mater; and a 'Black Shoe' is the regular sea-going officer. Towards the end of the summer in 1949 I embarked in the Queen Elizabeth to New York to join the United States Navy as an exchange officer. The trip across was somewhat different from travelling in the troopships that I remembered before. The company was great and it was an enjoyable passage. After New York, I was sent to Washington and put in a hotel, where the food was something I could hardly remember having had before, while I waited to see the Naval Air Attché in Washington and after that to be sent to Norfolk, Virginia, to the Staff of Commander Fleet Air Atlantic.

It was given a choice of how I could get from Washington to Norfolk. I could either fly commercial, I could go by train or I could go on the old Bay line, a stern-wheel paddle steamer riverboat that went from Washington down to Portsmouth. I am delighted to say that I had enough imagination to opt for the latter and I really couldn't believe myself as I stood on the stern of this ship, watching the huge paddle wheel turn, as we trundled off down the Potomac towards Portsmouth on a clear night with the moon shining. I could almost hear the banjo's strumming; what an introduction to the Deep South of the United States. It was magic, a magic that has never left me.

From Portsmouth I went across on the ferry to Norfolk to check in and find myself in the vast Naval Air Station, where the Mess was literally miles away from the headquarters. I had no transport, and hadn't locked on to the fact that you couldn't walk everywhere as you could in the United Kingdom; the temperature was now soaring up into the 90s, which I found very unsuited for my heavy, clothes-rationing woollen sports jacket and grey flannel trousers. So I bought myself my first kind of seersucker ice-cream suit to be cool, and in due course presented myself to the appointer on the staff, 'Dog-face' Smith. On entering his office I was surprised to see a full-blown

Commander with wings, lounging back in his chair, with his feet on his desk. I stood stiffly to attention and clicked my heels (a routine which was to stand me in good stead in the United States because it usually had the recipient of my attention wondering whether I meant it or was trying to be funny). 'Well, Lygo,' he said, 'we've decided to send you to Commander Fleet Air, Jacksonville, where you will join the staff of Admiral...' 'But, Sir,' I protested, 'I didn't come here to join a staff, I have never been on anybody's staff, I came here to fly jet aircraft.' 'Well,' said he, 'that's what we've got you down for.' 'Well, I'm sorry, Sir,' said I, 'I don't think that's acceptable. I think it would be a complete waste of my experience to be sent on the staff at my relatively junior stage.' He looked at me quizzically for a while and said, 'Well, what exactly do you want to do?' 'I want to fly in a jet squadron, that's what I came to do. I have a lot of experience and I would like to put it to good use in your Navy.' He looked at me silently for a moment, picked up the phone and spoke to somebody and said, 'Come back and see me tomorrow.'

I hitched my way back to the Mess and then hitched back the next morning to his office. Once again, there he was lying back in his chair and once again he greeted me in the same way. I clicked my heels and he looked at me rather quizzically and said, 'Well, you are going to join VF172 at Cecil Field in Jacksonville. Collect your orders from the Yeoman outside and report to the CO, Commander de Poix.' I was delighted and thanked him profusely and then, as I was about to leave, I asked, 'Flying what, sir?' 'They have the first jet squadron on the east coast,' he said, 'the FH Phantom, and they are about to equip with the Banshee F2H,' I was delighted and, thanking him again I departed, collected my orders, and the next morning boarded a miliary air transport service aircraft flying down to Jacksonville. I reported to the fleet headquarters in Jacksonville and then on by Naval transport out to Cecil Field, which lies about 30 miles outside Jacksonville, in towards the centre of Florida.

Next morning, I reported to the CO of the squadron and met the executive officer, the Operations Officer and everybody else concerned, and was told that I was now to be the Ordnance Officer of this Squadron and responsible for the Ordnance Engineering, since I was a qualified engineer. How this had got into my CV I am not quite sure, but it hardly seemed worthwhile denying. Then came lengthy briefings as to how and where and when and why and a quiz on the aircraft I was about to fly, all thoroughly professional if a bit over the top, and then I was let loose to fly. The FH was a very simple little aeroplane with two small Westinghouse engines very close to the centre thrust line, and it flew very much like a Vampire. I only spent a short time on this before being allowed to go off in a newly arrived Banshee, which was a delightful aeroplane similar to a Meteor in performance, although much lighter to handle with powered controls. After the third flight, when I was still being told more or less to fly straight and level, I decided that I would abandon the briefing and start to do some real flying. I therefore took the aeroplane up to a safe altitude and, closing one engine to idle, I then proceeded to put it through its paces of single-engine performance, finding out what its critical and safety speeds were and then, coming back to the airfield, I called and asked for a practice single-engine landing. I was greeted with the famous word, which seems to be universal from all towers when you ask for anything which is a bit unusual, 'Wait.'

As soon as the circuit was clear I proceeded to join to make a fairly wide one and then called downwind for practice single-engine overshoot. Again there was no reply, and then came a very surprising message: 'After landing, roll to the end of the runway, shut down the other engine and wait.' I found this to be extraordinary but it was

Being briefed in USS *Cora Sea*

their aircraft and their routine, so I duly came in, did not do the overshoot, landed, rolled to the end of the runway and shut down the other engine. I sat waiting while a tractor came out, hooked me up and towed me back in. When I approached the Squadron area, I was surprised to see the Captain, the Air Officer, my Commander Officer and most of the Squadron all waiting for me. I got out of the aeroplane as casually as I could and walked over, clicking my heels to the Squadron Commander. 'What happened?' he asked. 'Nothing, Sir.' 'How do you mean, nothing?' 'Well, I was just carrying out a practice.' He stared at me in disbelief, drilling me with his clear eyes, and then he said, 'Report to me in my office,' turned on his heel and walked in. I duly changed out of my flying gear (we used to wear pressure suits in those days) and then into my khaki uniform, and presented myself to him. My familiar routine of clicking my heels, standing stiffly to attention and staring straight ahead once again stood me in good stead. 'Stand at ease,' he said. 'Now, would you explain to me what you were doing?' 'What I was doing', said I, 'was to find out how this aeroplane performs on one engine, Sir, so that in the event that I have to face that situation, I shall know how to handle it, and will not be under the pressure that might otherwise occur, should I not be prepared.'

He stared at me in disbelief. 'Was this what you were briefed to do?' he asked. 'No, Sir,' I replied, 'It wasn't, but I was getting rather bored with the kind of things I was being asked to do and I thought it more important to test this aeroplane and my ability to fly it properly, so that I could be of more use to you.' His mouth fell open slightly and then, quickly recovering himself, he said, 'If you had damaged that aeroplane, Lygo, you would now have been on your way back to England.' 'But I didn't damage it, Sir, and neither would I.' He cleared his throat slightly and then, on a different tack, said, 'And how did it handle?' 'Oh, it handled extremely well,' I said. 'Its thrust lines are very close to the centre line, Sir. There is very little asymmetric difficulty with it and the safety speed is very, very close to the critical speed. The aeroplane can be safely brought in, I would have thought, with no problem, for single-engine deck landing.' 'I see,' he said. 'Well, in future, just do as you are briefed and not as you think fit to do.' 'Aye, aye, Sir,' I responded and turned smartly on my heels, having clicked them once more, and departed.

Amusing, you might think, but no – they were absolutely right, I was wrong. Their attitude was probably a damned sight more practical than some of the things I had been doing. But, my reputation in the Squadron had now taken off.

On the first weekend I decided that I would have to get myself a car, so I decided to go into town and buy myself a second-hand one. As I sat reading the morning paper before going into town, the dentist on the base came over to me and said, 'What are you doing this morning, Ray?' 'I want to go into town,' said I, 'I want to go to some second-hand car dealers to see if I can find myself some wheels.' 'I'm going into town and I'd be happy to give you a lift.' 'It would be a great pleasure,' I replied and got into his car, where to my surprise were a large number of paperback books. 'Are you a keen reader?' I enquired. 'Well, yes,' he said, 'in a way, but I'm actually returning these to the mother of a girlfriend of mine. She's an avid reader and has lent me these books and I need to return them, because I haven't seen her daughter for some time.' I was later to discover that this was a subtle way of reacquainting himself with the daughter.

We proceeded into Jacksonville and came to rest outside an apartment block, in front of which were a few people who were trying to put back in the ground various bushes and plants that had been torn out by the hurricane which had passed through in the preceding days. I was introduced to an extremely attractive, curvaceous young lady who turned out to be the young lady he was referring to. She escorted us into the house, informing us that her mother was away visiting her other daughter, took possession of the paperbacks, and then asked us if we would like some light refreshment. Coca-Cola was duly dispensed and as I lifted it to my lips I said, 'Cheers.' The young lady departed to the kitchen and came back and said, 'I'm sorry, we don't have any cheese.' This was my first meeting with Pepper van Osten, the woman to whom I have been married for over 50 years.

The work in the Squadron continued and we were finally to embark in the *Philippine Sea* to go down and do a sea work-up of Guantanamo, the US Navy base in Cuba. I bade a fond farewell to my new fiancée – yes, we met in September and were married in January – and departed for our first break, one of many more that were to follow.

The work-up off Cuba was proceeding satisfactorily when one day, when I was airborne and was flying as Section Leader on the executive officer, Pent Bluin, his number two ahead of me on the recovery (we were flying jets on the straight axial deck in those days) had his hook bounce up on landing. It locked up and he went straight into the Davis barrier. The Davis barrier had been designed to arrest jet aircraft when operating off an axial deck. A wire was stretched across the deck at about 18 inches or so above the level of the deck and this engaged the nosewheel of the aircraft which then automatically triggered a steel wire or barrier which shot up and engaged the main landing gear. When Ernie Brides exercised this in a Banshee (which had the linkage gear in the front of the undercarriage), the wire ran up through the joint between the linkage and the main strut. The strut acted almost like a wire-cutter, cut the wire neatly, and he proceeded straight forward to crash into the aircraft that had landed previously. Fortunately Ernie was not hurt, but the deck was a mess and they didn't seem to be very good at sorting themselves out. As I circled round and round, waiting to be recovered but without any clear instructions, I became concerned that there would soon come a point when I would not have enough fuel to divert. At about this time the red warning light of fuel low appeared in the aircraft, and I then told the ship that either I was to be recovered immediately or I was diverting. Since I received no reply to this other than 'Wait', I proceeded to tell them that I was diverting to Leward Point, the airfield for jets on the other side of the bay in the US enclave in Cuba. I was joined rapidly by a chap who was to become the best man at my wedding, who signified to me by using his thumb and clenched fist, to indicate a drinking motion, that he was running low on fuel. You are telling me nothing I don't know, I thought to myself, as we proceeded to head out into the direction in which I hoped would be Cuba.

Eventually the ship came up with a course to steer and so we settled down and hoped to see the coast come up. In due course, visibility being not all that good, about five miles or so, there it was, Leward Point. By this time my gauges were reading very low, but my companion was becoming even more excited so I signalled him to go in for a straight-in approach and land, and that I would come round behind him. This he did, but imagine my chagrin when I discovered that he had landed fast, jammed his brakes on and burst a tyre halfway down the runway. So there he was, slewed slightly on the runway and blocking it, or at least partially blocking it. I did a rapid calculation and figured that if Leward Point was as good at clearing its runway as the *Philippine Sea* had been at clearing its deck, I was going to be out of fuel before very long so I decided to come in and land. I called him on the radio and told him to fold his wings. We had electrical wingfold in the Banshee and I saw his wings begin to fold, which made a bit more space on the runway. I came in and touched as short as possible and, as soon as I had done that, hit the wingfold switch, folded my own wings and shot past him quite comfortably to finish up happily with some runway ahead of me. Now we were stuck at Leward Point.

After a stay of some 36–48 hours, it became clear that the rest of the squadron was going to be disembarked to join us. Banshee flying with the Davis barrier had been suspended until such time as measures could be taken to avoid a future disaster.

We worked to a tropical routine at Leward Point, starting early in the morning and finishing flying about 1 p.m., as it got so hot it became unbearable, and then all we had to do was lie on our bunks and perspire gently while the afternoon passed away until we opened the bar in the evening and had a drink. I was never very good at sleeping in the afternoons and would try teasing my companions with things which were perfectly true in those days, but which unfortunately today would no longer be possible. I would wait for about half an hour until they were all settled and then I would sing out, 'Who has the fastest train in the world? The British. Who holds the land speed record? Who holds the air speed record?' etc. It was a way of enlivening the debate and keeping my companions well informed until some well aimed boots caused me to desist.

With time on our hands, it was possible to have philosophical conversations and one of mine was to ask my companions how they intended to act as the world's policemen after they had assisted in the demolition of the British Empire. They of course fiercely denied the latter and felt embarrassed by my saying so, but I said, 'Not at all, I understand perfectly why historically and with all good reason, you assisted in the collapse of the British Empire, that is not my problem. My problem is how are you, who wish to be loved, going to conduct yourselves in trying to exercise the role of world's policeman? We've had a couple of hundred years of getting used to this and are quite used to the fact that you don't get any credit for this role and are generally speaking "disliked" for it and we don't mind being disliked. In fact, we quite like being disliked but you don't and I think you're going to have one hell of a problem.' Little did I know how truthful and how correct these observations were going to be. My companions were, as most Americans are, decent people who, because of their history of great success in their own country, can't understand why the rest of the world doesn't act in a similar fashion.

Soon it was time to be back in Jacksonville for our next deployment, which was to be in the *Roosevelt*, in which we were to conduct an exercise to demonstrate that the much-vaunted claim of the United States Air Force that its B36 bombers could fly so high that nobody could intercept them was not true, because the Banshee could and would. This was in the days of Senator McCarthy, and in the days of Johnson who, as Secretary of the Navy, was talking about closing down the United States Marine Corps! In the aftermath of the war he had people believing that they were now in a period of eternal peace, and the destruction of the US forces was about to begin.

It was unfortunate that the embarkation was to take place a couple of weeks prior to my wedding, which was to be in the local Anglican church in Jacksonville. One of the perks of being a foreigner in another country is that one usually gets one's home products duty free and I had therefore told my future mother-in-law not to worry about ordering grog for the reception, because I could get it so much cheaper, and that I would order all the champagne through the British Embassy in Washington, which I duly did. Because of the Federal Law, which required that you couldn't move duty free products across state lines, without incurring state taxes, I had planned to take an Expeditor, an SMB in US Navy terms, a twin-engined aeroplane not unlike a DeHavilland Dove, up to Washington to collect all the champagne and fly it back to Jacksonville. The embarkation for the operational development force exercise against the B36, however, meant that for the two weeks prior to my wedding, I was going to be embarked! We embarked and sat pitching and tossing off Cape Hatteras waiting for the United States Air Force to send out their B36s to attack us. Of course, they never did. For one reason or another they never came and thus we were unable to prove that we could or could not intercept them. Whilst these interesting inter-service war games were taking place, my champagne was languishing in Washington. Finally the trial was abandoned and we disembarked but, alas, it came to the day before the wedding and I still hadn't got the grog and so I had to go downtown Jacksonville and buy all the champagne again at over-the-counter prices since my Ma-in-Law to be

My first bonedome

had already paid me the duty free price. Not a bad deal but nevertheless one that left me completely strapped. Hardly the best way to start a marriage!

Our wedding, and particularly the reception, was a great success. I don't remember much of it but I do remember setting out to go down to Miami to catch the plane to Nassau, where we were to spend our honeymoon. Why Nassau? Because it was in the sterling area and, at that time, sterling was not a convertible currency; although I had money in sterling, I had very little in dollars, having bought my second-hand car and various other bits and pieces, including a decent outfit of clothes. So I wrote to my bank manager at Barclays Bank at the Orpington branch and asked him to transfer some money into the bank at Nassau for my honeymoon. I was under the impression that £500 would be a tidy sum of money for a week's holiday, but in his reply he said he was very happy to make the transfer but would respectfully point out that he understood that Nassau was a very expensive place and did I think that £500 would be enough. With the bravado of youth, I told him to transfer yet another £500.

Some weeks before, the Squadron had organised a "rum run" down to Cuba via Nassau, landing at Oaks Field, and there they had come with me to look at the hotel I was going to use for the honeymoon. I had discovered that there was a honeymoon package deal in a hotel in Nassau itself which I thought would be rather good, but the Squadron promptly said, 'You can't bring a Southern Belle to a place like this, Ray,' and had me finishing up at the Fort Montague Beach Hotel at the other end of the island, which cost far more money than I had ever envisaged spending anywhere in my life before.

The first night of our honeymoon was to be spent on the way down to Miami in the Ponce de Lion hotel in St. Augustine, now long since gone. All went well, the first night arrived, but at 3 o'clock in the morning there was a hammering on the door and the Squadron had arrived. I had been conned into telling one of my so-called Squadron mates where the first night would be, 'because,' said they, 'they wanted to send us some flowers'. Indeed they did, but they brought them themselves! I refused to be drawn by this and we stayed firmly in our room and let them go and drink themselves to pieces down below but perhaps as a result of this and other activities, we were later getting up and departing the next morning than we should have been to make the trip to Miami to catch the British West Indian Airways flight to Nassau. To make matters worse, I took the wrong turning out of St. Augustine and it was some time before I discovered that we were on the wrong road. The next thing that happened was I got a puncture and had to go back to a farmhouse where a barefoot lad in a Model T

Ford came down with a jack to help me change the wheel. As a result, I decided to stop and buy a new tyre with the remains of the money I had, in case something worse should befall us.

Adding all these things together, meant that we arrived in the traffic of Miami too late to catch the aeroplane only to watch it disappear into the distance; we were now stuck for the night. The problem was I only had enough money to pay for a room in the hotel or dinner, one or the other. This was long before credit cards! We decided that the only thing to do would be to call my newly acquired mother-in-law and ask her to wire some money via Western Union so that we could enjoy both. We booked in, had a meal and then sat waiting for Western Union to call and say the money had arrived. They didn't, and after many calls we decided to go down to the Western Union Office ourselves to see what had happened, having checked with my mother-in-law that the money had indeed been transferred. The languid attitude of the clerk in the Western Union office, who told me that there was no money for Lygo, infuriated me so much that I went round behind the counter and went through his file myself to find that it had been filed under Raymond. Furious as I was, I was glad to get my hands on the dollars so that we could quit ourselves of the hotel the following morning without being arrested!

The cast of Kongo, produced at NAS Jacksonville. I'm at the extreme right. Amateur dramatics once again!

140

Nassau proved to be as wonderful as all the brochures said it would; it was idyllic. Looking back on it of course, there was one mystery which now is clear to me. I had explained to Pepper that the cost of cigarettes in the UK was very high and that it would be a rather expensive pastime to smoke at the rate she was smoking. She promptly replied by saying, 'Oh well then, I'll stop' and can you believe it, stopped on our wedding day! I couldn't understand why, on the subsequent honeymoon when we were on the beach or wherever, she would suddenly say, 'Oh I've left my handbag back up in the room' and would disappear on some pretext or other to collect various lost objects and although I offered to collect them for her, she wouldn't hear of it. I now know why: she was having a quiet drag because she never did, nor ever has, given up – until 3 years ago!

After a few days in Nassau, I was cabling Barclays Bank in Orpington to send me even more money. I had begun to realise how expensive life could be. The best beach the hotel could offer was Rainbow Beach on Paradise Island, I believe. You took a boat across to it and there lay on the silver sands under the palm trees, but because of my ginger complexion I couldn't spend very much time in the sun, 10 or 15 minutes of exposure before the days of sunblock was all I could manage. What really riled me was having to rent an umbrella to keep the sun off when we were paying so much to have it! On one occasion my wife swam out to a float where she sprawled, only to be promptly chatted up by some bronzed Adonis who then asked her what she was going in Nassau? 'Well, I'm on my honeymoon'. 'Oh,' he said, 'where is your husband?' and at that moment I apparently arose from the lying position on the beach, covered in towels to keep off the sun, to sit up and return her wave. 'What's the matter with him?' asked the Adonis, 'Is he sick?'. 'No,' said my wife, 'he always looks like that!'

In my vague way, I had completely forgotten that having had no money on arrival, I would have very little on our return, in dollars that is, and so when we landed back in Miami, I found myself with just about enough money to pay for the full tank of gas that was necessary and to release the car from the parking lot, in order to get us back to Jacksonville! When all this had been taken care of, we had 13 cents left. On the way up to Jacksonville, Pepper said, 'Well, let's stop and get a hot dog and we can divide it between us'.

'Hot dogs' said I 'cost 15 cents, darling.'

'No, no,' she said 'you can still get a 10 cents hot dog' and so I was persuaded to stop at the first pull-in and walking in to the man I said, 'Do you sell hot dogs?'

'Yes Sir', he said clapping his hands together and producing a large weenie which he proceeded to throw onto the griddle.

'Just a moment' said I, 'How much are they?'

'15 cents,' he said, looking at me with some surprise.

'Thank you very much,' I said, and walked out. On the third occasion of doing this, I became exasperated.

'Darling,' I said, 'there's no such thing as a 10 cent hot dog'. We settled for some cheese crackers and by having her standing in orange groves while I appeared to be taking photographs of her, she nicked oranges off the tree. Unfortunately they were usually unripe. In this state, we returned from our honeymoon, still broke, still in debt. Later on the blackboard in the briefing room, I, by this time having collected the champagne and various other articles of drink, had 'bargain prices' chalked up and took the ready cash of my colleagues at duty free prices in order that we could buy our groceries.

The major event during my time in VF172 was to be the embarkation in the USS *Coral Sea* for a six-month deployment to the Mediterranean as part of the Sixth Fleet. I left Pepper, in the best Naval tradition, barefoot and pregnant. Mind you, being barefoot in Florida was not a particularly onerous experience and we were delighted with the pregnancy and the prospect of our first child.

After we had embarked and settled down and done some fairly gentle flying around the east coast (we were still flying off an axial deck with barriers), we proceeded to cross the Atlantic and enter the Mediterranean. Long periods of embarkation in an aircraft carrier become fairly boring in peacetime; you fall into a routine of flying (though not a lot of it, generally speaking) and endless days when you are really twiddling your thumbs or waiting for the evening movie. So one is left with a mish-mash of memories. The ship's doctor came on the broadcast to us halfway across the Atlantic and told us, with the amazing ability to spew out statistics that Americans seem to have, that the previous commission in the *Midway* had produced several thousand (I can't remember exactly how many now) 'exposures' which had resulted in rather less but still numerous (thousands indeed) cases of venereal disease. He told us we were going to beat this because our routine was to be that when you returned on board you'd be asked by the Officer of the Watch whether you had had an 'exposure' and if so you were to be immediately given a shot of penicillin. Of course it soon became a fairly raucous and amusing debate as to how many exposures we would each claim to have had in order to assist the statistics! This however could be dangerous because you then got stuffed full of penicillin, so it was decided it was best to be honest.

As the ship approached the first port of call, which was the then American base in the South of France in Villefrance, a notice went up on the crew notice board saying that the Squadron had arranged to

Banshees of VF 172 in formation. I'm flying No2 to the Senior Pilot in 206

rent a suite of rooms in a hotel, that several girls were going to be provided and a hire car, and this was going to cost quite a modest number of dollars per head for the Squadron to participate. Observing that we were divided into three watches for leave, I thought it was going to be an experience I had no wish to share in. Particularly so soon after I was newly married! In any case, I'd arranged to fly home to visit my parents and talk to them about the marriage and show them some of the photographs which they hadn't yet had an opportunity to see, and so it was that I escaped for that first ten days in Villefrance and was therefore unmarked by that particular experience but it did, to me, illustrate an extraordinary difference between the way in which matters were handled in the US and in the UK, or should I say between the US Navy and the Royal Navy.

Flying itself was fairly boring. It consisted of endless fighter patrols at altitude with endless crossover turns and just occasionally the opportunity to intercept something. It was a good illustration of the old saying, 'Twenty years of aviation, nineteen years in a left-hand turn.' On one occasion, when we did nothing but circle Vesuvius for two hours because the executive officer had a hangover from the night before we sailed that morning, I exploded in the crew room saying that, 'If we suddenly found ourselves in combat, I would not wish to be part of this team.' This led the CO to quietly take me away and say, 'In the event of a threat of any action, Ray, I can assure you that the experienced pilots of which you are one would be put in charge, and the more senior-ranking ones who have little flying experience will be relegated to flying wing.' 'This is all very well,' I countered, 'but it doesn't help to train them properly if they are put in a position where they don't know what to do and thus learn nothing because they haven't anybody to watch and follow.'

My faith in the humour of the United States Navy was restored towards the end of the commission when we were relieved by the *Roosevelt* alongside in Oran. *Coral Sea* was on one side of the jetty and we waited for the *Roosevelt* to arrive to relieve us on the other side. In planning for this Blackie Kennedy, who was the Squadron Commander of one of the other Squadrons, had come up with the bright idea of playing a joke on the *Roosevelt* by pretending to have a number of important Arab dignitaries arrive, at the moment she came alongside and almost the moment her gangway was out. All in a large cavalcade of black cars with suitable funny-looking flags flying to call on the Captain. Because I had a strange uniform, or at least it was different from theirs, I was deputed to become the Flag Lieutenant for this occasion and to indicate to the startled Officer of the Day in the *Roosevelt* who was, as they are in those enormous carriers, some distance away up this very long gangway, by holding up five fingers to indicate that the dignitary who was arriving was equivalent to five stars and should be treated accordingly. By dint of borrowing some of the Wardroom carpets and sheets and cork and various bits and pieces, and by the use of my somewhat strange uniform, we assembled a group which I must say at a distance passed reasonably well for Arab potentates led by a Liaison Officer. At the appointed moment the cavalcade of cars thundered down the mole and drew up alongside the *Roosevelt*'s gangway; they all got out and looked around and examined their feet and the sky and one end of the ship and the other end of the ship, while I indicated to the Officer of the Day by holding up my hand with five fingers (or four fingers and a thumb I should say) extended. The Officer of the Day leapt for the 'phone that was at the top of the gangway to summon the Captain down for this impor-tant visit and as we hung about there, finally we saw the Captain appear at the head of the gangway. At this moment, we decided to start up the gangway. Now you may have noticed, or if you haven't I'll tell you, there is a large number painted on the side of most warships and the United States Navy, and their carriers usually have a

40 number on them. Halfway up the gangway with everybody standing at attention at the end ready to receive us and buglers ready and a US Marine guard having fallen in, we stopped to have a long altercation, while I produced a piece of paper which we all surveyed; then we had a long conflab (this was halfway up this very long gangway) and then all the Arabs turned and departed down the gangway, and I shouted up to the man, 'Sorry, bud, wrong number!' and we left them. It was a great gag and well executed, and was complemented by the fact that the ship's bakers in the *Coral Sea* had baked an enormous cake while the band played 'We knew you were coming, so we baked a cake'. In all, a very amusing and well organised gag.

At the end of the commission we fell in on the flight deck and the CO came down with a bucket of medals which he handed out to every-body. When he got to me he said, 'I don't see why you shouldn't have one, Ray,' and when I looked at it, it was to commemorate the occupation of Europe. I have the medal to this day and of course it appears in a later episode.

My arrival home was to be greeted by the very pregnant Pepper. We had been away for Christmas and Brooke, our first child, was due in a matter of weeks; I was due to go back to England also in a matter of weeks, and so we began to sweat it out as to whether the child would be born in sufficient time for Pepper to accompany me or whether I'd have to go back and she would follow later. It turned out that the latter was the course we had to follow, and Brooke was born in the Naval hospital at Jacksonville which is actually in a small area called Yukon, Florida, an unlikely name for any town in Florida you might think. It was not an easy delivery for Pepper, and there were an inordi-nate number of children due to be delivered that same night. The senior nurse threw a wobbly, and I think Brooke was actually deliv-ered by the ENT doctor, but we were all delighted. After all too short a period I had to return to the UK, this time in the *Queen Mary* from New York, and back to duty – a severe shock to any system.

So ended my eighteen months of very happy service with the United States Navy. I learned a great deal; I learned to respect them for the differences that they had from the way in which we traditionally ran things in the Royal Navy. I made a number of friends and I enjoyed myself immensely, but best of all I had been united with a lady who was to be my companion henceforth and, together with that unique combination of American and British character, we have weathered many a storm.

8

The Naval Air Fighter School, Culdrose

I returned to the UK from my exchange tour in the United States Navy with more jet experience than any pilot then serving in the Royal Navy. Furthermore, it was embarked experience on an actual deck! The Royal Navy had yet to come to terms with jet aircraft; some years previously, 'Winkle' Brown had carried out some deck landings in a Vampire, after which he had, I believe, expressed the view that, with the engine control then available in a Vampire (which had a very slow reaction to throttle movement), the task would not be in the competence of the average squadron pilot. All human endeavour is sometimes set back by people who imagine they are so superior that none could match them and certainly never surpass them! This was to be proved wrong with the advances in reaction that were obtained with the next generation of engines, and within three years average pilots were doing it both by day and by night.

I was not debriefed on my experiences, and nobody asked me to talk to them. The so-called centre of jet excellence at the Naval Air Fighter School at Culdrose was 702 Squadron, but I was not invited to go and talk to them. In fact, I suspect I was positively resented because I might have more knowledge than they had. The only person who asked me to go to see him, ultimately, was George Baldwin who was then CO of the first Attacker Squadron at Ford, and I went down and talked to his Squadron about jet operations in general. No one else bothered, and this was a lesson that was to stick with me and serve me in good stead at a later stage of my career in coming to a judgement on the new anti-submarine helicopter for the Navy.

I went with my parents to Southampton to meet Pepper when she came over in the *Queen Mary* with Brooke, the most precious bundle of our first child, and I remember very well greeting her as she came off, looking like a movie star, in her outfit which might have been perfectly normal in Florida, but which in clothes-rationed Britain looked somewhat outstanding. I had left my latest automobile purchase, the Kaiser Fraser Manhattan, behind in America, to be shipped over by the US Navy on a contingency basis (I think it cost 10 dollars or something like it in those days, on a space-available shipment) and was there lovingly cosseting my 1937 AC drophead coupé. It was fairly low-slung, unlike the American cars to which Pepper was used, and it also enjoyed, or didn't enjoy, as the case may be, inflatable seats. These were rubber inserts in the seat which you had to blow up, but during the War and the period at either end these had somewhat deteriorated and although they were liberally supplied with Dunlop patches, you could never be quite sure that they would remain inflated for a long period of time. So it came about that when Pepper, complete with the baby in arms, lowered herself into the car expecting to meet a fairly high soft seat, she let go and fell a considerable distance before she hit an uninflated seat. She has never forgotten that experience of her introduction to the first British automobile.

I had been carrying out reconnaissance in the Helston area before she arrived, and had decided that the best thing we could do was buy a small semi-detached house on the Redruth road called Chybean. There had been a near disaster when the usual effervescing estate agent had taken me to see a very cutely converted cottage near by and I was tempted (although I was strapped for money) to buy it. As we walked back through the garden, however, I noticed some large galvanised tanks at the back of the house. 'What are those?' I enquired. 'Oh, that's the water,' he said. 'What do you mean, "that's the water"?' I enquired. 'Well, that's where you get your water from; it comes off the roof.' 'Are you telling me there's no mains supply?' 'No, no, no,' he said, 'quite unnecessary in Cornwall, it rains every day.' The thought of how much water the washing machine was going to use with the new baby, together with my American wife's attitude towards running water, put that firmly out of mind, but it was a close shave. At least the semi-detached had flushing loos and mains water and drainage.

The journey down from my brother's house in Petts Wood, however, was nothing short of a disaster. We travelled down on a Sunday, goodness knows why but we did, and it was pouring with rain. The drophead coupé had one small hole in the otherwise new hood and that happened, unfortunately, to be right over where my wife was sitting. The steady drip of water did not bode well for the rest of the journey, but worse was to come, because somewhere between Redhill and Reigate on the old A25 the car stopped. When I opened the bonnet, I discovered that petrol was pouring from the old glass petrol filter that used to be a familiar sight in those cars. It had cracked and fuel was just running out. I now had to leave Pepper in the dripping car while I went off to try to find a garage that would tow us in and repair the damage. As extreme luck would have it, I found a garage open that was prepared to come and tow the car in and very quickly short-circuited the filter so that we had a steady supply of fuel to the carburettors (all three of them).

As a result of this delay, it was going to be very late before we arrived at the Mullion Cove Hotel where I had booked in at special rates for Naval officers, in the rooms overlooking the dustbins at the back of the hotel, rather than the splendid views which are still afforded by that hotel at the front. The final calamity was when Brooke decided to give vent to her pent-up digestive system and it became necessary to change her in the middle of a remote part of Devon. I remember very well, pulling up at a petrol station and asking for some water, as there was no wash room there. The proprietor lived across the road and up a flight of stone steps, so I followed him up there and was given a very small pan of water. My wife appeared stunned when presented with the pan so I busied myself examining the engine and similar important components while she coped with the mess on her lap as she effected to change Brooke's nappy. It was not a happy introduction to the joys of living in the United Kingdom for my Florida-born wife. How she stood it, looking back on it, I just don't know.

We eventually arrived at the Mullion Cove Hotel and the proprietor, who had obviously been waiting for us in the bar, peered at the precious bundle and mumbled only one greeting 'poor little soul' – over and over again. We were exhausted, and to be greeted by a somewhat tipsy proprietor was not the best introduction to what were to be our living quarters for the next two months, while we sorted out the purchase of the new house. Nevertheless, it worked. I think the electric bill at the Mullion Cove Hotel must have gone through the ceiling, because the three bars of the electric fire were never off as my poor Florida wife shivered in her room, while I went about my business at Culdrose.

My appointment was to command 738 B Flight. It was an autonomous command looking at weapons evaluation for the Fury and the Sea Hornet, and one of the things I had to do was carry out and continue the dive-bombing trials of the Sea Hornet 21, when that aircraft had already been withdrawn from first-line service! The weather was Cornwall at its best, but to me, appalling. I had grown used to the weather in Florida, and coming back to the kind of weather that you get in the Cornish peninsula was a severe shock to the system. Do people really fly in this, I kept asking myself, and remembering of course that yes, we did. I'd just got out of the habit. In addition, getting into a large rotary-engined aeroplane, with swing on take-off and everything else, was also a shock as I had been used to the smooth ride of a twin-engined jet aircraft. There was nothing for it, however, so I persisted, wondering what the hell I was supposed to be doing most of the time. Fortunately, it was not for long.

The Fleet Air Arm had embraced centralised maintenance some years before, happily while I was out of it, and this had resulted in the most extraordinary lack of available aircraft. The whole of the maintenance had been placed in the hands of engineers who were solely concerned with maintaining the aircraft, not getting them ready for action. As a result, availability was low. Squadrons were manned by a skeleton crew just to put you into the aeroplanes and push them in and out of the hangar, but they were not responsible for the maintenance as this was done centrally. People in the central maintenance organization were not connected directly with the flying task and so were not particularly well motivated either. The memory of this came back years later during the debate on the Rationalisation of Air power. Fortunately, it had been decided that we should revert to Squadron maintenance, where the Squadrons were given the personnel to maintain and service, as well as fly, their own aeroplanes. Because of this we needed to form a new Squadron at Culdrose, within the Naval Air Fighter School, to carry out the task of conversion and Air Weapons Officer training, leaving the primary role of operational conversion of the then standard type, the Sea Fury, to the other two Squadrons, 736 and 738.

To my surprise and delight I was given command of a new Squadron, 759, and acquired four Firebrands, two Sea Fury Trainers, and four Hornets, as well as, eventually, 12 Seafires. The manpower for this was provided to me from the residue of the centralised maintenance team together with an air engineer officer, Geoff Long, who was at the time under Quarterly Report. I can't remember for what reason. My pilots included Bill Orr Cubben, an extraordinarily amusing and loquacious officer (who was then actually senior to me), as my senior pilot and an exchange officer from the RAF, John Pinnington. Eventually, I gathered around me those other pilots that were available to conduct the various tasks that I was given.

One of the first memories that I have is of a Leading Naval Airman coming to see me to ask whether he would be allowed to form a Squadron football team. I said, 'Of course, you can form as many Squadron teams as you like.' 'But what about time to play games, sir?' 'Well, if you've got a challenge and you want to take it on then we will. When we're ahead of the flying task, we'll have time off to do these things.' He seemed to be amazed by this reply. 'What's so surprising about this?' I asked him. 'Because we've never had time off for playing games.' 'Well,' said I, 'we intend to embark on planned flying as well as planned maintenance, and when we have achieved our task or are two days ahead of it, we'll close down and enjoy ourselves for a bit.' It was a great idea, but the first time I did it I was sent for and told to start flying again at once. The idea of rewarding your people who were working hard to exceed their target by giving them something in exchange seemed to the Navy at that time a strange way of operating. So I had to do something to show them that the system they were operating was entirely antiquated.

We flew on Saturday mornings in those days but no aeroplanes were available in the other Squadrons on a Monday morning because they were all on weekly inspection. We had aeroplanes available, however, as Geoff Long, who was an enthusiastic supporter of planned flying/ planned maintenance, so arranged our inspections that they were staggered throughout the week and generally took place when it wasn't possible to fly anyway because of the weather. By borrowing every pilot that I could lay my hands on I formed what was in those happy days known as a 'Balbo' and we flew 22 aeroplanes, all my aeroplanes bar two, over the field at nine o'clock on a Monday morning. They had never seen anything like this before, and it finally struck home that 759 had a method of operating that was better than they had seen up to then. It didn't, of course, make one instantly popular with other people who were operating less energetic routines, as I was soon to learn when I was hauled over the coals for failing to lead my Squadron past the saluting base on Divisions. With my shortage of pilots, I was also flying, and I left this task to my Weapons Electrical Officer. Not good enough, I was told, the CO should lead the Squadron by. But, 'I was flying, Sir.' That was no excuse, and probably it wasn't, but I learned my lesson and, because of the challenge to the Squadron, the lads, as usual, responded and were extremely smart on parade. 'OK,' I said to them, 'if we're going to do divisions we'll beat the rest of them at it, and beat them at flying as well.' Young men only need a challenge and the right kind of attitude and they will respond. They knew that most of the things I was trying to do were best for them, as well as best for the Service.

Gradually we established ourselves as a good Squadron, something to look up to, but it wasn't easy and there were several occasions on which I found myself sailing very close to the wind. We moved the Squadron, eventually, from the rather ramshackle quarters we had been given (I seem to remember that my headquarters were in a disused Link Trainer building) and proceeded to occupy a proper dispersal closer to the Control Tower. Also at about this time, Their Lordships decided that any officer in command of a Squadron of more than eight aircraft should be an Acting Lieutenant-Commander, and so I found myself an Acting Lieutenant-Commander! There were also

150

Part of the Balbo

some changes in the management at Culdrose at about this time. The Chief Flying Instructor was Willy Simpson who was not an instructor at all (but that was a peculiarity of the Fleet Air Arm), whereas I was an A1 instructor (not that that meant anything in the Navy!). A new Wings was appointed to us, Freddy Stovin Bradford, well known as a flamboyant Naval character.

One of the occasions which did not endear me to my colleagues and seniors was when the Squadron Commanders were asked to attend a gathering to decide how we could enhance the standard and status of Squadron Commanders. My colleagues started and one suggested that we should be piped on board ship: 'Very good, very good,' and this was duly noted as a good suggestion. Another one suggested that we should all have our own cars with drivers, so that we should be able to fly flags on them, I suppose. The suggestions covered this kind of ground and finally it was my turn to be asked what I thought. I have, unfortunately, a name that can be used almost as a term of reproach. 'And what is your view, Lygo?' 'I think, Sir,' I said, 'that we should all wear cocked hats.' There was a stunned silence. 'What do you mean?'

'What I mean, Sir, is it would make us look extremely different from everybody else and everyone would know that we were Squadron Commanders.' 'That's a ridiculous suggestion.' 'Of course it is,' I said 'just as ridiculous as trying to dress us up by some means other than our own personalities. We should be judged by our ability to command Squadrons, and demonstrate that we are in command by our performance. You cannot enhance a person's real character by just giving them baubles, and in any case my suggestion would be much cheaper than any of the others!' The meeting ended among the scowls of my colleagues.

Life progressed, however, and finally we were given the first of the new Vampire trainers in the Navy, to convert pilots to jet flying, and subsequently I gathered some eight or nine Meteors for the same purpose. So my jet days were back again and I was able to demonstrate that flying jet aircraft was just as simple, if not more so, than any other aeroplane, certainly as far as deck landing is concerned because you can actually see the deck.

Another episode I am reminded of at Culdrose is the preparations

759 Squadron, Culdrose in front of the 1st Vampire trainer

for Air Day 1953. Again Squadron Commanders were called together to discuss how we could run a successful Air Day and the question was asked, 'Did any of us have any bright ideas about how we could do something different?'

'Yes, Sir,' said I. 'When I was with the United States Navy we took part in an airshow in Chicago and they had a large articulated lorry which had been converted into a model aircraft carrier and this model proceeded up and down the runway while a Piper Cub did circuits and landings on it.'

'What a brilliant idea,' they said. 'Well, I see, yes that's very good, that's a very good idea, Lygo, thank you, h'm.' And the meeting closed with various other observations and arrangements. To my surprise, I heard no more of this until one day Stan Farquhar, who was then my senior pilot, came in and said, 'Have you heard, Boss, they're building an aircraft carrier like you suggested in workshops on an articulated lorry.'

'Are they really?' I replied. 'How very interesting. I hope they get it right.'

We had at that time one Auster in the Navy. Eventually the great day arrived when they trundled this model aircraft carrier out to practise with this Auster.

'Are you coming up to watch it?' Stan Farquhar asked me.

'No, Stan, I don't think so, I've got some work to do here but don't let me stop you or any of the other boys who want to go and watch this thing, by all means.'

When the civilian driver of the articulated lorry arrived at the end of the runway, he was then told he was to drive down the runway and that an Auster would be landing on his back. At this point the driver decided that that was not what he had been employed to do.

'Not to worry,' said Commander Air, 'I have a heavy goods driver's licence, I will drive it.' Bill Orr Cubben, my ex-senior pilot who was a batsman, was stationed on the upper part to bat the Auster on and to jump over the side into a net, which had been arranged, once the Auster had landed. On the first attempt with the articulated truck roaring down the runway, the Auster made a reasonable approach but not good enough and was waved off. Freddy Stovin Bradford then drove the truck to the other end of the runway and proceeded down it to attempt the next landing. This time it was successful. Bill Orr Cubben duly cut the Auster and the pilot closed the throttle, the aeroplane settled gently onto the deck of the model aircraft carrier, everything was immaculate.

'He's on,' shouted Bill Orr Cubben to Freddy Stovin Bradford, who promptly put the brakes on so forcibly that the Auster went straight over the front and deposited itself nose down on top of the front of the model aircraft carrier or truck, depending on your point of view.

When Stan came back and told me all of this, I said, 'What a pity they didn't really ask me a bit more about this idea, instead of just seizing upon it and rushing off to do it themselves, because if they had, I'd have pointed out that in recognising this problem, the US Navy had had a ramp fitted across the front of this flight deck which lifted up after the aircraft was on, in order to stop it rolling over the front when the brakes were applied.' I never knew what happened to the A25 on that particular occasion.

Another episode comes to mind. Stan Leonard, who had been shot down in the Korean campaign and had a damaged leg, wished to get back into full flying practice and was sent to 759 to be checked out. I said, 'There's no problem with this, Stan, we'll check you out in a Vampire trainer, you don't need any rudder control for a Vampire trainer and so that'll be absolutely fine. It's got hand brakes so no problem at all.' Stan duly went off solo in the Vampire trainer. No problem. When this was signalled through to their Lordships the answer came back that in order to be returned to full flying pay he would have to go solo in a Fury!

Now a Fury is not the easiest aeroplane to land if you've only got one effective leg but Stan fixed to have a strop made on the good side so that he could not only push on the rudder with his left foot but also pull through the strop on it as well. Which was a fairly effective way of controlling the aircraft. But with a large powerful radial, the swing on take-off or landing is fairly dramatic and it was not going to be an easy task. Once again, of course, this task fell to me as the senior instructor because the Chief Flying Instructor was not a qualified Flying Instructor! I was irritated by this, as I had been by many of the attitudes that I found in the Fleet Air Arm at that time, as you would have gathered.

'Don't worry, Stan,' said I, 'we'll beat the bastards at their own game.' I got him into the Fury trainer and decided that the only way to be really safe in this was to pick days when the wind was reasonably down the runway and strong, and I taught Stan how to very gently get the tail up on take-off and use the power slowly in application so that we could get the thing airborne without too much swing or excessive use of rudder. That equally in landing we should wheel it on and very gently let it come to rest rather than try to do a three-point landing. Stan was a good natural pilot and had no problem at all in mastering the techniques but it was worrying for me to send him solo without somebody sitting in the back to take corrective action if things went wrong. So we waited until we had a day when we had a strong wind straight down the runway. Off went Stan and whilst the lot of us held our breath, he came in and landed perfectly in the way described. I was therefore very pleased to be able to signal to the Admiralty that he had now gone solo in a Sea Fury, what more did they want? Stan was restored to full flying pay. Not a bad way to treat a Korean veteran!

We had some excellent characters. Spiv Leahy had joined me to run the AWO's course (we were destined to serve together twice more); Block Whitehead, who later became a test pilot for Vickers, was with me as an instructor; Barney Baron and Boot Nethersole, the terrible twins of Culdrose; Alan Hensher came to do a Firebrand course, I seem to remember, as did Corky Corkhill. The beaches were grand, the weather occasionally was lovely and we used to carry out reconnaissance on a Saturday morning in the Hornet to see where the wind was blowing and which were the best beaches to go to in the afternoon and on Sunday. Our professionalism was beginning to improve but old habits die hard and it was to be some years before we got the Fleet Air Arm up to the kind of standard that I thought should be the norm.

One Saturday morning there occurred an episode at Culdrose that provided me with the kind of lesson that I might need in my next experience of becoming a seaman officer. When I arrived in, Stan Farquhar said to me, 'Have you heard about the *Wave*?' I said I hadn't. The *Wave* was a frigate which was then under the command of a well-known Fleet Air Arm character, R.N. Everett, RN, who had made his name in part by running the 'batting school', and had introduced what was called 'personality batting' – in other words, making the 'Batting Officer' (Landing Signal Officer) less wooden and more responsive to the actual needs of the aircraft as it came in to land. He was already RN, as his initials at both ends implied, and so he was sent to command a frigate called the *Wave*. As I understood it, both the First Lieutenant and the Officer of the Day on the night in question were also aviators, the Officer of the Day being under training. The ship was on a goodwill visit to St Ives, and anchored off St Ives in an onshore breeze while the Captain and most of the officers proceeded ashore to a reception, leaving the aviator under training as Officer of the Day in command of the ship. They had one anchor out and were at extended notice for steam, that is to say, certainly more than four hours or so. During the course of the evening the wind freshened and turned to a gale, and the ship's anchor began to drag. They could not raise steam in time to get the ship under way, and letting go the second anchor failed to stop the ship continuing to drag.

'What's happened?' I asked. 'Well,' said Stan, 'she's gone aground in St Ives.' I jumped into a Sea Hornet and got airborne to have a look. I flew over to St Ives and flew round the harbour but there was no sign of a ship to be seen. I therefore returned to Culdrose, landed and said to Stan, 'I've looked all round the harbour but I can't see her.' 'Oh, but it 's no good looking round the harbour,; said he. 'You've got to look up the High Street!' I leapt back into the Sea Hornet and roared off once again, and there, sure enough, was the *Wave* practically up the main street in St Ives, so far on to the 'putty' had she been blown. It must have been a frightful experience for all concerned, not least for the people of St Ives, and sterling efforts were made to get the vessel off the 'putty' at subsequent high tides with the aid of tugs. I believe that R.N. Everett, RN, then made a somewhat famous signal, which was an interesting pun on his batting experience, to the Commander-in-Chief saying, 'Wave Off.' ('Wave Off' is the expression used when the batsman, on deciding that the aircraft on the approach was not going to make a satisfactory landing or had backed up too closely and the other aircraft ahead had not cleared the deck, waves the aircraft off by waving the bats crosswise in front of his face.)

There was a lesson in this for me, and I used that story to illustrate the point on several future occasions. The security of a ship, or a factory, or a business, is like the security of a lock on your briefcase – three tumblers, and they all need to be in the same position for the door to fly open. There were three aviators in direct line of responsibility and, whilst I have the greatest admiration for my fellow aviators, one has to recognise that, whether it is in the exercise of seamanship or the exercise of judgement in running a company, to have all people of the same persuasion in a straight line of responsibility is not always sound policy. What you need is a cross-section of experience, so that you have checks and balances in your locker.

The saddest moment at Culdrose was when our second child, born in Truro Hospital by Caesarean section, only survived 24 hours. It was a trauma neither of us will ever forget.

So Culdrose came to an end. I was to be 'desymbolised' and turned into a proper seaman officer as well as a Naval Aviator, and Pepper and Brooke proceeded back to the United States for their first visit. The way I had arranged for them to go was by the cheapest means then available: Icelandic Airways to New York and then down to Jacksonville. It was a much longer ordeal in those days than it is today and their journey was certainly an interesting one, particularly when they landed at Reykjavik in a howling snowstorm. Pepper and Brooke were literally lifted across the tarmac by two ground crew while the aircraft refuelled and went on its way to the United States. I have engraved in my memory bank the look that Brooke gave me as she turned back as she was carried off by her mother to the waiting aircraft at Heathrow. In those days there were no gantries; you walked out to the aeroplane on to the tarmac and away.

The life of a Naval wife in those days was never easy – long separations, a shortage of money because pay was poor (though the aviation pay did make a difference as far as I was concerned), and wives were left, by and large, to bring up the family. It was an awesome responsibility and a particularly difficult one for someone like Pepper who had come from a tropical climate of affluence to a so-called temperate climate in the grip of Socialism. You count yourself a lucky man if you made the right choice, but I am not too sure that our wives counted themselves always lucky in *their* choice.

9

HMS Veryan Bay

The heady days of my first command and the acting half stripe were soon to be forgotten. I was to be brought down to earth – well back to sea, really – with a bang. I was to become 'desymbolised', which meant that aviators, those who had transferred to the straightlaced 'A' branch, with the removal of the 'A' from in our loop, suffered a further indignity. This was replaced in the Navy List by a strange symbol which indicated that we were not 'seamen'. That is to say, we had not qualified as proper naval officers even though we were listed in the seamen's section of the Navy List.

In order to get this removed and to qualify as a seaman officer proper as well as an aviator, one was to be sent to sea to obtain a sea watchkeeping certificate, and normally it was expected that one would get this inside six months. Once obtained, the symbol was removed and there was nothing between you and the post of First Sea Lord – well, that was the theory anyway. So it was that in 1953 I found myself busted back to being a Lieutenant and appointed to HMS *Veryan Bay*, a Bay Class frigate which was destined for the West Indies.

I was completely green about what might or might not be required of me, so I wrote to the First Lieutenant to enquire whether there was any particular requirements that he might have of me. I had not met Tom Baird, the First Lieutenant, at this time, but our meeting was to be one of the more fortunate experiences of my Naval career. It is said that in his farewell speech at Lossiemouth, Rear Admiral Dennis Cambell, the man credited with inventing the angle deck, who had become Flag Officer Flying Training, made the following remarks: 'A Naval career is like a game of snakes and ladders, sometimes you land on a space which is occupied by a ladder and up you go. Other times you may land on a space which is occupied by a snake and down you go, but in all my experience of snakes and ladders, I have never played a game where there was a snake in the last three boxes.' He was, I believe, referring to his crossing swords with his senior at that time, the Flag Officer Naval Air Command, and failing to go on in the Service but retiring as a Rear Admiral, which must be one of the saddest oversights in recent Naval history.

HMS *Veryan Bay*

Nevertheless, I believe there is truth in this and I was to be fortunate in my Naval career in coming across more ladders than snakes, otherwise how could I possibly have arrived in the last three boxes? One such ladder was Tom Baird, but at the time I did not realise that he was gifted with a very similar sense of humour to my own which, of course, at times can be dangerous if you are serving together. When he asked me, therefore, to bring my golf clubs with me I was genuinely dumbfounded. I didn't play golf then, I don't play golf now, and I didn't possess a set of golf clubs, neither do I still. Little did I know that Tom was trying to obtain a set of golf clubs for the use of the Wardroom and thought that by inviting this wealthy aviator – remember we were getting flying pay and were considered therefore to be relatively wealth – that this was as good an opportunity as any!

I proceeded to Devonport to join my new ship, indeed my first frigate. When I arrived at Plymouth station it was dark and it was raining, so I hailed a taxi which deposited me at the dockyard alongside HMS *Veryan Bay*. I repaired on board, met the Officer of the Day, who got the quartermaster to help with my gear, and was taken to my quarters which were down below, one deck, where I shared a cabin with Lieutenant 'Nobby' Hall whom I was yet to meet.

It seemed that all the officers and most of the crew were ashore and I, having had supper and it being too late to be given anything to eat anyway, sat alone in the Wardroom and proceeded to read *The Times* which, of course, you will recall, my father had instructed me to read many years before. I had never got out of the habit. Imagine my surprise when the Officer of the Day came up behind me after some fifteen minutes or so and said, 'Oh Ray, I believe there is something you should know about.' I folded the paper down onto my knees and looked up at him and said, 'Yes, what?'

'Well,' said he, 'we have a Stoker on board who is under stoppage of leave and he has decided that he is going to go ashore. He has armed himself with a marlinspike and is barricaded down on the Stokers' Messdeck where he is causing a disturbance and is saying that he is going to proceed ashore and intends to beat up anybody who tries to stop him.' I looked up at him again and enquired, 'Well, why are you telling me?'

'Because,' said he, 'you are the senior Officer on board!' Indeed I was by some few days, being senior to the Officer of the Day concerned, but I must say I was stunned and, at the same time, slightly irritated by this delivery.

'Well,' I said, picking up my newspaper again, 'when the matter gets out of hand and you can no longer control it, be kind enough to let me know,' and I turned my attention back to the newspaper.

I didn't have long to wait however, before he was back again and said, 'The situation is now out of control.'

I said 'Right' folding the paper and dusting my hands, 'where is this chap and what is the situation?'

'Well, he is down in the Stokers' Messdeck and he won't let anybody come down, he won't let anybody come up and we don't know quite what to do.' I turned to the Duty Petty Officer, a young TAS man as I recall, and said, 'Turn out the whole of the Ship's Company that's on board.' By now it was something like 10 o'clock and lots of chaps were beginning to get ready to turn in for bed.

'All of them?' said the Duty Petty Officer.

'Yes,' I said 'every man jack of them on the Quarterdeck.'

'It's raining, Sir' he said.

'Yes,' I said, 'I am aware of that. In intend to make this Stoker the most popular chap in the ship.' We had no broadcast in that ship, messages had to be relayed by the Bosun's Mate who went round with a bosun's pipe and piped into every nook and cranny with the instruction or whatever the order was to be.

160

'Clear lower deck, hands fall in on the Quarterdeck. Clear lower deck.' The message echoed round the small ship which was of course entirely strange to me and I braced myself for the events which were to take place.

'Is the Coxswain on board?' I asked. The Coxswain is the man who takes the helm, the senior helmsman in the ship, but is also in charge of discipline.

'Yes, Sir.'

'Then I want to see him,' I said.

The Coxswain duly appeared.

'Now Coxswain,' I said, 'when we've cleared the lower deck and this chap hasn't responded and not come up on deck, you and I will go down into the Messdeck and apprehend him.' He looked at me with some surprise, 'But, Sir,' he said, 'he's got a marlinspike and he'll break the legs of anybody who comes down the ladder.'

'Well,' said I, 'you will be going first, Coxswain, so you will be able to let me know how you get on.' There was a look of pained surprise and horror on his face as he said, 'But, Sir, this is madness.'

'All right,' I said, 'Coxswain, I'll go down first.' He breathed an obvious sigh of relief. 'Since he has never met me' I said, 'and since I will announce to him that I have just arrived on board and don't know what this is all about, I think it is highly unlikely that he is going to break my legs.' As I prepared for this the Duty Petty Officer returned to say that the Engineer Officer, one 'Boots' Mocatta had returned onboard and of course was this particular Rating's Divisional Officer. I told the Coxswain, therefore, and the Petty Officer, that I would go and inform the Engineer Officer of what I intended to do and what had transpired.

The Engineer's office was at the end of a narrow corridor and having found it, as I walked down, I observed two men engaged in conversation, one on either side of the passageway just outside the Engineer's office. The one on the left looked to me as if he might be the Engineer Officer and the one on the right was a largish Rating. Walking up and standing between them I addressed the man I presumed to be the Engineer Officer as follows, 'Good Evening, my name is Ray Lygo and I am the senior officer on board at the moment and we have a problem with one of your men; I don't know what's wrong with him but I am just about to go down and apprehend him.' The Engineer Officer didn't reply but merely stared fixedly at the Rating opposite him, so much so that I transferred my attention from the Engineer Officer to the large Rating who was now some six or eight inches from me, to observe that not only was he large and considerably taller than I but he was holding a marlinspike just over my starboard ear.

There are moments in time when a glib tongue is better than anything else you can posses. 'Oh, you must be the laddie concerned,' I said turning to him, 'I understand you've got a problem, laddie. I've just arrived on board, don't know what it is all about but perhaps you would like to tell me.' He lowered the marlinspike and looked at me curiously. 'Come now' I said, 'I know absolutely nothing about you or what is your problem, so why don't we go and talk it over,' and turning on my heel I walked away down the passageway to be followed meekly by a large stoker who had lowered his marlinspike. I took him aft, down to the tiller flat and said to him, 'This is a place where we can talk quietly.' I already knew, of course, that this was where difficult Ratings were incarcerated since the ship had no cells or space in which to confine somebody who was violent or difficult and it was normal to put them in the tiller flat.

Down the ladder we went and I sat on a coil of rope and he likewise, while he told me his story. It was the usual one of misunderstanding and the fact that he had not been treated properly, or he thought he hadn't, that he hadn't been drunk when he was supposed to have been drunk, and there was no reason why he should be under stoppage of leave, and he was intent on going ashore, for what purpose I can't remember. 'But that would be breaking ship' I said 'and a serious offence, and I don't think you should compound the felony. What I think you should do is wait here and think about this while I go up and talk to your Divisional Officer and find out more about it, because you will understand quite correctly, of course, that I know nothing whatever of the case or the circumstances. I will, however, ensure that a proper enquiry is carried out.'

I left him and went up the ladder and then gave an order which I remember with sadness to this day, I said simply 'Slip the hatch' and the hatch crashed down on top of the companionway incarcerating the Stoker in the tiller flat. I say, with sadness because I had conned him into doing what I wanted him to do, but I suppose it was best for everybody that I had done that or we might have had a tremendous fight, violence or a striking, or something really serious on board. However, I didn't feel well about it and I still don't; nevertheless on reflection it was probably the best thing that I could do in the circumstances. I duly reported to the Officer of the Day and told him that he was now back in command unless he needed further assistance and told the Engineer Officer that his Stoker was down in the tiller flat and now banging furiously on the hatch and that perhaps he should go and talk to him. Certainly as far as I was concerned the matter was, for the time being, closed.

I then proceeded to unpack until several of my fellow officers returned on board. They included my cabin mate, 'Nobby' Hall, a benign-looking officer, pleasant, generally smiling except when he had the occasional contrived frown to make him look stern, a thoroughly nice man of about my own age, and as I remember, a short-service officer, as opposed to a permanent guy like myself. Next to appear, coming down the companionway at a rate of knots, was the First Lieutenant who had obviously had a good run ashore. He introduced himself and proceeded to laugh. Tom laughed at most things. He laughed his way through the Navy, I believe, and retired as a Vice-Admiral with the customary knighthood: a good friend of mine then and to this day. I remember, because I am somewhat sober of habit and rather straightlaced in my approach to Naval matters, being a little surprised by his general demeanour. He was, however, one of the finest seamen I met in the Navy and I was lucky to have come across him at such a moment in my career, particularly since we both got on so well together. His tolerance of some of my misdemeanours, and I perhaps would say mine of his, were the stuff of which lasting friendships are made.

Next morning it was time to meet the Captain, Wyndham Hare. Captain Hare was a four-stripe Captain because we were the leader of, I think it was, the Eighth Frigate Flotilla or Squadron, and he, of course had already been nicknamed many years before at Dartmouth, 'Bunny'. As if his name wasn't justification enough for this title, he had a habit of 'nibbling'. Whether this was in order to live up to his nickname or whether it preceded it I do not know; however it was a very distinctive feature of his manner. A very nice man, a very quiet man, almost I would say a recluse, he kept himself to himself, spent most of his time in his cabin reading, and occasionally appeared to do whatever was necessary and then would disappear again.

Next I was to be introduced to my boys' division; in those days we took boys in at the age of 14 and they went to sea as boys until I think they were 17½ when they became eligible to become Ordinary Seaman and were rated up accordingly. Prior to that, they were messed separately in a Boys' Messdeck and had special regulations laid down regarding their conduct. Leave, for example, was very restricted, they weren't allowed to go off wandering around late at night. The Navy was doing its best to both educate them and secure them in their indoctrination period in the Navy. Remember, it was quite common for youngsters then to sign-on for very long periods of time – seven, nine, twelve, twenty-two year engagements were the norm and once signed could not be broken. They could, of course, be changed by being 'bought out', but buying yourself out was only available after a certain period of time, or by discharge through unfitness of one sort or another, or in extreme cases, unfortunately only too common, by desertion, recapture, Colchester Prison and then discharge from the Navy with the stigma of being dismissed from the Service, having served in jail to boot.

My boys ranged in age from 15 to 17½ and of course the size of my division would reduce as the commission proceeded and boys reached the age of 17½ and were transferred to the Seamens' or Engineers', or whatever Division. Meantime I started off with some 14 boys in my division, a motley collection but it introduced me to a section of society I hadn't come in contact with before. Naval airmen, by and large, were brighter and better educated because they required higher educational qualifications to become Naval airmen whereas the Seamen branch was not quite so choosy. Many of the lads I had were from Ireland, south and north, and I also had a sprinkling of Geordies, a mixture I hadn't come across before. My other job was to be the Gunnery Officer!

Things moved apace in the *Veryan Bay* and we were due to go to sea and proceed direct to the West Indies where we were to come under the command of the Commander-in-Chief West Indies, who had his flag in Bermuda. It was a busy and fairly confusing time for me as I swotted up the *Seamanship Manual* and tried to understand many of the things that went on around me.

The Stoker who had misbehaved the night I arrived, was now of course, sober and a fairly contrite character but was to go through the full gambit of Naval justice in order to undergo his due punishment. I, of course, was a prime witness along with the Officer of the Day as to what happened, and had to give evidence at the First Lieutenant's Table and then at the Captain's Table. To my astonishment the Captain 'weighed him off' with 'cells', a punishment which only a four-stripe Captain could award and which could be awarded up to a maximum of 30 days. These were normally only awarded for very serious offences, although of course his offence had been serious enough, even though the evidence in mitigation was the usual one of stress and drink and all the other things.

I was curious to know how this was to be done; presumably we would leave him behind when we sailed so that he could serve his punishment in the detention quarters at Plymouth. However, if one thought about it this was almost an invitation to misdemeanour. How better to avoid going 'foreign'. Not so. The First Lieutenant had discovered a remote regulation in the QR&AI's which permitted you, in a ship which did not have proper cells, to rig a canvas 'cell' in a suitable part of the ship and the man could spend his time in there, supping on bread and water and whatever other kind of slops could be arranged for him, picking oakum, and being exercised under guard twice a day. Such a construction was now erected on P1 Gun Deck, which was up fairly high where the Bofors gun was situated just behind and below the Bridge, and my poor first acquaintance on board as a sailor, was incarcerated in this. I could hardly believe it. Coming as I had from the Fleet Air Arm and its very up-to-date and generous and friendly attitude between Officers and Ratings and the great trust between them, I found this an extraordinary event. Nevertheless, there it was and I was part of this scene.

The ship was in a disgusting state: there were rust flakes all over the upper deck, she hadn't been painted but merely duffed up by the dockyard, in engineering terms, to make sure that she was operationally fit. As a result she had come out looking decidedly rusty and a great deal of work needed to be done to get her looking shipshape. Number One had a very simple recipe for this. He said we should do nothing to improve the appearance of the ship until she arrived on station in the West Indies and after the Commander-in-Chief had seen the state in which the ship had left the Dockyard. He would then be in a good position to give the Admiral Superintendent the most regal blast for allowing a ship to come out of his custody in such a state. So we sailed off across the Atlantic towards Bermuda in the state in which we had found her, duly ammunitioned, fuelled and victualled, and ready (so-called) for action.

10

Arrival in Bermuda

The passage across the Atlantic in *Veryan Bay* was uneventful. I was immediately placed under the tutelage of the Navigating Officer for watchkeeping duties and, very quickly, once we were clear of harbour and into the ocean, was allowed to keep my own first full watch. This was really because there were only four qualified watchkeepers on board: the First Lieutenant, the Navigating Officer, Nobby Hall, and the Gunner, and two Midshipmen under training, one an engineer and the other a seaman. When we arrived off Bermuda, the Navigating Officer, as was and is the custom, on first detecting land or when within a couple of hours of approaching port, assumed the watch and took the ship in.

The first entry into Bermuda, or I guess any entry into Bermuda, is always fascinating because you pass so close along the shoreline and then into the Sound, following the channel as it takes you first toward Hamilton and then away round to the crescent-shaped end of the island to where we were going, Ireland Island where the Naval Dockyards were situated. The houses are a distinguishing feature of Bermuda and are unique for their white roofs, designed so I am told to catch the rainwater in the most efficient manner and, of course, I suppose to keep the houses cool. As a result they have a very attractive appearance and the whole place looks a bit like some large landscaped park. At the time we arrived however, the effect had been marred by a disease that had swept through the cypress trees and killed every one of them and, although great efforts were already being made to replant with a different variety, the stumps of the old dead cypress were like blackened fingers clawing into the blue skies, marring an otherwise perfectly idyllic scene.

My reverie observing what was going on from the back of the Bridge was rudely awakened when the First Lieutenant said, 'Right Lygo, go down and prepare to get the seaboat away because we are berthing starboard side to and I want the seaboat in the water for use while we are alongside.' This news was received by me with some consternation since I had never lowered any boat, seaboat or otherwise, and so I rushed to my cabin to pull out my copy of the Seamanship Manual and quickly ran through the terminology and routine for turning out and lowering the seaboat. The Naval jargon which must be used is almost like another language and as I am not particularly good at languages and really couldn't see much point in this strange way of giving fairly simple orders which could otherwise be well accommodated in standard English, it was an unbelievable burden for me. Fortunately when I got to the seaboat the Acting Petty Officer of the boys' division was also there and so with majesty I said, 'Right, Petty Officer, proceed to make ready the boat, turn it out and prepare for lowering away,' which he duly did, relieving me of the necessity of remembering all those strange nautical phrases! When the ship finally stopped we got the boat into the water and away and my duty therefore was done, apart from cleaning up the mess of the davits trailing in the water. It was a shattering experience for me nevertheless and a narrow escape and I resolved to apply myself more vigorously to the Seamanship Manual so that I should not be caught out again.

The Naval Base at Ireland Island was run down by this time and had ceased to be in active use. It was one of those outposts of Empire which had become a familiar feature of one's life in the Navy at that time. The buildings all looked the same, the rope yard, the head office, the victualling yard, the Portland stone glistening white – all were the same design whether you saw them in Singapore or Hong Kong or Gibraltar, or, indeed, Ireland Island – all the same pattern, all designed to fulfil the same role. It was sad though to see it now lying largely derelict.

At this time, as I have already said, there was a Commander-in-Chief West Indies, who had his house on the island, a very nice one with his own private beach and with a headquarters somewhere, I presume, in Hamilton; I don't think they were in Ireland Island. There was also a Resident Naval Officer who had a nice house in Ireland Island itself. The Commander-in-Chief's fleet consisted, as I recall, of two cruisers – one which was always away being maintained back in the UK, and the other one on station or cruising around, a large floating gin palace really – and a Squadron of frigates, mostly Bay Class or Bird Class which were also scattered throughout the islands carrying out their various duties of showing the flag and, I suppose, that we were still in charge.

The ship was to be inspected by the Commander-in-Chief, and as a preamble to this his staff came aboard on arrival to inspect the various parts of the ship for which they had functional responsibility. It fell to my lot as Gunnery Officer to be inspected by the Fleet Gunnery Officer. He came on board, immaculately turned out in his whites, into a ship that was hardly in a fit state for anybody to wear whites, and I had carefully informed the Gunner and also the Chief G.I. and the Chief Ordnance Petty Officer that they should stand close behind me during this inspection so that if I was asked any questions to which I didn't know the answer (which would have been practically 99 per cent of any questions he was likely to ask) they could whisper or interpose and answer for me.

I remember getting to the four-inch turret for'ard and having gone round the front, he turned to me and said, 'Where are your tampions?' Dismissing instantly the thought that these were sanitary devices, and in any case why mine, I had absolutely no idea what tampions were or their likely location, and casting my eyes nervously around the turret, I wondered what they might be and where they ought to be and also looked desperately around for advice coming along behind me, but they were trailing and didn't hear this. You have to be quick on these occasions and calling to the Chief GI, I said, 'Where are the tampions?' and he pointed out to me that they had been removed to be painted (they are in fact the plates that go into the muzzle of the gun to make them look rather tidy, and of course to keep out the sea water). Next we moved up to P1 Gun deck where we had a single Bofors gun mounted and as the Fleet Gunnery Officer stood there looking at the gun, I noticed that suddenly his white uniform was being peppered in bits of black. On looking round I saw that some of us were suffering too. I glanced up and there high above us was a stoker painting the funnel black, happily or deliberately oblivious to the fact that specks of paint were flying in all directions. I looked aghast as the Staff Gunnery Officer became more like a pepper pot, and hastily said, 'Sir, Sir, I'm sorry, you'll have to move away from here,' ineffectually dabbing at him with my handkerchief, only to make the spots of paint worse. He left the ship soon after, I don't think ever to return again. Tom had been wise in his decision to do nothing to the state of the ship but certainly the Staff Gunnery Officer must have had no doubt about his state.

It soon became clear that the celebration of the Queen's coronation, which was to be carried out throughout the West Indies on every British island, was going to depend to a large extent on the availability of ships to be present on the occasion of the celebration in order to add a little colour to the Lord Mayor's Show. To brighten up the affair even more, Their Lordships had decided that they would take the opportunity to use up out-of-date pyrotechnics that could be drawn from Naval Armament and which could be discharged as part of a firework display. There is not much that you can do with a bunch of red, white or green port flares except stand around and wave them, but there were also two-inch distress rockets that could be used quite effectively to brighten up the sky, though we thought it would be better if these could be fired in batteries. We therefore concocted, with the aid of the electrical department, a rack installing six of these which we wired up to electrical impulses enabling six rockets to be fired in one go. I decided that the thing to do was to get hold of some old, heavy, wire tennis-court netting, to form this into large screens and mount the port fires by poking them through the holes in the wire netting to form some traditional patterns – R Anchor N, and E Crown R. This was thought to be a jolly good idea and it was decided that we would be able to use these for our first display in Kingston, Jamaica.

The other chore which fell to my lot as Gunnery Officer was, to my surprise, to be in charge of the guard. To make matters worse it seemed that in every place we went, we would have to mount a Royal Guard, if the Governor was going to appear, which of course he almost certainly would, and that this Royal Guard which was required to be 120-strong took up practically the entire Ship's Company apart from the duty part! You can therefore understand that there was a certain amount of drilling necessary to get all the various miscellany of the Ship's Company to look something like a Royal Guard. To make matter worse, although in my case it wouldn't have mattered, the Gunnery branch had decided that they would change the way in which officers gave a salute on the march and I had to learn this new proce-dure, which in my case, because I have a fairly large nose, put me in severe danger of losing it. The drill required you to go from the position of holding the sword upright with the right forearm stretched straight ahead, up into a flourish which drew the sword across your face and down to the right as you marched past, as your eyes went to the right at the correct moment that you gave the order to the Guard. A slight mishap with the sword would, in fact, have caused some danger to anybody whose nose was big enough to bear witness to the event, and mine certainly was. Nevertheless behind the sheds in the old dockyard, under the tutelage of the Chief G.I., I was trained in this strange Naval art of saluting with a sword whilst marching past.

It was, and I suppose still is, a fond hope of Naval officers that they will effect a 'strangulation' in any port in which they might call. A 'strangulation' translated is to find some local who will take you out to dinner or entertain you, or introduce you to his gorgeous daughter and enable you to pass away your spare time in an entirely satisfactory and cost-free manner. We were, of course, in those days pretty poor and the married amongst us were sending money home to maintain wives or whatever and so 'strangulations' were desirable and acquiring them became a kind of art form.

Before we had left Plymouth we had been asked to take a new yacht out for the Trimminghams. Now you may not know about the Trimminghams but if you knew Bermuda, you would know about the Trimminghams; there were three rich and powerful families in Bermuda at that time, of which the Trimminghams were one. So we had carried this new yacht secured to the side of the ship, as there was no other place to put it, all the way across the Atlantic. After arrival in Bermuda one of the Trimmingham brood came on board to collect the yacht and we fondly expected that as a result of this there would be some 'strangulation'. Not a bit of it. However, what we were asked was whether we would like to compete in the Bermuda Cup, which was apparently what this yacht was destined to do, and if we wanted to use their old boat we would be welcome to make an entry. Sensing that this was a good way to a 'strangulation' we accepted and 'Boots' Mocatta the Engineer who, on most occasions, could hardly see through his glasses for the smear of lubricating oil but who, it was alleged, was a good sailor, and I, who was alleged to have no such ability, were detailed off to enter this particular race.

I well remember that afternoon. We went to the Royal Bermuda Yacht Club with its lovely lawns reaching down almost into the bay, and with its ladies sitting on them under large colourful umbrellas, watching their loved ones, and not-so-loved ones, depart for this famous race, in which a large Canadian contingent was taking part. Having located the boat we tried to get it sorted out, which eventually we did, but we were then running very late. We slipped and in full view of the assembled company, shot like a bow from an arrow from the Bermuda Yatch Club's steps and managed to go straight into a buoy with a resounding crash which brought the boat up all standing. Having sorted this mess out we finally found our way to the starting line only to discover that they had all gone! So we had a pleasant enough swan around the harbour and in due course came back to the Yacht Club with some transparent excuse which wasn't too transparent because it was actually true, that (a) we had been late starting with a boat which we did not understand, and (b) we didn't know where the starting line was. However, the main object of the exercise had been achieved, in that because we had entered the race we were invited to attend the reception which followed it!

So it was that both Boots, myself, the First Lieutenant and, I believe, one other, got ourselves invited to a reception which was given by some very charming lady in Bermuda, in a lovely house in a lovely setting, where the ability to sail was not apparently the main requirement, rather the ability to stay sober, or reasonably sober, while drinking large quantities of liquor. Here we were better qualified. Tom Baird, the First Lieutenant had several party tricks which he was trying to wean himself off because he had just become engaged and his fiancée, Angela, did not exactly approve of some of his more outlandish wardroom party tricks. The most impressive, however, was his ability to eat glass and as the evening progressed and got more boisterous and the men, as is the habit on these occasions, congregated at one end of the rather sumptuous living room with the ladies at the other, Tom was invited to perform this trick. Having been pressed upon enough times, he took a glass and proceeded with great relish to eat it. This was regarded with astonishment by all the present company and a great round of cheers went up when he had finished. At this point the hostess came over and politely enquired whether he intended to go on eating glasses. Tom looked at her in some surprise, but she continued, 'Because the one you have eaten is part of a collection of six Coronation celebration glasses and I would not wish any more of those to be eaten, but you may eat those over there if you wish.' This remark was sufficient to humble even the most riotous of us and soon after that we took our departure. It was to be, however, our first, last and only 'strangulation' worth having in Bermuda.

We set sail on the first leg of our cruise, having had the Commander-in-Chief's inspection in which he noted the disgraceful state of the ship and signalled the Admiral Superintendent Devonport, the Commander-in-Chief Home Fleet and everybody concerned about his dissatisfaction. Our route was to take us first to Kingston, where we would take part in the Coronation celebrations, then to Antigua, where we were to do the same, thence to Grenada where we were to do the same, then Pernambuco (now known as Recife) in Brazil, Montevideo in Uruguay and then, because we were not talking to the Argentinians, skirting the Argentine coast to Port Stanley in the Falkland Islands where we were to be guard ship for a period of three months.

I remember well arriving in Kingston, Jamaica, because we passed the spot where *Indomitable* had taken the ground, having completed a work up prior to a deployment to the East Indies via the Cape where she might have joined the *Repulse* and *Prince of Wales*. As it was, she had to go back up to Norfolk to be repaired. Who knows what otherwise might have happened?

Kingston, Jamaica, was fun; it was teeming with life. The jetty on which we were berthed was full of people as we arrived, selling all kinds of things and jostling for position one with another; a lively, colourful and entertaining scene. The first act was for the Captain to go ashore and call on the General Commanding the Local District, and with his sword and medals duly attached, he disappeared into the crowd. I was Officer of the Day and saw him go. He returned after about an hour and the routine then was that the General Commanding the Local District was to come on board, return his call and have lunch with our Captain at the same time.

In the fullness of time, therefore, as we waited for the appearance of the Brigadier, the teeming crowd of locals jostling each other on the jetty, the Captain somewhat nervous, nibbling to boot, a gentleman appeared up the gangway in civilian clothes.

'Take this fellow off somewhere,' said the Captain to me, 'and find out what he wants.' The chap looked at him somewhat surprised and said, 'Captain Hare?'

'Yes, yes,' replied our Captain sharply. 'Please stand aside, I'm waiting for the Brigadier.' Whereupon the individual drew himself up to his full height and said, 'But I am the Brigadier,' and indeed he was! I was left wondering why it was that our Captain did not recognise someone he had called on only a couple of hours before, but I have now reached the age when it could probably happen to me at a moment's notice!

After lunch, the Captain briefed us to say that there was to be a Tattoo on the parade ground above Kingston, and that the local band would be present. The Army were putting on a show as well as the local Police, the Boy Scouts and everybody else, and it was unfortunate that we could do nothing. I had already been required to lay a wreath and to give a salute with my guard in Spanish Town where we had paraded through the narrow streets of the old town with some dignity and saluted somebody – the Governor, I presume. Taxed, however with the fact that the Royal Navy was not going to be seen to have much of a part in this forthcoming Tattoo, I came up with the bright idea (with the aid of the Gunner) that we should illuminate the parade ground with star shell. The Captain thought this would be a brilliant idea and get the show off with a complete bang. However, it was decided that to fire four-inch shells into the middle of Kingston at night might be a little bit over the top, so it should be done with two-inch rocket flares which would have the same effect. These were flares designed for night engagements at sea, but would have the requisite range to actually get over the parade ground. In order to get ourselves into a position to do this and also to give the firework display, it was decided that the ship should be moved into the middle of the harbour and there secured at the correct angle so that we could illuminate the parade ground when the moment came and also give our firework display.

The great night arrived, the Ship's Company for the most part, apart from the Duty Watch, moved ashore to take part and watch the ceremony ashore, and the gunners and I were left on board in charge of the ship. The first act was to wait for eight o'clock, when the Tattoo was due to start, and precisely at that moment hand-train the four-inch turret onto the bearing of the parade ground which was marked on the chart, then get the elevation right for the range, and at the precise moment fire the rockets. I gave the order, 'Engage with rockets – Fire'. Oomph, off went the four rockets zooming into the middle of Kingston, and it wasn't until this moment that I suddenly thought, what happens if they don't all illuminate and if one drops into the middle of the crowd? To my relief, however, boom, boom, boom, boom – four burst of bright floodlight arrived precisely on time and, we assumed, in the right place. That completed, we loaded up our other distress rockets and I got my large steel netting firework displays rigged on the port side facing into Kingston, and proceeded to light the first of the port fires. I had overlooked one fact. You could only light the port fires from the front, and as you started at the top to light them to illuminate our displays, RN and the Anchor and then subsequently ER and the Crown, as the flares illuminated, they proceeded to discharge large volumes of hot sulphur which spewed forth and fell down on to the deck and on to those of us trying to light the lower ones. Apart from the danger of setting fire to the entire ship, it was a fairly hazardous operation to be standing there with the top ones spewing hot sulphur all over you!

It was an exciting experience but not one, I am glad to say, to be repeated. However, we were told when the Captain returned on board with the First Lieutenant that the whole thing had gone extremely well, that the Royal Navy was seen to be in business, that we had illuminated the parade ground at the precise moment the band struck up and marched on, and the whole thing was seen to be an absolute and outstanding success. The fact that I had nearly set the ship on fire we managed to avoid mentioning, and had scrubbed away the remains of the debris that littered the deck.

It was weeks later, after we had arrived in the Falkland Islands, when the mail, which came down in the *Fitzroy* from Montevideo once a month, arrived on board, that we learned of what had happened as a result of our display in Jamaica. The Captain received a letter from the General commanding local forces in which he said how much they had enjoyed having the ship and how much they had enjoyed the illumination of the parade ground that had preceded the Tattoo. He went on, 'It was unfortunate that one of your rockets had not finished burning when it struck a house which was subsequently burned to the ground.

Fortunately, it belonged to one of the locals who worked for the Army and we were able to hush the whole thing up!' A sad ending to an otherwise glorious occasion. One's mind boggles at the thought of what might have been the reaction should such an event occur today.

After Jamaica we then sailed down towards Antigua and there we lay off the main port whilst a working party was sent round to Nelson's Harbour. Once again we were to be used as the centre-piece for the celebration of the Coronation of Queen Elizabeth II. By this time we were getting pretty used to the routine and pretty much exhausted by the experience. Island hopping with nothing but cocktail parties and Royal guards was not the easiest way to see the world. Which reminds me, if you do want to see the world and you intend to do so by joining the Navy then let me explain that the bits of the world that you will see leave a somewhat kaleidoscopic view of the world as you look back on it.

For a start, one has duty on board for part of the time of a visit. Let's assume it is a three-day visit, which is fairly normal. On the first day there is a reception on board and most of the officers are certainly required for that, and the ship's company are busy getting the ship properly secured for the visit and made ready for Open Day, which almost certainly will take place and which will require their Messdecks to be clean and tidy; the galley and eating arrangements to be on display; the guns and equipment to be polished and ready for visitors.

On the second day there will probably be return calls for the Captain to make and an official reception ashore which will take up part of the time for the officers, banyans organised and general hospitality for the Ship's Company from those people who enjoy entertaining the Royal Navy. The last day is the day when we are thinking about preparations for getting away the next day and for our next visit and our next experience. If you throw in on top of this the necessity for a Royal guard which was 120 men (which out of a frigate company of 142 was the greater part of the entire Ship's Company) and that they all had to get their uniforms up to the highest standard and their guard drill to the highest standard possible, then of course the amount of time available for high jinks is extremely limited. Therefore the bits of the world that you are likely to see are those bits very adjacent to where the ship is berthed. Most of us don't get much farther than the first bar/restaurant/cafe where we have a quiet drink and sit down and enjoy the local ambience, which is extremely local to the port and to the ship itself. So much for the world!

The lunchtime session we had on the first day in Antigua followed a fairly similar pattern and we were expected of course to be ready for the ceremony the following day. One of the guests on board was one of the administrators in the government of the island and he very kindly offered to take some of us on a tour of the island after lunch.

Anything one does after lunch is fraught with difficulty if it is in the tropics and you have had a fairly liquid lunch, and the one in question was no exception. The invitees were four of us who managed to squeeze into a Hillman Minx, the First Lieutenant in front next to our host, me sitting in the middle at the back – I don't know why – between Nobby Hall and Bertie Howson.

We set off at about 2.30, I suppose, for this tour and the Administrator never stopped telling us about various interesting (to him) things as we travelled around the island. It wasn't long, however, before the effects of lunch and the heat and the droning voice of the well-intentioned Administrator had all my companions falling asleep and what was embarrassing for me was, that in the back seat I had both their heads falling one on either shoulder. Number One, who was in the front seat, was also having trouble keeping his head firmly attached to his shoulders and when his head lolled to one side it of course fell onto the shoulder of our host who was giving us some long explanation about how the water system was installed in that part of the island. I therefore felt it incumbent upon me to keep up the conversation by responding to the remarks being made by our host. In order to try to prevent us looking like a bunch of dodos, which of course we were. I had to keep addressing remarks to Number One: 'Don't you think so, Tom? Don't you think so, Number One?' to kind of bring him around so that he might say, '...well, yes ... I see,' and then of course he would fall back to sleep again, his head rolling over onto our host's shoulder! In this fashion we jogged around the island.

The first place of any importance we visited was Nelson's Harbour – which in those days was totally undeveloped and more or less as Nelson had left it – or it had been left in Nelson's time. The large capstans which had been used for heaving ships up and careening were still there, some spars still in place. The kedge anchors were still in place, rusted and enormous for warping the ships through that fairly narrow entrance and the rope yard and the various pools for spars, etc. were all more or less as they had been left.

A society had been started by the Governor called the Friends of Nelson's Harbour (which I believe still exists) to restore it and bring it up to the standard which has now been achieved. At this time, however, there was very little that wasn't original and every frigate that visited was expected to send a party of sailors ashore to help tart the place up. I experienced this on subsequent visits but this was the

very first time and there was very little to see except that which had
been left to decay for more than a century. It was a romantic place
and as we peeled out of this Hillman Minx, like sardines coming out
of a tin, we entered the only piece of the dockyard which was still
reasonably intact, which was the rope shed. There, in the middle of
this vast shed at a very small table, sat the Governor and members of
the 'Friends of Nelson's Harbour' who were having a meeting. The
Administrator said, 'Please excuse us, Sir,' and the Governor nodded
his agreement as we entered the room to look at what was there.

What was there was absolutely nothing, except the Governor and
the Friends of Nelson's Harbour sitting at a small table in the middle!
There was, however, one other item I remember – it was some kind of
sideboard of the period and on it was a large oil lamp with a large
tulip glass to it. One of us, I can't remember who, with a striking
gesture said,'This is a very fine,' and as he made the striking gesture he
knocked the only valuable piece of authentic glass on site off the top
of the lamp and passed it like a rugger ball in a line-out down the line
of us, being caught and passed with some considerable lack of
dexterity and total confusion until it finished in my hands at the end
of the row. I then, with trembling hands, placed it back upon the oil
lamp from which it had been dislodged.

The noise was indescribable inside this vast echoing chamber. The
whole of the assembled company of 'Friends of Nelson's Harbour'
stopped, transfixed at the sight of their only antique being used as a
rugger ball by these rather inebriated Naval officers who, of course,
were then overcome with giggles and had to beat a somewhat hasty
retreat out of the door. There is nothing worse than a bunch of
giggling idiots, because unless you are part of the syndrome that has
caused the giggles, it is not amusing, unless of course you happen to
be in a particularly light frame of mind and can inhale some of the
laughing gas that is being given off by the mob. This was not the case
and as we tumbled outside convulsed, and rolled about trying to stifle
our laughter, it was clear that the Administrator was not a party to
the joke.

We got back into the car and continued our trip around the island,
looking at various water taps, the hospital and various things that the
British Colonial Administration had done and improved within the
island; the schools, the road system, the telegraph and all those
typically British colonial introductions. Eventually the tour was over
and by this time we were beginning to sober up a bit – it was 4.00 or
4.30 – and we were invited to tea in the Administrator's garden. It was
a walled garden to an old stone cottage, as I recall, very charming and
tropical, and as we sat in the garden around the table a large-ish black

lady came out with scones and tea and all those things which the English are supposed to like at teatime and generally do, and proceeded to serve us.

The Administrator, I am bound to say, was still droning on about the island and the various things that had been done and it was obviously all his life's work. It turned out that he was a bachelor and really had spent his life devoting himself to the improvement of those people whom he found in his care. As we helped ourselves to the first scones and took our first sips of tea, he somewhat languidly rolled onto one cheek of his buttocks and without losing the pace of his remarks, which as I have said before were fairly monotonous and boring, let out the most enormous fart. We were stunned. We stopped with the scones close to our lips and exchanged glances and tried to believe that it hadn't happened. It certainly wasn't one of us. It clearly was our host but he had not stopped or been interrupted by this process of exhalation of wind and indeed then proceeded to roll onto the other cheek and let out another enormous fart. And again not a word was spoken and now, of course, the giggles were about to return and we were choking on the scones and tea and trying to appear to pay attention as our host literally rolled from one cheek to the other emitting the most thunderous farts. Not a word was said. Eventually tea was over, the farts had subsided, we were driven back by this kind gentleman to our ship where we made our adieus, thanked him profusely and staggered up the gangway.

I have never figured out whether the farts were to pay us for our lack of attention or whether he didn't even know he was emitting them, but I shall never forget being shown round Antigua the first time.

After this it was Grenada and here we faced a different situation. As we steamed into Grenada and fired our salute, little did we realise they had had a labour dispute and that a Mr Geary, who was the Labour leader, had been leading a riot as a result of which the local Police had opened fire. There had been casualties and Mr Geary had therefore taken to the hills inside Grenada and was in hiding. On our arrival my landing party, which in those days was still used in support of the Civil Power, was to be paraded as a demonstration of the intention of the British Government not to put up with any nonsense from Mr Geary, or anybody else. We were duly landed and exercised with the Police and my sailors were somewhat amazed to find that had they arrived a few weeks earlier we might have been standing there with our rifles loaded whilst the Police discharged their civic duty with us as back-up, and me with a drawn sword, although what I was supposed to do with that is difficult to pretend that I know. However the episode would come back to remind me in later visits to this island as we shall see. We made great friends with a local Scots couple who lived in a charming little house overlooking the harbour, who were very generous with their whiskey, and altogether it was a good visit.

The Captain stayed with the Governor in Government House and, indeed, stayed so well that he overslept his after-lunch nap on the day we were supposed to sail at 1500hrs., and although the ship was ready in all respects to proceed at the time stated we had no Captain. When he did arrive in his somewhat crumpled tropical lightweight suit and panama hat he came straight to the Bridge, because we were late, and proceeded to give orders to take the ship to sea.

One of the greatest nautical manoeuvres in getting a ship away from a jetty is "springing off". In this particular manoeuvre you leave a spring, that is to say a wire either coming from the fo'castle and going back aft to a bollard, or from the quarter deck and going for'ard to a bollard and assuming for example, as in this case, we had a wire from the fo'castle you then come slow ahead on the outboard engine, or if you've only got one engine, slow ahead, just for a tiny moment and the ship then moves ahead and the spring then brings the bow of the ship in towards the jetty and the stern swings off, out from the jetty and you are ready to make a 'stern board' away. Equally, if you wanted to come out head on and the wind was blowing a bit you would spring aft and then you would have sufficient movement of the bow off the jetty to get the ship away without scraping its side down the jetty. The Captain, who had obviously not quite recovered from his afternoon nap, was not quite as precise in his handling of the ship as he might have been and as a result he left the engines ahead a little too long. The ship, instead of coming gently towards the jetty and then springing the stern off, went straight into the jetty with a great thump. A colourful assembly of locals who had come to wave us off, including the Governor's driver who had brought our Captain down in HE's car, shrank back in horror as the frigate made a dirty dive into the jetty. But the jetty merely creaked, gave a bit and it became clear to them as the *Veryan Bay* bounced off that all was not lost. They began to enjoy the event. It was clear to them that this was quite a great departure and could hardly believe their good fortune when the Captain did it again. After the second bump we were well and truly sprung off and proceeded to make a stern board out into the harbour, turning and then departing from this very beautiful island and the lovely bay in which Georgetown is situated.

Our next stop was Barbados and here again we had to lay off as at that time there was no suitable jetty, and once again we had to rely on our own boat to get ourselves ashore. By this time the idea of doing a

Royal Guard and parading was getting somewhat monotonous; nevertheless we were expected to do it again. The ceremony this time took place on the racecourse, as I recall, and unfortunately the major-domo of the band, the local defence force band, was in prison and had to be let out especially for the celebration otherwise there would have been nobody leading the band. As you can imagine, he got more cheers than anybody else in the whole assembled company.

It was a tiring day for me and Bertie Howson, the Gunner, once again and we were late getting back on board ship. Then we had to get cleaned up to go ashore for the party at Government House that evening. Arriving late at Government House, tired as we were, we were struck by its beautiful setting with floodlighting in the garden and the reception taking place on the lawns outside the lovely house. Unfortunately they were just about to withdraw the 'grog' and this, of course was not going to do the Gunner and me much good. As we stood there I suddenly said to Bertie, 'Look, I think I can see where the grog is coming from – it's in that tent over there.' As I said this I happened to notice a rather charming lady standing by with an empty glass, not talking to anybody and alone. Walking over to her I said, 'Excuse me, but would you like another drink, it seems to be a bit short tonight.'

'Well,' she said, 'do you think you can get one?'

'Oh, yes,' said I, 'I don't think that is much of a problem, I can see where it is coming from. I'll nip in there and get us some.' So I promptly nipped off to the tent and came back out refreshed with two horse's necks for Guns and me, and a gin and tonic for our lady friend. We exchanged mutual cheers, took our first sip and then she said, 'Don't you think we should be getting down to the lower lawn where they are going to show a film of the Coronation?'

'Oh, no,' I replied, 'I really wouldn't bother with that if I were you. We've seen it three times already and I don't think we are in any hurry to go down there.' We chatted for a while and then she said, 'I really think I ought to go down.' So we followed her down to the lower lawn where the film screen had been erected and where the assembled company was sitting around waiting, and to my astonishment she proceeded to walk straight down to the front row and sit down next to the Governor! It seemed that I had done it again!

We watched the film for the umpteenth time and soon after, it was time to depart. As we queued up in the line of people making their manners before departure, there I saw our lady friend standing next to the Governor, bidding farewell to everyone and as she espied me coming she clearly nudged her husband to point out that there there was the young Lieutenant who had said that the grog was in short supply, but he knew where he could get one. Sure enough, when we arrived she was dissolved in laughter and introduced me to her husband, the Governor – Lady Arundel she was – and we parted the best of friends. Nevertheless it was another story to go round the Wardroom.

Now we started our long trip down towards Pernambuco, now known as Recife.

It had become patently clear to me by this time that my boys knew very little about sex and, in fact, had had no sex education at all. Here we were, exposed to the full glare of undesirable temptation and my boys obviously had not much idea of what it was all about. I therefore spoke to Dr Stewart, our doctor, and asked him whether he would give the boys a lecture or two on sex education.

'Not me,' he said, 'I wouldn't touch that with a bargepole.' And so I turned to the First Lieutenant and explained my problem and said, 'Well if he won't do it, I am their Divisional Officer, I'll do it.' The First Lieutenant said, 'Well, fine, but I think you ought to talk to the Captain first.' And so it was that I found myself on one of those rare occasions in the Captain's cabin, talking to this somewhat reclusive gentleman and explaining to him what I intended to do. He looked at me fixedly for a moment and said in his clipped manner, 'Well, if you must, Lygo, if you feel you must, then you must, but on your own head be it.' I didn't think this a very good preamble to my attempt to enlighten my boys into the sexual arts!

Nevertheless and nothing daunted I called them together on their Messdeck and started down the road on my explanation of sex and the sex act. It was very clear from the beginning that they hadn't the faintest notion of what it was all about and looked at me and listened intently with amazement. I explained the use of condoms, 'French letters' as they were commonly known in the Navy, where they were free issue. Nevertheless at the end of about an hour, the perspiration was pouring off me and it was clear to me, that I had taken on a bigger task than I had imagined. Several of my boys were from Southern Ireland, of Catholic persuasion, and one remark I remember very clearly was, 'Well the priest has told us that we mustn't use condoms because they cause cancer in women. They can give the woman cancer if we use them.' Faced with this kind of blarney, I was somewhat out of my depth. However when we reconvened I staggered on and hopefully had given them a fair grounding in sex and what it was all about, and the preventive measures that were necessary to be taken. Little did I know how much of the information I had given them they had absorbed.

As we approached the entrance to Recife the pilot boat met us and the Portuguese speaking pilot came on board. He had not one word of English, and we not one word of Portuguese. It was therefore to me extremely interesting to listen to the conversation and argument which proceeded between the Navigating Officer, the Captain and the Portuguese Pilot. As we thumped our way towards the entrance there was one marker buoy sitting right in the middle of the channel. The Navigating Officer turned to the Captain and said, 'We should leave that buoy to port, Sir.'

'Come you porty, come you porty,' said the Portuguese Pilot, clearly indicating that we should leave it to starboard.

'No, Sir, no we should leave it to port.' The Captain looked at the Portuguese Pilot indicating the direction of starboard.

'No, no,' said the Portuguese Pilot, 'Come you porty, come you porty.' The Captain was clearly faced with a dilemma and turning to the Navigating Officer he said, 'Well, he's the local pilot and I'm going to follow his instructions.' Whereupon our Navigating Officer issued forth the immortal words which always precede the events leading to groundings or collisions, if there is time, in which Navigating Officers want to exonerate themselves from all responsibility. Turning to the Yeoman he said, 'Take everything that follows down in writing.'

I nearly had to leave the Bridge at this point because the scene to me had been so comic, but indeed I did have to leave the bridge because the Captain who had his binoculars trained on the jetty some distance away said to the First Lieutenant, 'Do we have a guard, Number One?'

'A guard?' said Number One. 'No, Sir, we don't have a guard.'

'Well they've got a guard and we'd better have one too.'

'How do you mean, Sir?'

'They've got a guard on the jetty,' said the Captain. 'They are dressed in red uniforms with white bands and they are all fallen in and you'd better get a guard ready.' This was no easy task. I was the Gunnery Officer and the Officer of the Guard and so I was despatched to get the guard fallen in. We decided that a Captain's guard would be good enough but of course in that ship, as I have explained, there was no broadcast and the Quartermaster or Bosun's Mate had to go nipping round the ship, piping on the Bosun's whistle and shouting out the instruction, 'Guard fall in on the Quarterdeck'. This was received with consternation by the guard, and by me because I had to get changed into my no.10s (full whites) and buckle on my shiny black gaiters and get my sword out and medals. By the time I was just about to button up my no.10 tunic the Quartermaster came by and said, 'It's all right, Sir, you are not required. Guard stand down.' I changed back into my shorts and shirt and proceeded back up onto the bridge and by this time we were well inside the main harbour and coming towards our jetty. What the Captain had seen had in fact been stacks of red barrels of lubricating oil which the Chief had ordered in advance to be waiting for us on the jetty, and the barrels were all fallen in ready and had white bands round the middle. This was the guard the Captain expected us to salute!

The fun hadn't finished, however, because as we approached the jetty the Pilot turned to the Captain and said expressively with his hands pointed to his bosom, 'Me anchor.'

'What does he mean, me anchor?' said the Captain.

'I don't know,' said the First Lieutenant.

'I don't know,' said the Navigating Officer.

'Me anchor,' said the Pilot.

'I think, Sir,' said I, venturing for the first time to express an opinion on seamanship, 'I think he means that he has his own anchor.'

'What do you mean, he has his own anchor?' said the Captain.'Did you see him bring it on board?'

'No, Sir,' I said, 'I think what he means is that he has an anchor laid out.'

'Nonsense,' said the Captain. And we proceeded to thunder down towards our appointed berth on the jetty. Just then a small boat that had been laying off proceeded to come towards us, clearly trailing a line and the line was attached to an anchor which indeed was laid off the berth and could be used for letting the ship down onto the berth, or in the case of a strong wind for heaving it off. I was exonerated and leapt up in estimation of my knowledge of seamanship by all concerned!

Boys' leave started at one o'clock, as soon as they had finished their dinner, and ended at six, so that they could be back on board safely before the wicked happenings of shore life could affect them. However, by five o'clock the sirens were wailing and the 'paddy waggons' (Police vans) were coming back to the ship with most of my boys on board. They had in fact listened carefully to my instructions on sex; they now knew exactly how to do it and had got themselves into the first place where it was clearly advantageous knowledge and there they had disported themselves for a couple of hours, after they had managed to consume a considerable quantity of rum. So now I was landed with a bunch of drunken boys straight out of numerous brothels. I was appalled, but not half as appalled as I was going to be some few days later when the results of their encounters became apparent. Fools rush in where angels fear to tread!

During the course of the cocktail party in Recife, we met many expatriate Englishmen, because at that time the British were running the tramways, the railways, the cotton mills, and a whole raft of things in Brazil in those happy days. As a result there were a large number of expatriates to entertain us and to be entertained by us. During the course of the cocktail party, I commented to one that I noticed that when anybody came on board and was asked what they would like to drink, they immediately said Scotch. They all went for Scotch, they didn't go for gin or brandy, or anything but Scotch whiskey, that was what they all wanted.

'Yes,' said my guest, 'You see it is very difficult to get ashore here and extremely expensive.'

'How about your beer?' I said, because beer was difficult to get onboard, it was quite expensive in relation to what we had to pay for duty-free spirits.

'Oh,' he said, 'the Brazilian beer is very good and it is quite cheap.'

'What would you say would be a good price?' said I, my barrow-boy instinct coming to the fore at once. 'What would you say would be a good price for a bottle of whiskey, if you could get one?'

'Oh,' said the chap, 'if we could get whiskey at £6 or £7 or £8 a bottle we would think we were doing well because we often have to pay as much as £12 or £15.'

'Good heavens!' I said, bearing in mind that it was costing us something less than ten shillings. 'Supposing,' said I, 'I would be able to trade you a couple of cases of whiskey for an equivalent amount of beer, would that be a good deal?'

'Absolutely excellent,' he said. 'At what rate?'

'Well,' said I, 'Let's say £8 a bottle, shall we?'

'Oh, that would be a good deal,' he said. 'And you would wish to be paid in beer?'

'Yes,' said I, and thought no more about it.

The following afternoon I was the Duty Officer and was in the Wardroom reading quietly, with nothing very much going on, when the Quartermaster came down to see me.

'There is a lighter trying to get alongside, Sir,' he said.

'A lighter?' I queried, 'Are we expecting any stores?'

'No, Sir,' he said.

'Well, send him away,' I said and returned to my reading. A few moments later he came back and said, 'No, Sir, he won't go away, he is determined to come alongside and it looks as if he's got a whole load of beer on board.' I hastened up on deck. Sure enough, there was the lighter coming alongside with a grim-faced Brazilian driving it determinedly towards us and the whole of the lighter was covered in beer. This was the equivalent of two cases of Scotch at £8 a bottle, in terms of beer at the local price, and I had to get the entire duty part up to unload it. They were rewarded by having the first bottle of beer I suspect that they had had aboard ship for some considerable time, if ever. Of course in those days it was rum for sailors and nothing else. So we had beer at one penny a glass for the rest of the commission, which wasn't a bad deal!

After our visit to Pernambuco we again set sail down the coast of South America, plodding on at our steady 12–13 knots towards Montevideo. On and on we went until we came to the mouth of the River Plate, when doing a stint as officer of the watch, I observed what looked like a number of warships on the horizon. As we got closer it was clear that they *were* warships and I called the Captain to the Bridge. He came up and had a look and said, 'Hmm, it's the Argentinian fleet; we'll sail right through the middle of it.' Which we proceeded to do. The Argentinians appeared at that time to have some problem with finance and were rationed for fuel oil, so the fleet would go to sea, disappear out of sight, come to anchor in the comparatively shallow water off the River Plate and presumably conduct various exercises. So we ploughed straight through the middle, the customary exchanges of salutes were made between both sides, and a very friendly reception we received from the Argentinian Navy. Strange, really, because we were being sent down as a symbol of our determination to protect the Falkland Islands. We were all that was necessary to keep the Argentinians at bay; the White Ensign was enough – what a pity that seemed to have been forgotten at a later date. So we proceeded on our way round the corner and into Montevideo.

When the local Pilot came out to join us for our entry into Montevideo, he could hardly wait to point out to us the masts of the Graf Spee which were at that time still visible as she lay scuttled in the entrance. It was sad to see the only evidence of a one-time great ship sitting so ignominiously on the bottom. On the other hand, it had probably saved many hundreds if not thousands of lives lost if she had proceeded to sea and had had a fatal engagement with the British forces that were waiting for her.

Montevideo, in those days, was a fairly quiet backwater; the country itself was in deep financial trouble, and relations with Argentina were not entirely friendly, which was why we were welcome, I suppose. There was a small British community and they proceeded to entertain us, and we them, in the usual fashion. One amusing episode comes to mind from that time. As usual I was Officer of the Day on the first day of arrival when we gave a reception on board, and as I stood on the gangway seeing guests off, one chap was halfway down when he turned and came back and said to me, in halting English, pointing with his finger, 'You, me, lavatory.' I assumed that this gentleman wished to go to the heads so I asked the Bosun's Mate to take him and show him where the heads were, which he duly did. The man came back with the Bosun's Mate, both looking somewhat surprised, the man shaking his head and said again, 'You, me, lavatory'. I now became slightly concerned at the turn this conversation was taking, but being my usual polite self, as we are always bidden to be on such occasions, I said to the Quartermaster, 'I'll just take him along and show him where the heads are'. I led him to the officer's loo which was just forward of the gangway, and when I opened the door and pointed to it he shook his head again, and said, 'No, no, no. Lavatory you, dining lavatory,' and he was in fact inviting me to go and have dinner with him in a restaurant called 'La Vatori'. All that remained now was for me to rush to the quarterdeck and sweep up the remnants of any officers that were left behind who hadn't managed to get a 'strangulation', and Nobby Hall gallantly stood in for me while I disappeared with the gentleman, whose wife was waiting on the jetty I was delighted to find, and we proceeded to have a most enjoyable evening in 'La Vatori'.

Montevideo was the last civilised port of call that we were to enjoy prior to our period on duty down in the Falkland Islands, and so we set sail with some sadness and proceeded south.

We had planned to get into Port Stanley quite early in the morning, at about eight o'clock, and we therefore reached the vicinity of Port Stanley while it was still dark. The Navigating Officer took us towards the entry to Port Stanley harbour, and for the first but not the last time I went through that narrow entrance hard left then hard right into the inner harbour, to see the wreck of the old *Fennia* still sitting there on the jetty and the sight of the town of Port Stanley littering itself upon the bank that rose up on the port side of the harbour. We were there. In the distance we could see the Royal Marine camp with its radio mast up at the head of the port inlet on the rising ground, and as we had come into the outer harbour we had seen the oil depot to the right. This was the main reason for the Royal Navy's interest in the Falkland Islands – it was a fuelling depot (originally, of course, stocked with coal).

11

Exercising in the Falklands

Life in the guard ship in Port Stanley was a fairly boring affair so, in order to improve our operational readiness, Number One decided that we would carry out two distinct exercises. One was to practise laying out an anchor with the seaboat as part of "general drill", and to test the gas-tight integrity of the Citadel (the Citadel being that part of the ship which, when closed down, was supposed to be able to resist a gas attack). The second major exercise was to salvage a barge that was sunk alongside the jetty in Port Stanley, thus clearing the approach to the jetty; this would exercise our divers in effecting a repair and getting the barge pumped out, and then we were going to tow it out to sea and use it as a target.

The laying-out of the anchor was an interesting exercise but one which nearly cost us the seaboat, as I recall, because a frigate's anchor is a pretty heavy thing and it was quite a performance getting it underneath the seaboat so that it could be carried away to be laid out, but we did it. The exercise for testing the Citadel, however, was a little more interesting. Lachrymatory floats were to be laid out upwind of the ship, the gas (a type of tear gas) would drift down and we would then test to see whether we had the correct gas tightness. We were also able to get the gun crews and mortar crews to wear their gas masks and to check that they all operated properly. Tom duly got the lachrymatory floats away and lit them, and we saw the initial puffs of gas (just like smoke) coming off the floats.

The Captain had come up on the Bridge for this particular exercise, and after a while he turned to the First Lieutenant and said, 'I don't think this is working, Number One. I can't see any gas, I don't think there is any gas about.' 'Well, it's not visible, Sir,' was the reply, 'and we shall of course detect it soon enough, if all goes well.' 'Well, I think this is all a waste of time,' said the Captain but at that moment, sure enough, the first detection of gas from the detection devices began to operate and the rattles were sounded. 'On gas masks,' was the great shout, 'On gas masks,' and we all proceeded to put our gas masks on. Busily looking in the direction of the floats and around the ship in general, we failed to notice that the Captain, who had put his gas mask on, had quietly collapsed in a corner of the Bridge. In those days, when the gas masks were stowed, a large cork was inserted in the breathing part to stop dust and dirt getting into it, and the Captain had unfortunately failed to notice this and remove the cork. Having put on his gas mask, he was now in the process of suffocating! A hasty job of lifting him and removing the cork (though not removing his gas mask because otherwise he would have been attacked by tear gas) convinced him that Number One's test was at leats realistic.

The next exercise with the barge was much more exciting. The barge was duly patched up, the water was pumped out and it floated, so the first part of the exercise was complete. Now was the question of taking it in tow, which was done, and we started slowly to proceed to sea towing this very large and sluggish barge, which only had a free board of about 18 inches to two feet. The Captain had decided to invite some dignitaries from ashore to come with us, and so we had His Excellency the Governor, and various other characters, to watch this particular exercise. Having cleared Port Stanley harbour and got the barge out to sea, the idea was that we would then cut it adrift, lay off, and sink it with gunfire, thus exercising the guns. Having sunk it, as it proceeded to settle into the deep water off the Falklands, we were to use it as a submarine target, turn round and attack it with Hedgehogs, which were the forward throwing depth charges that we had in this Bay Class frigate. We lay off and, as the Gunnery Officer, I proceeded to attempt to engage this target. Unfortunately, with the ship rolling in the swell and the freeboard of the barge being as low as it was, there was no way we could get the shells accurately enough at that kind of range to actually hit it. We could get overs, we could get shorts but it was extremely difficult to get a shell to go into a two-foot-high target. Having failed to actually achieve this, I asked the Chief Gunner's Mate what he thought the solution to this was, and he said,' Lay and train by hand, Sir, one gun at a time,' so we closed and lay and trained one gun by hand (as in Nelson's day), 'bang', and missed it, and 'bang', missed it. It was almost impossible to hit. The Captain by this time was getting very scathing in his remarks about our gunnery. At one stage he actually ordered up the Royal Marines with their Sten guns to fire at it! Finally we were able to punch some shells into this thing but of course this was practice ammunition we were using i.e. it had no explosives in it – indeed we had fired nearly the whole of our allowance of practice ammunition – and all we succeeded in doing was drilling four-inch holes in it, and the water was slow to get in to make the thing actually sink.

However, at the end of this gunnery manoeuvre we finally did get it to sink and the ship then raced around in order to exercise its ASDICS and to carry out an attack on the barge as it sank. I was up on the Bridge for this performance and the TAS Officer, Nobby Hall, quickly got the ASDICS to detect this large lump of metal as it began to sink, and we were all delighted to hear the familiar 'ping', 'ping', 'ping', 'ping', as the ASDICS reverberated on the hull. We rounded onto the course to attack the sinking barge and the Captain, who clearly was new to this experience, said to the TAS Officer and to the First Lieutenant, as I recall, 'What do I do? What do I do?'

'Well, Sir, once contact has been gained, you say "steer by ASDICS".'

'I see.'

'Contact gained, Sir, contact gained. Range.'

'Steer by ASDICS,' said the Captain, and the TAS Officer proceeded to do this, and we steamed steadily towards where the 'submarine' presumably was located.

'In the bracket High, Sir.'

'What do I say now?' said the Captain.

'You say "engage with Hedgehog".'

'Engage with Hedgehog,' said the Captain.

'Fire!' said the TAS Officer, and away went the Hedgehogs in front, screaming up into the air in a bright arc to descend with a plummeting noise into the area in which the barge, presumably, was sinking. The ship now, the good old *Veryan Bay* with its 'up and downers' (engines) working really hard, was now worked up to its full 14 knots and charging straight towards the position where this 'submarine' was sinking.

Unfortunately everybody was so fascinated watching the dropping of the Hedgehogs that it took some time before the First Lieutenant reminded the Captain, 'Starboard 30, Sir, starboard 30. We mustn't overrun the...' Unfortunately we were a little late. Starboard 30 was ordered but at this time there was a shattering explosion as all the depth charges went off and the ship shuddered from stem to stern, the Captain's cap fell off, we had to hang onto various stanchions to regain our balance. As the ship moved out of the area we dusted ourselves off and went to see what damage had been done. We hadn't done much, a certain amount of water was entering the hull from various seams that had opened, but apart from that, with the judicious application of a little cement in the various leaks, we were rapidly seaworthy and returned to Port Stanley.

Whether we had actually impressed the assembled company with our prowess as the protecting force for the Islands in the face of both, at that time, Argentinian and Chilean aggression I am not sure. I am not sure that it convinced me. However, it's not what you can do but what you are believed to be able to do that adds up to deterrence.

12

The OAG

The ship spent most of its time in Port Stanley where there was very little to do at all. There was a pub and a couple of bars, there was one store run by the Falkland Islands Company, as I recall, and not much else. The local inhabitants were not exactly friendly, although to be fair it was a small community to entertain or involve the crew of a frigate, of which there was always one present, so we were really left to our own devices. There were trips to be made around the island in the ship but this was a fairly rare occurrence. We would go round to visit an out-station but our main task was to be there in case either the Argentinians or the Chileans decided to do something which our Foreign Office back at home would think to be unreasonable – to deter aggression, I suppose. There was a garrison of Royal Marines, about Company strength, the same as was there when the Argentinians finally decided to invade many, many years later – but when no RN warship was present.

We were there in the Arctic winter and this meant that it was too cold down south to go too far down before we met the ice packs and this restricted our activities even more than usual. The soccer pitch in Port Stanley was somewhat boulder strewn and not exactly flat, which didn't encourage too much sport, although we managed quite a bit. I had the problem, after the episode in Pernambuco, of trying to find something for the Boys' Division to do and I decided that I would only let them go into houses where I had personally vetted the inhabitants, which I proceeded to do. There wasn't too much entertainment for them, or hospitality, but I did achieve some; usually it was from fond mothers who saw the opportunity of getting their daughters married off to a sailor and thus a ticket back to the United Kingdom!

I discovered that there had been a Falklands Island Defence Force Band, a brass band which in more heady days had been used to celebrate various occasions and to provide some entertainment, and that most of the instruments remained. With a rashness that was driven, I suppose, more and more by despair at the lack of opportunity than anything else, I decided to form a Ship's Company concert Party and to put on a show for the Ship's Company and residents of

Port Stanley. The problem was that the musicians, such as remained, had become somewhat dispersed; some had left the island, and there was no music to speak of which we could use for a concert party. I had two pieces of good fortune however: one of the Midshipmen could play the guitar and could write and read music – whereas I couldn't – and the schoolteacher in the local school was able to play the piano. Further I discovered that two of the youngsters on board, coming from the north-east, had actually learned to play brass instruments and therefore we were able to form a kind of Frank Biffo's Brass Quintet, complete with pianist and guitar. Next was to write down the music and the words and at least get an introduction going so that we could get on the stage and eventually get off.

I had been involved in a quite good concert party at Culdrose before I had left there. The concert was due to be given on the night that King George VI died and so the whole place went into mourning and the concert was cancelled. But I did remember a lot of the words that had been written for that particular show, and the music and therefore I proceeded to hum the tune to the Midshipman who strummed it on the guitar, wrote it down and then got the pianist to play it. From then on we were able to write the parts for the various instruments and put the whole thing together. It is amazing how you can find people who can do things once you set your mind to it and we duly produced a member of the Ship's Company who could sing popular ballads; we had several skits which were fairly easy for us to manage, skits which I had remembered from past activities, and there was the usual kind of 'dress chaps up as women' to create the laughable spectacle of a hideous chorus line. The final and more fatal decision was that the Shipwright and I would do a song and dance act. I was to compere the show and tell jokes, which wasn't too difficult, but the Shipwright and I were to sing and dance to the Al Jolson tune 'Pretty Baby'. I had never sung or danced anywhere but the Shipwright apparently had, or said he had, and with suitable canes and two straw hats from somewhere or other we were able to attempt this particular act. It must have been quite dreadful and I blush at the thought of it to this day.

When the great night arrived, the entire Ship's Company except for the duty part was there, most of the Falklands Islands' residents of Port Stanley were there, the Governor and his wife were there, the Colonial Secretary was there, and by and large a riotous evening was had by all. Terribly amateurish, and I am sure badly performed but a miracle when one comes to think of the material we were working with. The stage was in the Town Hall at Port Stanley, the main civic centre, and it was quite a good stage as I recall; the curtains worked, which sometimes they don't, and – well to cut a long story short – we got by with it.

The major endeavour of that period, however, was the scheme dreamt up by Number One, Tom Baird, to play a joke on the frigate that was coming to relieve us. After the Coronation there was to be a Royal flight across the Atlantic, and the Navy had to station frigates along the Royal route. Thus there became a shortage of said vehicles because of this and instead of being relieved by a frigate from the West Indies station we were to be relieved by a frigate from the then South African station, Simonstown. These chaps, it was generally understood, were on the cocktail circuit, whereas we were on the icicle circuit. What a good thing it would be, therefore, to play a joke on these unsuspecting new arrivals when they arrived in Port Stanley having crossed the South Atlantic.

Number One's idea was that he should dress up as the Governor of the Falkland Islands and that I should accompany him as his ADC and that we would call upon the unsuspecting Captain and make them go through the various procedures of protocol which would be nothing more than a great big leg-pull. To prepare the ground, therefore, Number One wrote to his opposite number in the *Nereid*, the ship detailed off to relieve us, and told him that the Governor of the Falkland Islands, who was the Commandant of Local Forces, took his role very seriously and was often known to pay a visit to the incoming ship quite unexpectedly to make sure that they were fully briefed and aware of events and possible uses for the guard ship in and around the Falkland Islands. In order to make this story more credible he was also told that the Governor used the guard ship's boat which was already in the harbour, but flew his own Falklands Islands flag. Thus they would be aware that it was he who was approaching should this event materialise.

We then waited for the reply to the latter. To the horror of our First Lieutenant he discovered the First Lieutenant of *Nereid* had been changed, and the new First Lieutenant had been with Tom at Dartmouth, therefore there would be absolutely no prospect of him not being recognised when he appeared on board. As the *Nereid* was now approaching the point of departure and mail services from the Falkland Islands were somewhat unreliable, there was not much we could do about this and if we were to continue with the plan there had to be some changes. It was therefore decided that I should go as the OAG, the Officer Administering the Government, purporting to be Mr Colin Campbell, who was the Colonial Secretary and that I should have Bertie Howson, the Gunner, once again with me as my ADC. Now came the question of how we should dress ourselves to confuse the *Nereid* and carry the day. There were only three morning suits available in the Falkland Islands; one belonged to His Excellency the Governor, the other belonged to the Colonial Secretary and the third belonged to the Managing Director of the Falkland Islands Company, who was a very large and rotund man. As it was unlikely that we would be able to borrow the former and the latter would be far too big for me we had to find some other rig which I could don. It was discovered that one of the chaps ashore, who worked for the Falkland Islands Company I think, had been in the Devon and Cornwall Light Infantry and still had his dress uniform. He was about the same build as me and so when this uniform was duly produced and tried on, it fitted extremely well. The only problem was, that part of the regalia were spurs and I had to practise very carefully to go up and down ladders in the frigate in a way that didn't get my spurs entangled with the rungs of the ladder, which would have been a disaster.

In order to increase my status it was decided that I should borrow the Major of Marines' cap, which was the only Army-looking cap we had with gold braid on it, and furthermore I should be made up to a Brigadier by the addition of a crown and one pip to the two pips of the uniform I was wearing. I wore the insignia of the Falkland Islands Defence Force, which had just gone out of existence, on my epaulettes and on my cap. Now came the question of medals and we contrived to create some Army-looking medals because otherwise a row of Naval ribbons would have been a fairly obvious giveaway to a Naval Officer. A row of Army-looking ribbons was duly brought together from various sources and it was also decided that we would give them two clues to the fact that we were not genuine.

As mentioned earlier, I had been issued with an American medal when I had served in the United States Navy. Of course I wasn't ever entitled to wear this medal because it wasn't a decoration and so it was decided that I would wear this on the other breast so that my medals would be on the left-hand side, correctly, and the phoney medal would be hanging separately on my right side. The other clue was to stitch a double red cross over the Penguin which was the central feature of the Falkland Islands flag. This is a Union Jack with a Penguin in the middle and so we stitched a double red cross across the Penguin. These were the two clues for them to see that we were not genuine.

Meantime the Gunner had been fitted out with an Army khaki uniform complete with Sam Brown belt, which he had also borrowed ashore. We then had to practice Army salutes and not fall into the trap of using the rather different Naval ones. All was now coming close to the reality of doing this thing and it was decided that when

Bertie Howson and myself ready to board the *Nereid*

the *Nereid* arrived in Port Stanley at eight o'clock, we would have His Excellency afloat in his 'barge' and we would proceed directly towards the ship, arriving alongside just after it anchored, which would be the greatest moment of confusion onboard. In order to enhance our appearance it was agreed that when we passed the *Veryan Bay* they would bugle us and salute the Officer Commanding Local Forces and they would, furthermore, send a signal as we left the jetty in Port Stanley to the *Nereid* by light which said, 'OAG afloat, flag flying' – OAG, remember, stood for Officer Administering the Government.

Of course, as you can imagine, we spent many hours debating the best way to enhance and embellish this jape and I discovered that the

OAG would be entitled to a salute of seven guns. It was therefore determined that since they had been told how touchy His Excellency was about protocol we would expect them to actually fire a salute after I had left the ship and lay off to receive it.

The only thing we needed to do now, was to bring our Captain into this jape so that he would give us his tacit blessing and not frown upon such a venture. It was therefore decided that we would give a 'Dining In' night in the Wardroom of the *Veryan Bay* and that we would invite the Captain as our guest of honour. After he had been sufficiently lubricated we would let him into the story of what we were going to do.

During the course of the commission I had had certain trouble, not serious, but rather negative with the Surgeon Lieutenant, who had nothing else to do but treat a few sailors either for the common cold, gonorrhoea or syphilis. Apart from that he was supposed to be the Wardroom caterer; however the food became so disgusting that I blew up one day and the First Lieutenant promptly appointed me as the Wardroom caterer just to calm me down! As a result our doctor was left with practically nothing to do except to anaesthetise cockroaches, which became his daily sport, so I decided that I should also take this opportunity of having a joke at his expense and decided to design and produce an explosive cigar. I had seen explosive cigars used with great effect at many a Fleet Air Arm dinner and decided that we would have one as well. I duly obtained a cigar from the Wardroom stock, drilled out the end, remove the tobacco carefully and inserted a small quantity of black powder – remember I was Gunnery Officer– and then wrapped in tissue paper some yellow powder from the 'smoke puffs' that we had and inserted that as well. I then reinserted the tobacco at the end and the cigar was placed back in the box. 'Now', said I to the Petty Officer Steward, 'when we have passed the port and have toasted the Queen, you will pass the cigars and you will take the cigars to the Surgeon Lieutenant first. He, not being a particularly generous type of man will say, "No thank you," and you are then to say, "They are on the house tonight, Sir." Whereupon he will almost certainly take one – he will take the first one.'

The other ploy was to play a joke on the First Lieutenant and in order to do this I decided we would have an explosive gavel; I had also seen that before and when the First Lieutenant banged the table to bring people to order, the thing would blow up. Here I was less fortunate because I couldn't make the damn thing explode no matter what I did with it. My first attempt was to drill a hole in the end of the gavel, fill it with black powder and put a small cap out of a .22 into the end of it, covered with boot polish so that when he banged it

194

it would go off. However, no amount of banging could make the blasted cap go and ignite the explosive, so I decided the next thing to do was to cut the gavel in half and put the explosive in the middle so that when he banged it it would provide a better percussion on the cap. Still the blasted thing would not explode and I was left with a gavel which had not only been totally destroyed but had utterly failed to effect the aim. I had to confess to the First Lieutenant, therefore, that I had destroyed the only gavel in the ship, and to explain to him why. With his usual good humour, Tom merely told me that I would have to replace the gavel at my own expense and that he would use a spoon on the occasion in question.

The great evening arrived. Our Captain who, as I have previously described, was something of a recluse, duly appeared and was seated at the head of the table. The evening got under way and we proceeded to unfold to the Captain, after a period of time, our intentions with regard to greeting the *Nereid*. You must remember that our Captain was a 'four striper' and was a Flotilla Leader, and the chap coming was only a Commander and therefore we had the seniority edge on him as long as we could get the Captain on our side. Fortunately the Captain thought it was a splendid idea and thoroughly approved of the whole thing, except one part of it.

'No salute,' said he. 'You cannot allow them to fire you a salute, Lygo, because the salute will be heard by the Governor in Government House and he will immediately want to know what the firing is all about and we shall have a scene on our hands.' So it was agreed that, yes, reluctantly the Captain was right and there would be no salute. However, as I said to Number One afterwards, 'if they decide to fire a salute after I have left the ship, there is not much I can do about stopping it.' So it was agreed that we would depend on the good manners of *Nereid* to insist on firing a salute which I would not be able to stop!

There was one further thing that had to be done. I had to explain to the chap whose uniform I had borrowed, that there was every possibility that it would finish up in Port Stanley harbour with me inside it because if they rumbled what we were up to then I could expect a ducking. Indeed, I would have been rather surprised if they had dealt with me in any other fashion. So I warned him and told him that I was due to leave the *Nereid* at about nine o'clock and that he would know that all was well when he heard the salute fired because it meant that I was off the ship and his uniform was safe, 'and if by 09.30 you have heard nothing, I'm probably in the harbour inside your uniform!'

The great morning arrived. We proceeded down the harbour to wait

195

in the boat, resplendent, I may say, in our new uniforms, and at the *moment critique*, as the bows of the *Nereid* appeared through the gap at the entrance to Port Stanley, we set off down the harbour towards her point of anchoring. As we passed the *Veryan Bay* they sounded off and saluted us and, as we passed, they made the signal to the *Nereid*, 'OAG afloat – flag flying'. Of course it must be obvious to my readers now that it was highly improbable that the *Nereid* would have the faintest idea what all that was about; however that's another matter.

We duly arrived alongside the *Nereid*, which looked pretty battle-scarred from her trip across the South Atlantic, not in the best possible condition and no doubt the officers on board, who had been used to the cocktail circuit of South Africa, found Port Stanley slightly different from the ports which they were used to entering! There was no gangway and as I approached the ship, great haste was made to turn out the gangway and get it ready for me. In such haste were they that they let the gangway slip against the strop; the strop broke and the gangway then hung rather desolately over the side. I therefore climbed aboard the *Nereid* up a Mediterranean ladder which they had dropped for me. On arriving on the deck I was greeted by the First Lieutenant who gazed at me somewhat curiously and saluted stiffly, and the Officer of the Day and the Captain came bustling down the deck from the Bridge, the latter in his somewhat battered seagoing uniform which he had been wearing for the trip. I greeted him by saying, 'Good morning, Captain, and welcome to Port Stanley. I am Colin Campbell the Colonial Secretary and I am the OAG. This is my ADC,' introducing the Gunner at the same time.

We had not come empty-handed; I had decided that we should come bearing gifts. The water in the Falkland Islands is peat water, is brown in colour and when poured it looks very much like white wine. And so we decided to take six bottles of water, duly capped and corked, aboard and I had had (and there is a picture of the label) labels printed at the Government Printing Office, which read 'Old Tussac Table Wine – bottled at Goose Green for the Falkland Islands Company'. Tussac is, of course, the grass that grows in the Falkland Islands and Goose Green later became famous as a result of the Falkland campaign. The Captain took me forward to his cabin and the Gunner – my ADC – departed for the Wardroom, taking three bottles of Old Tussac Table Wine, while I took the other three up to the Captain.

On arriving at the Captain's cabin he invited me to sign the Visitor's Book, which I duly did with the signature 'Colin Campbell, OAG' and he asked me if I would like some coffee, which I accepted, and the steward was despatched to produced it. I was, of course, keen to keep

F.I.C.

OLD TUSSAC
TABLE WINE

BOTTLED AT GOOSE GREEN
FOR
THE FALKLAND ISLANDS CO., LTD,

The label I had printed for the 'wine'

the ball in my own court and to monopolise the conversation as much as possible. I asked him about the crossing, had it been comfortable?

'Not really,' he said, 'the weather was bad and it was long and tedious,' and he apologised for the state of the ship on arrival which had been badly affected by weather. I asked him about the length of time he had been in command, about the length of the commission and so on until he could contain himself no longer and said, 'Tell me, Sir, where is His Excellency?' I replied, 'Both His Excellency and Lady Clifford have gone to South Georgia to help resolve a whaling dispute with the Norwegians.'

'Ah,' he said, looking puzzled.

'Yes,' I said, 'it's something that occurs from time to time and His Excellency likes to take personal charge of things on these occasions.'

'But how, Sir, does he manage to get to South Georgia since the *Veryan Bay* is still here in Port Stanley?'

'Ah,' I said, 'quite easily. You obviously don't know of some of the advances that have been made in the Falkland Islands. His Excellency is a great innovator and has introduced an air service throughout the whole of the Islands and this, of course, enables him to use the aircraft to go as far afield as South Georgia.'

'Really?' he said, looking at me.

'Yes,' I said. 'He's done a great deal for the Island, as has Lady Clifford for the local arts, as you will have seen by the introduction of wine. He has just recently acquired for the Government a new aeroplane with longer range called the Upland Goose, it's made by de Havilland of Canada and he and Lady Clifford have flown to South Georgia in an Upland Goose.'

There are two types of geese in the Falkland Islands, the Upland Goose which lives strangely enough in the Uplands, and the Kelp Goose which lives on the kelp around the coast. He heard me in silence.

'You should look it up,' I said, 'in your Jane's *All The World Aircraft*, I'm sure you have one. A very interesting new development for the Islands.' He nodded his agreement. 'What do you think of Port Stanley?' I enquired, trying to regain possession of the ball. There is only one thing he could have possible thought about Port Stanley, to be honest, which was that it was pretty dreary, a collection of largely corrugated iron residences of no particular artistic value, or architectural merit, on the side of the hill that faced onto the Sound in which we were situated.

'Well,' he said hesitantly.

'Ah,' said I, 'I can see that you have been put off by the Admiralty chart. Please don't be put off by that. The new town of Port Stanley which has been built with the aid of the Colonial Development Corporation, is over the hill on the other side and there you will find, and your Ship's Company will find, much better facilities than you will have seen here. Of course none of this appears on the Admiralty chart which, of course, is somewhat dated. There you will find the new Civic Centre and a restaurant and various other things which will help to make your time in Port Stanley much more agreeable.'

'Really?' he said. 'That is interesting.'

'Oh yes,' I said, 'again down to His Excellency who has promoted all this.' On the other side of the hill on which Port Stanley lies is a vast open expanse of peat bog, nothing else; but that is not visible from a vantage point of the Bridge of a ship laying in Port Stanley itself.

I was now beginning to believe that it was time to make my farewells as all seemed to be going extremely well, too well really to last indefinitely, when there was a knock at his door and his First Lieutenant appeared with my 'ADC' close behind him.

'Yes, what is it, Number One?' said the Captain.

'I'm afraid we have a problem, Sir,' said Number One.

'What is it?' asked the Captain.

'Well, it appears that the OAG is entitled to a salute, Sir.'

'Yes,' said the Captain, 'well, well. . .'

'Well,' said the First Lieutenant, 'unfortunately we don't have any saluting charges made up.'

'Well, make some up' said the Captain, 'make some up.'

'But I'm afraid we can't do that in short order, Sir, because we cannot get into the magazine.'

'Why can't you get into the magazine?' asked the Captain.

'Because, Sir,' said the First Lieutenant with some exasperation, 'it is full of spuds. If you recall, the *Veryan Bay* told us there was a shortage of potatoes on the island and advised us to bring a good stock.'

At this point I was really only interested in one thing and that was getting off this ship in one piece and so I said, 'Well I'm sure that under the circumstances it is perfectly understandable, Captain, let's not worry about it.' To my horror my ADC then intervened, he obviously having had several 'horse's necks' poured down him in the Wardroom.

'But, Sir,' said he, 'you know how particular His Excellency is with regard to protocol and. . .'

'Yes, yes, yes,' I said, 'certainly, but I think under the circumstances. . .'

'Oh, but,' said the Captain, 'I'm sure that given time we can. . .'

'No, please,' I said, 'I wouldn't hear of it, it's quite understandable under the circumstances and I am sure that I can explain the whole thing to His Excellency quite satisfactorily when he returns, and now it is really time. . .'

'But Sir. . .' said the ADC again.

'No buts at all,' I repeated and glared at him. It was now clearly time to depart and we were escorted down the upper deck where I admired various fittings on the ship as I proceeded aft to the gangway where a bugler had been fallen in together with a piping party, to see me off more properly than had been the case on my arrival. My boat, resplendent with its Falkland Island flag with a double cross stitched over it, was waiting and promptly came alongside to collect me and my ADC. We bade our fond farewells to the Captain and I said that I hoped he would enjoy the wine which we had brought him and got down into the boat. The boat cast off, we motored out to about 20 yards or so where we stopped. Those on board were still at the salute. Then, as had been previously agreed, we produced some green port fires, lighted them and proceeded to wave them vigorously and make that well-known salute with two fingers. To our amazement they didn't move. They stood there still at the salute. I ordered the Coxswain of the motor boat to do a complete circle of the ship, which we did waving our green port fires and making rude gestures and shouting rather rude messages to them. Not once did they move; they stood there saluting, the whole ship at attention whilst this was going on and later I learned that they thought it was a Falkland Islands' custom that we were practising – like some Indian war dance, I suppose.

We now returned to the ship where we were eagerly awaited by the Ship's Company, and quickly told them what had happened and how we couldn't believe that it had gone as smoothly as it had. As I was recounting this to the Captain who was highly amused by the whole performance, he received a message from the *Nereid* which read as follows: 'In view of the Colonial Secretary's call on me this morning I presume our call on the Governor is cancelled?' Our Captain made back the following reply, 'Not at all, come as arranged.' And so an hour or so later whilst I was back as Officer of the Day at the top of the gangway, the Captain of the *Nereid* arrived, this time in his best uniform, sword and medals, ready to go with our Captain to call upon His Excellency the Governor. As he came up the gangway and I was saluting and he was, being piped, he addressed the Captain as follows: 'But Sir, Captain, ... I really don't understand how we can be calling on the Governor if he is in South Georgia.' The Captain looked at him, nibbling slightly, and then said,' That was one of my Officers, that was one of my Officers,' and led him away for'ard. He never recognised me, I don't know that he even saw me, the state he was in.

Is there an epilogue to this story? Yes, there are three tale-ends. It is alleged that when they opened the first bottle of Old Tussac table wine in the Wardroom and tried it, the Gunner of the *Nereid* said, 'Well this doesn't taste like anything to me, there's no taste in it at all.' To which the Sub Lieutenant, who was alleged to be an afficionado on the subject of wine, said, 'That's because your palate has been ruined by cheap South African sherry.' The second point is that the gentleman who had loaned me his uniform, at about ten past nine, when he still hadn't heard a salute being fired, thought that for certain, as I had predicted, I was in the harbour together with his uniform. He therefore rang the Falklands Islands Company and insured his uniform! I thought this was a very cute act on his part. And thirdly, the CGI in *Nereid* had served with the Gunner, Bertie Howson, in the gunnery school and recognised him but, through fear of making an ass of himself, did not chance his arm, believing him to have a double!

Soon after this we moved to the oiling jetty to have our tanks replenished so that we should be ready for the long trip back up to Rio de Janeiro, our first port of call on the ship's return to the West Indies. So certain were we that we would be paid a return visit by the *Nereid* to compensate for their embarrassment that we had fire hoses rigged to repel boarders and doubled up on security sentries. Nothing whatever happened.

On the evening of the hoax I found myself in the 'Upland Goose', the name of the pub in the Falkland Islands, recounting my story to some of the locals and as I was in full flight the double doors opened and the Captain of the *Nereid* came in; he clearly had been waiting inside the double doors listening to my story. I was somewhat nonplussed and could only offer to buy him a drink which I am bound to say he accepted with good grace!

Two days later as dawn broke we slipped from the oiling jetty and proceeded out of Port Stanley for the last time on our way back to the United Kingdom. It hadn't been dull at all – it had, in fact, been quite memorable; at least it kept the Ship's Company amused.

13

Departure from the Falkland Islands

Eventually the time came for us to depart from the Falkland Islands and proceed north to our first port of call, Rio de Janeiro. About a month before we departed, I returned on board to receive a signal which had been transmitted to me from my mother-in-law in Florida, saying that Pepper had undergone a successful operation and I was to send $2,000. Of course there was no means of communicating to find out exactly what was wrong and I had to wait for the kind of 'letter follows' which reminded me of one of Arnold Weinstock's jokes, the Jewish telegram which said, 'Start worrying, letter follows'. Of course I didn't have $2,000, or anything approaching it and the only thing I could do was to cable my brother in the United Kingdom and ask him to take the Kaiser Fraser that I had so lovingly brought back from Florida, to London and sell it for the best possible price, get the money transferred into dollars on the basis of the medical expenses, because in those days sterling was not convertible, and transfer the money to my mother-in-law to pay the hospital bill. It was not until a month later when the mail arrived that I learned the details of what had happened to poor Pepper in Florida. It had not been funny. Thank goodness for the Kaiser Fraser – it paid the bill. In these days of instant communication, it is difficult to remember what it was like waiting for news to follow a brief telegram – but there was nothing for it.

By the same mail came a notice to say that, if I had qualified as a Seaman by the time my six months were up (in about a month's time), I was to be returned to the United Kingdom to take up a flying appointment. The First Lieutenant and the Captain were really put out by this because it meant that they would be reduced to four Watchkeepers once again. The Captain was in a dilemma, and said to me, 'If I tell them that I can't spare you, the only way I can explain that is to say you have not yet reached the standard necessary to get a Watchkeeper's certificate, which is not true, because you have and that would affect your subsequent career, or I just have to let you go.' And so it was that I was to leave the ship in Rio de Janeiro.

By now I had been made the Fo'c'sle Officer in addition to my other duties, so I was able to stand right up in the eyes of the ship as we entered the famous harbour of Rio de Janeiro, having flogged our way steadily up from the Falkland Islands at 12 knots. I must say, it was a spectacular sight and an extraordinary position to be in to enter Rio, right in the bows of one's ships, observing all that was going on but without too much to do until we actually came alongside and then had to handle the wires.

We approached Rio de Janeiro, in some trepidation because of what had gone before. It appeared that the last frigate to enter Rio had been HMS *Snipe*, one of the Bird Class frigates I referred to earlier, in the command of Commander Hall-Wright. The story as we received it, which of course may not be entirely accurate, was as follows. The Ambassador to Brazil had staying with him a niece who had been invited by the Officers of the *Snipe* to a farewell cocktail party and buffet dinner on board before the ship was due to sail, and so insistent was this girl that they should do a tour of the nightclubs before she was returned to the Ambassadorial residence that they were 'prevailed upon' to take the young lady on such a tour in an open car and in mess undress uniform. Subsequently, when they arrived at the Ambassadorial residence at three o'clock in the morning to return the said niece, to the horror of the Captain, the Ambassador was waiting up for his niece!

They went back to the ship in some considerable state of unrest and early the next morning contacted the Naval Attaché, who happened to be a Naval aviator by the name of 'Chubbs' Randall, a Commander with Wings. His advice apparently was that they should call upon the Ambassador before the ship sailed to apologise for any inconvenience or distress that they had caused him. By this time of course the ship should have long since departed. According to our reports, upon entering the Ambassadorial study His Excellency asked Hall-Wright why he was there, to which the Captain replied that he had come to apologise for any inconvenience that he may have caused His Excellency the night before by keeping his niece out so late, and His Excellency is alleged to have replied, 'Your behaviour last night in Rio de Janeiro was not in accordance with the best traditions of the Service and you are already late sailing. You have missed your sailing date and therefore you are in contravention of your sailing orders and I shall signal Their Lordships accordingly, and the Commander-in-Chief West Indies, and I do not wish to see any Royal Navy ships in Rio de Janeiro again as long as I am Ambassador.'

Now this was all pretty fearsome stuff if it was true. Of course it meant that the Foreign Office would eventually have been alerted by the Admiralty to the fact that although there had been some minor disagreement in Rio de Janeiro it was not really up to the Ambassador to decide where Royal Naval ships should actually go. Time had passed and maybe some of the wounds had healed but the next ship to arrive in Rio de Janeiro was HMS *Veryan Bay*. So it was with some trepidation that we berthed alongside and prepared ourselves for the cocktail party which we were to give the next day. The Captain took himself off to make his calls on His Excellency the Governor and the Ambassador and I busied myself with the guard in order to lay the wreath which is always required in South America on these occasions, usually in honour of Almirante Cochrane who had helped the South Americans obtain their freedom from Spain, and who happens to be my particular Naval hero too.

As my readers may know, Rio de Janeiro is an extraordinary city, in that on the one hand there is luxury down to Copacobana Beach with untold riches displayed on every side, and on the other, up in the hills behind, the *hueva*, the peasantry who live in the most insanitary conditions in tin shacks without running water; surviving really by petty crime, I suspect, and more particularly from raking over the garbage heaps of the more fortunate.

The day for my departure was now coming nigh, and I was to stay back for a couple of days after the *Veryan Bay* departed in order to take passage in the *Andes*, the liner that was to take me back to Southampton for my next appointment. I was to be put up by the Naval Attaché for the day and a half or two days that I had to wait after the ship had departed. The visit progressed and the great evening of the cocktail party arrived. This was the first time that His Excellency had graced us with his presence on board and the first RN ship he had visited since the ill-fated *Snipe*, and we were all looking spick and span for this great occasion. Unbeknown to us, of course, and to me particularly, who was Officer of the Day waiting on the gangway – incidentally I always seemed to be Officer of the Day on these occasions – two of our staunch and loyal Hearts of Oak seamen had been on a run ashore in some of the less salubrious parts of Rio, and having had what is technically known as a 'skinful' had decided it was time they returned on board their ship. At about the time the taxi deposited them at the gates of the Naval establishment where we were berthed, at the end of a long mole, the Ambassador and his wife and niece were embarking in the Ambassadorial Rolls Royce to proceed to the *Veryan Bay*. Our two gallant sailors having arrived at the mole proceeded to stagger down the length of the mole to where the *Veryan Bay* was berthed, but unfortunately, it being unlit, they found themselves falling into a large hole which had been dug in the middle of the mole. They fell to the bottom of this hole. At about the moment they hit the bottom, the Ambassadorial Rolls Royce entered the gates of the Dockyard and turned down the mole.

Our two sailors proceeded to climb out of the hole in the mole, looking somewhat dishevelled and particularly disgruntled by this experience on top of their 'skinful', and as they peered over the edge of the hole, they came face to face with the headlights of the Ambassadorial Rolls Royce which illuminated them but of course did not enable them to see who was, in fact, illuminating them. The Ambassador in the back of the Rolls Royce then made his first mistake, he wound down the window to enquire what was going on. That provided the opportunity for one of the sailors, who had by now climbed out of the hole and was dusting himself off, to poke his head, with his Naval cap somewhat awry and on which was emblazoned HMS *Veryan Bay*, through the window into the back of the Rolls Royce and staring into the black and at the darkened figures inside – of course he had no awareness as to who they were, being blinded by the headlights – directed the following remark at His Excellency: 'You are an F-ing Arab'. He then fell back into the road as the Rolls Royce sped on its way with a fuming Ambassador, towards the *Veryan Bay*.

Meantime the Captain and I were waiting on the gangway to receive our principal guest. He alighted from the Rolls Royce, preceded by his niece and his wife, and then stormed up the gangway and addressed the Captain as follows: 'There are two of your sailors on the jetty who have just insulted me and my wife and they are to be placed under close arrest as soon as they return on board.' The Captain, to his undying honour, said 'Really, Sir, Your Excellency, what have they done?'

'I don't wish to discuss it now.'

'Then,' said the Captain, 'I can take no further action.' The Ambassador stalked aft to join the revelries on the Quarterdeck and I waited with some trepidation for the two sailors to return on board. By this time, realising the difficulties they might find themselves in, they had, in that marvellous way which sailors have, somehow contrived to sober up sufficiently to pass muster and get on board.

After enough whiskey had flowed and the Captain was sufficiently sympathetic to His Excellency's complaints, the matter was allowed to drop but it clearly did not heighten His Excellency's view of the Royal Navy, or those who served in it. Imagine therefore, my horror when I was told by the Naval Attaché who was on board, that His Excellency, his lady wife, the niece and the Consul General were all taking passage back to England in the *Andes*, along with Lygo. I shall not forget the Naval Attaché's briefing to me which was quite specific and to the point, 'Lygo,' he said, 'you must be extremely careful how you conduct yourself on the way home in the company of His Excellency. He does not like Naval Officers, or the Navy. He served in the Army during the last War and has a very low regard for the Royal Navy, which has been worsened by events that have taken place recently. Furthermore, you must not find yourself alone with the niece, lest it be seen or thought that you are attempting to compromise her, or she you in some particular way, and therefore you must, if you find yourself alone, leave the room immediately.' I could hardly believe my ears. I mean it had been some time, indeed a very long time, since I had been challenged in such a way and the thought of having to leave the room when somebody was coming on a bit strong was more than I could actually bear. I didn't believe it would happen anyway, it wasn't my kind of luck! Furthermore I was a happily married man who was returning to England to meet his wife who had suffered a not particularly pleasant operation and to welcome her back in her weakened condition to the rigours of the English climate.

Strolling on deck on board the *Andes* after I had been seen off by the Naval Attaché, and whilst we were waiting for the ship to proceed, I fell in step with a youngster of about my own age I suppose, a tall, fair-haired young man who turned out to be Swedish and who spoke very good English, and we started to chat and struck up a conversation and I thought, here's the obvious answer to the maiden's prayer. This unattached good-looking young Swede should be just the kind of person to entertain the aforesaid niece on the long voyage home.

After I had finished my stroll I went into the bar of the first-class lounge and to my surprise there was His Excellency and the Consul General sitting at the bar. 'Ah, Lygo,' said His Excellency, 'would you care to join us for a drink?' Here we go, I thought.

'Yes, Sir, certainly,' and I fell into my most ingratiating manner alongside them. We chatted away for some considerable time and I found him an entertaining and enjoyable companion, and so after a couple of drinks when he said to me, 'Do you play bridge?' I overstepped the mark slightly by saying, 'Yes I do,' not because I didn't but because really, if I had thought about it, it wasn't the kind of thing I would wish to enter into with His Excellency after all the warnings I had been given.

'Well,' said His Excellency, 'we've now got three with the Consul General here. Do you know anybody who could make up a fourth?'

I thought briefly and said, 'I've just met a young Swede and I'll ask him if he plays bridge and if so he could make the fourth.'

'Excellent, capital' said His Excellency, 'we'll meet here at six o'clock for a quick rubber.'

'Yes,' I said, 'by all means,' and set off to find my Swedish acquaintance. I asked him if he played bridge and he said yes, he did, so I invited him to make up the fourth and he said he would be happy to do so.

The moment arrived when we sat down and chose our partners and it so happened that I got the Consul General and His Excellency got the Swede. After the deal the bidding went something like this: I opened, or passed. His Excellency said, 'Two clubs.' My partner responded with three diamonds and my Swedish friend, examining his hand with some care, finally said, 'Three clubs.' We looked at him in some surprise.

'You mean four clubs,' said His Excellency, whereupon the Swede studied his hand with considerable attention and after a long pause said, 'No, I mean three clubs.' It was immediately apparent that his ability to play bridge was about as good as mine to play cricket. We were off to a good start!

The voyage proceeded. The fact that the niece had the next cabin to mine had me somewhat concerned to ensure that the communicating doors were properly bolted and everybody understood that I had bolted them, but nothing untoward happened, I am glad to report. In fact she could not have been more charming; the stories had obviously been more than a little embellished. I believe that she and the Swede spent a very pleasant passage home (as did the rest of us indeed) during which His Excellency confided in me that he was very disappointed in the bearing and conduct of Naval Officers who came to into Rio. I was able greasingly to assure him that, like very other aspect of life, Naval Officers were a variable feast and undoubtedly, on occasion, having been under some stress being at sea for considerable periods of time before coming into harbour, it was only natural that they should let their hair down.

On arrival in Southampton we parted the best of friends and I was now back home and ready to take up my next appointment.

14

Lossiemouth, West Raynham and Brawdy

After arriving in Southampton I went to see the Naval Appointer, to be told that I was to go up to Lossiemouth to take charge of two Vampire jet trainers with which I was to convert the then Sea Fury Squadrons based at Lossiemouth (802 and 804) on to jet aircraft, the Sea Hawk, with which the Navy was being re-equipped.

I parked Pepper and Brooke with my brother and sister-in-law, and proceeded to that then northern outpost of Naval aviation, Lossiemouth, which in those days was one of the most exciting and interesting stations to which to be attached. My first task was to find some accommodation.

It was always the case that those stations furthest away from centres of civilisation had the most life in them. Lossiemouth at that time was still a collection of wooden huts with old coke-fired stoves to keep you warm. The Mess was a rather larger wooden hut, and there was very little in the way of facilities on the base at all, apart from the flying facilities. Nevertheless, and perhaps because of this, morale and attitude to life were always of the highest order. The same was true of places like Brawdy in the remoteness of Wales, and Culdrose in the remoteness of Cornwall.

I was greeted with the usual story that there was absolutely no accommodation and no prospects of getting any, but I finally found out that there were flats to be had, or rented, at a place called Inness House (which was in the 'circuit' of Milltown, the satellite aerodrome to Lossiemouth), and a very imposing house it was. I saw the bailiff and was told, yes, there was a flat available over the stable, and this I could have if I wished. It was a bit like a railway carriage, with a long corridor running down one side overlooking the stable yard; branching off it, starting from the left, was a kitchen with a Rayburn cooker, and then a bedroom, and at the end a living room. Well, that would be good enough for us for my stay there, thought I, so I took it. On the next weekend available I went down to collect Pepper, who was making urgent nest-like noises that she wished to be re-accommodated away from my relatives as soon as possible. So it was, that I collected her and Brooke and the 1936 Buick Straight Eight, which my brother had traded against the Kaiser Fraser in order to pay for Pepper's operation whilst she had been in Florida and I had been in the Falklands. With this car loaded to the gunwales we proceeded north to Lossiemouth.

One thing that I had omitted to tell Pepper was that the Rayburn stove in the kitchen was the only form of heating in the entire flat, apart from open coal fires, that is. Pepper managed to survive by wrapping herself up in practically all the clothes she possessed, and spending most of her time actually sitting on the Rayburn. It was another great Naval experience. It really was freezing cold, and getting into bed at night was quite a performance since, although we already had a hot-water bottle, it was down in Cornwall and I was too mean (or skint) to invest in another! So the procedure we adopted was that I would get into bed and scream with pain as I warmed up the freezing sheets, and then roll over and scream again while Pepper leapt into the bit that I had warmed up. All part of the rich tapestry of life! Brooke, who was then four years old, proceeded to endear herself to the local Scottish gentry on the first morning by leaning out of the window and greeting a small, but obviously important youth who was being conveyed along by his nanny and who was wearing a kilt, with those famous words, 'Hello, little girl.' But we survived.

We still owned the house at Helston, near Culdrose, which is about as far away as you could imagine from Lossiemouth. It was rented, and until I could get the tenants out at the expiration of their tenancy we were not able to use it. Finally this was achieved, and I moved Pepper and Brooke back down to Helston and installed them in our little semi-detached house. I was able to get down there most weekends by flying one of the Vampire trainers, with long-range tanks attached, direct from Lossiemouth to Culdrose. None of the nonsense of airways in those days, you just got it up to 32,000 feet and flew in the direction you wished to go.

My flying companion in the task of converting the Squadron was Bill Newton, and we were both QFIs, and the Vampire was an easy aeroplane to fly. The pilots coming from the Squadrons were competent, so it didn't take long to get them through their conversion course, but the two Squadrons had rather different outlooks on life.

One episode comes to mind. The CFI at Lossiemouth at that time was a QFI, but of a lower grade than mine, and I was therefore surprised when the 'trappers' came round that I was put up for check. The 'trappers' were members of a team of QFIs from the Empire Flying School, who came round to check on the qualifications and flying training ability of Qualified Flying Instructors. As an A1, which is an exceptional rating, I don't think one was supposed to be

Briefing pilots of 802 Squadron at Lossiemouth

subjected to the examinations that these chaps conducted, but nevertheless I could hardly object and I duly flew with a Flight Lieutenant. After we landed he said, 'There's no doubt in my mind that you are still an A1 instructor but if I did have a criticism of your manner, I would say it was a little brusque.' To which I replied, 'Have you ever instructed Sub Lieutenants in the Royal Navy?'

'No,' said he.

'Then if you had,' said I, 'you'd be a little brusque too!'

After about six months the job was complete, in fairly record time, and I was then available for a further posting. I enquired of the Appointers whether it would be possible to get command of a Squadron, but was told, 'No, no, no,' I was far too junior for this, even though I had now collected my half-stripe on time, but perhaps I could get a job as a senior pilot in a year or so. Meantime, I was to be sent to the Naval Air Fighter Development Unit at West Raynham in Norfolk. This meant another move and another search for accommodation, and I duly departed to West Raynham to be greeted once again by the usual story. 'No, sorry old boy, there's absolutely no accommodation around here at all, you're wasting your time.' Nevertheless, I very quickly discovered that there were flats to be had at a price at Weasenham Hall, which was near Fakenham and not too far from West Raynham. I found a flat in what had been the nursery wing of the large, old and rather rundown house owned by Major Cooke. It was quite light and spacious and, apart from the fact that you could only bath twice a week, because that was when they flashed the boilers up, seemed to be as good as anything I was likely to get.

I sent for Pepper and collected her once again from Cornwall, but this time with all our American equipment: a deep-freeze, a refrigerator and an electric range, together with various other bits and pieces, including two barrels of china. Pepper was delighted that we were together again and expressed her pleasure at entering the flat and the nice light airy living room in which were two very large casement windows. It being a nice sunny day when she arrived, she opened one of the windows which promptly dropped straight into the courtyard below – it had rusted off its hinges!

The flat had its own separate meter and I connected up all our electrical equipment to the transformers that we had to carry around. I remember walking down the stairs after I turned everything on to see the meter about to behave like a flying saucer in a perspiration-line case, as it tried to revolve fast enough to count all the electricity that was now flowing through the circuit which, quite clearly, must have been totally overloaded!

There occurred at West Raynham one of those episodes which scars you and affects you for the rest of your life, if you're human. It was during this stay that Pepper once again became pregnant and I came home one day to find her looking very pale and wan, and she had taken to her bed. I asked what all this was about, and she had started to lose the baby. I therefore got hold of the local doctor, whose panel we were on, and he finally came out and said, 'yes, well, she'd better just stay in bed.' Pepper took an instant dislike to him. She and the medical profession have never been on the easiest of terms and for very good reason, from her point of view, but I must say this chap with his somewhat unkempt and unwashed appearance did not either inspire her or me. I remember that the bedroom was wallpapered in paper that was actually covered in coloured parrots. Not the easiest thing to look at if you are incarcerated, as she was, all day in a somewhat grey and gloomy room. Time passed and she clearly was getting no better and I was becoming more and more worried. I therefore sought out the RAF doctor on the base and said, 'Look, I'm very worried about my wife's condition.' I briefly explained what it was and said, 'I really would be grateful if you could tell me which of the local doctors you think is best qualified.' he said, 'I'm sorry, but it's unethical for me to give you that information.' I was stunned. He was a fellow serving Officer and here was a colleague who was clearly in some trouble, and the other guy was standing on ceremony. I glowered but then, realising that wasn't going to get me anywhere, I phrased my question slightly differently.

'Let me put it this way,' said I, 'If your wife was in a similar situation, which local doctor would you recommend.'

'Oh,' he said, 'in that case, I'd recommend Doctor So and So.' I called Doctor So and So, whom I recall came round in an old Bentley, and I promptly discharged the other one.

The new doctor took one look at Pepper, picked up the phone, the ambulance came and she was taken off to hospital. There, I am sad to say, we lost the baby, the second disaster in trying to have a family since the birth of Brooke. Not a happy occurrence. Pepper was very rundown after this and the weather really didn't help very much, even though it was a clear, sunny day elsewhere, there seemed to be a perpetual mist and fog hanging over that part of Norfolk. But time passed and I settled in to work at the Naval Air Fighter Development Unit, and weekly we would go into Swaffham or Fakenham to do our shopping. It was not a too unpleasant existence – no television, plenty of radio, and lots of card games. The tranquillity was broken after a few weeks, however, by a summons to go back to the Appointer in London who said, and surprise, surprise, to be told 'Lygo, we have a Squadron for you, a new Seahawk Squadron to be formed at Brawdy and destined to embark in the new carrier *Ark Royal*, and you will go as Commanding Officer.' And who should be my senior pilot but my old friend from Culdrose days, 'Spiv' Leahy. I was delighted, but I had to do the Day Fighters Leaders' Course at West Raynham before this happened, which was no particular difficulty except that, of course, it was run by a lot of what I called at the time, and still do, short-arsed Squadron Leaders who were absolutely ace at pulling masses of G, and destroying all the students by 'jumping' them and 'bouncing' them as we exercised in the fighter and fighter defence roles. In those days the RAF rejoiced in limit flying and we used to do a thing called a snake climb and a snake descent with sixteen Meteors leaping up through the cloud, out of the top to do aerial combat and then come snaking back down on VHF bearings to break out and come in a stream landing on the runway, usually with extremely little fuel left on either side, 30/30 being quite adequate, 20/20 and even 10/10 being the norm (gallons that is).

It was clear to me that before very long something rather nasty was going to happen. And it did. Sometime after I left the course, the weather closed in, those airborne didn't have enough fuel and a large number of aircraft were lost. Whilst I was there, another tragedy overtook the station. The Commandant was my old friend from Central Flying School, Group Captain Stevenson who, sad to relate, during my time at West Raynham, went off to the United States to fly some US aircraft and was killed, I think, flying an F84 or F86; another tragic occurrence in the annals of the Royal Air Force.

I survived the course and made many friends once again with my contemporaries in the RAF, who were to grow up with me, as I grew up in the Service, and finish up with various exotic appointments in the Ministry of Defence serving once again together; not always, it would appear, on the same side!

And so, leaving Norfolk behind, having traded the Straight Eight Buick for £150, which I placed on deposit on a secondhand Morris Minor, we proceeded once again via my brother and sister-in-law, having re-let the house in Helston, to Brawdy. Here again we faced the accommodation problem, but this time slightly better organised. As I was a Squadron Commander I was accorded a certain amount of priority and found myself in a Naval hiring in Langton Mansion, Fishguard. At this time the married quarters at Brawdy were just in the process of being built.

Soon after arriving at Brawdy I was invited to attend the commissioning of *Ark Royal* at Cammel Laird in Birkenhead where she had been built, and Pepper and I set off on this journey in the Morris Minor over the Welsh hills to Liverpool during a snow storm. It was an exciting journey clambering over the hills in this little motor car with the icy conditions that prevailed but we did make it into Liverpool and then Birkenhead and were finally there for the great occasion. The celebration of commissioning and the party afterwards was first class, but my meeting with the Captain, Dennis Cambell, the same Cambell I had told would have to stay back for some further flying after he arrived for a check at Lee-on-the-Solent, when I was an instructor in 759, could have been otherwise. He was not best pleased then, and when he saw me again he said, 'Ah, yes, Lygo, I remember you, you are the chap who practically grounded me.' I smiled meekly.'You're still here, Sir,' I said. He smiled back, not a man to harbour grudges, a charming and delightful man to have as one's Captain, to boot. Luck was with me once again.

800 Squadron forming with Sea Hawks was to be a twelve-aircraft F3 Squadron, a fighter Squadron, and we were to work up at Brawdy. We were destined to join HMS *Ark Royal*, the second of the large four-shaft, two-hangar aircraft carriers (the first being *Eagle*) to join the fleet since the end of the War. She was preparing to go on her first commission, operating out of Devonport. To form the Squadron the earliest Officers to arrive were 'Spiv' Leahy the senior pilot, Roger Heaton the Air Engineer Officer, and Sub-Lieutenant Berry the Air Electrical Officer. Spiv was an experienced, competent fighter pilot and an Air Warfare Officer to boot. Roger Heaton was a reasonably senior Air Engineer Officer, experienced and mature. The Electrical Officer was younger, a fairly reserved young Officer, and this was his first Squadron assignment. The four of us, therefore, went to the first dining-in night at Brawdy that I think they had had, with the new Captain and the new Commander. The Captain was Donald Gibson who had been the Commander Air at Culdrose, and this was his first Captain's Command. Commander Air was 'Winkle' Brown.

The dining-in night proceeded along fairly traditional Fleet Air Arm lines. We entered to the sound of the Royal Marine orchestra and took our places at table; my Squadron being placed at one of the wing tables from the head table, having my three Officers clustered around me. The other Squadron, 807, were on the other wing and they were fully manned under the Command of Peter Hutton. Soon after the meal had started the bread rolls began to fly and the Commander stood up and banged the gavel and said, 'Now look, settle down chaps, we don't want any more of this rowdy behaviour.' This only served to increase the volume of missiles that were whizzing about the place. This prompted Winkle Brown to come round to me, getting up from his place alongside the guest of honour, who was the Dean of St David's Cathedral, and to say to me, 'Keep your Squadron in order.' I was somewhat surprised; as I have described I had a fairly mature bunch sitting right under my eyes and we had not been responsible for the launching of any of the missiles at that stage in the proceedings!

The evening proceeded along well-worn lines with the speeches and fairly roisterous interjections coming from the members of the Wardroom. It wasn't long before the fireworks started going off; the thunder flashes were an extremely popular entertainment and diversion at dining-in nights at this time. The Commander, realising that things were getting even further out of hand, stood up at this point and said very firmly that there would be no more fireworks. His timing was immaculate because the firework that actually accompanied his final statement must have been thrown at the beginning of his statement and as he said the words, 'there will be no more fireworks' he disappeared with a loud bang as the firework exploded right behind him. Not exactly conducive to good order and Naval discipline.

The next morning I was asked to go and see the Commander and went down to the Wardroom to meet him. He was new to the Fleet Air Arm and new to the Station and he started by asking me for some advice. He said, 'I understand you are a very upright Naval Officer, Lygo, and I wish to have your advice as to how to handle affairs of the kind that we had last night. It was the most disgraceful dining-in night I have ever been to. Don't you agree?'

'Well, Sir,' said I, 'it's about par for the course these days.'

'Well,' said he, 'do you realise that the Dean of St David's was hit by a grape before he had had a chance to start on his soup?'

'Well,' I said, 'I think we should think ourselves lucky under the circumstances, Sir, that it wasn't a grapefruit.' He looked at me in amazement.

'But, I mean, how do you suggest I control this situation?'

'You can only control it,' said I 'through the Squadron Commander, Sir. You must make it clear to the Squadron Commander that his future, his career and his comfort depend upon him controlling the Squadron. You must allow them to let their hair down from time to time but when you say no, it is the Squadron Commander who must make sure his pilots behave.' He thanked me and I continued back to the Squadron to start the formation of 800 Squadron.

The pilots gradually began to arrive to make up the team that I was to lead for the next eighteen months. They were, of course, by then all straight-stripe RN Officers, some short-service but a good stiffening of general-list RN Officers, and we had a good and formidable team. I proceeded to apply all the lessons I had learned from my previous commands and also some of the experiences I had had watching other people in command. As an A1 qualified Flying Instructor, I was particularly concerned with safety. I did not wish to see anyone harmed in my Squadron, certainly not to lose anybody, and therefore I knew that strict discipline would be required to ensure that the highest possible standards were maintained. Because of my experiences during the War and thereafter, I was also very strict with regard to drink, and made it an order within the Squadron that there was to be no drinking at all when flying was to take place within twenty-four hours of flying, which meant that the lads could really only let their hair down and have a drink on a Friday or Saturday evening prior to starting flying again on the Monday. These were harsh rules by the standards of the time, but I was quite determined to keep a firm control on the amount of alcohol that was consumed in my Squadrons. I had seen enough death and disaster wrought by excesses of alcohol in the past to make me inflexible on the subject.

The aircraft arrived, the work-up proceeded, formation flying, combat patrol exercises, air-to-air firing, air-to-ground gunnery, low-level bombing, dive bombing, all the things of which the Sea Hawks was capable and, of course, instrument flying in all the kinds of weather that Brawdy and West Wales could throw at one. Meantime, the married quarters were being completed and the time came for us to move from Langton Mansion to our new married quarters in Haverfordwest.

Before this, on one special occasion I was Duty Officer in Command at the Air Station when a hurricane struck. Now we are not used to having hurricanes in the United Kingdom but I can assure you this was a genuine hurricane. Subsequent readings on the ammeter of the control tower showed winds of 130mph that night. It had started reasonably quietly with the ordinary kind of West Wales storm blowing, but as it progressed it got worse and worse and worse and the Nissen-hutted camp which was Brawdy began to disintegrate in the storm. Bits of accommodation huts flew off, the pieces of corrugated iron whipping through the air were lethal weapons and I finally ordered all Officer accommodation to be evacuated and for the Officers to congregate in the Mess, which was still standing. The First Lieutenant meantime was out running lashings over the top of the main dining hall, where we had assembled all the Ratings, whose accommodation was disintegrating, hoping they would be secure. I issued instructions that there should be no movement outside for fear of damage caused by the flying debris. We had, just before this event, completed writing the Squadron orders for publication, one of the mandatory requirements for a newly-formed squadron, and all the old-fashioned Gestetner purple duplicating skins were piled on my desk ready to be scrutinised by me the following morning before they were put on the machine and copies run off.

At about midnight or thereafter I was told that there was one Officer, Lieutenant Commander William Orr-Cobben, my ex-senior pilot who was the Lieutenant Commander Flying, still in his cabin which was disintegrating around him and he was refusing to move. I therefore decided to go and personally convince Bill that he should come into the comparative safety of the Wardroom itself and not stay in his rain-sodden bed. In order to protect myself, and I don't know why because it would be pretty useless, I put a wastepaper basket – one of those wicker ones – over my head, but I suppose it gave me some moral comfort rather than being of any practical value and I went out braving the storm with one other Officer and tried to get into the block into which Orr-Cobben was sleeping. The whole end of the building was in a state of collapse and we couldn't get the door open, but by walking round the outside of the building we were able to step over the walls which had collapsed at the other end and enter Orr-Cobben's cabin with comparative ease. Bill was fast asleep, tucked down into the bed under the remnants of the roof which had collapsed around him.

'Bill,' I said, 'you will have to get up and come into the Wardroom.'

'Why?' said he. 'I'm perfectly comfortable here.'

'You may be,' said I, ' but I don't think I can allow you to stay in these conditions at the moment; you will have to get up and come with me, Bill.' With great reluctance Bill dragged himself out of his pit and eventually accompanied me back into the comparative safety of the Wardroom.

Next morning the place was a sight to behold. The little village of Solva nearby had been badly damaged. On the aerodrome itself, most of the temporary buildings had been demolished or severely damaged and to cap it all when we got back to the Squadron the following morning we found there were numerous holes in the roofing of the office structure, one of which appeared directly over my desk and water had poured in onto the Gestetner duplicated standing orders, which sat as a soggy mauve lump in the middle of my saturated desk.

I ordered the Squadron into immersion suits and we proceeded to do such repairs as we could. Fortunately for us the hangars themselves, which were of a more modern construction, had withstood the test of the storm and so the aircraft themselves were not damaged. As I laboured up on the roof of my office block trying to get slabs of temporary material over the holes in the roof the 'phone rang and somebody in my office said, 'It's your wife, Sir' and passed the 'phone to me through the hole in the roof.

'Yes, darling,' I said answering the 'phone. Pepper sounded surprised, 'Did you know we had a dreadful storm last night?' she said.

'Yes, darling, I did know that.'

'Well, I can't get down the driveway, there is a tree blocking it and I am stuck in the house.'

'Well, I will be home as soon as I can, darling, but we have had quite a lot of damage here at the Air Station as well. As soon as I can get away I will be home.' Once again the division of time between the family and profession was hard to take but nevertheless I had to sweat it out until all was secure in the office before getting into my Morris Minor and weaving my way back to Langton Mansion where, indeed, the whole drive was blocked by an enormous tree. The house itself, however, had not suffered any damage and the inhabitants were safe. A tractor was procured and dragged the tree sideways so that we could get past it and up to the house. If you want to pick a day to have duty, try to avoid being the Duty Lieutenant Commander at an Air Station when a hurricane hits it and proceeds to blow it away.

It was now time to start formation aerobatics. In those days we were required to provide, or those of us who were keen enough, formation aerobatic teams to go to various Air Shows around the country, and we decided that we would have a formation six. The members of the team were Alastair Campbell, Mike Darlington, 'Tubby' Morse, 'Spiv' Leahy, Brian Toomey, and myself. My method of practising was to take them up to a safe altitude, say five or six thousand feet, and to carry out the manoeuvres at a set level of, say, 4,000 feet, and to make sure that every time we came out of the manoeuvre we had 500 feet in hand. In other words, we would start a loop at 4,000 feet and I would aim to finish it at 4,500 feet, so I knew that I had 500 feet in hand in every manoeuvre when I eventually brought them down to ground level. We did the usual things, loops, barrel-rolls, steep turns, and Spiv then decided that in order to brighten up the display, because when you were wheeling around with a formation six it took some time to get the aircraft back again to do the next manoeuvre in front of the crowd, it would be best if we broke the formation into a formation four after we had done a couple of simple manoeuvres, and then two would break off and do individual aerobatics in between the time in which I was turning the major formation back round to come in again.

This we proceeded to do and eventually Spiv said that he was ready to come in and do his solo act, low level, once he had finished it at a safe altitude. I said, 'Fine, get permission to do so from Air Traffic and then when you come in make sure, before you come over the airfield, that you have 500 feet in hand in every manoeuvre you do so that you know that you are perfectly safe if something goes wrong.'

We took off, the two broke away as previously arranged, we completed our practice and then came in for a formation-four landing. Having touched down and rolled to a halt at the end of the runway, turned off and started taxiing, I removed my oxygen mask because I was fairly hot, opened the hood and at that moment heard 'Spiv' call for permission to enter the circuit to carry out an aerobatic demonstration. This was approved. He came roaring in over the airfield, did a very slow roll, and as he was upside down, just about in the middle of the airfield, his engine quit. He pushed the stick forward, rolled the aeroplane out, shot up into the circuit, pulled around and called for an emergency landing. I was now barrelling along the taxi-way trying to get the oxygen mask strapped back on my face one-handed so I could

218

Seahawks of 800 in formation

call the tower because the answer he had received was, 'Wait', which was the kind of standard Air Traffic Control response to an emergency. Pan, pan, pan downwind for engine off landing. He brought the aeroplane round, blew the flaps down, blew the undercarriage down, and made a perfect landing on the runway.

By this time I was taxiing back into dispersal, and there waiting for me already hacking at the stones with his stick was the Captain, Donald Gibson. As I got out of the aeroplane he came over to me and said, 'What happened?' I said, 'I don't know, Sir, I know he had an engine failure and I think he has just conducted one of the most brilliant pieces of airmanship that I've seen and certainly something that thoroughly deserves a green endorsement.' 'I quite agree,' said Donald, and got into his car and disappeared.

'Winkle' Brown arrived. 'What happened, Lygo?' 'I really don't know, Sir,' I said. 'I only know that he had an engine failure inverted over the airfield and that he then carried out a most remarkable recovery and put the aeroplane down safely – an exceptional piece of airmanship.' Winkle looked at me and then said, 'Are you saying that you couldn't have done that?' I was taken aback. 'Well, I wouldn't wish to bet on it, Sir,' I said. 'Oh, really,' he said. 'I see. Well, I understand he wasn't authorised to carry out that display anyway.' 'Well, I heard him ask for permission, Sir,' said I, 'and it was granted,' 'Yes,

but I don't think the Control Tower knew what they were saying.'
'That may be the case,' I said, and he departed. Spiv came in and we
discovered subsequently that in the Seahawk at that time any period
of inverted flight with negative G could cause the fuel trap to fail and
the engine to be starved of fuel and the engine stop. Modifications
were then carried out to all Seahawks to prevent this occurrence.

The wheels of justice at Brawdy ground slowly and eventually I was
told that the Captain had decided to log Alan Leahy for disobeying
airfield standing orders in carrying out an unauthorised air display
which meant his name would be entered in the ship's log and would be
recorded against him in his record. I was astonished. Here was
something which deserved nothing short of a green endorsement and a
pat on the back for having saved an aircraft and performed brilliantly
and now the whole thing had been turned, through the intervention of
Mr 'Winkle' Brown, into something which was not particularly
pleasant.

When the moment came for Spiv to arrive in the Captain's office I
went with him to witness this occasion. We entered the Captain's
office where Donald was standing fairly nervously, ready to log Alan
Leahy.

'Well,' said he, 'I have decided to log you, Leahy, for a breach of
airmanship and airfield discipline and I want you to sign here.' I spoke
up for the first time, 'If you are logging Leahy, Sir, you will have to
log me too.'

'Why is that?' barked Donald looking at me. 'Why is that?'

'Because I authorised the flight, Sir, and if it was an unauthorised
flight then I should be logged as well because I have broken airfield
regulations also.' Donald looked at the two of us for a moment in
exasperation and then said, 'Get out the pair of you.' And we
departed.

The work-up proceeded apace and we had, I think, a first-class
Squadron. Spiv was a great innovator and decided that we would
emulate the example of the earliest 800 Squadron in the Fleet Air Arm
by painting our fins red. Without any authority, because to ask for
authorisation is always a dangerous precedent especially if you are
likely to be answered with a 'No', we painted all the fins red and Spiv,
who has a somewhat artistic touch, painted the 0 which was the letter
designate of *Ark Royal*, on the fin. We went further and had all our
drop tanks painted red. We had started something and in order to
identify each person's aircraft, mine being 100, instead of a one being
pained on the nosewheel door we had two-and-a-half stripes painted
on it to indicate the Squadron Commander. It was all good stuff, good
for morale and we had a first-rate team, strictly disciplined, so much so

that they got the nickname of 'The Hitler Youth'. Nevertheless I was determined that should we be called upon to perform we would be the best the Navy had.

One close call and a near miss, I recall, at Brawdy was when we were invited by Commander Air of *Ark Royal*, Mike Fell, to go down to pay a visit to the ship and make our number with the various Officers on board. The whole ship was being run in an extremely friendly and efficient and effective manner. *Ark Royal* had always had a reputation for high morale and it was easy to see that this was going to be continued throughout the life of this ship. In order to get down to Plymouth from Brawdy we borrowed the Station Domine, a de Havilland twin-engined biplane which carried about six passengers, and with Spiv and the Air Engineer Officer and the Air Electrical Officer as passengers and myself driving it we departed for Roborough. Before we took off Spiv asked me, 'Have you flown one of these before?'

'Yes,' I said, 'I flew one at West Raynham,' which would have been some time before, since when I had been flying slightly faster aeroplanes. On arrival at Roborough therefore, which at that time was a fairly short grass field and finished up sloping rather steeply down towards I don't know where, I completed my circuit and came in on the approach. It was only then that I began to wonder what the right approach speed was in a Domine! Well, I thought, if I come in at about 80 I'm bound to be all right, and slow down to about 65 as we come over the fence. The trouble was the Domine had no intention of slowing down and there wasn't much of a means of getting it to slow down once you had got speed. The net result was that I floated gracefully across practically the whole length of Roborough before touching down at the end, disappearing down the slope out of view of the Control Tower. As the hedge at the far end of the slope loomed up, I did the only thing that was possible, I applied practically full power on the port engine, full right rudder and the aeroplane then did a graceful ground loop finishing up facing back up the hill. Somewhat shaken by this experience I taxied the aircraft back up to the top and we all looked at each other and knew that disaster had not been far off – not a serious one but one that would not only have damaged the aeroplane but my reputation on arrival at my new ship, another life gone!

There are many stories I could tell about Brawdy, of the kindnesses of Donald Gibson and Marjorie, his wife. It was a gorgeous summer while we were there, of parties on the beach, of collecting wild bilberries on the Prescelly hills, of the amazing revelation I had when all the Form 206s (that is the Confidential Reports on Officers, which had to be written up before we embarked in *Ark Royal*) were returned to me for signature by the Captain's Assistant Secretary, only to discover that the last one in the heap was my own, which she'd sent back to me in error. I was thus able to read (of course I would, wouldn't I) all that had been said about me by my immediate superiors and the corrections that had been made by the Captain, and so I was fully aware of exactly what my report had actually been in the beginning, and how it had finished up, made all the more interesting some time later when I was promoted Commander to receive a congratulatory letter from someone who claimed a degree of responsibility – whom I knew didn't warrant it!

Memories of Tubby Morse coming back with a sack of cockles freshly dug out of the sands of Newgale Beach and the satisfactory progress made by Pepper through her third pregnancy under the unforgiving eye of the local doctor, who was a most conscientious man with very little sense of humour but a great dedication to his profession. I was very relieved to leave Pepper in his capable hands when the time came to embark. Subsequently, while we were in *Ark Royal*, she was safely delivered of our first boy, a Welshman to boot. The memory of our dining-out night, when the Wardroom dined us out on the night before we were due to embark and the Captain, Donald, made a somewhat impassioned speech during which he said, 'tomorrow we shall see the departure of the cream of the Fleet Air Arm,' a very flattering observation to be made about 800 Squadron, but the whole thing turned into an absolute hoot when the strident voice of Orr-Cubben was heard coming from somewhere at the back of the Wardroom: 'the cream of today is the cheese of tomorrow.' It brought the house down!

The embarked period in *Ark Royal* was a happy one and a busy one. We were the first Seahawk Squadron to embark in a carrier, and we had an active programme ahead of us. From a brief work-up in the Irish Sea we proceeded down through the Bay of Biscay into the Mediterranean, stopping at Gibraltar, and then it was almost continuous exercises in the Mediterranean until we returned to the UK after some six months, during which time Pepper was delivered of our third child, Derek. For the first time, when I left her once again pregnant and barefooted, I was at least relaxed because the doctor who was taking care of her was a very serious and dedicated man and I knew that she would be in safe hands. We were able to carry on with our formation aerobatics demonstrations from the ship from time to time, as well as carrying out good weapon-training exercises and air combat.

While the ship was in Grand Harbour at Valetta and we were disembarked at Halfar, we arranged to have an air-to-air combat exercise with the RAF Meteor squadron that was there. We agreed to meet over Malta at 30,000-plus feet and take it from there. We began the exercise but before long there was a cry of 'Mayday, Mayday, Mayday' from Stair Campbell, whose centre tank fire-warning light had come on. There had been some equivocal orders from Their Lordships as regards what to do about this, but I had told the Squadron that it was mandatory to bale out. He promptly did so, which brought the whole of the fighter combat exercise to a rather rapid conclusion! Fortunately, he was perfectly all right and the aircraft disappeared somewhere into the Mediterranean off Malta. It was, in my opinion, extraordinary to have an instruction which said that 'fire warning light' meant that you probably had a fire in your central tank but that you should wait to see whether in fact the fire developed! Can you believe it? He didn't, quite rightly, but it did put some pressure behind getting a modification out to ensure that we were not faced with this problem again.

We also started night flying and this was the first night catapulting and deck landing that the Squadron had done. The first night of the operation, and I recount elsewhere the episode that preceded it, I was the first one off to be launched; it was not quite dark at this stage, and when I came, back on again Spiv asked me what it had been like.

'Fine,' I said, 'no problem at all.' He was on the last detail and was launched just after midnight. When he came back (he is normally quite pale-faced but was looking slightly paler) I said, 'Well, how did it go?'

'Oh, no problem at all,' he said. The following night the order of launch changed, I was going last, he went first. After I had manned the aircraft and was ready for the launch, it was of course pitch dark; there was no light at all, and as the catapult fired and I felt myself hurtling into the blackness, I grabbed the head of the control column slightly tighter than I was used to and uttered one expletive, 'Jesus Christ!' and eventually climbed away. When I came back and landed, Spiv was waiting for me. We both looked at each other and started to laugh. 'What did you say?' he asked.

'I said "Jesus Christ",' I said.

'So did I,' said he.

The other Seahawk squadron was 894. Their gimmick was to wear bowler hats when they landed on, and to stir up the rivalry which existed between the two Squadrons, I came up with the idea of arranging for them, supposedly, to have a television interview in Naples. The Staff Aviation Officer in those days was Freddie Stovin Bradford and I knew he was coming out to visit us and would be joining in Naples, and I asked him if he could get hold of some notepaper from Italian television and bring it on board, which he duly did. How he managed it I'm not quite sure but knowing Freddie most things were possible. We then typed a letter to the CO of 894 purporting to come from the Italian television studio asking them if they would be prepared to appear on Italian television, complete with their bowler hats, which from an Italian point of view seemed to be synonymous with the way we Brits were supposed to dress. The date was set for the next ship visit to Naples and so I organised for a special boat to get Ted Anson ashore to organise a fleet of cabs to collect them to take them to the so-called television studio, but in fact to take them to the nearest whore-house where they were going to be welcomed by the local ladies and photographed in the process of going in there. I really couldn't believe my good luck when it all worked out. We got the boat away, Ted got them organised, they disappeared off, they were all duly photographed and a small piece appeared subsequently in the *Daily Express*, who happened to have a reporter on board. It helped to spice things up.

It was during this embarked period in *Ark Royal* that another special event took place: I was launched while the ship was turning at South Railway Jetty in Portsmouth harbour, the first time a jet aircraft was launched in harbour. I recount the episode because I had forgotten it until I found myself at a dinner party with a chap who said to me, 'I remember you being launched while the ship was turning in Portsmouth harbour.'

'Not me,' I said, 'I don't recall any such episode.'

'But I can assure you,' he said, 'I was the Launching Officer and you were in a Sea Hawk, and it was the first time we'd launched one in harbour while the ship was virtually stationary but actually turning off the berth.'

'Are you sure?' I said.

'Yes, yes, I'm quite certain,' said he.

'Was I launched straight towards the armament depot at Priddy's Hard?' I asked.

'Yes,' he said, 'you were.'

'Then I do remember it,' I said, 'because I remember thinking to myself, "if I don't make it and go in there, there's going to be the biggest bang Portsmouth's heard in a long time".' We did it again in Grand Harbour while we were moored just inside the breakwater, the whole point of these exercises being to demonstrate that an aircraft carrier's main task was to get her aeroplanes airborne. Both Mike Fell, our Commander Air, and the Captain, Dennis Campbell, had lived through a period when we had seen, as I recount in a later chapter, the tragedies that can overtake a carrier if it doesn't have its aircraft airborne. To be able to launch them stationary, or in a harbour, so that you could have air protection when you sailed, was an important feature of that time.

It was a great commission, a great and happy time, as time was always spent in *Ark Royal* and I was able to contrast it, to some extent, with my experience with the US 6th Fleet – both were happy experiences, but with a totally different type of training role for the aircrew embarked.

15

Staff Aviation Officer

One of my most exciting and enjoyable experiences was to be asked by Admiral Charles Evans, a distinguished Naval aviator who was Flag Officer Aircraft Carriers, to become his Staff Aviation Officer. We had, at that time, seven aircraft carriers: the *Ark Royal*, the *Eagle*, the *Victorious*, the *Hermes*, the *Albion*, the *Bulwark* and the *Centaur*, of which no less than four and sometimes five would be at sea and operating at one time. One would always be undertaking a long refit, sometimes as long as two or three years, and of the others one or two would be on short refits of six months or so. The complement of aircraft, at that time, were normally Sea Hawks, Venoms, Gannets and Whirlwind helicopters for air-sea rescue.

It was a super job in many ways, first because I was working for a delightful Admiral with a tremendous sense of humour and fun, and, second because it gave me as a professional aviator an opportunity to bring the standards of flying and combat readiness of the Fleet Air Arm up to the very highest. I had had one job as a Commander, having been newly promoted from serving on Admiral Evans's staff when he was Flag Officer Flying Training, and I had stayed in flying practice and had done a conversion course on to the Scimitar, the new, large, strike/fighter aircraft that was then the kind of flagship of the Fleet Air Arm.

The first ship in which the Admiral hoisted his flag was *Victorious*, which had come out of a major refit to be fitted with an angled deck and the new radar 984 CDS. She was an extremely well-run ship where many new ideas and innovations were introduced into the fleet. She was exceptionally clean; her Supply department was extremely well run; the Seamen department was well run, as were Engineering and Electrical, but unfortunately she didn't have a very good Air department, particularly important as they were to operate the Scimitar, just coming into service, the first aircraft we had that could carry a nuclear bomb. It was considered fairly normal, in those days, to put as Commanding Officer or senior pilot of a new aircraft entering operational service the test pilot who had been at Boscombe Down and whose responsibility it had been to get the aircraft accepted by the

226

Service. The problem with this particular concept was that it was not always possible for the chap concerned to remember that he was to stop test flying the aircraft and start flying it as an operational aircraft. It certainly was the case with Scimitar, which was the largest aeroplane we had attempted to operate but, as Dickie Reynolds put it quite succinctly to me at a later occasion, 'the Scimitar has not replaced the aeroplane.' It wasn't a happy situation and difficult for the Captain perhaps to grasp because it really didn't matter how good the rest of the ship was, if they couldn't operate their aircraft they weren't effective. As a result the Commander Air had to be relieved and when John Treacher came as the new Commander Air things began to improve. Having done my Scimitar conversion course, I was becoming a little concerned that if I didn't get to do some deck operation in it fairly soon I would be out of practice to demonstrate that the Scimitar was just another aircraft.

I managed to get some further practice in dummy deck landings at North Front at Gibraltar when the ship was there but I began to realise there was no clear incentive on the part of the ship to let me fly the aeroplane for fairly obvious reasons. Service aviation is a strange

Charles Evans hands over FOAC to Richard Smeeton

world. Some people become pilots in order to further their career – if that was a fashionable specialisation. Once having achieved promotion to Commander or Wing Commander they can be persuaded that they should no longer continue to fly for whatever reason suits their book. Wives sometimes come into it! Some, having volunteered for flying duties find they don't like it – and bail out at the first face-saving opportunity. Some are overtaken by events.

Classic examples of this were those chaps who were made prisoners of war early on, flying biplanes. When they emerged from the bag not only did they have to restore their general self-confidence but they found that aviation had moved on – jet aircraft were entering service and they found it impossible to make the transition. There was often therefore a resentment against someone who continued to fly beyond the period he was required to because he or she happened to like it and remained competent to do it.

There is always a way of solving problems if you refuse to let them beat you. I therefore asked the Admiral to make a signal to the ship to the effect that an aircraft was to be provided. This was done, and I shot off in the Scimitar to do my deck qualification. It was a great tank of an aeroplane but easy to fly on the approach because it had a good forward view, and once you had settled it down at the right speed it just sat there and you could motor it all the way in until you banged on to the deck and caught a wire. The advantage, of course, with an angled deck was that if you didn't catch a wire, or if you didn't want to catch a wire and just do some landings, then you could take off again straight down the angle without interfering with the deck park for'ard. I whistled round and did the necessary number of qualifying deck landings and then came in for a final landing.

The chap who had been designated as the first Squadron Commander of the Scimitar Squadron was one Des Russell, a man I knew very well and for whom I had a high regard, and tragically on the first embarkation after he'd landed he looked down into the cockpit to tidy things up before taxiing forward. The Scimitar had a fairly high nose attitude after landing and although visibility was quite good you were very high compared with the aircraft we were used to operating, and I think as Des cleaned up the cockpit he probably (almost certainly) failed to recognise that he was rolling steadily forward towards the edge of the deck, and he went over. Tragically he did not get out of the aircraft and was not recovered. Unusually for that period, he was already a Commander and unusual that he should be bringing the Squadron aboard as a Commander, but he had done all the work up ashore, had been promoted, and was going to have his stint embarked. In other words, he was one of those who enjoyed his flying.

228

I was the next Commander to land that particular aircraft on and after my final landing.

As I taxied out of the gear, I applied both brakes to stop the aircraft and the port brake failed. The aircraft swung towards the island. I called 'Chocks, chocks, chocks' over the radio, shut both engines down and the aircraft came to a stop just before it collided with the island. If, on the other hand, the starboard brake had failed and only the port brake had been operating, I would almost certainly have gone over the side and followed Des Russell! However, it didn't happen and that was the end of that particular saga. The exercise served to show to *Victorious* that a Scimitar could be thrown around the circuit just like any other aeroplane and didn't have to make a bomber-like approach from three miles astern.

Victorious was the first ship to be fitted with 984 CDS, the big searchlight radar that had been invented at the Admiralty Surface Weapons Establishment. It had a proper radar display in the ops room and the air direction room which enabled you to monitor the movements of aircraft and not rely on the old antiquated hand plot. With 984 you could actually plot the position of all the aircraft on the radar screen, with their symbols coming up as you selected them for whatever purpose you might have. Ian Eastern was the Air Direction Officer who had been the Direction Officer in *Indefatigable* with me during the War. Ian had been shot down in the abortive raid on Dakar in the early stages of the war and had been captured by the French; he was at the time, I think, flying a Skua. Like most people who had been captured by the French, he had not had a very happy experience. He had not flown operationally again since he had left the 'bag', but was now one of the most competent Air Direction Officers that we possessed.

This was still the time when the Navy was having to justify itself continuously for its possession of aircraft to the RAF, (has it ever been otherwise?) and it was decided that three carriers (*Eagle, Centaur* and *Victorious*) were to make a simulated carrier attack on southern England, coming up through the Bay of Biscay. The RAF's task was in the defence of the UK to detect and stop us. The idea that a surface force could get within striking distance of the UK without being detected was, to some, laughable. We decided that we would operate the fleet entirely silently, putting our tanker and supply force out to seaward as a group appearing to operate aircraft. The real carriers were to fly out aircraft to orbit them under radar and radio silence and to simulate flying off and on the tankers as if they were in fact the carrier force, and we would slip through as merchant ships undetected closer inshore.

We really could not believe how successful this ploy was. It was extremely frustrating for the Direction Officers to have this super radar and not have it working, but if it was turned on it became a beacon to tell everybody exactly where we were. The plot worked extremely well, and lo and behold we had still not been detected nor attacked, despite the best efforts of the RAF, until we were just about in range of Cornwall. I therefore decided that we should fly off a Scimitar at maximum range to carry out a nuclear attack on a simulated target, Predanock in Cornwall, which was to represent Plymouth. At what point should we fly the aircraft off on this mission? It was critical that we got it away before we were detected, and I could hardly believe that we were remaining undetected for quite as long as we were. I figured out that the aircraft would actually go quite a lot further than we were being told, and so the great moment came, the aircraft was launched with the Squadron CO at the helm and disappeared into the distance.

Meanwhile, we were still radar and radio silent and waited with bated breath for him to come up on his return, calling that he had

Victorious, Centaur, Hermes

actually achieved the mission. It was a long wait and as the time passed when the normal range and endurance of the aircraft would have been thought to be just about at its limits, I was getting some fairly searching looks from some of the ship's Officers, and it was clear to me that if something was to go wrong it would be down to my account. However, right at the end of the period, a call was received, we lit up and brought the aircraft back on board. He still had adequate fuel, but it was a remarkably good mission to have planned and to have flown, and of course we could hardly wait to get back for the wash-up in Plymouth to demonstrate that a large Naval force had been able to approach within striking distance of the UK mainland without being detected or attacked by shore-based aircraft.

Our Admiral, Charles Evans, was a consummate actor and when the Commander-in-Chief Strike Command gave the RAF's account of what had happened (they had a plot which showed or attempted to show that they knew where the carriers were and had them under surveillance all the time) my Admiral didn't say anything until right at the end of the presentation when the wash-up was about to conclude, when he stood up and said, 'Just one final word.' Walking over to the large screened chart of the tracks of what was assumed to be the carriers he said, 'That was very interesting, Air Marshal.' He pointed to the target which had been put up by C-in-C Strike Command and said, 'Unfortunately, as every Naval Officer here knows, you were attacking the wrong target. These ships representing a task force were in fact supply ships, and the main carrier strike force was way over here and you never detected it before we launched the attack on Plymouth.'

It had been a masterly performance but what was the purpose of it? Quite simply, its aim was to counter the claim that carriers and a carrier task force would be readily detectable at sea and attacked by shore-based aircraft long before we were a threat, so making the validity of carrier-based air no longer justified. In this exercise, however, we had certainly demonstrated otherwise, and we did this on many other occasions. Unfortunately the RAF's propaganda machine was always very much better than ours, particularly when one realises that not all the Navy was united in defending the actions of its carrier strike force anyway. It was a continually frustrating experience which eventually ended in 'the carrier battle'.

One of the anomalies, or strangenesses, that prevailed in the command structure in the Navy at that time, was that the Flag Officer Aircraft Carriers who rejoiced in the NATO title of Commander Carrier Group Two was not entitled to fly his flag or to operate his ships outside the NATO area and at that time we had two carriers permanently based in the Far East. This was a source of friction between my Admiral and others concerned and it was seen to be stupid to us that when the carriers had been worked up and went out to the Far East they should be commanded by non-aviating type staffs who had very little experience, or capability, with regard to carrier operations. Towards the end of Charles Evans' time as Flag Officer Aircraft Carriers, however, it was decided he could go out and fly his flag in HMS *Centaur* (one of the carriers that was then on station) and to conduct an exercise with the ship and some inspections, and in fact to command the flotilla of ships that was there stationed and the way this was accomplished was by having the Commander-in-Chiefs Far East, Flag Officer Far East absent on leave or some other excuse.

So we flew out to Singapore and there joined HMS *Centaur*, the Admiral and the staff, for a deployment through the China Seas up to Hong Kong. Emotions ran high amongst the aviators at the time and as the Admiral's senior aviating Staff Officer I had my fair share of concern and irritation at the way in which we were excluded from this important area of operations. We conducted flying operations and inspections along the route which I had established on the way up and the squadrons in *Centaur* performed extremely well. FOFar East's flag ship at the time was HMS *Ceylon*, a Colony Class cruiser, but of course her Admiral was not embarked. The Captain of *Ceylon* was one Frank Twiss, later to become Second Sea Lord, the Captain of the *Centaur* was Horace Law, later to become Controller of the Navy and Flag Officer Sea Training when I went through with *Lowestoft*. Frank Twiss in turn became Flag Officer Flotillas Home Fleet, under whom I served when I was driving the *Lowestoft*. Flag Officer Flotillas Far East was Varyl Begg who was later to become the First Sea Lord. A fairly formidable combination of up-and-coming Officers and it was against this background that, when we arrived in Hong Kong, I conducted myself in a way which I cannot describe with any pride.

The night before the arrival, Admiral Evans had been conducting general drill with the other ships under his command, making sure that all these 'fish heads' should learn that aviation Admirals could be just as difficult as anybody else. At one stage he had the *Ceylon* taking a destroyer in tow at night by the stern and various other enterprising exercises which I am sure had thoroughly endeared himself to everybody. He was, however, an aviator, an outstanding aviator and one who was held in great respect, revered almost by all of us who worked around him or for him.

When we arrived in Hong Kong we berthed alongside the long jetty that was then part of the Naval Base, *Ceylon* on one side and

Centaur on the other, and *Centaur* gave a large party in the Wardroom that night to celebrate the conclusion of the flying exercise and arrival in Hong Kong. I have never been a hard or strong drinking type but the relief of the tension that had preceded the exercises that we had conducted and the presence of so many aviators led to a very good party indeed. One of the Squadron Commanders was Paddy McKeown, who apart from trying to open fire on one of the escorting destroyers with a 20-millimetre gun, also came up with a bright idea that we should haul down Flag Officer Far East's flag which was flying in *Ceylon* and run it up inferior to FOAC's which was of course flying in the *Centaur*. Obviously at the time I thought this a great idea, which gives a fair indication of my condition, and together we went aboard the *Ceylon*, nipped up to the flag deck, hauled down the Admiral's flag, Paddy stuffed it inside his jacket and we wandered nonchalantly off the ship and subsequently ran it up inferior to FOAC's. This was considered to be an extremely good joke. It was in fact a very dangerous one; you muck about with Admirals' flags at your peril and a later episode recounts one of the consequences of this act at a later stage in my career. But worse was to come. It was discovered at about one o'clock in the morning when we went out to survey our handiwork that somebody (the Officer of the Day, in fact) had very kindly, as he thought it, returned the flag to the *Ceylon* and there it was flying again. Now we come to our worst mistake. We decided that this wasn't good enough and we would do it again. This time, of course, the *Ceylon* was somewhat prepared and Royal Marine sentries had been posted. Nevertheless we managed to get on board, find our way up to the darkened flag deck and Paddy actually again managed to haul the flag down. He also managed to get ashore and I threw the flag to him, which he retrieved at the run on the jetty and departed back to the *Centaur*. Unfortunately I was now left on board, hotly pursued by a bunch of Marines. In the happy state of partial intoxication which I then obviously was in, I was totally unconcerned by this and proceeded to belt up the forecastle of the *Ceylon* with the firm intention of walking across the headrope. I got there and this I proceeded to do, thinking 'well, if I slip off I shall grab the rope and go hand over hand down to the other end.' Of course I hadn't gone more than four or five paces before this is exactly what happened, I nonchalantly grabbed the cable only to find it had been well and truly greased, it slipped from my grasp and I plummeted into Hong Kong harbour, narrowly missing a catamaran. It was reasonably warm and I swam the few yards to the jetty steps and clambered out, of course in mess undress, to be greeted by an Inspector of the Hong Kong Constabulary who looking at me somewhat critically as I stood dripping on the wharf-side said, 'Are you all right, Sir?'

'Yes,' I said, 'fine, thank you very much.'

'Well, you are bleeding rather badly,' he said. I had apparently struck my head on something as I had descended into the water. 'This is not a very clean harbour, Sir,' said he, 'I advise you to go into Sick Bay and get yourself a shot when you get back.'

'Yes, of course, thank you very much, Inspector,' I said and marched firmly off back on board *Centaur*. The object of the exercise had been achieved and it was now time for me to divest myself of these wet clothes and go to bed.

Next morning I woke up with the usual and expected thumping headache but also with a dark realisation of all that I had been up to the night before. It must be nice to be one of those people who can never remember what they've done; unfortunately it was all too clear to me and I decided that the first thing for me to do was to go and make a clean breast of it to my Admiral. I duly presented myself to Charles Evans and told him exactly what had happened and he laughed raucously.

'Very good,' he said, 'very good, well, no harm done.'

'Well, I'm afraid there is harm done, Sir,' said I, 'I think it's going to be difficult for Captain Law to live through the next encounter with his Flag Officer Flotillas, and I think it would be appropriate for me to go and apologise to the Captain of *Ceylon* for my behaviour last night.'

'Not necessary,' he said, 'quite unnecessary but if you feel like it of course that's entirely up to you.' I duly reported to Horace Law and said that I wished to apologise for my behaviour, that I had gone beyond the bounds of reasonableness in the stress of the moment and that I intended to go over and present my apologies to the Captain of the *Ceylon*. Horace was and is a delightful gentleman; he nodded to me gravely and said, 'Well, I think that's a wise course of action, Lygo,' and so I rang up the *Ceylon* and fixed for an appointment to go and call on the Captain Twiss.

On my arrival in *Ceylon* at about six o'clock that evening, as I went up the gangway I was greeted by an aviator who was under training aboard the *Ceylon* who said, 'Welcome, Sir, bloody well done. Don't be put off by anything that goes on in this ship and good luck. We know why you've come,' so I proceeded somewhat encouraged by this encounter but warned by it also to go down and talk to Captain Twiss. As I walked in he was sitting in his day cabin and looking up to me, he said, 'Good evening, Lygo, why have you come to see me?' I said, 'You know perfectly well why I've come to see you, Sir, I've come to apologise for my behaviour last night.'

'Well,' he said, 'don't you think your behaviour was more in keeping with that of a Sub Lieutenant or Midshipman rather than a Commander?'

'I entirely agree, Sir,' I said. 'Unfortunately they don't seem up to it these days and somehow someone has to set them an example.' He looked at me again and said, 'How do you think my Commander is going to maintain discipline in this ship when Commanders from other ships and from Admiral's staff go running around the upper deck the way you were doing last night?'

'Whenever I have been in a position to exercise discipline, Sir,' I replied 'I have never found it difficult under any circumstances.' He looked at me again as I stood stiffly to attention looking at him.

'Would you like a drink?' he said.

'No, Sir, thank you,' I said, 'I have a date in Kowloon' (which I did have with a colleague of mine) but I thanked him profusely and withdrew. Frank Twiss had had a difficult War, a very gallant officer and a good seaman but he showed something else that night – to me, at any rate. A tolerance, a sense of humour and a degree of understanding that I really had no right to expect.

I did indeed have a date that night; it was with the Staff Direction Officer, Ian Easton, and we were going for a run ashore in Kowloon. This we duly did, finishing up in a bar called the Four Roses, I seem to recall, which was populated fairly sparsely by a number of ladies of the night who became increasingly aggressive as we completed our meal with no apparent intention of partaking of any of their charms. Ian, however, who was just coming out of a very messy divorce, decided that this was a good way to spend the evening. We were sitting, as I recall, in a booth with two forms either side and one of my purchases during the evening had been a lamp complete with a lampshade which was made, as far as I can remember, of rice paper. It was quite a large lampshade and I had it parked beside me on the bench. It was to prove to be a not inconsiderable impediment in making the journey home, but at this stage it was still in fairly pristine condition. When it became clear that the ladies of the night were not going to be fully employed, one particularly unattractive one decided that force was the best way of conquering my resistance and launched herself at me along the form, thus pushing me bodily along it towards the lampshade which was squashed slightly at the other end. I have never been able to satisfy Pepper that this is how the lampshade in fact got damaged despite all the things that happened to it afterwards but it happens to be the truth. I found my way back to the Commodore's house where we were then staying, a quiet and restful bungalow halfway up the side of the hill and turned in for a peaceful night.

We were departing the following morning from RAF Kaitak and went over in the Commodore's barge together with the Admiral. We must have looked a strange bunch of characters as we stepped out to be greeted by the Group Captain commanding Kaitak at the time, Ian looking decidedly the worse for wear and me with various parcels including this extraordinary lampshade. It took a long time to get back to England in those days and when we finally made it the lampshade, which had never been a thing of beauty and a joy for ever, was in a rather battered condition. Pepper looked at it somewhat ruefully when I opened it as my major contribution from my visit to the Far East; it never did find a place in the house and quite rightly, and she never did believe the story of how it got battered, but it happens to be true!

16

HMS Lowestoft

For my next job, in 1961, I was very lucky to be given a brand new ship, HMS *Lowestoft*, a Type 12 Frigate, building at this time at Alexander Stephens on the Clyde, to be my first sea-going command as a young Commander and as an aviating Commander, which was even more exceptional. I travelled up to Scotland and met the Officers that were then standing by, housed in the usual Portakabin on the dockside as the ship was being completed, and met Alistair McIver (First Lieutenant designate), 'Benny' Goodman, John Snow, John Webster (Navigator), Powys Maurice (Torpedo Anti-submarine Officer) and Peter Woods (Engineer Officer). Apart from the Engineer Officer they were a fairly inexperienced bunch, I suppose, and to find themselves commanded by an aviator who really didn't know all that much about driving a ship must have been for them a somewhat nerve-racking experience. They were a good young team, however, and backed me up tremendously.

The progress of a ship being built is slow and sometimes, for the Officer standing by, a little confusing – one has little control over what is going on, is there in an advisory capacity, and it was my first experience of a shipyard and some of the things that went on within it. It was, to say the least, enlightening. It was the period of severe union intransigence, not always helped by management lack of understanding and certainly not much sense of leadership. Hierarchical division of management and labour was absolute but I believe Stephens was, by the standards of the time, a more enlightened yard. It had not prevented them from suffering a rather debilitating strike, however, and any attempt to break the demarcation lines that were drawn between the various unions and were crippling British industry and were going to go on crippling it until Margaret Thatcher arrived on the scene, had to be seen to be believed. I suspect fewer and fewer people now can remember what it was like, but it was a time to get to know one's ship from the keel up and so a useful experience, particularly for somebody whose knowledge was as rudimentary as mine.

As we got closer to the commissioning date, I became concerned with the standard of finish that Stephens were achieving in the ship

On the bridge of Lowestoft

and decided to ask for an appointment with Sir Murray Stephens, who was then the Chairman, in order to register my dissatisfaction. A meeting was therefore arranged for me early one morning, but Alistair and I decided we ought to go to have a look at the *Brighton* which was being built on the opposite bank of the Clyde to see what standard was being achieved there. I remember very well going into Glasgow and getting on a tram which took us out on the other bank towards Yarrows yard and disembarking there, having made arrangements with the Officer standing by *Brighton* to go in and have a look. Having walked round the ship, we both agreed that we had nothing to complain of whatsoever with the finish in the *Lowestoft*! Nevertheless, I was stuck with the appointment the following morning to complain about it. When I entered the Boardroom of Alexander Stephens, I was confronted by the portraits of previous Stephenses of Linthouse who had been building ships for 150 years, and the models and photographs of the ships they had built, and here was I, a young upstart Commander, trying to tell them how to run their business. They were charming and listened to my rather modest complaints with some

238

sympathy, and promised they would do their best to rectify them. Stephens at Linthouse had been a company that had tried very hard to break the archaic working practices of the shipbuilding unions at that time but without success. Not long after the completion of the *Lowestoft* they went out of business. Admiralty policy at that time was competitive tendering, later believed to have been invented by other people, and the result of competitive tendering in a declining shipbuilding environment was that shipbuilders bid for work hoping that there would be an up-turn in their fortunes whilst they kept people busy in the yard at very marginal rates, if not loss leaders, but the orders never came. One of the biggest customers for Alexanders, I seem to recall, was the New Zealand shipping line, but again things were changing – Europe was coming closer and the Commonwealth influence and importance was diminishing. It was sad to see the demise of Alexander Stephens, along with so many other famous names on the Clyde.

The next shipyard to us at that time was Fairfields. It was then undergoing an experiment led by George Brown, the Labour minister, to see whether new working practices and a joint venture between unions and the yard's owners could produce a better atmosphere and cheaper and more effectively built ships. It was a great attempt but it too failed and Fairfields went the way of all the others, a monument to the weakness of management but regrettably, I fear, more to the intransigence of unions who in trying to protect their members' interests were destroying them at the same time.

Pepper came up for the commissioning ceremony, and we had the Flag Officer Scotland and Lady Copeman, who launched the ship, with her husband who had been the Controller of the Navy. In the usual parsimonious ways in which one had to operate I had booked us into some rather third-rate hotel and we were occupying a room that overlooked one of the grimiest streets in Glasgow – not the best place to leave my Florida hibiscus! We also had the mayor of Lowestoft and some of his attendants as guests, and I decided to break with all previous tradition in that we would have champagne for the entire Ship's Company, and so we did. It was one big party and thoroughly enjoyed by everybody and got the commission off to a good start.

Pepper has one abiding memory of the commissioning ceremony which, in accordance with tradition, was fairly formal involving a blessing of the ship by the Parson with the audience of visitors looking on on our somewhat cramped Quarterdeck. During one of the more silent moments in the ceremony, my wife enquired of the Mayor of Lowestoft what they did in Lowestoft and in a booming voice he said that they were mainly interested in and active in the canning industry.

Lowestoft entering Taranto – a thrill for any FAA chap

'Canning of pilchards', he said, 'canning of peas, canning of 'erring, canning of ...' and it was difficult for her to stop him waxing even more loquacious and to keep the volume down amidst the somewhat silent ceremony that was in progress.

Soon it was time to sail, the White Ensign successfully hoisted, and on the final acceptance day at sea before the commissioning I was asked to sign for the ship. There was I, who really could hardly be described as experienced, having to sign for a brand-new frigate, but I did and we commissioned it and got it away. I had had virtually no ship-handling experience; there were no simulators in those days, no carefully calculated advice, no course of learning, and I contrasted this with the way in which the Fleet Air Arm would have treated a seaman if he had come and asked to fly an aeroplane! When we arrived at Portsmouth, having come down around the west coast of Scotland and through the Irish Sea, the wind, as always, was blowing fairly hard. When our appointed time came to go up harbour I remember wondering whether I should wait outside until it abated, but we had a programme to keep and leave to be given and so, in a slightly nervous

240

state, I decided to go up. First the Nab and then the Warner, Block-house Fort and 'Shithouse' Corner is the well-known sequence of entry into Portsmouth. I believe the latter referred to the pub on the corner as you come through into Portsmouth harbour, which in the old days used to have as its heads simply a platform outside where it went straight into the water. Because of the way the wind was blowing, I decided to ask for a tug, and was gently nosed into the berth with the wind whistling around us. Afterwards I had a phone call from the Queen's Harbourmaster who said, 'Welcome to Ports-mouth. Is everything all right?'

'Yes,' I said, 'fine.'

'I don't suppose you took a tug,' said he.

'I most certainly did,' said I, as it irritated me to think that here was somebody prepared to be critical of someone who was doing something for the first time, he never having had instruction in how to do it! We ran in and out of Portsmouth for the first few weeks in the customary way, getting various things sorted out: compass swings and ammunition stowed, and gun trials carried out, then off to Portland for the work-up.

Portland in those days was quite an experience. I decided therefore to go in early, arrive on the Sunday morning instead of the Monday morning, and to spend the Sunday practising some manoeuvres along-side the Mulberry harbours that were located off Portland breakwater. I particularly wanted to practise stern boards into them to see how I managed this. Perhaps I didn't learn as much from this experience as I should have done! In a brightly over-confident manner I addressed my Ship's Company as follows: 'We're not to be put off by this Portland place. I give them 48 hours to start working us up or we'll start working them up.' It was a rather bold statement to make in the circumstances, but it worked. The Ship's Company came together with a bang and the work-up began, very tough and very tiring but enjoy-able in a challenging way. We were one of the first ships with the new long-range 177 sonar, so this was something that was new and inter-esting. We also had the advanced plotting table; the old pen-and-ink chart type of preview plotting tables had gone, and we had a chart table called the Cambria which projected a live radar image upwards on to the surface of the plotting table so that you could actually have a moving centre (which was your ship) and plot the others around it through the radar contacts. It was a tremendous advance and made the conduct of operations in the ops room very much more simple. It was easier perhaps for me to adapt to these conditions, working from the ops room, than it was for some Captains who had been used previously to running their ship from the Bridge. I enjoyed working

241

from the ops room and conning the ship from there on radar, but I suppose to an aviator it was a lot easier than to a seaman, so once I was in the ops room I was in my element.

We had all the usual near disasters, one in particular being when I had Pepper down for a weekend and we were going off to have dinner ashore with one of the staff (it may even haven been the Admiral) and as I was leaving the ship the Officer of the Day said, 'The First Lieutenant presents his apologies, Sir, but he's turned in and won't be able to see you off.'

'What's the matter with him?' I asked.

'Well, he doesn't look very well, Sir.' I promptly went into the First Lieutenant's cabin and he was looking far from well.

'You are to stay exactly where you are,' I said, 'and let's get the local doctor down.'

'No, no,' he said, 'I don't think I need that.'

'I'm sure you do,' said I and within a few hours I was to see my First Lieutenant carted off with what turned out to be pneumonia. Now for my next mistake. Instead of appointing somebody to replace him on a temporary basis, I decided that we would not do that but we would merely all move over one and we would split his duties between the Officers that remained. I told the "buffer" he would run the routine, told the Gunnery Officer he was in charge of all seamanship manoeuvres, and so on. This worked fine until I decided the time had come for us to exercise emergency breakaway while fuelling. This is a procedure that needs to be followed if you are hooked on to a ship fuelling and, perhaps in poor visibility or for some other reason, you need to separate and alter course very quickly and independently. So I waited until we had finished fuelling and called 'Benny' Goodman up to the Bridge and said, 'Are we ready to exercise the emergency breakaway?' 'Yes, Sir,' he said. 'Right,' I said, 'I'll wait until you get down there, dwell a pause and then I'm off.' He disappeared down onto the fo'c's'le; we were still hooked on to the tanker, although we stopped pumping fuel and I said 'Emergency breakaway, emergency breakaway,' sounded the siren and rang on the revs. Unfortunately, the chap who was to knock the shackle off the slip so that we could let go the jackstay couldn't get it to release, and before I knew where I was I had a tanker under tow on my starboard side. There were two ways that I could have got out of this. One was to have rung on 'slow ahead' or 'stop' and taken the way off the ship to take the strain off the stay so that he could get the shackle to clear, or to bore ahead, part all the wires, and get out of it that way. I chose the latter, and before I knew where I was steel wires were flipping around us like bits of string, one of which carved away the wooden railing around the top of the outer bridge right in front of me. We were clear, but it was a mess. The tanker was left with its hoses and all its gear dragging over the side, and I was with a slightly damaged ship but fortunately no casualties. I had just been a bit too keen. As I sat down to pen my signal to the Admiral, reporting what I had done, I was unaware of another episode that was then taking place with the poor old *Tidereach*, whom I had just savaged.

Her next exercise was to be with a frigate that was going to do a stern fuelling. This particular ship set the *Tidereach* on a course that, had they persisted with it, would have taken them right on to the Chesil Bank. Visibility by this time had dropped to about a mile, and in the end the tanker Captain had to do an emergency turn to avoid being driven ashore. The misdemeanour of this ship was so much greater than mine that mine paled into insignificance, and lucky Lygo had escaped a good wigging once again. All I was told to be was a bit more careful in future.

It was a great ship; we had high morale with high spirits combined, which I am bound to say I encouraged. We enjoyed ourselves. We were a Chatham ship and coming in and out of Chatham was always exciting, but it was a question of knack, and once I had mastered that it was relatively easy, in fact it was enjoyable.

Nevertheless, arriving in Malta was always something to be a little bit concerned about, however, because you were under the eyes of the Commander-in-Chief and his Staff, sitting up high in Fort St Angelo, and observed by everybody else of those times who had bases all round Grand Harbour. Furthermore, you eventually had to go up Sliema Creek, which you did stern first to get between two buoys. Not an easy task to perform under the eyes of everybody else who had already done it, or perhaps thought they knew better how to do it.

My first berth, however, was to be alongside in Dockyard Creek. We were going there for some replenishment or the other, I think, and I remember as we came into Grand Harbour the only signal I received was from the Captain of the Fleet, acting for the Commander-in-Chief Fleet in his absence, which said, 'there was a Chinaman looking out of one of your scuttles.' It irritated me; it would irritate me today. If you can't think of something substantial to say, don't say anything at all. It just demeans you, and it certainly demeaned this fellow to me. As my sarcasm and intolerance of pomposity was always close to the surface, I suppose I could have been standing into danger once again, when I called on him, to be told at the outset, 'I am sorry I couldn't say something nice, we're only allowed to make criticisms.' Can you believe it! I let it pass, which perhaps was fortunate.

My Captain 'F' (Frigates), had observed my alongside and asked me afterwards why I had gone into the berth by going beyond it astern and then coming into it forward, to which I replied, 'I prefer that, Sir. It gives me a better feeling of control.' I might have remembered this years later in Piraeus, although on that occasion there wasn't a choice! The moment eventually came for us to go up Sliema Creek, and I remember working at great lengths with John Webster the Navigator to make sure that we got it right. Poor John, he had his hands really full with this inexperienced aviator Captain trying to do all those things that he knew he had to do better than other people if he was to maintain the credibility which was so necessary for the aviation profession. We did it. It wasn't too bad; the wind wasn't blowing very hard, we managed to get the stern ropes out fairly quickly, the trick being to go at an angle between the two buoys putting your stern towards the shore, and then as the offshore wind blew it down, so you hoped that your boat which was already in the water would get the stern line out so that you could actually secure the stern, because if the stern slopped right across and you only managed to get the bow line on, then of course the ship would finish up swinging into wind or you'd be roaring around with the engines trying to get it lined up. Thank goodness it worked out all right, more by good luck than by good judgement, I am bound to say, and by the good seamanship of my crew. Then it was time to call on the 'Burning Bush'.

Admiral Bush was the Flag Officer Flotillas in the Med. at that time, under whose direct command we came. I had been told that he was a man who was very strict in discipline and very particular about the way in which people conducted themselves, or their ships, and that in addition he didn't like aviators. I was off to a good start, wasn't I? Number One was very agitated about the state of our boat that was to take me out to the Flagship *Blake*, to call on Flag Officer Flotillas, and he said, 'if the boat isn't right he'll send you round again. You will do it endlessly, and humiliate yourself in front of the entire fleet.'

'So,' said I, 'you'd better make sure the boat is all right then, Number One,' and indeed it was. So, the great moment arrived when resplendent in my No. 10s, I went alongside the gangway of *Blake*, the Admiral's flagship, and I nipped up the gangway and there was greeted by Admiral Bush. He was a tall, fair-haired man with bright blue eyes that stared at you, a good figure of a man who greeted me civilly enough; he took me to the "cuddy" where we chatted and he made a few oblique references to the way in which aviation was run, with some of which I could hardly disagree, others of which I parried, but we got on well. He was clearly a man after my own heart; I had a feeling that maybe this was going to be all right after all. In fact, some

244

days later I was invited to dinner aboard the flagship with wives, but of course my wife wasn't there, I could never afford to get her out there and she claims to this day to be the only Naval wife who's never been to Malta, and she still hasn't. After the dinner party, which was amusing and light-hearted and which I enjoyed, the Admiral said, 'Now, we will have horse riding.' Horse riding, I thought, what the devil is all this about? And a large wooden horse was produced in the middle of the Admiral's cuddy and he said, 'Now, I wish to see who can ride this horse. Right, Lygo, you're first up.' Now it was very clear to me that this was going to be a difficult performance. The horse appeared to have two sets of swivelling legs, so I got on it and promptly fell off backwards.

'Well, that's you down,' he said, 'next one.' But here for some hidden reason, I know not why, I said, 'No Sir, I am remounting,' and I remounted it, because the second time I almost had a feel for this wretched device and I was able to ride it quite satisfactorily, and then stepped off. So far the game was drawn, but I wasn't challenged again. Admiral Bush became one of my staunchest supporters and I am eternally grateful for his patience and consideration, and understanding and support I received from him. Had it been otherwise, this saga would have ended abruptly. I'll come back to him later.

During one of our self-maintenance periods in Gibraltar, we received that favourite signal that stirs all Naval Officers to action: 'From the C-in-C Home Fleet, sail with all despatch to Grenada.' That caused us all to get organised, I can assure you. Gathering the Ship's Company on board, we slipped and proceeded out and down towards Punto del Gardo in the Cape Verde Islands to fuel before crossing the Atlantic to Grenada. The reason for our sudden despatch was that Mr Geary, whom I had earlier met in *Veryan Bay* when I was in charge of the landing party, was now leading a somewhat troubled political life in Grenada and the Government obviously decided that it was time to do something about him. Arrival in Punto del Gardo was interesting because we had just thought it was going to be a quick operational in and out, take fuel and disappear again, which of course in effect it should have been, but as we rounded the corner and the jetty came in sight we saw that on the other side was a Portuguese frigate which had a guard and was ready to receive us formally. With great haste we assembled a return guard and the usual honours were exchanged, and while the ship was being fuelled we were invited by the Portuguese to come over and have lunch with them. It was an extremely pleasurable experience. Their frigate had been an old British frigate and, I must say, it was in gleaming condition. Every piece of brass in the old up and down engines was shining and the whole thing was a great credit to the Portuguese Navy, and we were very grateful (although very surprised) by their hospitality and sad that we didn't have time to return it. And so it was off across the Atlantic and arrival in Grenada with a salute to be fired to the Governor, and as we entered that beautiful bay once again I was reminded of my previous time there in the *Veryan Bay* as Officer in Charge of the Landing Party, and the connection with Mr Geary. As a result of our arrival and the salute that we fired, Mr Geary departed to the hills and subsequently was captured. Our task seemed to have been accomplished, and we sailed to rejoin our Squadron which was coming down out of the Channel to exercise in the Mediterranean. We knew we would be meeting them head-on and I was determined that we should be the first to sight them so, as the appointed hour drew near, we spent a lot of time searching the horizon with binoculars because I had decided to have radar silence so that they should not intercept our radar transmissions to see exactly where we were. Sure enough, we managed to see them first, gave the standard challenge, received the reply, then I was told to take station. My Captain F. had left a gap in the line for me astern of him and in front of number three, and taking station

Lowestoft alongside in Grenada

from ahead is always an interesting manoeuvre and looks good if it is done well. It was a great challenge to my Navigating Officer, I must say, more than to me, to get the exact point at which the helm went over, but we got it right, came round in a screaming turn and fell into position in the slot absolutely precisely. In order to make the meeting as light-hearted as possible, I had made a signal to my leader Captain Dunbar Naismith (affectionately known to my crew as Crowbar-Nuswift) which read, 'Delighted to find you at last, Sir, we've been looking for you ever since Gibraltar,' which I thought was quite amusing. What I got in return was, 'Proceed alongside for transfer for briefing.' So I took the ship alongside, went over on the jackstay (handing over command to my First Lieutenant), and I was then briefed by my Captain F. on the next set of exercises. No mention was made of the signal that I had made to him and when finally I departed, as he saw me over the side I said, 'Did you get my signal, Sir, on joining?'

'Yes,' he said, looking at me fixedly, 'I didn't understand it.' Well sometimes you win, sometimes you lose.

Another time when I almost lost was when we had a ship visit to Barcelona. The rest of the Squadron was there but with great enter-prise my Officers discovered that the Royal Ballet was performing in Barcelona, nipped ashore and invited the entire Corps de Ballet to attend a Wardroom dinner and dance. It was one of those rare occasions when I had Pepper out and we were parked in some rather second-rate hotel, not too far from the ship for the period in which she was to be there – not much more than a long weekend, really. Of course an invitation came from the Wardroom for the Captain and his lady to attend the Wardroom dinner, and Pepper when she discovered this said, 'Ooh, this is going to be the highlight of the visit. I'm really looking forward to that.'

'Well,' I said, 'I'm afraid we won't be going.'

'Why not?' she enquired.

'Because,' I said, 'it's only a formality. They're asking me because I'm not a member of the Wardroom and they have to invite me out of politeness, but I don't think we should attend.'

'Oh nonsense,' she said, 'I think this would be fun. I'm looking forward to this,' and there was no way with tact that I could dissuade her. The evening arrived and we repaired on board and down to the Wardroom for a supper and then into the Ante-room which had been suitably darkened and festooned with the usual Navy flags for the occasion, with soft music for dancing, and the fun began. I could see Pepper's eyes getting wider and wider in the dim light of the Ante-room as the evening progressed and as early as was reasonably

247

possible I made our excuses and we departed in the car that had been provided for us by the Consul.

As soon as she got me alone, Pepper started. 'Did you see what was going on?' she said.

'How do you mean?' I countered, knowing perfectly well what she was referring to.

'Well, I mean, did you see what so-and-so was doing, and he's a married man, and did you see the way he was carrying on with that girl?'

'No,' I said, 'I didn't see that.'

'And what about that youngster who's only just got married; did you see what he was up to?'

'Er, no,' I said, 'I didn't see that either.'

'But then did you see?' and so it went on. In the end there was a silence because I wasn't really responding very well.

'Is it always like this?' Pepper enquired.

'Certainly not,' I said.

'And when I am not there, do you behave like they were behaving?'

'Certainly not,' I replied. There was a moment's silence and then Pepper gave me the perfect squelch.

'What's the matter?' she said, 'can't you get one?' Sometimes there's no way of winning!

After a self-maintenance in Portsmouth, we were due to join *Berwick* with my Captain F. and proceed to Bridgeport, Connecticut, and then to Norfolk where we were to demonstrate the new Cambria table to the US Navy. My Captain F. was enthusiastic about this and told me how important the mission was going to be. With my experience of the US Navy and the way in which things were done, I felt I had to tell him that he shouldn't place too great an expectation on our achieving anything because they would look at it and say, 'Yes, this is much better than anything we've got but we intend to have something even better in the fullness of time,' and so we wouldn't sell it. This, in fact, was exactly what happened. The Naval Tactical Data System was on the horizon and it was decided that they weren't going to have an interim system.

The visit to Bridgeport was interesting in two ways. Firstly, before leaving Portsmouth when I returned on board from visiting a friend of mine, Chancy Parker, in a ship we were berthed alongside, I was met by my new Engineer Officer who was a submariner by training and therefore had most experience on diesels rather than steam engines and told that all was going well, the ship was being flashed up in order to be ready to sail early the following morning. I promptly proceeded to go to my cabin ready to turn in. Before I could do so, and indeed

248

before I could even get changed out of my Mess undress, he came to my cabin to say that we were going to have to shut down because he was worried about the fact that a valve in the boiler room that he thought should be passing steam, appeared not to be passing steam and he had therefore ordered the flashing up to stop, and the ship to be shut down while they looked into it. I was horrified; it meant of course that we were going to miss sailing and this duly occurred.

It was going to be an interesting evening. Secondly, I had been asked to take Harrison's No.4 with me in the *Lowestoft* to Bridgeport,

Harrison's No 4

249

so that it could take part in the New York Exhibition for which the French were lending the Mona Lisa. On this rather wet and windy evening, therefore, as we were berthed outboard of another ship, the Officer of the Day came to tell me that there was gentlemen from the Royal Observatory at Hurstmonceux who wanted to see me. When the chap was presented, he said he'd come with Harrison's No. 4 and had it in a car on the jetty, but how was he going to get it on board? To which I replied, 'Well, it'll have to be walked across the gangway to the ship inboard of me, and then across another gangway to my ship.' The man looked stunned at this and said, 'But that won't be safe. This is a very valuable, unique article and we can't allow it to be exposed to any risk.' 'Well,' said I, 'the only other solution is to have the ship moved under a crane alongside a jetty, so that it can be moved that way,' but I couldn't see how that could be effected in the time that was available. As we stood there looking at each other, there came a knock at the door and the Quartermaster stood there with a large wicker basket. 'What do you want me to do with this, Sir?' he said.

It was Harrison's No. 4. The problem had been solved. 'Where are you going to stow it?' asked the curator. 'Well,' said I, 'under my bunk, I suppose, or alongside it, so that it's as safe as it can be because if anything happens to me, it will have happened to it at the same time,' and with that sufficient assurance he departed. Harrison's No.4 was in fact safely transported to Bridgeport and then collected and on its way to New York. It was the first time it had left the UK since its original trials.

My Captain F. sailed and left the Squadron Engineer Officer behind to see if he could be of any assistance to us. My concern was considerably heightened when I saw these engineers and a new engine room Chief Artificer poring over diagrams of the layout of the steam system to try to discover where the steam was actually supposed to flow. I controlled myself for as long as possible but by the following evening I was totally at my wits' end. I phoned my old Chief, who was now up in Scotland at a shore establishment, and asked him what he thought, and he said, 'I don't understand what the matter can be. It's very difficult for me, unless I was on the site to actually know,' and he was the chap that had stood by when the ship was built so he knew every pipe and valve in it.

It was clear to me with the weekend now on us that we would be there for a week while the Dockyard crawled all over the ship trying to find out what was wrong, when I was fairly certain nothing was wrong at all. I went down to the boiler room to talk to the Petty Officer of the Watch who'd been on watch when we'd flashed up before. He and I stood on the plates there looking at the boilers and I said to him,

'When you flashed up yesterday, did anything happen that was different?'

'No, Sir,' he said.

'Were all the gauges coming up normally?'

'Yes, Sir.'

'There was no indication of any problem?'

'No, Sir.'

'Well then, why did we shut down?'

'I've no idea, Sir,' he said. I looked at my watch. I knew the moment for flashing up to sail the following morning, when I would only be 24 hours behind my leader, meant that if I didn't start flashing at about ten o'clock that evening we'd be in trouble. I sent for the Engineer Officer and said, 'Since we have not been able to find anything wrong with this ship, I intend to flash up normally and proceed to sea tomorrow morning.' He looked at me in a sort of stunned way and said, 'I can't recommend it, Sir.'

'Right,' I said, 'where's the Staff Engineer?' He came and was about as useful as Staff Engineers tend to be.

'Right,' I said, having changed for dinner, 'as soon as my supper is over we shall go below and we shall flash up and see what happens, and if the whole thing blows up then it'll be quite an interesting spectacle.' I was furious. Sometimes you smell incompetence; sometimes you smell a lack of understanding. Some people have a feel for machinery, others have no feel for it whatsoever. So I went down onto the plates at ten o'clock, said to the Petty Officer of the Watch (the same one), 'Are you ready?'

'Yes, Sir,' he said.

'Okay,' I said, 'flash up,' and we proceeded to raise steam. We raised steam very successfully, the kettles came nicely to the boil, the engines were turned and in the fullness of time the Engineer Officer came to report to me that the ship was ready for sea. We sailed the following morning and caught up my Captain F. in Bridgeport.

Command is about making decisions and the most difficult are when you don't have all the information you need but your gut tells you to act.

The second episode was of a quite different nature. It is customary when visiting the United States for the Navy League to be involved. The US Navy League is a body of well-meaning retired and associated people who sometimes enjoy Naval ranks because they have contributed to the welfare of sailors and look after them or make arrangements for them or subscribe to Naval charities. They also have an important political role for the US Navy. However they can be a fairly variable feast. In Bridgeport we were placed in the hands of these

251

worthies who proceeded to look after the Ship's Company and the Officers in, I believe, an entirely satisfactory manner but on about the second or third day of the visit, most of the official entertaining being over, I was alone in my cabin looking forward to a quiet evening meal and an early night with a book when I was told by the Officer of the Day that the boss of the Navy League in that particular area wished to come aboard and to see me. He duly arrived at something like six o'clock, I suppose, and when he saw me there he said, 'What are you doing this evening?'

'Well,' I said, 'nothing, I'm going to have a quiet evening on board.'

'You certainly can't do that,' said he, and he was one of those overpowering chaps that sometimes it's difficult to be polite in refusing. 'You must come ashore with me,' he said, 'come, we'll go off together,' and so I changed into some suitable civilian attire and accompanied him ashore and we drove off to his house somewhere out in the country. It was, as I recall, a very nice house and when we entered we were met by his wife who seemed to be a very gracious lady, who asked if we were going to stay for dinner; which I rather hoped we would be.

'No, no,' he said, 'we've got things to do.' At that moment his son came down the stairs and was introduced to me as well, and then, to my surprise, we left the house, got back into his car and went back downtown where we went into a bar. It was clear to me that one of the ladies of the bar or one of the barmaids, I suppose, was his girlfriend and he said to her, 'Right, I'd like you to fix Ray up with some other girl.' I was horrified. I had no desire to be fixed up with anybody and especially nobody from that particular bar. Fortunately, when the lady was produced and our eyes met I think she realised that this was going to be a fairly dull evening for both of us and so, fortunately, she had another engagement. It's sometimes nice not to be one of those chaps that has to brush the girls off; they tend to brush themselves off automatically, as far as I'm concerned. Not dissuaded, we proceeded to go ashore to have a meal in some café and my host was getting steadily more and more intoxicated. The result of this was that I became more and more sober. We then got into his car and he insisted on taking me back to the ship where I hoped I would be able to get out and say goodbye. No – they had purchased a present for me, a grotesque alabaster Toby Mug, and insisted on coming on board, and I had the intense embarrassment of having to come up the gangway leading someone who, if he'd been one of my Ratings would have been placed under close arrest. It is never easy to handle situations like this but one hopes that the Ship's Company, when the buzz gets round, and it does, would recognise that this is something over which the Captain had very little control. We went to my cabin where I offered him a nightcap and as politely and firmly as I could finally pushed them over the side.

The next morning, being Sunday, I was due to attend a service in the local Episcopal Church where again I was greeted by my host of the previous evening but this time with his wife! I then proceeded to go into a pew where I was put between them, where we sat and went through a traditional Anglican service. I have seldom felt so unclean as I did kneeling between those people that Sunday morning but then, I suppose, that's life, if you're not careful.

17

The Story of Two Admirals

During my time as Commanding Officer of HMS *Lowestoft* we had a 14-day period of self-maintenance in Gibraltar. We had finished work-up not too long before in Portland where the ship's appearance had suffered somewhat, and had come down to Gibraltar from Chatham where we had been giving Christmas leave in the usual grey, cold Chatham winter environment; this was just after Christmas, so it was a great relief, therefore, to be in the sun in Gibraltar. The whole time we were there the weather was absolutely splendid, enabling the First Lieutenant to get the ship looking really super.

Pepper came down to be with me, and in those days we stayed across the border in Spain, in La Linea de la Frontera, at the Hotel Universal. This was not only the cheapest accommodation in the area but also the most fun, because that was where things were a little more lively in the evenings. It was great to be able to sit on the pavement at a little table eating tapas and drinking La Ina, or Fundador, or whatever took your fancy at a price you could almost not resist.

Relations between the UK and Spain at that time had thawed a little, and it had been agreed that the Admiral in Gibraltar (Flag Officer Gibraltar) should be allowed to make a call upon the Spanish Governor of Algeciras even though the Spanish Governor was not allowed to return the call to the 'Fortress of Gibraltar' ('temporarily in the hands of the British', as the Spanish described it). Therefore it was decided that the best way to overcome this problem of protocol would be to have the Flag Office Gibraltar take passage in a warship to Algeciras where he would call upon the Spanish governor, and then the Governor could return the call aboard the British warship in a Spanish port.

It was therefore decided that the brand-new frigate, HMS *Lowestoft*, would be a suitable vessel to take Flag Officer Gibraltar on this rather august visit. As the ship would be having its 14 days self-maintenance and looking absolutely sparkling I wasn't worried about this event at all but in order to dress it up, I suggested that we get hold of the band of the Garrison Regiment to accompany the Flag Officer when he made his visit. The Regiment at that time was the Devon & Cornwall

254

Light Infantry and arrangements were duly made with the Commanding Officer to borrow his band for this particular call.

I carried on with our holiday in La Linea and, having seen Pepper off on her trip back to the UK from the airport at Gibraltar, I returned on board on the morning that we were due to sail, at about seven o'clock. We were due to sail at nine, the Admiral being scheduled to join at ten to nine.

When the First Lieutenant came in to make his morning report to me at 0800 hours he said that all the men had returned on board and everything was ready for our departure. The ship was under sailing orders and ready to proceed at nine o'clock and we would be welcoming the Admiral on board at about ten minutes to nine. I said 'Splendid'. Then he hesitated before he left my cabin and that was indication enough to me, that in this very lively ship, which I was lucky to command, something was up.

'What is it, Number One?' I enquired.

'Well,' he said, 'I think there is something you ought to know.'

'I see,' said I, 'what exactly is that?'

'Well,' he said, 'we've decided that we would play a prank on the Flag Officer Gibraltar's staff before we leave.'

I said, 'Yes, what's it to be?' and he said, 'We're going to run a *Lowestoft* pennant up on the yardarm of the signal mast at Headquarters as a kind of farewell gesture.'

'Well,' I said, 'that sounds fine.'

'Yes,' he said, 'but you should know that we have decided it will be attached to a gas balloon and that the pennant will be on a riding shackle so that they won't be able to haul it down.'

'What a splendid idea,' I said, 'when are you planning to do that?'

'Well, just about now, Sir'. So I said, 'Right, I will now go ashore to take some exercise and when the Chief of Staff to Flag Officer Gibraltar calls, I won't be here to take his call and you can tell him that I am taking my morning exercise and I will call him the minute I get back on board.' We smiled at each other and he departed and so did I to take a stroll on the jetty. As I returned to the ship I could see the *Lowestoft* pennant flying proudly from the yardarm at HQ.

I returned on board about half past eight and sure enough as I came up the gangway the Officer of the Day said to me with a broad grin, 'The Chief of Staff is anxious to speak to you, Sir.'

'Oh, really?' I said, and went down to my cabin and telephoned the Chief of Staff.

'Ah, Lygo, umm ... I don't suppose you know, but somebody from your ship has attached a *Lowestoft* pennant to the yardarm here and we can't get it down.' I said, 'Really, a *Lowestoft* pennant ... just a moment, Sir, I'll go and look!' and before he could reply I put the 'phone down. After a suitable pause I picked up the 'phone and said, 'You're absolutely right, Sir, there is a *Lowestoft* pennant on your yardarm.' At this point he exploded and said, 'Of course I'm right and I know that perfectly well, that's why I'm telling you. What I am also saying to you is, you put it up, you get it down.'

'Aye, aye, Sir,' I replied, 'I will look into it straightaway,' and sent for the First Lieutenant.

'Right,' I said, 'we have had our fun, whose idea was it?' It was almost bound to be 'Benny' Goodman's, the Gunnery Officer, and so I asked for him to come and see me. He duly arrived and stood smartly to attention as a good Gunnery Officer should.

'Well,' said I, 'it was a good jape but it is all over now, Guns. You put it up, you get it down.'

'Aye, aye, Sir,' he replied and came smartly to attention revealing a double-barrel shotgun, which he had been hiding behind his back, turned smartly on his heel and left. He disappeared ashore and later there was a double report of the shotgun and down came the *Lowestoft* pennant.

We were now ready for receiving the Admiral and he came on board at ten to nine when his flag was hoisted. He was a somewhat nervous man, or so it seemed to me; perhaps it was the *Lowestoft* that made him nervous – at any rate he came on board and was welcomed with full ceremony. It was at this point that I noticed the band for the first time; I had never seen so many bandsmen in all my life! I had not realised what an enormous band it was and as we couldn't accommodate them all on the Quarterdeck some had to be on the 'Seacat' mounting aft and others along some of the signal decks, so the ship was really well covered with bandsmen. The band played and played and at nine o'clock precisely we slipped and proceeded out of Gibraltar.

The trip across the bay was fairly uneventful and we were due to lay off Algeciras and fire a salute at ten o'clock. It was a lovely day, the sun was shining with just a little haze. We took up our position, sited the return firing battery and opened fire with the salute to the Governor of Algeciras. The Admiral was, at this point, displaying considerable agitation. He was on an enclosed bridge and I think perhaps this was something new for him; he was more used to being in the open air with all the noises of the ship to listen to, and as a Gunnery Officer he was in addition probably slightly deaf from guns in the past. We had been fitted with the new pattern Admiralty saluting guns, which we were using for the first time on this occasion.

The Admiral finally could not conceal his agitation any longer and said to me, 'I do not hear those guns, are you sure they can be heard ashore?' To which I replied, 'Well I hope so, Sir, it is the only piece of original ordnance that Their Lordships have given us since the end of the last War and if it doesn't work then there should be quite considerable consternation.'

In due course the puffs of the returning fire could be seen, although in the enclosed bridge you didn't hear them but you could see them, and we knew that our salute had been heard and was being returned. We were therefore due to proceed in and secure alongside so that the Admiral could go ashore to make his call. He kept looking at his watch and saying to me, 'Are you sure we are going to be on time?'

'Oh yes, Sir,' I said and began to play the very relaxed Captain, in fact slightly over-relaxed, ably assisted by the Navigating Officer, John Webster. Finally, as we turned in to enter the port of Algeciras I realised that we were in fact running a few seconds late and in order to make sure we came alongside at the precise moment I was coming in slightly faster than prudence would have dictated. Having lined up with the berth on the jetty I then went out onto the port wing to bring the ship alongside and there the full force of the Devon & Cornwall Light Infantry Band hit me. They were playing 'D'ye ken John Peel' at their usual 140 paces to the minute, a very stirring sound and fitting for the speed at which I was entering the berth!

Looking down the berth I perceived that where I was to stop was immediately astern of a Spanish banana boat and I couldn't help contemplating that if I did not manage to stop the ship adequately there would be plenty of bananas all over the upper deck. Keeping my voice down so that the slightly rising nervousness in it should not show, I proceeded to order astern revolutions, half-astern both engines, and then revolutions 110, revolutions 120, revolutions 140, full astern both engines, stop both engines. With a swirl of water we came up all standing immediately astern of the Spanish banana boat, precisely in our berth and exactly positioned for the gangway to go out. So far, so good. My luck was holding!

The day proceeded with the call on the Governor for which I accompanied the Admiral. Then a return match was held on board where a reception, organised by the ship, had been laid on for our guests. During the course of the reception I found myself talking to one of the local Spanish Generals – remember that in the Navy it was unusual to stay in an appointment for more than two years before you were moved – and so I asked him how long he had been in post in that area near Gibraltar, the Terra de la Frontera. I was astonished when he replied, '15 years'. This was the kind of stability that we could only dream about! However, I'm not sure that I would have wished to have had that kind of stability in some of the jobs I had had, although in the present one it wouldn't have been too bad!

The whole thing had gone extremely well. Our guests seemed well pleased and were taking their departure in good order. The Admiral was to depart back to Gibraltar by road, driving round the bay, and so the Governor having departed and all the officials gone, the Admiral was the last one to depart. Before we went to the gangway he said, 'I'd like a word with you Lygo,' and I thought, here it comes! I was taken behind the 4.5″ turret on the fo'c's'le. He looked at me slightly disapprovingly but not too much so, and said, 'I think this morning's performance has gone extremely well and I am very pleased with it.'

'Thank you, Sir,' I said, 'I'm pleased.'

'Yes,' he said, 'but what happened before we left, Lygo, could have done your career more harm than a collision and it is fortunate for you that I have a sense of humour.' I thought to myself, I'm beginning to see that.

'What exactly was the problem, Sir?' I asked.

'Well,' said he, 'I'm sure you weren't aware of it but just before we sailed, as my flag was struck, your pennant replaced it.' In Naval terms interfering with a Flag Officer's flag is really not done, it's the ultimate kind of 'don't do' syndrome and, of course, it was never the intention that that should be the way it worked out. I promptly said, 'Well, I'm sure, Sir, no disrespect was meant by this and it was just accidental that these two things coincided.'

'Yes,' he said, 'that may well be, but I think you should be more careful in future.'

'Aye, aye, Sir,' I said, and he departed over the side. We then went on our way to the West Indies and as we left there was no doubt that the whole Ship's Company knew that their joke and their subsequent good performance had both been noted equally and there was no particular affection for that particular Flag Officer.

The second Admiral was Admiral 'Bill' Beloe who was Flag Officer Medway when we returned to Chatham after our deployment to the West Indies.

The ship was secured inside the basin. It was winter, grey and pretty miserable in Chatham, not particularly attractive and very boring for those who had to stay on board. I was fortunate in that I lived not too far from Chatham and so was able to go ashore and come in on a daily basis.

One morning, I returned on board to receive the usual morning report from the First Lieutenant telling me that everything was under control and there were no problems. However, he hesitated as he was about to leave my cabin. 'What is it,' I asked.

'Well, Sir, I think you should be aware of an episode that took place last night. At eleven o'clock a signal was made to HMS *Chichester* – this was a ship lying opposite us on the other side of the basin – 'purporting to come from Flag Officer Medway, which said "from Flag Officer Medway, carry out Chatex One."' I smiled and then said, 'Did this signal go out live?'

'Yes,' he said, 'it was made on harbour intercom.' I said, 'Well, that's the first mistake, Number One. If you are going to pull a joke like this you must make sure that the signal has one copy only and that it is hand "disted". If it has gone out on the harbour network it could have been picked up by anybody and therefore, just a cautionary story, remember to tell the chaps, hand dist only. What happened?' I asked.

'Well,' he said, brightening up considerably, 'we could see a flurry of activity aboard the *Chichester* when the signal was received'.

'I bet you did,' said I. It transpired that the Officer of the Day, having failed to find any reference to Chatex One in Medway Orders, woke the First Lieutenant who said that the only thing they could do was to get the Captain out to open up the safe to look at the confidential orders to see if there was anything in the confidential books. This they did. By this time, and the Captain having returned on board, it was about two o'clock in the morning and they still hadn't been able to discover the origin of Chatex One. They had then called the Duty Staff Officer on the Flag Officer Medway's staff and asked him what the Chatex One exercise signal meant, but he didn't know. At four o'clock in the morning he called the Admiral and asked him what Chatex One meant. He had replied, 'There's no such thing. You've had your leg pulled. Go back to bed!'

I listened to this story with amusement – I would rather have a high-spirited bunch always up to something than a dull, disinterested lot. This is the stuff that morale is made of. It was quite a good jape, if only *Chichester* had not brought the Admiral into it. Then somewhat unnecessarily I enquired, 'I presume this was Lieutenant Goodman's idea?' 'Yes, Sir,' said he, 'it was.' 'Well I shall now phone the Admiral's secretary and apologise to him and ask if the Admiral would be good enough to see Lieutenant Goodman so that he may apologise for the inconvenience he has caused the Admiral. Meantime,' said I, 'Goodman is to get on to the Captain of the *Chichester*, who is a friend of mine, and ask if he can come over and apologise for the inconvenience he has caused him. The Captain of the *Chichester* is a good guy and will give Goodman a tremendous rollicking. That's all that will be involved and he will then have completed that part of the action which I think is necessary. In addition,' I said, 'I am going to tell the Admiral's secretary that I have stopped Goodman's leave for 14 days, except that I will rescind it; he will then effectively be under punishment and it is unlikely that he will be punished again for the same offence.'

Goodman duly went over to *Chichester* and, as I had forecast, the Captain gave him a thorough wigging and it was all over. More diffi-cult, however, was my problem with the Admiral because the secretary said, 'Well, the Admiral won't see Goodman, I am afraid, and he is very upset.' 'Oh dear,' I said, and sending for Lieutenant Goodman I told him that we must wait and see what happens.

We didn't have to wait long. A signal was received on board which said, 'To HMS *Lowestoft*, for Lieutenant Goodman. Intend to carry out Chatex Two on board *Lowestoft* with my entire staff at 11.30.' In due course they all arrived and drank on Lieutenant Goodman's wine bill until they had had enough and he had had enough, then they all departed. That Admiral, 'Bill' Beloe, became a hero in the ship. A quite different reaction to the way in which the other occasion had been managed.

He told me later, that at his staff meeting in the morning the episode had been regarded as a strong breach of security but he had then said to his staff, 'Come on, have none of you played a hoax?' Since no one wanted to be regarded as a wimp there was no reply. 'Right,' he said, how do we get even?'

It is through these simple basic understandings that leadership is exerted, morale is raised and people remain, or become, of high esteem.

18

Episode in Trinidad

During the course of a deployment it is customary to give a ship an opportunity to self-maintain; to complete the schedules of maintenance that have to be carried out and to provide the crew with some rest and relaxation. Such an occasion caused HMS *Lowestoft* to be detached to a Naval facility at the US Naval Base, Chaguramas, in Trinidad. Chaguramas was a classic kind of tropical US Navy facility, established as part of the offset agreement for the 50 destroyers during the Second World War. It was well laid out, had a jetty to accommodate destroyer-type ships and was, at the time we arrived, beginning to be run down and was only partially in use. Nevertheless, it did have shore power and those other facilities that enabled us to shut down our boilers in order to clean them and thus be able to maintain equipment.

Generally speaking, the weather while we were there was wet and humid, so the First Lieutenant was unable to do a great deal of work on the upper deck but as far as the Chief was concerned it was a blessing. We ran a kind of tropical routine, an early start and finish at lunchtime, so that we could give some rest and relaxation to the chaps who were doing the work. There wasn't really very much entertainment or activity for me while I was there and so apart form taking some exercise ashore I was for the most part staying on board. To my surprise, one evening early in the visit, the Officer of the Day came to my cabin and said that a lady had presented herself on board and wished to see me. I raised my eyebrows somewhat at this; it was unusual in any circumstances and the more so in tropical Trinidad, but who knows! I was even more interested, however, when he told me that she had arrived in a Rolls Royce. I asked that she be shown to my cabin and in the fullness of time the lady presented herself. She was an attractive middle-aged woman, well-dressed and well-presented, so conversation was not too difficult for me, although I had not had this experience for some few weeks.

Ultimately we came to the purpose of her visit. It transpired that her son had applied to join the Fleet Air Arm and had been told by the recruiting department in the Admiralty at that time, that he should present himself before an Admiralty Interview Board in the United

Kingdom. In order to get there he should take passage in the first warship (grey funnel line) that came into Trinidad, and we were it!

I said we would be delighted to give the young man a passage, particularly since he wanted to join the Fleet Air Arm, but that I would have to get clearance from the Commodore-in-Charge, West Indies, under whose operational authority we then operated, before I could agree to this. Having taken the details I then sent off a signal asking for permission to take the young man and parted from the lady telling her our sailing date and that she should present herself with the son on the due date. She thanked me profusely and invited me to dinner with them during the course of my stay, which I readily accepted. Subsequently I had a most enjoyable evening with the family and departed from them saying that I looked forward to seeing them on board with their son on the evening on which we were due to sail.

It is perhaps worth recording at this point that once again I had had one of my almost traditional run-ins with authority. The time taken for us to get back to the UK was a bit tight and it would have been better if we could have left Trinidad a day early so that we could get back in time to have a proper Families Day on arrival in Chatham. I was a great believer in Families Days. They are good both for the morale of the Ship's Company and for the families themselves. To be effective they had to be properly planned and given enough time and thought to be both instructive and fun for all. Our plan was to pick up families in Portsmouth, where most of the families resided, and take them up the Channel to Chatham on a day run whilst we demonstrated the ship's equipment, and put them ashore in Chatham along with their husbands or boyfriends when then they would all be able to go on leave. But the programme was tight if I was to avoid the disappointment of missing the pick-up point in Portsmouth. Having to go straight on to Chatham without them would have been a disaster.

However, my request to the local authority had been declined. I was told, 'No, you cannot sail a day early, you must sail on the date you have been given.' I therefore decided that I would sail one minute after midnight so that, in fact, I sailed as early on the day that was stipulated as possible, which was as close as I could come to ignoring the order whilst allowing me the freedom to remain serving!

On the evening of the night on which we were to sail, the Chief was preparing the ship for sea, as was the First Lieutenant and all the others of the Ship's Company concerned. In the Chief's case it means 'flashing up' the boilers and getting the engines warmed through ready for full power when we departed. The ship was berthed on a wooden jetty, that is to say the seaward end of this long jetty, pointing towards the shore; at the landward end of which was a large, typical US Navy clapboard grey painted building. The building was on the shore and the jetty led to the shore.

I dined alone as usual about 7.30 pm and by 8.30 or 9 o'clock was finished and ready at the appointed time for the young man to be delivered aboard by the loving parents. I was in the midst of having my coffee when they arrived and they joined me for a cup as we chatted. I told the First Lieutenant to take the young man away to his quarters and he having bid a fond farewell to his parents we continued to chat for a short while.

The Captain's cabin in the *Lowestoft* was blessed with two scuttles, or portholes as they are more commonly known, so that I did have the advantage of being able to look out on the port side of the ship, which was the side up against the jetty. This meant that we were pointing straight towards the end of the jetty and the building that I have already described.

To my surprise, whilst chatting I noticed the ship give a slight nudge, enough to make me jump up and look out of the scuttle. To my horror, I saw that we were underway and moving down the jetty towards the building! It was now pitch dark, apart from some lights on the jetty itself and to the intense surprise of my guests I shot from my cabin, up to the Bridge and hit it at the same time as Lieutenant John Webster, the Navigating Officer. However, we were some two and a half hours before sailing and there were no communications 'closed up' on the bridge and no way we could communicate with anybody; the Bridge was really the last place we should have gone, however natural an impulse it may have been, except that it gave us an excellent view of what lay ahead. One thing was clear, however, by the light of the moon we could see we were heading straight towards the US Navy building! Grasping this fact fairly quickly I shot from the Bridge down onto the main passageway and along to the top of the engine room hatch and hit it at about the same time as the Chief who had come out of the shower and was merely draped with a towel around his waist. We slid down the ladder together, hitting the plates simultaneously – he, by this time having lost his towel, stark naked, and me in my mess undress, so we must have been a somewhat incongruous looking pair. On the plates in front of the engines was an Engine Room Mechanician who was in charge of warming through the engines.

Now as an aviator I had been astonished to find that in most warships at that time, the drills of 'vital actions' for whatever emergency might occur, or whatever normal procedures that might be required to be followed, were not written down in a way which people could use as a check-off list when they were preparing for something,

The engine room controls of *Juno* being viewed by an Argentinian Admiral! Virtually identical to *Lowestoft*. Note the large brass throttles

or reacting to an emergency. For example, for man overboard, which was a fairly common exercise function, if not always for real, it was not done on a check-off list as you would in an aircraft, to run through the drills of 'vital actions' that you had to take to ensure the safe return of the man on board. I had, therefore, introduced check-off cards for any normal and emergency action, a system that is now in general use. As a result, above the position at which the Engineer Officer, or the Officer in charge of the engine room stood, was a check-off list of the drill which he had to go through to warm through the engines, so that we wouldn't be applying full power and steam to cold turbines. In order to do this he had to 'crack' the throttles of the two engines concerned. These are large brass wheels that have to be turned, above which is an indicator, the 'Chadburn' Indicator, showing the number of revolutions which you have now achieved on the propeller shafts.

Without more ado, and without waiting to see what had happened, I shouted, 'Full astern both engines,' and the surprised Petty Officer cracked one wheel to the astern position and the Chief grabbed the other wheel and opened it. I then stood there and counted one, two, three, and so on until I got to ten and then I said, 'Stop both engines', and ran back up the engine room ladder onto the upper deck.

It was a clear moonlit night and the sea was calm and black and we were at this point drifting comfortably off the jetty about 50 yards or so. A startled Ship's Company had started to crowd up on deck to see what was going on and it became fairly obvious that we had been to the end of the jetty and beyond, and back out again. To prove it there was a neat hole in the building at the end of the jetty! As we lay there in this dark still water, the prospects of a somewhat dramatic end to my career were flashing before me once more. In the heat of the moment I had forgotten all about the guests who had just delivered into my hands their only son. What on earth must they be thinking?

However, we had to get on and sort things out! I turned to a young able seaman who was standing by and said, 'Right, lad, take a line over the side, swim to the jetty and then heave in the first of the securing lines and we will get the ship back alongside.' He, being a well-trained young man, did exactly as he was asked. Over the side he went and we had the first heaving line ashore. There was nobody on the jetty, no US Naval personnel to see us off because we weren't expected to go for another two hours, and so gradually we got lines out and brought the ship slowly back alongside into comparative safety.

I sent for the Diving Officer, Lieutenant Powys Maurice, who was the TAS Officer, and said, 'Right, get the divers equipped, go down and see what damage, if any, there is to the ship'. We now had the gangway back, it being the first thing that we recovered as it floated rather drearily on the black surface of the water, and with as much bravado as I could muster I bade farewell to my guests and said, 'Well, all is secured, don't worry, we will be off at midnight as planned and your son will be taking his Board as soon as we get him back to the United Kingdom.' I don't know how reassured they were with all this and I rather suspect that they didn't really understand what had happened, which was fortunate! So they departed from the jetty with the Rolls Royce purring softly.

It didn't take Powys Maurice long to come back and report to me that there was a black mark about 6 feet up the stem and about 20 feet back along the bottom of the ship, a V-shaped wedge of black which indicated that we had been into black mud and out again, but he said, 'There's absolutely no damage, not a scratch on the ship.' My relief was profound and whilst he had been down there, I had gone forward to examine the 'bull-ring', the hawser ring at the top of the stem, which had been into the building and out again and found that the only damage appeared to be that some of the grey paint was missing. So far so good.

Now to deal with the US Navy. With the telephone lines reconnected I called the Duty Officer who was a Lieutenant, junior grade, and asked him to come down to see me. I invited him on board, offered him a drink and said, 'I am afraid we have had a bit of a scene here this evening.'

'Oh, really, Sir, in what way?' he asked.

'Well,' said I, 'I haven't quite worked out why, but the ship decided to take off by itself earlier on this evening and before we could stop it and get it back out again it actually went into that building of yours over there. As you can see there is a hole where we have entered it and left it again.'

'Which building?' said he.

'The one at the end there, that one there.' He looked at it.

'I don't see too much damage,' he said.

'No,' I replied meekly, 'it's just a kind of hole, that's all.' He said, 'I don't think we should worry, Sir, we've been trying to get that building demolished for some time. It's not used and will be demolished in any case one of these days. Don't worry about it.' I offered him, and he accepted, another large whiskey.

And so the episode was closed; except why had it happened? My subsequent enquiry showed why but, briefly, it was quite simple. My enthusiasm for checklists had required that a checklist for warming through engines and 'flashing up' should be set up in both the boiler room and in the engine room. In the engine room it was right in front of the ERM who was in charge of the 'flashing up' and who had been allowed to do it alone for the first time. In a sensible sequence in the series of events over which he had control, it read, 'When ready for warming through, action 1 – engage the Chadburn indicators'. They are not automatically connected, they have to be engaged. He had failed to engage them. So when it came to warming through the turbines and when the boiler room had told them they were ready, he had alerted the Officer of the Day for him to ensure the ship was properly secured, and then cracked open the port throttle. I should remind you that the port throttle on a Y-series-engined frigate in those days was an enormous brass wheel, a bit like a bit cartwheel. He had moved it, had looked up, had seen no movement on the indicator which, of course, wasn't engaged, moved over to the starboard throttle and opened that one. To his surprise there was still no movement and, said he to himself, 'Obviously I need to open these throttles further.' He went back and opened the port one further and still nothing happened so he opened the starboard one and still nothing happened and when he did it the third time the ship parted the wires and proceeded down the jetty. It was at the moment the wires parted that I had felt the nudge and appreciated what was happening! It was the subsequent action of going straight down to the engine room and going full astern both engines that saved the day.

It wasn't long before we understood what had happened, and so by midnight we were ready to proceed. At one minute past midnight, with three short blasts, I proceeded astern out of the berth and we turned the ship, waving a fond farewell to Chaguramas and the good JG who had done his duty well. Having said farewell to Trinidad we proceeded on our way to Chatham.

There is an old Naval saying, 'All debts paid on the first turn of the screw'; well, I believe that fitted the occasion.

I never reported this incident, I had nothing to report. I never made any mention of it either privately or publicly and so perhaps you are amongst the first to know; just another of my lives was lost and another saga of seamanship is closed. I never did know whether the chap joined the FAA!

P.S. It is no good having a check-off list if you don't use it!

19

By Hook or by Crook

During my time in command of *Lowestoft*, relations between the Irish Republic and the UK had improved sufficiently for there to be the possibility of a warship visit to Southern Ireland, the first since the British had left and abandoned Bantry Bay to the elements.

Events in Northern Ireland had been moving smoothly towards a more tranquil setting under the careful stewardship of Terence O'Neill, and we were quite used to using the facilities in Londonderry, which was the work-up base for anti-submarine exercises out into the North Atlantic.

Two ships of the Squadron, HMS *Berwick* and *Lowestoft*, were therefore detailed off and my Captain F., Captain David Dunbar-Nasmith, was briefed on how we should conduct ourselves while on this first, and very important from a diplomatic point of view, warship visit to Southern Ireland. *Berwick* was to go to Cork and I was to go to Waterford, and as you can imagine there were pretty stringent instructions about avoiding unnecessary incidents and behaving ourselves whilst we were on this goodwill visit.

The great day arrived and with the ship looking, as usual, spick and span we departed for Waterford. I hadn't appreciated until I arrived off Waterford that the original expression 'by hook or by crook' literally meant – to get to Waterford. Hook and Crook are two villages on either side of the entrance to the river which runs up to Waterford, hence 'by Hook and by Crook I'll get to Waterford.' We were duly met off Hook (or was it Crook?) by the Irish Pilot, who was a Lieutenant in the Irish Navy, who introduced himself in a very friendly fashion and proceeded to tell us that we should now move up the river, which I duly did. I became somewhat concerned as the river began to narrow until I could hardly see any water either side of the ship from my position on the Bridge, nothing but the green grass of Southern Ireland which was running down to the water's edge. The Irish Pilot showed no signs of concern at this however, and so we pressed on until I came to a fork in the river, with one reach running off to the right and the other stream, or mainstream it appeared to me, running straight ahead.

'Come round to the right here,' said the Pilot.

'Up there?' I enquired, looking at this rather narrow passage.

'Yes,' he said, 'up there'. And as we were too far into this situation to do anything but make a stern board out, I did as I was instructed and turned to starboard. At about this time there was a shrill whistle from a steam locomotive, which was chugging along the railway line, which ran parallel with the river, with people leaning out of the windows and waving to us. All really rather Irish, I thought, but pleasant and friendly and delightful, if you didn't have the responsibility for this warship on your hands.

Another bend in the river, however, took us into a broader expanse of water which was actually the main harbour at Waterford, with various jetties and quays, and we proceeded towards a position just in front of the bridge right at the end of the harbour and went alongside a wharf very close to the bridge itself and right in the centre of Waterford, which rose up on either side of the valley in which we were sitting with its houses clustered up the sides and around the waterfront.

After we secured, my first call at eleven o'clock was to be on the Mayor of Waterford, and so I dressed myself up in my best uniform, my sword and medals and, accompanied by the First Lieutenant and the Weapons Electrical Officer, Lieutenant Snow, we got into a car that had been provided for us and departed for the Town Hall. On arrival at the foot of the steps leading up to the Town Hall itself, I alighted and looked up to see the Mayor and his Councillors standing at the top of the steps formally arrayed in their Mayoral robes and badges of office. I climbed the steps and was greeted by the Mayor who said, 'Welcome to Waterford,' and I replied that we were delighted to be there and it was good to see him, etc. There was a moment's hesitation and then he said, 'Would you be after coming inside?' I said that that would be very pleasant so we duly entered the Council Chamber and found ourselves in what I presumed to be a side room with a trestle table and some forms on which we proceeded to seat ourselves. Soon after settling down the Mayor turned to me and said, 'Would you be after having a drink?' I said I would be very pleased to have a drink and he asked me what type of drink I would wish to take.

'Whiskey, of course,' I said, 'please'.

'Would you be having Scotch whisky or Irish whiskey?' he enquired.

'Well, Irish whisky, of course,' said I.

'You don't have to have Irish whiskey,' he replied, 'you can have Scotch whisky if you prefer it.'

'Oh no,' I said, 'I would much prefer to have Irish whiskey, thank you very much.' And so the bottle was produced, along with some glasses, and we proceeded to start a fairly healthy drinking session.

As time progressed, the atmosphere warmed noticeably and the Mayor decided that he would like to make a speech. He stood up and addressed us in the following terms: that Waterford was a prosperous city, it had a great industry, it was a marvellous opportunity for inward investment from foreign investors, particularly from the United Kingdom, and that he looked forward to my being able to return to the UK and tell my rich friends all about the virtues of investment in Waterford, because since the Revolution much work had taken place in order to restore it to its old kind of prosperity as a centre for glass.

I responded by saying that we were delighted to be in Waterford, that my Ship's Company average age was something like eighteen and a half and they would come to Waterford with completely open eyes and open expectations and would, I was sure, enjoy themselves because they would look upon it without any of the previous concerns which had bedevilled Anglo-Irish relations. They were too young to know what it was all about and they came with clear and open minds, and I was sure if they were dealt with by the local inhabitants in the way that I was sure they would be, they would come away with very happy memories of Southern Ireland, and Waterford in particular.

Naval Visitors To Waterford

At the reception at the City Hall, Waterford for the officers of the H.M.S. Frigate Lowestaff, which is on a courtesy visit to Waterford. Front (left to right)—Lt. Commdr. A. G. MacIver, Mr. P. Breen, President, Waterford Chamber of Commerce; the Mayor, Councillor J. Griffin; Mr. S. McClure, Vice-President, Junior Chamber of Commerce; Commander R. D. Lygo. Back (left to right) — Lt. A. W. Chapman, Slua Muiri; Mr. F. J. Cassin, Harbour Board Chairman; Lt. J. H. Flannery, Irish Naval Service; Supt. G. Butler, Garda Siochana; Lt. J. F. T. Snow; Mr. S. Gillain, City Manager. ("Examiner")

Calling on the Mayor of Waterford

270

As far as my going back and talking to my rich friends in England about the opportunities for investment in Southern Ireland, I had to tell him that we'd also had a revolution of a kind in the United Kingdom. Since the end of the war we had gone through a long period, and indeed were still in a period of Socialism, and this had caused many changes to take place, one of which of course was that I no longer had any rich friends and so I was afraid I couldn't go back and tell them, except of course I would be able to report back the findings of my visit which I was sure were going to be favourable. The whole thing became very convivial after this, and I finally departed at about 12.30 and arrived back at the ship about one o'clock, in order that I could have some lunch before the reception which was due to start at six o'clock in the evening.

I had hardly got myself unbuckled from my sword and medals when the First Lieutenant came to see me to report that there had been an unfortunate incident.

'What incident?' said I.

'Well,' said he, 'it appears that a couple of chaps came on board and told the Officer of the Day that there was a certain bar in town which was noted for its misbehaviour and whatever, and that it should be placed out of bounds.' I looked at the First Lieutenant with amazement.

'He hasn't put it out of bounds, has he?' I said. The First Lieutenant nodded glumly.

'I'm afraid he has, Sir, and furthermore he did it by broadcasting over the Ship's loudspeakers to the effect that Mrs Murphy's bar was out of bounds.' The broadcasting system of the frigate was loud enough and the situation appropriate enough to have that message echoing around every house in Waterford. I was appalled. The one thing never to do with British sailors, if you can possibly avoid it, is to put anything out of bounds for whatever reason, because they'll immediately want to go there.

'Oh dear,' I said.

'Mr Murphy is actually on board at this moment, Sir, protesting to us about this decision.' So I said, 'Well, perhaps Mr Murphy would come and have a word with me and I'll see if I can set this thing to rights.' Mr Murphy was duly persuaded to come. By this time it was moving towards two o'clock, and as he entered the cabin I warmly welcomed him and shook hands and said, 'I'm terribly sorry to hear what has happened, Mr Murphy. As you will appreciate I was away calling on your Mayor at the time and, had I been here, this thing would not have occurred, because we never ever do things like that. We never put places out of bounds.'

271

'But,' said he, 'that's as maybe, but I mean it's upset my wife terribly. She, poor woman, who runs the bar, doesn't understand why this statement was made and who has put this word about.'

'Mr Murphy,' I said, 'I can assure you that there was a mistake and we will do whatever we can to rectify it. How about,' said I, 'your having a drink first of all.'

'Well,' he said, 'I'm not sure that I should.'

'Come, Mr Murphy,' said I, 'surely you'll take a dram with me.'

'Well,' said he, 'indeed I will,' and so I proceeded to consume more of that golden liquid that had been passing fairly freely down my gullet since eleven o'clock.

After we had drunk ourselves a few drams, I said to him, 'Now, let me see how best I can put this to rights, Mr Murphy. Let me ask you, what time does your bar open?'

'It opens at five o'clock sir,' said he.

'Well, supposing I were to come and greet your wife and supposing I were to come in full uniform and have a drink with her, do you think that would put things to rights?'

'Oh, sir,' said he, 'she would be honoured by such a visit, and I am sure she would be very touched by your generosity.'

'Not at all,' said I, 'I can understand that she is upset and I wish to do my utmost to make amends.' We had a few more drinks and he departed, by which time it was now nearly three o'clock and I had been drinking fairly steadily since eleven. I should say I am not a great drinker under ordinary circumstances but the pressure of events can make one capable of consuming, it would appear, fairly large quantities without too much ill effect, whereas if you were to do it in a more convivial sense I am sure it would be damaging!

So I prepared myself, after a sandwich, to go ashore again at about half past four, which I did, and arrived in the pub at five o'clock to find it, of course, full of my sailors. As I walked in, the first questions they asked were, 'Hello, Sir, what's going on here then? Why has it been placed out of bounds? What's good about it?' Which was the kind of classic remark one would expect from a red-blooded tar.

'Don't ask me,' said I, 'I've no idea.' But going over to the bar I greeted Mrs Murphy warmly by kissing her hand and, she promptly offering me a glass of the local amber coloured liquid, we proceeded to cement the relationship. I stayed there until half past five and I returned to the ship to get cleaned up to stand on the gangway at six o'clock to start welcoming the guests, amongst whom was the Mayor, and many other local dignitaries, for the cocktail party which went on until eight o'clock and then I went ashore for an official kind of evening supper at a local house, and then back on board at eleven o'clock. By which time I reckoned I'd had 12 hours of steady intake of alcohol in the words of that song, 'drinking for the Empire, drinking for the Crown, drinking for the dear old British Raj'.

It had worked and the visit after that was a resounding success, everyone enjoyed themselves, the people were charming, we got on extremely well together. I remember going to one house where the chap told me how his uncle, I think it was, had hidden in the back of the sofa when the British troops came looking for what they regarded as malcontents at that time, and I was left with the firm impression that if only we could deal on the basis of openness, friendliness and living in the present, then the relationships between our two peoples would be and could be close and warm. There was so much that we had in common, particularly a liking for the amber liquid and, in addition, a perverse attitude to authority, which made for a true partnership.

Goodness knows who the characters were who started the story about the bar – presumably a competitor – little did they know of the reaction of British sailors!

When the morning came, prior to departure, the Mayor and some others with whom we had become friends came down to see us off. They had with them a large offering of spare ribs and other delicacies, which I was delighted to be able to take back to the UK. As we stood chatting, the Officer of the Day came into my cabin with a letter, which was addressed in Gaelic. I opened it and of course, couldn't read it so I passed it to the Mayor and said, 'I'm sorry I can't read this, it's in Gaelic.' He looked at it and said, 'I can't read it either. I should tear it up if I were you.' It was the standard protest about our visit I suppose, and certainly every night there was painted on the wall alongside the ship a slogan equivalent to 'Yanks Go Home' in the United Kingdom, and as soon as it had been finished the Guarda came and painted it out! We slipped and proceeded out of that quaint little harbour, down that narrow river and out through the twins of Hook and Crook to the expanse of the Irish Sea and away.

20

The Carrier Battle

My first appointment as a Captain was as Deputy Director of Naval Air Warfare in the Ministry of Defence. It is sometimes said, or was said, that the first job you had as a Captain didn't really matter very much because you were a long time serving as a Captain before you came up for Flag rank. So the time to enjoy yourself was in your first appointment, and the recommended place for this was to go as a Naval Attaché somewhere, or into a nice NATO job in some exotic foreign country to enjoy your well-deserved promotion. Nothing like that was going to happen to me, however, since I was appointed to the Ministry of Defence and it became clear to me, if it hadn't been clear already, that my career was going to be one of alternating between the Ministry of Defence and going to sea, which wasn't bad at all. It was good for, perhaps, hard work and experience but not much for family life and leisure. Nevertheless, there it was.

We had now grown out of the house we had built in Trottiscliffe and had gone from the sublime to the ridiculous in buying half of a large house, not too far away, called Mereworth Lawn, and we had exchanged oil-fired central heating and an insulated shoe-box, as I had described the house we built, for a large, draughty Victorian house with coke-fired central heating. We had moved in in the very severe winter of 1961, or should I say, I had left Pepper to effect the move, having myself sailed to Bermuda! She, poor thing, had to move in and face the rigours of a cold winter in Kent, in a draughty house, bringing in barrow loads of coke to stoke a boiler which didn't always want to stay alight, and to deal with an Aga which, as an American, she regarded as a somewhat unnecessary burden on society, which also never seemed to want to stay in. Naval wives have a lot to put up with! However, once again it was within reasonably easy commuting distance of London and also, of course, near to Chatham, where I had already had one ship and as we shall learn, fate was going to let me have yet another.

My arrival in the Ministry of Defence coincided with the defeat of the Conservative Government and its replacement by a Labour administration; Denis Healey was appointed Secretary of State for Defence with Christopher Mayhew as the Navy Minister. I was to relieve 'Winkle' Brown as Deputy Director Naval Air Warfare and my Director was George Baldwin, whom I had known previously and for whom I had a high regard. The man at the top of the Air Branch at that time was the Deputy Chief of Naval Staff and Fifth Sea Lord; this was Frank Hopkins, another distinguished Naval aviator and a charming man to boot. The First Sea Lord, also recently arrived, was Sir David Luce, again a charming and gentle Officer of the old school. None of us were prepared for what was to follow.

Immediately prior to my arrival there had been a fierce battle between the Navy and the Procurement executive, and the Royal Air Force, over the new fighter for the Royal Navy. We were looking for a replacement for the Vixen and Scimitar as a fighter, and the plan proposed was to collaborate with the Royal Air Force for a vertical and short take-off and landing aircraft (V/STOL), the P1154, which was to be a ground-support aircraft for the Royal Air Force and then fitted with a radar to be an interceptor fighter for the Royal Navy. The Navy had become concerned that the operational requirements for the interceptor fighter would be very much degraded by the Royal Air Force's requirement for a more simple ground-attack Army-support aircraft, and that the performance that we were going to get would be far lacking what was actually required. The preference was to go American, as was the fad at that time, and the Navy had its eyes fixed on procurement of the F4 Phantom. This battle had been won by the time I arrived and the decision had been taken that, provided the Navy could show that it could acquire the F4 Phantom within the same cost bracket as its share of the development of the P1154, it would be allowed to opt out of this joint development programme and go it alone with the Phantom.

It must be confessed that the Navy's argument had more to do with the length of the flight deck than the performance of the aircraft! This in simple terms meant that if the Navy were to opt for a V/STOL aeroplane it would be difficult to defend its decision to continue with the large fixed-wing carriers, which it was determined to do. The new aircraft carrier, CVA01, had already been approved in principle by the outgoing Conservative Government, along with the Phantom procurement, and the Navy was busy formulating its plans to build this new aircraft carrier.

Part of the package that I also inherited was to be a new anti-submarine helicopter to replace the Wessex 3, which was then about to enter service. The Wessex 3 was an uprated version of the Wessex 1 but with a much-improved sonar attack system which added so much weight to the aircraft that even with a different engine, it was unable

Artist's impression of CVA01

to provide us with any kind of endurance on task. So we were desperately looking for a better aircraft to deploy this much-improved weapon system, with the attack Sonar 195 and an integrated display for the observer in the back cockpit.

Here unfolds one of those incredible stories, which you can only experience if you have served in the Ministry of Defence and managed to preserve your sanity. The decision to go for a new big helicopter was based on the assumption that the Westland Aircraft Company was going to build it. Not many of us had much faith in Westland's ability, at that time, to build a completely indigenously designed big helicopter by themselves, but having read through all the supporting papers it became clear that there was no helicopter readily available that we could purchase off the shelf to lift our new anti-submarine system and give us the performance we required. Certainly all the

276

papers that were provided by the procurement executive came to only one conclusion: we would have to develop a new anti-submarine helicopter. The cost of this programme was, of course, large by any measurement but in my experience would almost certainly be even larger when the final bill was presented.

While we were debating this, one of my Staff Officers came in to see me to say that a young Lieutenant who had recently returned from exchange duty with the United States Navy was in the building, and would I like to see him? Remembering only too well the lack of interest shown when I had returned from my exchange tour with the US Navy, I was keen to see this chap.

He had been serving in a Sea King helicopter Squadron based at Key West and told me about the operations they had conducted and how they were getting on. I listened to him, asked him a few questions

277

and exchanged a few thoughts, and then I said, 'It's a great pity that the Sea King is not capable of lifting our 195 system to give us the endurance on task that we require.' He looked at me in some surprise and said, 'But I am quite sure it is, Sir.' 'Oh no,' said I, 'I have the figures here from the procurement executive showing that the aircraft, hot and humid, couldn't possibly give us the endurance we want with that load.' He looked at me again with some surprise and said, 'But I have just been operating out of Key West, hot and humid, and we have been doing three-hour patrols. Furthermore, I have the pilot's notes here which you can read and which will show you quite clearly that the performance you require is well within the capability of this aircraft.' I took the copy of the pilot's notes and looked at them and became first astonished and then irritated. It was quite clear that the performance figures of the Sea King for the United States Navy had been presented in such a way as to make it seem as if it could not perform the task that we required it to fulfil.

I am a qualified helicopter pilot, and this so incensed me that I asked George Baldwin's permission to go off to the United States and fly both the Sikorsky aircraft and also other contending US aircraft, the Bell Hewie, the Boeing Vertol 107 and the large Chinook (none of which had ever been used in the anti-submarine role). This created great consternation both at Westland and in the Ministry, and I learned as I went round that I was being followed, or at least tracked very closely, by John Speachley who was then Managing Director of Westland, to see what I was up to on my visits to these companies. I flew all the aeroplanes that I had come to see, and they all flew extremely well and handled easily. The difficulties that had been inherent in flying the early helicopters had been largely worked out of the system by this time and it was possible to almost fly, certainly the larger ones, as if they were fixed-wing aircraft.

During the course of the visit to the Sikorsky plant, I had the rare privilege of sitting at lunch next to Igor Sikorsky himself and exchanging views with him on the progress made in helicopter development and what the future held. At that time there was great expectations of a thing called the 'Tilt Rotor' and the 'Rigid Rotor', which he, over lunch, dismissed completely. Not surprisingly because he was the chap who had invented the flapping hinge which enabled helicopters to operate for the first time. I was also amazed to learn from him that he had been engaged in the design of 4-engine bombers for the Russian Air Force prior to the 1914-18 War. An extraordinary man and that meeting is something I cherish as a memory.

The conclusion that I reached on the way back was that, although most of these aircraft could perform the task, to try to do it in the

Chinook would be a mammoth task in some of our smaller carriers because the aeroplane was so large; that the Hewie was probably too small and Bell had never installed a hover coupler to the aircraft so that it could operate in the dipping sonar mode at night. This was also true of the 107, a slightly smaller Boeing aircraft, whereas Sikorsky had solved all the problems and had in the Sea King an aeroplane that was able to perform our task without expensive modification. It became a fairly natural choice for us. When I got back I started the ball rolling in this particular direction, and I remember saying to George Hiscock who was the Technical Director of Westland at the time, and also to John Speachley, 'If you take a licence to build this aircraft from Sikorsky and put the Wessex 3 weapon system in it, you will have one of the best products you have ever had and it will make you a great deal of money, because its export potential will be very large.' I was subsequently proved to be right; one of the most successful aircraft we have ever had in the helicopter field was this particular aircraft with this particular weapon system, and we had it for a tiny fraction of the cost of a completely new aircraft.

The emphasis, however, was not on anti-submarine warfare but on an interceptor fighter. Part of the package in getting approval for the Phantom was that it should be fitted with a Rolls Royce Spey engine, but an afterburner had to be put on the Spey to give the aircraft the performance we expected to get. Most of the Americans I spoke to were astonished that we should take out a perfectly good Pratt & Whitney J79 engine, which was already integrated in the aircraft, and put in a new one – but that is what we intended to do, and I remember saying that if any company could do it Rolls Royce could.

Mr Healey was now in full song in his new job and facing one of the difficulties, which all politicians faced on entering the Ministry of Defence, who the devil am I supposed to trust and who should I believe? Each of the three Services were geared and designed to produce and protect their own requirements and the experience of procurement had not been a happy one. Not that this always reflected on the Services themselves but more on the political changes that were the background to those procurement decisions. The withdrawal from Empire was in full swing and yet no one wanted to admit to the title of being a 'Little Englander'. We still had a string of outposts and bases around the world which were there to protect our interests and from which we could operate, and they in turn would require protecting – Singapore, Aden, the Gulf, Malta, Cyprus, Simonstown, the Falkland Islands, Bermuda, to mention a few.

At about this time Andrew Humphrey, who was to become Chief of the Air Staff and eventually Chief of the Defence Staff before tragically dying, was an Air Commodore in plans, who came up with the idea of what he called the 'Rationalisation of Air Power'. In this proposal, the manning and maintaining of aircraft, both Naval and Army, would be run by the Royal Air Force and manned essentially and primarily by them because they would have all the short-service backbone of the pilot requirement in RAF uniform, while the Navy would retain its general-list permanent branch Officers in aviation. So a Squadron would be made up of a mixture of RN General Service officers and RAF Short Service ones. These Squadrons were to be formed from a reserve of aircraft, which were primarily held ashore and were formed up into appropriate 'Squadrons' to embark and disembark as the Navy required. It was an original and ingenious attempt both to get some rationalisation in the total number of aircraft required to meet the likely operational task of all three Services, and thus reduce the cost, and also, of course, gave the RAF a secure and pole position in the flying business. The Navy saw this as a cheap attempt to undermine what they had struggled so hard to achieve, their own – their entirely own – Fleet Air Arm.

At about this time Captain Ian Easton came to take over from Captain Terry Lewin as a Director of one of the most important Divisions in the Admiralty, relating to planning. He and I were old friends, he having been the Air Direction Officer in *Indefatigable* when I was a fighter pilot in 887 Squadron during the War, and later when we had both served on the Aircraft Carrier Staff. A committee was set up under General Templar to look into this issue and make recommendations and the Naval Officer who was put on the committee was the most senior Naval aviator we possessed, Admiral Sir Casper John, recently retired Chief of Naval Staff.

The one aspect of this proposal which I found totally unacceptable, was the mixing of individuals and ground crew to form *ad hoc* Squadrons. I had previously been through this when I formed 759 Squadron at Culdrose from the remnants of the centralised maintenance system that had previously been operating. This system so undermined moral and took away the kind of Squadron, or Ship's Company, type of spirit that it produced the most appalling results in terms of both availability of aircraft and the performance of aircrew and ground crew together. It was only when we restored the 'whole Squadron' concept that we got back to something that began to look as if it would actually work in wartime. The idea, therefore, that you should send a bunch of RAF Short Service officers and some NCOs to mix with a few general-list Naval pilots to form *ad hoc* Squadrons operating in the demanding environment of an aircraft carrier was more than I could stomach. Furthermore, I didn't believe, and neither did any of my aviating friends, that you could really arrive at a peak of operational performance, particularly at night with all that that implied for deck operations, unless you had people who were devoted and specialised in doing it; to suppose that somebody could suddenly arrive and do this was an illusion. I remember giving a graphic account to General Templar and Admiral Casper John of my views of the difficulties that would be experienced by pilots landing a large and very fast aircraft at night – we were talking Phantoms at this stage, and Buccaneers – who hadn't had consistent experience in work-up to actually achieve this objective, on a deck the size of Hermes.

At the end of the day and after many months of argument the proposition was rejected by the committee but this caused Andrew Humphrey to make, as it turned out, an extremely prophetic remark, although whether it would have made any difference, who knows, when he said at the end, 'Well, you finally fixed it and that's the end of your carrier programme.' Who knows, it might have been the end of it anyway, but some things we shall never know. It will be interesting to see how Taskforce 2000 makes out.

Eventually we became engaged in what is known as the 'Carrier Battle'. I am bound to say that within the Navy, and certainly the Naval Air Staff, we didn't perhaps take this study as seriously as we should have done from the outset. To us it was just so incredible and laughable that it couldn't possibly be serious; it was. Mr Healey, faced with the difficulties of getting priorities right, had created a rather super class of scientist. If the Services couldn't agree on what they needed, why not bring in pure, abstract and separate scientific advice to give you the answer? Therefore scientists, who had no operational experience whatsoever and were unlikely ever to get any, or to have the responsibility of operational decisions, were elevated to the positions of judges and juries of the Services' requirements. They were then bolstered by the next illusion, 'Operational Analysis'. This meant that you were to analyse the operational requirements, starting with the threat, and come up with a theoretical technical solution to it; that, then, would be what you would go for. I mention elsewhere the problem of Sea Wolf in the protection of ships at sea, but it is as good an illustration of the nonsense that can result from operational analysis as is likely to be found.

If a ship needed to be protected against attacks from the air while it was in the ocean large, then it would need to have air protection; that protection had to be provided by either standing patrols or, if an aircraft carrier was available, then aircraft at standby that could be launched to defend the force. If these measures failed, then to counter the stand-off weapons that Russian aircraft were assumed to launch against us, incoming threats of this kind would need a point defence system which would be capable of intercepting the missiles themselves as they came into short range. The Navy had already decided that this threat could best be dealt with by Sea Wolf, a point defence missile system which combined a British Aerospace missile with a Marconi radar system and various other clever bits and pieces, which would actually home on to, lock on and destroy an incoming missile.

To justify any of these weapons you had to set a scenario in which a hypothetical attack would take place. It was therefore essential to understand what the Russians might launch in an attack: nobody knew what they would actually throw against you, we could only judge by looking at their exercises and determining whether there was anything there that could indicate the type of attack that might be made.

It was a closely argued debate based, of course, on a mass of assumptions. In order for the Services to justify any piece of equipment, they had to be able to satisfy the operational analysis teams that what they were proposing would actually meet the threat. Of course, it might well be that in producing something to meet that specifically designed threat you had something which was incapable of dealing with anything else, or certainly not much else! I honestly believe it is one of the most flawed methods of determining the types of weapon systems that one requires. It drives you in a particular direction with complete disregard for other alternatives, or other scenarios that might suddenly arise.

It was a commonly held belief by those of us that had served long enough in the Ministry of Defence to understand such things, that in the bowels of the Ministry of Defence were endless contingency plans for events which never materialised, but that there never had been and never would be plans for those events which actually did materialise. The responsibility of the Services and of Defence is to have sufficient flexibility and capability to discharge whatever threat suddenly materialises which you weren't expecting, and it is always the unexpected that floors you.

So it was that the threat posed through operational analysis of the type of attack that a frigate might have to withstand 'demanded' that four missiles should be ready to be launched against an incoming attack. Now Sea Wolf was designed to replace Sea Cat, a wire-guided system that had been mounted in our ships on two-barrel launchers. Almost every ship in the Navy had Sea Cat launchers and had magazines designed for stowing the Sea Cat missile. Because the Navy didn't want to rebuild its entire fleet around a weapon system, they had decided that the Sea Wolf missile should be of the same dimensions as the Sea Cat so that it could go into the same magazine. However, because according to Operational Analysis the Russians would launch four missiles in an attack, you had to have four missiles at readiness instead of two, as was the case with the Sea Cat mountings, these would not be adequate and a completely new launching system was required. It became large, cumbersome and difficult to install. Digging holes in ships to put in new equipment is always a costly business.

The opportunity to put two missiles on to the Sea Cat launchers was dismissed; it was not operationally correct. Furthermore (and this comes later in the story), when I had become Vice-Chief of the Naval Staff and asked why we couldn't put them on the Sea Cat launchers, I was told that they were not strong enough to withstand the weight of the missile and therefore could not be used. When I arrived in British Aerospace and was involved in the Lightweight Sea Wolf saga, I remarked at one meeting that it was a pity we couldn't use the Sea Cat launchers because they were not robust enough; this produced a gasp of amazement from my staff who said, 'But they are strong enough, quite strong enough. We have always argued that they could have been used.' Had we used the Sea Cat launchers then we could have had the Sea Wolf missile in service in practically every ship that subsequently went down to the Falkland Islands, instead of having only one ship that had been fitted with the four-barrelled launcher! And in any case, the Argentinean Navy and Air Force had not actually studied Russian tactics to the extent of being able to support the concept of our operational analysis team! Nevertheless, the task of arguing one's way through this kind of scenario-based procurement process was something which we had not experienced and if one dared to say such things as 'operational experience has shown this to be an absolute nonsense', then, of course, you became cast out as a Colonel Blimp and not having the correct type of analytical mind.

It was against this kind of background that we faced the 'carrier battle'. Essentially, this was about whether it was necessary for the Navy to have its own fixed-wing aircraft for defence and attack, or whether it was possible for the RAF to provide the cover from shore-based aircraft. There was a very important but understandable twist to this. If the RAF were to provide the fleet with its air power, then the RAF would decide on the priority it afforded to it. This was clouded in such terms as the 'Flexibility of Air Power' – a trap those of us who had fought long to avoid saw quite clearly. Our defence and attack would not be under our own control. The RAF maintained that they could provide all the cover necessary from their bases; in order to do that they had to demonstrate that they would be able to operate aircraft in protection of a force at sea continuously during the period of its passage, and be able to conduct the necessary surveillance operations that were also required. We maintained that they could not and more importantly, but difficult to prove, they would not.

The only Service which had experience in airborne early warning was the Royal Navy. We had it at first in the Sky Raiders and subsequently in the Gannett AEWs and this was to be replaced by a new joint staff target for an aircraft that was to service both the RAF and the Navy with non-rotating aerial arrays, as had been the case thus far, but with fixed fore and aft aerials similar to that which eventually was to be put into the ill-fated Nimrod. The RAF, however, at this time had never had airborne early warning (AEW) and therefore could hardly be arguing from the strength of its own experience.

When the first meeting with the RAF took place, I was sent to lead our team and found myself interfacing with six Air Commodores. There was an Air Commodore expert on fighter tactics, another on strike tactics, another on AEW, another on anti-submarine warfare, a chap who was an expert on air-to-air refuelling and the tanker force, and one other, I suppose to make up the team. I found it all slightly amusing, but in fact it was anything but. It was deadly serious! We were about to be outgunned, not with knowledge but with sheer weight of numbers.

The RAF was still reeling from the loss of most of its replacement aircraft programme. One of the first acts of the incoming Labour Government had been to axe the TSR2, the P1154 and the HS 681, which was the new transport aircraft. Paradoxically, the Navy had shown the way by adopting the Phantom in opposition to the 1154, and the RAF was told that it would have aircraft now procured directly from the United States, in the shape of the Phantom and the Hercules, but that the cherished TSR2, on which the RAF had built so much hope, was to be replaced by the F111, the new swing-wing aircraft which had been adopted for the United States services. Thus having lost the TSR2 and been promised the F111, the RAF's case for the most part was based on the capability of this particular aeroplane. We knew that the US Navy was fighting to avoid having to have the aeroplane imposed upon them by the then Secretary of State for Defence, Mr McNamara, as part of a rationalisation process for the provision of aircraft to the United States services. Once again we saw an argument taking place between an aircraft that was essentially designed for a land-based requirement being forced into a carrier environment for which it was not entirely suited. The F111 was the outcome, over a long period of time, of the Barnes-Wallis Swallow concept of a swing-wing aircraft. In order to try to get some detailed facts about the capability and performance of the aircraft, I was despatched to Washington to see the Head of Naval Aviation for a briefing. He was kind enough to see me and said, 'Ray, the aeroplane is a clunker. It will not do the things that we want it to do, we don't want it and in my desk here I have got a stack of information that will show all the things that are wrong with this particular aeroplane for our requirement.' I said that I would be delighted if I could have a copy of this, as it would be very useful in our particular fight. He paled slightly and then said, 'But I dare not show it to you, it is so sensitive here. McNamara is likely to go bananas if it were discovered that there had been any leak of any document which knocked an aeroplane to which he has attached his personal credibility.' I remember thinking at the time that it was strange that the man who had invented the 'Edsall' when with the Ford Motor Company, which had jolly nearly bankrupted them, had subsequently introduced the F111 which didn't do very much good to General Dynamics, which also proved to be a somewhat costly failure, to find that he was to go to the World Bank! I awaited the next world financial crisis with some interest. And so I returned empty-handed. Yes, I had been told the aeroplane would not perform in the way the RAF was claiming. Yes, I had been told that all the information that invalidated their claims was to hand, but no, I could not produce it.

One of the more difficult areas for the RAF to carry out Naval protection was in the Indian Ocean; this required them to build a base at Adu Atoll, where we had carried out some exercises from the very large sheltered anchorage that was there, but in order to operate their aircraft they would need to build quite an extensive facility. It was assumed that this would be built in order to support their operation; in the same way, bases in Western Australia would also be available for them to operate from, should they require them. Even so, the distances were quite enormous and would require aeroplanes operating to the maximum range and, in the case of providing fighter protection, for them remaining on task for exceedingly long periods, up to seven hours, I seem to recall, in a Phantom. We believed it was totally unrealistic to expect crews to remain in cramped conditions and on alert for seven hours; it also called for a massive tanker effort to supply them with fuel to keep them on station for such a length of time. The problem was that, no matter what you did with the bases in Western Australia and the Indian Ocean, there was a gap in cover that even the imaginative endurances that were being invented could not solve.

One evening, sitting quite late in my office, the Desk Officer concerned came in to me and said, 'I've been looking at the RAF's chart of cover for the approaches to Western Australia and I cannot reconcile this chart with any known projection'. It had been a long day and I looked at him somewhat puzzled.

'How do you mean?' I said.

'Well, it doesn't make sense, Sir. Australia is not in the right position'.

'Bring it to me,' I said. He did, and when we reconciled it with the correct Admiralty chart Australia had been moved 200 miles to the westward, in order to produce sufficient cover for the approaches to the Australian mainland. I could hardly believe it, and promptly the next morning this information was relayed to Sir Frank Hopkins and the Naval people that were intimately involved in the discussions that were taking place.

Even though all the evidence was presented by the Navy it was not believed by the Central Staff who were, I am bound to say, lock, stock and barrel behind the concept of knocking the Navy out of the carrier game, and it was covered up by explaining that it was some simple mistake which didn't really matter. It mattered a lot because it really should have given some grounds for believing that the Services were now beginning to go too far in their attempts to preserve their own case.

As the situation worsened, the United States Navy made an offer which I think was almost unbelievable. They offered to provide the Royal Navy with three carriers for I think it was $150 million. It would be the *Oriskany*, fully modernised to angle-deck standard, and two others, the *Leyte* and another of the same class which would have required modernisation. A team was assembled to go and look at these carriers, particularly the *Oriskany*. It did not contain one Naval aviator! It contained Naval engineers, constructors, seamen, but the one ingredient that was missing was a practising, active Naval aviator. The team came back and made a report which rejected the offer, saying that these ships would have been far too difficult to maintain in British Dockyards, and that their accommodation problems were difficult to overcome. It must be remembered that the United States Navy does not provide separate accommodation for its Petty Officer ranks!

At the height of all this, I came in one morning to be told that the RAF had decided that the escalating costs of the Rolls Royce engine in the Phantom had caused them to say that they no longer required it, and they would be quite satisfied to take the Phantom with the J79 engine. The Naval argument, strongly supported by the Procurement Executive, had always been that we needed the extra push of the Spey to give the Phantom an operational capability from our smaller carriers.

Faced with the withdrawal of the RAF from the programme, if this was to be endorsed, it meant that the whole cost of developing the

Spey for the Phantom would fall upon the Naval vote and we just couldn't face it. I asked Freddie Hefford to produce the graphs of performance for the two different engines off the short catapult of Hermes, which had become such a feature of the 'hot and humid' argument in the Persian Gulf. Whereas the Spey would have given the Phantom 32 minutes on task, the J79 gave it 28. I made a snap decision. 'Right,' I said, 'tell the central staff procurement executive, if the RAF is abandoning this engine so will we; we don't need it either, we shall go for the J79.' This communication was duly made.

At about half past two I was asked to go and see Frank Hopkins. 'What have you been saying about the Spey engine?' he asked. 'Well, Sir,' I said, 'the RAF have said that they don't really want it, they don't need it and they are prepared to have the J79 instead. This will place the whole of the cost of that development on the Navy, and I have said that if that is the case we follow suit because it only makes a slight difference to our performance, Sir.' 'Well,' said he, 'I have just come from having lunch with the Chief of Defence Procurement who has told me to call my dogs off.' 'Oh, really, Sir,' I said. 'Well, I have to tell you that these are the facts. What decision you wish to recommend, or make, is a matter for you to decide.'

It is interesting to note that the RAF was told that it had to have the Rolls-Royce Spey, and the Navy duly followed suit. The aircraft's performance with the Spey never met the expected performance of the graphs – it fell considerably short. It did mean, however, that Rolls Royce were able to develop a Spey engine with an afterburner, that their technology was improved and that their capability was enhanced, but it wasn't really an operational necessity, it was an industrial one.

The battle now shifted towards the requirement of the RAF to have the F111, or whether it could make do with an improved Buccaneer, the so-called Buccaneer 2 Star, which was to have an upgraded weapon system to meet its operational requirements. The Buccaneer, as a result of its escaping the axe brought down by Duncan Sandys when he said there would be no more fixed-wing aircraft, was proving, with the provision of the Mk 2 with the Spey engine, to be an outstandingly successful aircraft. It had been designed by the Navy to go a thousand miles and deliver a nuclear weapon against the Russian Fleet, and it was to do this by detecting first and then flying underneath the lobe of defensive radars. It employed 'loft' bombing, that is to say, looping the aircraft from low altitude and throwing the bomb, much like a sling shot, at the enemy thus enabling the aircraft to stay outside the then range of defence systems. There was no doubt that it was a first-class aircraft and likely to be perfectly satisfactory for the Royal Air Force. They, of course, did not want to know of it. Its great disadvantage, I suppose historically, must have been the fact that it had Royal Navy painted on the tail. If it had been designed and produced for the Royal Air Force, I am sure that it would have embraced it more enthusiastically, but in the heat of inter-Service battle and rivalry it was rejected out of hand.

We therefore had to turn our attention to proving that the Buccaneer 2 Star would satisfy the RAF's requirements, stand fast the ability to defend the fleet at sea, plus all the other things they wanted to do. What a complicated, overlapping mess this was all becoming, but it was clear that if the F111 were to be purchased then there would be no room in the total budget for carriers and the improvements that we wanted. The battle raged and I recall very well the debriefing session that David Luce gave us when he came back from the Chief of Staff meeting that had debated the alternative of the Buccaneer 2 Star or the F111. We crowded into the First Sea Lord's office and I, as a junior Captain, was somewhere at the back. David Luce gave us a brief rundown on the early stages of the meeting, and then said, 'The Chief of the Air Staff explained to us that the RAF was required to carry out very sophisticated reconnaissance missions, of which little was known outside the specialist intelligence sections that dealt with them. Part of the role was photographic reconnaissance, and the F111 was the only aircraft that could accommodate a camera of the correct focal length.' I really couldn't believe my ears, to such an extent that I shouted from the back, 'Prisms, Sir, prisms.' Several of my seniors turned round and glared at me and the First Sea Lord, pausing, continued thus: 'Well, gentlemen, there was nothing I could do to argue with the Chief of the Air Staff, it is his business and he knows what he wants.' Thus the decision was lost and the RAF was to get its F111! It was *almost* the final nail in the carrier coffin.

Now comes another episode I remember extremely well. A debate with the Secretary of State, with Mayhew as Minister of the Navy, was to take place on the outcome of the carrier study. Healey had made it clear, I believe, that he could understand the argument for four carriers but found it difficult to believe that three would suffice. George and I had a routine worked out between us in that I, because I could commute easily home, would stay late on Friday nights, whereas he who lived further away and used to spend the nights in digs in London during the week, would go home fairly early on a Friday, whilst he stayed later during the week. It was thus late one Friday evening when I received a message from Frank Hopkin's office to go up and see him. When I got there Christopher Mayhew was with him and Frank said, 'Well, Ray, we have just come from a meeting with the Secretary of State and we have another breathing space. We have a further one month in which to come up with arguments which can persuade him one way or the other. I thought,' said Frank ' that all was lost but we now have more breathing space.'

He and Mayhew had been celebrating with a drink and I was now asked if I would join them. I accepted and Christopher Mayhew then left for another engagement. Left alone with my Admiral, I said to him, 'If we are to win this battle, Sir, we must stop fighting it with one arm tied behind our backs. We must make sure that all the resources of the Navy are at our disposal.' I made this remark because George had reported to me previously that he had met three senior Captains the week before, all of whom had said what a shame it was that we were going to lose the carriers. There was also a belief in a large part of the Navy that if you got rid of these expensive aircraft carriers you'd have a bigger fleet in lieu, and therefore collaboration with the RAF was the sensible way to go. Whereas we knew that once you cut the head off the fleet the rest would wither.

'We need,' I said, 'to take the offensive against the RAF to show that so much of the evidence they have produced is false and phoney. We must do it by using Naval aviators to spearhead our campaign. With great respect to our seaman colleagues who have been fighting for us, they just don't have the necessary knowledge to conduct the affair.' And then I remember saying very clearly, 'If you put the knife in my hand, Sir, I will have their guts all over the carpet.' Frank looked at me and said, 'You are right, we are going to have to change the way we do this – you are absolutely right. You shall have the necessary strength and authority that you require to fight this last battle for us. On Monday we will make a fresh start.' I added one more thing. 'If you or your colleagues, Sir, are afraid of the sight of blood then don't ask me to do it.' He nodded and smiled and I believed that at this last moment we might have a chance.

I could hardly wait to call George and tell him what had happened. 'When you come in on Monday,' said I, 'you will be sent for by the Deputy Chief of the Naval Staff and given new riding instructions, and we can then get stuck into this thing in a way we haven't done so far.' George was delighted. Monday came, and Monday went, and he wasn't sent for. Nothing changed and although I produced a plan to show that we could actually do the whole thing, keep a four-carrier fleet going for less money than we had previously argued, by prolonging the life of the Gannet, doing away with a replacement AEW aeroplane, and by keeping the old carriers going. Despite the fact that this was all perfectly feasible, when Their Lordships went down to the corridor to see the Secretary of State, they went with the old three-carrier plan and no notice was taken of the proposal from the United States. No notice was taken of the fact that we needed a four-carrier fleet, and that I had produced one that we could afford; they reverted to a plan that had already failed. I remember watching them leave the First Sea Lord's office and I hung my head, because I knew that all was lost. When the decision was announced the First Sea Lord resigned, as did the Navy Minister. Frank Hopkins asked me privately whether he should go too, and I said, 'No, Sir, I think you should stay' (he was due to go as Commander-in-Chief, Naval Home) 'because we shall need senior aviators around to take care of the enormous problems we shall now face.'

David Luce gave his farewell party in Winston Churchill's old office in the old Admiralty building. It was a sombre affair and I was late arriving because I was still working hard trying to sort out some of the aftermath of this event. When I left, David Luce took my hand and said, 'I am terribly sorry about how this thing has turned out, Lygo.'

I said, 'Oh, well, Sir, it is over now.'

'Yes,' he said, 'we were robbed, Lygo.' I have to tell you that a most unfair thought flashed before my eyes: if you had recognised that we were being robbed earlier on, it might have been different.

'I know, Sir,' I said.

'Yes but, Lygo, we were robbed.'

'Yes, Sir,' I said, and turning reluctantly on my heel I walked away. The Navy had fought a battle which it thought, part of it, was unbelievable in its concept and therefore, perhaps, hadn't taken it as seriously as it should have done from the word go. It had not been united as the RAF had been in fighting the battle because more than half of it seemed to believe that if you did away with aircraft carriers and all the paraphernalia that went with them you could have more frigates and destroyers, even cruisers; a total and utter illusion.

The RAF had won, but what had they won? They had lost the TSR2, they were to lose the F111 and get the Buccaneer, whether they liked it or not, a reduced number of Phantoms, and an AEW aeroplane (the Shackleton) that went on for far too long while they struggled with the Nimrod, the successor to the original staff requirement for AEW aircraft. We never saw those overseas bases built; in fact, we were withdrawing from bases as fast as we could go while the planning exercise was actually being conducted. How sad and unnecessary it all was, and how much better it would have been to have concentrated on a maritime strategy that has served our country so well for so long and retained the flexibility that we require to respond to all types of operation. Perhaps after all Joint Force 2000 will provide it.

The net result of the Defence Review was the loss of the new carrier programme, CVA01 and all, and it is interesting to reflect on the tactics that helped to lead to that position. *Ark Royal* and *Eagle* were both laid down at the end of the Second World War and were completed after the War ended. They were contemporary with the American carriers *Midway*, the *Coral Sea* and the *Roosevelt*, which were about the same size. It is interesting to note that those three carriers were still in existence and continued to serve successfully for the whole of the period both before and after our Defence Review, yet the argument made by the Navy at that time to justify CVA01 was that both our ships were in fact coming to the end of their useful life. Why is there such a difference in the way in which the Americans can continue to operate their ships for much longer than we are able? In precipitating a crisis over CVA01, and if fact helping to bring about the Defence Review (although it is almost certain it would have occurred anyway), the Navy overstepped the mark.

What was particularly sad for those of us who were left in the Fleet Air Arm was to see the speed with which the remaining carriers were scrapped. *Victorious* went to the scrap yard within days of the decision being made, and others followed in fairly close order. It was as if the successors to the Naval heritage were determined to remove any trace of aviation history lest it come back to haunt them. So what were we left with? We were left with the procurement of a large anti-submarine helicopter, the very successful Sea King, which was done with minimum development costs by taking an existing American engine airframe combination and fitting an already well-tried British anti-submarine system. We were able to continue the development of Sea Dart to replace Sea Slug as the fleet's medium-range defence system, and we embarked on a short-range point defence system, Sea Wolf. One thing we did not have was any way of providing airborne early warning. The eyes and ears of the fleet, which was one of the origins of the Fleet Air Arm, was going to be phased out with the ending of the last Gannet Squadron to be embarked in *Ark Royal*. *Ark* and *Eagle* were to run on for a couple of years and then be phased out, together with their aeroplanes. The battle to keep *Ark Royal* going for a further commission was yet to be fought.

I left the Directorate of Naval Air Warfare to do the Senior Officers' War Course at Greenwich, the only staff course that I did during the whole of my Naval career. The Navy was left to examine how it was going to conduct its affairs in the aftermath of a Defence Review that had given its air defence to the RAF, only to find subsequently that that defence was eroded by the restrictions that the Defence Review placed upon the RAF, notably that it would not get the F111 and it would get a reduced number of Phantoms. The AEW capability was to be replaced by taking the same old radar out of the Gannets, and putting it into the Shackletons, already an old aeroplane, but this was still some way off. What a mess it had all been.

21

HMS Juno

After the tragic events of the carrier battle, I was delighted to be given command of a brand new Leander Class frigate building at Southampton, HMS *Juno*. The Senior Officers' War Course had enabled me to live at home near Chatham in Mereworth Lawn with my family for a change. The period of standing by a new ship means that you have to do a lot of courses, mostly in the Portsmouth area, and this involved travelling backwards and forwards to Portsmouth from Kent. I seem to have spent half my Naval career travelling along the A272 and bits and pieces attached to it.

I had originally been tentatively appointed to a ship, again a new Leander which was building this time in the Dockyard at Plymouth, and discovered there was another ship, *Juno*, which was due to be a Chatham ship and to be commanded by an old friend of mine who lived in the Plymouth area. I therefore called him up and said, 'Would you have any basic objection to swapping ships? If you took the one I'm supposed to take you'd be based at Devonport which is exactly where you want to be, and I would take the one you're supposed to get and that's going to be based at Chatham, which would not be good for you at all.' He readily agreed and said, 'Well, if you can get away with it, Ray.' Like most things in life, if you don't ask how do you know whether you'll be able to make changes? I asked the Naval Appointers and they had no rooted objection to this and so my appointment was changed and I was to have a second Chatham ship, very convenient for living in Kent.

I was to be the leader of the Fifth Frigate Squadron, although with the increasing pressure on the Navy and the cutbacks it was not always easy to get the squadron together to exercise as one group. Having mastered the intricacies of the Medway and getting in and out of Chatham, I was quite looking forward to having another Chatham-based ship. In addition of course the experience of driving an almost identical ship and again a brand new one meant that this time I was starting a fair way ahead of the ball game. In order to get home from Portsmouth while I was doing these courses, I decided that we should invest in a second car and I discovered an advertisement in the local

paper for an Austin A30. It turned out that this car had been completely rebuilt by a youngster with some enthusiasm, including putting in
a brand new engine, but there were one or two slight defects: (a) he'd
painted it by hand a kind of royal blue which didn't look all that good
and (b) it had no head lining inside except the kind of remains of what
had been there before hanging down like some scrofulous hairdo from
the overhead. However, it ran well and I was able to use it for the
trips backwards and forwards to Portsmouth.

Juno had been built by Thorneycroft in their yard at Woolston,
though the company had been taken over by Vosper during the course
of the building of the ship because Thorneycroft had virtually gone
into liquidation. John Rix, the Managing Director of Vosper at the
time, was a sterling character and it was clear that he was facing
various difficulties in the takeover of the Thorneycroft yard. I had
arranged to call on him to talk about the ship and its planned
handover date. On arrival in his office I asked him therefore in the
shortest possible time and way, whether he was confident the ship
would meet its planned handover date. He looked at me for a while
and then said, 'No, I'm not.'

'Perhaps you'd like to show me,' I said, 'the progress charts that
exist on the ship so that we can look at some of the critical items and
see what's on the critical path.' He looked at me again.

'I'm afraid I can't,' he said.

'You mean you don't have one?' I said.

'No, I'm afraid we don't.'

'Well, perhaps you have a bar chart,' I said, becoming sarcastic, 'we
can take a look at.' Again he looked at me rather fixedly.

'I'm afraid we don't,' he said.

'What, nothing?' I enquired.

'No,' he said, 'nothing. I'm afraid that's the state of the ship when
we took the company over and we are about to start to sort it out but
I'm afraid I can't give you any confidence or undertaking on dates
because we just don't know.'

'So,' said I, 'these dates of in-service are wish-lists are they?' He
smiled grimly.

'I'm afraid so.'

'Well,' I said, 'I shall have to report this to the Commodore
Contract Built Ships.'

'He already knows,' he said. There was not much more I could do at
this point, apart from express my concern, so off I went to the Portakabins alongside to meet the Ship's Company, such as it was. Most of
the key Officers were there and a few of the key Ratings, but the
build-up for a full crew would take some time. The First Lieutenant

was John Caughey, a friend of mine to this day, a fairly tough operator with a good sense of humour, who was ably supported by a good team of Officers. The Leanders were a new class of ship and, along with the standard 4/5 gun turret forward, *Juno* had Sea Cat, a wire-guided anti-aircraft missile aft, as well as the 'Limbo' or anti-submarine mortars. We had 177 sonar with which I was familiar, an excellent operations room and a neat and tidy ship in every way.

Eventually the time came for the ship to start her acceptance trials and for this a retired Captain is employed to take the ship to sea while she still flies the Red Ensign. I went down to Woolston to join the ship for part of these trials at the invitation of the Captain who was driving her. As I repaired on board at Woolston I noticed a rather strange flag flying, but since she was under the Red Ensign I didn't pay too much attention to it, and spent my time looking at the scenery as we proceeded to glide down Southampton Water, passing that famous hospital which it is alleged got its plans mixed up with one that was to be built in India. Two hospitals, it is said, were to be built for the military – one in India and one in the UK. The plans, however, got

HMS *Juno*

transposed and the one built on Southampton Water was designed for India with open balconies and no heating, and the one that was built in India was the one that should have been on Southampton Water. So one lot froze, and the other lot roasted. Whether it is true, I am not sure but it's a good yarn.

We entered Portsmouth Harbour to go to a buoy to pick up ammunition for the particular exercise we were to undertake which was 4/5 gun trials. After we'd secured, as I was standing on the bridge admiring the scenery, a very imposing-looking character arrived. He was wearing a yachting cap, a yachting blazer, white duck trousers and had flowing white locks. The Captain turned to him and said, 'I don't believe you've met Captain Lygo, who will be taking this ship over when she hoists the White Ensign.'

'No,' he said, turning to me and the Captain said, 'This is Mr Jack Thorneycroft.' As I shook hands with him there flashed in front of me that great Thorneycroft name, and I thought, when you were my age or younger, you inherited an industrial empire – Thorneycroft engines, diesels, Thorneycroft lorries, Thorneycroft ships, Thorney-croft South Africa, Thorneycroft Singapore, Thorneycroft South America – and when I shook hands with him what he had left was a herd of cows in the Isle of Wight. During the lunch which we had on trestle tables in a space that had been cleared, for the ship was by no means complete, he kept up a constant monologue with me which really, from his point of view, meant that everything that had gone wrong was the fault of the unions. I said nothing; there was no point in having a rather dispirited argument with him but I stored it away. Not untypical of the fortunes of so many great British companies at the time, where the management had seemed to believe that they could assume their men would automatically allow themselves to be led by them because of their social status, rather than their ability. In consequence they had abrogated their responsibilities for management in the face of militant unionism to professional personnel managers. Their concept of leadership was something which fortunately had rarely hit the Navy, Nelson being the classic example of someone who had risen to the top, but he was unique in having a total disregard for his own safety in the pursuit of his country's objectives and his respect for his people.

Many of the Officers and key Ratings were new to a ship of that kind, and I was therefore in complete control because I'd had a very similar ship before. The commissioning ceremony eventually went according to plan, I continued with my routine of having champagne for everybody (although how we managed to afford it I am not quite sure, but we did), and I hope and believe that a happy day was had by everybody. That's one of the few occasions in the early stages of a commission when you can bring it to life by having everybody on board enjoy themselves, including wives and families and girlfriends. I signed the receipt, we hoisted the White Ensign and we were away.

Juno had been well finished by Vosper Thorneycroft and was in excellent shape and remained so throughout my commission. We took such care of the ship and its appearance that it became nicknamed 'The Royal Yacht' because I believed that it was necessary to maintain

Old Juno's enjoying a day on board

and demonstrate the highest possible standards of efficiency and clean-
liness as a kind of benchmark for ships in the Royal Navy.

The Squadron I was to lead was fairly diverse, consisting of *Decoy*,
a Daring Class destroyer of a previous generation, *Falmouth*, a type 12
frigate similar to the *Lowestoft* that I had earlier commanded, and
AISNE. The programme for the ship, was to work up at Portland and
then, after a self-maintenance period in Chatham to collect the rest of
the squadron and a submarine, HMS *Walrus*, to proceed to the West
Indies to exercise en route and in company and to join up with Flag
Officer Flotillas. After my experience with the *Lowestoft*, the work-up
at Portland with *Juno* was fairly routine stuff, but it was again a
winter experience (probably the best way of learning about seamanship
in short order). We were to be accompanied for our West Indies
deployment by a tanker, the *Orange Leaf*, on which it was possible
(and I imagine still is) for wives to travel since the ship was flying the
Blue Ensign and not the White Ensign. I therefore set about finding
out whether I could get accommodation for Pepper to accompany me
on the voyage and since it wasn't policy to allow women to travel
alone I asked that my 16-year-old daughter, Brooke, should accompany her. This meant missing a bit of preparatory work for A levels
but I thought it was well worth the absence in order to gain a little bit
more knowledge of life at sea and a chance to get a look at the West
Indies. After a certain amount of difficulty and with the assistance of
the Captain of *Orange Leaf*, I finally got permission granted and so it
was planned that they should accompany me. The crew of *Orange
Leaf* were Chinese and this was to lead to some amusing experiences
during the course of the cruise.

Our first port of call was to be Flores in the Azores and as we
proceeded towards the islands the first mishap occurred. *Walrus*,
which was travelling on the surface, meeting the same bad weather
we'd had, had lost her gangway, which was secured on deck (or not
secured on deck in this case), over the side, and as it went down the
side of the boat it damaged her propeller. When we arrived in the
Azores it was necessary to get my divers to go down to have a look.
They found that the propeller had indeed been chipped, which made a
bit of noise as far as the submarine was concerned, when she was
trying to be quiet and submerged. However, I really didn't think that I
was justified in abandoning the whole exercise for this reason, and so,
after a conference with the Captain of the submarine, we decided that
we would make such temporary repairs by grinding away at the
surface of the blade that was damaged, as to make it serviceable for
the rest of the trip.

The Azores are beautiful islands and it would appear that one previous Governor had decreed that the populace would go out and plant flowers alongside the roads. As a result, everywhere was like driving through a garden. One of the major industries was growing pineapples under glass and enormous great things they became, to be shipped off individually in boxes to exclusive outlets in London, Paris and all over the world. The inhabitants were charming and friendly but most of the poorer class didn't seem to bother to wear shoes and we christened them all the Hobbits. At this time it was apparently policy for Canada to take a certain number of immigrants from Portugal and it was interesting to see the aspirants for visas to emigrate to Canada sitting on the kerbstones outside the Canadian Consul's office, cramming their feet into unaccustomed shoes in order to hobble in to take their interview. I'm bound to say it rained most of the time but then apparently it is a bit wet there, situated as it is in the middle of the Atlantic Ocean. But it was a good visit nevertheless and gave me a chance to get together with Pepper and Brooke again, who were of course in the *Orange Leaf* when she arrived a few hours after us. They had been accommodated in the Sick Bay, being the sensible place to put two ladies, and the doctor was able to use the facilities as required by having them absent themselves to the Wardroom, but for most of the time they were incarcerated in this space which looked straight out onto the fuelling deck so they were able to get a good view of us when we came alongside to fuel.

My daughter promptly went down with a rather bad case of influenza and the Chinese crew of the *Orange Leaf* took great pity on her, particularly the steward who was allocated to them, whose name was Lu Fuk (an unfortunate name to appear on the back of postcards that were sent to us from time to time from Hong Kong thereafter). The first port of call was Antigua where we were due to give the usual reception on board, but unfortunately at that time there was no berthing facility at Antigua and so we were at anchor some distance offshore; the *Orange Leaf* was anchored farther out still. The weather was blowing rather hard and the sea was running fairly steep around the *Orange Leaf*, and it became a great exercise in agility and seamanship to get Pepper and Brooke into the boat and brought over to the *Juno*. Pepper's description of the trip with a Chinese crew speaking an unintelligible language and becoming slightly hysterical with the experience on a pitch black night will be something, I think, that will remain in her memory for many years to come. The Chinese medicine that finally produced an immediate cure for my daughter's flu was when her steward suggested that the remedy for flu was to drink a glass of brandy in which a lizard had been placed for some weeks! The following day we had an official luncheon party, at which my guests assembled, and Pepper proceeded to tell the story as a joke. However, one of the ladies present listened straight-faced to the story, and at the end said, 'That's not the cure for flu – that's the cure for asthma.'

The trip was then a question of moving from one island to another. St Vincent which is a beautiful island, where we had the chance to visit Bequia, where Anthony Eden at one time had a house, and had retired to after his resignation as Prime Minister. It is sometimes difficult to get an adequate number of people for a reception from a small island and Bequia was no exception. However, fifty guests were duly assembled on the Quarterdeck for a lovely evening, and at one point the first Lieutenant came over to me and said, 'Please don't look aft at the moment, Sir,' and of course I asked immediately why not.

'Because,' he said, 'one of the guests is urinating over the side of the flight deck.'

Juno of course had a helicopter and as a helicopter pilot I was quite interested in flying it. I don't think the pilot was terribly keen on this idea and probably viewed me as I had viewed people of my age many years before as being somebody who really was a bit past it. The fact that I am still flying today perhaps indicates that I wasn't, but I still managed to fly the aeroplane from time to time although always with the Flight Commander in the aeroplane with me. Helicopters and small ships go well together for certain activities but not necessarily the one for which they were designed. The helicopter in *Juno* was part of the MATCH system which was a Manned ASW Torpedo Carrying Helicopter. The Americans had gone for an unmanned helicopter but I don't think the results would have been very much different. The problem was that to get the aircraft launched one had to have the wind in a fairly precise position coming at an angle across the flight deck. The purpose of the helicopter was to launch a torpedo into the vicinity of the sonar contact that you had on your long-range sonar, or to launch it into the attack against a submarine detected by another ship's sonar. The procedure was, as soon as a valid contact was established to call, 'Action, Match,' which meant for the helicopter, which was on stand-by, to be launched to attack the submarine. If the ship holding the contact had the helicopter, it had then to turn in order to get the wind in the right position to launch it and this sometimes meant losing contact, or a delay in getting the helicopter airborne, which was sufficient for the submarine, which was of course aware that it had been detected, to take evasive action and the sonar would then lose lock. It became an evolution and anything that becomes an evolution is not operational. If you have to spend more time worrying about a particular aspect of achieving a kill rather than getting in and killing the submarine then this can be a fairly pointless exercise.

There was at that time an alternative system, IKARA, which launched a torpedo on a drone, and I believe that even though this was not supported by the aviating community (as one can imagine) it would have been and could have been a more effective way of attacking a submarine contact. Nevertheless, the helicopter was useful for all other kinds of things, including collecting the mail from shore and generally taking casualties if you had an injured man, or effecting search and rescue operations if you were called upon to do this. On one occasion, much to the irritation of the Flight Commander, in thick fog when I was returning the Flag Officer back to his ship, I manoeuvred myself by radar to come up astern of the flagship, had the lookouts looking out for the wake in thick fog; came up on the port side of the wake until we saw the ship and then stayed alongside. We used the helicopter to transfer the Admiral's staff back to his ship, a fairly unique way of doing it and in my view much safer than getting knitting across between the two ships, because if you then found that there was some other contact that might be menacing you, you had quite a problem in manoeuvring two ships tied together or faced the alternative of having to cast off the lines while the two ships proceed independently with all the problems of getting together again.

Our next port of call was Barbados. At Bridgetown there was a mole alongside where we could berth and it was possible for the submarine to be berthed alongside us in order that we could supply her with electrical power so that she could shut down and do some self-maintenance. Unfortunately the jetty was particularly exposed and during the first night a long scend started which was noticeable in the middle of the cocktail party which, traditionally, we were holding on the first night. The Captain of *Walrus* had come on board to use my cabin to change into his best uniform and came out of my bathroom to find that all his clothes had disappeared. On enquiring of the steward what had happened, I found that Catania (my personal steward) had assumed that his best clothes were there to go to the laundry because they didn't look quite up to the *Juno* standard and that's where they'd been sent. We had a Chinese laundry which was common in the ships at that time, and very effective they were; they managed to get his uniform washed, dried and pressed in record time so that he was able to attend the cocktail party and the dinner afterwards. During the course of the evening the scend meant that the submarine began to bump gently against the side of the ship and then, as the evening progressed and the scend got worse, it positively thumped alongside. I could see that if nothing was done we would find ourselves looking a bit like a Coca-Cola bottle by the time the night was out. The submarine had shut down, and dismantled her diesels to do some

301

repair work, because we were now supplying power and she was thus unable to move under her own power. There was no tug instantly available and one had to be sent for, and finally, in the small hours of the morning, the submarine was towed away and put on the other side of the jetty. There, of course, she was not able to get power, but at least I was saved any further damage (two of the ship's side ribs had been pushed in about two or three inches as a result of this battering). I used the opportunity to submit to the Commander-in-Chief that it was high time we had some decent fenders on, other than the wicker ones that were the only ones available and which were completely ground to pieces by the weight of a reinforced submarine hull.

Our last port of call was Grenada, and here, can you believe it, my first call was on the Prime Minister, the same Mr Geary whose riotous behaviour I had been put ashore to stop as a young Lieutenant in charge of a landing party, and as a Commander in the *Lowestoft* had been sent with all despatch to stop his gyrations as leader of the Opposition; and now here he was – Prime Minister. Not untypical of events in the twilight of the British Empire. I called upon him, and although we hadn't met before, he obviously knew who I was and I was informed by the Governor, Sir Ian Turbot, a charming New Zealander, that he was to be taken on a nostalgia visit to Carriacou, the very island to which he had been banished when I had been there before, to call and see the people. I was told that he was also to bring with him his entire entourage which included not only his wife but another lady. Since the Governor was going to bring his wife, I then signalled the Commodore West Indies for permission for Pepper and Brooke to accompany me on this day only trip to Carriacou where we were to be accommodated in the only hotel on the island.

Quite innocently we had been looking for an opportunity to do a 4/5 gun calibration exercise and so, soon after we had sailed with all these people on board, and they were taking coffee down in my cabin, I had a call from the Gunnery Officer on the intercom asking me if he had permission to start the shoot. My answer was, 'approved if the range is clear.'

'Yes, sir, there's no evidence of any contacts on the range whatsoever,'

'Then go ahead,' I said. The first gun fired and Mr Geary turned several shades paler because I am quite certain that he was under the impression that the dear old Raj was going to incarcerate, him or take him off to some other place having inveigled him on board. It was not to be the case and we came to anchor off the island of Carriacou to await the arrival of the Administrator.

A small boat put off eventually, flying a large Grenada flag, which I think was the only one they had available, because it was so large that in the small boat it obscured the view of the Coxswain who therefore took some time before he was able to make out where the ship was and bring the boat safely alongside. Ian Turbot turned to me, as I stood somewhat stiffly and formally at the head of the gangway waiting for this fellow, to say, 'Don't be surprised at his appearance, Captain, he actually has a good knowledge of administration. His last job was as janitor of a block of flats in New York.' The evening's entertainment consisted of a dance and a kind of banyan at the local hotel. I had briefed my Southern Belle of a wife what to expect, and to be prepared for somewhat casual approaches, and sure enough one of these occurred when she was asked to dance somewhat informally by a gentleman. During the course of the dance, my wife asked him in what capacity was he attending the reception? He obviously didn't understand this question and she had to bring it down to, 'Why exactly are you here?' To which he replied, 'I heard the music and I came,' which I thought was as good a reason for attending any reception that ever I'd heard of.

The following morning we were to watch the launch of a boat which had been built on the island, a fishing boat, and a large part of the ship's company were invited to attend. The ceremony consisted first of all by the ship being blessed by the local preacher, the full ceremony – holy water and little girls, beautifully turned out in white dresses as the choir on board for the ceremony. As soon as this ceremony was finished, the little girls were thrown off the boat to be caught by their loving parents down below. Then up into the boat mounted the voodoo priestess, and as the drums that were assembled down below began to beat, the voodoo ceremony of commissioning the vessel got underway. This was accomplished by taking three animals on board, a cockerel which was placed in the bows as a lookout and then slaughtered, a sheep amidships for food and this was then slaughtered, and a ram at the stern to symbolise the push that was necessary to get the vessel moving, and this was then slaughtered. There must have been a fairly bloody scene on the upper deck, I imagine, although that was hidden from the view of us standing below. Next as the drums began to beat, a rum called Jack Iron was dispensed. It was pure white, like pure alcohol, and men with large machetes proceeded to shave at the props which were holding the vessel onshore and by reducing the size of them gradually began to get the vessel moving. We were told that a good ceremony sometimes lasted three days because presumably they didn't chop too much wood away at a time and kept themselves generously refreshed with Jack Iron, but because of the visit by the Prime

Minister and time being somewhat precious they presumably chopped away with a little more fire than they usually did and it only took a matter of hours before the vessel was gently eased down into the water. One of my Petty Officers came up to me during the course of the ceremony and said, 'I've just filled my lighter with this Jack Iron rum, Sir, struck the flint and a beautiful flame shot up.' It was a great occasion and a fascinating visit but one that was soon over and we returned the party to Grenada and once again bid farewell to that beautiful island. It was interesting to me afterwards to read all the gyrations about Grenada and of President Reagan eventually sending in US Marines to restore good order and, I wouldn't say Naval discipline, but at least some form of democratic government to overthrow the same Mr Geary that I had crossed paths with so many times before.

Our next visit was to join up with our Admiral (who was returning from the Pacific through the Panama Canal) and visit Venezuela. The purpose of the visit was for HMS *London*, the flagship, to demonstrate her Sea Cat system to the Venezuelan Navy in order to try to get a sale. Shorts manufactured the Sea Cat and the company's agent in Venezuela at the time was an expatriate Englishman married to a Venezuelan lady who lived in some luxury in a beautiful house in the suburbs of Caracas. We were all invited to stay up there in Caracas with them and I remember having an extraordinary day at the races where the horses, I seem to remember, were kept in velvet lined stalls whilst outside people sat begging on the ground in rags. A somewhat obvious contrast but a fascinating place to visit nevertheless.

The great day for the demonstration dawned and *London* embarked a large number of Venezuelan Naval officers and we took on board an equally large number. We were stationed by the Admiral one and a half cable's length astern of the *London* while the *Falmouth*, one of my ships which had some drones embarked, detached herself to an adequate distance in order to launch the drones against which the Sea Cat was to be used. Each drone had three flares and as we steamed along off the coast of Venezuela, the exercise began. We were spectators, of course, observing what was going to happen with some interest and as the first drone was launched we could hear over the broadcast, which we'd hooked up so that our guests could be aware of what was going on, the sequence of events.

'The first run will be a dummy run.' The drone began its approach to the *London* and the familiar gunnery cries began to ring out.

'Contact,' 'bearing,' 'range,' 'target acquired.' The drone was tracked overhead, turned and went back out again to start another run.

'The next run will be a firing run,' came the great cry. The drone was turned and started its steady approach to the flagship once again. The usual cries and then, 'light the flare'. The Sea Cat missile's fuse could only be triggered by a heat source and the flare was, of course, to provide this to simulate what would be the heat from the engine of an attacking aircraft. The flare lit and the drone came in.

'Check, check, check' was the next cry and the drone was turned and proceeded to retire for its second attempt.

'The next run will be a firing run,' came the cry and we all began to gaze expectantly as the aircraft approached once again. Again the familiar cries: 'target acquired,' 'light the flare,' the flare was lighted, the drone came in and then 'check, check, check,' and the drone was turned to go out again. It was now apparent, since there were only three flares on the drone, that this last firing run would have to be it. Again the little aircraft turned and came throbbing towards us and again the familiar cries and once again 'light the flare,' 'flare lighted,' the aircraft came in, 'engage with Sea Cat.' There was a tremendous whoosh from the stern of the *London* right ahead of us as the Sea Cat was fired and it went straight into the sea in a nosedive something like 30 feet from the side of the ship.

We all gasped in surprise and embarrassment but nothing like the embarrassment that was next to occur when from the flagship came the cry, '*Juno* fire next.' My Gunnery Officer's face turned a paler shade of white and he said, 'But there will be no flares, Sir and so the missile will not be triggered.'

'Understood,' I said and turning to the Yeoman, 'make to the flag: understand *Juno* to fire next but there will be no flare and the missile will not detonate.'

'*Juno* fire next,' came the order. Sticking my neck out a bit further, I made back, 'Understand *Juno* to fire next but please explain to our guests that we will not be able to destroy the target since it will not have a flare.'

'Engage with Sea Cat,' came back the order from an obviously somewhat irate Admiral. The little aircraft turned in once again, droning towards the *Juno*, and it was our turn now to say 'Target acquired,' 'tracking,' 'settled,' 'engage with Sea Cat.' Whoof, off went our Sea Cat and scored a direct hit on the little aircraft which spun down, narrowly missing the spectators on the Quarterdeck and plunged into the sea not 50 feet from our starboard side. A great cheer went up, we had scored a direct hit and had saved the day. I must say I was extremely relieved, although I felt very sad for the Gunnery Officer of the guided missile destroyer ahead. It transpired that it was one of those finger mistakes where a switch hadn't been made and the missile literally self-destructed, but then these things happen, or rather they shouldn't in peace and more seriously in war.

So now it was time to return our guests and sail on an exercise where the rest of our force was to be attacked by *Juno* acting as an Orange Raider. We were to be detached early in order to get ourselves in position to carry out the attack, and were supposed to be fitted with Russian missiles which gave us a considerable stand-off range. In order to complete the task a flight of Shackletons had been sent out from the UK to be based in Trinidad, or some suitable place, to support the force and to carry out anti-submarine surveillance against the *Walrus*. *Walrus* by this time was having all kinds of problems, and it was only by a deal of leaning on that I got the Captain to agree to continue with the exercise and submerge and do the things that submarines are supposed to do.

The arrival of the Shackletons reminded me of a previous occasion when I had been running an exercise out of Londonderry in Northern Ireland, where we had an anti-submarine school at that time. On this occasion it was a NATO exercise in which I had a small Norwegian submarine, the *Uthaug*, and a German frigate as well as my own ships. I gave a dinner party the night before the exercise started and the Group Captain running the RAF base told us that in his previous job he had been the Air Attaché in Bangkok.

'What was that like?' we enquired.

'A little different,' he said. 'Unlike your dinner party, Captain, when we had dinner with the Chief of the Thai Air Force we, of course, sat cross-legged on the floor with very low tables and we were fed by little Thai girls who came in to help us with our meal.'

'Literally fed?' we enquired.

'Yes,' he said. 'Yes, we were fed, and then between each course they showed us a blue film.'

'A blue film!' we said.

'Yes,' he assured us. The Germans, the Norwegians and the British were all astonished.

'Well,' I said, 'I don't know what to make of that but I tell you what, in the middle of the exercise tomorrow as we're out there pitching and tossing in a very unpleasant sea, there will come a moment when you're not sure what the hell is going on, I'm quite sure of that. If this is the case, we'll have a secret signal which is "show a blue film" and so if you make to me "Sierra, Alpha, Bravo, Foxtrot" I will know what it means.'

As the exercise progressed, sure enough there we were in the middle of the night with the little *Uthaug* making life very difficult for us, and my Chief Yeoman came over to me and said, 'Sir, this German has been making a signal on tactical primary fort the last half hour, and I can't decipher it and it's in no code book that I know of.'

'What is it?' I enquired.

'Here it is, Sir,' written on his signal pad – S, A, B, F.

'Ah,' I said, 'Chief Yeoman, yes, I understand exactly what that means. That's quite all right, just acknowledge.' He did and my reputation with the communicators in the ship went up 2000 per cent because it was quite clear that I knew something about signals that they didn't.

When we had detached from the force I was somewhat irritated to observe that one of the Shackletons was shadowing us so that they would know exactly where we were and from which direction we were going to attack. There was nothing I could do about it, however, and I just had to ignore the fact, although I did signal to the Admiral that I didn't think it would be a very good exercise if I was going to be tracked out by a Shackleton. When night closed in, we went silent (that is to say, turned off the radars) and proceeded to turn towards the blue force by picking up their radar emissions on our detector equipment. As we proceeded towards the force, and still having a feeling of frustration at having been shadowed by the Shackleton, I said to the communications team, 'Right, check through the frequencies and find out the frequencies on which the blue force are operating.' In a fairly short space of time they came back to me and said, 'We've got their frequency for their tactical primaries, Sir, and for their other frequency.' 'Good,' I said, 'is that the one the RAF Shackletons are on?' 'Yes.' 'Right,' I said, 'listen out and get his call sign.' After a while they came back and said, 'Yes, we have his call sign.' 'Good,' I said, 'give me the microphone.' I called the Shackleton and said, 'We have the raider now in a position which I would like you to illuminate. We can then engage with gunnery.' I then gave him the position of his own force and told him to illuminate. To our amazement, but delight, this he proceeded to do. My ops crew could hardly contain themselves and we could hear the consternation in the blue force as they found themselves illuminated by their own defending Shackleton. Before anything else could happen, I called the Shackleton again and said, 'That was excellent, that was first class. Now it would be great if you could do that again. Do exactly the same as before and that would be absolutely excellent.' Flattery goes a long way in any language, and the Shackleton duly came and illuminated them again. By this time the Admiral was getting somewhat het up, and I decided that, as we closed them to within technical range of my missile fire, I should wait for my next opportunity. Sure enough, we heard the well-known cry to form a surface-action group to come out to intercept me. As soon as that order had been executed and they had clearly turned out towards me, I came up on Tactical Primary with the call sign of the surface-action group and told them, 'Cancel my previous instruction. Rejoin the force.' Which they promptly proceeded to do. All this time I was closing. Again the order was given for the surface-action group to form and intercept me. Again I ordered it to return; by this time I was in theoretical range and engaged the blue force with my long-range missiles. We were now instructed to retire and conduct another attack from a different quarter, but I'd had enough of it by this time and said to my First Lieutenant, 'You can run the second exercise. I'm going to turn in. Let me know if anything happens.' At about three or four in the morning he called me and said, 'We'd like to have a go at doing that again, Sir.' 'What, trying to spoof them again?' 'Yes,' he said. 'It'll never work the second time, Number One, but if you want to have a go, have a go.' To their delight and amazement it happened all over again, so we had a rather amusing exercise.

Our next port of call for the wash-up was Curaçao in the Netherlands Antilles. After we had entered and secured, I made my way to the flagship to call on the Admiral and was greeted by the Captain of *London* who was looking very sombre. He said, 'Ray, I know you had a thoroughly good evening and you were spectacularly successful with that Sea Cat, but I should be grateful if you could try to calm down the Admiral who is really totally out of sorts with everybody in *London*.' 'Well, I'm very sorry,' I said, 'I certainly didn't intend to have that happen, but I'll see what I can do.' The Admiral, Peter Compston, was an aviator and when I met him he greeted me warmly and said, 'Well, you certainly managed to screw the whole of this organisation up last night, Ray, and congratulations on salvaging the demonstration of Sea Cat.' Despite my attempts to reconcile him to the fact that, although I was merely demonstrating that unless you're able to have a secure voice, then relying on voice to issue your orders is a dangerous way of conducting yourself, he could not bring himself to see the activities of his flagship as less than satisfactory, which was an unfortunate result and certainly one that wasn't intended.

We were now detached individually for various visits and recreation; *Juno* was allocated Cartagena in Colombia. Cartagena, of course, is where the enormous fort is located, which was regarded as the gateway to Spanish South America and to which Admiral Vernon was despatched with a large force to attack and take. Pestilence and disease ravaged both his sailors and the troops under his command and, although they laid siege to this enormous fort, the story is that the one-armed Nelsonian-type Spanish officer in command had reached the point when there was nothing left to eat and they were starved into submission. So in good Spanish dignity, he put on his best uniform, buckled on his sword and went out to surrender to the British, only to see to his surprise that they were actually packing up and about to withdraw. Cartagena did not fall, otherwise the whole of South America might have come under British rule and this was rather unfortunate for Admiral Vernon because he had victory medals struck before he sailed! It is an intriguing place to visit and we had a good and enjoyable rest. We then set off to our next visit, and the highlight of our tour, to Jacksonville, Florida, where Pepper and I had been married and where I was going to leave Pepper to go back in the *Orange Leaf* which was returning direct to the UK, not via Bermuda where we were going for a brief stopover. It was a great day for me to bring my own ship into Jacksonville, which I almost regarded as a home port. I turned her below the bridge, made a stern board through it, and berthed alongside the Prudential building, right in downtown Jacksonville, to be greeted by my in-laws, and where the ship was made extremely welcome.

Some had a better time than others, I suppose, because when I returned on board one evening the night before we sailed, I saw a large Cadillac convertible alongside the gangway and a young lady talking animatedly to the Officer of the Day in the company of one of the leading Naval airmen of the ship's flight. I was saluted as I came aboard and piped and went to my cabin. Soon afterwards the Officer of the Day appeared and said, 'I thought you might like to know what that was all about at the head of the gangway when you came aboard.'

'What was it?' I enquired.

'Well,' said he, 'the young lady came up to me and said, "I under-stand in your Navy they can buy themselves out." "That is correct," I told her, "in certain circumstances." "And I am told that it would cost £300 of your money for him to be discharged and that 600 of our dollars, and I've got it here and I want him!"' Unfortunately it wasn't as simple as that, and so she didn't get him but it was a good try, and it was a good visit.

So the time came for us to leave Jacksonville and Florida, and I asked my brother-in-law whether he'd like to come with me on the sea trip to Bermuda and spend a couple of days there while we were visiting, and then fly back to Florida from there. He was very happy to agree and so I took him off to Bermuda. I made the entry into Bermuda with that familiar trip along the inland sea towards Ireland Island at the far end where I put the ship alongside in dead calm conditions in a quite smart fashion. Then, putting on my sword and medals, I went to call on the Commodore. To my surprise, when I arrived at his office, he was sitting in his chair in a flowered shirt and shorts. There is an expression in the Services 'going bush' which means you are reverting to native style, and it looked as if that was what he was doing. We exchanged a few pleasantries. He had organised a reception and dance; I, in turn of course, was giving the usual cocktail party on board. It was a pleasant visit and, although we were to be there for about a week, my brother-in-law departed after day three having had a thoroughly good time. I suppose it was about the fourth day that I was awakened at about three o'clock in the morning by the First Lieutenant saying, 'I'm sorry to wake you, Sir, but I'm afraid we have a rather serious case on our hands.'

'What is it?' I asked.

'Well the Coxswain doing rounds has discovered photographs in one of the Petty Officers' Messes which indicate that certain of the ship's company have been enjoying the hospitality of a homosexual ashore.' I rubbed my eyes, sat up and he showed me the large photographs which left little doubt of what was going on, and identified the people concerned.

'What should I do?' he said.

'Well,' I said, 'you must proceed, Number One, straight down the middle of the road in accordance with the Regulations.' He looked at me for a moment and said, 'It's going to be a very painful thing to do, Sir.'

'I understand that,' I said. Homosexual acts were still illegal in Bermuda at that time so there was bound to be a civil case since there was a civilian involved.

'Where did these photographs come from?' I asked.

'We've discovered that the link man in this is the Confidential Books postman, the chap that brings them when ships arrive in Bermuda.'

'Well, in that case there's a possible breach of security and you have no option. And we have no option, whatever the consequences may be.' It was a sad occasion; we left three men behind to face civil charges in the courts of Bermuda and they were subsequently, of course, dismissed from the Service and the instigator was banished from the island. It transpired that he was in the custom of waiting for the last boat to leave from Hamilton and any Ratings that were stranded he would approach and offer accommodation for the night. The ramifications of this man's activity went right around the fleet and one Captain, who had Ratings in his ship who were identified as having been involved in this ring, said to me, 'I don't understand why you made all this fuss. My sailors can go ashore in East Africa and indulge their sexual activities with most undesirable and disease-infected women and this is all right, but to do what this chap was doing in Bermuda is considered not all right.' I could only

310

answer, 'The law is the law. I don't make it but out job is to uphold it.'

I had to call the whole Ship's Company in to explain what had happened and painfully to tell them that, unfair as it might be, the ship might well get a name for being a haunt of homosexuals when in fact it was nothing of the kind, and to tell them that many other ships in the fleet had been implicated and that the dangerous security implications of what had happened had been stopped by the actions which we, in *Juno*, had taken. That didn't stop the fact that during our next exercise on the intercom frequency when I was in the ops room, one of my Ratings said, 'We've just had a few whistles over the air.' I said, 'Well, if you can identify from whence it comes, there'll be trouble,' but we couldn't and it is one of the unfortunate facts of life that sometimes in doing one's duty the consequences are not always as they perhaps should be. A policeman's lot is not a happy one.

When I returned home the Commander-in-Chief, of course, wanted to know all about it and particularly why the whole of the events as they unfolded were covered by signals from *Juno* and not from the Senior Officer West Indies. It was an unfortunate affair from beginning to end, but as my young daughter when dancing with the Commodore had said in answer to his question, 'What kind of men do you like?' she replied, 'Young ones.'

311

22

After the Carriers

After I had left the Ministry of Defence, Admiral Sir Varyl Begg had come in as First Sea Lord to replace David Luce, and many other changes had been made. The new team was, quite naturally, expected to toe the new line, which was to be a fleet without organic air, except for helicopters, and to embrace the new relationship with the RAF.

A task force was set up to look at the way in which the Navy was going to be able to operate in the future, and the previously rejected V/STOL opportunity was now the best bet around. As the task force proceeded to examine the way in which it could operate, it was clear that the ability of shore-based aircraft to provide protection for the fleet was going to be an extremely difficult operation for the RAF to perform. This was particularly so since those bases that we didn't have, but were invented during the Defence Review, of course never materialised, and those that we did have were being disposed of as fast as the sale signs could be set up. The argument therefore began to evolve around whether the defence of the fleet when it was out of range of shore-based air could be best provided by an organic capability centred on the Harrier. This meant upgrading the Harrier from a pure ground-attack, Army-support aircraft to being an interceptor fighter, not an easy task for an aeroplane of limited dimensions. If this was to be the case, however, what kind of ship was going to operate these aircraft?

In the fullness of time the task force, under the leadership of Captain Ian Easton, came up with a ship which had a flight deck which stretched from one end to the other and looked remarkably like an aircraft carrier – they called it the 'Through-Deck Cruiser'. It was essential to avoid the impression that the Navy was embarking upon regaining what it had lost when it lost the carrier battle by producing another generation of aircraft carriers, a term that had never been all that enthusiastically received in Whitehall. I remember as a young commander, when I first arrived in the Admiralty, seeing a paper that was circulated about the time Duncan Sandys' axe was about to fall, saying that the term 'aircraft carrier' was not politically acceptable within Whitehall and the Naval Staff was encouraged to come up with an alternative to that name. It just goes to show how tenuous a hold aviation had on the true hearts and minds of the Navy and how badly the case had been sold to the mandarins of Whitehall. It didn't take long, of course, for the wags to christen the through-deck cruiser the 'see through' cruiser but in the meantime it progressed through the Naval Staff to arrive at the First Sea Lord's desk, where it was promptly rejected because it had a deck that ran from one end of the ship to the other; the task force was told to go away, so I believe, and come back with a proposition in which there was a Bridge right across the ship which prevented it from becoming an aircraft carrier!

It was at about this time that I was asked by Ian Easton and by the Assistant Chief of the Naval Staff involved to go into the Ministry of Defence and talk to them about the options that they had examined and whether I had any advice to give them. I was almost let in through a back door and was invited to go and see the ACNS(P) of the time, who was not an aviator but who certainly found himself in an impossible situation. He knew that what he should do was to recommend some form of restructuring which involved aircraft carriers but that his whole career might come to an abrupt end if he was seen to be promoting it! He shared an office with a common secretariat. I remember very well going into his office and being scrutinised by the secretary and one could almost get the feeling of being subversive in one's mere appearance in the Ministry at that time. I am glad I was to be out of it but the chaps who had to fight this battle did so over the next two years with great courage. They were assisted, of course, by the defeat of the Labour administration and the incoming Tory government who subsequently were partially to reverse the decision and keep *Ark Royal* in operation for quite a bit longer than had originally been planned.

My time in command of *Juno* was a very happy one, in part because the experience I had gained in *Lowestoft* meant that it was a re-run of a previous existence with all the experience I had gained now firmly tucked under my belt. Towards the end of my time in command of *Juno* I was asked to go and see the Naval Secretary and was told that my next job would be in command of HMS *Ark Royal*, the largest ship the Navy had ever possessed and the last of its major fixed-wing carriers. It was then undergoing a refit at Devonport, which was already beginning to run late. It was expected to cost over £30 million, which was a large sum of money at that time, and they wanted to get a Captain in position fairly early to ensure that the ship came out on time, because politically, if she was seen to be slipping badly, there would always be those who would argue that the Navy didn't need a ship anyway, so why bother?

The experience I gained in *Juno* and *Ark Royal* are the subjects of other chapters, but for the sake of completing the story about what happened after we lost the carrier battle I have to jump to the end of my time in command of *Ark Royal*. Not only had we suffered the disaster of losing Michael Le Fanu as Chief of the Defence Staff (and it was as much a personal loss for me as for anybody else in the Navy because he had been one of my greatest supporters), but now the Services had lost Andrew Humphrey who in turn had become Chief of Defence Staff. He was a man whom I had come to admire greatly and though, when we had first met, we had had a kind of remote running battle I wasn't senior enough to do direct battle with him, or to get to know him better, more's the pity!

Andrew's death at the top produced another great convulsion in the Naval system. My original new job on leaving *Ark Royal* was to go as Director of Public Relations on the suggestion of the Naval Secretary, my old boss David Dunbar-Nasmith. However, this appointment did not meet with the approval of the new First Sea Lord, Admiral Hill-Norton; I suppose it might have been thought that I may have been a little bit too aggressive and pro-Navy for the quietness of everybody concerned. However, the death of Andrew Humphrey catapulted Michael Pollock into the position of First Sea Lord, and Hill-Norton then became Chief of the Defence Staff.

After a bit of fumbling around, therefore, they decided that the thing for me to do was to lead a Naval Presentation Team, a public relations job which involved going around the country trying to explain to people the role and importance of the Royal Navy. Prior to this, however, I was asked to go and see the new First Sea Lord, Michael Pollock. Michael Pollock is a charming man and one I had got to know in the great carrier battle when he had been leading the Naval team and I was one of the supporting artists. I assumed that he would want to talk about *Ark Royal* and what had happened, as indeed he did, and after we had explored this subject for some moments I began to perceive that he was getting a bit nervous with this and clearly wanted to talk about something else.

'Well, now,' he said, 'I want to talk about something else. I want to get you on the Flag List.' I was somewhat taken aback, but of course flattered and happy to receive such information. I said, 'Well, Sir, thank you very much, I am most flattered by your confidence.' 'Yes, yes, yes,' he said somewhat impatiently, 'but what I need to know, Ray, is whether you support Naval policy.' I looked at him for a second and said, 'What is it, Sir?' The First Sea Lord looked somewhat nervously around the room and then, coming back to me, he said, 'As far as I can make out it is to proceed on the basis of a new class of through-deck cruiser. Do you agree with that?' 'No, Sir,' I said. There was an audible pause. 'Oh dear, why not?' he asked. 'Because,' said I, 'I regard it as a vastly too expensive way of replacing a lost capability.' 'How do you mean?' said he. 'Well, Sir,' said I, 'it seems to me that what we should go for is a class of larger aircraft carriers, built to commercial standards and therefore much cheaper, concentrating all their build into the flying facilities, leaving it to escort vessels to provide protection apart from point defence.' He thought for a moment, and I continued, 'But I understand, Sir, that we have recently got approval for the first of the new class of cruisers.' 'Yes,' he said, 'we have, and the contract has been let.' 'Then, Sir,' said I, 'I have spent long enough in this building to know that you never interfere with a programme once it is launched. I am therefore perfectly prepared publicly to support the new class of through-deck cruisers, but you will know and I will know, privately, that I don't.' 'That's good enough,' he said. The meeting terminated just after that. And that *children* is how I became an Admiral! Another example of how lucky I have been in my senior officers, who have been kind enough to tolerate my candour and directness and sometimes unconventional behaviour, but have backed me.

The through-deck cruiser is now a fact. I was privileged to go to the commissioning of the new *Ark Royal*, carrying on that famous name, but unfortunately these ships are a classic example of a product designed by a committee. Although great credit is due to all the people who persevered so hard to get that concept through (and perhaps it was the only way it could be got through), nevertheless it suffers from some major problems. First is the fact that, because it has gas turbines to propel it, the massive uptakes and downtakes that are required mean that the hangar itself is like a Coca-Cola bottle: it is narrow in the middle, which restricts movement of aircraft. The addition of Sea Dart forward of the island means that a large part of the flight deck is restricted for the use of aircraft; as a result of these particular problems, the ship carries far fewer aeroplanes than a ship of that displacement should be able to carry. In addition, of course, the logistics required for the support of the Sea Dart system are demanding on space. When these vessels first came out they had no point defence system; how much better it would have been if the lightweight Sea Wolf system had been fitted to the Sea Cat launchers on each quarter. For that matter, still would be.

23

Running Close Hauled

Life in a structured and disciplined service leads one to trim one's sails according to the prevailing wind, and to be careful with the language one uses under certain circumstances if it is not to stand one into danger. Nevertheless the ability to say what you really think without giving grounds for action, as opposed to grounds for dislike or grounds for irritation, are entirely different matters. I've often said to my wife that one day I would like to give a party to all the people who have been tolerant and kind to me during my careers. The beauty of it in part would be that once you had publicised the fact that you were having such a party, those who weren't invited would, or should, get the message. Unfortunately, as you get older, so do the people that were your superiors and in the ordinary course of events they begin to drop off the perch before you do! Thus, I suppose, if you hold on long enough you'd only have to have a very small party!

Quite recently, my eldest son said to me that all my children had been brought up to believe that I never compromised on any issue and went in guns blazing and sorted things out, but he said, 'It took me a long time to realise that you must have compromised along the way.' I said, 'Of course I did, but you can quite often avoid a compromise if people think that you are most unlikely to give way.' I don't know that it helps because life becomes somewhat confrontational and, at times, quite exciting but then we have to do things the way that comes naturally to us, whatever that might be.

The Navy, by and large, is a very tolerant society if you stick within the rules, or it was in my day. Unfortunately things change. In the book *Fabulous Admirals* some of them I wouldn't have regarded as being either fabulous or noteworthy; I would think some of them were extremely boorish and overbearing. It is true that the structure of the Service can lead you to believe, as you aspire to or achieve higher rank, that this somehow puts you into a rather different human category. It happens to politicians too!

I first met Admiral Frewin, or rather I first exchanged words with Admiral Frewin, when he came to address the Senior Officers' War Course which I was attending. The Senior Officers' War Course was a course for Captains for whom the Navy didn't know what employment to give, or were between appointments, or were pending appointment, and so a convenient kind of locker to stuff these people into was the Senior Officers' War Course at the Royal Naval College at Greenwich.

Having left the Ministry of Defence, and having been a party to losing the carrier battle, my next appointment was to go in command of the new frigate, HMS *Juno*, building at Woolston, and in the intervening period, because it was rather a lengthy one, I was sent on the Senior Officers' War Course. Admiral Frewin was a formidable character; he had a high reputation for being an extremely efficient and effective Officer, a strict disciplinarian but clever, and competent. He had been the Captain of the *Eagle*. In the aftermath of the loss of the carriers, however, it was not politic to be seen to be hankering too much after the lost Naval aviation, and there had been a popular belief in the Navy, in some quarters, that if you go rid of the aircraft carriers and their aircraft, the money released would enable you to have a much bigger surface fleet. Nonsense, of course, because once money is taken away for any purpose from a service or from anything else (the National Health Service if you like) it is never possible to get it back! The Treasury works on the principle of the ratchet. It was a sensitive time and one in which people had to toe the line in perhaps a way they didn't particularly like.

Anyway, the day came for Admiral Frewin, the Commander-in-Chief Fleet, to talk to the Senior Officers' War Course. His job, at that time, was to explain why the Commander-in-Chief's Flag was being shifted from HMS *Tyne* which had been the HQ ship of the Commander-in-Chief (it was a submarine tender) to go down into the basement of the headquarters at Northwood, which had always been the NATO headquarters, shared by the RAF, and run the fleet literally from a bunker. He did his best to explain how this was going to work but didn't, to me, seem to be very convincing in his argument. Perhaps, poor man, he wasn't convinced himself. Nevertheless, at the end, he asked if there were any questions. I raised my hand and he looked at me and said, 'Yes,' in a somewhat flat tone, piercing me with his very sharp eyes.

'I am not quite sure, Sir, how in a period of rising tension you're going to be able to exercise enough control from Northwood without delegating your authority to whoever is on the spot. How do you intend to solve this problem?' Admiral Frewin looked down at the dais and then looking up he gave an answer which I didn't find very satisfactory.

'Does that answer your question?' he said, looking at me again rather fixedly.

'No, Sir,' I said. There was a stunned silence amongst my colleagues that someone should actually dispute the Commander-in-Chief Fleet in such a manner. Frewin looked at me for a moment, then literally burst into flames.

'I know all about you, Lygo,' he said. 'I did not come here to be lectured by you. You've had your answer and that's an end of it.' There was another stunned silence. Many of my colleagues, I suspect, when they got back to their cabins took their Navy List out and put a line through Lygo. Once again, he's overstepped the mark. It was an embarrassing experience and it was interesting to see the way in which my peers reacted to this. Some wouldn't discuss it; some shrugged and said, 'Well, you asked for it,' and others smiled and said, 'Good for you,' but the latter were in the minority.

Weeks and months passed and I had to go to call on the Commander-in-Chief Fleet as the Commanding Officer designate of HMS *Juno*. With due trepidation, I arrived at the great Northwood headquarters and descended into the bunker, into the Commander-in-Chief's office which was quite small, as I recall, and there he was sitting behind his desk when I walked in and stood stiffly to attention. He didn't look up. His hands were working somewhat nervously at a pen he was holding and some papers, and then he put the pen down and looked up at me.

'The last time we met, Lygo,' he said, 'there was an unfortunate scene. It was my fault and I regret, it but you are an extremely irritating man.'

'Yes, Sir,' I said.

'Sit down,' and I sat down and we chatted about the work-up of *Juno* and what it was going to do. I had never had a doubt about his character or my respect for it but he went up even more in my estimation. He was right; I was irritating.

There were two other occasions when I had the opportunity to exchange words with him. Once, when he came on board my ship to pay a visit, as we turned from the gangway he turned to me and said, 'I can tell what a ship is like within the first 30 seconds, Lygo.' To which I replied, 'Then you must be an extremely perceptive man, Sir.' Checkmate! And another occasion was when he had to cross my ship to go to lunch in another, and as he was piped onto my ship and over the side to the other one I, of course, was there to greet him, and when he left and departed I was on the gangway again.

'I suppose,' he said, looking at me, 'you've been here the whole time, Lygo.'

'Naturally, Sir,' I replied, 'what would you expect?'

One of my first occasions to dine with him as C-in-C Portsmouth where he had been appointed after finishing as C-in-C Fleet, was a fairly sombre occasion, a little bit stiff and people were being a bit awkward in the way in which they were conducting themselves, which sometimes happens. I happened to be in a position at the table where I could see out into the garden at the back and I observed after a while a squirrel which was going about its business and to enliven the conversation I said, 'I observe this squirrel in the garden at the back of you, Commander-in-Chief, which reminds me of a member of the Board of Admiralty.' There was a hushed silence and they all looked at me. I said, 'they're very rarely seen but every now and again they nip out, grab a nut and disappear into their holes again.' The Admiral of course had his back to this performance and only smiled weakly at me and I could see that the pencils were out on the Navy List once again, but I have a feeling in life that if something is funny and makes you laugh, then you should laugh at it and not wait until an appropriate moment and then have a quiet giggle in the corner. I've always said that if I were Officer of the Watch and the Commander-in-Chief came over the gangway and it collapsed into the oggin, I would have a jolly good laugh as he went down at the same time shouting for the boats, crew and various other 'man overboard' procedures to be followed. Enjoy the moment!

Once again I was invited to lunch at Admiralty House. He had invited a wide collection of Captains and Admirals and he sat at the head of the table, and I was about in the middle I suppose, not below the salt but only just above it. I can't remember who was opposite me and what he said that sparked me, but something must have because I proceeded to give this chap, I wouldn't describe it as both barrels but certainly half a barrel. When I had stopped, I looked up towards the Admiral who had a slight smile on his face, and addressing the man to whom I had made my remarks, he said, 'Don't take it too hard. He's not a bad chap when you get to know him.' To me it was one of the greatest compliments that I could have been paid. He was a man after my own heart and I believe that he recognised some reflection of that in me. At any stage if he had been petty-minded he could have taken a dreadful revenge on Lygo's career. He never did. I had nearly lost another life but I hadn't.

Toward the end of my time in the Navy, I became increasingly concerned about the way in which we were promoting people in peace-time. The history of the Services in peace time is, generally speaking, that they have usually managed to promote the wrong people and when war has broken out they've had to get rid of them or suffer the consequences and then promote the people who have the right attitudes for winning rather than surviving in a spit and polish environment. It is a truism of any selection process, which I have enunciated many times, that one of the things you should be careful to be guided by is to promote the people who are competent and good but whom you might not like and pass over the people that you like when you know they're not really up to it.

Sadly Admiral Frewin died shortly after he retired and so, although he would be on my list to be invited, he is not available.

Sometimes one is constrained to say something which really conveys your feelings but you have to say it to people whom you would rather not have targeted. One morning as VCNS, the Head of Naval Signals came in to see me to tell me that despite the Government saying that we should sever all connections with South Africa he had discovered that we were maintaining an open radio link to Simonstown. I told him to close it down, which he did, but he went on to say that worse was to follow since the Head of Naval Transport and Logistics was still shipping oil into Simonstown as part of the global strategic reserve. I told him to stop, which he said was now being implemented.

That morning I went to see the Naval Minister, Pat Duffy, one of the nicest politicians I have ever had the pleasure to meet but Pat was understandably concerned whether this news, if it got out, would be of great embarrassment to the Government. I told him that I saw no reason why it should get out since I had stopped shipping the oil and I had shut down the link; so he then asked me whether I was sure that none of this would get out because of it did it would prove extremely embarrassing to the Government. This prompted from me a short burst on the banjo which went as follows: 'I now understand, Minister, why the Nazis were called National Socialists.' He looked at me in some surprise. 'Well,' I said, 'they were Socialists, weren't they, just like you.' He said, 'What a terrible thing to say.' I said, 'Yes, but you see when the truth became embarrassing they suppressed it, just like you.' 'That's a dreadful thing to say,' he said, 'I agree,' I said, 'but think about it,' and I left.

Political parties of any persuasion, once they get into power somehow seem to think they have a right to stay there and that anything that is going to be embarrassing or is going to somehow undermine their chances of being re-elected, or cause their leaders to be embarrassed in some way, shape or form, is something that must be gotten round (as the Americans would say). In simple language – suppressed or distorted, or to become economical with the truth which is a modern way of describing it. Whatever the persuasion, you can see it start to happen and to me as a democrat it's a very dangerous thing to see. It was sad that I picked on Pat, who is my friend to this day, to have to to make this remark and it wasn't directed at him; it was directed at the system and I believe it to be extremely telling.

24

Pride Goes Before a Fall

Pride goes before a fall! If you are to maintain any sense of proportion, I suppose you have continuously to suffer near disasters in your career to bring you back firmly to earth. It was fortunate that in my headlong rush to the top I came a cropper often enough to make me have a better balance, I think, than might otherwise have been possible. I give you three episodes which illustrate the point.

Episode one. My time at Lee-on-the-Solent in 759 Squadron had given me a great deal of confidence. I had enjoyed the CFS instruction course and felt myself, indeed must have been, a much better aviator having been through it, and I prided myself on my ability to fly in a much more professional way than I had heretofore. Finally the evil day arrived when, after doing some aerobatics, I came back to Lee-on-the-Solent, didn't pay as much attention as I should have done to the control tower signals and tried to land downwind. The tilley fired a red verey at me and I went round again and then realised to my intense chagrin what I had done.

I came round and landed the proper way, taxied in, went into the office where no one had known this had happened and presented myself to the Commanding Officer. I in fact, ran myself in.

'I have just carried out the most appalling piece of airmanship, Sir.'

'What have you been doing?' he said. I told him. 'Oh dear,' he said, 'well, it's just one of those things, I suppose.'

'No, Sir, it isn't. For somebody like myself it is totally and utterly inexcusable and I wish to be given punishment.' He looked at me in astonishment.

'What would you wish to do?' said he.

'I wish to take Duty Officer for at least 14 days, Sir, because I deserve it.' He smiled at me.

'Well, I imagine the others will be quite pleased,' he said, and so it was, but it served to set me right back on my haunches. No matter how good an aviator you might think you are, if you relax for an instant you can find yourself in trouble.

The next episode occurred early in my embarked time in *Ark Royal*, leading 800 Squadron. We had come to the point when night flying was going to commence. They had decided to practise loading the aircraft onto the catapults, going through the drill for night flying which was going to take place the following night. Spiv Leahy, my senior pilot, said, 'Do you want me to do this?'

'No, no,' I said, 'I'll do it, I'll do it,' and I was already in my mess undress, ready for a dining-in night, the same rig as when during the War I had tried to start a Seafire. In briefing my pilots for this episode, I had explained to them that once you were loaded on the catapult and ready for launch you flashed your navigation lights by turning the switch on and off, which was down almost behind you on the starboard console. One young Sub Lieutenant asked me, 'Do you not think, Sir, that this switch is very close to the unguarded drop tank jettison switch?'

'No,' I said. 'It is close to it but if any pilot mistakes these two switches it is an automatic 14 days Duty Officer.' That terminated the conversation. And so I clambered into the Seahawk and was duly loaded through the Cale alignment gear onto the catapult. Up came the advice over the RT, 'Go through the launch drill.' I put my hand down to flash the navigation lights and jettisoned both plastic tanks into the middle of the catapult. I was devastated. Commander Air came over, looked at me and used one word; it wasn't a pleasant word, it was perhaps not properly thought through in its application but it conveyed its meaning. Several hundred gallons of Avcat had gone straight down into the catapult machinery and all had to be cleaned up. I had really cocked up. I placed myself under 30 days stoppage of leave. It wasn't really possible for the CO to do Duty Boy, you see! But worse was to come, because the dining-in night gave the opportunity for everybody in the ship who knew what had happened, and particularly the other Squadron, to really have a good old go at Lygo! I felt absolutely dreadful. My Squadron rallied round me; they didn't laugh, some people may have said it wouldn't have been wise if they had done so. But the fact is we had to suffer through a formal dining-in night with every kind of jibe in the book being thrown at 800 Squadron. I had really fallen from a great height, or rather my drop tanks had, but it served to pin my ears back for a bit, that's for certain.

During my time in *Lowestoft*, under the leadership of Captain Dunbar-Nasmith, we had paid a visit to Athens, and he had told me afterwards how he had worked hard to get all the Squadron into Piraeus stern to the wall, when otherwise we might have been in the bay outside with a long boat journey to get ashore. So when the time came for me to take *Juno* in, I was equally determined that we would go stern to the wall in Piraeus.

322

After many signals to the Naval Attaché via the Commander-in-Chief and Flag Officer Flotillas and anybody else I could think of, we finally swung it and instead of being out swinging at our anchor in the middle of the Bay of Athens, we were allocated a stern-to berth in Piraeus.

The great morning arrived; we were ceremonially turned out and I came into the port of Piraeus, turned the ship, because by this time I had got the knack of coming astern into a berth, and readied myself for coming back into the berth. We had been followed in by the flagship of the French Squadron that was taking part in the ensuing exercise with the French Admiral's flag flying. He lay off because he was next to come in after me. I stationed the Gunner on the Quarter-deck and told him, 'I want you to call out distances as I approach the berth so that I can come to a stop in good time.' I positioned myself, lined the ship up and started back towards the stern berth. The figures from the Gunner came as follows: 200 feet – 150 – 100 feet, and then his voice rising an octave, 50, 40, 10 feet – bang! As his voice rose, so the revs ahead I rung on stopped us from doing something totally disastrous, but bang the stern into the jetty we did, and damaged it in the process. I was mortified. Here I was, at the peak of my time in command of this beautiful brand new ship and I'd actually creased it going astern into the berth. It was no good blaming the Gunner, although one could easily see how you could. It was I, with over-confidence, who had actually done it again. For the second time at least in this episode of events people began to write me off. Number One was very good, particularly since we had a reception and cocktail party that night, and he managed to cover most of the damage with bunting and flags, so that when the guests came on over the stern of the crumpled ship it wasn't too noticeable.

I was in black despair. I had also to call on the French Admiral because he was the senior officer in the trot and protocol required me to do so. He was charming and very considerate, having watched exactly what had happened.

'What will happen to somebody in your Navy who does something like that?' he enquired.

'I've no idea, Sir,' I said, 'I've no idea.'

'H'm,' he looked at me pensively. 'We have a saying in our Navy,' he said, 'it is simply this – things like what happened to you never happen to people who don't go to sea.' I was grateful for those few words of comfort but it made me pause in my tracks, it brought me up with a round turn, it made me a little less arrogant and for 24, 48 hours, I sulked a bit in my cabin although I forced myself to do rounds of the ship as usual. When the Navigator came to me and said,

'Shall we go through the Corinth Canal?' I had lost my nerve. 'No, Pilot,' I said, 'I think we'll go round.'

'I quite understand, Sir,' said he, and that was the end of it. Oh dear, another life lost.

We went into Malta on our way back and I had arranged to have the ship repaired. They cut away the damage, repaired it (Malta dry docks was then privatised), the work was quickly done and the ship looked just like new when we left, and, after I got back into Chatham, Admiral Bush, then C-in-C fleet, came to see me and said, 'Why did you report that episode?'

'Because it happened, Sir,' said I, 'I mean, I damaged the ship and I had to get it repaired in Malta.'

'Oh,' he said, 'but I would never have reported a thing like that.'

'I am sorry, Sir,' said I, 'I think times have changed,' but it just goes to show how lucky I was that I had an Admiral who took that view of what he considered to be a minor scrape, and so I breathed again. But all these episodes, spaced out as they were during a Naval career, kept me, I think, from becoming a bit more top heavy than some people will say I eventually became.

25

The Transatlantic Air Race

I had enjoyed *Juno*. It was my second frigate command and I had gained confidence, after experience in the first, HMS *Lowestoft*; with this one, life had been a lot easier. I had also mastered the art of coming up the Medway, in and out of Chatham, and although no one had actually bothered to teach me any of these things, I had picked up the necessary knowledge to ensure that I was able to make safe entries, exits and alongsides in a professional manner. One of the things I really began to enjoy was getting the ship into the lock at Chatham: coming up the River Medway and then getting into either the north or the south lock by aiming at the Bullnose, the piece in the middle, and then allowing the ship to drift off depending on which way the current was flowing. Or to aim it off if it was still, with no wind, and then slide it into the lock bringing it up with the riggers running around, getting the necessary wires on to the ship to restrain it. In fact, I had become so entranced by this procedure and the knowledge that I could do it that I conned the relief Captain, who was to take over command of the *Juno* into allowing me to take the ship out to demonstrate to him that all was well after the self-maintenance period, purely so that I could bring it in again!

I did this the last time with great aplomb and was watched, as usual, by the Admiral Superintendent, who came down to observe the entry and exit of all the ships that came in and went out of Chatham. On this occasion, so confident was I that I came in faster than ever and had to have a touch of full astern to stop the ship shooting straight through into the basin. It was a spectacular and quite arresting arrival, and he was kind enough to say, 'That was an extremely smart entry. You better not try that with your next ship.' By now, of course, it was well known that I was going on to drive *Ark Royal*, the crowning achievement of a career in the Royal Navy, because it was, and remains, the biggest warship that we ever had.

I was, however, looking forward to something rather different from the new challenge of command because I knew that there would be a gap of some six months between leaving *Juno* and taking up my command of *Ark Royal*, or at least standing by to get her out of the major re-fit she was undergoing in Devonport Dockyard.

Juno had hardly come alongside however, the telephone lines being connected, when I received a call from the Flag Officer Naval Air Command, Dick Janvrin. He first of all congratulated me on my appointment to *Ark Royal* and then went on to ask me what I was going to do in the intervening period. Smelling a rat the size of an elephant, I began to prevaricate and said, 'Well, I'm not sure, Sir. No doubt there will be several courses'

'Yes,' he said, 'but what I would like you to do, Ray, is run the Naval entry in the Transatlantic Air Race.' I'd never heard of the Transatlantic Air Race, I didn't know anything about it and didn't particularly want to. What I did know, of course, was that the Fleet Air Arm was in a very depressed state. The loss of the carrier battle had meant that the future of fixed-wing flying in the Royal Navy hung by a thread and that thread was the V-STOL Harrier, but that was still a long way off. We were in the throes of closing down fixed-wing squadrons, paying them off and de-commissioning air stations and vacating them just after they had been fully refurbished from the fairly squalid state in which the Fleet Air Arm had had to occupy them for so many years, only to see them, once refurbished, handed to the Royal Air Force! It was a sad and demoralising period for the Fleet Air Arm and I felt it as much as anybody else. Dick Janvrin continued, however, that he saw the opportunity to enter the Transatlantic Air Race as a great morale-booster for the Fleet Air Arm and that he wanted me to be the manager of the Naval entry. I tried to protest my innocence as it were, but to no avail and he asked me when and how soon I could take up this new task. I replied that my wedding anniversary was on the 21st January, and I really didn't want to do anything until I had at least had a chance of celebrating my wedding anniversary with my wife. He said, 'That's fine, so you'll be available on the 22nd,' and with the usual kind of inward sigh that one is used to heaving in the Service, I said, 'Yes, Sir, I'll be there on the 22nd.'

The next telephone call I received was from Flag Officer Scotland, Vice Admiral McGeogh, who again congratulated me on my appointment, and immediately proceeded to ask me what I was going to do in the intervening period. Before I could even answer him, he said, 'Because what I want you to do, Ray, is to go down and take charge of the Royal Naval Sailing Association.'

'But, Sir,' said I, 'I know nothing whatever about sailing, I'm not a sailor in that sense of the word; I've never been interested, I wouldn't know anything about it.'

'That's not the point,' he replied, 'and it doesn't matter; what I want you to do is sort out the administration.' It was with some relief, therefore, that I was able to say, 'I'm sorry, Sir, but you've been beaten to the post by Admiral Janvrin who has told me that I am to run the Naval entry in the Transatlantic Air Race, and so I'm afraid I will have to decline.' It did, however, indicate to me that any thoughts I might have had of having six months' gardening leave was not about to come to fruition.

My leaving of *Juno* was effected extremely well by the First Lieutenant, John Caughey, and the other Officers. The Wardroom and the First Lieutenant insisted that Pepper should come to the farewell lunch they were giving me before I left the ship. Having gone back home to Mereworth in Kent to give her this message, she accepted gracefully but said, 'They don't really want me,' and once she discovered that she would be the only wife there, she was quite certain they didn't really want her! She said, 'Thank them very much, but no thank you, I won't be able to be there.' When this message was given to John Caughey he was most upset and said, 'But I assure you it's important that she does come and we very much hope she will or it will spoil the little ceremony we have in mind.' This I duly reported to Pepper who agreed, somewhat reluctantly, to go to the lunch, still believing that it would be better without her.

It was a very pleasant lunch in the Wardroom on board the *Juno* with my Officers and at the end of it John Caughey made a little speech which went as follows:

'First of all, we are delighted that you are here today, Pepper, because it is to you we are going to address our remarks on this farewell occasion.

Nearly two years ago, when your husband joined this ship we met him and he met us and after about three weeks we, the Officers, had a meeting. We said to one another that it was not possible for us to spend nearly two years with this man in command. He is so demanding in the things he wants and the standards he is setting are so high that we really are not going to have a very tolerable existence. He is going to be difficult to live with. As we were debating what to do, we had that first cocktail party to which you came and we met you. After the party we had another meeting and we said to each other that as you had been married to him for 20-something years and had put up with him for all that time, then surely we could put up with him for two. And so the farewell that we are giving is for you.'

And with that he presented Pepper with a beautiful cut glass whiskey decanter which she accepted with pleasure amid much laughter.

327

He then turned to me. 'We haven't forgotten you, Sir, however, and we have something for you as well.' He handed me a small box which, upon opening, revealed one of those labels that you hang around the neck of decanters and on which was engraved, 'and another thing', which apparently had become one of my more familiar terms when addressing some particular aspect of ship's life. It was all very amusing and, to me, touching. I had always known I was a demanding superior but I'd also hoped that it was exercised with fairness and consistency, which is the only thing I had hoped to find in life when working under superiors.

The lunch over we were ready to depart. I had carried around with me in this ship, or had it moved by Midshipmen from place to place when that was not possible, the Austin A30 I had bought for £45 from a youngster who'd gone bust refitting it and repainting it a kind of Oxford blue by hand! It was, therefore, somewhat well known and it ran like a sewing machine. I was asked to get in this and Pepper was taken off somewhere else. Then, to my horror, the whole car was lifted up by the ship's company and they doubled smartly down the jetty with me sitting, surprised, at the wheel. I had been well and truly sent off! My ride home was therefore something of an anti-climax but we got there and celebrated our wedding anniversary.

I then got ready to depart for Lee-on-Solent, to fly up to Lossiemouth where I was to meet the Captain, one 'Winkle' Brown, to determine whether the Buccaneer Squadron wished to enter the Transatlantic Air Race. I was to be flown up in a Heron of the Communications Squadron at Lee-on-Solent and because it was going to be a long and boring flight, taking off at something like 9.00 am, I had Pepper prepare me some sandwiches to take with me and she included with those a large dill pickle. I happen to be very fond of dill pickles if you can get good ones and this was a particularly luscious example. So, with my sandwiches packed, I got into my little blue motor car and trundled off to Lee-on-Solent. On arrival I was given a great bundle of information on the Transatlantic Air Race, about which I still knew very little, and was ushered onboard the Heron aircraft.

The Heron was, and I suppose still is, a four-engined de Havilland aeroplane which was used at that time in the Naval Communications Squadron. It carried, as I recall, about 12 passengers, six on each side in single seats, and I was somewhat surprised to see, when the pilot came on board that he was an Air Engineer Pilot two and a half stripes wearing glasses! I merely made a mental note of this fact, no more. He was accompanied by a Petty Officer who was to be his radio operator during the flight.

The flight took off from Lee-on-the-Solent in not very good weather and we proceeded to climb through cloud and out at the top and trundle our way steadily north. The Petty Officer came back and told us that the flight was to go via Glasgow where a compassionate case Rating was to be dropped off, before proceeding to Arbroath where another passenger was to be delivered, and then the aircraft would continue up to Lossiemouth. We settled down then for the long flight and the aircraft climbed out from the cloud and rain, up into clearer weather above. I settled down to read all this bumf on the Transatlantic Air Race.

The Air Race had been organised by the *Daily Mail*, the original organisers of the London to Paris Air Race which was the background for the film *Those Magnificent Men In Their Flying Machines*. The idea was to race from the top of the Post Office Tower in London to the top of the Empire State Building in New York, and vice versa. There were to be many classes of entry; there were individuals who could enter by flying various airlines, making their own arrangements from the Tower to the embarkation point. There were the entries for people who wanted to fly their own aircraft, for example, but they would still have to make the transit from the Tower to the point of take-off at either end.

The sponsors hoped that they would be able to encourage the Royal Air Force, the Royal Navy, the United States Air Force, and the United States Navy to participate in the event and there was a separate category for military aircraft of various kinds. For example the Harrier would be in a class that was quite separate from the Phantom, the new Naval Fighter. The category which included the Victor Bombers would also be a separate one. So there were many different categories for entering and the plan had been for the Navy to enter its Buccaneers, which were a subsonic but long-range aircraft, in the category which would bring them into competition with planes like the Victor, whereas the Phantoms would be competing with other supersonic aircraft at the top end of the range.

The Navy had only just acquired the Phantom, the remnants of the original order which I had helped to obtain when I served in DNAW. It was originally intended to equip all the fighter Squadrons in the FAA. This, however, had been shrunk down to an order which would allow one Squadron only to be formed and that was to go into *Ark Royal*, the last fixed-wing carrier. The Squadron number allocated was 892 and they were only just receiving their aircraft. Crews had been training in the US for the arrival of the aircraft but they were at a very early stage in their formation and since the Air Race was to take place in the summer it was going to be pretty tight.

It was also clear from the correspondence of the Captain of Lossiemouth that he was not at all enthusiastic about the Buccaneers participating and was leading that rather sombre bunch of Naval aviators
who, quite understandably, saw the whole of their future crumbling.
This was particularly so for those, who at that time were called 'dry',
i.e. would not go to sea, as opposed to people like myself who were
lucky enough to have been cast into the 'wet' role, which meant that
we could go to sea in command of ships as well as Squadrons and Air
Stations.

The Heron droned on its way and eventually was about to descend
into what I assumed to be Abbottsinch. There was the usual kind of
bump, bump, bump of engines as the throttles were closed and we
descended into the cloud and continued to descend down, down and
down onto the approach to Abbottsinch. As it got closer to the
ground I looked out of the window to see whether I could spot the
ground below the cloud but I had not seen any by the time the engines
wound up to full power and the aircraft proceeded to climb up again
above the cloud. The first attempt to land had been aborted!

As we popped out of the top of the cloud the engines were almost
immediately throttled back and it was clear that we were going to
make another attempt to land. This time I began to take more than a
passing interest in whether we were actually going to see the ground
before we hit it! This is not an unusually pessimistic view for ancient
aviators to take and most of us do get slightly nervous when an
aeroplane is letting down on instrument conditions because we have
been through this process ourselves many times and know how easy it
is, without great care, for silly mistakes to occur. Once again I heard
the wheels go down as we approached the ground and as the engine
power was being steadily reduced I did catch a glimpse of some fields
and trees through the very low cloud before, again, the engines roared
into life and we climbed away up through the murk and into the clear.
This time the Petty Officer came from the front of the aeroplane and
told us they were unable to land at Abbottsinch and would be
proceeding direct to Arbroath. The aeroplane turned on to what was
clearly a north-easterly heading and I settled down to complete
reading my brief and to eat my sandwiches.

After a while the engines were closed again and we proceeded down
into a layer of cloud which soon cleared, into an area where there was
quite good visibility but there was another layer of cloud below us out
of which were sticking the two pylons of the Forth Road Bridge! I
looked at this with some surprise but we were still fairly high and I
thought, well perhaps this is a long approach into Arbroath, imagining
that we were still heading off in a north-easterly direction. The Wren

330

Officer in front of me turned round and enquired politely, 'Are those the Forth Road Bridge towers, Sir?'

'Yes,' I said. 'I have just come down from operating out of Rosyth and am very familiar with this area and you are absolutely right – those are the Forth Road Bridge towers.' The aeroplane continued to descend. As we got lower and lower I began to think that it was a very strange way of going into Arbroath; in fact, thought I, if we continue like this we shall be landing in Rosyth Dockyard! However, for the fourth time on that flight I told myself, 'Now steady, Lygo, you have been away from aviation for two years, driving a ship, and these chaps know what they are doing, you just mind your own business and it will be all right.'

At this point I had reached for the dill pickle and at that moment the aircraft descended into the low cloud beyond the Road Bridge towers. I was still curious but still mindful that it was none of my business. As I bit into my dill pickle there was an enormous crash and looking out of the window I saw that we were in a wood; trees were flashing by on either side, the engines leapt into a bitter roar of life and the aeroplane proceeded to screech its way out of the wood leaving a swathe of topped pine trees behind it together with eight feet of the port wing and six feet of the starboard wing. I now realised that, try as I might, it *was* my business and I got up, passing between the ashen faces of the passengers on either side, and went to the cockpit door. I opened it and there I saw the Lieutenant Commander struggling with the controls as the aeroplane climbed away into the cloud. I said to the Petty Officer, 'Has he got control, is he all right?' does he want a hand, can I come up there and help him?' – in other words, thinking that there might be a need for two of us on the controls to overcome some of the damage that had obviously been done to those controls.

'No, Sir, he's got it, it is all right,' he said. I turned back to the passengers who were staring at me with a kind of comic belief in the powers of seniority and said, 'We have a problem. I don't know now where he is going to try to land, it depends how badly the aeroplane is damaged, but he may decide to ditch it in which case we had better understand how to get out of the aeroplane should this arise.' And so I indicated to them the hatch in the roof, where the lifebelts were stowed and where the dinghy was stowed and as I settled down again the lad at the rear of the cabin said, 'Sir, there is smoke coming up through the floor!'

I turned and saw this wisp of smoke drifting up through the cabin floor and again went for'ard and said, 'I have worse news for you, we now appear to have a small fire aft – where is the fire extinguisher?'

The reply came, 'There is no fire extinguisher!' Even better, I thought, and even more reason why we should ditch. As I proceeded aft, however, I noticed that a hole had opened up in the low cloud beneath us and there, believe it or not, was the end of a runway! I shot for'ard again to the cockpit and said, 'There's a runway there, there's an airfield there, land on it.'

'Yes, Sir,' said the pilot, 'I'm going to,' and he was already beginning the turn to position himself to get onto the runway. As I went back to my seat another dreadful thought occurred to me; if this chap decides to put his undercarriage down, that's one thing, but if he decides to put his flaps down and one comes down on one side and not on the other this aeroplane is going to roll over and that will be the end. What a ghastly way to end an aviating career. I am bound to say that the one thought that flashed through my mind when the first accident occurred was, what a way to go after all these years of aviation and having managed to survive, to be killed in a Heron over the middle of Scotland through sheer incompetence. It was not a happy thought and I understand now about all these thoughts that flash before your mind in moments like this, and in particular the thoughts of your wife and family. What a way to die!

However, this was immediately pushed out of my brain by the realisation that having survived so far, we might be standing into even worse peril. I therefore went for'ard again and said to him, 'What have you got on the clock?'

'120 knots,' he said.

'Right,' said I, 'that is the speed you know this aeroplane flies at, do not put the flaps down, try to get the undercarriage down and land it at what you have got on the clock now, because that is the speed at which you know it will stay airborne.' I went back and strapped myself in and within a few moments we were approaching that runway which had appeared out of the gloom and the aircraft made a successful fast, flaps up, landing on the very long runway at Turnhouse.

Unbeknown to me it had been decided to land the aircraft at Turnhouse to disembark the compassionate case that should have gone into Abbottsinch and we were approaching not on a north-easterly direction but on a south-westerly direction. It was subsequently revealed at the Board of Enquiry that the pilot had over-read the altimeter by 1,000 feet and that we had ploughed into a hill-top on the approach to the runway. It was an absolute miracle and a tremendous credit to the de Havilland Company that the aeroplane was able to sustain such damage and climb out.

When we examined the aircraft after landing at Turnhouse, the port and starboard wings were almost in ribbons, a great deal of structural damage had been done to the underneath of the aeroplane and the fire that had started at the rear was clearly an electrical short circuit which did not, fortunately, manage to catch fire to anything very serious down aft because there was not much that could catch fire.

We were met by the RAF Group Captain Commandant, who looked in amazement at this wreck of an aeroplane which was then towed away. He asked me if he could provide any assistance to me and I said, 'Well, I need to be going on to Lossiemouth and I had better phone Lossiemouth and explain what has happened.' I 'phoned 'Winkle' Brown, the Captain at Lossiemouth, who said he would send a Sea Prince down to pick me up. I waited in the comfort and warmth of Turnhouse, ruminating over this recent experience of my return to the Fleet Air Arm and in the fullness of time the Sea Prince arrived. It was flown by a well-known Naval aviator, certainly well-known to me, Monty Mellor. I recounted to him the story of my adventures so far. He listened, puffing on his pipe and then said, 'Well, dear oh dear, Sir, what an experience. Anyway I think we had better go out and get into the aircraft and get on our way to Lossiemouth and I tell you what, Sir, see if you can spot my deliberate mistake on the way up there.' Such is the humour, always, of the Fleet Air Arm in situations like this, that nothing that was really dreadful could be taken seriously for very long. I entered this wreck of an aircraft, the Sea Prince, which hadn't been a good aeroplane at the beginning of its life and certainly was no better after several years of hard service in the Navy, and we throbbed and groaned our way up to Lossiemouth where I landed to be greeted by Captain 'Winkle' Brown, and we proceeded from there.

Lossiemouth was not a successful visit. 'Winkle' was suffering the withdrawal pangs of being told he wasn't going on any further in the Service, i.e. that he would retire at the end of his stint at Lossiemouth, and that, coupled with the news of the demise of the carriers, had led him to take a somewhat negative attitude. A Buccaneer Squadron was going to continue in service to go in *Ark Royal* and I think it was a shame that a damper was put upon their entry, but it was quite clear to me that it was not going to be well received in that place. I therefore proceeded south and duly reported to Flag Officer Naval Air Command.

My next trip was to Yeovilton to meet with 892 Squadron, the Phantom Squadron, to see what their attitude was. Here the attitude was totally different; it was one of enthusiasm for the undertaking and I began to feel that we had something that we could actually do. In parallel with this I was renewing my own flying qualifications by going up and doing a Hunter course at Brawdy. I then went on to fly the

With Brian Davies after my first flight as pilot of the Phantom

Phantom myself. All difficulties were swept aside to enable the Captain designate of *Ark Royal* to qualify on the Phantom, which I duly did thanks to the CO, Brian Davies, and Peter Goddard the Senior Observer, both of whom courageously sat in the back seat with me when I did my familiarisation flights.

As far as the Transatlantic Air Race was concerned, I suspect that Their Lordships had little concept of what was going on. It was something that was being organised by Flag Officer Naval Air Command. I was given a suite of offices in the Empress State Building at Earls Court and a staff to enable me to perform my task. They consisted for the most part of Officers, pilots and aviators who were about to leave the Service and who were filling in time until that occurred. Commander 'Shorty' Hamilton, a distinguished aviator, was about to emigrate to Australia and he was given to me as my kind of Chief of Staff. The next guy was an observer, Robbie Roberts to whom I allocated the New York end and who later finished up working for me in BAe. A couple of Naval airmen made up the team, plus Lieutenant Commander Fairweather to look after Public Relations.

334

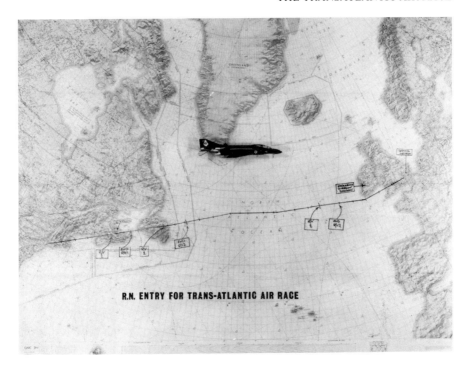

R.N. ENTRY FOR TRANS-ATLANTIC AIR RACE

The route of the Phantoms

The *Daily Mail* was taking the event very seriously and the team there was led by Brian Harper, who organised a get-together at the beginning of the episode to meet with the possible contenders. Brian, an effervescent, overflowing character had been strong in public relations all his life and was an amusing chap to boot. I think I startled him at the first meeting when he asked me if we intended to enter, and I told him we were considering it. He had with him the guy who was to do most of the leg-work and who subsequently wrote the book, *The Great Race*, and he said, 'Well I think you have a duty to the British public to enter this race.' This sparked a reaction in me which was genuine but to the point.

'We owe you nothing,' said I. The headline in the *Evening Standard* on the day in which the decision to scrap our Carrier Programme was announced read, 'End of the flying fools.'

'Let me tell you, Mr Harper,' said I, 'we owe you nothing and I will only do this if I believe it will be good for the morale of my colleagues in the Fleet Air Arm, and I will only do it if I am quite sure we are going to win.' This episode is well recorded in the book.

335

It became clear to me that there were two essential aspects to winning this race. It would not be so much the time taken to cross the Atlantic, as the arrangements made to get people from the top of the Post Office Tower to the aircraft and off the aircraft and up to the top of the Empire State Building, and vice versa. We decided that the best records could be achieved by flying from West to East with the prevailing wind behind us, so it was decided that our entry would be from New York to London.

I sent 'Shorty' Hamilton off to look at possible landing sites for a helicopter close to the Post Office Tower and he came back with two. One was the St Pancras railway coal yard which was not too far away, and the other was Coram Fields. In both cases, of course, we would need to get permission from the authorities to use them and only twin-engined helocipters would be allowed to fly over London.

It seemed sensible to go up the Post Office Tower myself and take a look at the various landing sites from there so we went up in the lift to the top of the Tower which now, regrettably, is no longer open to the public, and took a look around. 'Shorty' pointed out the St Pancras coal yard and the hospital grounds, Coram Fields, and as I stood there I looked down at the base of the Tower to behold right adjacent to it a big hole in the ground where construction was starting on a new building.

'Who owns that hole?' I asked. 'Shorty' looked down.

'I don't know,' he said.

'Well, find out,' I said, 'find out from the contractor who owns it and get them to give us the right to use it. Go and get an exclusive right to land there, get them to construct a helicopter platform in that hole so that we can use it, and then go and stitch up British Rail for the St Pancras coal yard and we'll be home and dry.;

After a few days 'Shorty' came back smiling with the good news that by liberal applications of Navy rum he had persuaded the building contractor to give us an exclusive right to the hole and to construct a 'helo' platform, and he had also managed to get an exclusive from British Rail. I now had under my control the most important parts of getting into the Post Office Tower. As I've said already, Their Lordships of the Admiralty had little knowledge of what was going on or inclination to care, I suspect, and so no classification had been placed upon our entry and I was free to do and negotiate as I wished. 'Shorty' also suggested that FLY NAVY be printed on the helicopter landing site! It was!

My Air Force colleagues, however, were in a different situation. The Board of the Royal Air Force had applied a classification of 'Secret' to their entry, so they could not go out and discuss with anybody how they were actually going to do it! This was, of course, a crucial point because the other vital element for our Naval entry was to get tanker aircraft to fuel our aircraft as they came across the Atlantic and this could only be from two sources – the Royal Air Force or the United States Navy. Whilst we had total regard for the United States Navy, we were not used to working with them in this area, whereas we were used to working with our RAF colleagues and so it was quite important that I manage to get Victor Tanker support.

One other element had to be put in place; the first refuelling was to take place off the coast of Newfoundland and the second in the South Western Approaches to the United Kingdom. In order to control the first one we could use the ground radar based in Newfoundland but to control the second one we needed a frigate stationed in the South Western Approaches that would actually take control and rendezvous the Phantoms with the Tanker. There was, therefore, a third element of success, to get the Commander-in-Chief Fleet to agree to release a frigate or to station a frigate in the South Western Approaches to do this task. Not very exciting for the frigate but essential if we were to be successful. Don't underestimate the problem of getting a frigate in that position: we had just lost the carrier battle and aviation was not a popular feature; to prise a frigate out of the Commander-in-Chief would not be easy.

The next thing to do was to ensure that the other end was going to be equally well organised and for this we were heavily dependent on support from the United States Navy. It was therefore arranged that I should fly to the United States to have talks with them, accompanied by my RAF opposite number whom up to that time I hadn't met.

I duly arrived at Brize Norton to catch the RAF aircraft that was to take me to New York and there met for the first time my RAF opposite number, Group Captain Peter Williamson. He was the Officer commanding the Harrier base at Wittering. Peter was a charming man, amusing, intelligent and easy to get on with. Sadly, having achieved the rank of Air Vice Marshall, he died at a far too early age, a sad end to what I am sure would have been an even more brilliant career.

'Can I have a word with you in private,' he asked soon after we had exchanged general pleasantries.

'Certainly,' I said, and we proceeded round to a quieter spot in the waiting room and sat on one of the benches while I waited for him to open up.

'Ray,' he said, 'I may call you Ray, may I?'

'Yes, of course, let's drop the formalities right off.'

Then, 'Ray, I don't know you and you don't know me, but I should

337

tell you in confidence that I was sent for this morning by the Commander-in-Chief of Strike Command who said to me, "We have just learned who it is that the Navy is putting in charge of their team. He's a chap called Ray Lygo and he is the most dangerous man in the Royal Navy – you must watch him like a hawk because he'll have you."'

I was rather flattered to receive such an accolade from the Commander-in-Chief of Strike Command and I said so. But I added, 'Well, that's very kind of him to describe me in those terms but I have to tell you that you don't have to worry about that. I will always operate absolutely as straight as a die and be absolutely clear and honest with you. However, Peter, if ever I suspect or have cause to believe that you are doing something behind my back then all bets will be off.' Peter said that he accepted this and understood it perfectly.

He then went on to say that because the Air Force Board had classified the entry 'Secret' he was having great difficulty making any arrangements for the arrival or departure from the Post Office Tower and similarly in New York.

'Well,' I said, 'I have a problem too, Peter. I have to have tanker aircraft to get my aircraft across the Atlantic and for that we depend on the Royal Air Force and I sincerely hope that you will be able to use your influence to get those tankers for me.'

'The difficulty is, Ray, we need an awful lot of tankers to get our own Harrier across.'

'I know,' I said, 'but there are enough to do both and it is absolutely crucial to my attempt.' I went on to say that I was sorry he had not been able to arrange for arrival in the UK or departure from New York, but if he found difficulty in achieving this he should come to see me and let me know and I would do whatever I could to help, knowing full well, as I did, that I had already got exclusive use of the two most suitable sites in London.

On arrival in New York we went out to the Naval Air Station, which was then a Reserve Naval Air Station but still operating, and met with the Operations Officer and the others who were going to be concerned with our entry. Unfortunately for them but perhaps fortunately for us, the Secretary of State for Defence had ruled that neither the US Air Force nor the US Navy would be able to enter the race because the administration was going through one of those periods of scrutinising public expenditure and he did not consider it was something on which the taxpayer's money should be 'squandered'. This caused a great deal of resentment within the US Navy and I am sure the US Air Force too. It rather badly reduced the competitive nature of the event for the *Daily Mail* but, of course, it did mean that it left the field fairly wide open for the Royal Navy! You might at this stage be wondering why it was that the Royal Air Force was not entering their Phantom in the race. They, too, were receiving Phantoms at about the same time as we were receiving ours but they had decided that it was far too early in the work-up and organisation of the Squadron for them to take part. As I shall reveal later they had also decided that for the same reasons the Royal Navy would not be able to enter its Phantoms!

One of the most active contributors to our arrangements in New York at the US Navy Air Station was a Commander in the US Naval Reserve. This chap was particularly incensed by the refusal of the Secretary of State to let the US Navy compete and told me that he intended to compete himself by running in one of the schedule flight sections of the race. I assured him that we would do everything possible to help him in his entry as a small way of saying 'thanks' to the US Navy for what they were offering us, which was the use of the airfield for the basing our Phantoms and, indeed, the Harriers, and also a US Navy helicopter to fly us from the helicopter pad in the East River to the airfield.

To get from the bottom of the Empire State Building to the East River Heliport we had organised Royal Marine dispatch riders to take our contenders down the route. The New York end looked pretty straightforward with a bike to the East River and a helicopter from East River to the airfield. Having fixed the details and left Robbie Roberts to organise it from that end we were then free to depart from New York the following day.

I had nothing to do that evening and my friendly Commander asked me whether I would like to go with him into New York to have dinner with his parents. It was a very kind invitation and I accepted. We got into his car and drove off into New York. My knowledge of New York was pretty sketchy but at least I could recognise Times Square when I saw it, and to my surprise we drew up round a side turning by a theatre in Times Square, where we got out of the car, secured it and went to the side door of the theatre.

I was still recovering from the shock of the conversation we'd had on the way in. He had told me that his entry was going to be different in that it had 'second sight'. He was clairvoyant and therefore he intended to make the run blindfolded! I expressed the usual kind of surprise at this suggestion but he assured me that this was the way he was going to do it and thus he would attract the maximum publicity for the US Navy. As I digested this information he pressed a button on the side of the door to the theatre and a voice answered. He announced himself and the door opened electronically and we walked into a small passageway, got into a lift and went to the top of the theatre. There we left the lift and came into a lobby, a door opened into a very beautiful apartment at the top of the theatre and to my surprise I found myself in the presence of the Lunts – Alfred and Lin Fontaine – the famous acting duo of the New York stage! Mrs Lunt welcomed us, wearing a somewhat diaphanous gown, and Alfred Lunt appeared subsequently, looking extremely dignified in his smoking jacket. I could hardly fail to notice that the decoration of the flat consisted, to some extent, of framed posters of their various Broadway successes.

I don't really think I took all this in at the time – I was probably still stunned by the idea of this chap running blindfolded – but it was a fascinating and entertaining evening which I enjoyed immensely and was most grateful for the kind hospitality that was shown. It turned out that the Commander was, in fact, the adopted son of the Lunts and a very close and affectionate relationship obviously existed between them.

After dinner, as he drove me back, I said, 'Well, if this is what you want to do we will lay on the motorcycle for you to take you to the East River terminal where you will have to catch a conventional civilian helicopter to Kennedy Airport,' from where he was going to catch a scheduled flight.

On the way back to the UK in the plane I again pressed Peter Williamson to confirm that the RAF were capable of providing tankers. I was able to tell him that all the facilities that we had organised were freely available to him, provided we got their tankers. While at the same time, in the United States, I had asked the US Navy if they would provide tankers for us in the event that the RAF were not able to do so. This was a somewhat delicate arrangement because, quite naturally, I wanted to ensure that the US Navy understood our appreciation for what they were prepared to do but, at the same time, I was very conscious that the tanking requirements in the South Western Approaches would be much easier and better handled by the RAF and that our crews were much more used to operating with the Victors than with their US Navy opposite numbers. Furthermore, if I revealed too readily to my RAF colleagues that the US Navy were prepared to provide the necessary tanking it might have been possible for them to use this as an excuse not to provide tankers themselves!

Preparations proceeded apace and I was now getting ready to move into the headquarters for the race, which was to be at RAF Strike Command. In the meantime, the *Daily Mail* had been busy stirring up interest in the race and one idea which I had was to have an electronic display in Trafalgar Square so that the public could see the progress of contestants in the race. Imagine my surprise when I was told that

A Victor fuelling one of our Phantoms

Trafalgar Square was reserved for demonstrations of a political nature and not available for this kind of display. It seemed strange to me that a Square with the name of Trafalgar with Nelson sitting on top of it, was not a suitable venue for advertising the capabilities of the Royal Navy! Of course the more one sees bureaucracy in action the less surprised one is by anything that they say.

All was now set for some rehearsals and for planning the details as to how the race should be attempted. Our idea was to run three aircraft in stages during the week of the race and my hope was that we should achieve a record-breaking run every time. I now had to think of a way of getting the interest of HMS *Nubion*, which had been detailed off to be the guard ship in the South Western Approaches, and struck upon the idea of sponsoring and paying for the entry of two of their Ratings to run in the race in the commercial aircraft sector. In order to get the necessary publicity I decided that we would do the first part from the Post Office Tower in a rickshaw drawn by another sailor and that the chap would run with a kitbag and a mock parrot on his shoulder. I was almost certain that this would hit the newspapers! Around the corner the chap would jump on a motorbike!

Where to get a rickshaw was a problem until we discovered that a submarine, believe it or not, had brought a bicycle rickshaw back from

341

THE TRANSATLANTIC AIR RACE
by Lieutenant Commander Brian Davies.A.F.C., R.N.

The crews of the winning Phantoms

Hong Kong. How it had managed to stow it on board I don't know but it had done so. We found out where it was, gained access to it and positioned it around the corner. Unfortunately, when the great moment came, the chap pedalled too vigorously, one of the wheels collapsed, and the rickshaw never got into position and we had to do without it – and we failed to get the photograph!

The subject of tankers now had to be faced and Peter was still unable to find any place to get the Harrier into London and the pilot into the Post Office Tower. I therefore told him that we had access to a helicopter platform which I had had built at the foot of the Post Office Tower, that he was welcome to use it and to use the St Pancras coal yard to which we also had exclusive rights but, of course, this could only be in exchange for them providing tanker aircraft. As a result, Peter was able to pull the necessary strings and subsequently able to confirm to me that RAF tanker aircraft would, indeed, be available!

Now we had everything in place. Our three aircraft were positioned in the US Navy facility in New York. The crews were trained and hot to trot. The ship, *Nubian*, was in the South Western Approaches and the stage was set for 'The Great Race'. Both ends were ready and I moved down into the operations room at Strike Command, along with Peter Williamson and some supporting staff in order to conduct affairs.

The Harrier, flown by Squadron Leader 'Leckie' Thompson was to make one attempt whilst we were going to make three attempts over the week's period of the race. Of the few places to land in the vicinity of London I had hit upon the idea of using Wisley and had approached BAC, which then owned and operated the aerodrome, as a satellite to Weybridge, for permission to operate there, and from whence a helicopter – Royal Navy, of course – was going to transport our pilots to the Post Office Tower. The helicopter would be positioned burning and turning alongside the runway so that as soon as the Phantom came to a stop, the observer leapt out into the helicopter and off to the Tower.

The first flight took off and all went like clockwork. The total time was 5 hours, 11 minutes and 22 seconds and we had broken the record for the Transatlantic crossing. The publicity received was stunning – overwhelming if you like – and we were delighted with the outcome. I now hit my first piece of irritation, or unpleasantness. We had arranged for two flights for the Ratings from *Nubian* and they were going to fly in commercial flights to Kennedy and would have had a good chance of winning because our arrangements from the Post Office Tower were so superior. I was going to pick them up and take them by helicopter direct to Heathrow. On the first run our chap, who had had the best time by far in London to catch the plane, arrived in New York, was picked up by our dispatch rider and taken to the Empire State Building where he arrived clearly first with very good time in hand. His most serious competitor in the race was Mr Clement Freud who was competing in the same section. When the Naval rating arrived at the Empire State Building, he leapt into the lift which was waiting with its doors open with a man in it.

As it started off towards the top of this great building, imagine his horror when he saw that all the buttons to all the floors had been pressed so that the elevator proceeded to stop at every floor. Mr Freud, when he arrived, luckily had no such problem and arrived at the top of the Post Office Tower well ahead of my Naval rating, thus beating him on time. When I met the lad afterwards I said, 'Why didn't you thump the chap in the lift who was doing this?' He looked at me and said, 'Well, I wasn't sure whether I should.' I said, 'I would have supported you if you had and I assure you the man deserved it.'

343

This meant that I was determined that we would really compete more severely next time and I decided to dispatch the next Rating myself from the top of the Post Office Tower. Mr Freud was also running in this race and we waited at the top as the seconds ticked by for the time to depart for Heathrow. I was determined that this time we would have a faster run. When the moment came for Clement Freud to depart everyone was looking very nervous but I hung on because I had stopwatched the time and then when I released the Rating I was quite certain he had a good couple of minutes in hand for any eventualities in New York. Unfortunately the aircraft in which he was flying was delayed landing in New York and as a result the time taken was longer than on the first flight and neither of the Ratings won their category.

Ah well, that's show business I suppose!

On the Wednesday the second of our aeroplanes was launched and, again, everything worked an absolute treat and they came in beating the previous record by some minutes and we had once more broken the Transatlantic record.

It was now the turn of the Harrier. In New York the Harrier had been based just on the East River on a derelict site from which it was to go direct to the St Pancras coal yard. It duly took off in a great cloud of dust from New York and proceeded to cross the Atlantic for its landing in the St Pancras coal yard.

'Shorty' Hamilton came into my office, because when we weren't flying I was in the Empress State Building rather than in the dug-out at Strike Command, to inform me of the imminent arrival of the Harrier.

'The Harrier is due to arrive soon,' he said, 'and are you going to go down and see it come in, Sir?'

'No,' I said, 'I think not, Shorty; I'll stay here.' He looked at me rather curiously and then departed to see the arrival of the Harrier, which was to be a great event.

An hour or so later he came back looking a bit like a black and white minstrel with tears of laughter having stained his cheeks. He said, 'You knew it, didn't you?' I decided it was best – and still do – to play it cool.

'Know what?' I asked.

'Knew what was going to happen,' he said.

'What did happen?' I enquired.

'Well,' said he, 'it was absolutely unbelievable, Sir. The whole of the Air Force Board was there to greet the Harrier, or it seemed so, and a Royal Air Force band. Of course they were all lined up, the Harrier arrived, went into the hover and visibility fell to 50 yards in coal dust. The whole place was covered in coal dust, including all the dignitaries who had come to welcome the Harrier and at the end of which they all said, "Lygo knew this, Lygo knew this, he knew this would happen."' Well, actually I might have done but it didn't matter, it was the best place for them to land but perhaps it would have been better if I had turned up, I would have been able to plead my innocence a little more genuinely. Nevertheless it was a great feat and some years later, out in the Middle East, I met Squadron Leader Leckie Thompson and we had a good laugh over all the events that went on around that time. He was, incidentally, no longer in the Royal Air Force, sad to report.

We were now running up to the last days in the race and the RAF had the Victor to come over and I had one last Phantom. It was during this period, in the office in Strike Command, that Peter received a 'phone call; it was clearly from somebody fairly high up, and he asked me if I would mind if he took the 'phone call somewhere else. Ho, ho, thought I, they are up to no good, and within the 15 minutes that he was out of the room I had had photostatted all the correspondence in his briefcase, amongst which was a fascinating document, a report to the Air Force Board as to why the Navy could not possibly enter its Phantoms. We just weren't as well organised, we just did it.

Now we come to the saga of my friend, a Commander in the US Navy. He was duly dispatched from the top of the Empire State Building, blindfolded. He went outside, got into the lift, no problem at all, down to the bottom, out of the lift, out of the doors to the waiting motorcycle, no problem, got on the back of the motorcycle and off they went to the East River helicopter site. He got off the motorbike, walked towards the helicopter that was burning and turning, nearly missed it but, I am glad to say, completed the whole event safely. A small recompense to the USN for all their help.

It was now time for the last aircraft to come over. I particularly wanted it to arrive on the Sunday, the last day of the race, so that we could get the full blast of publicity in the Monday *Daily Mail*. Unfortunately the weather was deteriorating and it wasn't going to be very easy to ensure the safe arrival of the aircraft. The last crew to arrive were the CO and senior pilot but they were clearly getting as worried as their Victor counterparts were, about the weather conditions. I had considerable difficulty holding them back from coming on the Saturday with the weather deteriorating, but the RAF had decided to have a large reception in London that weekend in the Banqueting Hall in Whitehall, and were anxious that the Victors should be there to complete the celebration.

345

Peter Goddard and Brian Davies, the final winners

Daily Mail

MONDAY, MAY 12, 1969

Greatest-ever air race
ends in blaze of glory

World beater by the Navy!

WHAT a finish! The Daily Mail Transatlantic Air Race ended last night in a blaze of excitement.

There was a most amusing conversation between Peter Williamson, at one end, and the Victor Captain, at the other, in which, although I was party to only one end of the conversation, it was clear that the Captain of the Victor was questioning the weather. The conversation had gone something like this:

'Yes, well, the weather ... well, the forecast is, oh 600 feet overcast, but there is a good diversion into Ballykelly in Northern Ireland and there the visibility is four miles and its 1200 feet, and ... the forecast? ... Well, the forecast is ... it really isn't going to get any worse, it's going to get a little worse at Ballykelly but we are having a big reception and the Board will be there and they are very keen for you to be able to partake. Yes, yes, 600 feet and ... yes, well, there's a diversion at Ballykelly and ... I do know the Chief of the Air Staff is going to be there and I think, you know, it is very important that you arrive. Yes, yes, 600 feet. Yes, yes,'

At this point I couldn't resist it, and walking over to Peter, I leaned over his shoulder and said into the microphone, 'But the decision, Pilot Officer Prune, is entirely yours.'

The last Phantom ran on the last day and came in beating the two previous records. I am sure it was a nail-biting exercise for Lieutenant Commander Brian Davis and Peter Goddard but it got us the headlines once again.

It was, therefore, a most successful episode. Three aircraft had flown the Atlantic with the essential help of the US Navy at one end, the Royal Air Force in transit, HMS *Nubian* in the South Western Approaches, and British Aircraft Corporation's use of Wisley, the Royal Marines' cyclist, the helicopters of the Royal Navy, a great team effort that had brought us not one victory but three. The object of the exercise, Dick Janvrin had said, had been to raise morale in the Fleet Air Arm – well, I believe it did, I hope it did. A little demonstration, once again, of the flexibility and capability of Naval aviation and its ability to rise to any new challenge in the shortest possible time with the guarantee of success. I have to this day in my office a very nice engraved ashtray which celebrates my success in managing this team effort.

It did something else. It introduced me to many more people in Fleet Street, whom I had not known before and this was to stand me in good stead at a later stage.

26

Ark Royal

My appointment to *Ark Royal* had been seen by many of my colleagues in the Navy as something of an exception because here was a
chap going straight from one sea command to another, which was
almost unheard of. Yet the task was pretty daunting: how to get the
ship out of Devonport Dockyard in one piece, having completed a
major refit. It was to be fitted with a new arrester gear that was necessary to enable it to operate the Phantom, a totally new system which
didn't depend on the usual kind of hydraulic rams that we had had
before. Instead it had a mass of knitting that went through many
pulleys and sheaths to achieve its purpose; it was called the 'direct-
acting gear', and it was certainly to provide us with some direct-acting
experiences during the course of the commission!

I was, of course, required to undergo the usual series of command
team training courses and, having come directly from one of the most
modern frigates, it was taking a step backwards in *Ark Royal*, in a
way, because her somewhat ancient operations room had only been
modified to the minimum standard. The idea was that she was to serve
one commission and that was to be it, and then paid off. Part of my
task, as an enthusiastic aviator, was to ensure that she served more
than one commission, and in this I was aided and abetted by the
Dockyard. The Admiral Superintendent at Devonport in those days
was a delightful Rear Admiral Engineering named Wildish, and in
their wisdom Their Lordships had decided to appoint me both as
Commanding Officer of *Ark Royal* and also to the staff of the Admiral
Superintendent Devonport, a dual appointment that was never, as far
as I am aware, to be repeated. It meant, of course, that I was a
Dockyard Officer in addition to being the Captain of the ship, and
therefore could have my say in Dockyard matters as an insider, not as
an outsider.

I remember going down the first time to see the ship as she lay
alongside in one of the basins and as I drove up to the Quarterdeck
gangway and parked my car under the shadow of this enormous ship,
I must say I was slightly overawed by the size and complexity of the
task that I now faced. She looked absolutely huge and as I walked up

the Dockyard gangway on to the littered Quarterdeck to be greeted by the Commander and the First Lieutenant, I recognised that another challenge lay ahead. I had been given, as you would imagine, a first-class team of Commanders to be my main management staff in this great ship: the Executive Officer Nick Hunt, who went on to become Commander-in-Chief Fleet, Guy Crowden the engineer, who carried an enormous weight during the period of the refit, Weapons Electrical, Francis Elvey, Surgeon Commander, Mike Boyle, the PMO, Instructor Commander, Tom Marshall, Derek Monsell as Commander Air, Pat Glennie as the Paymaster, and even a Dental Commander, Brian Robinson, together with the Chaplain, Bill Walter. A large team of professionals sometimes needs more careful management than a more mundane bunch.

The ship quite frankly was in a mess. They were just beginning to complete the compartments in the bowels of the ship but as far as the engine room and the main propulsion were concerned there was an awful lot to be done. In addition it was discovered that having taken hundreds of valves, and I mean great big bronze jobs, out of the ship to be refitted in the Dockyard, quite a number had gone missing! No doubt some had gone through that well-known hole in the Dockyard wall as part of the perks. Fortunately *Centaur* was still around, with the same type of valve and we were able to rob replacements from that ship, which was lying in reserve.

My first task was to get to know my new staff of Officers and Chief Petty Officers as quickly as possible, but this was difficult since we were housed in a couple of Portakabins alongside the ship while the Ship's Company, just beginning to build up and arrive, was housed within the barracks. My first act in my dual capacity was to suggest to the Dockyard officials that the weekly progress reports on the ship should be held in the ship, so my cabin was cleared out sufficiently for us to be able to hold our meetings there. I believe it served a point in emphasising that this programme was about the ship, not about the Dockyard. In addition, I had the Commander prepare a large placard which stood at the top of each gangway which gave the number of days that were left before the ship was supposed to sail on its shake-down acceptance phase. This was due in the first week of December and so each day a new figure appeared with the number of days to go before the ship sailed and after a while I think it became clear to the Dockyard officials and workmen, that in fact this is what I intended to do and so the ship had better be ready or everybody was going to be in trouble.

As part of my preparation I asked two of my contemporaries, John Treacher, who was then commanding *Eagle*, and Peter Austin, who was commanding *Hermes*, if it would be possible for me to come out and join them to get a feel for these big ships operating at sea and, indeed, if possible to make an entry in one of them up the Hamoaze so that I could get a feel at least of bringing in a ship of that size in this very complex and difficult entry to Devonport. Unfortunately it was not possible for me to make an entry in either of these ships, or it was not made possible, and as a result I spent a couple of days at sea aboard each of them but I didn't learn a great deal about the actual handling. This was to prove unfortunate as I shall recall in a later event.

The first problem that I faced was one morning early on, when Commander Crowden, the engineer, came to see me in a somewhat explosive state. Poor man, he was carrying an enormous load and he thought that he wasn't getting the support that he should have been getting from the Commander, who had a large number of chaps sitting around doing practically nothing, when the engine room department was working flat out. He obviously was coming to breaking point and I therefore had to ask the Commander to see me and to tell him quite bluntly that if he was not getting on with the Engineer Officer then he had better put it to rights because if I had to choose at that moment in time between keeping my Engineer Officer and keeping my Commander, there would be very little hesitation on my part; the Engineer Officer was more important. This seemed to have some effect and things calmed down but the stress and strain on technical Officers faced with a refit of this kind has to be experienced rather than imagined.

I had been given the use of a married quarter, temporarily, to accommodate myself and family in the Devonport area and we found ourselves in a Junior Officer's quarters overlooking the Sound. It was a small flat with a magnificent view but had not been designed to withstand the winds that sweep through the Plymouth area. As a result, when it really blew, it went in one side and out the other. Beneath me was my secretary, Roy Arthur, and his charming wife and those of you who know the Naval scene know how much Captains and Admirals depend on their secretaries for support. As the Ship's Company numbers built up, so my personal staff built up. I had managed to obtain the services of Petty Officer Rickerby who had been my Petty Officer Steward in the *Lowestoft* and with whom the whole family had formed a strong bond of friendship. We also had two cooks and another two stewards. Obviously if they were to stay in the barracks, when the Ship's Company fell in in the morning and if they had nothing to do, they would be detailed off for storing the ship or doing some other kind of manual duty which they didn't particularly relish. Therefore, quite clearly, they thought it much better to serve the Captain and his wife in the flat; the problem was that by the time the staff got into the flat with us, there wasn't room to swing a cat and I had to say to the secretary, 'I'm afraid this will not do. One steward is quite enough at a time in this flat.' Since Pepper enjoys cooking herself and the kitchen was so small it could only accommodate one at a time, or as Pepper puts it 'a one bum kitchen,' there didn't seem to be much point in having cooks in there as well. Too many cooks every day would spoil both the broth and marital harmony.

There was not much to be done out of working hours and Pepper and I used to go for walks. The two boys were in boarding school in Kent and Brooke was a weekly boarder, and so we attempted to get back home to prise them out of school for the weekend and spend the weekends back at Mereworth and then dash back to Plymouth again on the Monday morning – quite a trip in those days before the motorways were built. And so we were alone for the evenings and during the summer months took to strolling round the adjacent area and were fascinated to see that in a large number of the houses there was, hanging in the front window, a plastic parrot on a ring. It became a game to find a different walk on which we could count more of these plastic parrots, but they seemed to be a kind of feature of Plymouth's society at that time. So obsessed with this we became, and so amused, we recounted this story to our friends on board, and at one cocktail party we gave in the house the Dental Commander came with a gift of a plastic parrot in a ring which we solemnly hung in the middle of the living room. It became a test of the sense of humour of the people who came to visit us, if nobody asked, 'What the hell is that parrot doing there?' we knew they were somewhat inhibited. If they did, and were able to enjoy the story, then at least we knew they had a sense of humour.

The opportunity for public relations was enormous, the mere name *Ark Royal* was enough to get you onto any kind of radio or television programme you might seek to achieve and we made friends with local television and radio and managed to get a good coverage going. It was also essential to keep something in front of the Ship's Company while the ship was still uninhabitable, something on which they could concentrate as far as outside activities were concerned. So we were very keen to push forward our soccer team which, because of the sheer size of the ship, did extremely well even against the large shore establishments and these successes, with the great cheers that accompanied them, were one of the ways in which morale was built up. Morale in *Ark Royal* has always been good, there is something about the name,

Peter Cook and Dudley Moore

there is something about the ship that means that you are almost 'walking water' when you come on board. Nobody can think that there is anything bad about *Ark Royal*, everything has to be good, it is the best, it is the top, and therefore it was a pleasure to see the strength of the morale building.

During the commission I used to take the opportunity, from time to time, of inviting people, some of whom I had never met, to come and spend a few days on board to see how this ship operated. There were many who came and very few ever declined the invitation; it was something that was only going to be seen once, an operating aircraft carrier with these modern supersonic aircraft. Always they came to me afterwards and said what an extraordinary experience it had been and how impressed they were at the way in which people worked together. It enabled me to repeat what I had said before, and have said many times since, that the Navy is different from the other Services. The Captain is not a member of the Wardroom or the Chief's Mess, he is completely and utterly alone.

Everybody in a ship is of one company because we live together in a metal box and if somebody comes along and kicks a hole in that metal

Peter Cook and Dudley Moore

box and the water comes in, we all drown together, hence 'all of one company,' 'all in the same boat,' etc. It produces, or should produce and certainly can produce an electric effect on the community who work together for a common purpose. It is also easy to motivate a ship where every time the catapult launches an aircraft the whole ship shudders. As the catapult fires it reverberates through the ship right down to the boiler room at the bottom, and into the store rooms, up into the ops room, into the galleys where the cooks are preparing the

354

Peter Cook and Dudley Moore

food, into the guns, everywhere; and so the whole Ship's Company knows that they have done something, they have launched an aeroplane and as they hear the catapult thumping out, the number of aeroplanes launched is clear to them and they know that they are operating and doing their job. It is a very motivating effect which is unique to that type of ship and that also helps very much to give a sense of purpose to a Ship's Company and make them operate as a team.

In peacetime, officers in the Army operate with their men on exercises but then they separate. The RAF, when they go into battle, leave their men behind. In the Navy, we have our men with us all the time, and in peacetime the hazards, although much less than would be experienced in war and the risks much less, nevertheless they are there. A collision at sea, or a grounding, or an accident involving fire, or an explosion in a ship, all of which can happen from time to time, generates the feeling of being all of one company, and 'all together in the same boat' has a very significant meaning and an enormous effect on morale.

My Admiral at this time was Mike Fell who had been my Commander Air when I had embarked 800 Squadron in the *Ark Royal's* first commission, and he, along with a lot of other people, I am sure, was watching the progress that the ship was making in getting itself out of Dockyard hands. As time passed and gradually more and more of the ship became usable and available, we were faced with the usual choices of what we were going to accept in order to get the ship down the Hamoaze and out to sea on time. It was an unfortunate fact that the Dockyard maties who were to accompany us, had to be provided with separate accommodation more suitable for their standards! It was an irritation to everybody in the Navy that the accommodation provided for our sailors was not good enough for Dockyard maties, they had to be provided with individual beds in cabins. So great numbers of these were built – wooded structures, Portakabins erected in the hangar of the ship, in order to provide them with suitable accommodation. The number we required to take with us seemed to be growing daily and was approaching a thousand by the time we were due to sail. I imagine they all got paid rather special rates for this so it was therefore an attractive job.

As the days to run on the boards at the top of the gangways began to fall, however, and as Christmas was getting closer, it was fairly clear I think to everybody that I was determined to take this ship out, even if I had to carry it down the Hamoaze on my back, but the risk that they would run in going to sea so close to Christmas would be that if things went wrong, good heavens, they might be stuck at sea over Christmas.

We decided that we would go to sea with only part of the main steam range operating, the secondary part, I think it was the eight-inch range, and that we would be able to operate the four shafts of the ship. It had four engine rooms and eight boilers with all four engine rooms operating (although some might be still unlagged), though using only six of the eight boilers, and as long as we could circulate steam to the affected engine rooms through the secondary range, we should be OK. This meant that we would have limited power, but adequate for the purpose of getting the ship in and out of harbour – provided, of course, nothing went wrong!

One of the major restrictions we found on getting the ship ready was lagging, and it's worth recording with the light of later knowledge, that it was all asbestos. Towards the end when everything had been assembled, the laggers' turn came for the very difficult job of lagging all the pipework and these chaps were on 24 hours continuous working to complete the task. It had been my habit in previous ships and continued in *Ark Royal*, to make regular but unscheduled inspections of various parts of the ship by walking about at odd hours, sometimes quite early in the morning, or in the middle of the night. On one such visit I went down to one of the boiler rooms that was slowing down our progress to completion, to see how they were getting on. It was three o'clock in the morning and there was no work taking place at all. As I climbed the steep ladder out of the boiler room wondering what had gone wrong, I looked over my shoulder to see that laid out on top of the boilers themselves were a row of laggers all fast asleep. I continued on my way until I could get to a telephone and called the General Manager of the Dockyard, who was at home in bed, and told him that I had just found his laggers all asleep and required immediate action to get them back to work. Managers are supposed to manage, not stand back and let people do what they want.

As we neared the end of the refit period, we came closer to the time when I would have to take this hulk out of one of the most difficult channels in the world, and back again in one piece. So the Navigating Officer and I put ourselves in a tug from the Queen's Harbourmaster and went down the route so that we could familiarise ourselves with all the leading marks. During my work-up of *Juno* at Portland, Commander Cox, who was the Commander Sea Training, whose job it was to come on most Saturday mornings and debrief you on the way the week had gone, said to me on one such occasion, 'I hope you don't mind me saying so, Sir, but you do something which nobody else here at the moment does.'

'What is that?' I enquired.

'Well,' said he, 'you take your ship from the jetty and you take it

Ark Royal leaving the refitting basin

right out through the harbour entrance and it is not until you are well outside in the exercise areas that you hand over to a Navigating Officer. And, equally, when coming in, you take the ship from the Navigating Officer and you bring it in through the entrance and right up and put it alongside.'

I looked at him in some surprise, 'Well what do the others do?' I said.

'Well,' he said, 'it is normally quite common for the Navigating Officer to bring the ship in and the Captain only to take over at the last moment in putting it alongside. Similarly, when he has got it away from the jetty he hands it to the Navigating Officer who takes the ship out.'

'Really,' I said. 'Well, you do surprise me, because the bit I enjoy most is that bit and I have no intention of changing it.' However, in the case of *Ark Royal*, I did say to the Navigating Officer, 'I will get her down to the first turn and I will then hand over to you.'

As we started warming through the engines, it began to look as if the ship was actually going to steam out on the due day, and eventually, the great day arrived. As you can imagine, there was a considerable amount of media interest in this event and on the morning in question I went up to the Bridge to survey the weather. We had been watching it fairly carefully, and lo and behold we had a very strong wind indeed. Now with a ship of that size there were limits on the wind speed for entry and departure, and it was outside limits – particularly as Devonport is on one of the most difficult channels in the world. In addition, of course, I wasn't quite sure whether the engines would actually be working properly because they had been torn apart and put together again during the refit. It was also essential, of course, that we went at a time when the tide was high enough to get *Ark Royal* in and out satisfactorily. She was, at this stage, not fully laden and so wasn't drawing as much water as she did later on, but even so there were only a few feet underneath her keel when the moment came to be passing over some of the shallowest parts (6 – 8 feet was the maximum) so she wasn't the easiest thing to manoeuvre. I therefore reluctantly decided, looking at the rain sheeting down, with poor visibility and a very high wind, that I wouldn't go – a great anticlimax.

We had all worked ourselves up to a great anticipation but it didn't happen. I had taken into my confidence all the Engine Room Officers and at the briefing before sailing I had them in to explain to them the movements I was going to make on every engine to get ourselves out of the Hamoaze. We had to be going astern with some engines, ahead on the others, then stopping them and then going astern on them and I wanted the Engineer Officers to thoroughly appreciate on the chart where they would be, at what point, when those engine movements were made. All to no avail on the first day; of course there were some pretty pithy remarks in the newspapers to the effect that a little gust of wind had kept this great ship in harbour. It is sad, sometimes, that our media seems determined to make the worst out of any possible event. I don't mind exaggeration but that did hurt a bit, but what can you expect?

Although we had taken every precaution there was no doubt that there was a risk in taking the ship to sea in the condition in which she then was. I had received a signal from my Admiral, Michael Fell, which, whilst encouraging me to go, had asked me to be sure that I was quite confident that all was ready before doing so. We jolly well had to go; to have delayed with Christmas approaching would have meant, I am sure, weeks of delay. The determination to achieve the programme on time was absolutely essential, as far as I was concerned, to the future of that great ship. The following day the weather was slightly better; it was still windy and not very happy-looking – grey, overcast, showers – but I decided to go.

The great moment came, so at daybreak we slipped, the tugs pulled us off, the lead tug got itself into position, the stern tugs were nudging

A bit sad, particularly since I didn't have that many medals (© *The Sun*)

Ark Royal leaving Devonport after the refit.

at us, slow ahead both engines, and the great ship started to move down the Hamoaze towards the first bend. We didn't look a particularly impressive sight: it was a ship that was still virtually in Dockyard hands; it needed painting, it needed a lot of work done to it still, to the catapults and arrester gear, and we presented a somewhat barren and bedraggled appearance. Nevertheless, we were under way, she was moving, I had control of her, and I felt it in my bones, and so I never did hand over to the Navigating Officer but hogged that responsibility myself and took her all the way out into Plymouth Sound. I did it every time thereafter, and I believe I made more entries and departures from Devonport than any other Captain in that ship (easy to understand, since we were doing trials). Nevertheless, the first turn came, the first manoeuvre of the engines turning round that first corner, and then the short straight before turning again to run along under the Hoe, and then the dreadful (and often disastrous to ships of that size) Smeaton Pass, the turn that took us on the long run towards the breakwaters and out into the open sea. As we completed the turn and started down the passage towards the entrance and then made the turn towards the exit all was going well, my Commander said to me, 'Well done, Sir.' I knew he meant it, and I knew that the whole ship's company would feel proud of achieving an exit to time.

Some months later Ian Robertson, an old friend of mine, was sent

361

as Captain of *Eagle*. He wrote to me and asked whether he could make an entry in *Ark Royal* to familiarise himself with arrival in the Hamoaze and I readily agreed, remembering the difficulties I'd had before. In due course Ian came with me for a trip up the Hamoaze and subsequently took command of *Eagle*. We were alongside in Devonport at the time when we knew that *Eagle* was entering and arranged to salute them with a suitable broadside of cabbages, which when fired from a 4.5 shell case by dint of a large thunder flash at their base, and if you are clever enough, to insert another thunder flash in the cabbage just before you drop it into the cylinder, it will go straight up into the air and then explode with an enormous bang showering cabbage leaves everywhere. This was our welcome for *Eagle* but it was somewhat dampened by the fact that we subsequently discovered when we looked at the fairly sombre faces on board that she'd actually 'taken the ground' coming through Smeaton Pass, not the first time this had happened to a ship of that size.

I waited until she was secured alongside and called Ian and asked him if he'd like me to come over and have a chat, and he said he'd be very grateful if I would. I therefore went over and met him in his cabin where he had the charts with his navigator, and looking at the charts he said, 'I cannot understand how it was that we scraped the bottom of the ship coming through the Smeaton Pass, because we were in exactly the same position as you were in when I came up with you.' One glance at the charts was sufficient for me to see that he was almost certainly going to take the ground because he was slightly off-track to starboard, but of course my enthusiasm in asking him to come in with me had really compounded the felony. Whereas I drove the ship from the binnacle, I understand Ian's procedure was to have his Navigating Officer do this while he surveyed the scene by moving about on the Bridge. The difference between *Eagle* and *Ark Royal* was that *Ark* had a large kind of block of flats built on the starboard side outboard of the island which meant that the view from the Bridge to the waterline when looking slightly aft was of course quite different from *Eagle*, which had no such obstruction and therefore a buoy or a marker, which appeared from the Bridge looking slightly aft to be in the same position, would in fact be very much closer. It was a sad event and I felt extremely sorry for Ian and the fact that I had in trying to be helpful perhaps led him into thinking he was in a better position than in fact was the case. Subsequently, it transpired that one of the buoys was out of position – just to compound the felony! We sailed soon after for the Mediterranean and Ian was kind enough to ask me to be his defending Officer; however it would have meant me leaving the ship and coming back for this. This was not considered to be a good thing to do and so Ian subsequently had to face the Board of Inquiry with another defending Officer.

It is worth recording that at that time there were no lights for entry into Devonport, apart from the buoys, and of course one should never navigate by use of buoys because they might well be out of position, so running on a fix onshore which was not visible at night was fairly hazardous. One of the tracks that we had to take we used to run on the garden path running up to Mount Edgecumbe! It was only later, I think by the time I had finished with *Ark*, that they started putting proper leading lights in, can you believe it. On two occasions I came in at night because the tide was right for me to enter at that time and to have delayed would have meant difficulties in getting people ashore, and again as one felt one's way up the Hamoaze and finally turned the last corner to come into the blaze of lights of the dockyard, you knew that you'd taken your own life and career into your own hands once again in order to achieve some programme or to make a point. I suppose it's too much to expect to get any thanks for taking these chances and in fact one would only be criticised if something went wrong or court-martialled as the case may be, but I suppose that is what life is all about.

I have touched on several of the more spectacular events during the Commission in other parts of my memoirs but the task of completing the ship was a fairly all consuming one but when the great day of the commissioning came and the Queen Mother graced us with her presence, operating in her usual relaxed and charming style, we knew it would be all right. One amusing episode comes to mind during the rehearsal for the ceremony. The parson, who was sitting at the back ready to do his bit in the proceedings, moved his chair backwards and disappeared from sight as he fell off the stage – to the enjoyment of the assembed company!

It was during the lunch in the Admiral's Day Cabin on the great day of commissioning *Ark Royal* with the Queen Mother in her full splendour, that my wife had the following conversation with Dr David Owen who was then the Navy Minister. She said, 'And what do you do?' to which, somewhat suprised by this, he replied, 'I am the Minister for the Navy,' and she said, 'Oh well then, you're a Conservative.' 'No' he said, 'I'm a member of the Government.' 'Oh,' said my wife, 'but how can that be because I thought the Labour Party was against defence, so how can you be Minister for the Navy?' I must say I could have thought of better ways of putting it, or more tactful ways of putting it, but at that time the message, I think, got across – at least I hope it did. Certainly the Queen Mother seemed to enjoy it, and then she said, 'If you scrap the *Ark Royal* I

The Queen Mother arriving for the Commissioning

shall lead a protest march down Whitehall,' and I am quite sure that she would have done.

I was determined to have a Families' Day, which I had always had and this was going to be no different, except for course that we should have some two thousand or so people wanting to come to sea in *Ark Royal* for the day. I was also determined that every one of them should see a flying display and although this was considered to be almost impossible, nevertheless I said it should happen and it did. We divided everybody up into red, blue, green and yellow teams and moved them about the ship in such a way that every one had a chance to see everything that was going on inside and outside. Soon after leaving Devonport with everybody embarked, the Commander came on the bridge with a couple and said, 'Sir, I'd like you to meet Mr. and Mrs. ...,' and I must confess I wondered why he had suddenly singled somebody out to come up to the bridge at that particular moment. He continued as follows, 'Their son is serving at HMS *Raleigh* and they were coming to visit him today and when they got

Families' Day

down to the dockyard they got into the wrong tender and instead of going across to the other side to visit their son, they found themselves for the day in *Ark Royal*.' I don't think they were too disappointed!

Coming back into Devonport to return everybody ashore, I was just about to enter the breakwater, and was almost committed, when the sudden pipe of 'man overboard' was made and, with a quick look, I decided I could do a fast 360, which I did while the helicopter was scrambled, and picked the rating up who had been working in one of the boats and had managed somehow to fall over the side. I think a lot of the guests really thought this was all part of the entertainment, but I can assure you it wasn't. A great day was had by all.

During the work up period I was asked whether we would enjoy having the famous duo of Peter Cook and Dudley Moore on board to do one of their shows and I must say it not only was a great pleasure to have them but they did a remarkably good job of turning the aircraft carrier into a scene for their show. Towards the end, the final

365

act was going to be a replica of Dudley Moore playing the piano to be fired off the port catapult and as they prepared to do this and were loading the catapult and getting everything set up, I looked down and then called up the flight deck officer and said, 'I want a Fly Navy sticker on that piano.' There was a pause and the chap came back and said, 'The director says that he doesn't want that, it would spoil the shot,' and I said, 'Well tell him from me that if there's not a Fly Navy sticker on that piano, it doesn't get launched!' Subsequently I was told that when this message was transmitted, the director said, 'Can he say things like that?' To which the flight deck officer said, 'That man up there can say anything he wants and we do it.' The piano was launched with the Fly Navy sticker on it.

At about the same time we were carrying out calibration trials with the Phantoms, which were then operating from shore and in a classic 'fish bowl' environment day where the sea and the sky merge, one of the Phantoms was letting down for a low level run and just disappeared off radar. Search as we may, we had no luck in finding anything in the immediate vicinity. The BBC television team had gladly agreed to provide a concert party for the ship's company in the hangar that night, and very sadly I had to cancel it. What was even sadder, as a tail piece however, was that *Private Eye* ran a piece in their next edition in which they said the Phantom had in fact defected to Russia, or rather to Poland in the first instance. Although there was absolutely no possibility of any grain of truth in this story, it was not the kind of thing for wives of the crew to be reading about. Peter Cook of course was at that time with *Private Eye* but whether there was any connection I had no idea.

'Hands to bathe' became the usual regular feature which it had always been when I was driving a ship, and the first time we had over a thousand men in the water. Fortunately the Commander had taken the precaution of getting boats away so that if anybody got into trouble we could take care of them but the major problem came when the chaps who had got into the water all right tried to get out up the scrambling nets up the steep sides of *Ark Royal* and for some, who were not particularly fit, it was beyond them and they had to be pulled out and brought back to the quarter deck gangway by boat. I joined them, as I always did, and had a refreshing dip every time from the quarter deck while the escorting Kotlin (which we were never without) observed the scene with some amazement. On one occasion he made a signal to me which said, 'They all go Malta?' but when the Officer of the Day asked me if we should make any reply, I said, 'No, make no reply whatsoever. Whatever we say will probably be misunderstood, either accidentally or deliberately.'

Hands to bathe

Another event, which might have proved difficult but in the end turned out to be not so, was the absolutely correct decision by the then First Sea Lord, Michael LeFanu, to stop the issue of Naval rum. The Navy had moved on and it was traditional still to issue rum at 11 o'clock in the morning. It was therefore somewhat disturbing to go into a complex electrical department and find a Petty Officer or Artificer with a long screwdriver poking into a thing which said 'Danger – 3000 Volts' when as he turned to you and said 'Hello, Sir' the overwhelming smell of rum nearly knocked you back.

We had, in the Fleet Air Arm, partially overcome this by having rum issue after flying was completed but it was still an anachronism in a modern and highly complex service. When the order came down from the Admiralty, I fell the entire Ship's Company in and read the notice and told them that it was almost unavoidable that we should abandon this ancient practice, and substitute for it beer, which of course came in cans and I always insisted that it was opened on issue so that it couldn't be stowed away. The lads took all this in good part, apart from a general groan, and on the last day they constructed a

367

The last tot

coffin which they solemnly paraded round the ship as being the burial
of the rum issue and then ceremoniously consigned it to the deep.

On the more sombre side, we had a tremendous problem with the
new direct acting gear. When it worked it was fine, but after the trials
and when we started to operate it, we found that the arrestor wires
when they came out would not re-set and this meant that one of the
wires in the tangle of knitting that was down below had jumped off
one of the reeves, and now the whole thing had to be re-strung again.
This was a time consuming, tedious and tiring job for the flight deck
engineers and I sweated as we went into a major NATO exercise with
press representatives on board, wondering exactly how long the
knitting was going to last. Towards the end of the exercise when they
were re-reeving the wires for the umpteenth time, I went down to the
space where the flight deck engineers were working, just off the
hangar, at about 3 o'clock in the morning and were all looking totally
exhausted. I'd been down and chatted to them before and given them
some kind of a chuck-up, but this time all I could say to them was, 'I
have nothing further to say, we've just got to get the damn thing done

"Signal to Admiralty, 'You'll have your Ark Royal back the day we have our rum ration back'!"

(© *The Sun*)

again and fix this exercise,' which of course they did. I am glad to say after return to Devonport, the problems were sorted out

We visited Naples as one of our treat visits and I called on the Mayor of Naples as part of the ceremony. He was quite a small man and I arrived with sword and medals and was parked onto a rather low sofa where the grave danger is that, if you're not careful, as you sit down your sword will go straight up your left nostril. We chatted for a bit and I've never figured out why but I told him a not particularly funny story and since he spoke no English and I spoke no Italian, I told it to him in French which made it even worse! It is the simple one of how do you tell the difference between an American and an Englishman, and the answer is: an American lifts his hat in an elevator but an Englishman does not elevate his hat in a lift. Try that in French to an Italian and you won't be surprised that he looked at me with some amazement. I do remember, however, saying to him, 'It must be a great honour to be Mayor of such a beautiful city,' to which he replied,'Yes it is, but I wish the peolple would do as I say.' 'But surely, Mr Mayor, ' said I, 'you wouldn't wish to have a populace that was quick to do every thing you wish.' 'No,' he said, after a pause, 'but if only they would do some of them.'

On return to the ship, I was greeted by the Commander who told me that we'd had something over 1200 men ashore and there had been no problem, but he thought he should tell me that they were selling marijuana cigarettes just outside the dockyard gates. 'However not to worry, Sir,' he said, 'because in fact they're full of donkey droppings!'

And so to the end, with the traditional dining out for the Captain, and I stepped into a helicopter and was whisked off back to my home in Kent. It was a sad moment because I knew that there would never be anything like this experience for me ever again but then all good things must come to an end.

27

Is It True?

In the course of one's development, as life proceeds, certain events or certain stories have an impact on you that carry you forward, or you fall back on, as points of reference. Some of the stories, of course, are anecdotal to the extent that I cannot guarantee their truth but one that I have used many times is the reply which Field Marshal Montgomery is alleged to have given to Prime Minister Eden on the second day of the Suez campaign when the Prime Minister, having met him on some occasion, asked him, 'How do you think the campaign is going, Field Marshal?' To which Montgomery replied in his piping voice, 'If you tell me what it is you're trying to do, Prime Minister, I'll tell you how I think it's going.' I found myself repeating this sage comment endlessly in my business and Service life as a way of determining whether we were going in the right direction or not. It was a useful and amusing anecdote which helped to focus attention on a very simple question that so often should be asked.

A similar incident, or memory, served me well in another connection and of this I can at least verify the origin of the story, if not the truth of the exact event. The individual who told me, however, was sufficiently well known and distinguished I think, for us to assume that it was not too far away from the truth. Lord Louis Mountbatten was a much-loved character within the Navy; he had a particular affection, I think, for the Fleet Air Arm and for a while when he was Chief of Defence Staff, in combination with Sollie Zuckermann, in what Chapman Pincher named the 'Zuckerbatten Axis', he promoted the cause of the Navy and of Naval aviation to an extent that, looking back on it, was probably one of the highlights of the whole of Naval Air history.

After he retired he still retained contact with Naval colleagues and I remember that on one occasion when I was VCNS being asked to go and supervise a television appearance he was making because the production team seemed to be a bit reluctant to deal with the great man in a theatrical environment. I went over to the famous boardroom in the old Admiralty building, and there Mountbatten was, in the uniform of an Admiral of the Fleet, explaining to the television audience via the interviewer, the role of the Admiralty Board and the significance of the Admiralty Board table and where each member of the Board sat and what his function was.

As he sat in the middle on one side of the table so that he could indicate and be expansive about who sat where, he leaned forward and indicated the various members of the Board in the following way.

'There sits the First Sea Lord, that is where my father, Lord Battenburg, sat as First Sea Lord, that is where I sat when I was First Sea Lord' and so on. As he indicated the particular seat, his body moved up and down the edge of the table and as he leaned forward the buttons on his jacket went up and down the edge of the table, rat-tat-tat, rat-tat-tat. After the recording had been taken the director came over to me and said, 'I'm very sorry to say that although that was an excellent interview it was spoiled by the noise of his buttons rattling up and down the table.'

'What do you want me to do about it?' I asked.

'Well,' said he, 'I wonder if you would ask Lord Mountbatten to do it again?'

'Certainly,' I said, and stepping over to Lord Louis, I said, 'That interview, Sir, which was excellent, has been rather spoiled by the fact that your buttons were grating up and down the table and making a bit of a racket.'

'Really?' he said. I indicated to him the way in which this had happened. 'Well, we'll have to do it again,' said he and promptly started down that track. However, no sooner had he got into full flight than he was sufficiently carried away to start doing the same thing again and I really couldn't bring myself to ask him to do it a third time. Lord Louis's affection and regard for his father, Battenburg, was such that I believe the story which follows worth recording in its own right.

One of the yarns he told me while we were in Malta, when I was Captain of *Ark Royal*, was about his father and Winston Churchill. It appears that Winston, on appointment as First Lord of the Admiralty, before the Great War, appeared one Saturday evening at Sheerness in the Admiralty yacht *Enchantress*. He anchored in the vicinity of two battleships which were also at anchor. That evening he made a signal to the senior battleship, as follows: 'I intend to inspect Divisions in HMS *Blank* tomorrow morning.' This caused some consternation in each battleship because both had given the maximum leave and only had a quarter of each Ship's Company onboard. It was therefore decided to make up a Division-looking parade by borrowing men from the other ship and presenting to the First Lord an appearance of a fairly full Divisional turnout. This might have worked with some

Talking to Lord Louis with Des Cassidi on board *Ark Royal* in Malta

others but in the case of Mr Churchill it had an unfortunate reaction. When he appeared on board and approached the first Division he turned to the Divisional Officer and, indicating the first man in the rank, asked, 'What is the name of this man?' Since the Divisional Officer had never seen the man before in his life, since it was a made-up Division, he could only answer, 'I don't know, Sir.' Churchill marched onto the next one and asked, 'What's his name?' and he didn't know the answer to that either, and as Churchill proceeded to inspect Divisions he got a very definite impression that the Divisional system in this ship was not working. Well, it wasn't, because it wasn't the proper Divisional system, but nobody told him this.

As a result, so Mountbatten told me, Churchill made a signal to the Commander-in-Chief Nore – as it was at that time – saying that he had attended Divisions of such and such a ship on such and such an occasion and that he was most displeased at the way in which the officers had no idea of the names of their men and clearly could not be taking the proper interest in them that the Divisional system was designed to meet. As a result, the Commander-in-Chief Nore made a signal to Their Lordships in the following manner: 'On Saturday the *** of *** the First Lord arrived in your Lordship's yacht, *Enchantress*, improperly wearing your Lordship's flag and announced his intention of inspecting Divisions in HMS *Blank* the following Sunday. As a result of this inspection he made the following signal to me criticising the way in which Division were conducted; but Divisions had been organised in a way to satisfy his requirement to inspect Divisions in a ship in which three-quarters of the men had been given shore leave and this included the Captain.' The signal continued to be critical of the way Churchill had conducted himself and his subsequent remarks afterwards.

Mountbatten's story continues as follows:

'My father, Battenburg, was in his office when the First Lord stormed in and said to him, indicating the signal, "This man," – Commander-in-Chief Nore – "is to be sacked."

"Why is that, Sir?" asked my father. Because of this," Churchill replied, indicating the signal. To which, and at last I come to the point of the story, Battenburg replied, "But is it true, First Lord?" to which Churchill replied, "That has nothing to do with it." To which Battenburg was strong enough to respond, "But, First Lord, it has everything to do with it." '

This then became one of my standard anecdotes to justify that well-known question, 'Is it true?' The truth in this case, of course, was and still remains the case that the Admiralty Board flag may not be flown unless at least two members of the Board are present and since

Winston was on his own the C-in-C Nore was correct in saying that he was improperly wearing Their Lordships' flag. So, 'What is it you are trying to do?' and, 'But is it true?' were remarks I remember and am able to use within the setting 'anecdotes', and more often than not they make their point.

28

The Story of Three Carriers

When I first took command of *Ark Royal*, I was determined that the history of my *Ark Royal* should be different from those carriers which we lost during the War through various mistakes. This, the story of three carriers has, to my knowledge, not been told as one cohesive whole and I thought it important to weave it together in a way which would come across to my Ship's Company as a story with total relevance to their life and service on board this great ship.

Military Services are not very often interested in telling the stories of their mistakes but we learn as much, if not more, from these as we do from the great victories, some of which, of course, were not as great as people imagined at the time. It is understandable that during wartime, the lessons of incompetence should not be widely advertised because they would undermine morale, but it is important in the context of understanding the real lessons of war that they should be analysed afterwards and I put them in that context, because all of them have a lesson for all of us interested in the exercise of sea-power and, in particular, the importance of Naval aviation.

At the outbreak of war Britain possessed the largest Navy in the world – well just about – the US Navy was coming up fast but, and it's a big but, we had neglected air-power and had only begun to put it right in the late thirties. It was going to be some years before enough purpose-built carriers were going to be available for the enormous task that lay ahead. Just as importantly we had hardly any senior aviators – thus the task of commanding our carriers was totally in the hands of 'fish heads', the aviator's term for seamen.

So at the start of war there was HMS *Argos*, an elderly converted ship which had a small capability of carrying aircraft, no catapults, just some arrester wires. It was slow, it was old and it was not really an effective warship. Its main use was as a training carrier. There was *Eagle*, an elderly small carrier converted from a Chilean battleship which entered service in 1920; *Hermes*, again small but the first ship to be designed and built as a carrier but only carrying nine aircraft. Next we had the converted cruisers that had been turned into aircraft carriers, with varying degrees of success, with hangars exposed to the elements for'ard, as the flight deck had been built across the top of the original main deck. This class contained the *Furious*, the *Courageous* and the *Glorious*. As time had passed, improvements had been effected and *Courageous* and *Glorious* were adequate aircraft carriers by the standards of the time, although not in the same class as the new American carriers which were then coming into service. In addition, we had begun to see the fruits of the first purpose-designed carrier programme, that is to say new build from the keel up aircraft carriers, and in the forefront of these was HMS *Ark Royal*. Others of the same class still to come were the other three-shaft carriers, *Illustrious*, *Formidable* and *Victorious*, but these were yet to arrive on the scene, although they were nearly ready. Behind them, of course, came the new, larger class of carrier, the *Indomitable* Class – *Implacable* and *Indefatigable* – four-shaft, large two-hangar carriers, and the complementing smaller class of Light Fleet Carrier – *Theseus*, *Glory*, *Ocean*, etc. but all this remained in the future.

In 1939 the main carrier fleet consisted essentially of *Furious*, *Courageous*, *Glorious* and *Ark Royal*, three of which were to be lost in tragic circumstances during the early days of the War. My story of the three carriers starts with the loss of *Courageous*.

In the early days of September 1939, immediately after the outbreak of war, *Courageous* put to sea with her Squadrons embarked to go into the South Western Approaches to look for submarines. The story of *Courageous* was told to me by Lieutenant Commander Lamb, 'Pegleg' Lamb, who wrote the now famous book *War in a String Bag*. One evening in the Wardroom of *Implacable*, where he was Little 'F', he recounted the story to me over a glass of grog as follows:-

'We went to sea in a high state of enthusiasm, looking forward to the actual fact that, having waited so long, the war we all knew was coming had at last begun. A force consisting of *Courageous* and four escorting destroyers set out into the South Western Approaches on an offensive sweep to look for submarines. (A great deal of faith was at that time placed in the new ASDIC equipment. It was thought that this would find submarines and enable them to be hunted. In fact it provided a beacon for the submarine to home in on). In retrospect we really weren't very well prepared for this task. It was in the days when the Royal Marine orchestra was playing in the Wardroom for dinner and the ship was still incompletely darkened. Two of the escorting destroyers had been detached for other duties. In addition, we were on a steady course; there was no attempt to get onto an anti-submarine weave or an anti-submarine evasion course and on the evening of the 17th September, in a calm sea, *Courageous* found her first submarine. Rather the submarine found *Courageous* – she was torpedoed! Her scuttles were open and she rolled over and sank within 15 minutes.'

The emergency station for aircrew was on the Quarterdeck and so when Emergency Stations was piped we duly fell in on the Quarterdeck, along with the Royal Marines. The Royal Marines were fallen in athwart ships and the Squadrons, aircrew that is, were fallen in in various Squadron heaps dotted about on the Quarterdeck.

After a while the ship began to list and it was apparent that she was going down. A decision was made to start abandoning ship and a destroyer, HMS *Impulsive*, came alongside, a half cable or so away, ready to take off survivors. The water was not particularly cold, after all it was late summer in the South Western Approaches, and the aircrew – all of whom could swim – started to take across those Ratings who were prepared to leave the ship but who could not swim. At that time there were still a surprising number of sailors who had not passed the swimming proficiency test. So those of the aircrew who were good swimmers started swimming across, taking those who could not swim over one at a time, and each time coming back to find the

HMS *Courageous*

ship listing slightly more and the Royal Marines still fallen in athwart ship with a sergeant in charge. 'Peg-leg' asked the sergeant whether they were going to abandon ship, to which the sergeant replied, 'Not until I get instructions from the Royal Marine Officer, Sir. He's gone for'ard to have a discussion with the Commander.'

Time passed and the ferrying of Ratings continued across a fairly narrow strip of water and each time they came back the ship was clearly in a more precarious state. In the end 'Peg-leg' said to the Marine sergeant, 'I don't think your Officer is going to come back. I think he may be lost somewhere in the ship and I think the situation is now getting dangerous.'

'No, no, Sir,' said the sergeant, 'I'll wait for the Marine Officer.' Then with one of those flashes of inspiration for which Fleet Air Arm Officers are so famous, Lieutenant Kiggell, his CO, turned to the Royal Marines and addressed them in the following fashion: 'Royal Marines, turn for'ard, abandon ship.' The Royal Marines all fell-out and jumped over the side and made their way to the destroyer. Well, it's a good story!

He went on to say that most of the crew of the *Courageous* were saved, but 518 and the Captain perished. The survivors were all picked up from boats, either from *Courageous* or from the destroyers, or by going over the side in the calm conditions that prevailed and swimming to the destroyers. He recounts how sitting with a blanket around him in the destroyer's Wardroom and being given a clean, dry change of clothes, he watched the Commander of the *Courageous* lie on a settee in a state of utter dismay, and die; he didn't die because he was injured or because he was ill, he died because – as he put it – the enormity of the tragedy that had been suffered overwhelmed him.

Courageous was lost through total and utter incompetence, not entirely of its own making, although it had not been on an anti-submarine evasive course – in fact it had just turned into wind, its scuttles were open, it had no aircraft patrols airborne on immediate anti-submarine searches, it had only two destroyers as escorts and it found to its cost that the submarines were better at dealing with this kind of target than they were in finding them. The Admiralty policy of trying to find and sink submarines by providing them with a large honey pot relying on ASDICs in the escorts to defend them was fatally flawed. On the 14th September, *Ark Royal* on a similar mission narrowly escaped a similar fate to *Courageous*. We had lost one-quarter of our best carrier capability within a week of War being declared!

The second carrier was HMS *Glorious*. This, the newest and best of the converted cruisers, was operating out of Rosyth as part of the

Home Fleet and in the early days of 1940 had been in the Med. During the Norwegian campaign, she was made ready to go over to support the withdrawal from Narvik. In addition, she had just received a new Captain and my story of the *Glorious* was told to me by Lieutenant Commander 'Crash' Leggott who worked for me in the Ministry of Defence, or the old Admiralty as it then was, in the Directorate of Air Organisation and Training. 'Crash' was a very famous wartime aviator who had originally been a Petty Officer Pilot and later commissioned during the course of the War. He had, in fact, been my predecessor on exchange to the United States Navy in Squadron 172 based in Jacksonville, Florida. At that time, as the first post-war exchange officer with the United States Navy, he had flown the F4U Corsair and the first jets they had; I was the second and they had by then re-equipped to become the first Squadron of jet aircraft in the United States Navy.

It was something of an embarrassment to me, as a newly-promoted Commander, to have serving as part of my staff this famous wartime aviator, 'Crash' Leggott about whom I had heard so much and who was so much more experienced than I. 'Crash' was very generous in his relationship with me, however, and in fact called me up before joining me in the Admiralty to tell me how pleased he was that we would be working together and to ask what was I going to wear?

'What am I going to wear?' I repeated. 'Well, I'll wear a suit, I suppose.'

'Yes, yes,' he said, 'but don't you think we ought to wear formal Whitehall attire, pinstripe trousers and a black coat, and a bowler hat?' I thought about this for a moment and said, 'Well, 'Crash', I don't intend to wear any of that gear but, of course, if you wish to do so it is entirely a matter for you.' In due course he did in fact turn up complete with a bowler hat and black jacket and pinstripe trousers and a rolled umbrella and he wore that rig the whole of the time that he and I were together.

One morning he came in very late; I made no comment as five of us all shared the same office. Nothing was said. A week or so later the same thing happened; he turned up about eleven o'clock. This time waiting for a moment when there was a bit of peace in the office, he came over and said, 'Could I have a word with you?'

'Yes, surely,' I replied and he came over at lunchtime and told me this story.

'I have had a strange experience on two mornings now. As you may know, I live in Southend and commute to Liverpool Street and then I get the Underground to Charing Cross and walk over to the Admiralty.'

'Yes,' I replied, 'I understand.'

'But,' said he, 'on the two occasions I have been late I finished up in Richmond and have been shaken by the guard and told that the train had come to the end of the line, and I remember nothing of it.'

'How do you mean, you remember nothing of it?' I said.

'Well, I remember getting on the train but I don't remember anything thereafter, until I was woken up.' I thought about this rather briefly and said, 'Well, I think you should go and have a word with the doctor,' and he agreed so to do. I will come back to this story later but my information on the events in *Glorious* comes from ex-Petty Officer Pilot Leggott who was one of the very few survivors.

The new Captain, when he joined *Glorious* in Rosyth, apparently addressed the whole Ship's Company as follows: 'I intend to treat this ship just like a battleship and that is the way I intend to run it.' This attitude, of course, soon brought him into conflict with the Commander Air who disputed the way the Captain intended to run the ship and, indeed, the way he did run it, and the lack of understanding he showed for the whole aviation complement and its purpose. As a result there was an altercation which led to the Captain having the Commander Air put ashore pending court martial! As it turned out, lucky man!

The ship then sailed to cover the withdrawal from Narvik, and in particular to bring off the RAF Gladiators and Hurricanes that had been put ashore there and were now to be withdrawn. The operation of withdrawing the RAF aircraft was extremely successful, they were indeed all recovered on board, even though they had no hooks to engage the arrester gear, and were stowed ready for passage to the United Kingdom. The ship then set sail independently for Rosyth with a small escort of two destroyers. At the same time, south from Tromso, HMS *Devonshire* was leaving Norway, sailing with the Norwegian Royal Family to evacuate them to the United Kingdom.

HMS *Glorious* proceeded independently across the Norwegian Sea with an escort of two destroyers and the Captain announced that as it was Sunday they would clean the ship and get squared away to prepare for coming back into Rosyth where, no doubt, he was looking forward to the impending court martial of his Commander Air! No aircraft were airborne, no aircraft were ranged on deck ready to fly, the whole ship was being prepared for a kind of ceremonial formal entry into Rosyth and some well-earned leave.

At this moment over the horizon came the German pocket battleships *Sharnhorst* and *Gneisenau*. They fell upon the *Glorious* and proceeded to thump their massive shells into the hull of a ship the

Captain said he was going to operate as if it were a battleship, i.e. as if it had no aircraft. However, its main armament was its aircraft; its guns 4″ A.A.! There was an immediate panic to try to get some aircraft airborne, to get some Swordfish ranged with torpedoes that could go and attack the German ships, which they could have certainly attempted with every prospect of success, but it was too late and in any case most of the live torpedoes had been stowed below! The destroyers made one gallant attempt to attack the Germans and were blown out of the water in the process, and *Glorious* was sadly reduced to a sinking, burning hulk.

'Crash' Leggott told me that his emergency station was the forward port boat deck and when it became increasingly apparent that all was lost 'Crash' went back to the crew room, managed to get himself a 'Mae West' and some warm clothes and waited at the emergency station by the lifeboat. As the shells thudded into the ship and it began to list he said to the Sub Lieutenant in charge, 'I think we should turn the boat out, Sir, and get it away.' The Sub Lieutenant said, 'There has been no order to abandon ship yet, I'll go and see if I can find the Commander.' He never returned and so Petty Officer Leggott ordered the boat turned out and those who were there got into it and got away from the sinking ship. He told me that there were 22 men in that boat.

HMS *Glorious*

Most of the men that abandoned ship got into carly floats; carly floats which should have been equipped with survival gear in the shape of bully beef, water and tinned milk had no such supplies in them. It was alleged that they made the side of the ship look untidy and so they had been removed! Carly floats are open at base to the sea and in the freezing temperatures of the Norwegian sea when they became overloaded, or indeed normally loaded, with men, it meant that their feet or their legs were in the water. How much of you was in the water depended on how many men were on the float and most of them of course, and particularly those ones that were close to the ship, were grossly overloaded. 'Crash' had managed to swim to one that was quite a little way away and didn't have quite so many people in it, nevertheless he was the only survivor of his particular float and of the whole catastrophe just under 40 men survived, including one each from each of the destroyers. Despite the gallant performance of the destroyers in this action, there were no awards made and the enemy report that should have gone out from all three ships never reached, or was never received by, any of the authorities to whom it was addressed, if indeed it went out. There has been much debate on this since.

When the survivors were picked up some days later in the Norwegian Sea, freezing cold, out of 'Crash's' carly float there were only two alive – 'Crash' Leggott and one Royal Marine Corporal who was out of his mind. 'Crash' told me that most of the chaps had died within the first 24 hours. They just gave up and died from cold and the sheer magnitude of the disaster that had overwhelmed them. HMS *Glorious* was a total loss with all her aircraft, both Fleet Air Arm and RAF, and all the men who were serving in her. Only a few survived. 'Crash' was one.

The ship was lost because it was not operating as an aircraft carrier. It did not have its main armament, its aircraft, properly armed, ranged or ready or, better still, have them airborne because that is the right place for aircraft. If it had, it might have been a totally different story, as the Swordfish could have first detected and then attacked the battleships that were coming to sink their aircraft carrier home. So ended the saga of the second carrier, this time lost because it was not operating as if it were an aircraft carrier.

When 'Crash' came back from seeing the doctor he told me an extraordinary story. He said, 'The doctor asked me whether, when I sat in the tube train at Liverpool Street, was I sitting looking up at those hanging straps?' In those days there were large leather straps with a bulb at the end for hanging onto which were attached to rails which ran the length of the carriages and, of course, if there weren't people there they swayed back and forth with the movement of the train.

'I might have done,' he replied. The doctor then produced a watch and swung it in front of him – we have all seen these acts done on the stage. After a moment he said to 'Crash', 'I understand what happened to you, you were gazing at one of those straps and subconsciously you became mesmerised and lost consciousness, and,' said he 'that perhaps explains in part why you survived that ordeal in the Norwegian sea and why you have no recollection of arriving at Richmond. With the movement of the float in the Norwegian Sea you probably lost consciousness and were not aware of events around you for most of the time.' It was an amazing and remarkable story from a remarkable man who had a remarkable escape from a tragic and unnecessary loss of the second of our three aircraft carriers.

The third was HMS *Ark Royal*. Remember Lord Haw-Haw's cry, 'Where is the *Ark Royal?*' The Germans were constantly trying to pretend that the ship had been lost having claimed several times that she had been sunk. Just before the actual loss, *Ark* had emerged unscathed from bombing attacks, steaming down bomb alley in the

Ark Royal in the process of sinking

Mediterranean where her aircraft had been instrumental in supporting Malta and now having helped with the various activities that were then going on in the Mediterranean she was going back to Gibraltar. She was well clear of the danger zones from bombing aircraft, in the shelter of the Spanish coast and running in towards Gibraltar. She, too, was relaxing and she too was torpedoed! Can you believe that 'Crash' Leggott had just joined her having survived *Glorious*!

The crew were ordered to abandon ship. Once again there were destroyers available and the boats got away. There was plenty of time, in fact so much time that they were able to get the money out of the safe and take it with them, including the Ship's fund later to be used for striking the beautiful silver bell that hangs on the Quarterdeck of the present, and hung in the Quarterdeck of the previous *Ark Royal*. They had all but completed the abandonment of the ship but she didn't sink. She just sat there listing slowly and it was decided that the Commander should lead a party back on board to see if the ship could, in fact, be salvaged. By the time they had got back on board, of course, the water had got into the boiler rooms, they had lost steam, lost power, the pumps were not effective and it was too late. What an extraordinary spectacle it must have been. It must be clear that if the Ship's Company had had a thorough understanding of the damage control arrangements in that ship, or if she had been at the correct damage control state, she should have been saved – they didn't and the third carrier was lost.

So there is the story of how three of the most important ships that we had were lost for various reasons which do not bring credit upon the Royal Navy. I told this story to my Ship's Company much as I have told it here and then I added, 'We are never going to put our ship in a position where any of these things might happen to us. When we are at sea our aircraft will always be either airborne, which is where they are best suited to be, or at readiness on deck to go into action. We will know our damage control, we will exercise it and we will know how to save our ship in the event that it is damaged and is salvageable. We will never be on a steady course when submarines are about, or in exercises, we will always practise anti-submarine weaves and we will have the best anti-submarine protection available to us in the shape of our Sea Kings and our escorting destroyers, always alert the whole time.' And then I would add, 'And if any of you wonder why I go to action stations quite so often, or exercise all our systems so frequently and insist on the highest standards, no matter how badly they disturb the smooth routine of a peacetime warship, then remember this story and why we are doing it.'

29

The First Delivery of Mail to Malta by Balloon

One of the interesting things about an aircraft carrier is the flexibility that you have to do so many different things. In my opening speech to the assembled Company, including Her Majesty the Queen Mother, at the commissioning of *Ark Royal*, I was in some difficulty. Sitting in the front row was Dr David Owen, then Navy Minister of a government that had decided to do away with aircraft carriers. In fact the term aircraft carrier was almost enough to create a fire without fuel, and yet I was determined to make clear to people that what we had was an extremely valuable asset, and that the loss of it would, in my opinion, be nothing short of a tragedy. Therefore directing my remarks over the heads of the assembled Company, Admirals and in particular Dr David Owen, I said the following: "For those of you who came aboard up a covered gangway you might not realise exactly what kind of a ship you are actually in, but I have to let you into a secret. *It is an aircraft carrier*. There, I've said it! And because it is an aircraft carrier, it is also a frigate because its anti-submarine helicopters can operate in the same way as a frigate does. It's a guided missile destroyer because it has its air-to-air missiles which also can be used to attack other ships. It is also a cruiser because it has its Buccaneers with long range weapon systems that can certainly outrange any modern cruiser. It is a battleship because it is capable of engaging the enemy in any battle scenario that he likes to develop. It is a commando carrier; it can carry troops, it can carry supplies. It can do anything. It is the most flexible and versatile weapon system that the Navy possesses.' An absolutely accurate description of the capabilities of the ship, but not one which was calculated to endear one to people who were dedicated to destroying it.

The pleasure of being in such a versatile ship, however, goes beyond pure military capability because there are so many other things you can do. I have touched on the importance of morale and how easy it was to maintain morale in a ship of this kind when the catapults were launching aircraft and when aircraft were coming on. But also of course, it gave you scope for many other things. You were big enough to have your own television studio; you were big enough to have a

Clear lower deck

super collection of films and entertainments for your people on board, and all kinds of pursuits could be followed: archery, clay shooting, deck hockey.

Writing about the television studio reminds me of a way in which I dealt with it. When I first joined the ship, the Commanders aid to me, 'No doubt you will be addressing the Ship's Company using the new television system which goes throughout the ship from the television studio.'

'No, Commander,' I replied, 'I will not be doing so.'

'Might I enquire, Sir, why not?'

'You certainly may, Commander. When I fall the whole of this Ship's Company in, in front of me, I look at them eye to eye, and I can immediately sense from their demeanour what reaction they are having to what I have to say. It will not always be pleasant news and I need to know how it is being received, and I can only get that if I am dealing face to face with my people. If I go down into the television studio and give some talk or the other, some bright lower-deck lawyer in one Messdeck may decide that he would like to answer back and make some remarks as I am continuing my speech; whether this is well received or not it will undermine discipline in this ship and I will not have it. I do not intend to hide behind television.' I believe it's a point worth remembering whenever one is in the business of leading men in a disciplined environment. There is no substitution for a flesh and blood encounter.

One of the episodes I hadn't quite counted on when we started the commission, was the fact that one of the pilots in the Gannet 849 Squadron, Lieutenant Terry Adams, was a balloonist and he brought his balloon on board with him! Naturally he wanted to be able to fly it from *Ark Royal* and came up with the rather engaging idea that we should have printed special envelopes commemorating the fact that we were going to deliver the ship's mail, as *Ark Royal* approached Malta, by balloon. Now try to think of something that stops that idea! Well, of course, if you're a bureaucrat you could come up with something very quickly, but if you are concerned with something different and exciting that will entertain and enliven the ship's company and raise their morale, then why not? And so I said, 'certainly, let's do it'.

A sample of one of the envelopes

388

In order to do it, it was necessary to steam towards Malta from the upwind side of the island so that the balloon when launched would drift across the island, and it was also necessary to proceed at a speed which gave zero wind over the deck. So with a wind of about eight knots at sea, I was required to steam towards Malta at eight knots to provide zero wind over the deck while they flashed up the balloon.

We duly positioned ourselves not far from Filfa and proceeded directly towards the Island. We started the run from not too far away because we didn't want the balloon to have to go too far. However, delays occurred on deck while they were trying to get the right amount of flame, and laying the balloon out properly, or stop it blowing up with air or whatever was the problem, and we were getting closer and closer to Malta itself. Eventually my Navigating Officer, normally a calm and collected man, began to draw my attention quite forcibly to the fact that if we continued on this course for very much longer, we would run aground! I examined the chart as calmly as I could, and decided that yes, he probably was getting close to the truth but we could hold on for a little bit longer and so, we held on.

'Is the balloon ready to go yet, Wings?'

'Not quite, Sir, not quite, nearly ready'. By this time the Navigating Officer was looking extremely worried, and referring back to the chart and checking the position of the ship as accurately as I could, I determined that we were really out of time and that I'd have to turn bloody quickly if I was to avoid delivering the mail personally into the island, bow first!

Fortunately the great moment arrived.

'The balloon is airborne.'

'Starboard 35,' I ordered, and round we came to avoid being the first to deliver mail ashore directly by ship! The balloon looked marvellous as it floated away with its streamers flying with the celebratory letters on board, and as we watched it through our binoculars we saw it drifting straight towards the centre of Malta and hopefully towards the town of Valletta. It looked quite magnificent in the clear evening sky, but then something seemed to go wrong.

The balloon from our perspective, appeared to suddenly start to turn away to starboard, and it actually looked as if the balloon had missed the island and was now going to come back out to sea! My mind moved immediately to how the hell I was going to avoid having this balloon finish up in the 'oggin' with the consequent bad publicity this would produce: in addition how I would be able to explain to Their Lordships what the hell I was up to. It seemed to me that I might find myself manoeuvring this bloody great ship underneath the balloon, somewhere at sea, in order that he could land back on. This

Airborne

was going to be an interesting experience, fraught will all kinds of real and imaginary dangers. Fortunately for us, and for all on board, the balloon which appeared to be going out to sea had in fact just crossed the coast and was indeed veering towards the position where it would eventually go back out to sea. The balloon Captain, therefore, wisely stopped blowing hot air up into the envelope and the balloon subsided into some farmer's field not far inland.

Well, it hadn't made Valletta but it had made history and it had made it possible for us to celebrate without a Board of Inquiry! All's well that ends well.

30

We 'ad a Plan

While I was in *Ark Royal* in Malta, after the episode with the Russians, I was at a reception when I was approached by Rear Admiral Pighini who was then on the staff of Allied Forces Mediterranean based in Malta. He asked me if it would be possible to come and call on me in *Ark Royal* and of course I was very happy for him to do so. He came aboard in due course and having been shown round the ship, joined me in my cabin for a drink and then said, 'I want to tell you a story.' To the best of my memory, it went like this –

'In 1940 I was the Flag Lieutenant to Admiral Campioni, who was the Commander in Chief of the Italian Navy in the Mediterranean, and we 'ad a plan, an' the plan'a was that we would go to sea and we would wait to be detected by the British, an' then'a we would retire toward a line of submarines which would attack the British as they followed us, because we knew we 'ad the faster ships and we could stay out of range of your guns. As your ships came across'a the submarine line, the Italian Air Force would come and attack you. This was the plan. So we went to sea to put'a the plan into execution'. This must have referred to the action in June 1940 off Calabria, which took place before the Battle of Taranto, on the 11th and 12th November.

Admiral Pighini continued: 'We went to sea as planned, and sure enough we were sighted by one of your aircraft, and we knew your Navy heavy ships would come soon and they did, and we proceeded to put the plan into execution and retire towards Sicily. We were perfectly 'appy to keep you following us at a distance which kept you out of range, but then there came an attack by your Swordfish aircraft and although they achieved no hits, we had to stop to turn to track the torpedoes to stop the hits, and this slowed us down. As a result, it was possible for one of your ships [the *Warspite*] to obtain a hit on the *Vittoria Veneto*, which was the flagship in which I was serving, and this was a hit outside what we thought was the maximum range. [It was in fact, or must have been, a very lucky hit from the *Warspite* because she was out of effective range.] This caused considerable confusion in the flagship and we were now worried that the British Fleet would come soon in range, before we could make good our speed again to retire, and so the Admiral called for the Italian Air Force to come and attack the British ships.

The Italian Air Force came. They attacked us! Fortunately, they missed! So we say again to the Italian Air Force, come quickly, you attack the wrong ships, attack again the British. And they came again – this time we had large Italian flags spread out on the upper deck – but still they attack us! Fortunately nobody was hit but it was now getting very unhealthy for us, and so we changed our course and retired immediately towards Taranto, not taking the British towards the line of submarines. [In fact, it would appear as if the British also decided to withdraw at about this time.]

Admiral Pighini concluded, 'So you can see the effect of your Fleet Air Arm attacks, even though they were not successful, completely disrupted our plans. It also shows you that you cannot rely on shore based aircraft to protect you, and I come with one simple message for you: Never, never, never, abandon your Fleet Air Arm'.

'I was able to assure Admiral Pighini that some of us had absolutely no intention of so doing. A remarkable testimony from someone who actually did know.

31

The Fish War

If ever there was a campaign we couldn't win, it was the so-called Cod War. During my time as Vice Chief of the Naval Staff, we were faced with the appallingly difficult situation of trying to protect our trawlermen as they fished within international waters off the Icelandic coast, which the Icelandic government unilaterally had declared as part of their territorial waters by extending them from 3 miles to 15. It was a war we could not win because the whole of the international Press was bound to be on the side of the little guy who was standing up to this relic of an Imperial past in the shape of the Royal Navy. We in the Royal Navy, however, did not have to have our duty spelled out to us, we knew that it was as it always had been to uphold the policy of the government of the day, and to do our best to ensure that that was successful.

The problem was that the Navy was not equipped with the kind of vessels that would have been suitable for such an operation. We had come down from a large escort force to some 50 destroyers and frigates at that time, all of which were designed for the highly complex and demanding task of facing up to the Cold War confrontation with the Soviet Union. As a result, we had produced for the most part, thin-skinned vessels which were like the greyhounds of the sea, if you like, packed with sophisticated and very expensive equipment. Their vessels were robust tug-like craft with very little sophisticated equipment – they could take a few knocks without much trouble. To protect our trawlers and prevent the Icelandic gunboats from cutting their nets required us to interpose ourselves between them and the activities of the gunboats, led very successfully by the *Thor*, and to literally fend them off.

At the early stages of this confrontation, I attended a meeting in the Ministry of Agriculture and Fisheries, with John Rogers who was then the Minister responsible for the armed forces within the Ministry of Defence, and found myself ranged alongside him on the stage there confronting an audience which was composed largely of trawlermen, whose livelihoods were being threatened by the actions of the Icelandic government. It was an extremely rowdy meeting and I was very

393

surprised at the way it was conducted, and at some of the allegations that were being thrown about at Government ministers from the floor. What was very clear was that the trawlermen would expect the complete protection of their fishing fleet by the Royal Navy, and that anything less would be regarded by them as failure on the part of HMG to uphold their livelihoods, against what was considered by them and HMG to be an illegal action. As we walked back from the Ministry of Agriculture to the Ministry of Defence building, I said to John Rogers, 'I do hope that I shall never again expect to hear you criticise the conduct of affairs in the Ministry of Defence, because having seen what goes on in the Ministry of Agriculture and Fisheries I can only say you were extremely lucky, Minister, to be employed in such a well-disciplined department of state'. John, with his usual sense of humour, riposted, 'You're jolly lucky that we weren't there in the afternoon, after they've had their beer and sandwiches, otherwise it would have been much more rowdy'.

We then set in train the necessary actions to keep on station the requisite number of escorts to provide the protection which the trawlermen expected, and this of course also meant keeping a tanker there so that fuel would be available (without having to return all the way back to the UK) as well as a supply ship for victualling and stores. The task was clearly beyond the capabilities of the Fishery Protection force per se, although we had embarked on a construction programme of commercially designed vessels for this particular purpose, so the main brunt of the exercise was bound to fall upon the highly sophisticated frigate force.

Our tactics meant that the risk of collision was always there and also the sturdiness of the *Thor* compared with the frail nature of our frigates was bound to mean that we were likely to suffer more damage in any kind of 'touch and go' barging match than they would. Nevertheless, it was what had to be done, and it was done with considerable success by the ships that were stationed up there but it was always a question of how long we could continue to do this at fairly enormous cost in the teeth of the Icelandic intransigence. It was also clear to me, as I said at the outset, that it was a campaign that we could not win. However, I was quite determined that it was one we would not lose, in other words we would still be in possession of the field when the inevitable diplomatic compromise was reached which made our actions no longer required.

There was no doubt that in public relation terms the Icelanders were making much of the running, but that was inevitable. The David and Goliath syndrome was too strong. The whole effort was reaching a climax when I was due to go on leave, and I packed up on the Friday night and went home and handed over to the First Sea Lord. As usual, on the television that night there were the harrowing scenes of ships colliding, or near colliding, as we attempted to protect our trawlermen and there was little doubt that sooner or later lives would be lost. My concern had always been that they weren't going to be our lives; if the Icelandic gunboats were prepared to risk theirs that was a matter for them, but I didn't want to see any lives of British sailors lost, and in my view eventually that was going to be inevitable and must be the price we were prepared to pay to perform our traditional role.

Imagine my surprise therefore, when I returned from leave to be told as a result of what had happened on that Friday night that a decision had been taken to tell our ships to avoid damage or act in such a way as to avoid damage, which of course was tantamount to throwing in the sponge. This decision resulted from signals that came in from the officer in tactical command that he was concerned that casualties would be incurred if they persisted in the difficult weather conditions that prevailed to maintain our previous stance. It wasn't going to take, and didn't take, the Icelandic gunboats very long to realise that there had been a change in tactics and all they had to do as drive straight towards a British ship and it would give way. I really was furious because this meant in order to restore the situation and our credibility we were going to have to take far more risks than would have been the case if we had merely maintained our stance. I went to see the Secretary of State for Defence, Roy Mason, at his request, because he wanted to know what could be done to restore the situation, and I said that in order to do this we must be prepared to accept damage in order to protect our trawlers, if that was the Government's wish, but he must be prepared for casualties and potential criticism if the policy was to proceed for too long.

However, I was now fed up with the fact that we were sustaining damage and the Icelandic gunboats were getting away with it, and I therefore instructed Chatham Dockyard to fit two underwater projections to two diesel frigates which were then in Chatham undergoing maintenance, so that when they went up on fish patrol, if an Icelandic gunboat persisted in coming close across their bows they would hoist the International Signal 'U' which means 'you are standing into danger' and they would find that there was a large railway line sticking out ahead of the vessel which would somewhat impede their progress. Work proceeded to install these devices but fortunately for all concerned, a diplomatic solution was found, i.e. we had to concede the Icelandics' right to extend their territorial waters, with fairly dramatic effects on the fishermen from Hull and Grimsby. It was a sad day, and doubly so since quite clearly in international law we were correct in our stand, and we have seen since how the law governing fishing and fishery protection has made life extremely difficult for the fisher folk of our island.

Years later, I was invited to lunch by Harry Chapman Pincher who was writing a book about 'dirty tricks'. The reason he had invited me to lunch was to establish whether I had been involved in any during my time in the Navy. Can you imagine! I told him that of course I hadn't, but at the back of my mind amongst others were the events in Chatham Dockyard which might well have come under the heading which he was seeking to write about, but I refrained from revealing this to him; after all, it was one of the minor ones and hardly worth the title.

32

The Deterrent

The deterrent occupied a great deal of my time as Vice Chief of the Naval Staff because we'd got ourselves into such a mess. The Polaris missile system, which we had acquired from the United States as part of the Macmillan negotiations with the President of the United States after the cancellation of Sky Bolt for the RAF, was in need of updating or replacement and the job of doing this was given to the scientists in the Ministry of Defence and in the various establishments. After a while it was becoming perfectly clear to everybody within the Naval Staff that this programme was not going well and the chief Polaris executive, David Scott, was becoming more and more concerned about the delay in the updated programme named Cheveline.

Cheveline was a device to be equipped to the Polaris missiles which would effectively saturate the Soviet defences because it was believed that their anti-ballistic-missile systems would be able to defeat an attack by the straightforward Polaris system.

Here we come to another one of those operational, analysis and political judgements which, in my opinion, was flawed. It was based on the so-called Moscow criteria; that is to say, that we would not be in possession of a valid deterrent unless we were able to guarantee the destruction of Moscow. Only this would deter the Russians from attacking us. What was significant of course was that the Russian defence system around Moscow was apparantly able to counter the British threat. They were incapable of countering the American threat because it was so vast and overwhelming, and as Cheveline began to look as if it was getting into more and more trouble, it was right to question the whole concept of the Moscow criteria. Would not the destruction of Leningrad, Minsk or Vladivostok by a satisfactory deterrent? The political pressure egged on by the scientists who were intent on doing their own thing was so strong that it was extremely difficult to break through and, in addition, there was a campaign of disinformation which was almost designed to prevent ministers actually being aware of the truth. Finally, the crunch came when the Navy said it could no longer rely on Cheveline being produced if it remained under the control of the scientific establishment and it should be put out to industry. It was, to British Aerospace, although I didn't know this at the time; I only knew that it was to go to industry and that was a solution, the one that found favour. After I joined British Aerospace and spoke to the people who were concerned with the introduction of the management programme, there was no doubt in my mind whatsoever that had we not moved the whole of this programme into industry it would have been a disaster. However, times moved on and we were now talking about a successor for Cheveline, and one option of course was to look at the American Trident system, another was to look at Cruise missiles (a technology which we then possessed) and of course to develop the existing Polaris system to produce a British equivalent. Now in British Aerospace, lobbied quite hard for this latter option, indeed any option that gave British industry a chance to develop this capability and actually gave evidence before a Parliamentary select committee on the subject.

Soon after this evidence, I found myself in a Middle Eastern country where we were selling or trying to sell a particular system and John Nott had come out, who was then Secretary of State for Defence, to meet with the ruler to actually finalise the deal. The Ambassador had arranged a dinner to which I was invited along with various other people and John Nott himself. At the reception which preceded dinner, John Nott said to me, 'By the way, I've got to give you a rocket.'

'Really' I said, 'for what?'

'Well,' he said, 'you must know.'

I said, 'I certainly don't. It could have been any one of a number of things which you might object to. Which one have you picked?' He said, 'It's the evidence you gave to the select committee on the question of the deterrent.'

'Oh yes,' I said. 'What did I say that was wrong?'

'Well,' he said, 'how could you suggest that British industry could actually produce such a system?' I replied, 'You obviously haven't read the evidence that I gave, Minister, I said no such thing. I only said British industry had not been asked whether it could provide a system. That is something you will regret for as long as you remain in office.' He looked at me momentarily and then said, 'Let's talk about something else.'

'That's much more like it,' I said, and we talked about events that were going to take place the following day.

It is interesting to recall that his next visit was to another Gulf State, where we were also interested in developing military sales, but I wasn't allowed to fly in the same aircraft with him and my Marketing

Director had to charter a separate aircraft for us to fly in. At that time, it wasn't considered ethical for defence contractors to be seen travelling with Ministers! No wonder we lost a few! Contracts, I mean.

Some two years after I had left the Navy and was working for British Aerospace, I was asked by the then First Sea Lord, Henry Leach, if I could pop in to see him. The Navy were in the midst of a very severe defence review brought about by John Nott, which if it had been carried out would have decimated the Navy. When I appeared in his office, Henry outlined the situation and then asked me if I had any ideas of what the Navy could do to change the atmosphere in which they were operating. I could not forbear to say, 'How on earth have you got into such a mess in such a short time?' Not very helpful but it made me feel better. I told him that I could think of three things they might do. I honestly can't remember the first two but I remember very well the third because I said, 'If these fail then you have no alternative but to pull the plug on Trident.' Henry looked at me fixedly and said, 'I couldn't do that.'

'Why not?' I said.

'Because I believe in it, I believe we need Trident.' To which I replied, 'That has nothing to do with it. You asked me what measures I would take if I were in your position to secure the future of the Navy. Trident is a highly political issue; it would be extremely embarrassing for the Government if the First Sea Lord and the Board of Admiralty said "We cannot allow the purchase of the Trident to destroy the Navy." But Henry,' I said, 'you don't have to actually do this. I mean you just have to suggest that it might be the line you have to take if these policies are carried through.' I left him feeling very sad because it was clear to me that Henry was not a 'Whitehall Warrior' in the sense of being political but a straightforward, down to earth Naval Officer, which unfortunately is not always what you need to succeed in that environment.

However, the events in the Falklands changed all this and Henry was bold enough to go direct to the Prime Minister when all about her were preparing to surrender and say that there was still enough of the Navy left to make an assault on the Falklands to recapture them a possibility. Had John Nott had his way we would never have been able to recover them. In another chapter I talk about lightweight Sea Wolf and you can see how events are strung together through two careers. If lightweight Sea Wolf had gone ahead and our ships had been fitted widely with it, then our casualties from air attacks when they went down in the Falklands might well have been dramatically reduced.

399

33

The End

My last three jobs in the Navy were Flag Officer Aircraft Carriers Amphibious Ships, when I had all the large ships in the Navy under my command, and then Director General Naval Manpower and Training, and finally Vice-Chief of Naval Staff. With the death of Andrew Humphreys, and Edward Ashmore going temporarily as Chief of the Defence Staff, I became First Sea Lord as well as VCNS until the arrival of Terry Lewin.

The job of Flag Officer Aircraft Carriers was great, and being Commander Carrier Strike Group Two, which was the number two to Strike Fleet Atlantic, was a thrilling and exciting job. The major NATO exercises were always planned around the possibility, indeed likelihood, of a Russian attack on the West and it was marvellous to

The U.S. Navy's first AEW helicopter

be able to participate at such a high level in those particular games. Although we were a fast-diminishing force to be reckoned with, there was still much in my time that we could teach the Americans, particularly in the matter of air defence and in anti-submarine warfare.

I became fascinated by the American small carriers, their marine commando carriers, and the ability that those ships had to operate V/STOL aircraft, which was to be our only future after Ark Royal was paid off. I also became intrigued with an American experiment to put airborne early warning in a helicopter with a retractable inflatable dome underneath, which gave very good results. I relayed this message via the Commander-in-Chief of the Fleet to the Ministry of Defence, saying that I thought it was absolutely essential that we moved down this road. Had we had such aircraft in the Falklands, some of the events might have been entirely different. The danger to a ship at sea is always going to come from very low-flying or sea-skimming attacks, and these can only really be detected by airborne early warning under the control of the fleet. Suffice it to say that the wheels turned slowly, and that now we do have aircraft capable of exercising in this role.

My period as Director General Naval Manpower and Training saw yet another exercise in streamlining shore support in order to save money, and I had to overcome a very difficult battle with the Chief Wren to persuade her that we should close the Wren Training Establishment at Burfield and have the Wrens trained alongside our sailors down in *Raleigh*. I remember the climax of this argument when she came to see me at one point said, 'My girls are different from your boys, Admiral.'

'I am aware of that, Madam,' I said, 'but I suspect that although you may think and I may think that our boys are a pretty spotty collection at that age, your Wrens might find them quite attractive.'

'But,' she said, 'we must have walls high enough round the girls to make sure that they are not overlooked,' and this of course I readily agreed to. I also tried to get Their Lordships to agree to have Wren Officers trained as helicopter pilots, but they did not accept this. it was not long afterwards, however, that they were to accept Wrens going to sea with men; to be frank, I would never have agreed to this. I believe that one of the strongest arguments against allowing homosexuals to serve in the armed forces is undermined if you put women into the same combat units as men. By this you have accepted, it seems to me, the fact that you could have difficulties with the natural inclinations of both sexes when pushed too close together and this, of course, is precisely the argument that I would use against the introduction of homosexuals. It becomes a diversion which in war, or periods of stress, might prove quite damaging.

DAILY EXPRESS Monday September 26 1977

THE CHAPMAN PINCHER INTERVIEW

'The sheer size of Russia's naval effort is awesome—but for years they poured money into the wrong ships'

Admiral Sir Ray Lygo... believes in a future for surface ships

Britain can still rule the waves

(with a little strategic help from her friends)

TO rebut NATO's charge that Britain's defences are being cut below safety level, the Government claims that their superior quality makes up for the loss in size.

To test the truth of this, I went to see Admiral Sir Ray Lygo, Vice-Chief of the Naval Staff at the Defence Ministry.

I chose him not only because he is the most forthright Service Chief I know but because, as he is leaving next year, he can be even more outspoken.

DETERRENT

Surprisingly Sir Ray, who first achieved public acclaim by ramming a Russian destroyer which was harassing the Ark Royal when he captained the aircraft carrier seven years ago, supports the Government's claim — with one big proviso.

"The Navy has been quietly revolutionised and the results will make it Europe's most effective contribution to NATO and still the biggest — provided the Government completes the building programme and imposes no more cuts.

"Britain is no longer the third country of the world in trade or influence, but we will still have the third-biggest Navy, for we are only half way through the new build-up."

This one-time Fleet Street office boy who took over as a stop-gap First Sea Lord during a sudden reshuffle earlier this year, believes that a non-nuclear conflict is more likely than an H-bomb holocaust, provided the West keeps its deterrent.

"It is the American connection that sustains Europe, and Russia's prime objective would be to sever that jugular," he said. "So the Battle of the Atlantic would

nuclear-driven submarines from scratch. The Americans just didn't believe we could do

of sensors towed far behind a ship away from its own noise to detect lurking submarines.

However good new equipment may be, can surface ships really hope to survive in the missile age? The admiral is confident that they can.

"The performance of our new defensive missiles is so amazing that the public should know about it. With the Sea Wolf missile we can knock a 4·5 inch shell out of the sky and have done it repeatedly.

"Incoming missiles are bigger than that, and we do not have to hit them : getting near is enough.

MESS

"Our other missile, Sea Dart, an excellent anti-aircraft weapon, has turned out to be capable of attacking other ships—an unexpected bonus. We have other new weapons on the stocks."

Not long ago the Navy's torpedo programme was in such a mess that submarines were having to make do with obsolete weapons, and we faced the prospect of buying all-American.

Sir Ray told me that, thanks largely to the General Electric Company, the torpedo problems have been resolved.

"New torpedoes are now so effective that we are also putting them back on the decks of surface ships. With the Sea-King helicopters torpedoes can also be carried right to the target area."

Though the Government is denouncing the Labour Party's latest demand for enormous defence cuts, the admiral fears that an underlying Whitehall problem exploited by Treasury mandarins may delay the remaining building programme.

SCHEDULE

This is the Navy's inability to spend the money allocated to it each year.

Navy planners put in for a sum which is reluctantly voted to them.

Then, owing to labour disputes in shipyards and factories and to political post-

will be equipped with an invention which I believe will rank with the steam-catapult

An interview on taking over as VCNS

402

My greatest achievement at this time was, I think, to abolish the system of discharge by purchase. I introduced the notice engagement whereby, instead of having men locked into permanent engagements, they were given the option of transferring to a notice engagement in which they gave eighteen months' notice of intention of wishing to leave. This meant that, from a drafting point of view, they could still be used during that notice period for seagoing, though at a slightly lower level of pay. I remember being cautioned by the Admiralty Board at that time that we might have a tremendous run-out of men from the Service, but I countered with my usual argument: 'If we can't provide a Service in which men wish to serve freely, then we deserve to have them run out.'

In my time as Vice-Chief of Naval Staff, I think that I take most pride in the fact that the Naval share of the vote increased steadily the whole time I was responsible for it. When I was both VCNS and Acting First Sea Lord, I remember bumping into Edward Ashmore in

A meeting of the Admiralty Board in the old Admiralty Board Room

the corridor (he was now Chief of the Defence Staff, having been First Sea Lord) and I said to him, 'Remember we used to discuss the fact that there was one layer of management too many in the Ministry of Defence?' 'Yes,' he replied, 'Well, I've discovered which one it is,' I said. 'Which is it?' he asked. 'Yours,' I said, 'and since I am doing both jobs we certainly don't need both a First Sea Lord and a VCNS.' This has since come to pass.

Thirty-six years is a long time to serve anywhere, and I had achieved most of the things I had wanted to achieve. I could have stayed on as Head of Defence Personnel, but I decided that it was time for me to try something else. I was not suited for what I considered to be a fairly lacklustre-type job without direct responsibility, and I was very sad when I left the Ministry of Defence. You cannot help being sad when you leave something that you have devoted your life to for such a long time, but new challenges lay ahead. I had few regrets, and had achieved much in times of considerable difficulty, but a new chapter was about to open.

PART 2

BRITISH AEROSPACE

34

British Aerospace

Early in 1977 it became obvious that there would be nowhere for me to go when I had finished my stint as Vice-Chief of the Naval Staff in 1978. The premature departure of John Treacher had caused an upset in the sequence of appointments at the top of the Navy, and though I was subsequently to be offered what I thought was the non-job of Chief of Defence Personnel, technically one of the senior three positions within the Ministry of Defence, I decided that I would have to look elsewhere.

The question was, what to do? I had no immediate need of employment. My children were grown up and settled in their future occupations, the house was largely paid off, there was no onerous mortgage and I could have just settled down to 'grow tomatoes'. But I was only 51, one of the youngest full Admirals the Navy had made since the end of the War, and I believed I had a lot of life left in me. I also believed that I owed the system something for treating me quite generously throughout my Naval career and thought that I could make a contribution in the defence industry.

Having checked around with various people that I thought would have a good inside knowledge, like the then Chief of Defence Procurement, Sir Clifford Cornford, I was assured that industry was crying out for the kind of management talents that perhaps I could offer. The problem was, I knew very few people in industry. This was, in fact, to be an advantage when it came to getting clearance to work in the defence industry without having to go through a long period of sanitation. I had never, for example, been on the procurement side, the purchasing side of the Services. My knowledge and skills, such as they were, related to the management of small to large organisations culminating in the management of the Navy itself, being some 82,000 strong, excluding its civilian element, and my intimate knowledge of aerospace and shipbuilding from the sharp end.

It seemed to me that the shipbuilding industry was not one in which I would wish to find myself involved. I had seen some of the industrial relations problems that they had when I had stood by the building of the three ships I had been fortunate enough to command.

It was also an industry already in decline, whereas aerospace was a live and thrusting industry and was, after all, my first love. Such contacts as I did have were fairly tenuous. I had met and known at a distance, in the Navy, the then Chairman of Hawker Siddeley Dynamics, Captain 'Drunky' Lewin. I had met and sat next to, at an Admiralty Board dinner, the then Sir Arnold Weinstock. I knew Don Pepper who had worked for many years for Rolls Royce and was then on their board.

During a recent visit to the United States one of my ex-Squadron chums, Rear-Admiral Max Morris, had arranged a Squadron get-together; VF172 Squadron, in which I had served as an exchange pilot. At that gathering, Steve De Lamata, who had also been with the Squadron, asked me what I would do when I left the Service and suggested that I get in contact with Stan Harrison, who was then running the BDM Corporation, one of the 'Beltway Bandits' that had grown up around the Washington area.

With this somewhat sparse collection of acquaintances I decided to write to them seeking an interview and explaining that I was going to retire in about a year's time. I received replies from all of them in the affirmative, saying that they would like to meet me to discuss the possibility of my joining them. Don Pepper arranged for me to meet the then President of Rolls Royce America with a view to my taking over the marketing responsibility for military engines in North America, based in the USA. The interview Don set up, however, left me wondering what it was that I was supposed to be doing with them: the President himself was less than precise. Nevertheless, I was given the clear impression that, should I decide to throw in my lot with Rolls Royce, then that would be a possibility.

I met Stan Harrison on a subsequent visit to Washington, and later he and his family came to visit us, at our house in Kent. We all got on very well together and it was made clear to me that, should I wish to join BDM as an adviser on the military net, although I would be excluded from dealing with specific classified matters because of my foreign nationality, it was none the less believed that I could make a sensible contribution. This would be based in Washington.

Matters with GEC moved more positively, because Arnold was kind enough to say that they were sure they could find something for me, and put me in touch with Sir Robert 'Bob' Telford and Arthur Walsh, respectively Chairman and Managing Director of the Marconi Company. They subsequently came to visit me in my office at the Ministry of Defence and explained that they would like me to join them and possibly run an organisation based at Frimley. It was then arranged for me to go there to have a look at the place, in my Naval capacity, without indicating that I was likely to be the chap who was replacing the man who was showing me round! I found all of this a bit odd and, having been to the place and seen around it, was still left wondering what the responsibility and situation was likely to be. One chance remark by Arthur Walsh, in my office, somewhat turned me off, when he described Arnold as the hawk at the end of the chicken run. If everything was fine the chickens were left alone but if the hawk swooped, watch out! I thought this might be a somewhat uncomfortable relationship (and it certainly did not fit in with my subsequent more friendly knowledge of Arnold himself) but at the time, it was slightly off-putting.

'Drunky' Lewin invited me to lunch at Brown's Hotel, to be the venue of so many of the meeting and adventures that befell me at British Aerospace. Perhaps I should explain how he got the title 'Drunky'. It had nothing whatever to do with his drinking! It so happened that when he joined Dartmouth as a cadet there were two Lewins; one had the initials T.T., so it was pretty obvious that the other one had to be 'Drunky'. That name stuck to him throughout the whole of his Naval and subsequent distinguished career in industry. Unlike many of his contemporaries, however, Drunky never disavowed the name as he became more august, he stuck with it and was known, liked and respected as 'Drunky' throughout the Navy and industry.

I later received an invitation to lunch with three worthies that I had not met before. These were George Jefferson, then running the BAC Guided Missile Division, soon to be nationalised and form part of British Aerospace; Alan Greenwood, then Chairman of the British Aircraft Corporation, at the run-up to nationalisation, and Freddy Page, who was running the Military Aircraft Division of the British Aircraft Corporation at Warton. Again the venue was Brown's Hotel, and in my innocence, I didn't realise that this was in fact an interview. Indeed it was many years later that I recollected the episode and put it into some kind of perspective. The conversation over lunch ranged over the future of the military procurement process and the requirements for aerospace products, and I was outspoken in my criticism of the performance of industry.

I warned them quite specifically that unless industry improved its image and performance and its customer relations with the Ministry of Defence then they would find that the Services turned increasingly to overseas suppliers, American in particular, whom they judged would perform better. We had seen already the purchase of Exocet from the French and of sub-Harpoon from the United States. I warned them that, unless there was a concerted effort to improve the performance of the British aerospace industry, they would find this became the pattern. I was quite scathing about the lack of performance which the Services had had to suffer at the hands of the defence companies. Looking back on what I said to these three distinguished members of one of the largest defence companies we possessed, I wonder why they pursued me!

Time was passing, and Drunky arranged another lunch for me at Brown's Hotel at which he went over the opportunities that would be open to me on joining the Dynamics Group of British Aerospace, where George Jefferson had apparently expressed a desire to have me on board. The proposition was that I should become a Dynamics Group Director on appointment. There didn't seem to be any specific task that I was to perform, however; I found this rather strange and pressed Drunky for more information. He said that he would set up a meeting with George Jefferson to give me more specific details of what he had in mind, and as we left the hotel and were walking through the lobby he turned to me and said, 'Time is beginning to run out, Ray, and we do need to make a decision. If you are not going to join us we must look elsewhere, and I have it in mind to talk to John Treacher.' I replied that I knew John Treacher very well and if that was what they wanted then they must go ahead with it. At this, Drunky smiled knowingly and we passed out into the street and said goodbye.

In 1977 my only daughter, Brooke, announced that she wished to marry a Colonel in the El Salvadorian Army, who specialised as a neurosurgeon within the medical section. The wedding subsequently took place in Jacksonville, Florida, where Pepper and I had been married, and the reception took place at my sister-in-law and brother-in-law's home with the usual great kindness they always extended to us. As a result and with the passage of time my daughter, now pregnant, was living in El Salvador and we were anxious to be able to get out in time for the birth of their first child and our first grandchild, which was due in January of 1978. So the time was rapidly approaching when we would need to move if we were to be present for this exciting event.

In the discussions with British Aerospace, as it had then become, I enquired whether it would be possible to have, as part of my remuneration, a yearly trip to Central America so that we could visit my daughter. This was regarded as giving little problem. In the event it never occurred, but the interview with George Jefferson took place in the London offices of British Aerospace at 100 Pall Mall. This had recently been the headquarters of BAC, and it took place in the Chairman's office. George Jefferson was accompanied by 'Drunky' Lewin who explained at the outset that Jeff had asked him to be present because he could say things to me that Jeff couldn't. This left me slightly bewildered because I could not imagine what that was likely to be. We went over the now familiar ground of joining the Dynamics Group as a Group Director and doing such duties as were thought fit by Jeff in helping him to run the group.

The Dynamics Groups had been formed by the amalgamation of the BAC Guided Missile Division and Hawker Siddeley Dynamics. Whereas each had previously had both a Chairman and a Chief Executive respectively, the future organisation would have one Chairman and Chief Executive, George Jefferson, assisted by two Managing Directors running the subordinate divisions, the old BAC and the old Hawker Siddeley Dynamics. Drunky was due to retire in April and George Hough, who had been the Managing Director of Hawker Siddeley Dynamics before the time of nationalisation, had left. The old Hawker Siddeley Dynamics, therefore with Drunky about to retire, was running without top management, although this was not made clear to me at the time.

The conversation began to run out of steam and then Drunky said, 'What I can say to you and what Jeff cannot say to you is that what we are discussing here, Ray, is succession.' This left me completely confused, but they pressed me and assured me that it would be a great opportunity. For the life of me I still couldn't figure out how or why! Time was passing, however, and we were due to go off to El Salvador to visit my daughter. The night before we departed I still hadn't come to a decision. I had arranged to see Stan Harrison on my way back from El Salvador to discuss the prospects of joining BDM. I had not given an answer to the offer from GEC to run Frimley, neither had I made clear whether or not I was going to be involved with Rolls-Royce. A decision had to be made, and I was being pressed by British Aerospace to make up my mind fairly quickly.

The night before we left, I said to Pepper, 'I really don't know what to do, but I have to do something, we can't go on hedging our bets like this.' Did she wish to return to her native US? What did she think? Pepper was her usual direct self, 'Do whatever you think best. I don't mind where we live.' Almost at the toss of a coin I said to Pepper 'I think I'll go with British Aerospace; I don't quite understand what I am going to do but it seems more definite than some of the other prospects.'

Jeff had given me his home telephone number so that I could contact him when I came to a decision if it was out of working hours, so I rang him that evening before we departed and said, 'I have decided to join you.' His reply was, 'I am delighted, Ray, and I assure you that you will never regret it.' With that we completed our packing and left next morning on the first stage of our trip to El Salvador.

411

Before proceeding any further, it may be useful to give a brief outline of the origins of British Aerospace. When I joined in 1978 it had only just been nationalised, the nationalisation vote in the House of Commons having been passed by only one vote. The companies to be nationalised had campaigned vigorously against nationalisation. That part of the aerospace industry considered for nationalisation was the British Aircraft Corporation (BAC), then jointly owned by GEC and Vickers but managed by GEC; Hawker Siddeley Aviation and Hawker Siddeley Dynamics, parts of the Hawker Siddeley Group; Scottish Aviation, part of the Laird Group; Westland; and Shorts (though the last two were not in the event, nationalised). Shorts because of the peculiar problems of Northern Ireland, and Westland because the unions lobbied so vigorously against it that it was decided to exclude them from the act of nationalisation. The reason behind the vigorous opposition to nationalisation by the Westland workforce was the belief that Westland, when it was absorbed into the greater aerospace nationalised industry, would have difficulty in maintaining a separate existence. In other words, the viability of the whole Yeovil operation might well be called into question and it might be abolished or absorbed into other parts of the aerospace industry. This fear was, in turn, backed by management which, like the rest of the management of the aerospace industry, had no desire to become nationalised. It was rigorously opposed by the unions, fearful of job losses.

Of the four that were to become nationalised, the British Aircraft Corporation was the result of an amalgam of Vickers, the Bristol Aircraft Corporation and English Electric, designers and manufacturers of the famous Canberra. This was part of a rationalisation brought about the MOD in earlier years. BAC had through its antecedents developed many famous, and some infamous, aircraft, such as the Spitfire, Canberra, Valiant, Lightning, Scimitar, Swift and the ill-fated TSR2. It had also a fairly newly developed guided missile division, originally based at Luton, which had moved out to a new development site at Stevenage. Its main products were the Rapier missile system and Swingfire. On the commercial side, it had probably been the most successful of the aircraft companies to develop a civil or commercial aircraft product line, through the Viscount, Vanguard, the BAC1-11 and the VC10. All these aeroplanes, except the VC10, had sold in numbers which arguably could demonstrate that they had broken even, if not made a profit. The VC10 was an outstanding aircraft but did not sell beyond BOAC. The civil aircraft side of the business, however, was secondary to the desire to continue in the more profitable military side.

Hawker Siddeley Aircraft was also derived from a number of

412

famous companies: Hawker, de Havilland, Blackburn, Avro, Gloucester and, on the missile side, de Havilland Propellers, Armstrong
Whitworth, and Fairey. Its missile activities had produced Fire Streak,
Red Top, the Anglo-French Martell and, of course, the very
successful, perhaps the most successful large rocket, Blue Streak. On
the aircraft side it had produced a series of very successful military
fighter aircraft out of its Hawker, Avro, Gloucester and de Havilland
stables in the shape of the Hurricane, Hunter, Mosquito, Hornet,
Meteor, Vampire, Vixen, Javeline, Venom, Seahawk (part of the
Armstrong Whitworth acquisition) and, on the larger aircraft side, the
Lancaster, Lincoln, Vulcan and Shackleton. Perhaps its most spectacular product was the P1127 to be developed into the Harrier. It also
had its cancellations, the P1154, the 681 transport aircraft and the
AEW1166 to replace the Gannet AEW. On the civil side, they had
been less successful than the British Aircraft Corporation. The failure
of the Comet, that outstanding tragedy in the history of British
aviation, is well recorded, and the Trident which followed sold in quite
small numbers. It had been successful in the executive jet market,
however, with the de Havilland 125, which incidentally is the only
aeroplane of all those mentioned still in production to this day and
which had always made a profit.

Hawker Siddeley had also won a competition to produce the new
RAF advanced trainer, which broke new ground in terms of the
contractual arrangements. The contract was to be a fixed price for an
agreed specification to be built by the winning competing company.
Hawker Siddeley won with the 'Hawk' and that aeroplane and that
form of contract set the scene for the future arrangements for the
development and procurement of military aircraft within the United
Kingdom. It preceded any of the much publicised efforts that have
been made since to advertise competition and is an outstanding
example of how that policy could work. The aircraft has gone on to be
one of our most successful selling military trainers ever.

I have not covered the smaller end of the military market, trainers
like the Prentice, the Chipmunk, the Strikemaster, the Bulldog, etc.,
because by the time nationalisation had come, the companies
concerned had more or less decided to abandon that segment of the
market as being too expensive to develop and not all that commercially attractive.

There was one feature in common with all these designs, be they
civil or military: they were designed primarily for the British market.
In other words, the military aircraft were designed to fit the requirements of the three Services and the civil aircraft were designed, for the
most part, to meet the requirements of BOAC, BEA, and British

South American Airways. Vickers were the most successful in promoting their designs outside the United Kingdom, notably with the Viscount and the BAC111, but the designs that were totally constrained by the requirements of those rather special British customers were, in general, not suited for penetrating the world marketplace and were thus not commercially successful.

It must also be remembered that the aircraft industry had, since the end of the War, suffered the most extraordinary series of stop-gos, enough to destroy the will of any other than the most dedicated designers and producers. In the early 1950s we had the largest array of military and civil aircraft prototypes and developed types in the world. We had a substantial lead in jet aircraft design in terms of both engines and airframes, and the variety of aircraft that were coming off the drawing board was almost bewildering. During the decade that followed the Fairey Delta, the Rotadyne, the P177, the former two from that extraordinary Fairey Aviation, and many others followed. We were the envy and model for the world.

As decisions were being taken to replace the already very advanced aircraft in the inventory, like the Vampire, Meteor and Hunter, the Ministry of Defence of the day under the leadership of Duncan Sandys decided that there would be no more manned military aircraft because advances in weapon design had made feasible the possibility that everything could be done by guided missiles. As a result, funding stopped and a whole generation of new design fighter and attack aircraft was lost. We thus had no exportable fighter to compete in the largest market in the world: the interceptor fighter market.

The decision to switch to missiles produced a whole family of new guided missiles. The Red series: Red Top, Red Dean; the Blue Series: Blue Steel, Blue Jay, Blue Sky; the Green series for ECM: Green Parrot; and then, just as suddenly and without very much warning, the whole major missile programme based around Blue Streak, the most successful big missile ever produced, was abandoned and we reverted to manned attack aircraft! Out of this came the V-Force, the Valiant, Vulcan and Victor; and the need for them was so urgent that three separate designs were allowed to go into production at the same time as plans were being drawn up for replacement aircraft. Following the innovative design of the Buccaneer designed to go at low level came the TSR2, the development of the remarkable success in V/STOL to be the 1154, a new transport aircraft capable of operating from short fields, the 681, and a new AEW aircraft to replace the Naval AEW Gannets and to provide the RAF for the first time with an AEW aeroplane that they had never had before. This was to be complemented by a new class of aircraft carrier, CVA01, all based on a comprehensive worldwide defence plan.

At the change of government in 1968 which brought Mr Healey in as Secretary of State for Defence, all these plans were abandoned. After setting the services at each other's throats (where they did a better job of destroying each other than he could possibly have done had they hung together), the industry again lost a whole new generation of aircraft, except that the intervention of Harold Wilson which, I believe, saved the P1127 from extinction and thus the Harrier programme survived.

The new message was 'collaborate', and it was to be with the French. A whole programme of development was set in hand which resulted in the Anglo-French Jaguar and the Lynx and the other joint helicopter programmes. Most important was to be a new fighter attack aircraft, the Anglo/French Variable Geometry Aircraft. Unfortunately, whereas French industry was for the most part led by competent civil servants who had been seconded from industry, notably Ingenieur En Chef Rene Bloch, a nephew of Marcel Dassault, we were completely hamstrung by the need for the Procurement Executive to negotiate, keeping the Services at arm's length. As the Services also were devoting more time to fighting each other than addressing the real problem, the French were able to make much more significant progress than we were. For example, the French not only participated in the Jaguar but did not abandon their plans to produce their own aircraft, the Mirage, which it is alleged was based on the original designs of the Fairey Delta and thus were able to produce an aircraft that was saleable as a fighter when we were left with nothing with which to compete!

As the Anglo-French efforts foundered, however, attempts were made to switch to 'let's buy off the shelf, buy American'. The seeds for this had been sown by the Navy's persuasion of the MOD that it should be allowed to buy the Phantom to equip its existing and future carriers, instead of adopting the P1154 which it thought would not be a good fighter. That proved to be a rather shortsighted decision, driven by the desire to have aeroplanes that would justify large aircraft carriers, which the 1154 certainly wouldn't have done! As a result of the cancellation of the TSR2 the RAF was to get the F111, but in the event the F111 turned out to be not a very good aircraft to meet the RAF's requirement and it was forced to acquire Buccaneers, not only off the production line but from the Royal Naval squadrons that were disbanded at the end of the carrier programme.

Industry was also being chastised at this time for being inefficient, for being costly and for not producing the goods! I wonder why?

415

Experience with Blue Sky, Blue Jay, and subsequently Red Top convinced the Services that they should look to the Americans for the supply of guided weapons and Hawker Siddeley Dynamics were told not to develop their new agile air-to-air missile 'Shram' but instead to go and negotiate a contract for the purchase of the Sparrow missile, renamed Sky Flash. As Drunky Lewin told me, when they were sent to negotiate a contract with Raytheon, Raytheon looked at them in some surprise and said, 'What's to be negotiated?' Your Government has already decided that you will have our weapon and here are the terms under which you will buy it'. A classic example of the left and right hands not working together. As a result, American weapons were bought more expensively than they need have been and no one at that time was talking about 'off-set'. Indigenous manufacture was considered important, but not 'off-set'.

I hope I have painted a picture of an industry which was somewhat shell-shocked and which had been brought up to rely on Ministry fads and requirements and had often been forced to design and produce things for which there was no real commercial application nor a wider military requirement. I remember being told at one of the meetings at my early days at the Dynamics Group of British Aerospace that the requirement that we were studying was what the Ministry wanted. I asked, 'Who in the Ministry wants it?' and was told some designated sub-section of the operation requirements outfit in the Royal Air Force. I asked who exactly and was told, a Wing Commander in the RAF and I said, 'What the hell do you think he knows about the requirement? He has absolutely no idea of what weapons will be required. I know because I have tried to do it myself and it is a waste of time. Much better for us to ask them how much money they have got and see what we can design within the state of the art for the time-scale they specify and see whether they like it.' This was regarded as heresy not only, of course, by industry but by the Ministry itself. In other words, the industry liked being in the 'hind tit' of the Government and of the somewhat pompous and vicarious attitude of our then major national carriers. The result was a near disaster of a kind that few imagined because it had produced a generation of individuals in the industry who had very little sense of commercial value and were much better at reacting to the whims of the tied customers. I remember a discussion with the then Managing Director of Elliot Automation, Peter Mariner, after we had been studying designs of a new radar for umpteen years, who said, 'One of these days, Ray, they will make up their minds and I'll go down to the factory to see how we are going to build it and find that there is nobody left there who knows how to build anything!'

It was against this background that I entered industry. My knowledge of the Ministry of Defence, however, had convinced me that unless the aircraft industry was to mend its ways and to show that it could be commercially viable and internationally competitive, there would be no future for it, either in military aircraft, missiles or commercial aircraft. Indeed I entered Dynamics against a background of decisions to go for the Sub Harpoon weapon from the United States to equip submarines as opposed to developing the Anglo-French Martell into a sub-launched weapon. At a time when the decision had been taken to go for an Anglicised US Sparrow missile to be called Skyflash and the US Phantom was the main combat aeroplane; when American commercial aircraft firms Boeing, McDonnell Douglas and Lockheed were sweeping the board. What a significant moment!

My clearance to join British Aerospace had been forthcoming in fairly record time even though at that time, and still to this day, any 4-star who wished to enter industry had to get the Prime Minister of the day's personal permission. I had no difficulty since I had never been involved in the procurement side and also because people like Cliff Cornford, who was then Chief of Defence Procurement, obviously thought that it was a good thing that somebody as brash, perhaps, and arrogant as I was sometimes thought to be, should be given a chance to let a little air into the aircraft industry. In any event, I was cleared and actually joined Stevenage one day before my Naval service had come to an end. I was on leave so it didn't matter and I wasn't being paid by British Aerospace.

I remember driving up to the front of the building at Stevenage, which was then the headquarters of Dynamics Group, wondering what it was I was going to do. British Aerospace had been organised into an Aircraft Group and a Dynamics Group by the organising committee that had been set up to nationalise the industry. Theirs had not been an easy job, trying to get some sense of purpose and leadership into the organisation and bring together two companies that had fought each other tooth and nail ever since the end of the last war. The way they had decided to do this was to try to create a balance.

The chairman of British Aerospace was Lord Beswick, a Labour peer with a distinguished career in aviation, mostly commercial aviation, indeed sometime as a pilot, but he was, above all, a Socialist and persuaded of the virtues of collective bargaining, collective planning and of industrial democracy. His deputy, Alan Greenwood, had been for a time Chairman of the British Aircraft Corporation in its run-up to nationalisation. Alan was an experienced operative and a charming gentleman and ideally suited to bring together, or try to bring together, the warring factions. On the aircraft side, Freddy Page, who had been much involved in the Canberra and Lightning and a brilliant aircraft designer, finished up as Chairman and Chief Executive of the Aircraft Group; George Jefferson, who had run British Aircraft Guided Missiles, had emerged as Chairman and Chief Executive of the Dynamics Group – thus three ex-BAC men had succeeded to the most senior posts.

Bernard Friend, the Finance Director, had been brought in from Esso Chemicals. Drunky Lewin had joined the board as Chairman of the Hawker Siddeley Dynamics part of the organisation but under George Jefferson. Air Chief Marshall Sir Peter Fletcher with whom I had crossed swords in the Ministry of Defence over the carrier battle (although only marginally, since he was quite a bit senior to me), was a director of Hawker Siddeley and had been carried over to the nationalised company in charge of strategic planning. Eric Rubathon, who had run part of the Hawker Siddeley Aircraft Company, had become deputy to Freddy Page; and Tom Kent, who had been involved in the BAC Guided Missile Division, was on the Board as Managing Director of the Bristol/Stevenage Division. The Technical Director was John Stamper, who had been instrumental in the Buccaneer design and had come from Blackburn, run by Hawker Siddeley. The Company Secretary was Brian Cookson, who had been with BAC as Commercial Director, and Tin Pearce had been recruited from Esso as a non-executive director, as had Derek Gladwin, the Secretary of the General and Municipal Workers Union. There was no Board Marketing Director and no Board Commercial Director per se. The two groups, Aircraft Group and Dynamics Group, had been formed by the amalgam of the component parts of the predecessor companies that best fitted together. The Dynamics Group now had two major sub-divisions: the Bristol Stevenage Division, which had been the old BAC Guided Missiles and Hatfield, Lostock & Stevenage B, another site at Stevenage that had been the division of Hawker Siddeley Dynamics directly concerned with space and guided missiles. The space part of the Bristol Aircraft Corporation, which was located at Bristol, remained in the Stevenage/Bristol Division.

On the aircraft side there were six divisions! All reflected the previous owners' arrangements and locations, e.g. there was the Weybridge and Hurn Bristol Division of the Vickers and Bristol Aircraft Corporation locations. Kingston/Brough represented the previous Hawker Siddeley Military Aircraft Division; Manchester, which consisted of both Woodford and Chadderton, the old Avro location, formed another Division. Prestwick, which had been Scottish Aviation, formed another and Hatfield/Chester, the old de Havilland civil aircraft side, formed yet another Division. Warton was another division, previously BAC Military aircraft. Each of the Divisions in Aircraft and Dynamics had their own Board of Directors encompassing most of the functional activities, i.e. finance, marketing, commercial, technical, etc., each with its own secretary!

The two groups, Aircraft Group and Dynamics Group, were autonomous, the organisations being run from the top with little reference to headquarters which Lord Beswick had decided to move out of London to Weybridge as part of labour policy, retaining only one floor of the old BAC headquarters in 100 Pall Mall. The group Boards consisted of the senior functional members of the Divisions (Managing Director and Deputy Managing Director most usually), and each Division produced its business plan for the following year which was then approved by the group and subsequently passed up for consolidation at headquarters. Our political master was of course, the Department of Trade and Industry.

In deciding what standards to apply, the ratcheting up principle was used. In other words, rather than levelling down, everything had been levelled up. So because Hawker Siddeley Company directors previously at that level had had Jaguars, now everybody had Jaguars, even though previously BAC employees had had to be satisfied with Rovers! There was one major problem however, salaries were constrained by the Government's wages policy and the top directors were then being paid £20,000 per annum. You could not give an increase outside the Government's authorised increase for the year but wage restraint inevitably produced its own circumvention policies, notably promotion to newly established grades. Therefore we had many different levels of management completely unrelated to the management task, invented as a means of getting round the strict application of the wages policy. This was to lead to an even more difficult situation in the eventual management of the Company!

On my first morning with BAe I was welcomed by Jeff, who was his usual friendly and kindly self. He told me that there was to be a Board meeting the following day; I was to present myself to that meeting where I would be elected a director of the Dynamics Group, a position that carried an annual salary of some £15,000. My duties were unspecific and he would discuss those with me at a later stage.

Jeff told me that Lord Beswick, the Chairman, wished me to join the Board of British Aerospace as one of the three Dynamics directors, and I subsequently met with Lord Beswick and told him that I was very flattered with the offer that he'd made me but I could not accept because I had discovered that if I joined he Board of a nationalised company I would have to forgo my Naval pension. I was not prepared to do this as a matter of principle, even if my pension was only worth a pound a year. In particular, I stated that the rules were inconsistent because a member of the Civil Service or the armed forces who joined Short Brothers in Northern Ireland, for example, did not have to forgo their pension because although Shorts was wholly owned by the Government it was not 'nationalised' and therefore was not affected by the rule. I found this extraordinary and was not prepared to put up with it. Beswick said that he was sure that a way could be found around this but subsequently had to inform me that his exchanges with the Ministry had shown that this was in fact the case.

'Well,' said I, 'if you still want me to be on the Board of British Aerospace then one way round this would be for me to attend Board meetings but not to accept an appointment to the Board and continue as a director of the Dynamics Group but with Board duties, for which I would receive no salary.' This was agreed and so for the whole period of nationalisation, I attended Board meetings but was not a member of the Board, so that before the annual photographs were taken I departed!

I duly presented myself for the electoral process and was admitted to the Board of Dynamics. I noticed as I walked into the room that I was received with a somewhat blank stare by the other Directors who were there present; what I now know, but didn't know then, was that they probably had had very little by way of introduction or a chance to express any views on my appointment!

One item being discussed at the Board meeting that day particularly caught my attention. We were anxious to develop a lightweight version of the Sea Wolf missile system, lightweight because the Admiralty-designed weapon launcher, a six-barrel affair, was a very cumbersome and ungainly piece of equipment that cost a great deal and was therefore restricted in its fitting to only a few ships. This was very worrying because it was clear that the vulnerability of ships to low-level attack systems was such that we desperately needed something like the Sea Wolf to give them adequate protection. This was to be borne out later by the experience in the Falklands. The six-barrel system depended on a Marconi radar that was heavy and sophisticated but which we did not regard as being too reliable; it was also expensive. The BAe proposal, therefore, was to develop a lightweight launcher in conjunction with Holland Signale Apparaten, a subsidiary of the Philips Company in Holland, which had a long and successful history in the design of lightweight radar.

The debate within the Board of the Dynamics Group then touched on the investment that the company was making in the continuation of the lightweight Sea Wolf system, VM40, with particular reference to the fact that it was to be fitted to a modified and modernised Type 21 frigate. I knew that the first batch to be modernised had had to be cut from the Naval programme owing to the cost being more than the budget could stand, yet here was the company continuing to spend money on a development that I knew was unlikely to result in a purchase, especially in the role they envisaged. I sought a meeting with Jeff and told him that I was concerned to learn that they were pressing ahead with this programme because the installation in the Type 21s, to which he had been referring, was not going to happen. Jeff flatly disbelieved me and said that BAe had been assured by the Ship Department of the Admiralty that the modernisation would go ahead and therefore the weapons system would be procured. I was flabbergasted, and told him in unequivocal terms that the programme had been cancelled; if the company were to press ahead, it would be doing so at its own risk.

I think the lightweight Sea Wolf saga makes an interesting study. I have covered it already in Chapter 20 but it's relevance is such that I go over it again. In my days running the Naval Staff, the cumbersome nature and heavy top weights in the Admiralty-designed six-barrel launcher was a constant source of worry and the complicated nature of the radar was also an issue which was constantly being discussed. Most Naval ships of that period had been fitted with the Short Seacat system which was a four-barrel launching arrangement. Seacat was a wire guided weapon which was accurate against slow moving targets but the higher speed aircraft and Cruise missiles were clearly outside its capability. BAe had developed the really remarkable Sea Wolf system which was an autonomous system guided by a Marconi tracker and capable of intercepting a 4.5″ shell, which was the target used for the development trials. It was, and still is really, one of the only guided missile point defence anti-missile systems in existence in the West. Why had it grown to such an enormous top weight and size? One of the reasons for the complexity of the launcher was the assumption that any future attack on the fleet from the Russian side would require a minimum of six missiles to be able to adequately defend a ship and therefore there had to be six missiles ready to fire.

Here we come to one of the nonsenses that became prevalent at the Ministry of Defence as a result of introducing science into the operational requirements area. Before long everybody gets carried away with bogus arguments based on assumptions which have never been tested. How did we know that Russian aircraft or missiles were going to come in flights dispersed in such a way as to require six missiles? Because Intelligence told us so. Where did they get their information from? Mostly, I suspect, from reading Aviation Week which was usually a better source of intelligence than our own! Here was the rub

421

however: in order to get weapon systems or ships, or aircraft, or tanks, or anything through the scrutiny of the Ministry of Defence operational requirements committees at that time, which were dominated by scientific input, it required that you were able to satisfy the theoretical requirements or your programme would not be endorsed and since you were almost certainly talking about a period out of sight, in terms of technical competence, you had to go for a very advanced and sophisticated system in order to justify the expense that was then going to be incurred.

Now, of course, it would have been a very much simpler question if we could have hung the Sea Wolf missiles onto the existing Seacat launchers; we would then only have had to incur the expense of the missile and radar development and not the development and installation of the very heavy six-barrel launcher. I had personally raised this question at a staff meeting in the Ministry of Defence and had been assured by my 'experts' that this could not be done, that the existing Seacat launchers were not strong enough to take the Sea Wolf missiles and that we had to have six barrels, not four, and this meant that most ships could not take the system. Also, no money could be found for modifying the four-barrel launchers and even if it could, it could not be justified in operational terms. This clearly was cloud-cuckoo land but it was the one in which we had to operate.

British Aerospace quite rightly wanted to produce a lightweight system because it saw that it would not be able to export the existing six-barrel launcher. They were looking for something that would be both capable and exportable. Soon after I joined there was a meeting in Holland to discuss this matter with Holland Signale Apparaten at which Marconi Radar were present. It was Jeff's understanding that agreement had been sought and gained from Marconi to participate with Holland Signale in the development of the lightweight radar and for Marconi to stop opposing the programme which they had been doing. Marconi felt that if the Navy turned to Holland Signale for this radar there would be an end to their monopoly of Naval radars and that a very dangerous precedent would be set. They also believed that their system was better and more capable than the Holland Signale system and used a great deal of their talent to persuade the Ministry of Defence that this was so. Jeff, having struck the agreement, thought that the way would now be open for a joint development with Holland Signale, funded by both companies, in order to interest potential customers. He was wrong, Marconi never acknowledged the agreement. There was, however, one further barrier. The Sea Wolf system was so effective and efficient that it was unlikely that it would ever be given an export licence to other than NATO countries, most of which had either already opted for, or were in the process of opting for, other systems!

It was at this juncture that I had arrived in Dynamics and it was this message that I as trying to convey to Jeff, but it fell on stony ground and I realised that I was not in a position to go any further than that without betraying even more confidence. Since the company knew the commercial world better than I, there must have been some reasons for pressing ahead. It was at this same meeting that I asked Jeff what my primary task should be. His answer was to advocate the VM40 lightweight solutions and he would also like me to take a look at the old Hawker Siddeley Dynamics business located at Hatfield, Lostock and Stevenage, with a small offshoot at Chiswick.

Since I could not see much point in pursuing the former, I asked Drunky to organise the necessary visits to Dynamics. He said that this would be fairly straightforward but he thought the most important meeting would be with Bill Neil and Mac Smith who were respectively Director in Charge and Finance Director of the Lostock Factory. These two were affectionately known as 'The Robber Barons of the North'. My first visit, however, was to be to Hatfield and I duly presented myself there to receive a presentation on the affairs of that particular site from Laurie Evans who was the Director in Charge. Using a flip-chart he went over the various projects they had going at that time. I was introduced to the management team – at Director level, that is – and taken for a visit around the factory. I was not greatly impressed; but then since I was so new I thought I should wait and see.

The visit to Lostock was more complex because it was quite clear that Drunky wanted to be present and introduce me to the major players. It was arranged, therefore, that we should meet for dinner at The Last Drop Hotel, just outside Bolton, a favourite venue for events in that part of the country, and a very interesting place to boot. Pepper and I duly set off to find this place and having managed to get hopelessly lost around the Manchester area we only just arrived with enough time to change before appearing in the private room reserved for our dinner to meet both Drunky and his wife, and the other two couples. It was a convivial occasion and we all seemed to get on very well. Both Bill and Mac were Scots and had many of the characteristics of that great race. Bill was an experienced engineer, having come from a background of mechanical engineering, and had great pride in the way in which Lostock had been turned round.

It was alleged, and I believe with some truth, that the working practices and standards at Lostock were in a terrible state when he had been brought in to turn it around, and he achieved this. His method and style of management was one of direct involvement, and he was a staunch supporter of the social club and the various activities that went on inside the factories to make it more of a family. Mac Smith was a Finance Director who, although having an office down in Hatfield as the Finance Director of the Hatfield Lostock Division, in fact spent nearly all of his time up in Lostock where he enjoyed the atmosphere and the camaraderie that undoubtedly existed at that plant. He was a skilled financier and a canny Scot to boot.

My last visit was to Stevenage 'B' site where the space activities were concentrated. This site had been built originally by Hawker Siddeley for the assembly of the Blue Streak rocket and the assembly halls were, and are, still there. After the collapse of that programme it was largely an empty building with a few bits and pieces going on as they attempted to build up their space activities, mainly around the European Space Agency (ESA), which had been conceived to set up a consortium of several companies across European boundaries, each backed by an American expert in the space business. In the case of Stevenage it was a grouping that went by the mnemonic MASH, which stood for Matra Air-Italia Saab and Hawker Siddeley, and their American supporter was TRW. The man that ran the space activity was Peter Hickman, clearly an enthusiast in the space business and a very nice man also. He struck me as being a somewhat lost soul at the time, since little activity or management attention was really directed towards our space involvement. They had been successful in winning competitions for communications satellites for the European Communications set-up. They were a young and enthusiastic team with a lot of very highly qualified people, but seemed to be lacking some direction.

After I had completed my visits, and it had taken less than two weeks to arrange and go round, I wondered what I should do next. I assumed that the thing to do was to go and tell Jeff what it was I had discovered, and duly asked for an appointment and met with him. I said, 'You asked me to do two things, one to do with lightweight Sea Wolf, and the other regarding the Hawker Siddeley divisions. I have made my view clear on lightweight Sea Wolf; what I would now like to tell you is what I have found out in the Hawker Siddeley Dynamics Division.'

'Yes,' said Jeff, 'what is it?' 'Well,' said I, 'you have a problem.' 'What is it?' he asked. 'There's nobody running it,' I replied. 'Drunky has retired as Chairman. This post is no longer necessary in the new set-up since you are the Chairman of all the Divisions but there is no Managing Director. Since the departure of George Hough there has been nobody running it. It is run as two separate entities, one at

Hatfield and one at Lostock; as far as I can see they don't readily accept the leadership of either as being primary, and the Space Division sits out as a somewhat neglected entity by itself.'

To my surprise Jeff said, 'Yes, I know.' Well I thought, if he knows and he is the Chairman and Chief Executive, that is the end of my involvement, but this was not to be. 'What do you think we should do?' asked Jeff. We, I thought. We! I've only just walked into the place. 'What you have to do,' I countered, 'is to appoint a Managing Director.' 'Yes, I know,' said Jeff, 'but who?' 'Well, you must have half a dozen chaps you could nominate to do the job,' said I. There was a pause and then he said, 'I'm afraid that isn't true.' 'You must have somebody.' 'No,' he said, 'I don't. 'What, no one?' 'No one' said he.

There was an even longer pause and, because I cannot stand long pauses, I said, 'Well, would you like me to have a go at it?' He looked at me for a moment and said, 'Why don't you do that, Ray?' To which I replied, 'Jeff, I'm flattered that you think that you would allow me to do such a thing but I can give you no guarantees. Although I have run large organisations before I have never done anything quite like this, so I cannot guarantee that it will be successful. I shall do my best.' Jeff looked at me for a moment through those poised hands and said quietly,'That's good enough. I'll go down on Friday and talk to them, and I'll call a Board meeting for Monday at which you will be appointed'.

I know that Jeff went down to Hatfield on the Friday, and so I was expecting a fairly straightforward entry into the appointment on the Monday. George sat at the head of the Boardroom table with me on his left-hand side. He opened the meeting by saying, 'Chairman's remarks. I have decided to appoint a new Managing Director. It is Admiral Sir Raymond Lygo. He's here on my left. It's all yours, Ray,' and he got up and walked out. As I glanced around the table at the faces that were confronting me, I suspected (later confirmed) that this was the first they had heard of it! I made a statement then that I believed at the time, which was as follows: 'I do not believe that the Admiralty Board would regard it as acceptable to have somebody brought in to run the Navy from outside because they hadn't got anybody they thought fit to take over from the inside of the company, and I make you a promise that as far as I am able to ensure it, this will not happen again,' but it had happened and I was on my own.

I think it is probably correct to say that my arrival as Managing Director of British Aerospace Hatfield Lostock Division was not viewed with universal approbation. I think it was welcomed at Lostock and the Stevenage B site, once they got to know what it was all about, but the situation at Hatfield was not easy because the management there really thought that they had a right to run the whole show and I was clearly perceived as an outsider. There were minor skirmishes to start with when I insisted on having the best office, having been told that I could have a perfectly good office at the back of the building! I was fortunate to have acquired Drunky's secretary, Olive Tregelles, who was a tower of strength to me in those early days.

Soon after my arrival, I got hold of the General Manager and said that I would like to talk to everybody. His response was that he would call a meeting of the Board of Directors. This was not what I meant but I let him go ahead, and outlined to the Board what I believed to be the way ahead for the part of British Aerospace for which I was now responsible; that we had to meet our targets to achieve our budgets and, if possible, beat them, and that in order to be competitive we had to look at ways of reducing our costs. We should also begin a strong political struggle for the adoption of Sea Eagle as the stand-off weapon for the Royal Air Force and the Royal Navy against a ship target. This was in opposition to the American air-launched Harpoon which was then the preferred option. Sea Eagle was to be an indigenous design of a Cruise missile, a very important development for the future of the missile division within British Aerospace.

After this, I again told the General Manager that I wished to address everybody and he said he would arrange for a meeting of the management club. The pay system that had been brought about by pay restraint had generated various levels of management which were guarded jealously by the occupiers. People ate in different places depending on their status; their motor cars, of course, reflected their status. Everything had been designed to get round the pay restraint by giving people material advantages which wouldn't be counted against their salary. I agreed to meet the management club and duly addressed them in the same vein. This completed, I again said to the General Manager, 'I wish to talk to everybody.'

'Well,' he said, 'I'll get the union representatives together.' I was becoming amused by this dialogue and said, 'Yes, certainly, I'll talk to them.' Which I duly did. There was no different message, and then again I said to him, 'Now I need to talk to everybody.' He said, 'I don't quite understand. We have over two thousand people on this site; how do you mean you wish to speak to everybody?'

'Well,' said I, 'I intend to speak to all of them, to address them, all together in one great big heap.' He looked at me in some surprise.

'I don't think we have a space big enough to accommodate them,' he said.

426

'Well, I would've thought if we cleared the main canteen we could probably do it in there,' said I. 'Otherwise I shall do it in the open air; we'll wait till we have a nice day and then you'll arrange for the necessary broadcasting equipment and I shall do it in the open air.'

'Do you really mean you're going to talk to everybody in one group?'

'Yes,' said I. 'When I was Captain of *Ark Royal* I used to speak to all of them, fallen in in one great heap, and this is what I intend to do here, and furthermore I intend to do it throughout the company in all those parts for which I am responsible.'

Eventually the great moment came and it had been decided that I should do this on a Friday at four o'clock, just before they all packed up, but I was warned by the General Manager again, that the secretaries were entitled to go fifteen minutes early and if they got up and walked out in the middle of my talk I should not be surprised. I said, 'I should be very surprised if they did this because I am sure they don't have bad manners.' And so, at about ten to four one Friday afternoon, I went over to the canteen where a small dais had been erected and a microphone stood in the middle of this vast empty space. There was my secretary, there was the General Manager, and there was nobody else. At five to four there was still nobody and I began to wonder whether for the first time in my life if I had really blown it. But at four o'clock they began to emerge from their various places of work and come over to the canteen, and by ten past four or thereabouts they were all assembled. I addressed them in the following manner: 'My name is Lygo, L-Y-G-O, Ray Lygo or Admiral Sir Raymond Lygo Knight Commander of the Bath if you want the whole lot, and I have been appointed Managing Director of the Hatfield Lostock Division, and I intend now to tell you what my first impressions are of you, and to tell you something about me, and then how together we can work to make this a successful and profitable business.' I was to go on throughout my career in British Aerospace addressing, in turn, everybody in the company on the same theme, but this was the first attempt. Nobody walked out, it was all over at four thirty, and I received a round of applause as I left the canteen.

My next port of call, for the purpose of addressing people, would be Lostock and here Bill Neill insisted it was done in the theatre which was part of the canteen, and I should be on the stage and that the audience should be seated. In view of the fact that we had some two thousand people at Lostock, and the canteen only enabled something like two hundred to be sat down, I was facing ten separate sessions. I couldn't believe it but I didn't argue and Bill Neill started off by saying he would introduce me. I think they were all wondering what on earth was going to happen, and so for a whole day I solemnly went through ten speeches to ten different groups of two hundred each. After the first three, Bill soon realised that he didn't really need to introduce me at all, and the theme I followed became standard.

One amusing episode comes to mind. Part of my spiel was to say that my contribution was that I knew the workings of Whitehall and was used to walking the corridors of power. At one stage in one audience, a chap with his arms akimbo shouted out, 'I should think you do. That's how you got this bloody job.' I looked him straight in the eye and said, 'If you think that I have got this job by that kind of influence, and that I am prepared to work the kind of hours I am prepared to work, for the money that they are paying me, purely because it was a soft number, then you've got another think coming.' Some years later I met again on one of my walkabouts and he said kindly, 'I was wrong and you were right.'

There then followed Stevenage B site and Chiswick, and my series of introductory talks had come to an end. To my surprise, it appeared that this had never been done before and I was at pains to point out that if you fell everybody in in front of you and talked to them, you were talking regardless of rank or position, or whether they were members of unions or not, you were talking to everybody and you got your message across quite directly. The next ploy was to start walkabouts and go into various departments and just talk to the people I met about themselves, about their families, about the holidays they'd had, about their position in the company, what their views were, what their ambitions were. As the scope of my responsibilities extended and as I began this walkabout system all over the company, usually going by helicopter in the end, to various far flung corners of the empire, I became used to people saying to me that they had never spoken to a Director in the company before, leave alone the Managing Director and Chief Executive as I became. It never ceased to surprise me how easy it was to communicate with people once they understood what you were about. I was always received with great courtesy, and sometimes I would be near to tears when a man who I had been talking to said, for example, 'I've been here for forty years and this is the first time I've spoken to a member of management.' In one particular site, I found a certain nervousness amongst the people I was talking to and as I sat on a bench chatting to a chap, I noticed he kept looking around him.

'What's the matter?' I enquired.

'Nothing, sir,' he said.

'I said, 'Come along, there must be something wrong, you look extremely uneasy. What's the problem?'

428

'Well,' said he, 'we've been told to report all the questions you asked us, and the answers we've given you.'

'Really,' I said. It was not my policy to announce my arrival at sites when I went walkabout, but it was invariably my custom to go to see the General Manager before I left. On this occasion, I said to the General Manager, 'I have been told you wish to be informed of all the questions I asked your people, and the answers that they gave. If you are concerned about whether your people are going to tell me things which you would not like me to hear, then you have every cause to worry, and if I ever find that you are conducting yourself in such a way in future you will be removed from your position forthwith.'

My days as Managing Director of Hawker Siddeley Dynamics were, I think, probably the happiest of my time in British Aerospace. It was a small enough division to get your arms around, you could get to know most of the people in it, and there was an opportunity to start to do some of the things that I thought were very necessary. First, the rain was coming through the roof at Hatfield and money needed to be spent on improving the general working conditions and this I succeeded in getting authority to do. I was surprised to find there was very little social or sporting activity going on there, and decided that we would have an Open Day. The reaction to this was typical of the kind of resistance to anything that smacked of change – this was something that infected the whole organisation. We cannot have an Open Day, I was told, because so much of the stuff we have is secret and we can't have the general public walking about. 'Then we'll lock all the secret stuff away, or cover it with blankets,' I said, 'put it behind screens or have sentries posted, but we're going to have an Open Day, and we're going to have fun. We're going to have a band, and we're going to have a fair, and we're going to have a good time.' And we did. The weather was lovely, it was a beautiful, sunny day, the crowds turned out in great numbers. For the first time, most of our employees' families had a chance to see inside the compound at Hatfield. We shared an air day with the aircraft group on the other side of the runway, and all in all it was a splendid occasion. It cost us a few bob, but then, you don't achieve high morale without being prepared to spend a bob or two in areas that some people might think were not material.

Next I looked around for the sporting activity, and decided that we should have a young men's sports team and a girls' hockey or netball team, and again ran into the problem of how were they going to get time off to do it. I merely called them together and said, 'If you are prepared to play for an hour after work finishes, we'll have an hour off before work finishes for the apprentices to have sport.' And this

Inter site sports

again we did, every Wednesday as I recall, and it worked a treat. Why shouldn't it? This led me to start a series of apprentice sports days which eventually, when I became Managing Director of the entire company, spread throughout the entire company. We divided the company up into areas, and each area had a finalist, and the finalists finally came together for a grand finale. It was a great occasion and the youngsters thoroughly enjoyed it. We got T-shirts to commemorate the events and I, on finishing presenting the prizes on one occasion, said I was short of a T-shirt, and when it was presented to me I proceeded to strip off and put it on. This in full view of several hundred young apprentices. They thoroughly enjoyed it and it became a fixed ritual at every subsequent prize giving. The spirit was marvellous but it always is when young people are given a little bit of encouragement and made to feel that they're part of a team.

Time was passing, however, and a general election was looming; the Conservative Party in its manifesto had stated the intention of returning British Aerospace to the private sector, the first large company to be privatized. As a result of these intentions, I started asking my companions on the Board whether it was something we

430

were going to debate because if there was a change of government, and it seemed extremely likely that there would be one, how were we going to face up to the fact that the incoming government was determined to privatise us. None of my companions on the Board at that time wished to raise the subject. 'It will upset the Chairman,' said one. 'Well, he's going to be upset soon,' said I, and so in desperation, as the imminence of the election came closer, I decided to raise the matter myself. Remember I was not a full member of the Board. So at the conclusion of one Board meeting under 'any other business' I said to the Chairman, 'Yes, Chairman, I have one thing I'd like to raise and that is the attitude that this Board is going to take towards privatisation.' Lord Beswick stared at me a moment in utter disbelief.

'I don't wish to discuss that subject,' he said.

'Then you are wrong, completely wrong and utterly wrong,' I said, somewhat perhaps overstating the case in my desire to make the point, 'because all my experience of these matters in Whitehall is that if the recipient of attention which is forewarned is not going to take certain precautions and actions and get himself ready for the inevitable, then things may be forced upon him which he will not like.' There was a long silence and then Alan Greenwood spoke up.

'I think Ray has a point,' he said. 'I believe we should think about this very seriously,' and then Tin Pearce added, 'I believe so, too.' There was another pause.

'What do you propose?' said Beswick.

'I suggest that each member of the Board,' said I, 'should be asked to state his opinions in writing.'

'I want nothing in writing,' said the Chairman, 'except from you,' he said, looking at me fixedly.

'Certainly, Chairman,' I replied, and so the meeting ended.

I went back to Hatfield to ponder on how I should present a case to the Board. In the end, it was a very simple one. What I said was this: 'In a capitalist society, the only way in which you can measure efficiency is by the profitability of the organisation. It may be regrettable that this is the only way it can be measured, but so far no one has come up with a better scheme. This being the case, it is important that the whole of the company has to be competitive, and we live in a contracting environment in a contracting world, and unless we are competitive we shall not survive, no matter how we are structured. So I believe that there is no alternative for the future well-being of British Aerospace other than that it should be returned to the private sector and become competitive in world terms. I am therefore fully in favour of privatisation.'

The fact was that few of my companions on the Board, if any, were really as enthusiastic for privatisation as I was, but their point of view was entirely logical and understandable. Their view simply was that since the rest of the aerospace industry in Europe was not privatised (it was government-owned) it would be impossible for us as a private company to be competitive with them. I also suspect that it was rather comfortable for them. Some of them, who had been in the private sector for many years and seen the difficulties that they had faced, preferred to be within the folds of the Government so that they could expect to be financed and looked upon in a more benign way than would have been the case with the harsh reality of dealing with the stock market and the banks in London. So it came about that we were privatised; many of the problems that my companions foresaw came to pass, but I remain firmly of the view that there was no other way.

We were the first major company to be privatised, and much has been learned of the process with the passage of time. Looking back, there were aspects of the privatisation process that were to prove almost fatal. Our advisers should have ensured that the obligations entered into during nationalisation were retained by the Government, not passed to a private company. Thus our liabilities to our partner in Airbus needed to be ring-fenced, as did some guarantees of launch aid, without which we were saddled with massive potential liabilities. In more recent privatisations this has been recognised, but not then.

It was a difficult time. We progressed from nationalisation through to privatisation, and the change of emphasis and the change of culture that was required was immense. You cannot change overnight the attitudes and behaviour of eighty thousand people who have been brought up to believe that the Government owed them a living.

35

Weapons Procurement

My arrival at the Dynamics Group of British Aerospace coincided with the loss of the possible Martell joint venture with the French for a submarine-launched surface missile, against Harpoon, the American equivalent, and the loss of Shram to the purchase of what became Sky Flash, the modified American Sparrow air to air missile. It is interesting to reflect historically on the way in which the competition between Martell and Harpoon was decided. As I understand it, and this all took place before the time I arrived in Dynamics, the staff requirement originally set out by the Navy required a missile that would exit the water, having been fired from a submarine submerged, and then do a very sharp turn to turn it into a low-level Cruise-type missile for the rest of its journey. This was a very difficult manoeuvre to complete and a task to solve and had undoubtedly affected the timescale and cost of the joint Franco-British proposal which was based on an existing Franco-British missile, an air launch missile called Martell, in order to be able to meet the Naval specification. After the Navy had looked at Harpoon, there was a certain enthusiasm for the American solution, though Harpoon did not really meet the naval requirement. The battle between the two contenders continued and the pro-American lobby won the day on the basis of the lower cost of the Harpoon system. Once the decision had been made, however, the Navy then proceeded to have the Harpoon weapon changed so that its profile would more nearly match its staff requirement, thus adding to the post-acquisition cost and causing the missile to be redesigned. It is possible, therefore, that the true comparative costs of the two missiles would have been much closer than at the time in which the decision to proceed with the American missile was taken.

Another blow had been the Royal Navy's decision to buy Exocet. Exocet was a weapon being developed for the French Navy and was enthusiastically pursued by the Royal Navy to the extent that it became the lead Navy to acquire the missile. In other words, it was the British requirement that was largely responsible for funding the missile's development for the French Navy and the Argentinian Navy, and everybody else's Navy. Furthermore, with the procurement of a foreign missile or system you are never quite sure of exactly how the system is going to work, or whether the system you have acquired is exactly the same as that which is being fitted to the Navy that is selling the system. It is so easy to slightly modify the guidance or final fusing systems of missiles to be different and also be capable of interruption or jamming, and it is therefore difficult to establish when you buy a weapon, unless you are entitled to open up the entire system and examine it (which you probably are not because it's covered by a country's industrial property rights, and has a classification on it which forbids this) how actually to jam that missile. This was to prove extremely worrying during the Falklands crisis.

Against this background, it was clear to me that we really had to win the next weapon system coming along or our ability to design indigenous, complete weapon systems would be severely impaired. The next system to be debated was the requirement for an air-launched anti-surface missile to replace Martell. The competitors here were Harpoon once again, Exocet, or a Cruise missile from the United States. The task of actually getting the Ministry of Defence to go for our indigenous design, Sea Eagle, rather than its alternatives, was very demanding indeed and I spent many hours and days lobbying hard with Ministry officials and politicians to promote the case for a British weapon, led by the Dynamics Group of British Aerospace. It had, of course, many essential components from other parts of British industry that were just as enthusiastic as we were to obtain an order: Marconi, Thorn EMI, Sperry and so on. It was an uphill struggle but we were greatly assisted by the very positive attitude taken by Geoffrey Pattie, then Junior Procurement Minister in the Ministry of Defence, in supporting our programmes, and at the end of the day we won. The way in which we won was, however, interesting. Towards the end of the competition, we had discovered that the price that was being quoted to the Ministry of Defence by officials in defence procurement was a figure we could not recognise. It was very much higher than anything that we had put forward, and as I recall bidding under the old procedures for the Ministry of Defence where we put forward our costs for development and the production run and then there was a formula that enabled us to take a profit, we were coming in at something like £140 million, and we had information that the figure quoted inside the Ministry was much higher and that this was going to put us out of court when compared with an 'off the shelf' buy of a foreign missile. No matter how we tried, we could not get behind the figures because the Ministry would not reveal to us either their budget price for ours or our competitors' prices; although we knew what our prices were, what was being compared and how like was

434

John Knott announces the purchase of Sea Eagle. On the platform: Hugh Metcalf, me, Dougie Lowe

being compared with like was not available to us. It therefore became important to me that we tried to resolve this issue, and I therefore sought a meeting with the Controller Aircraft, my old friend Sir Douglas Lowe, in order to try to force this issue into the open.

When we met with the officials from the Ministry of Defence I had with me Laurie Evans, who was then the Deputy Managing Director at Hatfield and in charge of the overall design of the weapon, and we finally managed to elicit from the conversation around the table that a figure of something like £180 million was being quoted as our price. The way in which the Ministry arrived at these figures is worth reflecting on. Because of the overruns in costs which the Ministry had experienced through the various levels of incompetence in British industry at that time and before, they had to safeguard themselves when putting forward a price which had been quoted by a manufacturer. In order to protect themselves if the missile finished up costing more than was thought to be the case, they added a contingency to it;

435

thus if a missile was being quoted at £100, you added a 20% contingency, or a 50% or a 100%, and said, 'No, it will actually cost this much'. This, of course, sometimes put the missile of the indigenous manufacturer clearly out of court, and if you were comparing the cost of design and development and production with an 'off-the-shelf' purchase which could be quoted at a fixed price (unless, of course, you were subsequently going to modify it, as had been the case with Harpoon), then almost certainly the cost of the 'off-the-shelf' item would be less than the indigenously designed and produced one.

In order to break this log-jam, I turned and in a low voice said to Laurie Evans, 'We don't recognise this price, do we?' To which he said, 'Not at all.' 'What', said I, 'do you think would be the total price, if we were to go fixed and firm for this programme?' He thought for a moment and said, '£120 million.' Admittedly it was a figure off the top of his head but I took it and added a slight margin, and then interrupted the conversation to say, 'I am prepared to make you a fixed-price bid for this contract, design and manufacture, and for a price of £130 million, and I'll sign up for it today.' The effect on Dougie Lowe was traumatic. Nevertheless, the meeting concluded with us arranging to put in a fixed-price bid for this contract at that price.

A few weeks later I received a 'phone call from Dougie Lowe one evening at home, in which he said, 'I've just come from a meeting, Ray, and you'll be pleased to learn that you are going to be awarded the contract for the Sea Eagle missile.' 'Is it a fixed-price contract?' I asked. 'No,' he said, 'it will be an incentive cost-plus programme.' 'Then I don't want it,' I replied. There was a silence. 'Are you serious?' he asked. 'Yes, I am serious,' I said. 'I want a fixed-price contract, that's what I want. That's what I need to have if I am to turn this cost-plus-mentality company into a competitive machine.' 'Well,' he said, 'you'd better discuss that with the Permanent Under-Secretary.'

I called Sir Frank Cooper and told him that I had just had a conversation with the Controller Aircraft, in which he informed me that it was not to be a fixed-price contract but that it would be a cost-plus incentive one. 'I don't want it, Frank,' I said, 'I want a fixed-price contract.' 'Well,' said he, 'I think perhaps if you were to take a little more off your price, Ray, then we might be able to move.' To which I countered, 'I am not taking a penny more off my price. I've already come in £50 million under what you thought it was likely to cost, or what your officials were telling you it was likely to cost, and which could have cost me the whole contract. But the reason I want a fixed-price contract is to stimulate people in my organisation to start working under the disciplines of fixed price, because if it's a cost-plus incentive programme we shall run rings round your contractual people because I can pay mine more than you can pay yours, and at the end of the day we'll finish up getting more money than you think you're going to pay, and that is not the object of my exercise. I want to get my company as lean and hungry as it possibly can be so that it can compete overseas.'

The long and the short of it was that I couldn't get it. I had to accept that incentive cost-plus contract, which of course pleased my people but did not entirely please me. But we had won it! Drunky Lewin, my predecessor in the job, was kind enough to call me to say, 'Congratulations, Ray, I could never have done what you've done.' Basically, it was because I knew how to walk the corridors of power in Whitehall, and had a burning determination to win this one if we were to begin to turn the corner.

The next one up was Alarm. This was a radar-suppression weapon which was designed to go on the Tornado so that it would keep the heads down of the various defending system while Tornado penetrated. Again, the competition was against an American weapon of a similar kind that was already being produced. We also had (as we had had in Martell) in this intelligent weapon, the weapon's ability to determine, in a pre-set mode, which particular order of preference it should go for in competing radar emissions. In order to get the performance, both in range and speed, we needed a completely new rocket motor; the competition for this was fairly severe between Bayern Chemie in Germany and Royal Ordnance in the UK, as well as Aerojet General in the United States. The rocket motor that came closest to the performance required, and to a guarantee of development timescale, was the Royal Ordnance motor, and it was also made clear to me that to select Royal Ordnance to provide the motor would be a benefit to us in competing for this contract, rather than by choosing an American or German motor. I was concerned, however, that the pressure on Royal Ordnance would be too great and the task too difficult, and I was particularly concerned when a friend of mine from Aerojet General, who was retiring, came to see me in my office in London to say that he was bidding farewell to his contacts in industry and as a farewell message to me to tell me that they did not believe at Aerojet General that the motor that was being talked about by Royal Ordnance was capable of production. This to me was extremely worrying. The guy had no particular axe to grind, he was leaving the company, and I therefore asked Hugh Metcalf to come and see me (who was then running Dynamics, I having moved on) to determine whether he thought there was danger in the Royal Ordnance design. Hugh said that he had complete confidence in the ability of Royal Ordnance. Against my better judgement, I therefore allowed the selection of

437

Royal Ordnance to go forward and eventually, after much debate and very nerve-racking trials and tribulations, we won the contract.

Development started, during the course of which British Aerospace bought Royal Ordnance as is explained in another chapter. But we were on a very tight timescale, and as development proceeded I began to see the graph of achievement for the rocket motor rising more steeply every month that passed. Finally we came to the firing trials and although the first, I believe, and perhaps the second were successful, we then started to tun into trouble as the motor was put into more stringent tests. I suggested to Bernard Rosser, who was then running Hatfield and responsible for the programme's overall performance, that we ought to have a second string to our bow by inviting Bayern Chemie (the German company which had a slightly different solution to the problem) to start developing at our cost in parallel as a fall-back situation. As time passed it became clear that while most of the components were working to time and everybody else seemed to be achieving their set task, the motor was becoming critical and the path of achievement was getting steeper. Now I was asking for fortnightly reports and also, of course, informing the Ministry, our customer, that we were having problems. There was no point in trying to hide it but the Ministry, because we were on a fixed price for development and production programme, merely said, 'That's very interesting but it's down to you.' By this time, Air Marshal Harcourt-Smith had taken over from Dougie Lowe as Controller Aircraft.

Finally the day arrived when I could stand it no longer; I called for Rosser to appear before me.

'Let's face it,' I said, 'Bernard, we have failed.'

'No, Sir,' he said, 'we haven't failed. Royal Ordnance have failed.'

'I am sorry,' I said, 'whose name is on the prime contract?'

'Well, ours, British Aerospace.'

'Then we have failed. We have been unable to manage our sub-contractors adequately in order to achieve the programme, and I know what you want me to do. You now want me to go in and try to re-negotiate a contract. It is not like the old days of cost-plus when this thing could be dealt with over a long period of time and nobody would get hurt. Here we are standing to lose a great deal of money, if we are not extremely careful. And to gain any sympathy at all, I need to be absolutely honest with the Ministry of Defence because to attempt to shrug my shoulders and pretend it was not the fault of British Aerospace would have me thrown out of the building, and quite rightly so.' I decided to go and see Peter Levine, the new Head of Defence Procurement, to see whether we could renegotiate the contract because it was becoming apparent to us that Bayern Chemie's solution was looking very good indeed, and likely to be able to solve the problem, although in a slightly longer timescale.

My interview with Peter was along the usual fashion of a polite interchange of general ideas to start with, and then I got round to the subject of saying that we were now in trouble with Alarm and in fact British Aerospace had failed. Peter acknowledged this and said, 'Well, of course, it's a fixed-price contract and of course any extra costs will fall to you. We may also be entitled,' said he, 'to liquidated damages in the event of failure, if we have to go elsewhere and buy an alternative system.' 'If you go against me,' said I, 'I shall merely go against you.' 'But you can't,' he said, 'it's nothing to do with us.' 'On the contrary,' said I. 'At the time this missile contract was signed, you owned Royal Ordnance, and you were responsible for putting forward the proposals that have turned out to be false. Therefore, if you persist in going against me, I shall have no alternative but to go against you to recover all my costs because one of your own companies misled us into believing that it could actually solve this task and must be held responsible for the failure. Furthermore,' I said, 'I have the writ already prepared if you wish to proceed on this matter, and I shall serve it to you now if that would suit you.' There was a pause, and then Peter said, 'Well, perhaps we can think about ways of solving this problem,' 'I am sure,' said I, 'that we can.' And we did – with the Bayern Chemie solution.

As I have said many times before and since, a fixed-price development and production contract is the best and only way to go if the Ministry is to get value for money. The contract has to be placed in a sensible way with sensible conditions on a responsible contractor, but if he fails, for reasons or measures over which the contractor has little or no control, particularly if you are nudging against the limits of scientific and technical knowledge, you have to recognise that endemic in the system is the possibility of failure and therefore you must face up to the resulting consequences. Driving the contractor into bankruptcy does not solve your problem, and certainly doesn't solve his.

One of the weapons which was being talked about at an early stage when I arrived in Dynamics, was ASRAM, the advanced short range air-to-air missile, which was to complement the medium range air-to air missile that was to be produced by the Americans. ASRAM was to be a European missile, produced by a consortium of companies, prime amongst them being Matra in France, BGT in Germany and British Aerospace in the UK. The problem really was that, whereas both Matra and British Aerospace had produced missiles, the Germans had not produced anything other than Sidewinder under a sub-contract from the American manufacturer. So their design and development capability was untried. Nevertheless, there was a burning desire on the part of the Germans, who were seeing themselves as funding one third of this development, that they should be given a very important part to play. It's difficult with a small missile to see how you divide it up: the guidance system and the fuse system are two component parts, and the motor and body another, but the clever bit of course is the detection and guidance system and most of the major companies wanted that particular part of the missile.

The programme had been rumbling along in the way in which these joint venture multi-national programmes tend to do, when I received a call from my opposite number in Matra who said that the French were going to pull out of the programme and he would like to come and explain to me the reasons for this in person. We therefore agreed to meet at a hotel near to Heathrow. When he arrived he told me with great simplicity that the reason they were going to withdraw was because multi-European programmes always took an age to come to fruition; their concern was to achieve the ability to export the missile into world markets, for which there was a great demand to replace Sidewinder, and that the best way of achieving progress and success was to have a single nation programme and this would go ahead faster and be in the marketplace quicker and would scoop the market. I listened to him politely, and said that nevertheless I was very sorry to learn that the French were going to leave the programme because the only way in which European collaboration could work would be through the very long production runs that would be possible by combining the requirements of three, four or five nations as opposed to the inevitable short runs that one nation only could justify. He looked at me for a moment and said, 'I agree, I think it's sad but the fact is we will have our missile developed before you get yours; it will be in service; it will be available for sale and we shall scoop the market.' He then went on as follows: 'Of course, your missile might have a little better fuse, your missile might have a little better guidance, but at the end of the day when you sell to an Arab, poof! what does it matter?' I was shocked. In the first place the missile we were talking about was for the Royal Air Force and the Royal Navy. It was a missile that was designed to be used in the Cold War, at that time at its height, and the thought that we should go for a second rate missile purely so that we could sell it in large number to the Third Nations was to me scandalous. Nevertheless, it is the way that our partners and henceforth competitors saw it, and that is the way they went. It did, however, teach me a lesson about the motivation behind French production of weapons. It would seem that where our Services came first, and exports followed if they were permitted, in their system the weapon was designed for export and the French Services took it whether they liked it or not.

I am reminded of a presentation which was made by the French Air Force on the Force de Frappe to then colleagues in NATO, of which I think at that time they might still have been members. As we sat in the old Admiralty cinema while there was being outlined the way Jaguars were going to be used to drop nuclear weapons as a defence in the Cold War against the Russians, I nudged my companion and said, 'Keep an eye on that German general down there because it's only a matter of time before he realises that the only place they can drop that weapon is in the middle of Germany.' It's great to have what people believe to be an effective force, but you must be prepared for the whole thing to fall apart if somebody really tests it.

36

Up Where We Belong

Soon after the election that brought Margaret Thatcher into power in Downing Street, I was approached by Kenneth Warren, an old friend of mine from industry days when he had worked with Marconi, and asked if I could meet with him. He was then the Parliamentary Secretary to Keith Joseph, who was running the Department of Trade and Industry. Ken said he wanted me to meet a very important man but it would have to be done very quietly and secretly, so I arranged to have lunch with this unnamed person, together with Ken Warren, in a private room at the Stafford Hotel. At the appointed hour Ken duly appeared with the mysterious guest, who turned out to be Adam Butler, who was then Minister of State in the Department of Trade and Industry. After a drink we settled down for lunch and the main purpose of the meeting became apparent.

British Aerospace was still nationalised and was clearly one of the front runners for privatisation. The question I was asked was, 'Who do you think would be most suited to become the Chairman of a privatised British Aerospace?' Of course this was all in confidence, and in order to be helpful I ran through the list of possible contenders. Freddie Page I ruled out on the grounds of age and his impending retirement: Alan Greenwood, the Deputy Chairman, on the same basis. It really narrowed the field considerably.

'Now let us discuss Lygo,' I said. Adam responded, 'No, no, I don't think. . .'

'No,' I said, 'please don't misunderstand me because I am going to rule him out on the basis that he doesn't yet have enough commercial experience. Maybe he would be suitable for the next time round.' This was accepted without comment, and I proceeded, 'The logical man to take over the Chairmanship of British Aerospace is George Jefferson. He is a skilled engineer, understands the business thoroughly, is a good negotiator and wily operator.' This suggestion was greeted in silence. 'What about Tin Pearce?' asked Adam. Tin was a non-executive director, and at that time, Chairman and Chief Executive of the Esso subsidiary in the United Kingdom. 'I really cannot comment,' I replied, 'because as a non-executive director I've only seen him at the occasional Board meeting; he often arrives late because of other commitments and often has to leave early because of other commitments, so I really can't offer an opinion.' The meeting was, however, to set the stage for what was to happen.

We had only just moved into the new headquarters in Stevenage for the combined Dynamics Group, and as a result of this move I relinquished my job as Managing Director of the Hatfield Lostock division and was ensconced in headquarters as Deputy Chairman. Tom Kent, who had been running the other division, was brought in as Deputy Chief Executive. My new office was at the back of the building overlooking the dustbins, as I recall, but it was perfectly adequate and I concentrated my attention on supporting Alex Sanson, the Marketing Director, and the marketeers because I didn't believe that they were getting as much support from the top as they probably should have done.

Soon after moving in, I was visiting Jeff on a routine occasion and he asked me how I liked my office. 'Well,' I said, 'you know, if you like a view of the dustbins it's not a bad office but I'm quite happy.' 'You don't have to worry, Ray,' he said, 'because very shortly you'll be occupying this office.' I looked at him in some surprise. 'How do you mean?' I asked. 'Well,' he said, 'I am going to become the Chairman of British Aerospace and I shall want to you take over the running of the Dynamics Group.' I told him I was very flattered by this and encouraged, but how did he know that he was going to become the Chairman of British Aerospace? 'Because,' said Jeff, 'the Board has decided that I should become the Chairman.' 'But,' said I, 'have you checked with the Permanent Under-Secretaries' Club in Whitehall?' 'How do you mean?' he asked. 'Well,' I said, 'the decision as to who is going to be Chairman of British Aerospace will be largely in the hands of the Permanent Under-Secretaries' Club in Whitehall, who will advise Ministers and Secretaries of State as to who they think the most suitable person would be. What the nationalised Board of British Aerospace thinks about it will have very little to do with it.' Jeff looked at me in some surprise. 'Have you checked any of them out,' I asked, 'to find out how they're likely to react?' 'No,' he said, 'I haven't.' 'Well,' I responded, 'I know all of them by name and, generally speaking, personally, and I'd be happy to go and make a few soundings for you if you like, to see how the land lies.' 'I'd be very grateful if you'd do this,' said Jeff.

I left his office and started down the corridor, thinking about who I would approach first, when there was a patter of feet behind me and Jeff came scurrying after me to say, 'Ray, on second thoughts, I'll approach them myself.' There was nothing really I could say to this, much as I would have liked to have said something, because I thought to myself, and indeed knew, 'You've now blown it, Jeff,' because those chaps will never tell you what they are going to recommend. They will tell you that they think you would be a very good candidate and highly qualified, and give you all the kinds of assurances that you might wish to receive, but that wouldn't affect the way they would advise Secretaries of States or Ministers for one moment. In other words, whereas they might have let drop a hint or two as to the way the wind was blowing if I asked, they would certainly not give any indication except a favourable one (misleading as that may be) to Jeff.

Events showed that I was absolutely right. Tin Pearce was selected to be the Chairman of British Aerospace to take it into privatisation. The outcome as far as I was concerned was pretty nearly the same because Jeff, exasperated by what he saw as an illogical selection, was offered the post of Chairman of British Telecom, which he took – a far larger job than running British Aerospace! Good to his word, however, I took over from him as Chairman and Chief Executive of the Dynamics Group.

A word now about the attitude at that time towards people who came out of the oil industry. By and large, they were all thought to be exceptional businessmen. The development of North Sea oil had been and still was an enormous undertaking but the fact that they were all, for the most part at the time, selling a product in short supply to an avaricious marketplace seems to have bene overlooked. Furthermore, in the case of Esso UK it was a subsidiary of Esso Europe which was in turn a subsidiary of Exxon in the United States. Therefore the knowledge and experience in running a PLC was not something of which Tin Pearce had enormous experience, yet that was the perceived truth: that all oil men must be geniuses in running businesses. Tin having accepted the Chairmanship of British Aerospace then asked me if I would take over and run the Dynamics Group, as Jeff had recommended. I gladly accepted because I liked the Dynamics Group, I liked its products and I believed there was a great future for that organisation; but there was a problem. I pointed out the situation which had prevailed since I joined British Aerospace, i.e. that I attended Board meetings as if I were a Director, but in fact was not a Director because the effect it would have on my Naval pension, was an impediment to my taking the position. Tin said he was sure this could be overcome and indeed I made it clear that it had to be, and that when it had been solved they could call me and I would accept the position.

Time passed; it was becoming clear as it had been before, that it was not going to be easy within the bureaucratic morass of Whitehall, and it wasn't until the very last moment before privatisation, which of course swept all these previous restrictions away, that it was accepted that I could join the Board without losing my Naval pension. The fact remained that as a team neither Tin nor I in particular had experience in running a PLC.

The Government's intention was to sell off 49 per cent of British Aerospace, and this they proceeded to do. Kleinwort's was appointed as broker to British Aerospace for the flotation and we proceeded, however inexperienced the majority of us were in this matter, to go down that route. The executives on the Board now consisted of Freddie Page running the Aircraft Group, me running the Dynamics Group, Eric Rubathon being the deputy to Freddie Page, Tom Kent being my deputy, John Stamper as Technical Director, Peter Fletcher as Strategic Planning Director, and Bernard Friend who had been brought in from Esso, as Finance Director. Brian Cookson was Company Secretary. Peter Fletcher retired almost at the same time that privatisation took place and Tin Pearce invited a number of worthies to join the Board as non-executive directors to join Derek Gladwin, who had been put on the Nationalised Board by the previous Government. These were Harold Hitchcock, deputy Chairman of the Westminster Bank, Sir Jack Wellings, Chairman of the 600 Group, Sir Ken Dunham, Chairman of ICI, and Ken Bevan, Deputy Chairman of Royal Insurance. It was a well-balanced Board, or it should have been, with all the necessary skills to run a successful company ,but as things turned out it wasn't as straightforward as that.

In the way the Board was constituted the real power remained in the hands of the two groups, and Tin Pearce decided to set up a committee under the chairmanship of Ken Bevan to advise on the organisation of the Company for the future. On this committee sat Ivan Yates (who had replaced Freddie Page), John Glasscock (who had replaced Eric Rubathon), Brian Cookson (the Company Secretary) and myself. I suppose the committee sat for about three months deliberating which way we should go and called before it all the Directors and the senior executives of the Company to take evidence. I was surprised when Bernard Friend, the Finance Director, in his evidence said that there was no way in which the headquarters could control the company because the information that they received was at the behest of the Chief Executive and Chairmen of the individual groups and that as a result he had no control over the finances of the company. I found this extraordinary and said so. 'If you are the Finance Director, why don't you control the finances? Whatever information you ask for from Dynamics Group you will receive because it is your right to receive it.' It was clear, however, that the way in which we were organised was not the best way forward, and the committee's eventual recommendation was that the two groups should be reduced in status by not having Chairmen but just Chief Executives, and that a new Managing Director of the Company should be appointed to run the Company as a whole. This position Tin Pearce offered to me and I accepted. The division of responsibility was that I would run the Company and that he would handle external affairs. As a result, I handed over the control of Dynamics Group to Hugh Metcalf and moved myself in with Tin Pearce and Bernard Friend to the one floor we occupied in the old BAC headquarters at 100 Pall Mall, along with Brian Cookson and one or two supporting ancillaries. The main elements of control remained bedded out in Stevenage and Kingston respectively. Having created the post of Managing Director, therefore, one could only manage through the two Chief Executives of the respective groups; it was clear to me that this was something that had to be changed. The trauma of the introduction of a Managing Director was probably bad enough, so the changes that had to be made had to be handled with some care.

At the very early stage of my involvement as managing British Aerospace as a whole and having looked with astonishment and surprise at the aircraft side of the business as it then was, I concluded that there would have to be a massive rationalisation. I therefore went to see the then Secretaries of State of the various departments concerned – Employment, Trade and Industry, Defence and the Scottish Office – to tell them that there would have to be severe rationalisation in British Aerospace and that basically we could not go on manufacturing low-added-value products in high-value sites.

Remember at this time land values were rising steeply and fortunes were being made by land speculators. British Aerospace was sitting on some extremely valuable property, in the shape of Kingston, Weybridge and Hatfield, and had enormous manufacturing facilities in the north of England that could easily absorb the work that was to be done, but the policy of nationalisation had been to spread the work around all the sites so that there was employment for everybody who wanted to be employed. Thus bits of everything were being made all over the place and having set up the manufacturing facilities required it was going to be an expensive business to rationalise them and furthermore, disruptive to programmes that were essential if we were to keep the business running smoothly and profitably.

Although we were now firmly embarked on the Tornado programme, we desperately needed to get ourselves back into the single-seat fighter market, which is the world's biggest defence market. Air Forces all over the world are interested in high-performance,

446

single-seat, interceptor fighters which can go crackling off their runways and satisfy the ego of the Air Forces that wish to use them. There is little logical argument to defend the concept of an interceptor off the deck fighter but nevertheless that is what people want. They also want supersonic speed because that's a fairly macho thing to have, although once you start to load the aeroplane with external stores or a reasonably high G, it's going to go subsonic anyway. That's if it hasn't run out of fuel in the process of going supersonic! The last aeroplane we'd had that filled the bill or part of it, and this a long time before, was the Hunter and now we needed something to replace it, and this had to be the key objective in our military aircraft activity. Collaboration with our European partners had been set by the Tornado programme, so it was logical to see development in that area on the aircraft side. For the civil side, there was already an undertaking to embark on the development of the 146 and I have devoted a separate chapter to the history of this aircraft, but by the time I took over we were committed to it.

We were by now a 20 per cent partner in Airbus Industrie but, shorn of nationalisation, had to rely on Launch Aid in order to match the kind of capability that our European partners enjoyed, since they were all nationalised, and were dealing with Continental 'funny' money. On the missile side there was a distinct threat that we would go American. Sky Flash was an adaptation of the successful Sparrow missile in the United States, but the decision to go for Sea Eagle had stemmed the tide but we had an uphill fight ahead of us to get all the business back firmly into British hands. On the space side we had been made to exist on the back of the European Space Agency which, to be fair, most other European countries were doing, but had lost a lot of ground in the process of becoming more commercial.

I therefore set about preparing the first strategy paper for British Aerospace with my new perspective and majored on the theme that, if and when peace broke out, what were we going to do to fill the loss of the military order book? Diversification out of the aircraft business would be a dangerous course to take; it seemed, therefore, that we should develop the skills that we already possessed and build up our commercial aircraft capability to meet the ever-growing demand for civil aircraft which all the forecasters agreed would occur. My recommended course of action was to develop and strengthen our Dynamics business by going flat out to get work in on British missiles; to develop our commercial aircraft business on the back of our military skills; and on the military side to go flat out for a new interceptor fighter for the year 2000. In addition, I suggested

447

that we should develop the spin-off businesses that we had acquired to the best of our ability.

The Board endorsed this broad strategy and we proceeded to adopt it. It was flawed, however, and I was misled in one essential respect. While we should have had the knowledge to build successful commercial aircraft, in fact we did not. When Hawker Siddeley and BAC had been nationalised, the best people in the commercial aircraft side of BAC based at Weybridge (which had the best stable and success rate in building civil aircraft: the One-Eleven, the Viscount and the Vanguard) left when they saw the centre of activity moving towards Hatfield and the 146. After months and years of delay a decision to launch the 146 had been made. This was essentially a political decision in order to keep Hatfield open, but by this time the skill levels and expertise had fallen to a low level and this could only be made up by bringing in people from the military side of the business. Here was a problem. Military designers had little concept of commercial reality and certainly didn't understand the extreme pressures under which a commercial aircraft would have to operate. We were not talking here about 60 per cent availability, or 70 per cent availability, but 98 per cent availability or more, and it took some time for me to understand that despite all the words that were being used and the statements that were being made, we just didn't have the commercial attitude to solve the problem. Nevertheless, we were to a large extent committed and had to make the best of what was in fact a bad job. It is not a game for the weak-hearted. There is an expression within the industry which runs, 'If you want to make a small fortune out of commercial aircraft, then start with a large one.'

One of the other problems, although a minor one, which I'd inherited was the Jetstream. This was produced up in Prestwick, one of the most depressed factories we'd inherited from Scottish Aviation during nationalisation. The Jetstream 31 which was a re-engined version of an older aeroplane which had been around for some time, was not selling and didn't seem as if it ever would sell. Despite changing the management at Prestwick and putting Brian Thomas in to take charge of it, there didn't seem to me as if there was going to be a future in making that site profitable and I therefore called on the Secretary of State for Scotland to tell him that I intended to close Prestwick.

George Younger protested, of course, that it was the only manufacturing facility for aircraft in Scotland and I said I sympathised with him but I couldn't afford to keep a factory open that was losing money. He countered by saying that we'd had development aid, regional development aid that is to say, and I, having looked at the books said, 'Yes, and I'll give it all back to you, but I'm going to close

Prestwick.' It was a sad day, particularly since Prestwick was in George Younger's constituency, but nevertheless a necessary one and when I got back to Pall Mall I set the wheels in motion for the notice to be given and all the correct procedures to be gone through for closing Prestwick.

Suffice to say, that before those steps could be implemented the efforts of Brian Thomas and his team at Prestwick had transformed the order book and the appearance and morale of the site, and before I knew where I was, I wasn't looking at closure so much as expansion as the order book shot up. The Jetstream 31 happened to hit the deregulated market in the United States at precisely the right moment. FAA rules required a steward to be on an aeroplane with more than nineteen seats, and the Jetstream 31 had nineteen and it also had a stand-up cabin and a loo, and this was just what the emerging commuter business was looking for. So our order book climbed and at one point peak production of the Jetstream 31 reached over forty a year at Prestwick, when my original break-even figure had been twenty four!

Our success in the short term, however, had a very nasty sting in the tail. As a result of intense competition in the commercial aircraft market, Macdonnell Douglas had introduced a system of 'turn-back' – that is to say a customer could sign an agreement with the Company whereby he would take the aircraft and commence making payments in some form of arrangement but at any stage he might decide he didn't want the aircraft and could turn it back to the manufacturer giving 60 days notice. It was a killer for the manufacturer, but once one manufacturer had started to offer this it was difficult for others to avoid offering the same terms if they were to remain competitive. It was to prove almost the undoing of British Aerospace in the much longer term, and long after I had left. One of the points to make at this stage, I think, is that in my experience it is not always the best thing to have a marketing and salesman put in charge of running an organisation. His ability to sell the product will be unquestioned but his commercial judgement in so doing may well be impaired!

37

Airbus Industrie

As a result of the British Government's desire to see anything that was in government hands removed and put into the private sector, a committee was set up (on the urging of the Prime Minister, I suspect) to examine ways in which Airbus Industrie could move into the private sector (which of course BAe was already in). A committee of three wise men was called upon to judge whether this was possible or not, and our representative on this was Jeffrey Sterling, now Lord Sterling.

He and I discussed the possibility and I fear I must have been somewhat negative in my response because I just did not believe that the Germans and the French, in particular at that time, were ever going to countenance a move towards the private sector at this stage in the development of Airbus Industrie. Furthermore, the way in which the accounts were kept made it a perfect vehicle for hidden subsidies. In other words, if for example the ATR-72 (which was a joint Franco-Italian enterprise at that time) was included inside the commercial accounts of Aérospatiale together with Airbus Industrie, I could believe (and so did my colleagues) that the ability to establish where that aircraft's costs were being allocated would be almost impossible to discover. One of the ways in which this is done is by not apportioning the overheads of a particular project to that project but by sweeping it up in the general overheads, whereupon it becomes extremely difficult to discover. It would require something like the National Audit Office to get in there to actually find out what was going on, and I had absolutely no doubt that the French would not permit this.

Several meetings were held over a period of some weeks to see whether there was any possibility of getting a better organisation. All that Airbus Industrie knew were the partners' prices. It had no means of knowing what their costs were, so it could never determine which was the most efficient of its partners or what profits that particular partner was making. So when all the prices were added together they almost inevitably came to a price larger than the market would bear, in which case Airbus Industrie had then to apply a blanket reduction across the board to get the aircraft to a price at which it could sell.

The major players in Airbus Industrie: me, MBB Aerospatiale, CASA

This didn't mean making profits because that was not the object of a *groupement industriel économique* (GIE).

I remember in particular one dinner party, in Paris I believe, with our partners present. I was sitting next to my French opposite number and in the end I said quite bluntly, 'Why can't we agree to open up our books to Airbus Industrie so they can see what our cost base is, because everybody agrees that until we know what the cost base of the partners is, we cannot begin to move towards a truly commercial proposition.' He said, 'I agree with that, but this is not possible.' 'Why?' I enquired. 'Because', he said, 'the commercial and military business of our company is intricately involved and I don't see how they could be separated.' 'But I've separated it,' I said, 'I've separated the commercial activities from our military activity and I can open the books of our commercial activity tomorrow, and I'm sure that given an opportunity to do so you could do the same.' He looked at me quietly for a moment and then he said, 'But there would be no point in this.' 'Why would there be no point in it?' I asked. There was a long pause as he looked at me fairly closely, and you could almost see the

451

balloon coming out of his head in which was engraved 'perfide Albion' and then he said,' Because everybody would have two sets of books!' In my simple English way, that never occurred to me! The only thing I said, I think, at the time was, 'Well, it's a jolly good job the Italians aren't part of this group or we'd have three sets of books!'

It was not a waste of time because it revealed, I hope, to people who had not believed this to be the case before, that the attitude of our then partners in Airbus at that time was totally opposed to anything that we wished to do and we were considered to be extremely naive, rash and I suspect 'American' for taking the route we had taken. It has taken fifteen years to get Airbus Industrie to a point where it is prepared to take the plunge but even now it is difficult to see, with the enormous investments that governments have made, how politics can be kept out of the business so that it can be run as a truly commercial enterprise. Work was allocated on the basis of the shareholding. It will be interesting to see how this develops and to what extent it will be possible for the new Chief Executive of the organisation running it to actually move in the most cost-effective way when the vested interests of countries, nationalities, flags and governments are all involved.

The decision for British Aerospace to join, or I should say rejoin, the Airbus Industrie Partnership was taken by the outgoing Labour Government during the period of British Aerospace's nationalisation. The decision basically was to decide whether to go with Airbus Industrie as a full partner once again, or to make some arrangement with Boeing that would have effectively put British Aerospace in the position of a subcontractor.

I believe that the origin of Airbus Industrie was a British concept of what could be done to spread the enormous financial load required to launch a major commercial aircraft. Having launched the idea, however, the UK withdrew, apparently going through one of those funding crises that countries experience, when they have no long-term strategic plan. Unlike the rest of Europe, France did have a long-term strategic industrial plan, part of which was to develop its aerospace industry, and it has been remarkably successful in achieving its objective. The British having abandoned the idea, the French then continued the partnership with the Germans and brought the Spanish in for a minor shareholding. When the British decided to return there was not, of course, the large share that might otherwise have been available which would have given us equal status to the French and Germans, and we were accommodated to the extent of 20 per cent of the total shareholding.

The Board, under the chairmanship of Lord Beswick and with the strong preference of Sir Freddie Page who was running the Aircraft

452

Group, took the decision that we should rejoin Airbus Industrie, but unfortunately the terms and conditions that were negotiated were not done in the light of the future privatisation of the company. Had that been the case, or had British Aerospace then been privatised, certain undertakings and safeguards would have been sought from the Government that were not deemed necessary to be given to a nationalised company. In short, whereas a nationalised company could expect to receive government backing for a partnership arrangement that had a large political dimension, it was by no means certain that a private company could expect the same advantage (even though we had the concept of Launch Aid, which had been designed soon after the war to provide the long-term funding that is absolutely essential for the development of major aircraft programmes). Quite simply, without something like a 20-year finance plan at interest rates that are acceptable in the competitive market of aerospace, then it was just not possible to have private companies invest their money successfully in new long-range programmes; the cash impairment curve, which is horrific in the early years, would just not be sustainable.

As it was, no guarantees of government support were included in the agreement but the French having been bitten once by the British withdrawal, quite rightly, insisted on terms which would make it very difficult for any company to leave the consortium without carrying all the costs of its continued membership that might fall upon it. This was a precedent set by Concorde where, again, the British decided to withdraw, only to discover that the agreement with the French meant that if either partner withdrew from the programme they would have to continue to discharge responsibilities they had previously accepted without the benefits of partnership until the programme ended. I believe this clause was introduced by the British in the event that the French decided to withdraw!

The first major aircraft that Airbus Industrie embarked upon was the A300. There had at the beginning been considerable scepticism about the ability of a loose industrial arrangement as was envisaged in French law, a GIE, to be able to come up with anything other than a clunker – in other words, a horse designed by a committee. To the astonishment of the Americans, and to a lot of other people as well, this proved not to be the case, and the A300 started a brand of products that were destined to become world-beaters.

The British participation in this aircraft, after the withdrawal of the British Government from the programme, had been vested in Hawker Siddeley which had continued to work under a subcontract to Airbus Industrie. It had been allocated work on the design and production of the wings and was well advanced with the task. Thus, when the new

Addressing employees of Airbus Industrie at Toulouse

partnership was established, the precedent, if you like, of British Aerospace producing the wings was established. The final assembly plant at Toulouse had already been created by Aérospatiale on French territory. The Germans were given the task of producing largely the fuselage, which is not a particularly exciting part of the aircraft; by default, therefore, the British had managed to get the really clever aerodynamic part, the design of the wings, but did not have the advantages that final assembly and the manufacture of the front of the aeroplane gave to the French.

The partners who built a particular part of an aircraft were responsible for subcontracting the various pieces that were required for the part they were manufacturing, in our case largely the undercarriage, some hydraulics, electrical activations for the operation of flaps and undercarriage, but nothing very spectacular such as the French could command by being the manufacturer of the front end where the bulk of the electronics and avionics equipment was to be installed. Thus, in bringing British Aerospace into the partnership at 20 per cent, the safeguarding of the electronics and avionics industry in the United Kingdom was really left to market forces. This is all well and good if you have the capital to make the long-term investment, but it placed British companies at a disadvantage compared with their continental partners who, generally speaking, were nationalised companies with funding the like of which we would never see.

The manufacture of wings was eventually to be based at Bristol but under the policy that was then adopted by the company, and in particular the Aircraft Group, work was allocated around the company to fill the facilities available, rather than looking at concentrating work into the most economic facilities and thus reducing the spread of overheads and capital employed. This was to produce enormous problems after the company was privatised.

Airbus Industrie was organised on a typical pattern of the French GIE, which literally means that it is the bringing together of a group of companies to perform a certain function and the administration, which is vested in this case in Airbus Industrie itself, has no control over the partners' costs; indeed it was not aware of the partners' costs! The programmes were launched on the basis of marketing and technological assessments, then the work was divided up between the partners in what was known as the 'Liars Club'. This consisted of officials from various companies meeting together to decide what share of the work they were going to get in order to match their shareholding in the enterprise, and then they would submit the prices that they intended to charge to Airbus Industrie, who would then attempt to negotiate those prices down if they thought them unreasonable, but they had no lever with which to do this because they were not aware of the partners' costs – and could not place the work elsewhere. As a result of our rejoining somewhat late, our initial share of manufacturing work was short of the 20 per cent that we were entitled to under our shareholding and it was the long-term plan to adjust this by an increase in work share for the UK on subsequent models to compensate for this.

Airbus Industrie operated from the top under a Supervisory Board which consisted of the President of Airbus Industrie, his Technical Director, (not his Financial Director), and the Presidents (or Chairmen in our case) or Managing Directors of the partners. When I first became involved, Tin Pearce was our primary representative with Air Chief Marshall Peter Fletcher, a previous director of Hawker Siddeley, continuing the Hawker Siddeley connection by being on the Supervisory Board. As British Aerospace evolved then the membership changed to represent the most senior figure in the Commercial Aircraft enterprise to be alongside the Chairman; for a while this was John

Glasscock. The other members of the Supervisory Board had been with their companies for some considerable time and were basically aerospace people. This, of course, was not true of our Chairman and it was a widely felt view within Aerospace that it would have been better if someone more senior from the aerospace side, particularly the aircraft side, could have been our representative. However, the Aircraft Group was much more concerned with its military activities than its commercial ones, and the commercial aviation business was a bit of a Cinderella at that time.

The first major new programme that we faced under privatisation after the launch of the A300 was the A320. The A310 had just managed to be agreed with the previous administration, but the A320 required us to invest an enormous sum of money over many years in order to participate in the 20 per cent to which we were 'entitled'. To have borne the entire cost of the programme, which we reckoned was going to cost something in the region of £400 – 500 million of investment by the company in order to get it off the ground, would have produced a cash impairment curve which would have been intolerable; it would, in fact, have bankrupted the Company!

We therefore sought Launch Aid. There has been much talk, and there still is, about operating on a level playing field in Europe; I am bound to say that I never saw one in my time and I suspect it is still not there. It was clear that our partners were going to get 100 per cent of all the money they required. For France it was part of their industrial strategy to build up their aerospace industry, so there was no question about not doing it; Airbus Industrie was perceived in France as a French invention. The Germans were there because they also wanted to build up their aircraft industry again, they were nationalised, and they wanted to be seen to be a good partner and were prepared to go ahead. And here were the British, the only PLC, whingeing about finding the money at commercial rates. It was just impossible, and so we had to make Launch Aid work. We went through endless presentations to the Department of Trade and Industry in order to try to make a case, and we examined our own future with great care to think to what minimum level of funding we could accept from the Government in order to participate in this programme.

By this time we had become the recognised wing manufacturers of the Airbus consortium, and although I had argued earlier, from my position in Dynamics, for us to bid for final assembly of the A320 at Bristol, my colleagues on the Board did not believe that would stand any chance whatsoever. Here I believe the Board made a mistake. I argued forcibly at the time that it was for Governments to decide whether they wished to fund a particular activity, since they were going to have to foot half the bill, not the Board of British Aerospace. We could say we wanted to have final assembly, and if we were told we couldn't have it, that was a decision that the Government had taken but we should not take that decision for them. However, I was not then running British Aerospace and my arguments were not sufficient to carry the day. You can argue, and I often do, that the wings are the clever bits of a commercial aircraft and that if you look out of the aeroplanes as you fly in them today you will find that as the carrying capacity gets bigger, the wings seem to get smaller! This is because of the advances in aerodynamics that have been made in wing design.

Bernard Friend and I believed that we would need at least £250 million of Launch Aid if we were to stand a chance of coming out of this thing without difficulty, but Norman Tebbitt at the Department of Trade and Industry was not prepared to agree more than about £220 million, leaving us some £30 million short. In the end we were gearing ourselves up to go ahead at £220 million when I had a private meeting with Norman Tebbitt. I pointed out to him that at the same time we were talking about entering the A320 programme, we were coming to the crunch on a decision whether to proceed with the advanced turbo-prop that was the successor to the 748, which was in production at Woodford and Chadderton, or to terminate that programme. 'If', I said, 'we terminate that programme I shall have to close Woodford and possibly Chadderton, and there will be a massive loss of employment. It would be most unfortunate', I continued, 'if we were to make this statement after you'd stood up in the House and said the Government was prepared to give us £220 million worth of Launch Aid, and I then said, 'Thank you very much, but as a result of that we'll have to cancel the advanced turboprop.' Norman saw the force of this argument and managed to persuade his Cabinet colleagues to go to £250 million.

Therefore a presentation was made to the Cabinet, with the Prime Minister in the Chair, and I missed one of the best opportunities I've ever had of saying something which I really believed. Towards the end of my presentation, the Prime Minister said to me, 'Are you sure that this project will make money?'

'I am sure it will make money for you, Prime Minister,' I said, 'and I hope that it will make money for us too.'

'Because,' she said, 'Sir Raymond, I do not want another Concorde.' It flashed through my mind at that moment the best possible riposte.

'Prime Minister, there are only two things in this country to which people look up. You are one, Prime Minister, and Concorde is the other.' I didn't say it; the moment passed, and I have lived to regret that

Presenting the case for launch aid

I never had the moment's courage to make this statement. It was of course true. One of the great tragedies of the British is that they seem somehow determined to set themselves down when they have something to be proud of. Concorde was a magnificent achievement; it is our equivalent to the Space probe and the men on the moon, and yet it never got, it seems to me, the credit it deserved because it was looked at in a narrow commercial sense which it could never have hoped to fulfil. It was a massive and extraordinary achievement, and still is. To think that that aeroplane, old as it now is, accumulating daily more super-sonic hours than the rest of the world's Air Forces all put together is indeed an astonishing achievement. We got the Launch Aid.

After the successful launch of the A320, time moved on and the next programmes would be the development of an A330 and 340. The A330 would be a direct competitor to the MD11 being actively consid-ered by Macdonnell Douglas. The 340 was to be a four engined aircraft of even longer range.

The prospect of asking for even more launch aid for the 330

programme, and the inevitable perils that would arise from competing with both Boeing and Macdonnell Douglas caused me some sleepless nights. In the end, and without any kind of notice to anybody, I went over to the United States to talk to Macdonnell Douglas. I had a very convivial meeting with both the Macdonnell brothers. My suggestion was that we should take the fuselage of the MD11 and put the newly designed wings for the A330 on it and thus we would share the total cost of development. I had asked our designers whether this could be achieved and they said they thought that could be a possibility. During discussion, however, the problem that was going to arise became very obvious. The Airbus family of aircraft had a completely newly designed cockpit which was far in advance of anything that was then in the market place. If the two designs had been put together, we would have insisted that the Airbus design would have to be the one that went into this combined aircraft. If this had happened of course, it would have meant that all the existing Macdonnell Douglas aircraft would have been obsolescent in terms of front end design. There was of course another, and perhaps even more important, problem – how could Macdonnell Douglas as a PLC become involved in an organisation that was a G.I.E. I believed that this could be overcome, but I think the major problem was the powerful drive on the part of their head of commercial aircraft to be seen to be going it alone. Not always the best way to satisfy your shareholders interests, as subsequent events confirmed.

At the end of the meeting I remember Sandy Macdonald saying to his brother, 'Ray has made a profound statement.' I am bound to say this came as somewhat of a shock to me but nevertheless I listened. 'Ray has said, unfortunately this thing will be resolved within the market place.' It was.

Most of these activities had been at my instigation and, as a result, I was not entirely persona grata with Airbus Industrie. On the other hand, I knew that if I had asked Airbus Industrie to have a look at this, it would have been turned down out of hand. I felt it was something I had to do to protect the interests of our shareholders. But alas, it came to nothing. The A330 went ahead, and a splendid aircraft it has turned out to be and there is no MD11 to compete with it and, sad to say, no more Macdonnell Douglas either.

It was becoming clear to me that if I wanted to effect the kind of changes that would be necessary to enable British Aerospace to survive, then I didn't have much time in which to do it. There are two ways of effecting change in any organisation: one is by persuasion and explanation, a somewhat lengthy performance whereby you may be overtaken by the events you are trying to forestall. The other method is by the judicious application of gun powder; here results are instantaneous, but you are left to clean up the mess. I decided that the only course for me was to use gun powder but to prepare people for it by a series of strategic reviews, where we gathered all the heads of the various sections together. I remember putting up a diagram in which I depicted the current organisation with the two Group Chief Executives, and an alternative one in which we went to a functional organisation at the headquarters with power devolved to the individuals who were running component parts of the company: Commercial aircraft, Military aircraft, Dynamics, Space, Communications and Miscellaneous divisions. I set about persuading the two Chief Executives that this was the right way to go and that their roles in a functional capacity, one as Head of Engineering and the other as Head of Operations, would give them the necessary status that they required and bind together a more cohesive management team. I don't know that they were convinced, but they accepted it and then to give this the Good Housekeeping seal of approval McKinsey was asked to come in and conduct a review of the organisation but I was careful to tell them before they started what my solution would be.

The task of turning an organisation with a cost-plus mentality, that had been on the receiving end of government support and contracts for most of its existence, into a profit-oriented commercial one was a steep task. To put profit upfront was not too difficult. On taking over the role of Managing Director of the whole company, I once again employed the tactics that I had used when I ran the Dynamics Group, of having every one fall in in front of me to receive a simple message: that we would together make this the best and biggest and most successful aircraft company in Europe. I asked them simple questions. What are we in business to make? No, it is not aeroplanes or missiles or spacecraft I would answer: it is money, it is profit, it is dividends for our shareholders and, said I on every occasion, if there is any man or woman here who doesn't believe that that is what we're in business for, then leave now. If we can make money by making those things that we all believe we know how to make, then so be it. If we can't, then we'd better think of something else we should do. I enjoyed it; I believe the people did. They'd never had direct communication from the top of the company in such a fashion before and it was interesting to see the different ways in which the various sites handled the situation. I well remember at Warton the thousands in the vast assembly hall when I addressed them from the balcony, a bit like Mussolini. Afterwards I would talk to the union representatives but I had in fact done what managers should do, communicated my message directly to

Addressing the troops at Warton

all the people and not through the unions. It is not the job of unions to conduct management messages, that is not their function and management which has allowed this to happen has stood into danger.

At the end I remember going home and saying to Pepper one evening, 'I have, for the first time in my life, to face a terrible moral dilemma.' She looked at me curiously; could it be that I was about to reveal some terrible secret? 'What is it?' she asked. 'I am telling all the people I speak to', I said, 'that if they follow me and we work together as a team, I shall make them into the best aerospace company in Europe.' 'Well,' she said, 'what's the problem?' 'What I am not telling them', said I, 'is that in the process half of them will have to go.' With her usual pragmatic and direct approach, she said, 'What's the alternative?' 'They'll all go,' I said, 'and so shall I.' 'Then you don't have a

461

Same again, Stevenage

moral dilemma,' she said, 'You just have to get on with it.' But getting on with it was not going to be easy. We were in a period of expansion; the order books were rising, our marketing successes were consider- able, and in order to satisfy our customers we had to keep the produc- tion lines flowing. Therefore, to shut down whole lines for the period of time it would take to move to another location was a massive undertaking, and extremely costly. In addition, costly industrial action would have been totally counter-productive. Best to wait for a natural break in the production run, and to have prepared yourself by making an investment in an alternative source. Thus it was that a second line for the 146 was started at Woodford on the back of the very large order that we received from TNT for what we called 'Quiet Trader'. But getting people to say they understood the need to make profit was one thing, making the company into a genuine commercial entity was another; I believed that this could only be done by turning the various

462

activities into profit centres, with the management boards responsible directly for their own profit and loss, and accountable to headquarters for the same.

I started this with Royal Ordnance after we had acquired it; it worked extremely well, and I continued to move in that direction, but time was running out for me. I was approaching 65; although I had renegotiated my contract when Roland Smith came in as Chairman, and I was passed over for the job, I knew that there was a body of opinion at Board level that would be anxious to see me depart as soon after my sixty-fifth birthday as they reasonably could contrive. To get things done one had to act in a fairly autocratic way, and one of the things that I did was to bring all the power to the centre. I made it impossible for anyone to actually do anything under the old system unless it had my approval, and I believe many people thought that power had gone to my head, and that I intended to keep it that way. What I had decided was that the quickest way to apply the gun powder was to bring power to myself, restructure, and give that power back again to the new organisation; that is what I did, but in the process one didn't make as many friends as one would have liked.

The danger in all these operations is that people will tell you they understand because they know there's not much point in saying they don't, but in fact they don't understand.

I remember very well, in my early days at Dynamics when I called together all of what were then called 'the management club' after about three months as Managing Director, and I told them that I had asked them to do certain things, to stir up the organisation and to set about their work with a sense of purpose and urgency which I had thought was lacking, and I told them that I hadn't seen much of this happening. The senior guy had the courage to stand up and say, 'Sir Raymond, we understand what you want us to do; we know it is the right thing to do; I have to tell you we don't know how to do it.' The problem really was that very few of them, if any, had received any formal management training, and certainly none in leadership. So it was an uphill struggle but the order books were booming. The 146, despite all its problems, was beginning to turn the corner. The Experimental Aircraft had been launched and had flown and, although the single-seat Hawk was not there, Farnborough 1987 was for me the height of our success. Our public relations department had come up with the idea of using the music of 'Chariots of Fire' at the Farnborough Air Show to herald our own aircraft, and we had persuaded the SBAC to let us have a parade of British Aerospace aeroplanes, all together down the runway, and then the flying display. It was a tremendously emotional event. Unfortunately the single seat Hawk wasn't there, but everything else was and it was a great tribute to all of the people in British Aerospace and a great fillip to all of them to see the parade and hear the stirring music of Chariots of Fire, and to have the display culminating with the spectacular Harrier doing something that only the Harrier had ever been successful in doing – vertical take-off and landings, and safe transitions. When I asked Tin Pearce to go out on the balcony and acknowledge the salute as the Sea harrier bowed, I felt immensely proud of all that we had achieved in a relatively short space of time. It looked to me as if it was beginning to work. Westland was behind us, but Rover and Arlington lay ahead.

38

Takeovers, Mergers and Acquisitions

During the period of nationalisation the company had been particularly constrained by a clause in the act which required that we only operated in those areas in which we were already engaged. In other words, we could not enter into adjacent areas of our business, even if we wanted to, but were restricted to those things which we were already engaged in doing. This is what I called 'the steam engine syndrome'. In effect, it meant that when what you were making went out of fashion you weren't entitled to make anything else; this was ridiculous and one, but not the major, driving force to get us out of nationalisation and into the private sector. The minute we became part of the private sector we would be able to do our own thing and bid for whatever came along, and be bid for; the former we looked forward to with considerable anticipation.

The first business that became available and which was in an area where we had expertise – an overriding factor for acquisitions – was Sperry Gyroscope UK. Sperry had decided to divest itself of its UK operation and had placed it on the market to the highest bidder. Sperry at that time was, for the most part, engaged in the manufacture of mines and mine-hunting equipment. It also had its traditional gyroscope business but this had become small during the post-war period; most of the work was now concerned with advanced underwater mining systems, a far cry from those spiked objects which we all familiarly associate with mines.

It was Ministry of Defence policy, as a result of the Rayner Review, to stream contractors into various areas of expertise, and one was not allowed to bid outside those chosen areas. For example, we were allowed to bid for military work within the aircraft framework – missiles, space and the associated businesses in which we were involved and had been nominated – but we were not, and had been removed from the list of contractors who were qualified, to bid for sonars, anti-submarine systems and mine warfare systems. This was a shame, because the Stevenage division of British Aerospace had been responsible for the development and fit of a successful sonar for conventional submarines but on complete of that contract, as a result of the Rayner

Review, the company had been removed from the bidders' list. Of course, we were not alone in this; other companies were not allowed to bid in areas in which we were regarded as having expertise, and the Rayner Review recommended this because it concluded that having every company in the aerospace industry bidding for everything was a waste of scientific resources and tied up too many people pursuing too small an objective (in monetary terms, that is). To acquire Sperry, therefore, meant that we would automatically enter the underwater business, because as long as we kept Sperry as a separate entity, wholly owned by British Aerospace, it would be able to bid for underwater programmes in the mine warfare field, along with Marconi.

The question of whether we should bid was raised first to me by Hugh Metcalf at one of the Dynamics Group meetings. I therefore raised the issue at a Board meeting, where it was debated by my colleagues. In the end, somewhat reluctantly, Tin Pearce said, 'Well, you can go ahead and bid for it.' This was accompanied by a subsequent remark to the effect that takeover bids very rarely ever worked out in practice. History, I am sure, has proven him right on this point, but it was hardly encouraging for me. Here I was, just out of the woods, looking at this strange, new, private-enterprise world (which, of course, I had been enthusiastically in favour of), but I had very little idea of how to go about this particular activity!

I collected Alan Smith, the Finance Director of Dynamics, and together we went to London to meet the owners of Sperry who had come over from the United States and were being advised by their own merchant bankers. En route we concocted something like fourteen questions that we wished to have answered to clear our minds about the possibility of a bid. At this stage we had not involved Kleinwort Benson, our nominated merchant bank advisers, or Hoare Govett, the stockbrokers for British Aerospace at that time, because this was merely an exploratory meeting. Nevertheless, it was something completely new to me and on arrival at some office premises in London, the two of us were finally ushered into a room in which there was a longish table with a rather splendidly groomed merchant banker sitting at one end and a bunch of characters on the other side of the table. These were the Sperry owners and in the middle was the gentleman who had come from the States to make the deal. On entering the room and viewing this scene my sense of the ridiculous overwhelmed me once again and I said, 'What is this, an adoption society?' I could very well have said, 'I refuse to say when I last saw my father,' because the set-up was very reminiscent of that famous painting. I don't think my light-hearted approach to this found tremendous favour at the time and probably somewhat confused the sellers. However we proceeded to go through the questions we had raised, one at a time, and when we got to about question number eight the well-groomed financial adviser to Sperry interjected, 'My client has to leave by such and such a time to catch a plane back to the States so I do hope you're coming to the end of your questions.' To which I replied very abruptly, 'He's selling, I'm buying, I'll ask the questions.' It really slightly irritated me to believe that we were expected to pay several millions of pounds – tens of millions as it turned out – for something without the preliminary questions having been thoroughly examined. It was also my first experience with merchant banks – I was not impressed.

The meeting proceeded to the end and, satisfied as to the questions we had asked, we returned to British Aerospace to digest the information and discuss matters now with our lawyers, bankers and stockbrokers. It was clear that the competition was going to be fairly extensive and in the end, of course, it became a question of how much we were prepared to pay. Here I had another shock – the first one having been the kind of upstage attitude of the merchant bank advisers of the opposition. This was that no one, it seemed to me, was prepared to give me any indication of the price we should pay! No figure was mentioned, no matter how much I probed our advisers, and this rather undermined my confidence in them. It was very clear that I was on my own; I was going to be held responsible, and I would have to do it. So of course we did it. We were given a bracket of figures and I picked one that I thought was not too much, not too little and, like the three bears' porridge, just right, and that was the offer we made. It must have turned out to be the best because we were informed that Sperry was prepared to discuss our offer in detail. There were of course, the usual questions about pension rights and transfer of terms and conditions of service and so on, but in the end we had a final meeting. It was fairly late at night when the issue of the value of the pension contributions arose – whether the pension fund was properly funded or not – and I seem to recall that we required a concession of some kind, not a great deal, in order to consummate the deal. To my surprise my American opposite number said that he would have to phone New York and get clearance from the lawyers – it was a new experience for me to see how American business is lawyer-driven. Whereas I would have been empowered within broad authority to have negotiated all the terms, together with my legal adviser (and if he had not been present I would have pressed ahead anyway), it was clear that my American opposite number was not in a position to do that. Finally the deal was done and we acquired Sperry.

Now our misfortunes really began, although it was some time before

467

it became clear how serious they were. I have already mentioned the cost-plus attitude of British Aerospace that I found on arrival, the attitudes towards competition which were fairly non-existent, and the lack of an entrepreneurial, aggressive attitude towards bidding – in other words, a good market-driven attitude. The acquisition of Sperry produced a management that was very much in the same traditions of British Aerospace, if not worse, and my mistake was in leaving that management intact in order to run the business, looking at the profit forecast and believing that it would be all right as long as the work that was planned to come to them actually came to fruition.

There was another major contract within Sperry that we inherited at the same time, a container-examination system. The problem of smuggling arms and drugs had become a major issue, and Sperry had proposed a very complex and expensive system of examining containers that passed through an examination system that had to be specially built and which it was claimed would detect drugs and munitions. The first of these contracts had been let to the United Arab Emirates in Abu Dhabi, and a very large fixed-price contract it was. It transpired that the contracts were drawn in such a way that it guaranteed to find *all* drugs and *all* munitions that were secreted in these containers. You can imagine that such a guarantee was almost impossible to meet, and the tests that the customer eventually asked us to carry out involved looking for ounces of detectable material and the odd gun hidden in very difficult places, rather than the kind of large-scale smuggling activities that the system was actually designed to detect. Thus it was that the only trials carried out were of such minuscule detectable quantities that it was almost certain that the system would fail, and it eventually became clear that we had acquired a contract that was not deliverable. To make matters worse, no sooner had we bought Sperry Gyroscope than the Ministry of Defence changed its procurement process and said that it was now possible for everyone to bid for everything! So the exclusivity that we thought we had acquired by buying Sperry, in accordance with the Rayner guidelines, were swept away overnight.

To make matters worse, mine warfare had never been top of the pops in any Naval activity. I remember entertaining the United States Navy Defence Committee on one of their visits to the UK and at the end of a breakfast meeting the Chairman asked me what I thought was the best way, the most cost-effective way, of defeating the Russian fleet? I said that the most cost-effective way of defeating the Russians would be to look at their geographical situation and mine the buggers in. They looked at me in some surprise. I pointed out that their access to the sea was limited and very mineable. If we were to make a reasonable investment in mine warfare and in mining, and in the new guided mine systems, then we could ensure that they never got out of harbour and therefore ceased to become a threat. Our mines would be just as effective against their nuclear submarines as they would be against their surface ships.

'Why then,' asked the Chairman of the Armed Forces Services Committee, 'why, Sir Raymond, have we not made any investment in mine warfare?'

'Because,' said I, 'you cannot give a cocktail party on a mine!' This brought the house down and I used that expression many times afterwards to illustrate how difficult it was for mine warfare to become sexy; it was dirty, it was somewhat dangerous but it was an extremely effective way of dealing with an opponent, particularly one such as the Russians. Not nearly as glamorous as destroyers, frigates or aircraft.

It never came to the top of the agenda, and the many programmes that we had to develop very clever mining systems were never funded while I was with British Aerospace. So Sperry, for a combination of reasons, turned out as Tin Pearce had forecast, a not very good acquisition. Fortunately, we acquired with it a site at Bracknell, in the heart of 'Silicon Valley', that was extremely valuable and when we were able to finally close it down and dispose of it, the actual price we got for the land and buildings squared the books. We didn't have to show a loss that might otherwise have occurred, as we had transferred the work to other parts of British Aerospace because the business itself in Bracknell was just not capable of sustaining itself any longer. So much for our first acquisition and my baptism of fire.

At the time of the privatisation of British Aerospace the statement made in the House of Commons by Norman Tebbitt, who was then Secretary of State for Trade and Industry, was that it was 'the Government's present intention' that they should retain the 49 per cent of the shares that remained for sale. There was no time limit given to this 'undertaking', and it was a lesson to me, because it became obvious that a 'present intention' can disappear as soon as the statement is made! I became sarcastic in my reference to present intentions thereafter, and still am, because arriving one morning in Pall Mall, as, usual very early, having had my swim at the RAC just down the road, Tin Pearce appeared, also a fairly early arriver, and asked me to go round and see him, saying that Peter Laister had come in to see him. Peter Laister was then Chief Executive of Thorn EMI. Thorn EMI had an interesting piece of military business, mainly concerned with fuses and electronic devices of a fairly sophisticated nature, and he had come round to say that he had approached the Secretary of State, Norman Tebbitt, to see whether Thorn EMI could buy the remaining shares in British Aerospace and had been told that there would be no objection to this!

Looking back on it, it is surprising to see that it was agreed so readily when competition and the need for having an open bid was later to become the rule or the road. I was just as taken aback as was Tin, but I was due to go off on a visit overseas and as we debated this I said, 'Well, I had better go and see Peter Laister and see what he has to say because if I'm off in a few days' time I need to close with this issue as soon as possible to see whether I think it is feasible.'

My concern in all these takeovers, mergers or acquisitions was quite simply to determine whether the structure of the combined operation was workable; in other words, if the two were put together was it capable of being run as a central organisation or did it have to remain devolved, or how was it going to be organised so that it could be integrated and work profitably?

The question of whether it would happen was a different matter – one for the Board as a whole, and centering on price. I therefore went round to see Peter Laister at his offices in Thorn EMI, where it transpired that Peter had worked previously for Tin Pearce when Tin was running Esso. It was therefore an interesting reversal of roles to think that Peter Laister would acquire a major shareholding in British Aerospace through Thorn EMI and, of course, would expect to become Chairman of the combined companies (certainly Chairman of British Aerospace), thus dispossessing Tin Pearce who had previously been his boss! The subtlety of all this was not my main focus of attention, but in the discussions with Peter Laister it transpired that this opportunity to reverse roles was one he did not find entirely disagreeable.

What Peter Laister effectively said was that when the two things were put together and he became Chairman he could see no proper role for Tin Pearce, apart from, perhaps, as Deputy Chairman, if he would accept this role, but that he would require me to run both parts of the business. I was both surprised and, I suppose, slightly flattered by this approach and went back to Pall Mall to report to Tin Pearce. Looking back, I suppose my mistake was to have been quite so honest. I told him I hadn't realised that Peter Laister had worked for him in Esso. Tin confirmed this and, in his quiet and somewhat deprecating way, made it fairly clear to me that he, in turn, didn't have a particularly high regard for Peter Laister whom he thought to be a bit of a fly-by-night. I then informed him that his intentions, it would seem to me, were quite obvious, that he would wish to become Chairman of the combined group and had asked me whether I was prepared to become the Chief Executive. I don't think this went down extremely well with Tin, but nevertheless it was the truth and it was the exact truth.

470

Tin, Bernard and I at the AGM

I then proposed that we should have some meetings with the members of the defence part of Thorn EMI and its Board to see what their total ambitions and capabilities might be. The first meeting took place in Thorn EMI's offices and I had with me both Ivan Yates and Hugh Metcalf, who respectively ran the two groups in British Aerospace – Aircraft and Dynamics – and quizzed them on what we thought would be their capabilities and attitudes in any combined operation. I am bound to say that none of us were particularly impressed. It was quite clear that this was an opportunistic move on their part (later I was to defend such an attitude in our acquisition of Rover, but that is another matter!). More importantly, the calibre of management and their capability did not strike me as being particularly high and I just was not impressed with the quality of the Board. I also thought that Peter's own attitude to it was rather peripheral, shall I say, not central, and it seemed clear that this was, for him, a stepping stone to bigger and better things.

It was my first experience with this wheeler-dealer type of approach and I suppose that, because it was so foreign to me, I didn't really realise the full import of it. It was to be an event and an attitude of mind, that I was to see in my subsequent career many times. We had several meetings and discussions with their Board at this time, when the value of British Aerospace shares, which had been floated at 150p, were sitting just a little over that figure, which valued the company fairly low. It would then have been a fairly cheap acquisition on the part of Thorn EMI, particularly if they used some of their paper which was very highly rated at the time. The Board of British Aerospace was not particularly enamoured of this prospect and indeed, was hostile to it, but Tin proceeded to deal with the matter in the same way that he dealt with most things – that is to say, he appeared not to deal with it. In other words, he pursued a policy of almost benign neglect. His line was that, since we were coming up to an AGM and as a result were in the 'closed' period, it would be very difficult to reveal any of the information on our future profitability, which Thorn required, without breaching confidentiality. Nothing could therefore be done until we had got the AGM out of the way, and then he would be prepared to discuss the matter further, along with our advisers, Kleinwort Benson. It was, I must record, a very shrewd policy.

The day of the AGM dawned. As we sat there on the podium, the Board solemnly ranged for everybody to see, the Chairman's opening statement was that he wished to report that we had had an approach from Thorn EMI to buy the remaining shares in British Aerospace. To say that pandemonium broke out would not be an exaggeration, and the Smith New Court analyst, Brian Newman, was the first one to race out of the auditorium to 'phone the news through; by the time the AGM was over, the share price had risen to heights that seemed unreal at that time. They continued to rise on the speculation of a bid and this, of course, meant that the task of Thorn EMI doing this alone at a low price was rapidly receding. Enter Arnold Weinstock.

I received a call from Arnold Weinstock, Chief Executive of GEC, to say,' What was all this about? Wouldn't it be much more sensible if there could be a rapprochement with GEC?' It should be remembered that GEC had been the joint owners of the British Aircraft Corporation, together with Vickers, but that GEC had the management of BAC and this, of course, had affected the relationship with GEC post-nationalization. In other words, I believe that many of the people who had previously worked for Arnold. and had come under his strict financial controls, felt greatly relieved that this was no longer the case and they now were more free to pursue their own particular endeavours, not necessarily with profit in mind, and were against any thought of doing a deal with GEC if it involved Arnold. So from both parts of the predecessor companies, Aircraft and Dynamics, there was hostility to GEC. I did not have any prejudice of any kind in the matter, so it was possible for me to be a little more objective in my approach towards GEC – not that it was to do any good!

The two parts of the Dynamics business that then existed would have fitted together with GEC Marconi like a glove on a hand. Whereas GEC Marconi was the one who, for the most part, made the guidance systems, British Aerospace was the vehicle manufacture, that is to say made the missile bodies, the motors, the way in which the whole system was designed. There was very little overlap so it would have been, and could have been, an ideal match, and has since become so.

Arnold was also very interested in the military aircraft side because GEC's radar and avionics were fairly dependent at that time on the success of the military aircraft products of British Aerospace. What he was not keen on was the commercial aircraft side and he believed that this was something he could do without. It was always clear to me, however, that there would be no deal unless it encompassed the whole of British Aerospace and we could find some way of putting the two pieces together. Meetings were therefore held between Arnold and his Finance Director, Tin, myself and Bernard Friend, to see whether there were any grounds for a joint venture, or a takeover, or a joint company of some kind. The structure Arnold had in mind was that the Dynamics part of the whole business would be run by Arthur Walsh and that I would be Chief Executive of the combined business, embracing military aviation, avionics and the Marconi empire. It would have been an extremely effective and efficient union. There was, however, great hostility to this idea within British Aerospace. My friendship with Arnold was, of course, a reason for regarding me with some suspicion within the corridors of British Aerospace. I liked Arnold. I admired him for what he had done and for what we could do together for the combined companies. It seemed to me to be an extremely sensible arrangement if sensible commercial solutions could be found.

There remained, of course, the problem of what the actual Board structure would be, and here Arnold was prepared to be much more flexible than Peter Laister had been because Arnold ran GEC from the centre and it seemed to me regarded the Board as an appendage to his authority. He therefore didn't place too much emphasis on the importance of the Chairmanship and was perfectly prepared to accommodate Tin Pearce in some role or other, although the two men were by nature so different that it was difficult to see how they could ever relate.

We then came to a BAe Board meeting at which Tin outlined the discussions had taken place with Arnold Weinstock and that he and his Finance Director were coming round that very morning to have discussions on the values that could be placed on the various component parts of the business to see if some arrangement could be achieved. This generated a pretty furious reaction among the non-executive directors, led by Ken Durham, who demanded to know what right Arnold had to discuss prices and values with us without the full authority of the Board. Tin backed away and said, 'Well, it is just an exploration,' but this merely produced an even more violent reaction from the Board which, with the weight of opinion against Arnold within the executives (apart from me) and the hostility that had been generated in the non-executives led by Ken Durham's outburst, meant that the approach from Arnold was to be rejected. I protested that this was extremely rude, he was actually getting ready to come round to have a chat when the Board meeting was over and had been prepared to talk to the Board if necessary. I was overruled and a message had to be sent to Arnold to say that the meeting was off and that no further discussions with GEC were to take place.

It was a tragic and lost opportunity to put two great British companies together and make one of world-beating class, but the narrow-mindedness and the prejudices that existed within British Aerospace at the time and the weakness of Tin Pearce meant that this opportunity was lost. My personal view was that Arnold should have made a bid for British Aerospace, to hell with it, and gone ahead and done it, but Arnold was not that kind of man. He had always made it clear that he would only do a deal if it was an agreed takeover, or an agreed joint venture, or an agreed combination, but not anything that involved hostility. If this was a correct interpretation of his attitude, and subsequent events have shown that it was absolutely correct, then I believe it was a mistake not to have entered into discussions to see what could come out of it at that time. As I have made clear already, the question of whether or not it was a sensible commercial venture was a separate issue. My concern was solely to see the tremendous advantages that could flow from the integration of the resources of the two companies to produce what has now been achieved, a very significant player in the world of aviation. I think that was wrong, on reflection, and have always thought it was wrong, but nevertheless that was the view that was taken. It is strange looking back to see the reverse actually occurred.

There was, of course, an aftermath to this. My position within British Aerospace was not strengthened by this episode, because quite clearly it was believed that my friendship with Arnold had affected and could affect my judgement. It had, but only with the best interests of the two companies in mind. Not for the last time in my business career, I saw personal ambition and prejudice stand in the way of shareholder and business interests.

My relations with Arnold had not always been as friendly as they have become over the years, and I well remember the first time going to see him with Tim Pearce and Freddie Page as one of a kind of general 'get together with GEC' meetings. Arnold opened the discussion by saying he couldn't understand how and why Dynamics were getting into the electronics business and trying to muscle in on Marconi's part of the defence operation, and why didn't we stick to the things we were doing. I fired on all cylinders immediately and said, 'Sir Arnold (as he then was), we are in the electronics business, we intend to stay in the avionics business and we intend to grow in the avionics business and if you can't accept that this meeting is now at an end.' I think this somewhat robust approach surprised Tin and possibly Freddie, but Arnold merely said, 'Well no, if that's what you want to do I accept that,' and the conversation continued. Afterwards I heard from Dick Clayton, an ex-Naval colleague of mine who was on the Board of GEC, that Arnold had asked him to go see him to ask about this fellow Lygo. According to Dick, Arnold said, 'He's a very tough character, isn't he?' to which Dick, one of my best friends in the Navy, had replied, 'He's very tough indeed.' And perhaps because of that approach and that beginning we have managed to get on pretty well ever since.

The problem with GEC at that time was, in my view, that it was too big and, since Arnold controlled the company through the balance sheet and not necessarily with any deep technical insight into what was going on, it meant that he could often be misled by the people who were making the technical decisions: certainly in some areas this became very serious. Quite early on I went to see him in a friendly way to say, 'You should be aware that we are standing into danger on three programmes, and this all down to a shortfall in the performance of Marconi Avionics and Marconi. One is the Nimrod. If you don't do something about this programme it's going to be a disaster. Second is the radar for the Tornado variant, which is running extremely late and we shall be producing aircraft without radars.' (In fact, the joke within British Aerospace was, because we had to put ballast in the front of the aircraft because we had no radar, to describe it as the Ferrocrete radar.) The third was for another Dynamics weapon system. Arnold listened to me and said he would look into it and do something about it. Soon after this I was on an unscheduled visit to Woodford and went into the hangar where the AEW Nimrods were being prepared.

As I walked up the ladder to go into the rear of the aircraft, a British Aerospace engineer came out and greeted me and I asked him, 'How's it going?'

'Terrible,' he said, 'when are we going to take over Marconi?' I looked him, smiled and said, 'We really have quite enough to do at the moment without that,' but it was reminiscent of the time when I had been on board the first Type 42 that we were selling to the Argentinian Navy. The Captain, who rejoiced in the name of Nelson Castro, was kind enough to give me lunch on board, at the end of which he made a small speech thanking British Aerospace for its contribution to the efficient running of his ship, but then saying, 'I hope you will not take it amiss but I do wish you would take charge of Marconi,' so it was a familiar story. I later went back to Arnold and told him that things were getting worse with the Nimrod, and that unless drastic action was taken the programme would fail. He assured me that he had taken action and I said, 'No, you haven't. You fired the chap in the middle of the heap – you should have gone to the top.'

One of the major problems with the Nimrod programme was that neither British Aerospace nor Marconi were prime contractors for the whole programme. This was vested in the Ministry of Defence so co-ordination could only exist through the Controller Aircraft – A very bad way to organise a programme. I am told that the Aircraft Group were very surprised when the original decision to proceed with the AEW Nimrod was made and they hadn't really placed much hope on actually achieving the contract. As a result, I think the preparatory work was probably less detailed than it should have been. The problem was that the weight of the equipment that the aircraft was being asked to take in order to meet the specification meant that it was going to reach a situation where we would have to change practically the whole undercarriage. In the end a fierce rearguard action was fought by GEC in order to try to save the programme when the Ministry of Defence finally got to the end of its tether, and I found myself appearing on a platform with Jim Prior in front of Members of Parliament and various people of supposed influence to support the programme. I must say I felt it a difficult role to perform since the statements that were being made about the success of the programme were to me, not founded on a very accurate base of achievement. Nevertheless, we loyally supported GEC in its attempt to recover the programme. We failed, and AWACS was purchased instead. It was a sad end to a radar that had started life as part of a programme to replace the AEW Gannets in the Royal Navy, so a rather dark curtain was finally drawn on the whole of that programme.

It was about this time that I received a call from Dick Clayton, an old friend of mine who was then on the Board of GEC who said he would like to come and chat about the possibility that the two companies take an interest in the shipbuilding industry. At the time I was looking at a fairly smallish possibility of acquisition of a company that was building the offshore patrol vessels up in north east Scotland, but Arnold (it transpired) had bigger fish in mind. Dick and I agreed that the company that we should go for, if we were to go in a combined sense, would be Vickers, but Arnold did not appear to favour this. The next best option was Yarrow, and Arnold discussed the matter with me while our own discussions with the potential shipbuilder in north east Scotland somewhat faded away. Arnold went ahead with a bid for the acquisition of Yarrow. He phoned me afterwards and said I'm prepared to allow British Aerospace to come in for 50 per cent of the action at Yarrow for the same price that I paid for it. I put this matter to the Board and like so many of the things that came on offer from Arnold it was viewed with extreme suspicion. Because I could see that if I got personally involved in this it would damage the prospect, I allowed the matter to be referred to a committee under the auspices of the Secretary, to look at the legal implications of this, and the Dynamics Group to have a look at the way things could be fitted together since they had the shipbuilding interest down at Bristol.

Matters dragged on for nearly a year and although I kept probing the answer was always, 'Well, we haven't quite resolved this issue,' and 'we haven't quite resolved that issue,' and in the end Arnold called me and said, 'I can't hold this offer open any more. The actual price of Yarrow is now rising, and has risen and I cannot, in all honesty, keep the offer of 50 per cent of the original price open for British Aerospace,' and so we dropped out. Another lost opportunity based entirely on prejudice, but of course it's all come right in the end since with the takeover of Marconi, British Aerospace will finish up acquiring the whole of it anyway!

39

How Not to Manage Property

Over the years of my stewardship of British Aerospace, the more I discovered about the way in which our real-estate assets had been managed the less happy I was until I became positively furious. In fact, I said at the time, if I could have laid my hands on some of the people who were responsible for disposing of some of our assets, or making arrangements for the disposal of some of our assets, I would have them sued, or better still shot!

The first site that was going to be redundant to our needs that had any value to it was Weybridge. Here the old BAC had title and possession of a very valuable acreage right in the middle of a desirable part of the London suburbs. Prior to nationalisation, half of the site on the other side of the river had already been sold to developers and turned into an industrial park. We had been left with the other half, including remains of the famous Brooklands racetrack, the Weybridge museum and the buildings on the factory side. Property developers at this time were making an absolute fortune, and I was becoming increasing tired of the fact that we didn't seem to be participating in this bonanza. Two episodes come to mind.

Soon after I took over the whole of British Aerospace, and having decided that all the sites in the south of England would eventually have to go, I looked at the Hatfield aircraft site and decided that, in order to maximise the value, we should acquire the freehold of the houses that were dotted around the perimeter of Hatfield on the main road. Most of the owners of these houses were anxious to dispose of their properties anyway, since they were no longer the desirable residences they once were, being crowded in by an airfield development on the one hand and major roadworks and development in the centre of Hatfield on the other. Quite a number of them were keen to sell and get out, and I instructed the local management to deal with these people as the sites became available, so that we acquired all of them and tidied up the entire site. This we had proceeded to do but in the process I discovered that someone had leased an acreage of British Aerospace land to provide a car park for the hotel which sat on the main road in the middle of the development site! Furthermore, the terms at which this had been let were hardly commercial!

Another episode was at Kingston, where I discovered that land down to the River Thames had been allowed to pass into the occupation of a gentleman who owned a house next to the recreation ground alongside our site in order that he could build a garage on his property, and that no rent that was reasonable, or any arrangement that was commercially satisfactory, had been agreed. When I suggested that we should change this arrangement there were quiet protests because these were all part of a gentleman's agreement that had been made in the past. It made me wonder what else had gone on and taken place of which I was not aware.

The management of real estate in British Aerospace had passed, I suppose, by default or history to the Secretariat which had the Legal Department within it but which, of course, had no expertise within the property development side. I therefore insisted that an Estate Manager should be appointed and we eventually obtained one with a small department to look after this mass of real estate which we were accumulating. In discussion with various friends however, it became clear that there were only two ways in which we could properly manage our real estate; one was to employ highly qualified people to do it. The trouble here was that the kind of entrepreneurs one wanted to oversee our property development potential were not readily going to work for a great bureaucracy like British Aerospace, despite what I was trying to do to blow it apart. The alternative, therefore, was to go out and acquire a property development company which would become a wholly-owned subsidiary of British Aerospace. Here the trick would be to lock in the management in such a way as to ensure that they didn't all disappear the minute the acquisition was completed because in this area, as in many others, you are buying people as goodwill. I therefore began to draw up a list of the likely property companies that could possibly fit the bill. As usual there was resistance within British Aerospace to this particular activity because the Secretariat believed that they were perfectly capable of managing the estate we had without going this route, when it was perfectly obvious to me that they were not capable of so doing. A cobbler should stick to his last, we had no in-built flair for property development, we just knew we had a hell of a lot of potentially valuable real estate and we needed it to be managed in such a way as to enable us to generate the kind of funds that we would require in order to pay the costs of refurbishment and movement and redundancy that would undoubtedly result from my long term strategy. For over a year this issue was debated and for over a year

479

we toyed with the idea until at last, with the arrival of Roland Smith, the nettle was grasped.

One of the companies we had concentrated on was Arlington. They seemed to possess the right range of skills and the right expertise for developing the kind of estate that we had inherited and so a dialogue was started between Roland and Kenneth Keith, who was then Chairman of Arlington, as to how this deal could be structured and done. A particularly imaginative scheme was concocted to ensure that Raymond Mole and various other top executives would remain as part of the management team and have a substantial minority interest in order to keep them motivated after the deal was done. All this was taking place in 1988 when property companies were booming and the prices that were set were those which related to the market value as perceived at the time. There has been much criticism of British Aerospace's purchase of Arlington in the years that have transpired since, but events must be judged in the time-frame in which they took place and against the background of why they were done. I believe that what was done at that time was wise and correct although nobody could forecast the collapse in the property market that was to follow so soon afterwards. The fact remains that we took too long reaching a decision.

It was at about this time that we had acquired Royal Ordnance and with it a vast amount of real estate that already was known to be surplus to requirement. This mainly concerned acreages at Enfield and Waltham Abbey, both areas that were just outside the Green Belt and highly desirable for further development. All this is covered in the chapter on Royal Ordnance.

The Arlington team seemed competent and acceptable and we found it quite easy to work with them. The whole of our large portfolio was given into their care and, of course, it was about this time that the largest take-over of all began to appear possible, i.e. Rover.

40

The 146 Saga

Whenever we are not where we would like to be, we are always where we are. That is true of any situation in life, I suppose, and certainly it was where we were when I took over the management of British Aerospace, because the decision to launch the 146 had already been taken. What was not clear to me then, and only became clear after the passage of some considerable time, was that the history of procurement of civil aircraft in British Aerospace was much more complex than I had imagined.

The decision to proceed with the 146 was entirely political. Lord Beswick, then the Chairman of British Aerospace in its nationalised capacity, decided that the only way that they could continue to keep Hatfield Aircraft in business was to continue with the 146 programme, which had been devised by Hawker Siddeley but put on the shelf because they could not see a way of commercially financing the programme. At this time I was running the Dynamics part of the old Hawker Siddeley business based at Hatfield, and as part of my learn-in I had been invited by Mike Goldsmith who then ran Hatfield Aircraft to go over and meet with his people. I remember going across the airfield into a somewhat gloomy dining room, as I recall, with an even gloomier bunch of directors. I was not impressed. Goldsmith was a tall, well-presented and energetic man, but the team he was working with, it seemed to me, were not of the highest calibre. I was glad that I wasn't involved in that part of the business; in fact, I said so when I went back to the other side of the airfield. Little was I to know that within a very short space of time their problems would be mine!

The decision to proceed with the 146, therefore, had been taken during the period of nationalisation. George Jefferson, my Chairman, was not going to be available for that Board meeting, so I was the representative of the Dynamics Group. I thought at the time that this was a 'diplomatic' absence. Jeff, I suspect, did not want to be seen to be opposing the wish of the Chairman – whom he wished to succeed! I had received no briefing as to how I was to conduct myself at the meeting, but there was no doubt that we had considerable misgivings within the missile business about the wisdom of proceeding with the

146. The presentation of the case for the 146 was well handled and, I think, based on the assumption that a decision in favour was going to be taken anyway! The one question I asked was whether an independent survey of the market prospects of the aircraft had been undertaken. The Chairman dismissed this as irrelevant. 'We have the best market surveying organisation in the aircraft industry and there is no reason to believe that it is wrong, and therefore I don't think there will be any point in spending money on getting a second opinion.' Like many Board decisions, I suspect that this was taken on the basis that the people who wanted it were strong enough to get it and the people who were hesitant were really not in a position to force a strong disagreement.

Shortly after the decision I had occasion to have a discussion with Alec Sanson, then Marketing Director of Dynamics, an old engine man who had learned his trade with Napier. He said, 'Why have they ever decided to put those Avco Lycoming engines on that aircraft?' I confessed that I had no understanding of this either, but Alec's concern was rather more deep-rooted. As an old engine man he held firmly to the belief that aircraft were hung on engines rather than engines hung on aircraft, and how right he was. 'That company', i.e. Avco, said he 'has never been in the commercial business, they don't understand the pressures and requirements of the commercial sector, and I just don't see how they are ever going to be able to support that aircraft.' It was a fact, of course, that the engine, or the core of the engine at any rate, had originally been a tank engine for the United States Army and had been procured under Defence Procurement procedures. As events unfolded, Alec's words were to prove very prescient.

The programme for the development of the 146 was already well under way. The cash-impairment curve of a newly developed aircraft is a frightening graph; it dips down steadily to bottom out at some hundreds of millions of pounds of total expenditure at peak, or bottom trough, and then rises to pass through the magic zero line to produce those marvellous profits in the life hereafter. It is, of course, for the most part a total con – there is no pot of gold at the end of the rainbow. Once the cash-impairment curve begins to recover, at about 300 or 400 aeroplanes, and begins to move into profit, you can be absolutely certain that the aeroplane is now obsolescent and therefore much more money will be needed to be pumped in to bring it up to the state of the art. That will mean that the profits that you have hopefully looked forward to will turn into another cash-impairment curve, and if that isn't bad enough, when you think, right, we shall now close down and enjoy the profits, the cost of closing down and redundancy more than offsets any profits that you might have expected. It is, in fact, a roller coaster of almost certain commercial disaster. Nevertheless, the commercial aircraft industry, for the most part, is based on the heady prospects of profits to come.

There was one important aspect of the development that had totally missed me. As I have said, the expertise in developing commercial aircraft (such as it was) had resided in the old British Aircraft Corporation. When the decision was made to proceed with the 146 it had, of course, to be at the expense of developing the Two-Eleven, the successor to the One-Eleven. Many of the people who were best skilled in marketing, building, designing and maintaining commercial aircraft left or were shunted off into various backstreams of the old BAC, and Weybridge, its headquarters, was gradually showing all the signs of beginning to be run down. Hatfield, which had been a kind of empty morgue, was now full of life, but the only people who could be found to work in this new environment were people who were, by and large, not the first-rate team; they had already departed. To build up the team, people were drawn from the military side of the business because expertise in designing, building and maintaining large civil aircraft had largely passed – if it had ever indeed been achieved – with the ending of the Trident line.

I believe that if the decision had been made to proceed with the Two-Eleven, rather than the 146, that aeroplane would have been a worldbeater and still have been in production today. Of course, events that have developed with the 146 since my departure and the updating of the engine and the ability to get the engine company to stand behind it has had a dramatic effect on the prospects of the 146, but much of the trauma, lost money and credibility would have been avoided had we proceeded with the Two-Eleven rather than the 146.

The first large order and the one that excited us all at the time, was the sale of some 18 aircraft to Pacific South West Airlines, a California-based airline operating in the Californian corridor out of San Diego. It is perhaps worth recalling at this point the original concept of the 146. Here was a highwing, medium-size aeroplane, up to 120 seats – starting out at something in the region of 80 – with a very soft undercarriage and shortfield performance given by its four engines. It was designated to be an aircraft that would be the Dakota of the 1970s and operate from unprepared fields or not very good airfields in the Third World. Pacific South West Airlines was essentially a commuter airline operating in the most intensively competitive and demanding commercial corridor in the world. Sales were trickling in from other small airlines, which I later termed 'dodgy' airlines on account of their delicate balance sheet health, but Pacific South West seemed to be a key to the golden future. The design authority and the prime contractor, if you like, for the design and final assembly of the 146 rested with Hatfield but they, in fact, were only to build the front section; the centre section was to be built at Bristol, the tail section at Woodford and the wings by Avco Aerostructures in the USA. This arrangement had been designed by the Aircraft Group to spread the work about. This was the philosophy of that period; you moved work to fill factories, and there was no proper control of price. In fact, factories did not operate at arm's length, and therefore costs plus profit were what was passed back to the central authority. The net result was (and this, of course, was a military procurement process) that costs were not of prime consideration, the prime consideration was filling the factories with work!

The first review of the 146 that I had carried out showed that our costs were such that we could not break even at exchange rates in excess of US $1.30 to the pound. At this point I should digress into the exchange rate problem. All commercial aircraft are marketed in US dollars; if you want to buy a new civil aircraft it is priced in US dollars. You may pay for it in French francs, or Deutschmarks, or Sterling, but the price is set by the US dollar benchmark. Quite simply this is because at that time 80 per cent of the world's commercial aircraft were being produced in the United States so the competition was always in dollars. The most proficient producers of commercial aircraft were companies in the United States and therefore if you are to sell competitively you have to produce a product that is better and which, without subsidy, can compete on a dollar equivalent price. At the time this review was made the pound was sitting at about $1.50/1.60 and it was quite clear that we had a problem. However it was in the very early stages of production of the aircraft and the conventional wisdom at the time was that if you plotted the relationship between the pound and the dollar from 1890, when it was just over $5, to the year 2000 it would decline to a parity of $1 to £1. You therefore had a very comforting graph which showed that given the passage of time all would be taken care of and you really didn't have to worry! Of course there were occasional blips but by and large this didn't matter in a long term business. It was fortunate that already a large amount of the contents of the aircraft were bought in and sourced from dollar areas – the engines and wings and some of the avionics were sourced in dollars – and so there was a dollar element but it wasn't enough to cover any eventuality.

A few months after my arrival the first aircraft were being delivered to Pacific South West, and I began to ask the usual questions about whether the customer was satisfied and whether all was going well.

Although the reports indicated that there were problems I was assured continuously by management that these were just teething troubles and, in fact, the customer was very satisfied. After a while I became less satisfied, and insisted on monthly reports on how things were going at Pacific South West; despite the reassurances that I was receiving, however, I became more and more concerned until at last I decided that the only way to find out was to go over there and talk to the management myself. This I proceeded to do; I met with the then Chairman of Pacific South West in San Diego. It was a salutary experience. The engines, much as Alec Sanson had predicted, were not performing to specification. Furthermore, there were four of them, so in comparing the performance of the aircraft with conventional McDonnell Douglas twin-engine aeroplanes we had a built-in headwind.

Never shall I forget the Board meeting that I was invited to attend. To my surprise there in the Boardroom was a full-scale Avco Lycoming engine on a stand, looking very clean and proper. At the outset they welcomed me politely, as Americans do, and then said that they were delighted that I should come because perhaps I would be able to help them carry out some of the recommendations that were being promulgated by British Aerospace to assist with some of their problems.

At that time they were having tremendous problems with the Plessey starter, which was failing at such an unacceptable rate that Plessey had reduced the frequency of oil-change in their starter to something under 20 hours! This meant that every 20 hours the oil on those particular motors – all four of them – had to be changed. I was asked to demonstrate to them how this could be achieved in the way that had been indicated. I was taken under the engine stand and shown the problem. The starter sat a long way forward in the engine, so a very long spanner was required to undo the four bolts that secured it to the engine casing. The clearance at the top of the starter was only something like two inches and the oil-filter cap was at the top (and this was the only orifice in the starter), so the instruction to drain the oil out of the four motors very 20 hours or less could only be achieved, according to them, by an amusing diagram that showed them turning the aeroplane upside down in order to drain out the oil, the alternative being to remove all four starters every 20 hours! I was frankly, ashamed. Here we had been promoting a product that I had been assured was performing, and here was a graphic indication that it was very badly wrong.

When I got back to the UK I immediately rank John Clark, who was then running the Plessey company, and was most direct in requiring him to sort out his starter motors. I followed this with a blistering note to him, pointing out the way in which I would hold Plessey responsible. John, I am sure, was as upset as I was and action began to be taken, but these things all take time and meantime our reputation was going down the drain.

We were also having trouble at that time with noise coming from the door. I discovered that door seals on commercial aircraft were a traditional problem and that within the predecessor companies BAC had solved the problem with the One-Eleven and the Viking – but no one had asked them to design the door for the 146!

To be fair to British Aerospace, most of the problems came from the component manufacturers, mostly engine, but of course the aircraft was produced, marketed, serviced and maintained by, and the project liability lay for the most part with, British Aerospace and the answer, 'That bit has got nothing to do with me' was not really good enough. I came back determined to make some changes in the management structure. I did, but it was only the beginning of a very long haul. Avco Lycoming just refused to accept that the expectations of the commercial operator were realistic and required attention from the engine manufacturer to improve the reliability of the engine. The saga continued, and I shall come back to it.

Meantime, the high wing configurations and low noise levels of the 146 led one to believe that it could become an ideal freighting aeroplane. We tried, unsuccessfully, to market a military version with a rear-loading ramp, because it was ideally suited for this, but the cost of doing it on company funds was just not on. What we could afford was a big double door at the back in order to facilitate the loading of freight and the installation of rollers to ensure that containers could be positioned with a minimum of trouble. This led us to the marketing of the 146 freighter, and it was a short step from that to the concept of a combo, an aircraft that could move freight by night and passengers by day.

The one company that seized upon the idea of the versatility of the 146 was TNT. Its CEO, Sir Peter Abeles, had decided that the era of using clapped-out, second-hand, gas-guzzling old passenger aeroplanes for moving freight was passed – they were noisy and they polluted the atmosphere. He therefore saw that if he could develop the 146 exclusively for freight business he could use it at night out of noise-sensitive airfields and it would be effective and efficient. The studies that his chaps carried out for him in TNT confirmed this, and it began to look as if the freighting market was one on which we could well capitalise.

About this time Pacific South West Airlines was acquired by US Air, by my old friend Ed Calodney. He had already acquired

Allegheny, and the result was a rag, tag and bobtail bunch of aircraft that actually undermined the commercial viability of the entire combined force. Early on he voiced his view that the availability of the 146 was not good enough – we were talking about 98 per cent availability, he was talking about 99.5 per cent. In a highly competitive commercial environment, this shortfall was crucial to the viability to the airline itself. He threatened, early on, to take the aeroplanes out of service and park them or try to get rid of them, which would have been a tremendous blow to the 146 and our prospects for selling to other customers. I therefore took myself off to see Ed, to see if there was any way out of this problem.

I had by this time become Chairman of the American end of British Aerospace, which was directly responsible for the in-country service of the 146. Ed's main problem was with the engine, and I therefore sought one final meeting with Avco Lycoming and its superior, Textron, to try to bring together the engine manufacturer and the user so that we could try to come to some arrangement whereby Textron would stand up to their responsibilities for the maintainability of the engine. Ed Calodney agreed to attend such a meeting and we met in Textron's offices in New York.

I have never been so disappointed and so ashamed of our standing as I was on this occasion. Ed Calodney put forward his case which amounted to an indictment of the way Avco Lycoming were standing behind their engine and their ability to guarantee in-service availability. In the end the Chairman of Textron, Ed Nolan, said to Ed Calodney, our customer, in front of me, 'You must have known about these aeroplanes when you bought them, you knew about the engine reliability, don't expect me to pull your chestnuts out of the fire' – or words to that effect. It was to me unbelievable, but it was fact. For my part, and not before time, I had completely lost faith in the willingness of Textron to support the engine and to drag them into an acceptance of their commercial liability and responsibilities in relation to its serviceability. We proceeded to look much more vigorously for alternatives to the four engines we already had and, although we looked at a two-engine configuration using a large Snecma engine, and talked to Rolls Royce about the prospect of them producing a smaller engine that we could hang on in lieu of the Avco Lycoming, whichever way one turned we were stuck with that engine. If ever there is a lesson to be learned in the design of commercial aircraft it is the one that Alec Sanson had indicated: 'Commercial aircraft hang on the engine – not the other way round.'

The advantage that the 146 had, which was undeniable, was its quietness and its ability to operate out of noise-sensitive airfields without causing unacceptable interference, so it did open up the possibility of moving freight particularly, or passengers for that matter, in and out of noise-sensitive airfields when otherwise it would have been impossible to operate aircraft. The difficulty was getting people to recognise that this was so; no matter how often you told people that you had a very quiet aeroplane, you couldn't possibly convince them unless you gave them a demonstration.

One such demonstration was at the new London City Airport. Mowlem had decided to develop an airfield in the old docklands east of London, and I therefore sought an early meeting with Phillip Beck of Mowlem to discuss with him the prospect of using the 146 at this airfield. All my previous knowledge indicated to me that the grave danger that would probably arise would be that they would put the runway right up against the local gasworks, or some other obstruction, which when they came to extend the runway (as they would almost certainly be required to do) would prevent it. Phillip and I met, therefore, and he brought with him the plans of the airfield that they were proposing to build. To my delight, I saw that it wasn't going to run up against the gasworks; it was going to have a completely clear run and therefore the room for extending the runway existed, if that was what was required. It was obviously an ideal location for the 146, but before we could get permission to get the 146 in there, many objections had to be overcome. Phillip was not keen to press the case for the 146 until he had got clearance to operate some less exciting aeroplanes, and so we wasted a lot of time (as it turned out) waiting for things to go 'softly, softly' when in fact they could have been expedited if we had made a case of it early on, because two things were to materialise; which just goes to show the peril of trying to plan anything in a complex world – or how easy it is to delay action.

The first objection that raised its head was the new river crossing. It was proposed that there should be a new river crossing – a suspension bridge with towering piles that would have been right on the approach or take-off path from the airfield! It was to be regarded as the gateway to the Port of London, which of course had ceased to exist due to a combination of the weakness of management and the obduracy of the unions! That great port, which for most of my lifetime had been the largest in the world, was now reduced to practically nothing, and having a gateway to it was a bit of a fallacy; so one area of activity had to be to get the design of the bridge modified in such a way that it would not obstruct the approach path to the airfield. But there was yet another development that had gone ahead through another department, the enormous tower block that had been approved to go up in the Docklands development. Canary Wharf, the largest tower in the whole London area, was within a few degrees of the approach path, and the only way around this problem was to get the angle of approach changed so as to make it safe. These were the kinds of hidden problems that surrounded that particular project but eventually, on a windy day, we brought the 146 into Docklands with the whole assembly of various pressure groups around, and they all had to confess that it could not be heard. It is a very quiet aeroplane.

One of the other objects of my attention was National Airport in Washington. This very busy airfield is constrained by noise to daylight hours only, and is fairly short at that, yet any attempt to get a demonstration in during night hours was fraught with difficulty. I was reminded very much of the attempts to get Concorde into New York. If Americans don't want something to happen, they have an amazing ability to prevent it. I even remember saying that I would be prepared to fly the aeroplane myself up one night and then call for an emergency diversion, go into National, open up and take off and then have full page advertisements in the local papers the following morning saying 'did anybody hear the 146?' This was considered to be far too outrageous a proposal to be taken seriously. It is frustrating when you've a vehicle like Concorde for example, or the 146 at the other end of the spectrum, which have special capabilities which could make them worldbeaters and yet the bureaucratic and commercially obstructive attitudes towards anything that might be different or compete with other people's interests, get in the way.

The real saviour of the 146 turned out to be TNT: I was told by Brian Thomas, the then Marketing Director, that Sir Peter Abeles, then Chief Executive of TNT, wished to procure up to 72 'Quiet Traders' (as we had named the freighter version of the 146), and that he was prepared to operate them or lease them out through his leasing company because he had a firm belief that the aircraft was going to be the most successful in the rapidly expanding night freighting field. I was told that I should go to Monte Carlo to meet with Peter Abeles, and that if we got on together he would almost certainly go with us; if not, it would be the end of the deal. Not a very good briefing for the start of a friendship! I duly flew down to Monte Carlo and met with Peter in his hotel.

I remember sitting waiting for him in the ante-room as he walked in, the larger than life figure that he was, with the, at that time, almost inevitable cigar in his fingers. We went through the polite formalities and then started talking about the aeroplane. Peter's idea of using the quietness of the aircraft to enable it to move freight at night in and out of noise-sensitive airfields was clearly a correct one. The problem that he had was the price we were asking for the aircraft. This debate continued for some time, and he assured me that he could buy alterna-

489

tive aircraft from Boeing or McDonnell Douglas at cheaper rates than we were asking for the 146. I countered this by telling him that I was well aware that this might be the case, but if he wanted an aircraft that was capable of operating inside the noise limits there was only one that could do it. Peter chastised me about the costs of British Aerospace, and I had to agree with him. I said, 'Yes, I know that we are not as competitive as we ought to be, and I'm working on this, but it's a long process and it cannot be something that's going to be achieved immediately and overnight. In the meantime, I have to charge the price at which I cannot make much money but at least not lose any.' We got on well together and at the end of it he said to me, 'Well, I think we'll go for it,' and that was it. We never had a written contract, as I recall; we never had anything but a gentleman's agreement that he would take our delivery for the next three or four years of the 'Quiet Trader', and he honoured it to the letter.

Even the deal with TNT was still not enough, but it did provide me with the opportunity of proceeding to do by stealth what I would not have been able to do by direct confrontation. It enable me to open a second line for the 146 Quiet Trader at Woodford; my aim then was the eventual closure of Hatfield, but the problems of closing and managing the way ahead at this time must be the subject of a separate chapter.

Thus I met Peter Abeles and struck a friendship with him that lasted until the time of his death. He had started TNT, Thompsons Nation-wide Transport, in Australia with two trucks – Samson and Delilah – and from that humble beginning this extraordinary Jewish refugee from Hungary had built up one of the largest transport companies in the world. Sometime after I returned from British Aerospace, he came over to England and asked me if I would become the Chairman of the UK and European companies. I accepted, and there began a relationship with the company which has lasted to the present time, although I ceased to be Chairman when the company was taken over by the Dutch Post Office.

The saga of how this happened and why and his subsequent death deserves its own book. As a result, I met with Alan Jones his Managing Director in the UK and now of the whole European activity and was introduced to a company that he had virtually created with a culture that I have yet to see matched elsewhere. One of the first British companies to win awards for quality, both in the UK and Europe, the National Training award, Investor in People and endless other Transport Awards. This was one of the happiest periods of my life: I was with a well-run, enthusiastic company with no barriers, and an example to all who aspire to create something for everyone based on success.

41

The Space Saga

On my arrival at Hatfield, one of the more depressed areas for which I found myself responsible was the Space and Communications Division at Stevenage. It seemed clear to me that here was an enthusiastic bunch of mainly young people in a most important part of our business, one certainly with a future, and yet they were not receiving the support that they should from the top management of the company. I therefore devoted some of my energy to improving the prospects of business in this area.

The first major opportunity was to be a new communications satellite for the armed forces, and it had been decided by the Ministry that this should be a competitive tender between Marconi and British Aerospace. Up to this point, Marconi had been responsible for the payload in the satellite, and British Aerospace for the vehicle. Thus, if we were to compete, each company would be required to find a partner that could produce the other part. In both cases, this almost certainly meant finding an American partner. In our case it was TRW, the one with which we were closest associated; in Marconi's case, I think it must have been Ford Aerospace. We worked very hard on getting together a solution that would meet the requirements of the Ministry of Defence in timescale and cost, and our bid was duly submitted. You can imagine my surprise when, on a visit to the United States, I received an urgent call from Peter Hickman, the Managing Director of the Space Division, to say that I was required to return to have a meeting with Lord Trenchard, then the Minister for Defence Procurement and Geoffrey Pattie's boss, to discuss our bid. I flew back and landed at Heathrow to be met by Roger Dance, Peter's deputy, and I remember changing into something more suitable for the visit as we travelled in my car from Heathrow to the Ministry of Defence building.

Our meetings with Lord Trenchard always opened with a warm welcome and a greeting that embraced the fact that he knew the problems of industrialists because he had himself been in industry. Indeed he had, he had worked for Unilever, and he didn't seem to realise that on our Board was Kenneth Durham, who had been the

Chairman of Uniliver, and knew all about Trenchard's involvement (much of it, I gather, trying to run the Mars business). Nevertheless, one always had to go through the preamble and listen to this, but imagine my surprise when he said that they were very concerned at the way in which the competitive tender was developing. 'How come?' I enquired. 'Well,' said Trenchard, 'I cannot bear to see two great companies tearing each other apart.' I was astonished, and said so: 'But I thought that's what you wanted,' I said, 'I thought you wanted competition, and in order to win a contract we had to produce the best possible bid at the best possible timescale.' 'Would it not be possible', he said, 'for you to collaborate with Marconi?' I was even more astonished. 'Of course we could', I said, 'but then there wouldn't be competition, would there?' I left the meeting somewhat confused, not for the first or last time I am bound to say. When competition looked as if it would serve a particular purpose it was encouraged, but if it was suddenly discovered that somebody was going to be disadvantaged and they put up a howl in response to this; then of course sometime the rules were changed. They certainly were in this case, and as Dougie Lowe said to me as we left Trenchard's office and went down the corridor, 'If you don't collaborate, Ray, you won't have a programme.'

So it was that we came to collaborate with Marconi on the first communications satellite for the British armed forces, and subsequently we worked together for a bid for the NATO IV satellite. NATO had always acquired its satellites from the Americans, and for us to break this monopoly was going to be quite a task. The foundation had been laid, we had a good solution, and there was much sympathy among the other NATO nations for a change away from the Americans now that there was an alternative available. It did, however, take an awful lot of lobbying and a lot of hard work; the margins we were using to compete were extremely slim but, to cut a long story short, we did win the programme and the first ever NATO communications satellite to be procured outside America fell to the consortium of British Aerospace and Marconi, led by BAe.

At about this time I was asked to go to a meeting chaired by Kenneth Baker, then the Junior Minister of Technology and in charge of communications. He had put forward, or somebody had put forward to him, the idea of exploiting the geostationary orbital position allocated to the United Kingdom by the International Regulatory Body for Space, of 31° west, from which position a satellite could be used to span the Atlantic. In other words, its footprint would cover the whole of the east coast of the United States, and the whole of Western Europe from its unique position. The idea put forward by the

Department of Trade and Industry was that we should build a satellite that would be both a telecommunications satellite for British Telecom, and also used by the BBC for broadcasting to the east coast of America and into Western Europe. It was a good idea, and the basis for this attempt was to be the joint venture between Marconi and British Aerospace that had been successful in winning the NATO IV contract. So a consortium was set up, consisting of BT, the BBC, GEC (in the shape or Marconi), and British Aerospace, and eventually a company was formed to promote the product called United Satellites. From the outset, trying to reconcile the requirements of BT for a satellite to be in service by a certain date and the desire of the BBC to get the kind of service they wanted was going to be a major difficulty. Furthermore, there was little spirit of compromise or reconciliation among the partners.

I had not realised that, in entering this consortium, we were the only company that had not been directly involved with either the BBC or British Telecom; Marconi had, and not only was there a lack of sympathy between the BBC and BT but also between Marconi and BT, and also between Marconi and the BBC, for whom they had already worked. What a happy combination! The progress of United Satellites was slow, cumbersome, frustrating and irritating to an extent that I have seldom experienced before or since.

In order to meet the required in-service date, it was necessary for the two manufacturers to start spending money; while we were prepared to spend some money on preliminary studies, the moment would come when we would be required to start purchasing equipment and booking slots for a launcher, and incurring quite substantial costs. Try as we might, it was difficult to get all the parties to come to an agreement, and as a result the spend curve began to rise without any commitment to proceed. Every time we decided that we would stop production, our two customers indicated that if we did they would withdraw from the programme and we would be left high and dry, whereas if we would only hold on, they were sure that an agreement could be reached. Finally events reached a climax in which agreement seemed to have been achieved, and in fact a party was held at the BBC in which some champagne was broken out, indicating that the BBC (the Board of Governors, that is) had agreed, or were about to agree, or would agree to the programme as defined, and so it was a green light to go ahead. We assumed that it was and proceeded to spend even more money, to be absolutely shocked at a later stage to be told the BBC was withdrawing. BT then decided that it did not wish to go it alone, and British Aerospace and Marconi were left holding the baby.

493

I reported this matter to the Board; they were fairly sanguine about it but our share of the losses was, by this time, quite considerable. Arnold, on the other hand, called me and said, 'I intend to sue the BBC.' I duly reported this to the Board, but they were not inclined to join him; Arnold, however, made it clear to me that if we weren't going to join him he was going to proceed alone, and I finally convinced the Board that we should go with Arnold and claim substantial damages from the BBC. Matters dragged on for several months until finally the BBC agreed to an out-of-court settlement that cost them many millions of pounds. It was a pyrrhic victory. I would much rather have seen the whole programme proceed. As we now see it, Rupert Murdoch has acquired most of the capability that the BBC could have had, and BT would surely have welcomed the use of a satellite that could transmit so many bits of information backwards and forwards across the Atlantic at this time.

At a meeting of industrialists in 10 Downing Street, Margaret Thatcher (then Prime Minister) asked us what we thought we had going for us in the United Kingdom, and I replied 'Our geographical position which is still of immense importance, the English Language, and 31 west' and I knew she wouldn't understand the last point and would be curious to find out what it meant, as indeed proved the case, but I am afraid we never really managed to carry either the BBC or the Government along with us in a programme that was essentially launched by the DTI and that could have been of immense benefit to this country if we had the wit to proceed. In my opinion, another and tragic lost opportunity, resulting from a failure of government to recognise the need for an industrial strategy. I am the first to state that subsidies lead to inefficiency but, in a case like this, a little leadership at the time from the DTI could have brought the BBC to heel – some slight discussion about licence fees perhaps? An indication to BT of what was in the national interest? If every partner is left to pursue his own individual short-term, short-sighted requirements, then no longer-term programme of any substance would ever be achieved.

By this time, advances in telecommunications had made it possible to replace point-to-point communications with person-to-person communications. In other words, we were beginning to see the possibility of the mobile telephone. Space and Communications were now enthusiastic to embark upon this particular venture, and we proceeded to enter into partnerships that could result in us becoming a player in what we saw to be an immensely important and emerging market. This was the origin of Orange. I remember suggesting that we should approach the Church Commissioners to get permission to put an aerial on every church in the United Kingdom to give us complete coverage and then a considerable income. By the time I left British Aerospace things were going strong, and by now we have seen that the value of this particular activity as it has developed is enormous – but you have to have the guts to stay in the business and not quit, as UK Limited had done with United Satellites.

42

The Single Seater Fighter

'Twas when the war had just been fought
A Great One had a sudden thought
We must have a single seater fighter for the Fleet.'

So begins the first stanza of, to me, a quite telling poem written by some anonymous Fleet Air Arm pilot in the 1950s.

Long before those who came much later and gained much credit from it, we had had competitive tendering within the aerospace industry, and one of the most successful examples of the way in which this can work was the Hawk trainer. When the RAF required a new advanced trainer aircraft in the 1950s, it put out a specification for which the two then premier aerospace companies, Hawker Siddeley and BAC, competed. It was to be a fixed-price, firm-specification aeroplane for a set number to be produced, and it was to go to the most competitive and cost-effective company.

The competition was won by Hawker Siddeley with its proposal for the Hawk Trainer. The Hawk carried forward the traditions of Hawker's wing design and innovative general aircraft concepts, and some would regard it as the last to come out of the famous Hurricane, Hunter and Harrier design team. It carried the name of a much famed aeroplane produced between the wars, and it turned out to be a worthy successor and a first-class aeroplane. In my opinion, this was largely because the aircraft manufacturer was left to design the aeroplane to meet the fixed specification within a cost and time frame that compelled him to exercise the kind of disciplines that the aerospace industry so sadly needed. For those of us who came later and were trying to continue this trend of fixed-price competitive tendering, the increasing political antics of the Ministry of Defence in proposing competition for everything, as if it was something that had never occurred before, was irritating, to say the least.

The competition won by Hawker Siddeley meant that the industrial property rights of the aeroplane rested with the company, and of course, became the rights of British Aerospace in the fullness of time.

One of the greater acts of arrogance that was perpetuated by the then officials in the Ministry of Defence during my time was to try to put the update and modification of the wing of the Hawk out to competitive tender. The Hawk wing had been designed to survive for a certain flight life, which had been handsomely exceeded, and its use in low-level training had placed stresses on the aircraft that the wing was not designed to take. It was therefore having a much harder life than anyone had envisaged when it was first put out to contract. The main spar and parts of the wing that were carrying most of the stress were being subjected to excesses that meant that the wing would need to be reworked. This work clearly belonged to the successors of the Hawker Siddeley design team; I was in no mood to allow it to go anywhere else and became increasingly irritated as I saw the antics of the Ministry of Defence attempting once more to override the legitimate rights of industry and put this work out to competitive tender, when quite clearly, since we held the industrial property rights, it could not be placed anywhere without our agreement. I cannot remember the exact number now that was required to be reworked, but the price that we started with was something in the order of £160 – 180 million, and by a process of 'salami slicing' we had been forced back through, in my view, idle threats of competition to a position where we were prepared to accept £130 million but had actually stuck at £140 million.

A final meeting was therefore to be held under the Chairmanship of the then Minister for Defence Procurement, Lord Trefgarne, to see whether this issue could be resolved. Lord Trefgarne is a nice, cuddly type of man who was, as many ministers are in that position, perhaps less comfortable with the opinions of his officials than he might have admitted. A meeting was therefore held in which on my side I had the people from my aircraft company, including Dick Evans, and on the other side the Chief of Defence Procurement, the Controller Aircraft and the Deputy Controller Aircraft, along with whatever official there was. It was my policy, and always has been, never to take papers into a Ministry meeting. It always seemed to me to give you a psychological advantage when they looked across from behind the piles of briefing papers they had, to a bunch of chaps who had nothing in front of them whatsoever and presumably, and indeed did have, the information necessary inside their brainbox.

Lord Trefgarne started by saying that he understood that there was a problem, and I said, before he could continue, 'There certainly is a problem, Minister. You are in breach of your contractual obligations to British Aerospace, and if you persist in this course of action, I shall have no alternative but to sue the Ministry of Defence.' Even my own chaps were a bit taken aback by this rather brusque approach, but it was my honest view. There was no way in which I was going to allow the Ministry of Defence to bully British Aerospace. Cutting a fine deal is one thing; using improper pressure and improper methods is quite another.

Trefgarne looked at me and smiled and said, 'Well, I'm sure we've no need to get to that position,' to which I replied, 'I am also sure we shouldn't get to that position, Minister, but I wish to make my position perfectly clear.' He acknowledged this and said,' Well now, surely there is a way in which we can compromise.' 'Indeed,' I said, 'there must be.' 'Now let's see,' said he,' what is the price difference?' 'Well,' I said, 'our price is a £160 million and your price, I understand is £130 million.' 'Why don't we just spilt the difference.' he asked. 'Done,' I said, and walked out with a contract worth £145 million, that he could have had for £130 million and that we should have had for £160 million. Nevertheless, it was a good deal, so good that the Chief of Defence Procurement had to leave the meeting lest he became overcome with rage. Both the Controller Aircraft and the Deputy Controller could hardly conceal their smiles, because both these chaps realised that we were perfectly within our rights to take a very strong and robust line. When we got outside, my chaps were gasping with amazement. 'Yes,' I said, 'we've won that one, but you'd better watch it because they will have us on the next one and the next one and the next one, if we're not jolly careful.' Meantime, we had struck a blow for freedom.

The Hawk was British Aerospace property but I could not understand why, in the words of that first stanza of that Fleet Air Arm song, since we didn't have a single-seat fighter, we couldn't produce a single-seat version of the Hawk. Even if it did not sell to the RAF it should certainly be able to be sold to many emerging nations as an excellent cheap subsonic fighter.

On my first visit to Dunsfold, after taking over British Aerospace, I walked into a hangar and there saw a Hawk with a Sea Eagle missile hanging underneath it. This was guaranteed to catch my attention, because Sea Eagle was my first success in achieving business for British Aerospace since I joined. 'Very impressive,' I said, 'I like the look of that. What I don't understand is why we've never built a single-seat version.' The chaps that were showing me round stopped and looked at me. 'But we've always wanted to, Sir.' 'Then why haven't you done it?' I asked. 'Well, because no one's ever agreed with us higher up.' 'Well, I agree with you,' I said, 'How much?' They looked at me in surprise. 'I tell you what,' I said, 'if you can produce a demonstrator single-seat Hawk for less than £30 millions, you've got a job. Go back, put your heads together and come up with a proposal to me, and say I want it.' There was a scurrying of feet as they departed. This led, in the fullness of time, to the demonstrator we built, the Hawk 200, with our own money but with the collaboration of many of our industrial partners in aerospace in Britain, including Rolls Royce. There was much talk of fitting an afterburner to the aircraft because, as I have said many times, the most saleable product is a single-seat fighter that makes a great cackle as it roars down the runway. What it does after it gets airborne is anybody's guess, and certainly it can put on a good aerobatic display – fifty years of aviation, forty nine years in a left hand turn.

So it came to pass that the Hawk 200 was produced and the demonstrator flew at Dunsfold. A great sales campaign was launched, and an Air Day was to be held at Dunsfold for the launch of the aircraft; we had invited most of the aerospace and national Press, and potential customer representatives in the United Kingdom, to witness the demonstration. The whole thing was going to be geared around the attack and air defence capability of this remarkable little aeroplane. It was to be flown by Jim Hawkins, and the day was fast approaching when I should appear, dressed in flying overalls with a special kind of badge with Hawk 200 on it, to open the ceremonies. I should add that

The Hawk 200 Single-Seater

499

I had flown the Hawk trainer on several occasions before and had thoroughly enjoyed the way in which the aeroplane flew. I don't think that anyone who has enjoyed flying a Hawk would forget the aeroplane. It is a classic out of that famous stable.

A full dress rehearsal was to be held the day before the demonstration, and coincidentally I was to take part in a competition that had been organised by the CBI in the Albert Hall. They had organised three competing teams to build a polystyrene castle. One was a team of industrialists, led by the then Chairman of United Biscuits, Hector Lang, in which I was a competitor; three groups of trade unionists, amongst whom I remember, was Brenda Dean; and three engineering students. I was on my way to the Albert Hall when the car 'phone rang. It was the General Manager at Dunsfold. 'I'm terribly sorry to have to tell you, Sir, but the Hawk 200 has just crashed.' I was stunned. The history of aviation is one of immense success and tragic setback, and this was one of the most tragic setbacks of my aviation career. I learned that the pilot had been killed, that the aeroplane had not come out of a particular manoeuvre that was part of the aerobatic display, and had flown straight into the ground. We had lost one of our most experienced test pilots and our demonstrator in a matter of seconds.

We cancelled the next day's performance, and the necessary Board of Enquiry was set in motion. I had two difficult tasks to perform. The first was to phone my office to tell my secretary as gently as possible that the man to whom she was very close was no longer with us. The other was to go to the Albert Hall to take part in the competition, with that news banging about in my head. Not one of my happiest days. The graduates won, the industrialists came second in the competition, I am glad to say, and the trade union officials came last. So I suppose, in a way, honour was satisfied on this particular front if on no other.

Having thought about what had happened and having sat in the Hawk 200, though I had not flown it, I was fairly certain that one of the problems was that when you're conducting complex aerobatic manoeuvres, the fact that you're sitting with such clear all round visibility as the Hawk 200 gives you, means that unless you rely totally on your instruments, particularly your artificial horizon, it is impossible to look back at the wings well enough to get a sense of whether you are right way up or not. It is very easy to become disorientated in a fish bowl effect, and many aircraft have been lost, particularly over the sea, by becoming totally disorientated when the sea and the sky merge together, and the same is true of a clear blue sky if you are conducting aerobatics and you cannot actually keep checking the position of your wings. Every instructor will tell you when you start your first loop 'throw your head well back and watch for the horizon to come up as you go over the top and make sure your wings are level'.

Sad and tragic as the whole thing was, the insurance on the aircraft expired at 12 noon that day, and the accident occurred just before noon. As a result we had the money to build another prototype and the aircraft has gone on to become the great success it deserves and a fitting epitaph to Jim Hawkins.

So we built our single seater fighter; regrettably it wasn't for the fleet.

43

Up the Down Escalator

I once heard Margaret Thatcher use the expression 'up the down escalator' in one of her television interviews and it reminded me that that was what I was originally going to call my own story because when I joined the Royal Navy in 1942 it was the largest Navy in the world. By the time I had left, it had shrunk under successive administrative cuts (and of course after the ending of the Second World War) and the beginning and prolongation of the Cold War. During that time the number of people in the Navy had declined dramatically, as had the number of Flag Ranks! Therefore, looking back on it, I suppose one would not have placed very good odds on anyone who started as a Naval Airman Second Class finishing up as a full Admiral. Nevertheless it is a reflection on the openness of the system that it actually happened.

Her remark was coupled with some other things she said which reminded me how right she was in her assessment of the way in which our country's affairs were being run during the time in which I found myself in the Ministry of Defence. It is also, I think, worth remembering how desperate we had become under successive years of Socialist Old Labour. It clearly wasn't working. In the end, all political parties cling to their dogma when their dogma has ceased to be fashionable. It might be right but it isn't timely, and the concept of nationalising everything, which the Socialists embraced with such enthusiasm, had been demonstrated to be a failure, yet they clung to it. The Conservative desire to privatise everything willy-nilly must also have its limitations. It seems to me there ought to be a balance, but perhaps that is just being too much of a simple sailor.

One of the things which depressed me most about my experience in the Ministry of Defence and in Whitehall, was the readiness with which our officials seemed to concede before they had started; they were essentially defeatist. I suppose history shows that at the end of all great empires there is a great wave of defeatism which sweeps across the whole establishment. Again I come back to the point of how much and how desperate we were to see a change of administration and the new fresh wind that was promised to be brought in by Margaret Thatcher.

At one particularly depressing period of our history, towards the end of the Socialist reign as it were, I remember a Board dinner given in the old admiralty dining room to which we invited a bunch of industrialists; I will not be indiscreet enough to mention their names but at the end of the dinner and as we were having our coffee and brandy, one of the industrialists present said, 'When are you chaps going to take over? The situation is desperate, this country is approaching a precipice; when are you going to start doing something about it?' There was a moment of shocked surprise and then some of my colleagues responded very positively. Then it was my turn to be shocked because the constitutional position of the Services was perfectly clear to me and therefore I thought it necessary, looking at the strained expression in the eyes of the Deputy Under-Secretary (Naval), that I should intervene and say light-heartedly, 'Well, thank you very much for your confidence in our ability, gentlemen, but I have to tell you that the Navy is not very good at this kind of thing. Our normal policy is to proceed promptly to sea and to stay there until we find out who is going to win and then come back again. So if you really want to make any progress you should talk to the General commanding the London district, not us!' This was sufficient to take the moment of potential tension out of the conversation. I then went on to say that in my view the situation was much more serious than approaching a precipice, because if you came to the edge of a precipice you could at least look over and recognise that it was a hell of a long drop. But if we were to go into decline by stepping down a never-ending footpath that led us eventually to the rocks below then each step would be different, each step could be justified. And, indeed, on one particular evening at a reception at the Ministry of Defence after a particularly difficult day, I said to Frank Cooper, then Permanent Under-Secretary who happened to be at the same party, 'I now understand, Frank, why the Jews went voluntarily to the gas chambers.' He looked at me in some surprise and then said, 'How do you mean?'

'Well, it's perfectly clear to me that they were led by people like you.' He looked even more surprised. 'What do you mean, Ray?'

'Well, not you personally, Frank,' I said, 'of course, but your ilk, your contemporaries I think will lead this country to its destruction, walking backwards in front of it and apologising for every step they take.'

I believe Margaret Thatcher to have been absolutely right when she said there was a feeling of defeatism throughout the whole institution. Success is relatively easy to achieve, you just have to be determined to achieve it; once you give up then you might as well forget it. All those management boards on which I sat and on which we were interfaced

The Prime Minister and Denis at the Farnborough Air Show

with our colleagues from the Continent, or the United States, it didn't make the slightest bit of difference, our civil servants always seemed to start from the premise that they would have to finish up by reaching a compromise. They therefore proceeded to the position of compromise by moving their pieces into the centre of the table while the people on the other side hadn't moved anything at all, and furthermore had absolutely no intention of moving anything towards us and so, for the most part, we were seen off.

504

There are always buzz words going around and they generally have a double meaning. The one I remember most was 'flexible' – one had to be flexible in one's approach; one had to be realistic – what this meant was, in fact, to be prepared to be flaccid – be prepared to surrender. Margaret Thatcher changed all that and one must not forget the great relief it was to see the opinion polls swinging so decisively in her favour to form the first of that long succession of Conservative administrations. I remember the night before the election, or a few days before, I was invited by an ex-Naval colleague of mine to the Mud-suckers and Dredgers Ball – no, I am not joking, I think it actually was that – and I, as the guest of honour, had an opportunity to harangue these characters. I remember saying how much I looked forward to the new dawn that was coming and we could forget decline and all the nonsense that had been preached for the last twenty years, almost continuously, and start to concentrate on the regeneration of wealth in this country so that we could hold our heads up high once again and proceed to get better. It was interesting for me to note that my speech did not generate a great wave of support. There are a vast number of people who seem to relish decline or certainly don't relish being disturbed on the way down.

Given the right environment and the right kind of government backing, and a change of attitude, there was no doubt that great things could still be achieved and the aerospace industry was the one great intact capability in which we could be amongst the top three in the world, and it was my ambition to make British Aerospace the greatest aerospace company in Europe. It was this kind of attitude that I adopted when it came to the promotion of the European fighter programme.

44

The European Fighter

It was quite obvious to my colleagues in the Military Aircraft Division of British Aerospace that unless we managed to get a new combat fighter into our programme then the business would slowly fade away. We had seen, as a result of the successive failures of government to pursue any consistent aerospace policy, that our markets were being eroded by the French who had the great virtues of consistency: a determination to protect their aircraft industry and to make it the largest and best in Europe.

As a result of changes in government policy over the years we had no aircraft for sale, which was desirable as far as emerging nations were concerned. There is a great deal of nonsense talked about aircraft performance, and it is important to set the record straight, or straight as far as I am concerned. At the end of my time as Vice Chief of the Naval Staff in the Ministry of Defence, and just prior to my retirement, I walked down the corridor to see my opposite number, the Vice Chief of the Air Staff. I said goodbye to him formally and then asked him if he would like 36 years of Naval aviation experience for free. Of course everybody looks a gift horse in the mouth and he was no exception.

'How do you mean, Ray?' said he.

'Well,' I said 'would you like to hear my views on aircraft procurement policy for the future as a result of my experience?'

'Of course,' said he, and I knew that he was merely being polite. What I said was, 'Quite simply, supersonic speed is an illusion; put your money into V/STOL and you will have the support of the Navy, the support of the Army, and most of the world's Air Forces. Except, probably, of the Royal Air Force.

The fact is that supersonic speed in a fighter can only result in an excessive usage of fuel: the aircraft very rapidly proceeds to run out of it and has to return to base. Furthermore, if you hang external armaments on it and it cannot go supersonic anyway! What is most important in confrontation and in readiness to defeat an enemy is endurance. Aircraft with long endurance can be airborne and be held airborne without constantly returning to base (which involves

506

turnround and the risk, of course, that they will go unserviceable; there will be crew fatigue and so on) to be ready for combat is what operations require. Just as the correct place for ships to be is at sea, not stuck in harbour – witness Taranto: ships might be sunk if they go to sea, but they will almost certainly be destroyed if they stay in harbour – the same is true of aircraft: the easiest way to destroy them is on the ground. Nevertheless, the market demands supersonic aircraft; the market demands what I call the 'Biggles' approach, the fluttering of the red scarf out of the cockpit as the aeroplane crackles down the runway to thunderous applause from the audience who really don't understand what it is going to do. In the same way, I used to remark when large number of people came to watch the wonders of aircraft being launched from aircraft carriers, or from anywhere else for that matter – and the subsequent recovery, 'Doesn't it look grand, but I wonder what they have been doing in between?' Thirty eight years of aviation, thirty-seven years in a left-hand turn! However, the first lesson of marketing is, give the customer what it wants; for the most part, what was wanted was an interception supersonic fighter, and our only chance of getting one was if we could get it on the back of procurement by the Royal Air Force – the good news was the RAF thought that it wanted one too!

The bitter experience of the aircraft industry in attempting to get any logical programme out of Government, however, led us to question whether we would ever get there. So a group of aerospace companies came together to form a potential lobby under the leadership of Ivan Yates who was then beginning to rise up in the organisation of the Military Aircraft Group, as it was then called. He eventually took over from Freddie Page. Ivan is an extremely intelligent and able aeronautical engineer, and understood very well the importance of such a project to the future of British Aerospace. He therefore devoted his considerable energies to getting the industry to club together to make a proposal to the Government on the basis that we would fund half of the cost of developing a demonstrator to meet the RAF's operational requirement for such a fighter. He managed through the auspices of the Society of British Aerospace Companies to bring together groups that were often engaged quite fiercely in competition – Smiths Industries, Marconi Avionics, Dowty, Rolls Royce, EMI, Ferranti and so on – under the leadership of British Aerospace. The plan was to offer to part-fund the development of the Experimental Aircraft Programme by industry, but we needed government support. Intense lobbying softened up the natural resistance of the MOD until we finally reached the crunch meeting with the Controller Aircraft, Dougie Low.

Dick Evans and I were kept hanging about outside his office while he conferred with a mass of officials, and when we were finally admitted there were no seats for us! After some shuffling, we were asked by Dougie whether our estimate of the cost would be £60 million. I replied, 'Of which you would provide two thirds.' At this point, Dougie had a massive nosebleed! As he sat clasping a handkerchief to his gushing nose with his head thrown back there was a deafening silence, only to be broken by my saying to relieve the tension, 'If I'd known you would react this way, I'd have settled for less!' Dougie recovered – he was apparently subject to these attacks but his timing was impeccable. After the meeting reconvened, we struck a deal. It would be 50/50 – or so they thought – but we had a programme! Much credit must go to Dougie – without his support we would not have succeeded. As a result of our work we were able to persuade John Nott, then Secretary of State for Defence, to agree to make a statement at the Farnborough Air Show in 1986 to the effect that we intended to go ahead with the production of a demonstrator in conjunction with our continental partners in the Tornado programme. It was the success of the Tornado venture that led us to believe that this would be the most successful way ahead for our programme.

To my considerable surprise, the statement was made and we were ready to roll. The usual debate then started with our European partners about the way in which we should divide the programme up, and it was finally agreed that the UK would produce the front end of the aeroplane and one wing, while the Italians produced another wing and part of the tail unit, and the Germans would be responsible for the remainder.

We started down this route, and soon discovered that what we could do as a private company and what our German partners MBB could do as a government-owned company, was quite different. Our Italian partner, on the other hand, with the mysterious and wonderful way in which Italians seem to work, was able effectively to do what it wanted with the full support of its government. MBB, however, found difficulty in persuading the German government to fund their requirements because at the time they had no stated operational requirement; since technically they had no money of their own, they couldn't do what we had done. In the end, after considerable anguish, they had to pull out. It was not only bad news for them, it was even worse news for us becaue we then had to fund the rear of the aeroplane. Ivan, not to be deterred, came up with the idea of putting the rear end of a Tornado into the demonstrator, which made it look a bit hump-backed when it finally flew but at least enabled us to overcome the problem! Of course, all this took years to bring to fruition and as they passed so changes in administration brought Michael Heseltine in as Secretary of State for Defence. The impact of the demonstrator had achieved two things: first, it had impelled the Government forward in its contemplation of a new generation of fighters for the RAF, and second, it had brought the French to realise that for the first time in recent history they were going to be left at the starting post unless they started to do something themselves. They reacted by announcing that they were going to go ahead with the design of the Rafael; this would also be a demonstrator, and it would be competitive, of course, with ours. It was widely recognised in Whitehall that there would be considerable merit if we could have a consortium which included the French, but it was fairly clear to industry that Dassault had absolutely no desire to join a consortium and I refer you back to the remarks made to me by Matra at the time they left the consortium which was then trying to produce the successor to Sidewinder for the European Air Forces.

There ensued a continuous dialogue between the various UK industrial parties, and we would appear together regularly in Michael Heseltine's office in order to press the points of view for which we wanted Government support in the negotiations that were then beginning to take place about the future of the European Fighter Programme. Meantime the demonstrator was coming along well and, despite the setbacks we had received as a result of the withdrawal of MBB, we were able to look forward to a successful demonstration at the 1988 Farnborough Air Show. Unfortunately, at a critical moment towards the run-up to the show there was a strike at Warton, and it was fairly clear that it was thought by the unions that the way to extort more money and conditions from the management was to hold up the demonstrator and make it miss Farnborough. I therefore reacted with a fairly simple instruction: 'I do not care whether this aircraft goes to this Farnborough, next Farnborough, or never at all, it is not to be allowed to enter into any consideration in our negotiations with the unions.' I am pleased to say that through the dedication of various supervisory staff and management the programme was kept on target; once it was realised that the threat was not going to work, the strike was resolved and we were able to meet the original target date.

There now began a regular series of meetings under the chairmanship of Michael Heseltine, designed to keep everybody on target and to make sure that we were all speaking with the same voice because the inter-governmental discussions that were taking place were more important than the deliberations of the individual partners. Michael proved to be a great ally; he listened carefully to what we had to say, always had a reasoned point of view to put forward, and in general was supportive of our cause. The Ministry's team was led very ably by

Donald Spiers, who was now the Controller Aircraft, and he was supported by the Vice-Chief of the Air Staff. It sometimes seemed to me that the Air Force itself was somewhat equivocal in its support for the new fighter, presumably becaue it knew that if it was not to go ahead they would have to find something else. This would probably be the F-18, or even the F-16, and therefore it did not wish to tie itself too firmly to this project lest, as history had shown so often, it should be lost. In other words, it didn't want another TSR2.

The meetings were normally conducted with myself, Ralph Robins from Rolls Royce, and sometimes one other, usually Derek Alan Jones from Ferranti leading the equipment side. The programme was, of course, one of top priority for British Aerospace, and on my taking over as Managing Director of the company I became more and more caught up in the political battle for this particular product. All seemed to be going well until one day I was asked to go to see Michael Heseltine on my own, which I duly did, and I found him lounging on the chaise longue, which was one of his habits, and he addressed me in the following fashion: 'The European Fighter Programme is going to fail because of one particular person.' I fell straight into the trap, of course, and said, 'Who might that be?' 'It is you,' said he. I was genuinely shocked and asked what he meant. 'It is because you will not do a deal with Dassault,' he said. 'If we could do a deal with Dassault we would have the European Fighter, but if you cannot do a deal with Dassault then we won't get one.' 'But Secretary of State,' said I, 'I assure you that if I thought it were possible to do a deal with Dassault I would bend over backwards, well almost, in order to achieve that objective, but I do not believe that it is possible. I believe they are set in their ways and determined either to lead the consortium, which is unacceptable to us, or to go ahead on their own; but if you think it is due to my intransigence I assure you that I am prepared to go over to talk to Dassault tomorrow.' 'I think that would be a very good thing, Ray,' he replied. And so I duly presented myself at the famous Dassault headquarters just outside Paris, a rather lovely house, where I met with M. Valliase, supported by his then Managing Director, Revlon Falco, a very competent and level-headed potential partner. However, it was clear that it was not he who was going to call the shots, but Papa Dassault in the background. My meeting was pleasant enough and covered much of the ground that was necessary in order to understand the position of each partner.

The French position was quite simply that the size of the European Fighter that we had come up with was too large, that it would therefore be too costly, and that their model of Rafael would be best and preferable for them. Underlying all this was the necessity on the part

510

of the French to design an aircraft that was compatible with the capability of their then aircraft carriers. If the aircraft was to exceed 40,000 lb in weight it was difficult to see how it could feature in the armament of the French Navy, whereas we had no such constraint after the demise of the British carriers (although ours would have been able to operate aircraft of weights greater than this). Nevertheless, that was a restriction which obviously affected their vision. They were also obsessed with the idea, not unreasonably, that weight and cost went together, and that too many partners spoilt the broth. They would rather have seen the thing developed as an Anglo-French programme with them leading, with the requirements of Rafael paramount in their mind, rather than anything else. This, of course, was a position that would be totally unacceptable to us.

We did, however, have to be quite sure that the aeroplane we were designing met the RAF's operational requirements. If it didn't it was not a runner, if it did then at least one could argue that it was what the RAF wanted. What was just as important was what the Luftwaffe wanted and what the Italian and Spanish Air Forces wanted, and after months of wrangling and debate and study they more or less came to the same conclusion that the RAF had come to. The specifications were slightly different for the various Air Forces, but all agreed that an aircraft that looked more or less like, and weighed more or less what our projected aircraft was designed to do, would be the one they wanted and that anything less than this would be neither acceptable not, at the very least, desirable. My previous experience of the way the Services could shift their operational requirements to meet the political whim had me less than confident that they would be able to sustain this but they did insofar as it went, certainly the RAF did, and so we were on fairly firm ground in rejecting an aircraft based on Rafael which clearly was too small to meet the requirement. Nevertheless there became a problem when the Germans thought that the aircraft was too large and began to argue for a smaller aircraft.

The key to any successful aircraft programme is, of course, the performance of the engine, and Rolls Royce had nailed its colours firmly to the mast of a new and more simplified three-spool engine that was to be designed to meet the requirements of the aircraft. As the requirement for making the aircraft smaller became more strident (the Germans began to have second thoughts) so it became necessary to explain to our political masters that if you started to make a very small high-performance engine it was almost of necessity going to be a very hot engine and thus prone to the usual kinds of problems that we had seen in the past. All these arguments had to be trotted out in front of Michael Heseltine and the Permanent Under-Secretary, Clive

511

The unveiling

Whitmore, and it is fair to say that they listened with care and responded responsibly. I felt fairly certain that if we could keep the thing on the rails then we would be successful. I have gone over these events with Ralph Robins recently. They, Rolls Royce, met all the requirements though I doubted this at the time.

I duly reported my first meeting with Dassault to Michael Heseltine, but said that we had arranged to have our officials look at the various differences that existed and come back and report; I would then go back and have another meeting with them. These meetings were always amusing because it took me a little time to realise that when M. Valliase asked to be excused for a moment, it was nothing to do with the strength of his bladder but the fact that he was going out to have a telephone conversation with Papa Dassault, sitting somewhere in his château, who was desirous of knowing what this bloody Englishman was up to.

It was clear from the last meeting, very sadly to me, that there was no way ahead. I had been invited round the Dassault factory where a prototype Rafael was in construction, and one of the things that M. Valliase emphasised to me was that collaborative programmes produced more money for the people who made the connectors than for anybody else. This was a subtle way of saying that he didn't think that it was sensible to have collaborative programmes, but that the aircraft should be designed and built in one place with the partners contributing. There was much strength in his argument, if this meant Dassault; it also meant, of course, that the final assembler and designer would be in a dominant position, and this was clearly unacceptable to us.

After my second meeting with Dassault, I again reported back to Michael Heseltine and this time I said to him, 'I have done what you asked me to do. I have explained to you why I do not believe it is possible to collaborate with the French, but if you would like me to explain to you, or give you my view of what French defence policy is, then I would be happy to do so.' He looked at me quizzically and said, 'What do you mean?' 'Well' I said, 'Would you like me to give you my view of what French defence policy effectively is.' 'What is it?' 'Well,' said I, 'it is, retire gracefully to the gates of Paris, roll over and surrender.' I put it in somewhat more graphic terms than that. 'If you wish that to be British defence policy then, of course, you only have two things to do, Secretary of State. One is to stand up in Parliament and say so, and the second, having got their endorsement, is to ask me to produce a really sexy-looking aeroplane at low cost, which will not meet the operational requirement. And that, of course, I would be able to do, but you have to tell me that that is what you want.'

Eventually Michael suggested that the only way of resolving the deadlock between the potential partners, but not the partners in the demonstrator aircraft, was to get somebody other than the British to arbitrate. He approached Manfred Werner, who was then the Secretary of State for Defence in Germany, who very kindly offered to hold a meeting with the so-called disputing partners, myself and my French opposite numbers. I therefore proceeded to Bonn to meet with Manfred Werner, a charming, erudite gentleman who never failed to impress me by his ability to understand questions and come to a positive answer in a fairly short time. I sat with him alongside my French opposite number, M. Valliase. He had with him M. Revlon Falco, and I had with me, I think, Ivan Yates. MBB were only to be seen in the distance, and one of the difficulties that we experienced in the whole of this negotiation was the equivocal position that our German colleagues took. Not, I am glad to say, the Italians. But the Germans, as a totally state-owned company, were very nervous about being seen to be trying to lead their government, rather than the other way around. All our experience was that if we didn't lead our Government we would have nothing at all!

Werner started the meeting by saying, 'Well, I understand that there are two opposing views. On the one hand the British, and on the other hand the French, and therefore there is a disagreement between you two.' I was quick to respond. 'I wish to correct that impression, Minister. In fact, of the five partners, four are agreed and one disagrees. The Italians, the Spanish, the Germans and the British are decided on a model; the French have decided on another, so it is not one against one, it is four against one.' It was important to get this point across. 'There is really, therefore, nothing for me to defend,' I continued, 'I am merely here as a representative of four partners, it is for the odd man out, the French, to explain why they cannot agree.' The French proposal clearly failed to meet the operational requirements of the other four, so the outcome of that meeting, therefore, was a very firm decision that the four would have to go ahead without the French and that the French would have to go ahead without the four. It was a shame, but it was almost inevitable. I felt, as I sat there, that this confirmed all my experience on the management board of the Anglo-French variable-geometry aircraft, that had come to nothing, and various other programmes that had come to the same end: this was the inability of the French to be able to move away from a preconceived idea that was essentially based on the fact that they were determined to lead the programme and that exports were their first priority. It was thus possible for our Secretary of State, as a result of this meeting, to recommend the go-ahead of the European Fighter based on four nations but without the French.

Many battles were to follow in order to keep the thing on track but thanks to the single-mindedness of Ivan Yates in the beginning, and the courage of our commercial partners in the UK under the leadership of British Aerospace, we had done that which we had set out to do: get ourselves a programme that would enable us to have an aircraft that we could sell into the most prolific market for military equipment in the world, the interceptor fighter market. We hadn't had one since goodness knows when – the Hunter, I suppose – whereas the French with the Mirage and the Americans with the F-16 and F-18 had been able to hold sway to their entire satisfaction. Only the Hawk, that amazing little aircraft that had resulted from a competitive tender long before anybody who subsequently gained fame for such activities had thought of it, only that was able to represent us at the bottom end of that particular area of activity.

45

Royal Ordnance

After my experience with Sperry, we approached the next opportunity for acquisition with caution. However, the more we looked at Royal Ordnance the more we recognised that it would be a very sensible and complementary business. I was determined, nevertheless that it should be operated as a separate and independent company and not become embodied in and over-bureaucratised by British Aerospace.

The $64,000 question, of course, was how much we would have to pay in order to win it; we knew that it was going to be an open competition, and we thought that GEC and GKN at least, and possible Trafalgar House; would all be bidding, though for different reasons. Trafalgar House's bid would be mainly on account of the very large property assets that Royal Ordnance owned in the shape of Enfield and Waltham Abbey, two vast acreages that were no longer required to satisfy the requirements of Royal Ordnance and which, in fact, had already been declared by them as being surplus to their requirements. They had sought planning permission to develop the Enfield site, which had been turned down. All these facts were known to the bidders and to the general public, as well as to the press at large.

I knew that the Board would not be enthusiastic to support the acquisition, purely on the basis that they didn't seem to me to wish to support anything that I wanted to do, but nevertheless the case was made and put to them and once again actively supported by the executives of the company, so I wasn't alone. Roland Smith, who had just been appointed as a non-executive director, sat next to me, and when the question of the bid for Royal Ordnance came up he began to take a keen interest. I was asked what price I thought was required to get it, and I said that I thought that it would be somewhere between £150 million and £180 million, and closer to £180 million if we really wanted to get it. A long debate then proceeded to take place among the non-executives and the Chairman about what the true value of Royal Ordnance was and what was the view of our financial advisers. Generally speaking, the view of financial advisers on these occasions is hardly worth having becaue they never wish to commit themselves. It can, however, be interesting to listen to a debate among well-qualified people discussing a subject of which they have no detailed information but in which they wish to partake so as to demonstrate their ability to make a contribution! None of our non-executive directors had any inside knowledge of Royal Ordnance, what it made or what it was about, and I therefore found this type of debate rather frustrating.

Towards the end of the debate Roland nudged me and said in his good Mancunian accent, 'We want this, don't we?' To which I replied 'Yes, we do.' He bided his time. I was then told that we should not bid more than £150 million for Royal Ordnance. 'In which case,' said I, 'we won't get it.' Roland then came to my assistance and suggested that if we really wanted it, and he believed that it seemed on the face of it to be an ideal thing for us to go for, we should give the Chief Executive some broader band in which to operate. I finally managed to screw out of the Board authority to go within a budget of £150 million to £180 million, but no higher. As soon as the Board meeting was over I formulated with our advisers a bid at £180 million.

In the meantime we had been dealing with the disposal of the site at Weybridge, and we had taken on board a joint-venture partner in the shape of Trafalgar House. Towards the end of the run-up to the final bids for Royal Ordnance, Trafalgar House decided that, having looked at the business as a whole, it was not interested in progressing. I was interested, however, in the continuing development of our sites and suggested, or at least Eric Parker did, that in the event that we were successful he would hope that we would continue to be their partner in developing some of the Royal Ordnance sites.

One of the more worrying aspects of bidding for government contracts or for bits of establishments at this time, was that you were never sure how many 'last and finals' there were going to be; in other words, you would think that you had actually won a particular competition only to be told that a further round was to be held because other people had come up with some interesting ideas. In fact, it became part of the policy to come up with interesting ideas if you thought you were losing the competition! As a result, Tim Pearce and I were asked to go to see the Minister in charge of Procurement, Lord Trefgarne, to have a chat with him before the bids were finally assessed. He greeted us in his usual friendly and comfortable way and proceeded to tell us that they had had some very interesting and competitive bids for Royal Ordnance from highly regarded companies of which, of course, ours was one, but that it was going to be a very tight issue and he wanted to give us an opportunity to revise our bid upwards if we thought that was something we should do. Tin and I had of course discussed this before we went in and, apart from the fact that we had no authority from the Board to go beyond £180 million, I didn't believe that this was something that we would particularly want to get involved in; it would become a Dutch auction and you never knew where it would end. So we agreed that there would be no movement and so, when asked by the Minister whether we wished to increase our bid in any way, the answer was 'No'. He smiled and cocked his head on one side, which was one of his mannerisms, and said, 'Are you quite sure, because it's going to be very tight and I wouldn't want you to think you hadn't been given an opportunity to rethink your position.' 'No,' we said. Tin was quite firm. 'We do not wish to increase our offer, which stands.' And so it came about that we won and GKN lost.

It was quite accidental that I had a luncheon engagement the day of the announcement at which the GKN top management were present, along with myself, as guests, and they were kind enough to congratulate me on my acquisition. We knew, however, that they were in fact very disappointed because their Board had not given them the flexibility that they required to go up to what they thought would be the winning figure.

We then proceeded to look at the development and reorganisation of Royal Ordnance, and the first thing to do was to get the top management sorted out. We agreed satisfactory and sensible separation terms for the management which was going to be replaced. It was unfortunate for them that what they had been led to believe, that a management buy-out was the preferred option, had not proved possible and therefore they were effectively left out in the cold. I put in Dr Maurice Dixson, who was the Commercial Director of the Military Aircraft Division, to run Royal Ordnance, and he chose as his second in command, Peter Kenyon as his Operations Director.

As always in these cases, once you get in there you begin to find things that are not going as well as they should; in particular, we found that we had three massive problems. One was the production and delivery of the Army's light gun, for which there was a fixed price contract; second was the arrangement for and the contract that had been signed with the Ministry for the development of the new automatic weapon which was produced at Enfield; and the third was the motor for the Alarm missile, which is covered in a separate chapter.

I became Chairman of Royal Ordnance as part of the devolution process that I have described earlier. It was not long before Maurice had to get stuck into sorting out the organisation – a difficult task, as I remember him showing me the existing organisational chart which he described as looking like an aerial view of Clapham Junction. All this needed to be straightened out as well as the major contracts which, if they were not taken care of, would cause grave losses.

As a separate issue there was the question of what to do with the

Top and Bottom – reaction to the purchase of Royal Ordnance. Middle – my attempt to get Macdonnell Douglas 'MacDac' into partnership with Airbus

redundant sites at Enfield and Waltham Abbey. We therefore asked Trafalgar House to help us look at ways in which we could perhaps do something with these sites, and it was my clear belief that any realisable value of the real estate would only pay for the cost of moving and restructuring the organisation. For example, it was our belief soon after the acquisition that, in order to make the small arms contract achievable, we needed to completely restructure and automate the manufacturing line and move it somewhere else. The existing facilities at Enfield were just not capable, even at peak production, of satisfying the contract that Royal Ordnance had signed! As far as the light gun was concerned, eventually we had to start with an audit from the bottom up, to find exactly what was in the factory! There had been no proper records kept since almost the beginning of time, and stuff was lying around on the factory floor without anyone being quite sure what it was and where it was supposed to go!

It was therefore somewhat galling to find that an analyst had looked at the total acreage of Enfield and Waltham Abbey and, by the simple process of multiplying the acreage by the value of building land in that area, had come to a figure for the value of the land which was far in excess of anything that we had ever heard of or certainly were ever likely to achieve. This was particularly so since planning permission on Enfield had already been rejected once, and the ground at Waltham Abbey was polluted by explosives being stored there and would cost quite a lot of money to have it cleaned up. Nevertheless, in the way in which these stories are handled, it became a common belief that we had ripped off the Government in the purchase of Royal Ordnance. We had, in fact, bid more than anybody else, and had been in possession of no more information than was available in the public domain and to all our competitors and to the analysts alike, if they had cared to look at it. The belief that we had somehow managed to pull one off was not true but certainly not conducive to dealings with the Government if they were to believe such a story. Fortunately they didn't but it didn't stop them getting almost as much stick as we did for failing to get the proper price for Royal Ordnance!

The other side-effect of this kind of story is to distort the share price, and it is very difficult to see how these statements can be corrected. If you say that it is not true, the sites are not worth this much, then people will merely say that you are trying to play down the story and in fact, of course, there is a great bonanza sitting there. It is almost impossible to disabuse people of something they wish to believe. This episode did, however, serve to bring to a head a matter which had been wrangling in my bosom for many years; that was, how we managed the property assets that we actually owned.

One of the conditions that had been part of the negotiations for the purchase of Royal Ordnance was to give the new owner time to turn Royal Ordnance from a wholly-owned government subsidiary designed to produce all its armament requirements to a company that would be able to be competitive in a world sense. It was recognised by everybody that this would not be a simple task, and there would therefore need to be a gradual phasing out of the main contracts for shells and bullets and general explosives, which had been the prerogative of Royal Ordnance. Negotiations thus centred on the way in which these orders would be phased out over the first few years of the new ownership, and the eventual amount that would remain within Royal Ordnance's exclusive right. It was recognised that it was essential to maintain some permanent capability within the United Kingdom.

As soon as we became the owners, we therefore also became subject to competition on a worldwide basis. One of the newer companies that had sprung up to compete with us was ASDA, which had moved quickly to acquire a Belgian manufacturer and thus enabled the company to be more competitive than it might otherwise have been. It was soon clear to us, however, that we were beginning to lose contracts to our competitors and we couldn't really understand why. Of course, we had no clear evidence of the prices that had been charged, but we were surprised that, having had long runs and the experience of producing various basic commodities and products, we were being undercut by start-up companies. We could only assume that they must be losing money in the process, although that is always a dangerous assumption to make in a competitive world.

It was to be some years before we discovered that some of the reasons why we were losing contracts was undoubtedly because certain inducements were being offered by some of our competitors in order to win contracts. It is a paradox that competition, which is held to be of benefit to everybody and, for most of the time, probably is, can have some unforeseen consequences. For example, when Royal Ordnance was the exclusive provider of all ordnance for the Services there was no possibility of kickbacks or inducements being offered to officials, civil or otherwise, in order to influence the outcome of a contract because it was coming to Royal Ordnance anyway. The minute you introduce competition, however, you introduce at the same time the possibility of corruption. It would seem, therefore, that, like most things that involve a step change in procedures, it is necessary sometime to think beyond the simple benefits that might flow from a policy, to consider some of the unfortunate side-effects that might result, and be prepared in advance to secure the system against abuse.

I do not recall that any of the officials who were trying to evade the contractual terms under which we had bought the company by forcing us to compete for products that were contractually ours, were ever brought to book for dealing with such people. Unfortunately, certain chickens never seem to come home to their proper roost.

46

Rover

One morning in early 1988, Roland (who had taken over from Tin Pearce as Chairman) popped into my office to tell me that he had been to a reception the night before where he had met Graham Day, then I believe Chairman and CEO of Rover, and in the course of conversation had asked him what the plans were for Rover. Subsequently he had asked whether he thought that if a bid was made for Rover it would be acceptable to the Government. Apparently Roland had received an indication that any offer for Rover would probably be considered. Roland then asked me what I thought of this idea. I said that I didn't know what to think because it was a bit difficult to get one's mind around it. Nevertheless, as I was off for a Far Eastern visit shortly after this event, if he wanted to think about it then we could talk again when I came back, because presumably there was no particular hurry about this idea.

Roland was fairly expansive about the idea that the Government would probably have to pay somebody quite a lot to take Rover away and that it would be on the basis of it effectively being recapitalised. I said it was all a question of whether Rover was in a fit shape to be privatised and whether it looked as if its future as an independent operator was sustainable. Leaving him with the thought of what might be, I proceeded to depart for the Far East. During the course of my tour I had several 'phone conversations with Roland in which he informed me that he had had discussions with David Young, then Secretary of State for Trade and Industry, in which it was fairly clear that if we wanted to proceed, we would be pushing at an open door. However, Roland said he had refused to commit to anything until I was available to have a look at it and discuss it with him. 'I will not do anything without my Chief Executive being present,' I remember him saying. I then suggested that if it was that urgent I could break my visit and come home so that we could get stuck into this opportunity, but we both agreed that if I were to suddenly cancel my visit and return home it might raise speculation that we would rather do without. So it was that I finished my tour and returned to the UK to face up to this new opportunity.

Collusion. Roland Smith and me

It was during the Far East visit that I met Mr Kim, the Chief Executive of Daewoo Industries, at that time a very successful Korean company, and over dinner he gave me the story of the growth of Korean industry, and Daewoo in particular, and all that it had achieved. I listened to what he had to say and then I said, 'I think you have achieved remarkable success; which, however, do you think is the more difficult task, starting with a clean sheet of paper, as you did, or taking a group of companies that had previously been fiercely competitive and had achieved great reputations in their own particular fields but which were then overmanned and overgeared in terms of the number of projects they had, and imbued with all the historical ideas of their own value; and to take this group, in the midst of a decline in the manufacturing base in the country, and turn it into a profitable private-enterprise culture?' He said he had no doubt that the latter was the most difficult task.

When I returned I suggested to Roland that the first thing I needed to do was to meet with Graham Day but that this had to be kept fairly low key lest anyone locked on to what we were up to. Graham was therefore invited to come to our house in Eaton Terrace, and he duly appeared. I asked him whether he felt comfortable with the idea of working within the framework of British Aerospace and he countered by saying that he had worked for an Admiral before. This had been Tony Griffin at the time of the nationalisation of the shipbuilding industry, and I did say that there were, of course, different types of Admirals, as there were different types of shipbuilders and motor manufactures. I little realised how his experience with British Shipbuilders had coloured his views of senior Naval personnel! This was to be revealed at a much later date. I also asked Graham Day whether he believed that the situation was as we had been led to believe, that is, that the massive injection of government money that had been put into Rover had been put to good use, that it was now at the bottom of a trough of capability and, with the investments that had been made and the association that had been struck with Honda, whether the company was really, in his view, at the point of take-off and recovery? He said he believed that it was.

I then asked him the third part of the equation, which was whether he could give me some sort of guarantee that he would remain associated with Rover for a period of three years. He said he could give me that undertaking; he was not particularly concerned with continuing in the demanding role of Chief Executive; he was more intent, at this stage in his career, on taking on the Chairmanship and non-executive role in various companies, rather than staying at the coalface. We talked about a possible successor and I think it was at this meeting that he mentioned his ideas about bringing George Simpson back from Daf, where he had been sent to straighten out the Daf/Leyland enterprise, to be his effective successor. I took him at his word on this, which subsequently was proved to be extremely sound in all respects, and he certainly honoured his agreement to remain associated with Rover. I believed it was important because he had established a reputation in the eyes of the Government and industry at large as being a man who had done a great deal for Rover and whose success was associated very much with the fortunes of Rover. Of course, one can argue that the turnaround at British Leyland took place much earlier under previous Chairmen and Chief Executives who laid the foundations for the relationship with Honda, the streamlining of the operation and the massive investment programme, but nevertheless, Graham was important to our successful acquisition of Rover at that time.

The next move was to acquaint the Board as to how far we had got and then move to the second stage. The information that we had gained on Rover and the information imparted to our colleagues had

524

been restricted to Roland and me because the dangers of leaks were all too obvious. And so it was that the Board was duly acquainted with the conversations we had had and the opportunities as we perceived them, and we sought their authority to enter into formal negotiations. As you can imagine, there was a very lengthy debate about the merits of this endeavour but Roland was his most persuasive self and convinced the Board that we should proceed to the next stage. This was a meeting with David Young and his advisers on the one side and Roland, Bernard Friend and me, with Dudley Eustace now in attendance; he had arrived to take over from Bernard Friend who had agreed to stay for what I thought was an unnecessarily long period of indoctrination.

The meeting proceeded in the usual David Young bright and breezy fashion; not a man for hanging about in any event, he was keen to do the deal. He saw that it was a great opportunity for the Government to divest itself of what had been a long-lived white elephant and to discharge part of his remit of getting rid of as much of the nationalised industries in Britain as could possibly be effected.

The question hinged on the terms and conditions under which the deal could be done. As I recall, at the time the deal was struck it was on the basis of the Government injecting £850 million into Rover and we would pay a notional £150 million to acquire the assets that were then on offer. This seemed like a good deal, but of course it depended on whether you believed that Rover was viable and likely to remain so for a reasonable period of time. Part of the condition was the agreement that we should not dispose of Rover for five years from the time of purchase. This seemed not unreasonable if we had got our figures right, and at the conclusion of the meeting, after leaving David Young's office, Roland turned to me and said, in his broad Mancunian accent, 'Ooh, this is a grand deal. This is a great opportunity. Ooh, it's a grand deal, Ray.' To which I said, 'Yes, but we have to think about the figure at which the deal will actually be done and what our walk-away figure will be.' He looked at me in some surprise, 'No, no,' he said, 'the deal has been done at that figure, or will be done.' 'I'm afraid', I said to Roland, 'that we have done a deal with somebody who believes he can deliver that deal but who will find as the thing progresses that it is not possible to deliver at that figure. All my experience in this area shows that there is bound to be some clawing back during the process of negotiation. What we have to decide is what our walk-away figure would be, and mine is if they were to drop the injection of cash to £650 million; at below £650 million I don't believe we could do it – we couldn't actually make the arithmetic work.' Bernard Friend agreed with me in principle and so, even though Roland was shaking his head in disbelief, we left the meeting to start the actual detailed negotiations, subject of course to Board approval. The Board duly took note of what was on offer; I made my statement about believing that we had to have a walk-away figure in mind, and that mine was £650 million. This was noted although not taken too seriously, because I think, no one believed that it would come about.

The history of the thing showed that I was right. As the officials of the DTI looked at the deal, they thought about what was likely to be acceptable to the European Commission in Brussels, and slowly the amounts were being looked at under a magnifying glass. Indeed, in the end Brussels stipulated that no more than £650 million should be injected into Rover in order to get it away. There were many meetings and long examinations by our lawyers and our advisers which went on and on and on and on, but the discussion had to be reached ultimately as to whether or not we were going to do the deal at that price or not. Finally we reached the crunch point and at a Board meeting to discuss the final terms of the offer, which was £650 million – we having to put in £150 million – a decision had to be made.

Roland, to my surprise, expressed his disappointment. I remember being fairly slumped in my seat opposite him as we went through the preliminaries, and suddenly it dawned on me that he was actually taking this as a matter of principle and would recommend that we walk away from the deal at that figure. I remember saying, 'Are you saying, Chairman, that you do not think you can support this at that price?' to which he replied, 'I've got to think of my own personal position.' I countered by saying, 'No, Chairman, I think you must think of the position of our shareholders and our employees. I believe it is a good deal at £650 million.' 'Yes,' said Roland, 'but it is not the deal that was struck.' 'No,' I said, 'but then I did warn you at the time that I doubted whether that full amount would ever be deliverable.' I believe Roland was very close to walking away from the deal at that moment, and if I had given any encouragement I think it would have been off, or he would have been off. Perhaps, as later events were to show, I should have encouraged it! The fact is the moment passed and it was decided that we could accept it but that we should try to get some of the lost benefits back if that were possible. I undertook to try to negotiate with the officials in the DTI some way of improving the bottom line by getting agreement on certain issues that had been hanging over us for some time. For his part, Bernard attempted to negotiate a deal whereby, although the £150 million would be paid over by us to them in the financial year, we didn't pay until the end of the financial year, thus saving a considerable amount of interest.

Together with Bernard, I had been concerned for some time about the assessment of our tax liabilities with regard to our partnership in Airbus Industrie and how this was to be treated. The matter had been resolved successfully with the inspector of taxes concerned, but a new inspector was seeking to reopen the entire question. We had had to make provisions in the accounts, therefore, against the eventuality that the thing went against us. Although it had already been found in our favour on one occasion, we needed some government support to see if we could get an early resolution of the tax liability. In addition, we had been negotiating, or trying to negotiate, a deal whereby we got more money for the involvement of British Aerospace's Space and Communications Company in the European space consortium. There were various things that we wanted to do if certain programmes went ahead that would give us some injection of government money – I seem to recall something like £3.5 million was at stake – and if we could get a favourable outcome it would effectively save the company that much money. Taken together, this and other bits and pieces of issues yet to be resolved, we came to a figure that was much bandied about – the so-called sweeteners. What had totally been lost sight of was that the original deal that had been informally agreed was no longer the deal we were being offered, and it was reasonable in my view for the company to find ways of getting the Government to provide funds for other programmes that it thought were appropriate and which had nothing to do with Brussels.

We put all these proposals together and submitted them to the Secretary of State. He replied in the affirmative but unfortunately made some remarks in the letter, which was leaked, which were to lead to untold difficulties for him in the future. It was even more unfortunate that something like that should be leaked and become public knowledge, and the whole thing began to look like some kind of dreadful conspiracy, which it was not. In fact, it was no more than the normal negotiation of contract terms and conditions, and we had acted in the interests of our shareholders in attempting to obtain the best deal possible for the company, although still far short of the deal that had tentatively been agreed. In all this, David Young did his best to support the original figure.

We now awaited the final draft of the agreement that was coming from Brussels as to what we should be allowed to do, or how the deal was to be struck. I was due to go to a luncheon in Downing Street, and at drinks beforehand I found myself chatting to David Young; we were congratulating each other on the fact that we had actually got a deal, and he was due to make a statement in the Lords on it that afternoon. I was therefore more than surprised when I was told by one of the Prime Minister's aides that I was wanted on the telephone; it turned out to be Bernard Friend and the Company Secretary. They said that they had just received the terms and conditions attached to the deal from Brussels and that they were unacceptable. I was stunned. 'How do you mean, unacceptable?' I asked. 'Well, one of the conditions they are imposing upon us is that we should give an undertaking not to dispose of, or change any of the agreements that we enter into, during the five-year period of our agreed tenure of ownership.' Quite clearly no PLC can give that precise undertaking. We could be subject to events over which we could have no control. It really was a stopper. 'What are you saying?' I enquired. 'Well, we're trying to get hold of the Chairman,' he responded, 'but he is away at some luncheon somewhere and I'm afraid we're going to have to pull it.' 'But I've just been talking to David Young,' I said. 'Well, don't say anything more to him,' was the reply I got. 'How do you mean, "don't say anything more"? I can't go back in there and face the man and not tell him we've got a problem.'

I went back into the reception which was about to empty into the dining room for lunch, and taking David aside I warned him that we were standing into danger and there appeared to be some problem which wasn't very clear to me. During lunch I was called out again to take a 'phone call from the office to say that, having looked carefully at the whole thing with their lawyers, they had decided there was no way round it. To which I replied, and I remember Charles Powell was in the room at the time, although whether he actually heard what I was saying I've no idea, 'I'm sure there must be some way round this. Let's not get in a panic.' But it was too late, they had decided and the deal had to be postponed for 24 hours while various assurances were obtained that the conditions we would be unable to meet were withdrawn from the Brussels requirements. No company can guarantee that it is going to do all the things it says it is going to do at any particular time. Neither can any individual guarantee that he will conduct himself in a certain way for the next five years. It is an impossibility; circumstances alter cases. Nevertheless, it didn't improve relations with the Government, but then these things happen. Finally the deal was announced in Parliament, we then held a Press conference, and of course circulars had to be sent out to our shareholders informing them of the deal.

Here we came to another one of those dilemmas that one faces when presenting a case of this kind. Much play was being made of the lack of synergy between British Aerospace and Rover, but that was not entirely true. Rover had, through its association with Honda, learned a great deal about 'just-in-time' techniques, and that would clearly be something that would be an advantage to British Aerospace. The

THE TIMES

AST WEEK'S VERAGE DAILY SALE 43,000

No 63,134

FRIDAY JULY 15 1988

Aerospace group 'absolutely happy' after clarification of terms

BAe purchase of Rover cars to go ahead

By Sheila Gunn, Colin Narbrough, John Bell, Daniel Ward and Michael Dynes

Professor Roland Smith at the joint press conf

DAILY MIRROR, Thursday, December 7, 198

Rover: BAe in deal on brands

Andrew Cornelius
Industrial Correspondent

Shareholders asked to back MG sports car revival plan

PAUL FOOT reporting

The company they keep

BRITISH AEROSPACE

LOUD and long were the Tory cheers when British Aerospace took over the aircraft industries nationalised by the last Labour government.

NORMAN TEBBIT   SIR RAYMOND LYGO   LORD YOUNG and PROFESSOR SMITH

TORY TANGLE OF AEROSPACE SELL-OFF

Some of the massive coverage

529

manufacturing cycles were different; they were much shorter at Rover, and if they could be phased out of sequence with British Aerospace's major investment requirements then you could make a case for a smoothing of the actual combined business operations. It was a question of how we could use some of the techniques we had developed in aerospace structures in the manufacture of cars. A case could well be made for synergies, but the analysts and the Press were very sceptical about this. At the end of one Press interview I remember one young gentleman saying to me somewhat sarcastically, 'Wouldn't you say, Sir Raymond, that this was an opportunistic move?' To which I said, 'Yes, I would say it was opportunistic, wouldn't you? Isn't that what business is all about?'

The major benefit, of course, was that it had the enormous effect of cleaning up our balance sheet. It was never our intention at that time to make it a long-term holding, and this turned out to be verified by events, but opportunistic, timely and effective it certainly was. Roland had a nose for things like that – most of the time.

There is a footnote to the Rover saga that is worth recording. It was difficult to persuade the analysts and institutions that it was other than an opportunistic move, which of course it was, but we had to play to the conventions of the Stock Exchange and the *Investors' Chronicle* in trying to come up with some excuse to make it sound as if it was more plausible than they might think. They were synergies, of course, in the 'just-in-time' techniques which had been introduced into Rover, in the disciplines that Honda had brought to the partnership, and there were other things that the aerospace industry could bring to the car industry. For example, I had the idea of using all our aluminium swarf to be turned into forgings. We also had the unique ability in British industry of managing very large, extremely complex networked programmes, and all this could be used to illustrate that it wasn't an entirely stupid arrangement. Another important factor, of course, was the different cycles. If the cycle of investment in new car models could be massaged to not coincide with the large rises in development costs of new aircraft then we would be able to have a smoother financial outlook.

In presenting the case to the institutions and to interested parties, one had to be fairly bullish. The share price was looking good, and so it should have been at that particular time; the five-year forecast when I left was looking healthy – not exceptional growth, but we had taken steps to minimise the effect of the ending of the Cold War by developing alternative avenues. What was not, of course, forecast at that time was the collapse of the civil aircraft market, coinciding with the end of the Cold War, then you had at once to face the terror of two cycles coming into the same timescale. After one talk to analysts at which I had been quizzed on the Honda connection, I said that we were very enthusiastic about it, that it was extremely valuable to us and that we also considered that it would be something on which we would certainly wish to develop. These, to me, somewhat innocent remarks produced a tirade from Graham Day.

He wrote a letter to the Chairman and all the directors, executive and non-executive, saying that by my remarks about Honda I had undermined a relationship that he had been careful to build up, that the Japanese, and Honda in particular, were people who did not like to have their relationship advertised so widely; it placed the whole relationship in peril and he asked that I should be instantly dismissed. To say that such an outburst was unbalanced was, in my view, putting it mildly, but what was interesting at the time was the reaction of my colleagues to this event. It is interesting to see how people tend to put their heads down when the bullets start to fly. The Chairman was somewhat equivocal; he said that Graham Day was essential to the fortunes of the combined group at the time and that, while he thought his letter and the way in which he conducted himself was unbalanced, there was not much he could do about it that was not damaging to the company. I had to ask him, therefore, whether he was actually saying that I should resign on the strength of my remarks, which were merely to set the record straight in relation to how we, British Aerospace, viewed the Honda connection. The only chap who was quite unequivocal about it was a new non-executive director Ronnie Hampel, who expressed the view that the letter was outrageous, uncalled for and should be withdrawn at once – and it was. All copies were asked to be returned and destroyed, and I insisted on a formal apology, which I received from Graham personally in my office. A most extraordinary event and one that scarred me at the time (or should I say added one more scar to a well-beaten back), but for the time being the cat was returned to the bag.

47

Managing Change

There have been many learned dissertations on the subject of managing change and there are many books written on the subject, but when one is faced as the person responsible with actually managing change it can be quite a different matter.

As soon as I took over as Managing Director of British Aerospace, I set about matching the future prospects and manufacturing base of the company and it was very clear that we had too many sites and too many people producing too great a variety of products. We therefore had to concentrate and streamline.

As I have already said, there are two ways of effecting change in any organisation. One is by a carefully laid-out programme of consultation and agreement by all the parties concerned in which you move along a certain path. However, that path is bound to cause problems for people who will be made redundant or have to shift their jobs or otherwise become disadvantaged, and in that process of consultation the resistance to change has its greatest opportunity for frustration. The other method is by the judicious use of gunpowder. Here you blow the thing apart, and then you have to spend a considerable amount of time cleaning up the mess. Whichever method you choose is dictated as much by the character of the individual concerned as by anything else, but there is also a time factor.

My problem was that the amount of time I had to effect the dramatic changes that were required in British Aerospace was going to be relatively short. If I was to retire at 65 then I had something like six or seven years in which to carry out the massive changes that were needed, and this really wasn't going to be long enough, for one very simple reason. We had a full order book and it was expanding! Was this good news or bad news? If you have a full order book and you have your manufacturing spread all over the country, as had been the previous practice under nationalisation, then trying to shift anything and disrupt the people concerned is going to cause grave difficulties; if disruption in one plant brings the whole of the rest of the organisation to a grinding halt because they are making a component part that is essential to the construction of the whole, then it is even worse. One therefore had to proceed with stealth as well as with the judicious application of gunpowder.

At the time of my taking over, Home at Spalding Moor, Bracebridge Heath and Hurn had all been earmarked for closure. They were, for the most part, units that did not have a great effect on the rest of the company, so the closures could be effected without great disruption. Soon after I took over and had a look round, I told the Chairman and the Board that in my view every manufacturing facility in the south would have to go. We could no longer afford to make low-value-added products in high-value sites and at that time, with the property boom in full surge, the value of our real estate was climbing every day. It thus was very difficult to see how one could navigate one's way through this situation with ease. Much debate took place about whether Kingston or Weybridge should be the next one to close, and I had inherited a plan which identified Kingston for closure. However, having looked again at the scene, it was decided by the Military Aircraft Division that in fact it should be Weybridge, even though this had become the headquarters of the rump of British Aerospace, the main headquarters having been established now in the Strand in London. We must remember that Lord Beswick had decided to move the headquarters to Weybridge as part of the then Labour Government's policy of moving activities out of London, and we had been left with one floor in Pall Mall. Once the company had been reorganised, however, and the power of the two individual groups broken to the extent that we now had one centralised management under me, then it was clear that the key participants in the management had to be in one place; because of the need for us to be constantly interfacing with Whitehall, both Tin and I believed that it was sensible to continue to keep the headquarters in London and as close to Whitehall as possible. It was therefore decided to vacate Pall Mall, much to our disappointment because we would have liked to have reverted to the original situation in which the company had access to most of the building, but this couldn't be guaranteed. We therefore looked elsewhere and chose the new development at the corner of Charing Cross station, designed by Sir Hugh Casson. Weybridge, therefore, would only be required to house a few of the people that were required, and it was decided to develop a new office block there in order to accommodate the rump, as I called it somewhat unfairly; items like pensions, real estate, and some of the audit functions could clearly be well carried on from there, whereas the essential requirement for currency control and hedging would need to be done in the Strand. This meant that we could sell the rest of the Weybridge site.

533

The major difficulty in concentrating facilities was with the major programmes. The establishment of a second 146 line at Woodford would enable me eventually to close Hatfield; I had already taken the precaution of acquiring all the private houses that surrounded the airfield site, so that we could have a clean site for disposal when the time came. It was logical to concentrate all military aircraft production at Warton, but the Harrier was embedded into Kingston and Dunsfold and that would have caused grave disruption, even thought the actual number of aircraft being produced at that time was very low. The Hawk was clearly another candidate. On the commercial side, Bristol was seen to be the logical place for wing production for the Airbus Consortium and, since it also had a military capability in terms of repair and overhaul and a Dynamics facility as well as a Space Centre, it seemed to me to be a banker in the future distribution of our sites. One thing was clear; in my view the redundancy payments that we were to offer had to be as generous as we could afford for two reasons. The first was because people were being made redundant through no fault of their own but because of distortions that had been caused by events since the end of the war and the policies of nationalisation; the second was because, with full programmes running at all our sites, we could not afford disruption. Generous severance payments were thus in fact, a wise investment. Hopefully, these costs would be repaid by the release of the assets in the sites that were no longer required. This proved to be the case, though there was some distortion in the public's and analysts' minds of the value of what we were doing.

As it was, to effect the changes I needed to make was inevitably going to take longer than desirable, unless there came a downturn in the requirement for aircraft or a falling-off in trade which would enable us to move swiftly. Fortunately (or with hindsight, I suppose, unfortunately), it didn't happen during my time in office and thus progress was remarkably slow.

The other option, of course, in a programme like the 146 for example, was to get out of it altogether, and I remember being challenged by the non-executive directors, quite rightly, as to whether there was a prospect of ever making any money from the 146, and if not should we not get out of it straight away. The problem with civil aircraft is always that if you have actually sold some, you are responsible for supporting those aircraft for as long as they remain in service and this might be ten, fifteen, twenty years; you therefore have a responsibility and an obligation in financial terms whether you like it or not. There is, however, the cost of redundant material and the cost of making redundant the people that were employed on the aircraft, and in the case of the 146 it was spread around many of our factories. I remember going through the figures for the Board and saying that my estimation of the cost of withdrawing from the 146 programme at a time when we had sold, or had been committed to sell, something like 100 aircraft, would have been £350 million in 1985 money. This would have been enough to have brought the company to its knees. We were therefore on a roller coaster, but if the prospects of selling the aircraft are good enough then at least you are capable of deferring the evil day and you might even be able to manage your way out of it. If we could have got rid of Hatfield early enough then that would have helped but, as it happened, the order book for the 146 began to rise steadily towards the magical figure of 300; in fact, in the last year of my term of office, the Commercial Aircraft Division, as it had then become, made a small profit – at least on paper!

My experiences in the closure of Hurn, Bracebridge Heath, Spalding Moor and Weybridge had taught me that, even with the high property values that we were then experiencing, to expect to make a profit was unrealistic, especially so since I had introduced a generous redundancy scheme. I firmly believed that it was better if people who had to go went in a good state of mind, than to have hard feelings and industrial unrest that might have spread throughout the whole company. This proved to be the case. We never had one example of industrial action as a result of closure.

When it came to Hamble this was a different matter. Hamble was a factory that had been famous for the production of the Folland Gnat, a remarkable aeroplane that came out of the argument as to whether one should continue with light, cheap aircraft in large quantities or move down the sophisticated large-aircraft route. The argument raged for many years and had fierce protagonists on both sides, but although the Folland Gnat had sold to the Indian Air Force in largish numbers, it didn't actually win the argument at the end of the day. It is interesting to speculate with all the experience of hindsight whether this was the right decision to have taken.

Nevertheless, Hamble was a bit out on a limb. In order to clear the minds of management from concentrating on peripheral activities to the exclusion of the core ones, I had created British Aerospace Enterprises which took under its wing all those activities that were not central to the tasks of British Aerospace. I recruited, or rather he recruited himself to me, Ian Fraser who, with Richard Hooke, collected a raft of small enterprises. One of the difficulties was the reluctance on the part of the original inventors or people that had the ideas of creating these spin-off businesses to let them go. Nevertheless, by brute force they were wrenched away for the most part and given to Enterprises to develop, with the object of floating them off as soon as they became profitable enough to justify flotation. Hamble fitted neatly into this mould, if it could be made viable on its own account, and this was a much better option than closing the factory with the inevitable redundancy costs which would have exceeded the value of the real estate. I fell the people at Hamble in and explained the situation to them. The management was competent and in place, and we set them off along a road by which they could achieve independence and eventual flotation. Some 90 per cent of their work was coming from British Aerospace, so it was important to get some guarantee from British Aerospace that this work would continue on a declining basis so that they had a chance to go out and get subcontract work from other manufacturers, not only in this country but from overseas. They had one special capability, which was acrylic stretching of cockpit canopies, and we invested in new equipment to improve their capability. All this was then proceeding well at the time of my retirement. What went wrong since then I have no idea, but it was very sad for me to see Aerostructures Hamble come to such a sorry pass so soon after what had been, in my opinion, a great idea to save the jobs of the people there and give them something to look forward to. Certainly, the opportunity to give the workforce a chance to save their own futures instead of being made redundant is always something that should be examined. However, they are still there and good luck to them.

48

Strange Customers

My warning to young Commanders joining the Naval Staff while I was running it was, 'You are now entering a jungle, and in any jungle there are various snakes about and it is sometimes difficult to find your path. Be very careful where you put your feet.' The same, in a way, is true of the commercial world. There are some strange customers about.

Early on in my days in British Aerospace, I was approached by Wing Commander Checketts, who had been an equerry to the Prince of Wales, who said he wished to introduce me to an interesting man who wanted to expand his business in the United Kingdom and get his company registered on the London Stock Exchange. This company was called International Aerospace, and the gentleman concerned was Mr Guirin. In due course, I took him to lunch at Brown's Hotel and we chatted about his company which, he assured me, was in the high-technology end of our business, that it had many interesting developments in which he thought we, British Aerospace would be interested, and he was seeking a listing for his company on the London Stock Exchange. I was surprised at this and asked him why he thought it was necessary. His answer was that the security requirements operating within the UK were less strict and severe than was the case in the United States. I was dubious and left it at that, but I did agree that next time I was in Washington I would take the opportunity to fly up to his factory in Pennsylvania and meet with him again.

In due course the moment arrived and I remember flying in a helicopter from Washington up to Pennsylvania and across Three Mile Island, the place where the first nuclear power generating station accident occurred. On arrival, I was met by Mr Guirin and taken to the factory, a fairly smallish-looking affair, as far as I could see; I was not invited to walk around it because I was told that it was working on classified material and, of course, non-US-cleared personnel were not allowed in. I was given a fairly obscure description of the work they were carrying out, and saw projections of turnover and profit and loss which had my eyes opened. I thought to myself at the time, 'I'm the first to admit we're not very efficient in British Aerospace and are not getting the return on capital employed and profitability that I would like to see, but this chap's projections are astonishing.' I concluded that there must be something wrong with this. Was he doing something or trading with someone he was not strictly allowed to do at that time?

I discovered later that Mr Guirin, having been turned down by British Aerospace (I didn't even bother to take it to my Board or to discuss it with anybody, I just thought it a bit too outlandish to be true), went to practically every major company in the UK and finished up with Ferranti. They bought his story, and in the fullness of time it caused the collapse of Ferranti. Just before this, Derek Alan-Jones came to see the Chairman and me in Pall Mall; he was looking for £30 million of equity to replace that which he had lost in this scam. There was no way it could be forthcoming from British Aerospace but we did agree to look at the possible takeover of Ferranti, in conjunction with Thompson CSF. I flew to Scotland for a meeting with Malcolm Rifkind, who was then Secretary of State for Scotland, and explained to him what it would be like if we were to take over Ferranti, or attempted to do so, and to explain to him that this was an early stage but that we would ensure that it remained in Scotland and under British control. Unfortunately, when we started our investigation, every page we turned over revealed a worse state of affairs than we thought so we decided not to proceed with it in conjunction with Thompson. Thompson, however, which was dealing with state money and not investors' money, decided to go ahead and finally acquired the company. It has acquired many more since. It is not difficult to do, if you have the full backing of your government and are dealing with taxpayers' money!

The next strange character to appear on the scene was Mr Boaskey. We were interested in expanding our business in simulators at that time, and had acquired Reflectone in the United States. We were looking at the possibility of acquiring Singer Link Miles in Shoreham, which we knew might be available. Mr Boaskey eventually took over the whole of Singer Link Miles and then appeared in my office, and afterwards to lunch, when he said that he knew we were interested in the simulator business but he intended to keep it because it was going to be part of their core business. I remember thinking to myself, 'Mr Boaskey, you've never had a core business in your life. You are a financial manipulator, and to tell me you think that you are going to keep this just in order to make my appetite grow more voracious is simply not going to work.'

Some three months later he came to see me again. In the meantime, we had had regular contact with his man in the UK and I was able to say to Mr Boaskey, I think it was one of my better lines. 'Are you asking me if we are interested? Well, the answer is yes, we've always been interested in Singer Link Miles but I have to tell you that as every month passes, your company becomes worth less than you thought it was when you last came here. So if you want to do something, I advise you to do it fairly quickly.' He didn't and finished up in jail. Mind you I don't think it was anything I said that caused it. Once again the company went to Thompson CSF. You meet some funny people in business!

The first time I met Robert Maxwell was at one of those large dinners that are organised from time to time; I was at a circular table near the rostrum and found myself seated next to Robert Maxwell. To say he was larger than life was an understatement; I was certainly impressed by his girth and general demeanour. He was a big man, it would seem, in every sense of the word. I introduced myself to him and he responded by saying, 'Yes, I know who you are, and for an Admiral you're not a bad businessman.' I have never worked out in my mind whether that was a compliment or a criticism. We chatted for a while but he had bigger fish to fry at the table than he could have hoped to cook with me and I remember him getting up in the aftermath of the dinner and getting hold of the microphone himself and making a speech about something or other on which he was prepared to hold forth.

Time passed and the prospects of doing some business or getting an interest in the United Satellites programme caused me to want to talk to him again. In passing, when we had first moved to the Strand I had asked the administration staff to look into the possibility of getting a helicopter platform on top of the building. The answer, of course, was the usual one, 'Oh no, we'd never get permission to do that,' to which I replied, 'How do we know if we don't ask?' It was a difficult one because I could see that my aviation experience would lead people to believe that the main reason for my wanting a helicopter platform was so that I could fly a helicopter on and off it myself. As far as I was concerned it was a genuine enquiry, as we would then be able to use helicopters to move rapidly to Farnborough and some of our other business locations. I was told in the course of enquiring that the only authorised helicopter platform was on top of the Mirror building, so when the moment came for me to call on Robert Maxwell, I was ready to ask him how he had gained permission for this facility.

As part of my briefing before meeting him I was told that he would almost certainly interrupt the conversation we were having to take an important telephone call from some head of state somewhere in the world, and this seemed to be a feature of any meeting with Mr

Maxwell. I duly presented myself at the Mirror building and was shown up to the eyrie at the top that was Robert Maxwell's lair. It was, as I recall, an octagonal room and certainly one that would have been a good set for a Whitehall farce in that it had enough doors in it to facilitate entry and exit of various characters. Robert Maxwell was accompanied by Peter Jay, who seemed to be his bagman at that time. It seemed a strange change of occupation and on being introduced I said, 'Yes, last time we met was when you were Ambassador in Washington,' and he acknowledged this but whether he actually remembered me is neither here nor there. The conversation about how we could operate together in the field of communication satellites was under way when of course the telephone rang and, true to form, Mr Maxwell asked to be excused and walked over to his desk; it was the President of some African country who was on the 'phone and he had to take the call. I found this somewhat amusing after the briefing I had had but even more interesting in view of later developments was when one of the doors opened and one of his sons appeared to see whether he could raise some matter with his father. He was most brusquely dismissed. 'No, no,' said Maxwell, brushing him away with his arm, 'I'm busy. Come back later.' I thought it a fairly strange relationship. We didn't do any business with Robert Maxwell, and perhaps it is just as well.

I did, however, ask him how he managed to get permission to have a helicopter platform on top of his building. His answer was quite simple. He said, 'I didn't. I found a building that did have permission and bought it!' Well, I suppose that is one way of solving a problem.

49

HOTOL

The history of aviation has been determined by various major steps that have led to a plateau of performance which has lasted for some time until the next development occurred. The move from biplanes to monoplanes was one; the knowledge that enabled us to penetrate the sound barrier was another. One of the most important factors in solving these problems, and many of the others, was the supply of an adequate propulsion unit; power was the key to many of the advances. At one time it was thought that the continuous advance in aeronautical performance was to be unending. It was assumed that once we had broken through the sound barrier then speed and performance would continue to rise thereafter. What was not fully recognised was the importance and significance of the heat barrier which was the next threshold of achievement. The barrier places a great restriction on the way in which aircraft are manufactured; indeed, no aircraft, other than some experimental aircraft, have actually solved this problem within the atmosphere and the cost of doing so is astronomic.

It had been clear for some time, however, that if one could get a vehicle into outer space, that is to say, outside the restrictions of the earth's atmosphere (exo-atmospheric) – and, of course, all the Sputniks and space probes and the trip to the moon were based on getting clear of the earth's atmosphere – one could overcome many of the problems. From a commercial point of view, to have to throw away the major launch vehicle in the shape of an expensive vertical launch rocket every time you became airborne was hardly likely to be viable; until we could come up with some way of having a reusable vehicle independent of a launcher, the idea was stillborn.

In the mid-1980s, however, my chaps at Stevenage Space and Communication came to me with the idea of 'Hotol', based on an engine design by Alan Bond. The name was derived from 'horizontal takeoff and landing' and instead of pointing the aircraft or vehicle vertically upwards, the idea was to launch it horizontally down a conventional runway. The massive amount of fuel required to get the vehicle outside the atmosphere and into the stratosphere was a tremendous penalty on the aircraft in overall weight terms and had an

541

enormous effect on the structure. In order to mitigate this, the idea was to launch the vehicle on a trolley or an undercarriage that was not part of the aircraft, and which was left behind on the runway as the aircraft got airborne and departed. Thus the aircraft was able to carry a much lighter undercarriage that would be perfectly capable of withstanding the load on landing because the weight of the beast had been much reduced by the consumption of the fuel required for the mission. Once again, we very much depended on an engine that would not only be capable of providing the necessary thrust within the atmosphere but would be capable of going supersonic and into the stratosphere and performing equally well there. It was thought we had such an engine.

I was impressed by the arguments and fascinated by the possibility. The initial studies we carried out showed that a prototype might be built for something in the region of £30 million, in 1985 money, which would be a scaled-down version of the vehicle to be used as the passenger carrier. From experience I mentally doubled this. When one realises that, freed from the earth's atmosphere and capable of speeds of the order of Mach 8 or 9 or greater, the trip from England to Australia could be accomplished in under the hour, one began to see the enormous strides that would be possible if this concept were feasible.

There was another reason for me to be intrigued – my memories of Barnes Wallis and his Heartland theory. Barnes Wallis, more famous to the general public for the invention of the bouncing bomb, was experimenting with a model aircraft called the Swallow at a disused airfield at Predannick, when I was based at the Naval Air Fighter School at Culdrose, where the track for launching the Swallow is still in existence. A remarkable man, he was kind enough to expound his theories once after a dinner at Culdrose. He was concerned with launching variable-geometry aeroplanes (swing-wing aeroplanes that could sweep the wings back for supersonic speed, finally brought to realisation in the F-111 and the Tornado) but his preoccupation with supersonic speed and a belief that you could go on flying ever faster led him to expound his Heartland theory. Quite simply it was that, in his mind, the centre of the earth's mass in terms of population and geography was somewhere in the middle of the North Sea and therefore if one could develop an aircraft that was fast enough then, in the same way as the railways in the United Kingdom radiated from London, making it quicker if you wanted to go from Cardiff to Edinburgh to go via London, a major hub could be created for air travel by any country that was adjacent to the heartland; it would then be cheaper and more effective and efficient to travel from Tokyo to

San Francisco by way of the North Sea hub, rather than going direct. His theory was fine, but the practical ability to get the speeds required to make this a possibility were, of course, not within reach at that time. Hotol, however, provided a possible solution. I believed that there was sufficient merit in this proposal for some preliminary funding to do some design work to find out how the thing was going to operate; although it was the brainchild of the Space and Communications Division at Stevenage, it was essential that they brought our conventional aeronautical experience into play, so Warton was involved in the project.

After much argument and passage of time, a design team was set up and it was important to involve Rolls Royce in this venture; in my conversations with Ralph Robins, therefore, it was decided that both companies in parallel would fund some preliminary feasibility studies into this concept. Discussions with the Department of Trade and Industry were also held, and they also received the idea with considerable interest. It was agreed that we should jointly fund it, 50 per cent by private industry and 50 per cent by government.

It was important to get a head of steam behind this in terms of publicity, and we made a great point of playing this up on our stand at the Paris Air Show which featured Hotol to some considerable extent. Funding, however, was obviously going to be a problem; there was no way that the project was going to be funded by private enterprise; the airlines were hardly likely to want to spend the kind of money that we were talking about against the vague possibility of success, but work continued. The pre-feasibility studies were completed, which showed that the idea was feasible but that a considerable amount of money would now be required to develop a demonstrator to prove that the theory worked in practice; here we faced a change of gear in terms of the funding requirements. We were now in the midst of a period when government funding for this kind of activity was becoming less and less likely, and the prospect of raising the necessary private finance was, quite frankly, remote. We managed to get a number of supportive articles in the press, but nothing like the groundswell of opinion that was necessary. People at that time were more interested in making money out of property development than in the long-term prospects for the step change in air travel that Hotol promised. Prince Charles became extremely interested in the concept and talked at great length about the possibilities, his imagination being seized by the prospect, but the timing was wrong; by the time I left British Aerospace we had had to accept that we weren't going to get any serious funding. To continue to trickle-fund it was hardly justifiable on the part of British Aerospace alone, and so the project came to a halt.

Looking at a model of HOTOL at the Paris Air Show

Alan Bond still advertises his engine and the advantages that it will produce and, like so many great ideas, may have to take it to America to see whether they can find the necessary imagination and funding to put this programme into practice. I do hope it is not another example of our imagination being less than others who may reap the benefit.

Now there is talk of a replacement for Concorde. Concorde, a quite superb aeroplane, also hit a plateau, but pollution and the environment is becoming more and more of a problem. The cheapest replacement for Concorde would be an updated Concorde, but who is going to produce the money for that? Sometimes nations need ideas to inspire them to achieve things that otherwise they would never have attempted but, with our great history of innovation in transportation, I really did believe, and still do, that Hotol was something that could have been and certainly ought to have been tested a little further.

50

The Way Ahead

It was clear to me by 1987 or so that the most important step for British Aerospace to take during the 1990s would be to establish itself on the basis of European partnerships. We already had one in the civil field with Airbus Industrie which was beginning to look as if, despite all the administrative problems with it, it would be successful, and we also had the joint venture with the Tornado and the European Fighter with MBB, Aeritalia and CASA. What was desperately needed, in my view, was an arrangement with another weapon procurer to make sure that we had a future in the design of weapons for all three Services. Another important area to look at was the commercial aircraft range below Airbus. Here it was clear we needed to find an arrangement with someone in order to spread the cost and risks.

It was early in 1988 that Alan Gomez of Thompson CSF came to see me to have a chat; his theme was that we should co-operate. I responded by saying, 'Why don't we put the two companies together and make one?' He looked at me with some surprise but then smiled and said, 'Why not?' We were to find out why not with the passage of time, but that was my solution to the Dynamics side of the business's problem at that time. If we had looked for a UK partner it would of course have been Marconi, where we would have fitted together like a glove, but unfortunately, because of the problems that had developed within British Aerospace in relation to anything to do with GEC, I had come to the conclusion that at the time this was a non-starter. However, we had to do something if we were to move ahead, and it was also a fact that Thompson CSF was very much involved in the onboard electronics part of weapons design and manufacture; in a way they matched Marconi, and would have been a complete and whole partner for us. There were one or two problems. The first was that Thompson CSF was partly owned by the French government, and the first thing that they stated was that the proposed joint venture or joining together of the two components could only proceed if we decided to take a weapon that the French were then designing as a point defence system for their ships. But we already had a point defence system, Sea Wolf, and it wasn't logical that we should take another system at that time. Nevertheless, that was one of the conditions, and it was difficult to overcome. One of the other difficulties at the outset had been to estimate the realisable value or the actual value of the assets of both companies in order to effect a proper share. I had come to a conclusion long before this, and I hold it to this day, that if two enterprises want to get together, and they are roughly equivalent, stop arguing about the relative value, accept that each is as valuable as the other, make it a 50/50 share, put them together and sort the mess out afterwards. If you don't then the danger is that you will fall into the hands of committees of subordinates who will not be motivated so much by putting the companies together and making savings as to preserve their own jobs, and you will get nowhere. Because of the pressure of events I decided that, whether I liked it or not, I would have to delegate this responsibility to the Dynamics Group; having put a new managing director in there in the shape of Norman Barber, I was fairly confident that we might get some progress.

It really wasn't to be. We began to lose momentum towards the end of my tenure of office, and it was getting too late for me to effect change because nobody knew what the attitude of my successor would be, or what events would unfold after I had departed that would make it less likely that this thing would go ahead. In my view, it was another missed opportunity. The two companies would have fitted together beautifully, although as Arnold said to me on one occasion, 'I don't understand why it is that you get on so well with this chap; after all, he jumps out of aeroplanes, you've always stayed in them.' He was referring, of course, to the fact that Alan had been a parachutist whereas I was, and still am, an aviator.

The next opportunity I saw was to solve the problem of the bottom-of-the-range civil aeroplane market – that is to say, the 146, ATP and Jetstream – by doing a deal with Fokker. In 1986 I had been asked to pay a visit to Dornier to discuss the possibility of doing some kind of collaborative programme with them. I was delighted to meet Klaus Dornier himself, who was more interested in telling me about seaplanes and flying boats than anything else, but his managing director was clearly enthusiastic about the idea of getting into the civil aircraft market, particularly the 40-seat market. I remember very clearly saying to him, 'If we were not in the civil aircraft market, I would never dream of entering it. And if I were going to enter it and had taken a sufficient overdose to have me think that that was a sensible solution, I certainly wouldn't get into the 40-seat market. It's the most competitive market in the whole of the civil aviation business, with very slender margins, and you'll lose your shirt.' He looked at me in some surprise. 'But,' he said, 'our military business is going to decline, and is in decline, and I've got to replace it with something.' 'Well, don't replace it with that, ' I replied. 'It's much better that you close the factories and make everybody go home and find other employment.' 'But the German government', he said, 'wouldn't like us to do that.' 'Then the german Government', said I, 'had better pay for it, because I cannot see any way that a private company could start up and get into that particular market without having an extremely long purse indeed.'

The logical partner for us, in many ways, was Fokker, but I found that there was a hostility towards Fokker within BAe and a belief that it was only a matter of time before it went out of business. History has proved this to be correct, although it had an amazing ability to survive. Early on in my custody of British Aerospace, I found myself sitting next to the then managing director of Fokker, Frans Swartouw, and thought that he was behaving in a rather offhand fashion. After a while I said to him, 'Is there some problem that I'm not aware of?' and he said in his direct manner, 'Yes, there is. British Aereospace has always acted abominably towards Fokker; we have had nothing but hostility and rudeness from your people, and that rather colours my attitude.' I turned to him slowly and said, equally slowly, 'But I have no history in British Aerospace; I am an outsider, a relatively new boy, and if you have some legitimate objection or if you have a better idea I would be more than willing to listen to it.' 'Nobody', said he, 'has ever visited Fokker from British Aerospace at a senior level.' I made a mental note of this, and when I got into the office next morning I said, 'I wish to go to Fokker. I need an aeroplane as soon as possible, tomorrow will do, and I'll nip over there and have words with Frans Swartouw.' I therefore had much pleasure in arriving, flying a 125 myself into Valkenburg, to enter Frans's office announcing myself by saying, 'You said no one had ever come to visit you, well, here I am! What have we got to talk about?'

Fokker had been very successful with the Fokker 50, and was now talking about a Fokker 100 which would be a direct competitor to the 146. There was little doubt in my mind that they had the better design for the commercial market than we had. The Fokker 100 was not all that different to the way a BAC One-Eleven would have developed if we had gone down this route, but that was water under the bridge. It was clear, however, that at that time Fokker thought that they would be able to beat us in the marketplace and so they were not terribly keen to pursue any arrangement. However, with the passage of time I went back to Fokker, which by then had new management and was facing some of the problems which we were beginning to face ourselves, and discussed with them the possibility of putting the two companies together. I recognised, if nobody else did, that the 146 had found for itself a niche in the cargo market and, that it was not a direct competitor to the Fokker 100, and that we could actually keep them both in production while we talked about a successor aeroplane to replace both of them. I went further than this, and said that I believed that MBB were also interested in entering the civil aircraft market and that it would be sensible to include them as a triumvirate in this particular package.

The Dutch were not very keen on this because they had had a bad experience with a large shareholding that Dornier, I think it was, had taken in Fokker; this had not worked out and had left them with a rather bitter taste in their mouths. They also thought that it would be politically difficult for them to be seen at that time to be coming together with a German company. I suggested, therefore, that we should form a relationship with Fokker with a tacit understanding that we would give a third of the company to MBB as soon as the dust had settled, but that we would initiate the moves with the Germans. I therefore opened up a dialogue with both Reuter and Schremp who were then running MBB and, in the case of Schremp, just taken over Deutsche Aerospace. By this time Schmidt, who I had met earlier at Dornier, had now joined up with them as part of the amalgamation of German aircraft companies and I had a meeting with Reuter, Schremp and Schmidt.

I asked whether they were anxious or keen or wanted to enter the civil aircraft market and it was made clear to me that they did, but also that they would wish to design an aircraft. They were going to do this anyway, so joining a partnership as a subcontractor was not to them particularly attractive. I pointed out that starting off with a new design was going to be crippling expensive; better to join forces and talk about a next-generation aircraft after we had shared out some work within a partnership with existing capability. They listened to this and seemed to be prepared to listen. I then set up a separate meeting with them, introducing Roland Smith, who had by then become Chairman, to them, and we had a very good meeting in which I outlined my plans for a three-party agreement that we would lead with Fokker, bringing the Germans in later. I shall never forget the conversation between Roland and me on the way back in the 125 from this meeting. In his usual style he said, 'Ee, that was a great meeting, Ray, that was great. I can see that we'll form a joint company; I'll be the Chairman, you'll be the Chief Executive, they'll put in their money and we'll have the design and production.' I looked at him with somewhat pained surprise. 'You have just been talking', I said, 'to one of the most powerful teams in Germany. They're certainly not going to roll over in the way that you suggest. If we start talking about who's going to be Chairman and who's going to be Chief Executive, and as far as I'm concerned I'm retiring in the not too distant future and so it doesn't really apply, but if you start talking along those lines I can assure you there'll be no deal whatsoever. The only way to do a deal is to do it honestly and openly, not to discuss who's going to run it, and not really pay too much regard to who's going to run it, but to hire the best person from whomsoever and wheresoever he or she becomes available.' That was the plan I had in place for the development of our below-100-seat market. One can only rely on the personalities involved and good faith in these matters; suffice it to say that it did not happen after I left. Why, I don't know, but deals of this kind depend on goodwill, an understanding by the partners of what is involved and a desire to get things moving. Events moved on, and the collapse of the civil aircraft market with the recession that was soon to follow – which led eventually to the collapse of Fokker – overtook all these ideas. It was fascinating to see senior people in Germany being keen to enter the civil market; all the evidence before them was that it was a disaster field if you weren't very well established and did not have full government support, as I am sure the Franco/Italian combination that produced the ATR had and still has. You can make all kinds of profit with funny money but very little in hard currency at the bottom end of the aircraft market.

I should add that I had excluded the 125 from this proposed development because I believed that that was something with which we could be successful in its own right. Whether that might or might not have been true, I cannot now say, because the only commercially successful aircraft that spanned the whole of this period has subsequently been sold to an American competitor.

Just before I left British Aerospace at the end of 1989, I handed over the review of the budget for 1990 and the five-year forecast to my successor in October and gradually wound down towards the end of the year when I took a semi-sabbatical by going round the world saying goodbye to people I had known. I did not leave with any fear for the future of British Aerospace; the five-year forecast that I had seen didn't predict spectacular growth but a period of steady consolidation as we brought together the new arrangements in Europe that I believed were necessary. Furthermore, we actually turned in a notional profit on our commercial aircraft business out of Hatfield for the first time ever. The European Fighter programme had been launched; Airbus Industrie was becoming more effective and efficient, after much goading by British Aerospace. The Rapier 2000 had been secured, Alarm was in production, and a new air-to-air missile was in the offing. The Harrier programme, with the assistance of the Navy, looked as if it was going to be all right and, although our space activities had had to be cut back to a small and modest capability, the possibilities of using point-to-point communications were exciting. True, I hadn't been successful with Hotol, but that really was something else. It was disappointing not to have been offered the chance to become Chairman, and I wasn't very happy about the way in which this had been arranged. But it had happened, and I was glad to be going – yet another life beckoned. I had been asked to join James Capel as a director of corporate finance, and the London & Edinburgh Trust had invited me to become non-executive director of this very thrusting and dynamic company. Another life was over and another was beginning. I was proud of what I had achieved, and sad at what I had not been able to do for lack of time and, in some cases, support, but by now this was once again yesterday's story.

GLOSSARY

sea cabin	day cabin, usually near the bridge
3 point attitude	landing attitude
AFTS	Advanced flying training school
aircraft spotted	aircraft put in position
Asdic	echo sounding system for detecting submarines – "Anti Submarine Detection Investigation Committee"
Balbo	large aircraft formation named after Italian airman
binnacle	compass stand on the bridge
blow the flaps down	pneumatic system for lowering the flaps
'buffer'	slang term for a Chief or Petty Officer, head of Seamen department
cables length	200 yards
CDS	Chief of Defence Staff
CFS	Central flying school
cuddy	Admiral's cabin
EFTS	Elementary flying training school
elevator control	means of controlling attitude around the horizontal axis of an aircraft
ERM	engine room mechanic
FLYCO	the control position in a carrier for controlling aircraft
guard ship	ship stationed to guard a port or possession
lease-lend	wartime American scheme where equipment was available without charge
MADDLS	mirror aerodrome dummy deck landings
Mediterranean ladder	vertical ladder up ship's side
OAG	officer administering government
oleos	undercarriage legs
putty	the ground
QR & AI	Queen's Regulations
quarterly report	disciplinary measure which requires a report to be filed every quarter
round down	aft end of flight deck
SAVO	staff aviation officer

shakedown cruise	working the ship up operationally
SP	senior pilot
stick	compositor's small tray for holding type in printing
Tasman	anti submarine specialist
tilly	utility vehicle
wound up	aircraft engine brought to full power

GENERAL INDEX

Bradford, Captain Freddy Stovin 151, 153, 223
Brides, Ernie 135–6
Bristol 455, 484
Bristol Aircraft Company 412, 418, 472, 478
Bristol Stevenage Division 418, *462*, 534
Bristow, Alan, Westland affair 26, 44
British Aerospace 417–551
  Airbus Industrie 450–64, 546
  Aircraft Group 418–19
  Alarm production problem 437–9, 550
  Arlington 480
  Commercial Aircraft Division 535
  Dynamics Group 410–11, 416, 418–19, 423–34, 477, 546–7
    sports activities 429–30
  European fighter 506–14, *512*, 546, 550
  GEC 472–6
  Hotol 541–5, *544*, 551
  London City Airport 488–9
  Military Aircraft Division 506, 533
  nationalisation 465
  Orange 494–5
  origins 412
  privatisation 431–2, 442, 444–5, 465, 469
  property assets 519–20
  purchase of Rover 522–31, *529*
  purchase of Royal Ordnance 515–21, *518*
  real estate 378–80
  satellites 493
  Sperry Gyroscope UK 466–9
  Thorn EMI 469–70
  Westland affair 4, 9–14, 25–9, 33–4, 38, 40
British Aerospace Enterprises 535
British Aircraft Corporation 409, 412, 496
  Guided Missile Division 418
British Leyland 524
British South American Airways 414
British Telecom, satellite 493
Brittan, Sir Leon (Sec State for Trade and Industry), Westland affair 3–4, 9–11, 29, 34–5, 41, *42*, 43
Broom, Sub Lt Philip 16
Brown, Captain 'Winkle' 146, 214, 219, 220, 328, 333
Bush, Admiral Sir 244–5, 324

Butler, Sir Adam 442

C
Calodney, Ed 486
Campbell, Alastair 218, 223
Cambell, Rear Admiral Dennis 125–6, 158, 213, 224
Campioni, Admiral 391
Canada 75–7
Canary Wharf 488
CASA 546
Cassidi, Admiral Sir Des *373*
Castro, Nelson 476
Caughey, Captain John 295, 327
Central Flying School 123, 127–9
Chadderton 418, 457
Chapman Pincher, Harry 38, 371, 396
Charles, HRH Prince 543
Checketts, Wing Commander 537
Chiswick factory 428
Churchill, Sir Winston 372, 374
Clark, Sir John 485–6
Clayton, Admiral Sir Dick, GEC 475–7
Cod War 393–6
Compston, Vice-Admiral Sir Peter 308
Constable, Lieutenant 84
Cook, Peter *353–5*, 365–6
Cookson, Brian 418, 445, 446
Cooper, Sir Frank 29, 436, 503
Copeman, Lady 239
Corkhill, Corky 155
Cornford, Sir Clifford 407, 417
Cox, Commander 357
Crossman, Jimmy 117
Crowden, Commander Guy 19, 350–1
Cubben, Bill Orr 149, 153
Cuckney, Sir John, Westland affair 3, 13, 26–8
Culdrose, Naval Air Fighter School 146–57

D
Daewoo Industries 523
Daily Mail 335, 340, 345
Dance, Roger 491
Darlington, Mike 218
Dassault 509–10, 512–13
Davies, Brian 334, *334*, *346*, 348
Dawson, Geoffrey 56–7
Day, Graham 522–4, 531
de Havilland Propellers 413

556

INDEX OF SHIPS

INDEX OF AIRCRAFT